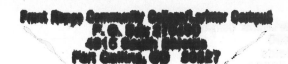

Developmentally Appropriate Programs in Early Childhood Education

Marjorie J. Kostelnik
Anne K. Soderman
Alice Phipps Whiren
Michigan State University

Merrill, an imprint of
Macmillan Publishing Company
New York

Maxwell Macmillan Canada
Toronto

Maxwell Macmillan International
New York   Oxford   Singapore   Sydney

Cover photo: PhotoEdit
Editor: Linda A. Sullivan
Production Editor: Jonathan Lawrence
Art Coordinator: Peter A. Robison
Photo Editor: Anne Vega
Text Designer: Jill E. Bonar
Cover Designer: Crit Warren
Production Buyer: Patricia A. Tonneman
Illustrations: Precision Graphics

This book was set in Univers and Century by Compset Inc. and was printed and bound by Book Press, Inc., a Quebecor America Book Company. The cover was printed by Phoenix Color Corp.

Macmillan Publishing Company
866 Third Avenue
New York, NY 10022

Macmillan Publishing Company is part of the Maxwell Communication Group of Companies.

Maxwell Macmillan Canada, Inc.
1200 Eglinton Avenue East, Suite 200
Don Mills, Ontario M3C 3N1

Library of Congress Cataloging-in Publication Data

Kostelnik, Marjorie J.
  Developmentally appropriate programs in early childhood education/Marjorie J. Kostelnik, Anne K. Soderman, Alice Phipps Whiren.
    p. cm.
  Includes bibliographical references and index.
  ISBN 0-675-21327-4
  1. Early childhood education—United States. 2. Early childhood education—United States—Curricula. 3. Child development—United States. I. Soderman, Anne Keil. II. Whiren, Alice Phipps. III. Title.
    LB1139.25.K67   1993
    372.21'0973—dc20   92-32718
                                        CIP

Printing: 1 2 3 4 5 6 7 8 9 Year: 3 4 5 6 7

Photo credits: pp. 4, 171, 172, 383, 409 by the authors; pp. 23, 201, 259 by Bruce Fox/Michigan State University; p. 167 by Gale Zucker; all other photos by David Kostelnik.

Preface

We're pleased that we've connected with you! That means that we've forged an avenue to another person who is interested in early childhood education and that we have a chance to share our ideas with you. Those ideas have to do with building qualitatively better educational contexts for young children. We believe this requires viewing young children from a developmental perspective, rather than as passive vessels to fill with already collected pieces of information.

Young children face a bigger task than simply getting ready for preschool, kindergarten, first, second, or third grade. They are in the process of building the bedrock of concepts, information, skills, and dispositions that will determine their capability to live in and contribute to the 21st century. Lauer (1990) has suggested that the main objectives of general education for postsecondary students should be self-knowledge, critical thinking, and community. We believe the same is true for preprimary and primary children. The best support for this comes from adults who philosophically believe in and have the skills to implement developmentally appropriate practices in the early childhood classroom.

What constitutes developmentally appropriate curriculum and practice in early childhood education? This question is somewhat easier to answer today than it was 10 years ago when early childhood faculty at Michigan State University sat down to do the hard work of defining desired educational outcomes for the children attending our laboratory school. Since that time, the well-grounded paper on developmentally appropriate practices from the National Association for the Education of Young Children has been produced. There are now excellent curricular and evaluation guides from visionary states such as Maine, Connecticut, California, Michigan, and Florida. In addition, a critical mass of early childhood research and application has been articulated in a growing number of publications. All of this has been geared toward advocating for appropriate curriculum and practice—in essence, respecting children's developmental levels as we plan more effective activities and experiences for them in early childhood settings.

Despite increasing resources available to practitioners, a number of myths about what appropriate practices are all about have led to confusion about what is needed to restructure programs, or whether they should be restructured at all. As professionals in a variety of educational settings across the country are reassessing their early childhood programs, certain questions are commonly posed: What kind of research base supports the fairly significant educational shift being proposed? Does everything have to change about the way classroom teachers are working with children? What makes this effort different from other educational bandwagons? Is there only one right way to do what has to be done? How are teachers supposed to construct the physical environment and manage children? What part should parents and the community be playing? Most importantly, how can we tell whether children are really learning?

As an outgrowth of our work with increasing numbers of educators probing for answers, we saw the need for a coordinated guide to support their exploration, planning, and implementation. Our goal in writing *Developmentally Appropriate Programs in Early Childhood Education* was to bring together the best information currently available for developing an integrated approach to curriculum and instruction in the early years. We also hoped to create a bridge between the worlds of child care and early education, as well as between preprimary and primary programs. The resulting volume is targeted toward teachers in training and professionals working in formal settings with children from 3 to 8 years of age. Although there is now widespread agreement that early childhood education spans birth through 8 years of age, the preponderance of formal educational programs are centered in the early years on preoperational children. Moreover, infancy and toddlerhood are special ages within early childhood which require additional specialized knowledge that goes beyond the scope of this text.

The Format

Developmentally Appropriate Programs in Early Childhood Education is divided into three parts. Part I, which comprises chapters 1 and 2, addresses the philosophical basis that has been the driving force behind educational changes being advocated and explores the principles and myths related to suggested programmatic practices that follow in later chapters. In Part II, chapters 3 through 10, curricular aspects have been explained in terms of six developmental domains and the two primary processes by which children learn, rather than by subject matter. There is individual focus on aesthetic, affective, cognitive, language, physical, and social

development, as well as the learning processes of pretend play and construction. The domains, which provide the structure for curricular design, encompass traditional school subjects but extend the usual content of education to a broader, more integrative perspective. In each of the domains, the reader will find a discussion of theory, research, and educational issues related to children's development in that particular arena, a suggested outline of ultimate goals and objectives, teaching strategies for supporting children's development, and examples of classroom activities that teachers may use to support development. Part III, chapters 11 through 17, suggests guidelines for managing time, space, and materials; for creating learning centers; for devising and implementing themes; and for promoting self-discipline in children. Parent involvement is also considered in this section, and a comprehensive look at testing and evaluation in the early years is included.

To the Reader

We believe that the information contained in this book will be valuable to both novice and master practitioners and that you will find that it goes beyond any other single source currently available in early childhood education. We are aware that there are many fragmented approaches that describe what to do or not to do with preschool and elementary children, or about why we should be making changes in curriculum, instruction, management, or evaluation. We wanted you to have a cohesive view of not only the "what" and "why" but also the "how"—that is, realistic and comprehensive strategies for achieving developmentally appropriate practices. We think it's important to tell you that all of us have had a number of years working directly with young children and also with educators in preprimary and primary settings. Also, while the ideas presented have been field-tested and are known to be effective, we know the information gathered here is just a beginning point and that knowledge about most effective early childhood approaches will continue to evolve. You will play a part in that evolution.

ACKNOWLEDGMENTS

We would like to recognize the major contributions to this text by four of our colleagues at Michigan State University: Barbara M. Rohde, Department of Family and Child Ecology, contributed chapter 3, "The Aesthetic Domain;" in addition, she supplied artwork in the form of classroom floor plans in chapter 11 and pictographs for chapter 12. Sheila Fitzgerald, professor of teacher education, created chapter 6, looking at "The Language Domain." Crystal F. Branta, associate professor in physical education, wrote chapter 7, "The Physical Domain." Laura C. Stein, Department of Family and Child Ecology, produced chapter 8, "The Social Domain."

We also appreciate the generous assistance received from David Kostelnik, photographer, for the excellent pictures taken at a number of preschool and elementary school sites; the teachers in the Michigan State University Child Development Laboratories, for their early work on the curriculum and also for providing continuous and easy access to their classrooms for observation; Beth Bellemer of the Scarborough, Maine, School District, who unselfishly contributed the bulk of longitudinal data on developmentally appropriate programs that appear in chapter 2; the Maine Department of Education for allowing us to print their normative sequence presented in chapter 17; Mary Stevenson-Brandau, Ellen Kotlus, Sue Palmer, and Cornelius Vonk, who reviewed the chapters on themes, parent involvement, discipline, and change, offering numerous insights from an administrative perspective. We also acknowledge the various school districts throughout the state of Michigan—especially Traverse City, Battle Creek, Forest Hills, and Kentwood—who provided us with thoughtful feedback, enhancing the curricular base.

We would also like to thank the following reviewers for their comments and suggestions: Jeri Carroll, Wichita State University; Rhoda Chalker, Florida Atlantic University; Karen Colleran, Pierce College; Barbara Foulks, State University of New York–Geneseo; Linda LeBlanc, Whittier College; Ann Marie Leonard, James Madison University; J. David Mohler, Slippery Rock University of Pennsylvania; Linda Reiten, University of Mary; Mary Snyder, Mount St. Clare College; Mary Ann Waldon, Texas Southern University; and Loraine Webster, Franciscan University of Steubenville.

During the preparation of this work, we discussed our ideas with and received feedback from a number of Michigan State University students, Head Start, Chapter I, child care, nursery school and elementary school administrators, and other early childhood educators. We heard the concerns of many parents of young children and listened to the children themselves as we observed them responding to diverse programmatic practices in early childhood classrooms. We are especially grateful for all of these contributions in shaping our vision of what appropriate practices ought to be and in motivating us to share that vision with others.

About the Authors

Marjorie J. Kostelnik is a professor of Family and Child Ecology at Michigan State University and is the program supervisor of the Child Development Laboratories on campus. Her background includes teaching and consulting experiences with a variety of elementary school, nursery school, child care, and Head Start programs in the United States and abroad. Editor of *Teaching Young Children Using Themes,* she has also coauthored *Guiding Children's Social Development: Classroom Practices* with Laura Stein, Alice Whiren, and Anne Soderman. Dr. Kostelnik has just completed a 2-year term as president of the Michigan Association for the Education of Young Children.

Anne K. Soderman has had 14 years of classroom experience working with children in both public and nonpublic educational settings prior to joining Michigan State University, where she is currently a professor of Family and Child Ecology. In addition to carrying out teaching assignments in a number of international settings, she consults with public school systems in early childhood curriculum, instruction, and evaluation and also trains Michigan State University Cooperative Extension staff in aspects of human development. For these efforts, she has received the John A. Hannah Award.

Alice Phipps Whiren teaches curriculum in early childhood and child development to undergraduate and graduate students at Michigan State University. Early in her career she taught young children in an inner-city public school in Michigan. She has also served as a Head Start assistant director and has provided a variety of training sessions for preschool teachers. More recently she has been a consultant to public school systems as their staff implements more developmentally appropriate programs for children.

THE CONTRIBUTORS

Crystal F. Branta is an associate professor in the Department of Physical Education and Exercise Science at Michigan State University. She is a specialist in the motor skill development of children and has over 15 years' experience as director of two children's laboratory programs on campus. Most recently, she has begun to work with classroom teachers in urban public schools regarding incorporating objectives and activities for motor development and physical fitness in the curriculum of pre-K through sixth grade.

Sheila Fitzgerald is a professor in the Department of Teacher Education at Michigan State University. She is a former elementary schoolteacher, and she is frequently asked to give teacher inservice sessions on language arts instruction for school district faculties. Dr. Fitzgerald is a former president of the National Council of Teachers of English, and she has published numerous articles and chapters on language learning in professional journals and books.

Barbara Rohde teaches preprimary classes at the Child Development Laboratories of Michigan State University. A former elementary art teacher in public schools, Ms. Rohde has an art education degree which has formed her interests in vocal and instrumental music, drawing, printmaking, and illustrating.

Laura C. Stein is a Head Teacher in the Child Development Laboratories at Michigan State University. Her role includes training teachers as well as teaching 4- and 5-year-old children. She has coauthored a textbook on children's social development, has contributed numerous chapters and articles to books and journals, and speaks extensively to professional audiences.

Brief Contents

Contents

CHAPTER 12
Implementing Learning Centers in the Classroom   292

CHAPTER 13
Theme Planning and Implementation   313

PART I

Foundations

CHAPTER 1

Early Childhood Education Today

EARLY SCHOOLING: THE NATIONAL DEBATE

WHY 180 DAYS AREN'T ENOUGH

CHARTING A NEW COURSE FOR EDUCATION

RECAPTURING KINDERGARTEN FOR 5-YEAR-OLDS

Today's headlines herald increasing concern about how we educate our children. Nowhere is this concern more striking than at the initial phase of children's educational experience—the preprimary and early primary years. Annually, millions of young children in the United States are engaged in group educational experiences outside the home. What awaits them there—the content of their lessons and how they are taught—will have a profound effect not only on their own lives but, ultimately, on the whole of society as well.

During the early years, as children make the transition from "home child" to "school child," children develop the dispositions and attitudes that will stay with them throughout their academic life. Educators report that by the end of second grade many children have reached one of the following pairs of conclusions: "School is exciting/challenging/fun. I am a good learner." or "School is boring/difficult/painful. I can't learn" (Kostelnik, 1989b, p. 24).

Youngsters whose conclusions affirm their self-worth as well as the value of their educational experiences have a strong foundation for subsequent life success. However, the future for children whose self- and school evaluations are negative is bleak. These are the children most likely to require extensive remedial assistance, encounter mental health problems, endure academic failure, and drop out of school (Doyle, 1987; Elkind, 1987). Which opinions children form has much to do with the kinds of educational experiences they have early on. As a result, America's interest in early childhood education is burgeoning. Families, educators, politicians, business leaders, and the public at large are becoming increasingly aware of its significance in young children's lives.

At one time only children in nursery school or center-based care were thought of as being in early childhood education. Today, early childhood education refers to a much broader array of children and settings (Jorde, 1986). Its scope is being redefined to include children from birth to

8 years of age, with the vast majority of them participating in preprimary, kindergarten, or primary programs. These children attend programs that may be half-day or full-day, public or private, enrichment or remedial in focus, targeted at low-, middle-, or high-income families. Such programs are administered by a variety of institutions in differing community locales. Currently, more children than ever are involved in early childhood education.

THE EXPANSION OF EARLY CHILDHOOD EDUCATION IN THE UNITED STATES

A broader view of what constitutes early childhood education is the result of two major factors. First, we have expanded our notion of the age range encompassed under the title "early childhood." In the not too distant past, the term *early childhood* was used only in reference to children 5 years old and younger. Parents and educators alike recognized that such youngsters differed significantly from older children. Using this traditional demarcation, it was entry into primary school (usually first grade) that served as the dividing line between early and later childhood. Thus, preschoolers were categorized as one group, school-age children as another (Smart & Smart, 1972). Following this line of reasoning, one might assume that first and second graders would be more like fifth graders than like kindergartners. However, research and practical experience reveal this to be untrue. Evidence related to children's intellectual, social, and physical powers suggests that significant shifts in young children's development are more likely to occur around 7 or 8 years of age than age 5 (Brewer, 1992; Safford, 1989). Consequently, psychologists and educators have conceptualized early childhood as extending through the 8th year of life (Bredekamp, 1987). This period crosses traditional programmatic boundaries including preschool children, kindergartners, and students in the early primary grades.

Second, the actual number of young children enrolled in group education experiences is rising. One reason for the increase is that more and more families with young children have adults who work outside the home. It is esti-

Increasing numbers of children below the age of 5 are participating in early education programs outside the home.

mated that by the turn of the century a full 70% of all children below the age of 5 will have both parents employed or live in a single-parent household with a parent who has to leave home to work (Children's Defense Fund, 1991). Moreover, research findings emphasizing the learning potential of young children have become increasingly prolific throughout the past several decades. Attention to these findings by the popular media has contributed to a growing national sense that the early learning years must not be squandered. These circumstances have combined to prompt a phenomenal increase in the demand for early educational services. Parents, once satisfied with informal arrangements in which their children were simply kept safe, are now demanding more stimulating programs in which children's learning needs are also addressed. Consequently, child care centers have experienced record registrations and now account for 25% of all prekindergarten experiences. Likewise, the proportion of 3- and 4-year-olds signed up for nursery schools has nearly doubled

within the past decade, from less than 21% to 40% (Hymes, 1991).

Additionally, reports documenting the long-term benefits of early childhood education, for poor children in particular, have been numerous and convincing (Lazar, Darlington, Murray, Royce, & Snipper, 1982; Schweinhart, 1985). Head Start, a federally funded preprimary program for low-income families, currently serves 450,000 youngsters each year with plans to extend enrollments to significantly higher levels. However, at its current level of funding, only one in five eligible children can take advantage of the program (Zill, 1989). As a further attempt to reach the children of the poor, 28 states have initiated efforts to provide educational experiences to disadvantaged 4-year-olds (Mitchell, Seligson, & Marx, 1989). Similar programs for 3-year-olds also are on the horizon (Geiger, 1991).

Furthermore, as a result of parents' needs for child care and their growing understanding of the benefits of early schooling, kindergarten, still noncompulsory in most states, now reaches about 95% of the children eligible to attend (Day, 1988b). Few children, consequently, enter first grade with no previous group education experience. Finally, as children proceed through the early primary grades, many of them are simultaneously involved in additional early childhood services such as after-school child care or other planned educational activities (Grossman, 1992).

All of these developments have increased the scope and impact of early childhood education throughout the United States. In summarizing the trends, Hymes (1991) notes that "the field of early childhood has moved from the fringes of the education 'establishment' to center stage" (p. 2). The result is that a variety of institutions and professional groups are moving quickly to accept new levels of responsibility for educating young children (Warger, 1988). Such efforts have led to heightened interest in how to best create optimal programs in which children from all family backgrounds, economic sectors, and cultural groups can flourish. To better understand what is happening in the field, it is logical to next consider the central figures in this movement, the children.

CHILDREN'S INVOLVEMENT IN EARLY CHILDHOOD EDUCATION

Meet Kevin, Phonecia, Ronald, Angela, and Erich

Kevin, 3 years old, attends a cooperative nursery school 2 days a week. He likes to build with blocks, look at picture books, and dress up in the pretend play area. Because of a serious speech impediment, the other children find it hard at times to understand him. Kevin has become increasingly frustrated at their inability to grasp his meaning and of late has been striking out in anger. Kevin's parents, concerned about his aggressive behavior, make an appointment to discuss it with his teacher.

Phonecia's parents were divorced last year. She now lives with her mother and two older siblings. A generally quiet youngster who enjoys coming to the Head Start center, Phonecia is just learning to read and write. She can identify her own nametag and point out the word

McDonalds in the newspaper. Yesterday, she wrote out "Skl is fn" all on her own. Today, she asks the teacher to help her write "Daddy, I miss you."

Ronald is enrolled in the morning kindergarten session at Peabody Elementary. At noon, he is transported to the district-sponsored after-school child care program where he stays until 6 o'clock. Later, during supper with his family, Ronald excitedly describes all he did that day. He is most proud of being able to count. At the end of the meal, his father asks him to get eight spoons for dessert; he comes back to the table with five. He counts them out, double counting some, and comes up with eight.

This is Angela's third school in 2 years. A first grader, she began school eager to learn but has become discouraged over having to "start over" in each new classroom. Lately, she has complained, "I can't do it." Angela is behind most of the other children in her skills and seems a likely candidate for retention. Her parents are worried about her schooling but have had to move often in search of work.

Erich walks to school with his grandmother, who cares for him while his parents work. Upon entering the classroom, he joins the other second graders in the large group area for greeting time and a story. After the teacher dismisses the class for the free-choice period, Erich studies the center activity choices that are posted on a board and chooses three: retelling Knots on a Counting Rope at the flannel board, playing with unit blocks, and observing the hamster babies and then recording their characteristics. He also notices on the "Have To" board that the teacher has assigned him to read Animals Born Alive and Well silently, then aloud with her. For the next 90 minutes Erich makes his way around the room, working at each of these activities in turn. The teacher reminds herself to send a note home with Erich telling his family how well he is able to handle independent learning.

Kevin, Phonecia, Ronald, Angela, and Erich are just a few of the millions of youngsters who participate in early childhood programs across the United States. In thinking about them, three

TABLE 1.1
Developmental Tasks throughout Childhood

Task	Infancy and toddlerhood (birth to 2–3 years)	Early childhood (2–3 to 5–7 years)	Late childhood (7–9 years to pubescence)
Achieving an appropriate dependence-independence pattern	Beginning the establishment of self-awareness	Becoming independent physically (while remaining strongly dependent emotionally)	Moving beyond primary identification with adults
Achieving an appropriate giving-receiving pattern of affection	Developing affectionate feelings	Developing the ability to give affection Learning to share affection	Forming friendships with peers
Relating to changing social groups	Establishing a concept of alive versus inanimate, familiar versus unfamiliar Developing rudimentary social interaction patterns	Developing the ability to interact with age-mates Adjusting to family expectations regarding one's social behavior	Establishing a sense of belongingness in the peer group
Developing a conscience	Beginning to adjust to other's expectations	Developing the ability to take directions and to be obedient in the presence of authority Beginning to develop obedience in the absence of authority as conscience substitutes for authority	Learning more abstract rules and developing a true conscience
Learning one's psycho-sociobiological sex role		Learning to identify with adult gender roles	Beginning to identify with one's same-gender peers

conclusions can be drawn regarding the similarity of their involvement in early education. First, children ages 3 to 8 share common needs and characteristics. Second, all young children function within an ecological context in which the family plays an essential role. Third, the term *early childhood education* is applicable to a wide array of programs that share mutual aims. Let us examine each of these inferences more closely.

Common Needs and Characteristics of Children Ages 3 to 8

The children just described differ in many ways. They live in different communities, exhibit diverse skills, come from distinct family back-grounds, and participate in varying settings outside the home. Yet they are more alike than unalike. For instance, all have a common need for nurturance and affirmation (Curry & Johnson, 1990). Access to safe, supportive environments is likewise a universal necessity (Short, 1991). In addition, between the ages of 3 and 8, children work through several developmental tasks characteristic of the period that represent essential milestones in social, cognitive, physical, and language development (see Table 1.1) (Havighurst, 1954; Mussen, Conger, Kagan, & Huston, 1990).

As can be surmised from Table 1.1, the periods for accomplishing particular developmental tasks are not absolutely discrete but often over-

TABLE 1.1
continued

Task	Infancy and toddlerhood (birth to 2–3 years)	Early childhood (2–3 to 5–7 years)	Late childhood (7–9 years to pubescence)
Accepting and adjusting to a changing body	Adjusting to adult feeding and cleanliness demands Adjusting to adult attitudes toward genital manipulation	Adjusting to expectations resulting from one's improving muscular abilities Developing sexual modesty	Reorganizing one's thoughts and feelings about oneself in the face of significant bodily changes and their concomitants Accepting the reality of one's appearance
Managing a changing body and learning new motor patterns	Developing physiological equilibrium Developing eye-hand coordination Establishing satisfactory rhythms of rest and activity	Developing large-muscle control Learning to coordinate large and small muscles	Controlling and using a "new" body Refining and elaborating small-muscle skills
Learning to understand and control the physical world	Exploring the physical world	Accommodating to adult restrictions on exploring and manipulating an expanding environment	Learning more effective ways of studying and controlling the physical world
Developing an appropriate symbol system and conceptual abilities	Developing preverbal communication Developing verbal communication Developing rudimentary concepts	Improving one's use of the symbol system Developing more elaborate concepts	Learning to use language to exchange ideas or to influence one's listeners Developing an understanding of real causal relations Making finer conceptual distinctions and thinking reflectively
Relating oneself to the cosmos		Developing a logical, though uncritical, view of one's place in the cosmos	Developing a scientific approach to problem solving

Adapted from *Marriage and Family Development* (5th ed., pp. 172–175) by E. M. Duvall, 1977, New York: J. B. Lippincott.

lap, with variations in how dominant a particular issue is at a given time. However, such delineations provide a general guide as to what tasks will likely absorb people's energies during a particular life phase. Those representative of the early childhood period form a foundation for the concepts, skills, and dispositions children carry forward into later phases of development. Note, too, that these years are linked not only by *what* children learn but also *how* they learn. Because youngsters this age share thinking patterns associated with the preoperational period described by Piaget, they acquire knowledge in ways that differ significantly from those of older children and adults. Direct sensory encounters with the world, not abstract academic processes, are the primary means through which they expand their understandings and skills (National Association of Elementary School Principals [NAESP], 1990). Young children do not yet have access to the deductive and inductive reasoning powers that emerge in adolescence and early adulthood. Their world is more bound by the here and now, the tangible, and the motoric. Such needs and characteristics represent common developmental threads binding Kevin, Phonecia, Ronald, Angela, and Erich into a kindred group. Understanding these developmental similarities is a key variable in developing effective educational programs for children from preschool through third grade. Implications for early childhood programs related to this conclusion include the following.

Implications:

1. All educational programs in which children participate between the ages of 3 and 8 should be considered *early* childhood education.
2. Although some early childhood programs may emphasize either care or education more than the other, all have the responsibility to meet both children's nurturance and stimulation needs.
3. Early childhood education programs must be designed to accommodate young children's unique developmental abilities and understandings.
4. Because children in the early childhood period are more alike than dissimilar, continuity *between* prekindergarten, kindergarten, and elementary programs as well as *among* those programs children attend simultaneously (e.g., child care center and elementary school) should be as natural and well planned as the continuity between any two grades in later childhood and adolescence.

The Ecological Context of Early Childhood

Children are born and carry out their lives within an ecological context. This context includes both the biological makeup bestowed on them by their parents and the environment in which each develops. That environment encompasses both the nuclear and extended family; extrafamilial settings such as neighborhood, center, or school; and the culture and society. These contexts often overlap and are embedded within one another, influencing persons in complex, interconnecting ways. Subsequently, the contexts of young children are best represented as a series of concentric rings, with each ring influencing and being influenced by the others (Bronfenbrenner, 1989). A graphic representation of this conceptualization is offered in Figure 1.1.

The Biological Context.   At the contextual core is the child endowed with a particular biological heritage. Genetic givens include gender, temperament, and a timetable for the emergence of intellectual, emotional, and physical capacities. In addition, young children are born with a predisposition to act on the environment, learn, and seek social stimulation as well

as form bonds with other people (Sroufe & Cooper, 1989). Yet, because each child comes into this world a unique being, all these factors combine to create a singular context for his or her future development.

The Immediate Context.   Development is further influenced by the immediate environment—all the people, objects, settings, and resources with which the child has direct contact. At birth, this context is dominated by the family. Eventually, additional settings (e.g., family child care home, child care center, school, playground, neighborhood, or 4-H group) become increasingly influential.

The Socioeconomic Context.   All the immediate settings in which children sometimes find themselves are further embedded in a broader socioeconomic context. The impact of social and economic factors on children's development is frequently indirect but profound. For instance, the materials provided in a classroom and the curricula children encounter at school are shaped by educators, parents, and school boards using resources within a particular community. General economic factors and community-based

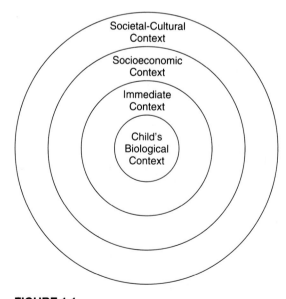

FIGURE 1.1
The Ecological Context of Child Development and Learning

beliefs also contribute to the educational program offered students. Indirectly, all these factors have an impact on each child even though the parties may have no direct contact with one another or the children.

The Societal-Cultural Context.   Individuals, families, schools, and communities exist within a society and a culture and are greatly influenced by these, the broadest of all environments. The societal-cultural context, the outermost ring in Figure 1.1, is defined by the belief patterns shared by groups of people. These beliefs shape the structure of various societal institutions (e.g., legal, economic, religious, and political systems) and other social structures such as social class. In addition, within and across societies there exist cultural groups who share more narrowly defined beliefs, norms, and values and who differ from one another in their basic approaches to living. Essential cultural variations exist regarding the way human beings relate to one another, the significance of time, personality types most valued, how humans relate to nature, and fundamental notions of whether human beings are innately good or bad (Berns, 1989). As a result of how different groups approach these issues, some children learn that cooperation is more highly valued than competition, and others learn the reverse. One cultural group might interpret a child's assertive behavior as a positive sign of independence, while another would be dismayed at the child's lack of deference. In some groups children are encouraged to revere nature; in some they are taught to control it. Which belief system prevails for children is a function of the cultural context in which they find themselves.

Contextual Relationships and Impacts.
None of the contexts described here exists in isolation or exerts its influence apart from the rest. They are all interdependent, both influencing and being influenced by the others. For instance, children are not passive recipients of environmental impacts. They actively contribute to their own development and to the creation of the contexts in which they live and learn. Knowing this, for example, we may observe that a "resistant" child frequently elicits rule-related

confrontations from adults and that such behavior, in turn, prompts the child to become increasingly resistant. Similarly, the family environment may be strengthened or weakened by changes that occur in the socioeconomic context surrounding it. However, because influence is bidirectional, families also affect socioeconomic forces, demanding alterations in services and community organizations to support their changing needs. This interdependence among contexts makes it clear that intervention with the child will have an impact on the other contexts within which he or she functions, such as the family. Also, what goes on in the family or neighborhood will influence the child's behavior in the early childhood program.

The Nature of Families within the Ecological Context.   During the early childhood period it is the immediate context of the family that has the greatest influence on the child. The family is responsible for meeting children's physical needs as well as for socializing the younger generation. Family members provide children with their first social relationships, models for behaviors and roles, a framework of values and beliefs, and intellectual stimulation (Bobbitt & Paolucci, 1986). All such functions take place through direct and indirect teaching, in constructive and sometimes destructive ways, more or less successfully. In addition, all the environmental influences discussed earlier are channeled to some extent through the family. For instance, it is via the family that children gain access to economic resources and learn the customs of their cultural group. The first attitudes toward education, work, and society that children encounter are in the family. Parents arrange for out-of-home care and make the initial entrée into a school for their children. They also promote or inhibit opportunities for peer and community contact. If parents are stressed by the hardships of poverty, the uncertainty of losing a job, or the prospects of marital dissolution, their ability to meet the needs of their young children is jeopardized. If such parents receive help or support from relatives, friends, or social institutions, the home environment they create for their children may be enhanced.

In short, the significance that biological variables, other immediate environments, socioeconomic, and societal-cultural factors have for young children is always mediated by decisions and interactions within their families (Sroufe & Cooper, 1989). Thus, to better understand what is happening to young children in America, it is relevant to review the current status of children and their families. As a first step in this process, the reader is invited to take the self-quiz on family trends presented in Figure 1.2.

The trends highlighted in Figure 1.2 can be summarized as follows:

- After remaining level through most of the 1980s, the child population of the United States is on the rise. Children from low socioeconomic groups (black and Latino children) are the fastest growing segment of that population.

- Few children live in a two-parent family of breadwinner father/homemaker mother. Dual-career families and single-parent families account for the majority of living arrangements in which children find themselves today.

- The lives of U.S. children have been greatly affected by divorce, remarriage, unmarried parenting, and delayed childbearing. Each year, over 1 million children experience the hardships of divorce. Approximately 75% of all parents who divorce remarry, causing their children to experience a transition to a blended family. The number of adolescent pregnancies is increasing dramatically. Most of these moth-

---

1. Is the birth rate in the United States going up or going down?

2. Will the children to be served by early childhood programs in the next 20 years be mostly white or nonwhite?

3. What proportion of preschool-age children have mothers in the work force?
   25%   50%   65%

4. How many children annually experience a change in family structure through divorce or remarriage?

5. How many American teens gave birth last year?
   175,000   350,000   472,000

6. Were the majority of teen parents black, white, or Latino?

7. Who makes up the poorest age group in the United States?
   children   single women   the elderly

8. How many children live below the poverty line?
   2 million   7.5 million   32.5 million

9. Which group of families is most likely to be poor?
   Young families (18–24)   Middle-age families (40–50)   Families over 65

10. Are the majority of poor families black, white, or Latino?

11. Are the majority of poor people working or on welfare?

12. What is the most common reason why children run away from home?
   disagreements with parents   family violence   divorce

FIGURE 1.2

What Do You Know about Children's Families?

Answers: 1. going up 2. nonwhite 3. over 50% 4. 1 million 5. 472,000 6. white 7. children 8. 32.5 million 9. young families 10. white 11. working 12. family violence

Sources: Children's Defense Fund (1991), Jenson & Warstadt (1990), Washington (1988), and Zill (1989).

ers are unmarried. Every 31 seconds a child is born to an unwed teen. Simultaneously, a rising number of women are postponing childbirth until their 30s and 40s.

■ Children are more likely than any other age group to live in poverty. Young families have been hardest hit by the past decade's economic stagnation, and the fastest growing segment of the homeless population is families with children. At the current rates, by the year 2000 one in four children in the United States will be poor.

■ Physical and sexual abuse, along with family violence, have increased significantly in the past few years. Every 14 hours, a child younger than 5 is murdered. Every month at least 56,000 children are abused.

While it should not be inferred that every family raising young children is in crisis, these demographic trends indicate that pressures on families with young children are great. In addition, the interrelationships among contexts and the dynamic nature of their influence on child development suggest important implications for early childhood educators.

Implications:

1. Professionals must take into account many dimensions when considering children's early education and determining appropriate methods of intervention.
2. The collective influence of the ecological context is unique for each child. Although some effects may be shared among a group of children, the total milieu for one youngster is unlike that of any other. This means each child is distinct from all others and requires individual consideration at all times.
3. Early childhood programs not only influence children and families but are themselves influenced by the contexts within which they operate. It is neither possible nor desirable to try to work with children in isolation.
4. Educators should expect to plan programs that address the needs of all kinds of families—single-parent families, dual-career families, blended families, traditional families, young families, older families, and families in crisis. Sensitivity to economic, religious, and

multicultural issues must also increase. There is no one "correct" family form, value system, tradition, or lifestyle.
5. Early childhood education programs provide direct services to children as well as support to parents in their parenting role.
6. Early childhood programs are in a position to provide children with a stable, predictable environment at times when they and their families are experiencing discontinuity and stress from other sources.

The Variety of Early Childhood Education Programs Today

The field of early childhood education is comprised of multiple services. Programs for young children operate under different auspices (public or private) and vary in location and size (private home, church, small-group center, or large school). They encompass a wide range of educational philosophies and curricula (from much free choice for children to limited opportunities for making decisions, from child-centered to adult-centered activities and routines). Early childhood education programs also vary in the target audience for whom they are designed; in their scope (full-day to half-day, full-year to partial-year, every day to some days); and in the training background of key personnel (Caldwell, 1986). An overview of the vast array of services currently available is offered in Table 1.2.

These variations in programs serving young children have evolved from distinct needs and traditions. For instance, modern *child care* programs have come about in response to societal demands for protected environments during parents' working hours and historically have emphasized the health and safety of the children enrolled. Although some involve government subsidies, many rely on corporate or private sponsorship and parent fees.

Supplementing the learning experiences children have at home has long been the function of the *nursery school* movement. Usually financed through parent fees, nurturance, enrichment, and school readiness have been their primary aims. More recent early intervention programs, such as Head Start and Chapter I, are the result of federally mandated and supported efforts to

TABLE 1.2
Early Childhood Education Programs for Children Ages 3–8 Years

Program	Children Served	Ages	Purposes	Funding
Nursery schools	Mostly middle class	2–5 years	Enrichment experiences aimed at "whole child" development	Parent tuition
Parent cooperative preschools	Children of participating parents	2–5 years	Enrichment experiences aimed at "whole child" development and parent education	Parent tuition and support services
Church-related preschools	Children of church members and the church community	2–5 years	Enrichment experiences aimed at "whole child" development as well as spiritual training	Church subsidies and parent tuition
Group child care programs	All	6 weeks–12 years	Comprehensive care of children covering all aspects of development	Varies. Some sources include employer subsidies, parent tuition, state agencies, and the federal government via Title XX funds, USDA Child Care Food Program, child care tax credits, private and charitable organizations.
Family child care homes	All	6 weeks–12 years	Comprehensive care of children covering all aspects of development	Varies. Some sources include employer subsidies, parent tuition, state agencies, and the federal government via Title XX funds, USDA Child Care Food Program, child care tax credits, private and charitable organizations.

Program	Population	Age	Purpose	Funding
Head Start	Children from low-income families, children with disabilities	3–5 years	Comprehensive development program addressing children's educational, nutritional, and medical needs, also parent education	Federal funds
Even Start	Children and parents from low-income families	1–7 years	Integration of early childhood education and adult education of parents	Federal funds
Follow Through	Children from low-income families	5–8 years	Continuation of educational support for former Head Start participants	Federal funds
Chapter I	Educationally deprived children (migrant, disabled, neglected, and delinquent children)	4–12 years	Supplemental education for children and parents	Federal funds
State-sponsored 4-year-old programs	Children identified as at risk for economic, developmental, or environmental reasons	4–18 years	Development of readiness skills for future schooling	State taxes and special allocations
Developmental kindergarten	Children identified by school or parents as "not" ready for regular kindergarten	5 years	Development of readiness skills	State and local taxes or, in the case of private schools, parent tuition
Kindergarten	All	5–6 years	Introduction to formal schooling	State and local taxes or, in the case of private schools, parent tuition
Transitional rooms (pre- or junior first grade)	Children identified by school as "not" ready for first grade following a year or more of kindergarten	6–7 years	Development of readiness skills (most likely related to reading)	State and local taxes or, in the case of private schools, parent tuition
First, second, and third grade	All	6–8 years	Transmission of society's accumulated knowledge, values, beliefs, and customs to the young	State and local taxes or, in the case of private schools, parent tuition

remediate unfavorable developmental or environmental circumstances. These *compensatory education* programs focus on a segment of the population, disadvantaged children. They are designed to change such children's life opportunities by altering the course of their development for the better. *Primary education,* on the other hand, reflects a history emphasizing the commitment of public funds to mass education. The goals of primary education have focused on transmitting society's accumulated knowledge, values, beliefs, and customs to youngsters of all backgrounds and educational needs.

Compulsory in some states, not required in others, but available in all, *kindergarten* straddles the two worlds of early childhood. Long considered a transition into formal schooling, kindergarten programs have been the center of much current controversy. Should they be structured more like nursery school or more like the upper elementary grades? Traditionally more similar to the former than the latter, today's kindergarten programs have experienced a shift in emphasis. Awareness that many children have attended early education programs previously and concern over children's subsequent school success have resulted in increasingly adult-centered, academic kindergarten programs (Morado, 1990). This trend has ignited renewed debate, not yet resolved, over the real function of kindergarten and its role in children's lives. It has also spawned new early childhood programs like developmental kindergartens and transition rooms.

All of these programs have evolved as though on divergent rather than interrelated paths. Although focused on children within the same age range, childcare, nursery school, compensatory, primary, and kindergarten programs have frequently operated in isolation with few physical, fiscal, or social ties among them (Mitchell et al., 1989). Even when conducted under the same auspices, it is common for preprimary, kindergarten, and elementary school programs to have little contact with one another (Grossman, 1992). Such segregation is reinforced by the fact that not all early childhood programs are regulated by the same governmental agencies, nor are early childhood personnel all educated in the same way. In fact, the training of early childhood professionals is often segregated along traditional lines. Child care and nursery school personnel

take one course of preparation, compensatory personnel another, and primary school teachers and administrators yet another. Even when they have similar training, educators find that the remuneration for their efforts also varies along program lines. That is, the same individual, doing basically the same job, will be paid more as a primary teacher than as a child care provider or Head Start teacher (Willar, 1992). Such disparities have served as effective barriers in uniting the field of early childhood education.

Yet, because early childhood programs exist in an ecological milieu, their paths actually do interrelate. All have a commitment to the well-being of young children. Many function within similar socioeconomic and societal-cultural contexts. This means they share many common aims, practices, and concerns. In addition, as children move from one setting to another, the youngsters themselves create a juncture at which programs intersect. Recognizing their common bonds and the need for continuity among children's experiences, teachers and administrators in all facets of early childhood education are becoming more sensitive to the interrelated nature of the field. As an outgrowth of this awareness, professional organizations have published position papers advocating better integration and coordination of early childhood services. Among these groups are the National Research Council, the National Association for the Education of Young Children, the National Association of Early Childhood Specialists in State Departments of Education, the Association for Childhood Education International, the National Association of Elementary School Principals, the Children's Defense Fund, and the Council for Exceptional Children. The implications for educators in this regard are many.

Implications:

1. Regardless of their unique mission, all early childhood programs share an ethical responsibility for enhancing the quality of life of children and families.
2. There is no one early childhood program that best meets the needs of all children and all families.
3. Increased professional communication among the many and varied colleagues within the

field of early childhood education is essential if greater cohesion among children's services is to be established. Such communication involves information pertinent to individual children as well as to the field.

4. Early childhood programs could benefit from sharing certain program resources, such as in-service training.

5. Children benefit when early childhood educators strategize practices to ease their transitions from one program to another. Such local coordination also could help programs address unmet needs without unnecessary duplication of efforts.

FOUNDATIONS OF EARLY CHILDHOOD EDUCATION

Although the variety of early childhood education programs is great, there are three dimensions they all have in common: *philosophy, organization,* and *personnel.* Throughout the last several decades, researchers have investigated which factors within each of these categories can be associated with the most positive educational outcomes. What has been discovered so far provides a foundation for program design and evaluation.

Philosophy in Early Childhood Education

Teachers and administrators make judgments every day about what to teach, what goals to institute, what strategies to use, what standards of achievement to establish, and how to assess achievement (Kostelnik, Stein, Whiren, & Soderman, in press). With these ideas in mind, they continually ask themselves questions such as the following:

What should be the goals for each child?

Is a goal that is suitable for one child also appropriate for another?

What should be done if pursuit of one goal undermines another?

Which strategy or set of strategies will be most effective in achieving a particular goal?

What should one do when a strategy proves ineffective?

How much time should be devoted to addressing certain content or goals?

What standards of achievement should be upheld?

Should the same standard apply to all children in the class?

When or why should standards be changed?

What is the most valid way to determine whether or not children have achieved the standard?

Not all educators answer such queries in the same way. Each bases his or her decisions on personal assumptions about how children learn and the nature of early childhood (Schickedanz, York, Stewart, & White, 1990). What adults believe about young children ultimately determines the way they interact with children, the kinds of environments they create for them, and the expectations they generate for children's behavior (Newman & Newman, 1978). These ideas comprise their philosophy of education. Educators glean educational philosophies from many sources: classes or workshops they have attended, books and journals they have read, and past or present experiences they have had inside and outside the classroom. Their conclusions may rest on evidence that is systematic or unsystematic, objective or subjective, explicit or implicit, comprehensive or fragmented (DeVries, 1974). Regardless of their origin, such philosophies reflect basic beliefs and values about children and learning and have a profound effect on programs for young children.

Although the exact amalgamation of beliefs and values each person adopts is unique, four different philosophical orientations have dominated the field of early childhood education throughout the past century: psychoanalysis, maturationism, behaviorism, and interactionism (Brewer, 1992; Weber, 1984). Each is based on a different theory of child development. Many teachers and administrators, deliberately or unconsciously, subscribe to one or a combination of these. Basic premises relevant to all four perspectives are presented in Table 1.3.

The four perspectives differ in their relative emphasis on the influence either biology or environment has on children's development and learning. Although some purists cling to one

TABLE 1.3
Theoretical Influences on Early Childhood Programs

Psychoanalysis	Maturationism	Behaviorism	Interactionism
Fundamental beliefs about human development are:			
the human being is not rational but is governed by emotion and internal drives.	the human being's physical, social, emotional, and intellectual development is genetically determined from birth.	the human being is an empty organism at birth. The human being is passive and only responds to external pressures.	human beings are active in determining their own course of development.
development is a process of continual compromises between the individual's needs and societal expectations.	development results from internal biological factors in a benign and supportive environment.	development is determined totally by experience with the environment.	development occurs as a result of interactions between the individual (inherent human characteristics) and the environment (experience).
Learning is the result of:			
internal drives that cause children to act on the environment to gain satisfaction.	maturation.	quantitative changes in the organism.	qualitative changes in the organism.
The tempo of instruction is determined by:			
the child.	the child.	the teacher.	children and the teacher.
The role of the teacher is:			
therapeutic guide.	nurturer.	purveyor of knowledge.	stimulator and resource.

particular point of view, in practice there are few advocates of any single position exclusively. Moreover, early childhood education as a field is not represented by a sole philosophical orientation or a uniform set of practices (Brewer, 1992; Roopnarine & Johnson, 1987; Spodek, 1982). Indeed, child development theory alone does not constitute an adequate educational philosophy. Pedagogical knowledge as well as a clear notion of one's ultimate aims for children's educational experiences are also necessary ingredients (Spodek, 1973). Yet such theories do serve the useful function of providing a viewpoint through which practitioners can interpret their observations of child behavior. They also influence educators' practices. That is, teachers and administrators who consciously espouse a particular set of beliefs can use them to gauge what actions to take in the early childhood program. Examples of the relationship between theory and practice and how it impacts the way children are taught are illustrated in Table 1.4.

All of the theories just described have been more or less popular at varying times within the past century, and all continue to be influential today. A brief historical review shows that the philosophy of early childhood education reaches back hundreds of years to philosophers like

TABLE 1.3
continued

Psychoanalysis	Maturationism	Behaviorism	Interactionism
Teachers view children's mistakes as a sign:			
of conflict between the child's urges and social expectations.	that the child is not ready for the content or skill.	of insufficient instruction.	of children's current thinking.
Teachers respond to children's mistakes by:			
giving children coping strategies such as venting and symbolizing.	withholding further instruction until the child is older.	breaking the task down further or giving the child more practice.	offering children experiences to broaden or alter incomplete or inaccurate concepts or skills.
Current thinking is influenced by:			
the value of play.	the value of play.	the value of teacher-directed activity.	the value of play and children learning by doing.
creative expression and significance of children's feelings.	sensitivity to the uniqueness of the early childhood period.	sensitivity to the possibility of altering the course of child development.	the significance of child-constructed knowledge.
the acceptance of the child as an individual person.	group norms.	task analysis in the microteaching event.	the integrated nature of learning.
the importance of classroom climate.	the importance of matching instruction to current abilities.	the importance of instructional technology — modeling, positive reinforcement, punishment, shaping.	the balance between child- and teacher-initiated activities.

Comenius and Rousseau. In the later part of the 19th century and the first quarter of the 20th, Froebel, Montessori, and Dewey, among others, advocated particular methods and techniques based on their own interpretations of child development and the goals of early schooling. By the mid-20th century, public interest in early childhood education was high. New ideas from the field of psychology were coming on the scene that still permeate our thinking. Since the 1940s each decade has had its dominant themes, concerns, and preferred explanatory theories. In reviewing how these perspectives have emerged, one gets a clearer picture of where we are today regarding the education of young children.

The 1940s and 1950s. Based on Arnold Gessel's work of the previous 20 years, the notion of maturational readiness permeated early childhood programs of the 1940s and 1950s. According to this school of thought, teachers were expected to support the natural unfolding of children's developmental capacities. The proper curriculum for each child could best be determined by referring to the norms for that age range. Attempts to train children before they were "ready" for certain kinds of learning were be-

TABLE 1.4
How Theory Influences Observation and Practice

Situation: Jamal has been working on a puzzle much of the morning. Although he gets the puzzle halfway completed, his frustration begins to mount as he struggles to find a way to make the last few pieces fit. Finally, he shoves the puzzle away, crying out, "I can't do it."

Psychoanalysis	Maturationism	Behaviorism	Interactionism
	The teacher observes:		
the child's facial expression and muscle tension.	the child's use of fingers and palm in picking up the puzzle pieces.	the cues the child is using to place the puzzle pieces correctly and incorrectly.	that the child repeats the same unsuccessful strategies over and over again.
	The teacher infers:		
internal conflict.	that the child's hand coordination is inadequate for the size of the pieces.	that the child is distracted by so many pieces and needs more practice recognizing color and shape as cues for placement.	that the cognitive characteristic of centration and the child's increasing stress are inhibiting his ability to consider alternatives.
	The teacher responds by:		
taking Jamal over to the workbench where he can pound as a way to vent his frustration.	inviting Jamal to try a different activity more suited to his abilities.	giving Jamal fewer more differentiated pieces to work on.	acknowledging Jamal's frustration and talking with him about what he could do when such circumstances arise, e.g., take a break, ask for help, use the colors on the pieces as a clue for which one goes where.

lieved to be, at worst, harmful or, at best, ineffective. Children not deemed ready to embark on a certain task were left to wait until they had matured sufficiently to master the task rather than being offered prerequisite skills to facilitate achievement. This practice eventually became known as giving children "the gift of time."

During this same period, Freud's contributions to understanding the significance of early personality development gave impetus to the view that childhood education could serve as a means to prevent mental illness. This, coupled with Dewey's (1938) focus on the importance

of providing opportunities for the growth of the individual and an awareness of the interdependence of persons in society, paved the way for centering on children's emotional well-being. With the publication in 1950 of Erikson's (1950) *Childhood and Society*, awareness of the importance of the child's socioemotional world was ensured. Primary education continued along traditional patterns but with increased attention to children's mental health. In many early childhood programs the expectations for emotional and social growth became maximal while those for academic performance became minimal.

The curricular focus was on readiness activities and ones aimed at supporting children's sense of well-being rather than direct instruction or an emphasis on cognitive skills. Because of both these influences, the climate of all early childhood programs (especially nursery schools and kindergarten) became more democratic and child centered. Unfortunately, in too many schools as the social environment became richer, the intellectual climate became more sterile. Afraid of frustrating children, teachers refrained from offering challenge. Afraid of repressing children, teachers removed all restrictions. Afraid of inhibiting children, teachers withheld all direct instruction and guidance (Spodek & Robison, 1973). The result was a teaching mode in which teachers practiced a minimalist philosophy. This model is one that educators still refer to as the "traditional" approach to early childhood education.

The 1960s. When the Soviet Union launched *Sputnik* in 1957, pressure for increased performance in education mounted. With the advent of the sixties, a gradual shift in focus from children's emotional needs to one of how to teach basic academic skills effectively took shape. Much research had accumulated from behaviorist theory that provided the technology for efficient learning of highly specific tasks. The role of the school was viewed as that of creating an environment where the production of appropriate behaviors could be supported and the child's accessibility to specific stimuli controlled (Spodek, 1973). Behavioral technology was applied to shaping children's actions. Such shaping involved first targeting a desired behavior, then fixing a baseline, next selecting reinforcers, then analyzing the task and sequencing the instruction, and finally systematically applying the reinforcers (Pellegrini, 1989). As a result of the popularization of this point of view, a movement in elementary education to teach skills and specific behavioral objectives at each grade level began. Many preschools also adopted the new technology.

In 1965, Head Start was initiated to ameliorate the alleged deficiencies of young children of poverty prior to formal school entry. The goals of Head Start were broad, emphasizing all aspects of child development. Parent education and health promotion were integral parts of the program from the start. Initially, most Head Start programs were closer in philosophy to the traditional approach of the previous decade than to the more behavioral perspective taking hold in programs for older children. Eventually, the skills approach associated with behaviorist theory permeated many Head Start programs as well. In addition, because Head Start children who made early gains did not continue to progress in elementary schools as had been anticipated, Follow Through was developed in the last years of the decade. The aim of Follow Through was to sustain positive Head Start outcomes as children moved through the early elementary grades.

By the time the sixties came to a close, greater numbers of children and professionals had entered the field. Much turmoil accompanied this rapid expansion as professionals holding various philosophical perspectives became advocates for their point of view. This set the stage for the decade to come.

The 1970s. Conflict between the traditional perspective of the 1940s and 1950s and the more recent behavioral orientation was inevitable. It resulted in practitioners being confronted with two opposite views of what was "best" for children. On the one hand, direct instruction, external rewards, and adult-centered activities were seen as an efficient means to achieve certain behavioral outcomes. On the other hand, proponents of play, child-centered activities, and internal motivation emphasized process-oriented goals. In common practice, the two polar approaches tended to divide by age group. The primary school adopted a more behavioral philosophy, becoming increasingly dependent on workbooks, drills, and adult-centered activities. Programs aimed at children below the age of 5, such as nursery schools and child care centers, continued to be dominated by a play-oriented philosophy.

Eventually, people wanted to know, Was one perspective right? Which outcomes were best? What model of early childhood education should dominate the American scene? To answer these queries, planned variations of curriculum models were developed. Supported by federal dollars, scholars had opportunities to construct curriculum based upon particular theories and test them out (Evans, 1975). Studies of this kind were carried out for several years. Ultimately, it was discovered that no one theory was exclusively successful. Furthermore, effective models, regardless of their theoretical base, shared certain elements in common: a theoretical or philosophical guide for action, clearly defined goals, committed and well-trained teachers, parent involvement, an openness to continuing change, and systematic evaluation (Consortium for Longitudinal Studies, 1983). Knowing that neither of the polar approaches espoused in the 1950s and 1960s were unilaterally successful, educators next became interested in how these perspectives might be integrated.

The 1980s and 1990s. Based on experiences of the previous years, it no longer seemed useful to create dichotomies between maturation and environment, child-initiated and adult-initiated activities, exploration and skill acquisition, or socioemotional and cognitive development. In the 1980s, early childhood professionals wanted to know how to implement programs in which there was a balance between self-discovery and instruction, children had chances to play but also participate in teacher-directed activities, and children's self-esteem was enhanced along with their physical, language, and cognitive skills.

It was in this atmosphere that educators became increasingly interested in the work of Jean Piaget. Although it is true that some teachers, administrators, and program designers had known about Piaget long before (e.g., Kamii & DeVries, 1978; Lavatelli, 1973; Weikart, Rogers, Adcock, & McClelland, 1971), it was not until the 1980s that popular interest in his ideas burgeoned. Piaget's fundamental propositions were that children are cognitive beings who pass through a series of stages throughout childhood and adolescence. These stages are influenced by *both* biology and children's interactions with the physical world (Forman, 1987). Piaget also rejected the passive view of children espoused by the maturationists and the behaviorists. He believed that children play an active role in their own cognitive development. In these ways, Piagetian theory offered a middle ground between the primary perspectives of the past.

Yet, because Piaget was a researcher, not an educator, it was left to others to devise early childhood programs using Piagetian notions of child development and learning. This led to many variations and interpretations. Some educators focused on Piagetian theory alone (Forman, 1987; Lavatelli, 1973; Yawkey, 1987); others integrated Piaget's cognitive development theory with additional theories in an effort to address all aspects of child development and learning (Hendrick, 1992; Weikart & Schweinhart, 1987). Examples of the latter include Erikson's emotional development theory, Dewey's theory of play, social learning theory as described by Bandura, Gardner's theory of multiple intelligences, and Vygotsky's theory of language and culture (all of these are described in more detail later in this volume). This amalgamation of theories and practices, emphasizing the interaction between biological and environmental influences, became known as the interactionist philosophy.

Although the interactionist perspective had proponents prior to this time, it was during the 1980s that increasing numbers of practitioners in the field heard about it and wanted to know how to translate interactionist principles into effective classroom practices. In 1987, the NAEYC offered an answer to these queries when it published a position paper on developmentally appropriate practices in early childhood (Bredekamp, 1987). This document articulates an interactionist philosophy of early childhood education. It also identifies classroom practices congruent with that philosophy as well as examples of incongruent ones. The publication of these guidelines was quickly followed by a series of position papers from other groups, such as the National Association of State Boards of Education (1988) and the NAESP (1990), that underscore the active nature of childhood learning.

As it became more well known, the interactionist philosophy led educators to reconsider the use of materials in the classroom, the role of the teacher, and the ultimate aims of education. It also brought about a renewed interest in the integrative nature of learning. Early childhood professionals now are exploring ways to integrate learning across the school day, across educational settings, over subject matter, and between grade levels. In contrast to the previous decades' theoretical divisions along program lines, professionals in child care, nursery schools, compensatory programs, kindergarten, and first and second grade are in agreement that the interactionist philosophy has great utility for them. Although not without its critics, the interactionist point of view has the potential to unite the early childhood education field as few theories in the past could do. Only time will tell whether or not that will happen.

All of the philosophical orientations and trends just described have had a tremendous impact on the field of early childhood education and still suggest important implications for practitioners.

Implications:

1. All professionals involved in early childhood education, regardless of their theoretical orientation, have contributions to make to the field.
2. Specific philosophical orientations are more or less useful in thinking about children and their development, not right or wrong.
3. Educators benefit when they consider the following questions regarding their own theoretical biases (DeVries, 1974):

   ■ What theories do I hold concerning young children and their development?
   ■ What do my behaviors with children imply about my theoretical beliefs?
   ■ Are my behaviors with children consistent with my theoretical beliefs?

4. Effective early childhood programs have an articulated philosophy, goals, and activities that relate to that philosophy and program personnel who share the program's perspective.
5. The theoretical developments of the 1980s and 1990s are not simply retreads of prior approaches but rather a synthesis of previous views along with new conceptualizations that go beyond those espoused in earlier decades.
6. Professionals in early childhood education can expect to work with increasingly diverse populations in increasingly integrated ways.

Obviously, philosophy is an important dimension of any early childhood program. Another element to be considered is how the program is organized.

Organization in Early Childhood Education

All early childhood endeavors must be organized to provide effective services for children. Numerous attempts have been made to determine if one type of program organization is more effective than another. These investigations have focused mostly on how children are grouped in the program, group size, and the numbers of children per adult.

Grouping Children.   When educators talk about grouping children, they are usually focusing on how the makeup of a class is determined or how small group instruction is delivered. Should children be clustered together by like characteristics in homogeneous groupings, or should the composition of each group be more heterogeneous? Should children move through the educational system along a particular track as determined by age, ability, or interest, or should class and group assignments be more diverse and fluid? These are questions that have been debated for many years. The discussion has become increasingly intense as educators grapple with the broad range of capacities and skills characteristic of students in early childhood programs. Consider Harry and Miriam, for example.

Harry is an outgoing youngster who has just turned 6. Only yesterday, he wanted to count the days left in the school year by 13s. Most of the children in his class are just learning to count to 100 by ones, but Harry has little difficulty with skip counting. He also enjoys simple math operations and is usually accurate in deriving the answers.

Miriam, also age 6, is very quiet. Though it is close to the end of the year, she has made little progress in working out the simplest number combinations. Her counting has improved, but she still finds it confusing to go beyond 20.

In deciding where to place Harry and Miriam for the year, the principal debated whether they should be in the same classroom or in separate classes with children of similar abilities. Ability tracking or the practice of grouping children by IQ or level of demonstrated skill in a prescribed area of the curriculum (e.g., reading or math) has been common practice since the early 1900s (Barbour, 1990). The foundation for grouping like children together is sometimes based on the maturationist view that certain children are simply too immature to do the work expected within a particular classroom or grade. Within this mode of thinking, children considered "too young" are frequently placed in alternative programs (e.g., developmental kindergarten or transitional first grade), placed in groups that move at a slower pace, or delayed in proceeding through the system (e.g., asked to wait another year before entering the program or to repeat the current year's instruction) (Holloman, 1990). An alternate rationale for grouping like children together is the behaviorist notion of targeting one's teaching to the specific learning needs of the children. It is assumed that instructional delivery will be more efficient when children are more alike (Weaver, 1990). Three typical methods for grouping by ability involve (a) creating groups based on screening and assessment prior to program entry, (b) grouping children according to formal or informal assessment of math or literacy skills once they are in the program, and (c) creating groups based on special services or funding sources such as ones related to children with disabilities, children labeled gifted, or children eligible for Chapter I pullout programs (Knapp, Turnbull, & Shields, 1990).

The results of numerous studies offer overwhelming evidence that long-term ability grouping fails to improve children's academic achievement and simultaneously damages many children's self-concepts. For instance, higher achieving children do not do better when together, and lower achieving children do much worse in homogeneous classrooms (Glickman, 1991). These results are partially due to unequal treatments of the groups by teachers and to low-achieving students developing self-perceptions of being "behind" or "slow" (Allington, 1983; Johnson & Winogard, 1985). In addition, ability grouping frequently has the side effect of decreasing other aspects of diversity in the classroom with children of color, males, and those coming from poorer families more frequently tracked into lower achieving groups (Dawson, 1987; Soderman & Phillips, 1986). In contrast, groupings in which children are mixed in terms of ability, cultural differences, gender, and socioeconomic background offer many benefits. With this kind of organization, educators are better able to accommodate children's diverse learning rates and learning styles as well as varying interests. Gifted and talented, above-average, average, and less able students are all able to find challenges and to work comfortably. Consequently, all children's achievement is enhanced under these circumstances (Barbour, 1990). Such results have led many educators to believe that heterogeneous rather than homogeneous groupings are the structure of choice.

Despite research evidence supporting mixed-ability groupings, many programs maintain their efforts to achieve homogeneous ones. Some do so because such groupings are easy to organize and fit traditional notions of program structure. This is as true for nursery schools and child care centers (in which groupings often revolve around age) as it is for elementary schools, in which both age and abilities are determining variables. Other educators fear losing financial support for certain categorical programs such as Chapter I. In response to these concerns, professionals are actively seeking organizational alternatives to ability grouping. Some programs have created heterogeneous groups through ungraded primary plans, cross-grade groupings, or continuous progress plans (Braddock & McPartland, 1990). Others allow learners to remain in heterogeneous groups most of the day, then regroup periodically by ability to address certain goals. However, once the skill or content is mastered, these groups dissolve and other newly constituted groups form around another learning goal (Rutter, 1983). Cooperative learning groups in which children of mixed abilities work together toward a group goal have also been found to enhance children's learning (Manning & Lucking, 1990). Furthermore, there now are school districts that have discarded ability grouping while successfully maintaining categorical funding. They have done so by applying for exceptions and by using the resources for children across classroom groups or to reduce class size (Glickman, 1991).

Including children with disabilities in regular classrooms is another way in which mixed-ability groupings are becoming more common in programs for children 3 to 8 years of age. This movement began in 1975 with the passage of PL 94-142, which mandated that children have access to education in the least restrictive environment. More recently, PL 99-457, passed in 1987, extended educational services to special needs children from birth to the age of 6. Both laws authorize services for special needs children and encourage the use of programs where less abled children have opportunities to learn and grow in the same settings that more abled children use. Similarly, for several years, Head Start has been required to include disabled children in its programs. At least 10% of all Head Start enrollees must meet this condition, regardless of family income. Investigations regarding the impact of including children with disabilities in mixed-ability classrooms have yielded positive results. Though teachers often must make adjustments to the physical setting and adapt activities somewhat, mainstreaming special needs youngsters in early childhood classrooms has proven beneficial to disabled and non-disabled children alike (Lawton, 1988; Meisels & Friedland, 1990).

A third way in which heterogeneous groupings are created is through mixed-age groups.

This kind of classroom organization has been explored in "family-style" child care configurations (siblings are placed together in the same classroom), ungraded primary units (e.g., children ages 5–7 grouped together), and mixed classes spanning two grades (e.g., a first- and second-grade split). It has proven successful in the United States, Canada, Great Britain, and Sweden (Katz, Evangelou, & Hartman, 1990; Ministry of Education, Province of British Columbia, 1988). In a comprehensive review of mixed-age grouping with young children, Katz and her colleagues report the following advantages to having children in classroom groupings where the age range spans at least 2 years:

- Mixed-age groupings resemble the neighborhood and family groupings of the past in which the socialization of children by other children occurs normally. These days because of parental employment, many children spend much of their time in programs supervised by adults rather than in the informal social milieu of a neighborhood. Mixed-age groupings in these programs give children natural opportu-

Early childhood education programs are inclusive, enhancing the development and learning of all the children enrolled.

nities to interact with children whose ages span the early childhood period.

■ Older children in mixed-age groups have opportunities to learn leadership skills and prosocial behaviors in interactions with younger children not possible with age-mates. Younger children have older ones to imitate and are able to learn new, mature social play skills.

■ Children's cognitive skills may be enhanced as they work on problems with others whose knowledge or abilities are similar but not identical. Opportunities for "cognitive conflict" that challenges but does not exceed children's capacities stimulates the thinking of all the participants.

■ Research related to peer tutoring and cooperative learning indicates that both novices and experts benefit from shared learning experiences.

■ Mixed-age groupings serve to relax the rigid, lock-step curriculum with narrowly defined age-graded expectations, which are inappropriate for many children.

The positive outcomes listed here hold true for children and programs throughout the prepri-

mary and primary years. However, there is strong evidence that the impact of heterogeneous groupings on children 6 years old and younger is especially beneficial (Katz et al., 1990). In statements regarding signs of quality in early childhood programs, various organizations have supported the concept of heterogeneous grouping for the majority of children's experiences (National Academy of Early Childhood Programs [NAECP], 1991; NAESP, 1990; National Research Council, 1991). Their positions are summed up as follows: "Children are heterogeneously grouped in each classroom but may be homogeneously subgrouped for portions of the day, based on the nature of the activity. These subgroupings may change to meet varying rates of child growth and development" (NAESP, 1990, p. 10). The implications of the body of research related to grouping children in the classroom are obvious.

Implications:

1. Children benefit most when programs are organized for maximum heterogeneity. Admin-

Children benefit when class size and adult/child ratios allow for more personal interactions.

istrators and teachers should carefully group children to ensure a mix of abilities, cultural and socioeconomic backgrounds, and genders.
2. The organization of the entire early childhood program may revolve around mixed-age or cross-grade groupings.
3. Homogeneous grouping is most appropriate when children are briefly grouped together within the classroom for a specific task based on their learning needs. However, such groupings are best when temporary and flexible.

Group Size and Numbers of Children per Adult.   Class size and the adult-child ratios maintained in each classroom are issues of keen interest to educators. Common sense would indicate that fewer children in a class leads to more individualized attention from the teacher and higher levels of achievement attained by children.

When it comes to the early childhood period, this conventional wisdom holds true. Smaller class size and more favorable adult-child ratios have been found to be strong predictors of enhanced interactions among staff and children and more positive educational practices (Bredekamp, 1991; Ruopp, Travers, Glantz, & Coelen, 1979). Such conditions benefit children 8 years of age and younger, children from disadvantaged backgrounds regardless of age, and children with disabilities in all settings (Shaffer, 1989). In keeping with these results, two national bodies have offered suggestions related to the number of children for whom each adult should be responsible in an early childhood program. For instance, the NAESP (1990) makes the following recommendations regarding overall class size and adult-child ratios:

3- to 5-year-olds	Maximum class size of 20 Adult-child ratio of 1:10
6- to 8-year-olds	Maximum class size of 20 Adult-child ratio of 1:20
At-risk children	Adult-child ratio of 1:15

The standards for accreditation of early childhood settings established by the NAECP (1991) put forth similar recommendations:

3- to 5-year-olds	Maximum class size of 20 Adult-child ratio of 1:10
6- to 8-year-olds	Maximum class size of 24 Adult-child ratio of 1:12

Finally, regulatory efforts to promote quality in child care centers and family child care homes have also addressed group size and staff-child ratios. Although the numbers vary from state to state, all states regulate these elements of child care via licensing standards. Based on findings from the National Child Care Study completed in 1979 and a recent study by the National Research Council (1991), the following ranges are suggested:

3-year-olds	Class sizes from 14 to 20 5–10 children per adult
4- and 5-year-olds	Class sizes from 16 to 20 7–10 children per adult

Numbers such as these are based on the idea that young children grow and learn in close relationships to adults. Youngsters are particularly responsive to individualized instruction and personal feedback about their learning experiences. Opportunities to engage in meaningful, firsthand interactions with informed adults are necessary for children's continued achievement. In addition, to maximize child access to the grown-ups, children throughout the early childhood period benefit from group configurations in which two adults are present (Albrecht, 1991). This might be achieved through use of paid staff as well as volunteers. Although the preceding numbers have yet to be realized in many early childhood programs, they suggest certain implications for educators and goals toward which programs may strive.

Implications:

1. The issues of class size and adult-child ratios are related to educational outcomes.
2. Children in all types of early childhood settings benefit from low class size.

The organization of early childhood classrooms continues to be investigated. To date, the evidence suggests that how children are grouped in a program, the numbers of classmates they have, and the ratio of adults to children in each setting affect the quality of outcomes children are able to achieve. One other key dimension all early childhood programs have in common is a need for qualified people to implement the program.

Personnel in Early Childhood Education

Traditionally, just as children whose ages span the early childhood period have not been considered as a whole, neither have the teachers or administrators who work with them. Instead, preprimary teachers, kindergarten teachers, and teachers in first and second grade are often viewed as functioning separately from one another, with few collegial ties (Grossman, 1992). Additionally, teachers' self-perceptions of their role in the program and the degree of autonomy they enjoy are frequently differentiated along conventional program lines.

Preprimary Teachers.   Adults who teach children between the ages of 3 and 5 years (including nursery school, childcare, Head Start, and Chapter I programs) are usually expected to plan programs that support a broad range of developmental goals including social skills, language, cognitive, and physical development in a comfortable, play-based program (Hendrick, 1990; Hildebrand, 1990). They are also expected to help children develop good health habits, confidence in themselves, and the ability to learn from their experiences with others in a supportive environment. Many teachers of children this age also assume that part of their job entails facilitating parental learning about their children and parent-child interaction skills (Berger, 1991).

In prekindergarten classrooms, there is generally more than one supervising adult, and so a pattern of staff differentiation exists among them. Head teachers and assistant teachers share responsibilities for program planning, providing leadership to aides and volunteers, and implementing the curriculum. Teacher's aides support the efforts of the teachers, implementing program plans, guiding children, and assisting with many management tasks. Members of the teaching team may work simultaneous hours part of the day as well as some separate hours to cover the 10 to 12 hours of service offered by many child care programs. Thus, estab-

lishing continuity for the children and among themselves becomes another facet of responsibility to which they must pay attention (Bredekamp, 1991). All of these adults, regardless of their level of training and official title, are perceived by children as teachers in the ongoing daily interactions, and all share responsibility for maintaining appropriate standards of safety, nurturance, and instruction.

Kindergarten Teachers.   Teachers in the kindergarten see themselves as having many of the same responsibilities ascribed to preprimary teachers. Such teachers historically also have been responsible for helping children make the transition to formal schooling (McKee, 1990a). With the emergence of nearly universal kindergarten education being available, the flexibility and autonomy of the kindergarten teacher has been called into question. New demands for preparing children for first grade or focusing on narrowly conceived subject matter has placed many kindergarten teachers in considerable role confusion and personal stress (Whiren, 1990). As one teacher with more than 20 years' experience in the kindergarten recently lamented:

> They [the administration–curriculum committees] keep asking for more and more. I don't think it's a matter of educational methodology anymore. What I'm being told to do is increase the pressure on children. This is becoming an ethical issue, not just an issue related to curriculum. I'm beginning to think that my kindergarten may actually be harmful to some of the children; I want no part of that. (Whiren, 1990, p. 276).

This teacher, with many others, has expressed concern that her responsibility for determining appropriate program goals, content, structure, and instructional strategies is being jeopardized. This loss of autonomy has become a critical, substantive, and divisive issue in the area of kindergarten education (Warger, 1988).

Early Primary-Grade Teachers.   Traditionally, the teacher's responsibility in the early primary grades has been to provide instruction in reading, writing, and arithmetic (Safford, 1989). Over the years, however, curriculum expansions have been made to include social studies, science, the arts, health, self-esteem programs, and physical education. All of these expansions have occurred without commensurate increases in instructional time. In addition, many teachers at these grade levels are under pressure to complete the book or meet specific grade-level objectives that have been selected and approved on a programwide or even statewide basis. Though they have maintained autonomy in establishing relationships with children and in selecting some of the strategies or teaching methods they will use for instruction, teachers of children at the older end of the early childhood period often experience less flexibility in deciding about curriculum or the content and skills to be taught (Lessen-Firestone, 1990).

Common Ground among All Early Childhood Teachers.   On the surface, it may seem that teachers at different levels within early childhood education are expected to carry out their jobs in very dissimilar ways. Certainly, many teachers believe this to be the case (Kostelnik, 1990). However, the reality is that all early childhood educators share many common roles. They all *provide instruction* to children, *nurture* children, *comfort* them, *offer medical assistance, keep records, work with parents,* and *cooperate* with support staff (paid or volunteer) in the organizations where they work. All *contribute to the socialization* of children in the role of student and *support* children in their ability to interact with others and understand and control their own feelings. Increasingly, early childhood personnel are expected to *inculcate moral values* of the society and try to *eliminate negative attitudes* the children might have about race, gender, age, or disabling conditions.

In considering all the demands made on early childhood educators, there is little doubt that they have responsible and demanding roles to perform. From this other issues arise such as how teachers are selected, who might be expected to do the best job, and what knowledge and behaviors characterize a well-qualified person in the field.

Preservice Education for Early Childhood Teachers.   The skills and experience that early childhood staff bring to their jobs, as in any profession, are presumed to affect the quality of their performance. Both the specific

substance of their education as well as the amount of advanced training they receive contribute to quality of performance. Educators who have specialized training in early childhood education tend to demonstrate greater responsiveness to children, increased efforts to stimulate children, promotion of children's verbal skills, encouragement of children, and more effective adult direction (Berk, 1985; Howes, 1983). Teachers who have had training in child development and learning also are more likely to use indirect guidance, be less restrictive in the classroom, and be more supportive of children's verbal expression and self-initiated activities (Berk, 1985). Other studies have indicated that teachers' more formal knowledge of child development and early education methods is correlated with children's displays of greater social and cognitive competence. These positive training effects have been found for all staff, not just head teachers (Phillips & Howes, 1987).

In an attempt to influence the content of teacher training programs, the Association of Early Childhood Education International (1983) and the NAEYC (1982) have made recommendations for the training of teachers at all levels of early childhood education. Content and skills fall within the following clusters:

Broad liberal arts education

Family life and human relations

Child development and learning

Educational philosophy

Early childhood curriculum and development

Technical study in the methods of teaching

Practical experiences with young children under appropriate supervision

Recommendations have been made that early childhood teachers have from 4 to 6 years of professional education. Often this involves some type of teacher certification or accreditation.

Certification and Accreditation of Early Childhood Teachers.   The type of certification and the competencies that are included may or may not be congruent for the training and experience needed to be optimally effective in an early childhood program. Some states provide a general elementary certificate with a broad focus, other states have a specific early childhood certification designed for the teacher of 3- to 8-year-olds, and still others provide the option of either an endorsement or a minor in early childhood for the general elementary certificate. Currently, only those teachers with specific qualifications meeting the early childhood guidelines of the National Council for Accreditation of Teacher Education (NCATE) are granted the right to teach in public elementary schools at the primary level.

There are, in addition, many early childhood professionals who have the knowledge and skills to act with effectiveness but who are not certified by their states. Because these professionals are prepared for the community-based early childhood programs, they specialize in the design of programs outside the traditional scope of public education. For example, the standards for school-age child care specify training in child development related to the age group with which the teacher works and training in program development that goes beyond academic considerations alone (Albrecht & Plantz, 1991). Conventionally trained elementary teachers who have not acquired specialized knowledge and skills in child development are less suited for working with young children than either certified or noncertified professionals who have such a background.

Similarly, alternative training programs have been designed for assistant teachers focusing on the skills they will need in daily practice. Such training may be obtained via an associate's degree or through the Child Development Associate Certification program, also known as the CDA. This latter form of training centers around teaching people specific observable competencies related to the following six goals (Perry, 1990):

1. To set up and maintain a safe and healthy learning environment
2. To advance children's physical and intellectual competence
3. To support children's social/emotional development and provide positive guidance
4. To establish positive and productive relationships with children's families
5. To ensure a well-run, purposeful program responsive to participant needs

6. To maintain a commitment to professionalism.

Continuing Education. One's training as an early childhood educator does not end upon attainment of a degree or certificate. In-service training also plays an important role in maintaining high-quality programs for young children. Such training may be delivered through support staff, consultants, specialized training, or peer coaching (NAESP, 1990). Novice teachers need support as they put into practice the knowledge and skills acquired in their preservice education. Experienced or veteran teachers, unaccustomed to the particular needs of young children and unfamiliar with the practices necessary to accommodate those needs, also require in-service support. They need intensive and sustained staff development attention as they deal with the formidable task of rebuilding classroom routines; cope with shifts in concepts, values, and beliefs that undergird teaching practices; and inevitably face anxiety about change in their professional lives (National Association of State Boards of Education, 1988). On-the-job training in some systematic form is also necessary for teacher assistants and other adult members of the teaching and learning environment so that intervention efforts may be cohesive and coordinated (Phillips & Howes, 1987).

Program Supervisors and Administrators. No matter what the size of the organization or where it is housed, the best early childhood education programs are characterized by strong administrative leadership (Mitchell et al., 1989). The early childhood supervisor's responsibilities include taking the lead in articulating the philosophy of the early childhood program and the rationale behind it, assuring the availability of appropriate curriculum and assessment materials and techniques, assembling an appropriately trained and qualified staff, and stimulating parent and community involvement in the program (NAESP, 1990, p. 43). Educational leaders also have to remain alert to incongruent practices that threaten program integrity, such as standardized testing, and take steps to rectify them.

To carry out these duties well, administrators must be knowledgeable about the early childhood teacher's role and the unique characteristics of early childhood programs. They must also be respected by and able to influence those in power positions relative to the program (e.g., board members, the superintendent, etc.) (Mitchell et al., 1989). The best way to gain such knowledge and influence is through formal preparation and experience with young children. That is why accrediting bodies such as the NAECP require that anyone directly supervising kindergarten or prekindergarten programs be a qualified early childhood specialist. The NAESP (1990) recommends that administrators responsible for supervising children between the ages of 3 and 8 have a background that includes

- course work in child development specifically covering the early childhood period,
- demonstrated knowledge of how young children learn, and
- broad expertise in instructional and management strategies specifically applicable to young children as opposed to children in general or focused on children in the middle and upper grades.

As is true for teachers, administrators must keep informed by constantly exploring new ideas and practices in early childhood education. Their role in the program is a critical one, including both leadership and support to others in an effort to create the highest quality programs for young children and their families. Implications related to the roles and qualifications of teachers and administrators in the early childhood program follow.

Implications:

1. Prekindergarten, kindergarten, and early primary teachers are all early childhood educators who require specialized knowledge and skills related to young children.
2. Early childhood programs are enhanced when program administrators have a strong background regarding young children's development and learning as well as early childhood teaching practices.
3. To remain effective, early childhood educators and program administrators must keep abreast of developments in the field throughout their careers.

SUMMARY

Early childhood education is an expanding field both in terms of the number of children served and in the conceptualization of the early childhood period. Once treated as mutually exclusive, nursery schools, child care programs, compensatory preprimary programs, kindergarten, and the early primary grades are integrating perspectives and practices to provide greater continuity for young learners. Thus, early childhood education encompasses a broad array of services developed in response to children's needs, family requirements, and community characteristics.

In an attempt to determine how best to develop particular programs for particular communities, variations in philosophy, program organization, and personnel have been assessed as to suitability and effectiveness. The four philosophical perspectives having the greatest impact on programs and eliciting the most investigative research have been the psychoanalytic, maturationist, behaviorist, and interactionist points of view. Based on these orientations, model programs have been designed, implemented, and evaluated longitudinally in an attempt to put the competition among theoretical perspectives to rest. No one model can lay claim to being the most effective overall. However, the integrative nature of the interactionist perspective holds promise for bridging the philosophical disparities that have traditionally divided the field. In addition, it seems that congruence between philosophy, goals, and activities, as well as commitment and involvement in the program by both parents and staff, are the variables that yield the most positive outcomes for children and families.

How children and adults are distributed within a program also has been scrutinized. In attempting to target instruction more efficiently, it has been traditional to group children homogeneously based on some common characteristic such as age, ability, or entry criteria for especially funded intervention. Unfortunately, homogeneity has not proven to be the most effective means of constructing classroom groups. The benefits of heterogeneous grouping appear to be much stronger. Furthermore, examinations of the effects of class size and the ratio of children to adults indicate that small class size and a relatively small ratio of children to adults result in greater learning among children during the early childhood period.

Well-trained personnel are another key element in creating effective early childhood programs. Qualified staff may emerge from several different avenues, but all must have a strong background in child development and learning, an understanding of early childhood teaching practices, and skills in working with parents. Additionally, teachers and administrators must remain current in the field throughout their professional involvement with children.

In reviewing these known facts about early childhood education, it seems obvious that the field is evolving toward a more unified perspective that crosses traditional program boundaries. That perspective has centered around the notion of providing high-quality educational programs to young children. "High-quality programs are ones that meet the needs of and promote the physical, social, emotional, and cognitive development of the children and adults—parents, staff, and administrators—who are involved in the program" (NAEYC, 1984a, p. 7). In trying to describe how to achieve high-quality programs, educators have focused on the concept of developmentally appropriate programs. The remainder of this book is devoted to exploring what it means to be developmentally appropriate. In chapter 2, a definition of developmentally appropriate programs and the rationale that drives decision making in such programs is described. Chapters 3 through 10 specify sample goals for children and suggested strategies and activities educators might use to reach those goals. The remainder of the book, chapters 11 through 17, focuses on methods of practical implementation required to enact developmentally appropriate early childhood programs on a day-to-day basis.

CHAPTER 2

Developmentally Appropriate Programs for Young Children: Definitions, Principles, and Myths

The children were sitting with their teacher in a circle. They had been studying dinosaurs and were now deeply involved in the subject of paleontology.

Teacher:	*"How did those dinosaur bones get down there in the ground?"*
Eze:	*"They died in the ground. The dinosaurs laid down in the mud, and then they just died in the ground."*
Chris:	*"Quicksand—it was quicksand that got 'em."*
Carlos:	*"Somebody put the bones there; I think it was the sandman."*
Sarah:	*"There was a big hole and the dinosaurs fell in and they got all buried up."*
Nathan:	*"After the dinosaurs died, then the people came and buried up the bones."*
Teacher:	*"It sounds like you know a lot about dinosaurs and how they became fossils. Remember, there were no people alive when the dinosaurs were on earth."*
Nathan:	*"Oh, yeah. That's right. That's right. I know! It was a front-end loader. That's it—a front-end loader buried 'em but it didn't have no driver."*

Conversations like these reveal children's efforts to grasp new concepts: What is a fossil? What do bones found in the ground have to do with huge creatures who lived long, long ago? Children build concepts by extracting bits of information from their experiences. Gradually, over time, they create linkages among the bits, combining them to create new ideas. Sometimes, as was true for Nathan, they readjust their thinking to accommodate new information that doesn't fit their old notions.

Listening to the children, one cannot help but notice the parallels between their efforts to further their conceptual understandings and the struggle taking place for adults within education circles to do the same. The concept educators are trying to formulate is that of "developmentally appropriate programs" for children from birth through 8 years of age. We are developing this concept just the way children do—bit by bit,

not all at once—building on what we know and what we are learning. Our real-life experiences with children and families, as well as theory and research, all contribute to our increasing store of knowledge. As the years go by we are expanding our breadth of understanding and our level of sophistication about what we mean when we say "developmentally appropriate."

Simultaneously, we keep readjusting our ideas to accommodate new information as it becomes available. Sometimes this is a highly personal process, as when individuals reflect on their work with children. Sometimes it involves a group effort, as happens when several practitioners from the same community, center, or school get together to examine the early childhood programs for which they are responsible. And on occasion, professional organizations such as the National Association for the Education of Young Children (NAEYC), the National Association of Elementary School Principals (NAESP), and the National Association of State Boards of Education (NASBE), have pooled their collective wisdom to develop position papers on the subject. Regardless of who is thinking about it or how it is being considered, anyone contemplating what it means to be involved in developmentally appropriate programs must first create a working definition of *developmentally appropriate*. That, too, is where we shall begin.

WHAT DOES IT MEAN TO BE DEVELOPMENTALLY APPROPRIATE?

In reviewing the wealth of material currently available describing individuals' and groups' perceptions of developmentally appropriate programs, it becomes clear that no two are exactly the same (Bredekamp, 1987, 1991; Elkind, 1989; Katz, Rath, & Torres, 1987; Michigan Department of Education, 1986; Minnesota Department of Education, 1989; NAESP, 1990; Peck, McCaig, & Sapp, 1988). However, three principles are common to all:

1. Developmentally appropriate means taking into account what is known about how young children develop and learn and match-

ing that to the content and strategies they encounter in early childhood programs.

2. Developmentally appropriate means approaching children as individuals, not as a cohort group.
3. Developmentally appropriate means treating children with respect—understanding children's changing capacities and having faith in children's continuing capacity to change.

In other words, we must first think about what children are like and then develop activities, routines, and expectations that accommodate and complement those characteristics. In addition, we must know more than a few descriptive facts about a child, such as birthdate and gender, to design meaningful educational programs. We have to look at children within the context of their family, culture, community, and past experience to create age-appropriate as well as individually appropriate living and learning environments. Finally, we must recognize the unique ways in which children are children and not simply miniature adults. Experiences and outcomes planned for children should reflect the notion that childhood is a time of life qualitatively different from adulthood.

EMPIRICAL SUPPORT FOR DEVELOPMENTALLY APPROPRIATE PROGRAMS

What began as a feeling for many people is becoming a documented reality. Flexible curriculum models that incorporate principles of child development and learning into their philosophies and practices are likely to produce long-term gains in children's intellectual development, social and emotional skills, and life-coping capabilities (Peck et al., 1988). Children's curiosity, creativity, and independence are also enhanced (Walberg, 1984). For instance, children participating in developmentally appropriate reading programs (ones that are process oriented and individualized) demonstrate better independent listening comprehension, better understanding of what they have read, and a greater ability to apply and generalize knowledge in problem-solving situations (Palincsar & Brown, 1989). Similar results have been reported for children from varying backgrounds, including youngsters described as likely to have difficulties learning to read (Klein, 1981).

Similarly, when compared with children taught mathematics via traditional methods, children in developmentally appropriate classrooms have been found to be more involved in the process of understanding mathematics. They tend to display a better grasp of concepts and are more adept in generalizing computation skills across a variety of circumstances (Nicholls, Cobb, Wood, Yackel, & Patashnik, 1991). Interestingly, these children also have been found to know significantly more number facts than children who endure drills and ditto-style practice, even when the latter's teachers spend twice as much time on the material (Peterson, Fennema, & Carpenter, in press).

Social learning also shows positive influences as a result of teacher application of developmentally appropriate practices. Children who are the recipients of such practices exhibit better social problem-solving skills and more cooperative behaviors than their counterparts in more traditional classrooms (Bellemere, 1991; Fry & Addington, 1984).

A review of research recently presented at the National Forum on the Future of Children and Families (1991) suggests that developmentally appropriate practices are successful with children of varying ages and backgrounds. However, they may be particularly powerful tools when used with children traditionally labeled "poor achievers." Newman and Church (1990) suggest that children who have difficulties in school, no matter the reason, "are the very ones who benefit most from a learning context that encourages them to take risks and to experiment. For so many of these children, their problems have been exacerbated by the fragmented, right-answer skills-based instruction they've been receiving. Many of these children have stopped believing they can learn" (p. 23). Within a developmentally appropriate learning environment, such students perceive themselves as successful learners for the first time.

Related to the preceding observation, data show that children whose teachers enact developmentally appropriate practices exhibit significantly fewer stress behaviors than children whose teachers rely on strategies described as developmentally inappropriate (Burts, Hart, Charlesworth, & Kirk, 1990). Although children in the former group are not completely stress-free, the number of incidents and the total amount of stress they display is far less than that exhibited by children whose time in school is dominated by whole-group instruction, paper-pencil tasks, and oral drills. Not too surprisingly, children's self-esteem is influenced for the better when teachers treat them in ways congruent with developmentally appropriate practice (Curry & Johnson, 1990; Fry & Addington, 1984). Student attitudes toward school and teachers are apt to be more favorable as well (Walberg, 1984).

Longitudinal studies of the past decade reveal that children in highly academic preschool and lower elementary settings demonstrate early gains in mechanical skills such as reciting letter sounds and number facts when compared to children from developmentally appropriate programs. However, by the middle elementary grades these gains disappear and both groups perform equally well, academically. Unfortunately, by this time children subjected to rigid instructional practices exhibit more negative social skills and aberrant behaviors than youngsters not subjected to these conditions (McKee, 1991; Schweinhart, Weikart, & Larner, 1986). In the long run, researchers report that developmentally appropriate preschool programs produce children who continue into their teens to have high achievement in language, reading, and arithmetic (Schweinhart & Weikart, 1980). Such effects result in not only children's improved scholastic performance but also lower delinquency and unemployment rates for those youngsters in later adolescence (Schweinhart et al., 1986).

Equally positive findings are also coming in at the elementary level. For instance, a 5-year study of traditional versus developmentally appropriate classrooms has been conducted in the Scarborough, Maine, public school district. Evaluators report that the children involved in developmentally appropriate classrooms outshine their peers in more traditional classes in many ways (Bellemere, 1991). Teacher observations reveal that children in the former group are highly cooperative, confident, self-motivated learners. They display excellent problem-solving and decision-making skills and are flexible in adapting learning strategies across settings and situations. Anecdotal records and portfolio materials support the conclusion that these youngsters are highly interested in reading, fluent in their expressive writing, and knowledgeable of the resources available to them for gathering information and finding answers (including, but going beyond, asking the teacher). Parents report that children in the developmentally appropriate classes are more apt to be excited about reading and writing and better able to make connections between what they are learning in school and the real-life problems they encounter at home and in the community.

Standardized tests given at the end of second grade elicited scores that correspond to these favorable outcomes. Children in both the traditional and developmentally appropriate classrooms scored equally well in general reading skills. However, while traditional classes yielded students who scored higher on tests of spelling and reading mechanics in isolation, youngsters in the developmentally appropriate groups scored significantly higher in terms of vocabulary, reading comprehension, expressive language, and reading and writing mechanics in context. Likewise, the two groups showed similar scores in overall mathematic skill. Children participating under developmentally appropriate conditions, however, scored significantly higher in conceptual understanding and problem-solving skills than pupils not assigned to those kinds of classrooms.

A statewide assessment of fourth graders (now in their 5th year of developmentally appropriate practice) indicated that the positive second-grade trends continued. In addition, children in developmentally appropriate classes scored significantly higher in reasoning and problem-solving skills than did children experiencing more traditional teaching practices.

Perhaps the most telling data of all involved children's self-assessments of their progress and themselves as students. Children in developmentally appropriate classrooms reported great enthusiasm for school and high involvement in the learning process. That kind of excitement is in contrast to a second grader in another district who was overheard to tell a kindergartner angrily, "Stay in kindergarten! Don't go to first grade. First and second grade is awful. All

Children in developmentally appropriate classrooms are excited about school and eager to learn.

we do is work, work, work. We never get outta our seats. It's awful!" (McKee, 1986, p. 24).

The favorable findings associated with developmentally appropriate programs offer a strong empirical rationale for schools to adopt a corresponding philosophy. However, to be truly effective, that philosophy must be reflected in the curriculum children experience each day.

THE RELATIONSHIP BETWEEN A DEVELOPMENTALLY APPROPRIATE PHILOSOPHY AND CURRICULUM DESIGN

Curriculum can be conceived as having three sequential components: *antecedents, transactions,* and *outcomes* (Goodwin & Driscoll, 1980; Stake, 1967). Antecedents are the conditions existing prior to the operation of the program. In early childhood programs, antecedents involve what the children bring with them to the classroom: their culture and family background, the influences of their community, prior experiences and knowledge, and the ways in which they develop and learn. Transactions are the ac-

tivities that constitute the program. As such, they encompass all the processes that go on inside of it: lessons, routines, adult-child interactions, and children's interactions with one another. Outcomes consist of the effects of the program. These include intellectual, behavioral, and attitudinal outcomes, anticipated as well as unintended effects. Considering all three components is essential to each phase of program installation: design, implementation, and evaluation (Provus, 1972). Taken altogether, they constitute a comprehensive overview of the many factors involved in educational programming. To overlook one or more of these components leads to faulty decision making because potential variables and influences are not adequately considered.

Unfortunately, in many schools the emphasis is on only one of these—outcomes. For instance, a typical approach to program design is for committees to create "curriculum guides," usually for individual strands of the curriculum such as science or mathematics. These guides involve a compilation of objectives children are expected to achieve at each grade level, with no mention of antecedents or processes. Consider-

TABLE 2.1
The Effect of Addressing Outcomes First in Designing Early Childhood Curriculum

Step 1: Focus on Outcomes—Develop goals via task analysis. This analysis usually occurs in a "top-down" fashion with outcomes for each level dictated by what is expected at the next higher level.
Step 2: Focus on Transactions—Generate teaching strategies that support the stated outcomes.
Step 3: Focus on Antecedents—Identify what learner characteristics best predict success relative to the teaching practices chosen and the expected outcomes. Screen children for these characteristics and track them accordingly.

Outcomes	Transactions	Antecedents
Example 1:		**Children must be:**
Each preschooler must recite his or her telephone number correctly to proceed through kindergarten screening into "regular" kindergarten.	The teacher says the numbers aloud one at a time; the children echo in response. The teacher recites each child's telephone number two numbers at a time; the child echoes in response. The teacher says each child's telephone number; children raise their hands when they recognize their number.	passive, quiet, attentive, auditory learners.
Example 2:		**Children must be:**
Kindergarten children must identify and name 20 consonant sounds and 5 short vowel sounds to proceed into the first grade.	The teacher points to a letter and says the sound; the children echo the sound. The teacher points to a picture in which the sound is depicted; the children say the sound. The children circle all the letters that correspond to a certain sound. The children trace dot-to-dot representations of letters that correspond to a particular sound. The children circle all the pictures on a page that begin with a given sound. The teacher says a series of sounds, children touch their noses when they hear a particular one.	passive, attentive, visual learners able to control a writing tool.

ation of how the objectives relate to or impact other facets of the curriculum are usually ignored. Often, too, the objectives cited are simply a reiteration of the scope and sequence put forth by a particular textbook series (Kostelnik, 1990). Because of a commercial desire for universal applicability, publisher-based objectives fail to take into account the characteristics of particular learners in specific classrooms or communities. For instance, a recent review of several kindergarten basal manuals revealed that none of those examined helped kindergarten teachers provide instruction to children based on their individual needs (Durkin, 1990). Expected outcomes were the same for all participants, and it was assumed that children would move from objective to objective en masse.

Teachers, handed a curriculum guide in which outcomes are the only identified curriculum component, get the message that program effects are the sole variable to consider in selecting teaching practices. The same is true for districts in which such guides are not center stage but the outcomes on the report card serve the same purpose. This impression is further reinforced when schools use end-of-unit test scores and grade-level achievement tests as the primary measures of program effectiveness. In such cases, teachers "teach to the test" or "teach to the card" regardless of how well the content and skills demanded suit individual children in their classes.

When outcomes are emphasized to the exclusion of the other two curriculum components in these ways, they ultimately drive the entire program. That is, outcomes determine the processes teachers enact as well as the antecedents necessary for children to experience success in school (see Table 2.1).

Early childhood programs that focus on goals alone and those that begin program development at the outcome end of the sequence make two mistakes: they are incomplete in their conception, and they are formulated in a backward fashion. This leads to programs that are unresponsive to differences among children. Youngsters who fit the antecedents required by the outcomes achieve success; those whose behavior, knowledge, and attitudes are incongruent do not. A typical programmatic response to the mismatch between children's characteristics and program needs is for children to be siphoned off into special classes in the hope that their performance will be influenced in the desired direction. Another is to withhold services or retain children in a grade in the belief that the following year a better match will be achieved. Either way, children are expected to fit a predetermined mold that often fails to reflect their needs and best interests. Such programs are by their very nature developmentally inappropriate.

A more effective result occurs when educators consider all three curriculum components and design curriculum by thinking about relevant antecedents first (see Table 2.2). As evidenced by the sequence depicted in Table 2.2, the task of determining appropriate early childhood curriculum hinges on understanding the nature of children. Thus, the most appropriate curriculum results when planners have thorough knowledge of child development and learning (Leeper, Witherspoon, & Day, 1984; Williams, 1987). This kind of knowledge is also a key ingredient in program implementation.

THE EDUCATOR'S NEED TO KNOW

The need for educators to have specialized knowledge about child development and learning is well established in the literature (Bredekamp, 1986; Elkind, 1989; Goffin, 1989; NAEYC, 1986; Peters & Kostelnik, 1981; Ruopp, Travers, Glantz, & Coelen, 1979). Studies consistently find that adults who have such knowledge are better equipped and more likely to engage in developmentally appropriate practices (Snider & Fu, 1990). Instead of treating their interactions with children as wholly intuitive, they bring factual information to bear on how they think about children and how they respond to them in the classroom. For instance, understanding child development provides practitioners with insights into student behavior and helps adults better grasp the context within which those behaviors occur. Teachers' notions of what constitutes normal child behaviors are expanded. They are more likely to accept typical variations among children as well as accurately recognize potentially problematic conditions that may require specialized intervention (Kostelnik et al., in press). Familiarity with child development

TABLE 2.2
The Effect of Addressing Antecedents First in Designing Early Childhood Curriculum

Step 1: Focus on Antecedents — Identify general characteristics that describe how children develop and learn.

Step 2: Focus on Transactions — Generate teaching strategies that match and support child development and learning.

Step 3: Focus on Outcomes — Identify long-range outcomes that build on antecedent behavior and incorporate community and societal expectations.

Antecedents	Transactions	Outcomes
Example 1:	**The teacher:**	
Children are active learners.	gives children opportunities for gross motor activities each day.	Children engage in meaningful activity.
	includes a free-choice period in the daily schedule during which children can move about the room freely.	
	creates a daily schedule in which quiet, inactive times are followed by longer, more active periods.	
	keeps inactive segments of the day short.	
Example 2:	**The teacher:**	
Children are curious.	builds activities around children's interests.	Children develop problem-solving skills and the disposition of inquisitiveness.
	provides many chances for children to explore materials and concepts.	
	encourages children to pose problems and investigate solutions.	

offers clues to practitioners about the order in which activities might be presented to children and the degree of developmental readiness necessary for children to achieve program goals (Spodek, 1986). Development also provides one standard by which programs can assess their goals for children. Expectations that exceed the typical developmental range for children of a certain age in relation to particular content and skills can be modified using child development as a guide.

Similar benefits accrue when educators have a strong background in how children learn. Although we are far from having unanimous agreement on how learning takes place, there is increasing evidence that children in the 3- to 8-year age range think and acquire knowledge in ways that differ significantly from older children and adults (DeVries & Kohlberg, 1987; Kamii, 1985; Siegler, 1991; Sulzby & Barnhart, 1990). Reviewing both theory and research, teachers and administrators can develop informed beliefs relative to young children's learning, which leads to educational judgments that in turn influence the physical environment of the classroom and school, how children are taught, what content and processes are valued, and how program effectiveness will be assessed.

Although awareness of child development and learning principles alone are not sufficient to create effective early childhood programs, they serve as the cornerstone upon which such efforts build. With this in mind, let us now turn our attention to basic principles of child development and learning and the implications such principles have for early childhood programs.

PRINCIPLES OF CHILD DEVELOPMENT

Children Develop Holistically

Aesthetic, cognitive, emotional, language, social, and physical development are all interrelated. No *one* facet of development exists independent from the others, nor is any *one* most valuable. For example, adults observing children engaged in a vigorous game of dodgeball might categorize their activity as purely physical. Yet the children's ability to play the game is also influenced by other developmental processes:

- *Aesthetic*—appreciating the grace of another player's movements, enjoying the rhythm of the game
- *Cognitive*—figuring out the sequence in which the game is played, determining how many children can fit in the space available, remembering who has had a chance to be it and who has not had a turn, analyzing the best angle for hitting a fleeing player
- *Emotional*—coping with the disappointment of being out, accepting compliments and criticism from other players, expressing anger over a disputed call
- *Language*—determining what "scripts" to use to get into the game or out of it, using words to describe the rules, responding to the teacher's directions
- *Social*—negotiating the rules of the games, signaling others about one's desire to have a turn, making way for a new player, working out disagreements over boundaries and teams

Likewise, reading and computing not only are intellectual functions; they have social, emotional, aesthetic, language, and physical elements as well. The same is true for any task in which children engage. Social processes shape cognitive ones, cognitive processes promote or restrict social capabilities, physical processes influence language and cognition, and so on. Consequently, when thinking about children, it is best to remember that they are integrated human beings whose development is enhanced when educators concern themselves with all aspects of their development (Santrock, 1990). This orientation is referred to as focusing on the "whole child" (Hendrick, 1990; McKee, 1991).

In support of the whole child philosophy, it has been found that serious problems arise when one facet of development is emphasized to the exclusion of all others. For instance, infants who receive adequate physical care but whose social and emotional needs are unmet fail to thrive. Similarly, as children reach school age, those who participate in classrooms in which academic achievement is the only priority suffer from lack of attention to social and emotional development (Spodek, 1986). For some of these children, whose limited social skills lead to rejection by peers, the devastating effects are long lasting. Such youngsters are more likely to engage in delinquent acts or succumb to mental health problems (Bierman, 1987; Parker & Asher, 1987).

Equally negative effects result when intellectual skills are promoted to the detriment of physical development. Children exhibit increasingly poor fitness and health-related behaviors over time (Reuschlein & Haubenstricker, 1985). This state of being is problematic both in the short term (children fail to develop optimal cardiovascular functioning, physical strength, endurance, and physical skills) and in the long run (children grow up to be sedentary adults at risk for heart disease and other physical ailments). So important is the notion of whole child teaching that in early childhood education, the curriculum and the whole child tend to be seen as indivisible (Williams, 1987). This has important implications for early childhood programs.

Implications:

1. Activities and routines are designed so that all aspects of child development are addressed each day. A sample of developmental processes associated with whole child learning is offered in Table 2.3.

TABLE 2.3
Developmental Facets of Whole Child Learning

Aesthetic	Affective	Cognitive
Developing sensory awareness	Developing a positive, realistic	Developing thinking processes
Imagining and visualizing	self-concept	(observing, recalling,
Exploring	Accepting and expressing	comparing, patterning,
Creating	emotions in socially	classifying, generalizing,
Responding	appropriate ways	integrating and evaluating)
Interpreting	Coping with change	Constructing knowledge
Developing critical awareness	Developing decision-making	Developing memory skills
Expressing and representing	skills	Acquiring facts
through a variety of forms	Accepting challenge	
	Developing independence	
	Feeling pride in	
	accomplishments	
	Increasing instrumental know-	
	how	
	Enjoying living and learning	

Adapted from *Kindergarten Curriculum Guide and Resource Book*, 1985, Victoria, British Columbia: Ministry of Education; and *Teaching Young Children Using Themes*, M. Kostelnik (Ed.), 1991, Glenview, IL: Scott-Foresman.

2. Educators think of subject matter (e.g., spelling or reading) in terms of how it supports child development, not simply as an end in and of itself. Thus, reading is viewed as an element of language development. As such, it is considered relative to listening, speaking, and writing, not in isolation. Likewise, handwriting is treated as a product of fine motor development and visual perception. Instructional strategies and expectations for children are created in that context.

3. Consideration is given to how time is allocated in the day. Since all facets of child development are equally important, huge amounts of time are not devoted to some areas (e.g., reading or art and crafts) to the preclusion of others (e.g., science or social studies, problem-solving activities or games).

4. Integration of experience rather than segmentation is emphasized. This includes integration across developmental domains, subject matter, and traditional lines of responsibility. For example, children participate in activities that incorporate language, physical, and social processes simultaneously. They have experiences that combine reading and science and math. The adults with whom they come in contact often work in teams. The responsibility for creating an effective learning environment is shared among students, teachers, specialists, administrators, and parents.

Child Development Follows a Normative Sequence

Development is sequential, and changes over time occur in an orderly fashion. Children around the world share remarkably similar patterns of development across all domains. Normative sequences have been found relative to locomotion; use of the hands; language, social, and personality development; graphic and symbolic representation; problem solving; logical-mathematical understanding; and moral development (Smart & Smart, 1982; Sroufe & Cooper, 1988). For instance, in order to move from place to place, a child first learns to lift his or her head, then sit up, then stand with assistance, then crawl, then stand unassisted, then walk, then run. Similarly, children's earliest attempts at putting pencil or marker to paper in order to write a message is to create scribbles. In cultures in which the alphabet is used, scribbles gradually give way to linear repetitive movements, then to letterlike forms,

Language	Physical	Social
Responding and communicating through listening, speaking, writing, and reading Experimenting with language Representing through language	Developing competence in using large and small muscles Taking care of and respecting one's body Being aware of and practicing good nutrition habits Developing physical fitness Appreciating and enjoying human movement	Developing internal behavior controls Helping Cooperating Respecting and accepting others Learning from others Seeking and giving companionship Developing friendships Becoming a responsible citizen Appreciating and respecting the cultural identity and heritage of others Respecting the environment

then to single consonants representing entire words, then to combinations of letters in phonetic attempts at spelling, until eventually more and more standard spelling is used.

Such changes are often uneven rather than smooth. Individual children may spend more or less time involved in a certain behavior; they may move forward a bit, back a little, then forward again. Some children may even skip some phases that are less relevant to their circumstances. However, the sequences tend to remain predictable, with the increments for each one emerging in the same order. An understanding of the importance of normative sequences holds certain implications for early childhood professionals.

Implications:

1. Reading about and observing young children carefully helps educators identify various normative sequences.
2. A knowledge of developmental sequences is used to figure out how to challenge youngsters appropriately in the classroom and to determine reasonable expectations for individual students.
3. Teachers avoid unduly accelerating children's progress through certain normative

sequences such as those associated with spelling, number recognition, or handwriting.
4. An ability to articulate normative sequences to others helps those persons better understand child development and how the practices and goals of the developmentally appropriate classroom support children's learning.

Child Development Proceeds at Varying Rates within and among Children

Every child develops according to his or her own "biological clock" (McKee, 1991). No two children are exactly alike. Differences in development manifest themselves in two ways: intrapersonally and interpersonally.

Within every individual, various facets of development are dominant at different times throughout childhood. For instance, infancy is a time of rapid physical growth; although language development also is progressing, it is at a relatively slow pace. The same trends reverse themselves as children enter the preschool and elementary years; physical growth slows down, while simultaneously children make spectacular strides in using language. These are examples of *intrapersonal* variations in development. Such internal variations explain why the same child may be easily moved to tears, have difficulty with verbal expression, climb nimbly to the highest part of the jungle gym, recite the alphabet backward, and have moderate success cutting with scissors. Such unevenness in development is to be expected.

Interpersonal variations in rates also occur. Even though the normative sequences still apply, the pace at which youngsters move through them differs. Hence, children the exact same age may exhibit behaviors and understandings quite unlike one another. And, if one were to chart the normal development of an entire classroom of children, the time at which each child reached certain milestones would vary considerably. For instance, one could expect some first graders to come to school in September reading words and phrases. Other children might just be starting to make the association between various letters and sounds. At the same time, certain children in the class may group objects by function only,

others by more than one property at a time, and still others may be exploring how to regroup objects in different ways. All of these variations are normal, and similar differences could be found across all domains.

Readers familiar with age-level expectations or norms may be wondering how those correspond to the variation-in-rates principle. Profiles of typical age expectations for certain skills such as walking, speaking, counting, and participating in games are commonly available for the early childhood years. However, readers are cautioned that the ages identified do not represent exact points in time. Such figures are based on averages. So, even though skipping may be listed at age 6, sometimes this capacity emerges later, say, at age 8, while occasionally it can be seen as early as age 5. Norms guide us in understanding the order in which certain behaviors appear and approximately when they may occur. They are not meant to be used as absolute standards or rigid timetables for growth and development.

These second graders share the same birthday but vary in their rates of physical, language, cognitive, and socioemotional development.

There is always a range of variation in human development. Also, when a milestone is achieved it is not necessarily predictive of proficiency over time. By age 10, there may be little difference between children who began skipping at 5 and those who mastered this skill later. Likewise, children who began talking early in their 2nd year do not necessarily talk more or less or with greater or lesser skill than youngsters for whom age 30 months marked the beginning of fluent verbal communication.

A vivid example of how variations in rates of development continue throughout the school years is provided in Table 2.4. This chart depicts differences in children's thinking abilities as established through scientific studies of human brain growth and cognitive functioning. The headings at the top of the figure correspond to stages of cognition as described by Jean Piaget, each representing a shift in children's intellectual capacities. (Readers unfamiliar with these stages are referred to chap. 5, "The Cognitive Domain," for a summary of each stage.) As the reader can see, it is normal for different children the same age to be functioning at different levels of cognitive understanding. Additionally, variations in rates actually become more spread out as children mature. Finally, maturity comes at different times for different people. Not all children will move into the most advanced stages of cognitive functioning at the same time. Some children will achieve cognitive maturity in adolescence; others will do so much later. Variations like these are typical in all areas of development. Understanding the wide-ranging variations among children is a key consideration in the creation of developmentally appropriate educational programs.

Implications:

1. Children in early education classrooms exhibit a wide range of abilities.
2. Professionals avoid focusing on a single index (e.g., IQ, reading test score, child's ability to draw a man, etc.) as a measure of children's overall potential or achievement.
3. Careful observations of children uncover patterns of behavior for individual children

TABLE 2.4
Percentage Distribution of Thinking Abilities in Children by Piagetian Developmental Stages

Child's Age (Years)	Preoperational Thinking	Onset of Concrete Operational Thinking	Achievement of Mature Concrete Operational Thinking	Onset of Formal Operational Thinking	Achievement of Formal Operational Thinking
5	85%	15%			
6	60	35	5%		
7	35	55	10		
8	25	55	20		
9	15	55	30		
10	12	52	35	1%	
11	6	49	40	5	
12	5	32	51	12	
13	2	34	44	14	6%
14	1	32	43	15	9
15	1	14	53	19	13
16	1	15	54	17	13
17	3	19	47	19	12
18	1	15	50	15	19

Adapted with permission from "Brain Growth and Cognitive Functioning," by H. Epstein, Fall 1979, *Colorado Journal of Educational Research*, p. 19.

within various developmental domains. Practitioners use this knowledge to individualize their instruction rather than teach all children the same thing in the same way at the same time.

4. A daily schedule is helpful in which children have opportunities to pursue activities at their own pace, rather than being required to rotate from activity to activity on a predetermined schedule. Educators may adjust or change their plans to meet the current needs of individuals in the group.

5. Developmental norms are not used as rigid standards against which children are labeled "ahead" or "behind" others in the group.

6. Classroom activities that encompass multiple learning objectives versus a single desired outcome allow children more than one opportunity to be challenged and to experience success.

7. Teachers repeat activities more than once during the year so that children can gain different benefits from the activity according to their changing needs and capabilities throughout the year.

8. Parents and colleagues may need assistance in recognizing children's individual patterns of progress rather than simply comparing children with others in the class.

Development Is Epigenic

Development is based on a foundation; past, present, and future are related and build on each other in succession. New capabilities and understandings arise out of and elaborate on what is already there. This process is called *epigenesis.* The idea that children develop a sense of independence only after having established an adequate sense of trust illustrates the epigenic principle. So, too, do the facts that children's writing evolves from scribbling, that expressive language is founded on earlier babblings, and that children's understanding of numbers is based on their first achieving such milestones as object permanence and one-to-one correspondence. In all of these instances, certain developmental threads are carried forward over time, providing continuity from one phase of development to the next. The implications of epigenesis for practitioners are obvious but essential.

Implications:

1. Interacting with children and observing them carefully reveals what they know and can do.
2. Instruction is planned based on each child's level of performance and understanding.
3. Ample opportunities are available for children to explore and practice what they have learned prior to expecting them to learn something new.
4. The teacher helps children make connections between new and past experiences and support their progress toward more elaborate concepts or skills as they exhibit interest, mastery, and understanding.
5. Concepts and skills are not addressed in isolation or out of a context relative to children's experiences.
6. Children will not exhibit behaviors and understandings that are far beyond the current developmental foundations on which they are building.

Development Has Both Cumulative and Delayed Effects

Beginning at birth, children accumulate a history of repeated, frequent experiences that may have positive or negative effects on their development depending on the circumstances. How this happens is illustrated by infants who usually have their needs met and so develop a sense of trust in themselves and in the world. Youngsters whose needs are often ignored or thwarted develop mistrust. These outcomes result from not one or two incidents but rather a long-term pattern of interactions that children come to view as typical. Consequently, children who occasionally see a violent television program may not experience long-term deleterious effects. However, children who spend hours, weeks, and years watching violence depicted on television eventually demonstrate increased levels of aggression in their daily interactions (Friedrich & Stein, 1973; McHan, 1986). Likewise, when schoolchildren frequently receive tangible rewards, such as stickers or treats, for complying with school rules, they come to rely on these kinds of external behavioral controls to guide their actions. Efforts to instill more positive internal feelings of social responsibility meet with increased resistance (Kostelnik et al., in press). Once this occurs, such cumulative effects are difficult to reverse.

Most recently, Lillian Katz (1987; Katz & Chard, 1989) has made an eloquent case for considering the long-term negative effects of such traditional school practices as flash-card drills and daily worksheet sessions. She points out that the sporadic use of such techniques may be harmless. However, the cumulative result for children who receive a steady diet of such experiences seems to be lack of confidence in their intellectual abilities and an erosion of inquiry and problem-solving strategies. Her concerns are echoed by other educators who fear that traditional practices such as these undermine children's conceptual development, participatory skills, grasp of essential meanings, breadth of knowledge, and interest in school (Cummings, 1991a; Kamii, 1985; Parker, 1991; Steinberg, 1990).

Development not only is the result of cumulative influences but can also trigger delayed effects. That is, early experiences may influence children's functioning in ways that only become obvious later in life (Radke-Yarrow, 1987). For instance, some children of abusive parents may appear remarkably well adjusted while growing up yet experience serious mental health problems in adolescence and adulthood as a result of their tumultuous past (Ney, 1988). In a similar vein, the short-term outcomes of school retention may appear to have positive results for a particular child. However, a line of evidence extending back more than 50 years reveals that for many children, the eventual aftermath of retention is delayed progress in reading, decreased motivation to achieve, and an increased tendency to drop out of school prior to high school graduation (Doyle, 1989).

Implications:

1. Long-term goals are as valuable as short-term outcomes. Expectations for children are considered relative to ultimate program aims (e.g., increased literacy) and not simply how they support children's preparation for the subsequent grade (e.g., knowing 10 prescribed sight words).
2. Methods match aims. For instance, if a curricular goal is to help children develop self-control, then school personnel take the time to reason with children and teach them alternate ways to meet their needs. Short-term strategies such as rewards and punishments that get children to comply but keep them dependent on adult controls are not the sole strategies used. In this way, immediate instructional strategies that actually undermine long-term goals are discovered, supplemented, or replaced.
3. Longitudinal studies of children in the school system, focusing on the extent to which conceptual learning and children's motivation to learn are enhanced, are conducted.
4. Developmentally appropriate practices are explained to parents, colleagues, and decision makers in terms of how they support children's learning over the life span.

There Are Optimal Periods of Child Development

Throughout the early childhood years, there are opportune times during which significant changes occur in children's development. These changes are related to complex interactions between children's internal structures of body and mind and their experiences with the physical and social environment. During optimal periods, children are more receptive to both positive and negative environmental influences than at other times (McKee, 1991). Outside those parameters, it is of little value to pressure children toward cognitive, emotional, social, or physical functioning that structure does not allow. Conversely, if children are denied the kinds of experiences that enhance development at an optimal time, they may be unmotivated or unable to reach potential later in life without expending inordinate amounts of energy.

As one example, preschoolers and children in the early elementary grades are biologically inclined to develop fundamental motor skills such as catching, throwing, hopping, and running that they can later combine into more complex skills. During this phase of their lives, most children are open to instruction and willing to spend much time engaged in physical activity, thereby increasing their skills. However, youngsters for whom such opportunities are unavailable become less willing to initiate learning and practicing fundamental motor skills in the later elementary grades. By middle childhood, many conclude that they do not possess the talent necessary to succeed. Lack of skill and reluctance form a proficiency barrier that causes children to shy away from further involvement in physical activities and games. The cumulative effects of these reactions often last a lifetime. This makes the early childhood years an optimal period for children's achievement of motor proficiency (Haubenstricker, 1991). It is then that children's basic attitudes and skills related to their physical selves are either enhanced or discouraged.

There is increasing evidence that early childhood marks an optimal period for a variety of developmentally based processes and capacities (Hendrick, 1992; Katz and Chard, 1989; McKee, 1991). In addition to motor skills proficiency, some of these include the following:

Prosocial attitudes and behaviors

Communicative competence

Affiliation skills

Self-esteem

General problem-solving strategies

Logical-mathematical thought processes

Coping strategies

Emergent literacy

Aesthetic awareness

Attitudes toward authority and rules

Attitudes toward work

Attitudes toward oneself as a learner

This list is not meant to be exclusive or exhaustive but to give the reader an idea of the importance of the early childhood years and areas that deserve particular attention in early childhood education. The reader may also note that the period of early childhood is *not* identified as an optimal time for the development of isolated academic skills.

Implications:

1. The principle of optimal periods of development is reflected in instructional programs in which the processes and capacities mentioned here are explicitly addressed in ways that enhance children's development.

2. Educators should be able to articulate to others the critical nature of the early childhood years in relation to all aspects of child development.

PRINCIPLES OF CHILDHOOD LEARNING

Children Are Active Learners

When we say children are active, it is important to recognize the multidimensional nature of their activity. First, young children are motoric beings. They are genetically programmed to reach out, pull up, stand upright, move forward, move about (Haubenstricker, 1991). As children move, they seek stimulation, which thereby increases their opportunities for learning.

Second, children use their whole bodies as instruments of learning, taking in data through all their senses. Young children are compelled to taste, touch, hear, look at, and smell objects and spaces in order to find out about them—what their properties are, how they function, how they fit in with the rest of the world. It is in this way that children connect thought with action.

Third, children are active participants in their own experiences. They are not empty vessels passively waiting to be "filled up" with information and experiences determined by others (Bredekamp, 1991; Sroufe & Cooper, 1988). On the contrary, they energetically seek ways to achieve their maximum potential in both structure and function. Left to their own devices, children explore, learn, and discover (Mussen et al., 1990). In addition, if the usual avenues are unavailable, children search for substitute sources of satisfaction (Smart & Smart, 1982). Consequently, youngsters find alternate ways of satisfying their needs when ordinary paths are blocked. A child who is deprived of approval from adults may seek it from peers instead; a student who finds seatwork boring may rush through it, heedless of accuracy, in order to gain satisfaction from moving on to another kind of task.

Implications:

1. Children are provided many multisensory opportunities to explore and handle objects directly every day. This kind of hands-on learn-

ing dominates the teaching strategies implemented.

2. Substantial segments of time are planned during which children can move about the classroom freely.
3. The teacher creates schedules for the day in which quiet times are followed by active times and in which times when children are to remain passive are kept to a minimum.
4. Opportunities for gross motor activities are made available to children each day, both indoors and outside.
5. Educators observe children carefully to see if some of children's "unacceptable" behavior may be the result of blocked goals. If such is the case, teachers and administrators work with the child to determine better alternatives for meeting his or her needs. These strategies sometimes involve assisting the child in adopting new behaviors or restructuring some aspect of the classroom that is developmentally inappropriate.

Children's Learning Is Influenced by Maturation

Heredity not only provides the initial equipment with which human beings are endowed (e.g., gender, temperament, intellectual capacity) but also establishes a general timetable for the emergence of new capabilities and understandings throughout life (Thomas, 1985). This timetable can be retarded by environmental insults such as malnutrition and slightly accelerated through environmental stimulation. However, the rate of maturation is *not* completely elastic (Kaplan, 1986). Instead, it represents the orderly sequence of change dictated by one's own genetic blueprint.

As human beings mature, new possibilities for learning are created that could not have been realized earlier. This is illustrated by the fact that children's ability to exercise self-control increases with age. As children progress from toddlerhood into the primary years, their cognitive capacities mature to the point that they are able to recognize linkages among behaviors, events, and consequences. Thus, a preschooler might see no connection between the act of hitting and the act of biting, whereas a gradeschooler would recognize both as "hurtful" behaviors. Conversely, if suitable maturation has not taken place, it is futile

to demand that children demonstrate mastery of particular knowledge or skills. For instance, to walk, children must first develop strength and balance. Trying to make a 4-month-old walk results in failure because the child lacks the prerequisite structures necessary for success. Similarly, most young children do not have the ocular control to accurately shift from a near focus (e.g., the paper on their desk) to a far one (e.g., words or numerals on a blackboard). Such coordination tends to develop sometime after the 7th year, which makes the task of copying work from a blackboard generally inappropriate for kindergartners and first graders (Soderman, 1991).

Likewise, comprehending the conservation of substance seems to evolve around age 7, of weight around age 9, and of volume around age 11 or 12 (Phillips, 1975). Although some children may exhibit aspects of conservation earlier or under very particular conditions, the general notion that conservation tasks are beyond the capacities of most young children remains true across cultures and socioeconomic groups (Kaplan, 1986; Thomas, 1985). In all these ways, the biological characteristics of each child place some limits on the order and speed at which particular competencies appear.

Implications:

1. Early childhood professionals learn about how children mature and what might reasonably be expected of children over time and communicate this understanding to other significant adults in children's lives.
2. Children enjoy learning activities that are within their ability to master.
3. The teacher should simplify, maintain, or extend activities in response to children's demonstrated levels of functioning and comprehension.
4. School curriculum is designed so that there is some flexibility in the grade placement of learning goals. For example, no single grade level should encompass both the introduction and mastery of particular knowledge or skills. These should be spread out over more than one grade. Also, the accomplishment of certain milestones such as counting to 100 or being able to carry out a forward roll safely should fit into the expectations for

more than one grade. Restructuring school schedules and grade configurations to allow children to progress at a more self-determined rather than calendar year–determined rate would also support flexibility.

Children's Learning Is Affected by Environmental Variables

Although children cannot profit from certain experiences without the appropriate neurological and physical structures, neither do they gain knowledge and skills from maturation alone. Environment plays a critical role in the learning process. The environment runs the gamut from one's biological environment of nutrition, medical care, physical exercise, and drugs, to the physical environment of clothing, shelter, materials available, climate, and energy, to the social environment of family, peers, schools, community, media, and culture (Santrock, 1990). Such environmental aspects either enhance or detract from children's ability to learn. We know, for instance, that children who are well rested, fed, and physically comfortable get more out of school than children for whom these basic needs are an issue (Maslow, 1954).

In a like manner, children learn best when they feel psychologically safe and secure (Bredekamp, 1991). For young students, this translates into knowing that they are in a place where routines and expectations are predictable and suited to their capacities. Security also comes from being in the company of adults who respect and like them, tolerate mistakes, and support children's efforts to explore and experiment. Children's learning is further enhanced when the school environment is stimulating but not overwhelming. If the latter conditions prevail, children tend to shut down cognitively, becoming less sensitive to environmental cues, less likely to encode information, and less able to transfer information from one situation to another. They give clear signs that they have had enough of a situation or are having trouble making sense of something by acting out or withdrawing in some way. Professionals, sensitive to such indicators, must then adjust the environment and their expectations to better match children's needs.

Another important environmental dimension is continuity. All of the settings in which children participate are interrelated. Children do not live and learn in a vacuum. The influences of one setting continue to be present as children participate in another. Thus, the home environment affects children's learning at school and vice versa. Within this holistic context, family members, educators, peers, and the general culture have a profound influence on what children learn, how they learn, and what motivates them to learn (Ceci, 1990; Siegler, 1991). Children's learning, therefore, is enhanced when children perceive a connectedness between home and school, when what is valued in one system is honored in another, and when the learning expectations in each setting are compatible.

Implications:

1. Teachers and administrators highlight the importance of the environment on learning by making sure that the school or center facility is safe and secure and complies with the legal requirements of the appropriate licensing or accrediting local or state agency.

2. School programs are structured to ensure that children's biological and physical needs are addressed. For instance, children may use the toilet whenever they deem it necessary, they may rest when they are tired, and they receive snacks and meals as appropriate. Classrooms and outdoor areas offer ample space for safe, unencumbered movement. Adequate ventilation is provided, and room temperatures are maintained at a comfortable level. Children's wet or soiled clothing is changed promptly.

3. A daily schedule is established that is relatively stable and predictable to children. Changes in routine are explained in advance so that children can anticipate what will happen next.

4. Educators design activities, transitions, and routines keeping in mind children's attention span, physical development, and needs for activity, social interaction, and attention from caring adults.

5. Consistent adult supervision is provided so that children can readily identify a specific adult from whom to seek help, comfort, attention, and guidance.

6. Children are treated with warmth, respect, and caring (regardless of socioeconomic, cultural, ethnic, or family background, appearance, behavior, or any disabling condition).
7. Early childhood professionals use positive discipline techniques aimed at enhancing children's self-esteem and self-control.
8. Two-way communication is established between home and school or center. Home events are considered in planning children's educational experiences, and those experiences are communicated to families.
9. Teachers and administrators work collaboratively with children's family members and others in the community to develop shared goals and otherwise create an optimal learning experience for children at school and beyond the classroom.
10. Educators make clear the value of each child and his or her family and cultural group via school practices and activities.

Children Learn through Physical Experience, Social Interaction, and Reflection

Children have a powerful need to make sense of everything they encounter. From birth, their efforts focus on organizing their knowledge more coherently and adapting to the demands of the environment by directly manipulating, listening to, smelling, tasting, and otherwise acting on objects to see what happens (Kamii, 1986; Shaffer, 1989). From such investigations children generate a logic or knowledge of the properties of things, how they work, and how they relate to one another. This knowledge comes about not simply from the passive act of observing but from the more complex mental activity of interpreting and drawing conclusions about what happens (Beilin, 1989; Thomas, 1985). Such conclusions either add to children's existing ideas (assimilation) or cause children to reformulate their thinking (accommodation).

Children's experiences with physical objects are further influenced by their interactions with people. As youngsters play, talk, and work with peers and adults, they exchange and compare interpretations and ideas. In doing so, they often face contradictions in the way people or objects respond, and those discrepancies force

children to abstract new understandings from what has occurred.

It is through such experiences that children construct increasingly elaborate and complete notions of the world and how it functions. These understandings develop from the inside out. That is, children use their own activities to acquire, structure, and restructure knowledge. For example, although children can learn that a spoon is called a "spoon" by being told its name, they will comprehend the "threeness" of three spoons only by constructing that concept internally. Threeness, in this case, is not a physical property of the spoons themselves but rather represents a construct that exists in the child's own mind when relating the spoons to another child or other spoons and objects in the world. Such abstractions come about gradually through children's experience and experimentation in day-to-day circumstances as a result of their own mental activity. Consequently, number concept cannot be taught to children directly. Simply telling children that there "are" three spoons does not ensure that children will recognize the threeness of the situation. Nor will paper-pencil exercises or verbal recitations of number combinations get to the fundamental constructs needed for understanding.

In this same way, much of the essential knowledge children acquire throughout childhood is not directly taught. Instead, children receive feedback from the physical and social environment that either confirms or challenges their way of thinking. Thus, children learn on their own what no one can teach them: making relationships among objects, grouping and ordering them; structuring time and space; understanding number; understanding causality; conserving the physical aspects of objects. Elkind (1976) refers to this kind of learning as *operative learning*. Dominating the preschool and elementary years, operative learning encompasses all the operations and conceptual knowledge children require to get about in the everyday world (Beilin, 1989; Kamii, 1986; Katz & Chard, 1989; Mussen et al., 1990). It requires children to do, observe, think, interact, and communicate (Ministry of Education, Province of British Columbia, 1988).

A second type of learning identified by Elkind is *figurative learning*. Referred to as social-con-

Physical experiences and social interaction enhance children's learning.

ventional knowledge by Piaget, it involves knowledge that has its source in conventions created by people. Examples include language labels, historical facts, customs, rules, and certain skills (such as how to form the letter *A* or how to throw a football correctly). Because figurative learning is arbitrarily determined, children cannot reconstruct it or discover it on their own but instead must copy or memorize it. And, since there are right and wrong answers, children's source of feedback regarding the accuracy of their understanding is always other people. Figurative learning is important to children's education because it provides the way children learn what is valued by their culture and the society in which they live and thus helps children develop a sense of belongingness. They acquire it through modeling, reinforcement, and direct instruction.

Yet, for figurative learning to be meaningful to children, it must eventually be incorporated into the operative relationships they have constructed. To understand who Sally Ride is, for instance, children must place her in a category (astronaut/scientist/woman), a place (the United States), and a time (current). Categories,

place, and time are all operative constructs. Similarly, if children are to understand the importance of looking both ways before crossing the street, they must first have constructed notions of danger and safety, boundaries, speed, and so forth. If the child can make no such connections, the information becomes irrelevant and will be discarded.

Connotative learning, as described by Elkind, is the third type of learning in which children engage. It is the conscious conceptualization of one's own mental processes, or what is sometimes described as metacognition or reflective thinking. Although this kind of learning emerges most prominently during adolescence, there is evidence that its beginnings are evident during the early elementary years (Thomas, 1985). Educational strategies aimed at helping children reflect on what they have done or how they know what they know support increased self-awareness and recognition of potential learning strategies. Children who make a plan of how they wish to proceed with an activity, then later recall and analyze how closely their actions matched the original plan, are involved in connotative learning. So, too, are children who generate ideas for how to remember a list of items (e.g., chunking, making associations, using imagery) and then use one or more of those strategies to aid their memory at another time.

Educators demonstrate an understanding of the importance of physical experience, social interaction, and reflection in relation to children's learning when they do the following things.

Implications:

1. Articulate to others the value and differences among operative, figurative, and connotative learning.
2. Attain a clear idea of children's operative capabilities and how to enhance these in appropriate ways.
3. Emphasize operative learning throughout the preschool and early elementary years.
4. Work to achieve a balance between actively guiding children's learning and providing opportunities for children to explore on their own.
5. Support operative learning by encouraging children to explore and act on the environment as well as by providing experiences that stimulate children to discover and construct knowledge for themselves.
6. Interact with children, posing questions and introducing new elements to challenge children's current thinking.
7. Provide daily opportunities for children to interact with their peers.
8. Introduce figurative learning in a context relevant to children.
9. Offer information, ask questions, demonstrate, point out, and explain in an effort to help children acquire knowledge or skills they cannot discover on their own.
10. Provide experiences that enable children to make linkages between new information and what they already know and understand.
11. Give children opportunities to reflect on their experiences and help children develop strategies for doing so.
12. Use assessment strategies that address all three types of learning: operative, figurative, and connotative.

Children's Learning Styles Differ

If we adults were trying to get directions to a place we had never been, some of us might prefer using a map, others would like to hear the directions several times aloud, and certain others of us would need physically to go through the motions of orienting our bodies to the left or right as we went over the directions in our minds. These differences in how each person might best process the directions are due to the fact that every human being has a preferential modality that works best for him or her (Kovalik, 1989). Modalities are the sensory channels (visual, auditory, kinesthetic, and tactile) through which people perceive the world. People who are primarily visual learners, for example, respond best to what they see. Often they envision things in their mind as a way to recall them. Youngsters who rely on hearing and talking as their primary means of learning are referred to as auditory learners. For them, sound is the message. These youngsters sometimes move their lips or talk themselves through tasks. Kinesthetic/tactile learners are children who must move and constantly touch things in order to grasp concepts. It is not unusual for them also to have to touch themselves in some way to remember or process information. All people use all four modalities to learn; however, all people also function more effectively in the context of some versus others.

Howard Gardner of Harvard University has taken the idea of preferred modalities further than the four modalities described here by expanding the construct beyond simple perceptual processing. He believes that everyone possesses at least seven intelligences, or "frames of mind," and that a person's blend of competencies in each area produces a unique cognitive profile. The seven intelligences are as follows:

Linguistic

Logical-mathematical

Musical

Spatial

Bodily-kinesthetic

Intrapersonal

Interpersonal

Gardner's theory suggests that "each of these (intelligence/competency) areas may develop independently (in the brain). Individuals may be 'at promise' in some areas, while being average or below average in others" (Hatch & Gardner, 1988, p. 38).

How these seven intelligences influence children's learning is summarized in Table 2.5. Gardner (1983) emphasizes that people possess varying degrees of know-how in all seven categories. Yet there are certain ones that eventually dominate, which makes those the ways in which a specific person learns best.

In addition to the learning style variations described so far, further differences among children may exist as a result of cultural factors. Research exploring variations in learning style among Euro-American, African-American, and Mexican-American children suggest the existence of two basic styles, field dependent and field independent (Anderson, 1988). Field-dependent learners are socially oriented and so work best cooperatively and in groups. Collaboration among peers and between children and teachers are common ways in which these needs are satisfied. Such learners are most attuned to verbal tasks and appreciate figurative learning that has social content characterized by fantasy and humor. Their attention is captured by general principles rather than minute facts. Field-independent learners, on the other hand, value individual achievement and enjoy competition. They are goal-oriented learners who do best on analytic tasks and most easily learn figurative content that is inanimate and impersonal (Reed, 1991).

Studies across cultures indicate that many Western cultural groups of mainly European descent tend to be field-independent learners, while non-Western minority groups are more likely to be field-dependent learners (Anderson, 1988; Gilbert & Gay, 1985; Little-Soldier, 1989). Such results suggest that educators must be careful not to handicap children by demanding that they accommodate a learning style that is foreign to them. Furthermore, when considering these cultural characteristics, one must use qualifying terms such as *may, many, most,* and *tend to* to indicate that not all children of a particular cultural group possess these characteristics and to avoid stereotypes. Children are at all times individuals and must always be regarded as such (Reed, 1991).

Implications:

1. Educators should provide activities that represent a variety of modalities and address the same concept or skill in more than one modality.
2. An array of activities is provided each day, from which children may choose, so that students can self-select ones that best suit their learning needs.
3. The value of each different learning style is highlighted in various ways rather than focusing on the importance of some (e.g., music or math) and ignoring others (e.g., intrapersonal or kinesthetic).
4. A variety of experiences that suit the learning styles of both field-dependent and field-independent learners is offered, with particular care not to utilize methods characteristic of only one style.

Children Learn through Play

Play is		
	fun.	It is pleasurable.
	symbolic.	It is not constrained by reality.
	meaningful.	It connects and relates experiences to one another.
	active.	Children are doing things.
	voluntary.	No one has to force children to play.
	intrinsically motivated.	Curiosity, the desire for mastery or affiliation, are some reasons children play.
	rule-governed.	Rules may be implicit or explicit.
	episodic.	Play involves shifting goals that children develop spontaneously.

TABLE 2.5
Children's Frames of Mind: Corresponding Learning and Teaching Practices

Type of Intelligence	Child enjoys:	Child excels in:	Child learns best by:	The classroom should provide opportunities for:
Linguistic Learner "The Word Player"	reading, writing, telling stories.	memorizing, names, places, dates, and trivia.	seeing, saying, and learning language.	many language-based materials, which should be print rich.
Logical-Mathematical Learner "The Questioner"	doing experiments, figuring things out, working with numbers, asking questions, exploring patterns and relationships.	math, reasoning, logic.	looking for patterns and relationships.	handling objects, exploring new ideas, and following the scientific process naturally.
Spatial Learner "The Visualizer"	drawing, building, designing, and creating things.	imagining things, sensing changes, doing mazes/puzzles.	visualizing, dreaming, using the mind's eye.	children to work with art and construction materials and to create "projects."
Musical Learner "The Music Lover"	singing, humming, whistling, listening to instruments, responding to music.	picking up sounds, remembering melodies, pitches/rhythms, keeping time.	rhythm, melody.	information to be presented via rhythm and melody.
Bodily-Kinesthetic Learner "The Mover"	moving around, touching and talking, using body language.	physical activities (sports/dance/acting), crafts.	touching, moving, interacting with space, processing knowledge through bodily sensations.	role playing, drama, creative movement, gross motor, and other whole-body activities.
Interpersonal Learner "The Socializer"	having lots of friends, talking to people, joining groups.	understanding people, leading others, organizing, communicating, manipulating, mediating conflicts.	sharing, comparing, relating, cooperating, interviewing.	cooperative, collaborative activities and projects; children to express selves to others.
Intrapersonal Learner "The Individual"	working alone, pursuing own interests, self-imagery.	understanding people; focusing inward, on feelings/dreams; following instincts; pursuing interests/goals; being original.	working alone, individualized projects, self-paced instruction, having own space.	self-paced activities, individualized projects, private space, and time for children to work on own.

Adapted from H. Gardner (1983), *Frames of Mind: Theory of Multiple Intelligence.* New York: Basic Books; and "Seven Styles of Learning," September 1990, *Instructor Magazine*, p. 52.

Children play at home, at school, and everywhere in between; with people, things, and ideas (Whiren, 1991). When more fundamental needs are met—when children are not sleeping, eating, or seeking emotional support from others—children choose to play and can remain occupied that way for hours at a time (Sutton-Smith, 1971). Play is the province of children from the time they are born throughout the elementary school years.

All areas of development are enhanced through children's play activities. Play is the fundamental means by which children gather and process information, learn new skills, and practice old ones (Spodek, 1986; Sroufe & Cooper, 1988). Within the context of their play, children come to understand, create, and manipulate symbols as they take on roles and transform objects into something else. Children explore social relationships too—experimenting with various social roles, discovering points of view in contrast to their own, working out compromises, and negotiating differences (Spodek, Saracho, & Davis, 1991). Play enables children to extend their physical skills, language and literacy capabilities, and creative imaginations (Fromberg, 1987). The safe haven play provides for the release of tensions, the expression of emotions, and the exploration of anxiety-producing situations has also been well documented (Santrock, 1990). Furthermore, there is convincing evidence that children's general social, communicative, and cognitive functioning in play tends to exceed the level expected of the same children in academic subjects in school (Chance, 1979; Fromberg, 1987). In fact, the research touting the value of play in children's lives is substantial, and most scientists agree that play is central to children's learning. Why, then, is there such resistance to letting children play in school, especially, in elementary school?

Some educators suggest that the problem comes about because adults in our society have traditionally considered play the opposite of valuable work and therefore the opposite of learning (Fields, Spangler, & Lee, 1991). Others believe adults are unaware of play's benefits and so categorize this essential activity as "just playing," equating it with frivolous or extraneous endeavors (Eiferman, 1971). Still others claim that adults confuse educational play (supported by the teacher with educational aims in mind) with random activity (which results when teachers fail to support play properly) (Spodek, 1985). The first two misconceptions are best addressed through better communication about how play helps children develop and learn. This means early childhood professionals, who already believe that play is essential for children, have to become more knowledgeable and eloquent in defending play to colleagues, parents, administrators, and other program decision makers (Fields et al., 1991). The third misperception will only be rectified when teachers and administrators understand the ways play can vary in the classroom and how to support educational play.

Bergen (1988) has developed a schema of play and learning consisting of four categories of play depicted along a continuum. The play categories progress from child centered to adult centered, from discovery learning to rote learning. Briefly, the four kinds of play are as follows:

1. *Free play*—This is the most child-centered, discovery-oriented category of play. Children choose whether to play, how to play, what to play, and when to play. Such play requires the teacher to provide a safe environment, supported by a variety of props, and minimal restrictions regarding how the play will proceed. The children creating a grocery store out of a refrigerator box or turning the outdoor climber into a spaceship could illustrate this type of play. Making up their own card game or playing with language sounds, of their own volition, are other possibilities.

2. *Guided play*—This kind of play has many of the elements of the above category, but the experiences are carefully structured by the teacher so that certain discoveries are more likely to occur. Thus, guided play has more rules, fewer alternatives, and closer adult supervision than free play. Examples might include play at the workbench or computer or in a pretend grocery store in which the teacher asks questions or models behaviors aimed at helping children focus more closely on the roles of customer and employee.

3. *Directed play*—When the adult designates that children may choose one of three

Play is the primary medium through which children learn.

board games or asks all the children to play "duck, duck, goose," he or she is directing the play. The children's participation is required, and the means by which the children play is often adult determined. The primary kind of learning that takes place within this mode of play is receptive, with the emphasis on verbal instructions and explanations.

4. *Work disguised as play*—This category describes task-oriented activities that the teacher attempts to transform into directed or guided play episodes. Playing a spelling game or conducting an addition facts race are typical examples. Most work disguised as play involves rote learning. Although it may be a more enjoyable way to engage in practice and drill, it no longer contains the elements of play described at the onset of this section.

Bergen (1988) points out that the school day for preschoolers and children in the lower elementary grades should include many opportunities for free play and guided play. There are limited benefits to devoting much time to directed play and even fewer for the fourth category. Teachers who transpose these desired emphases by focusing on the last two categories to the exclusion of free play and guided play are not promoting the kind of play from which children benefit the most. The same is true for teachers who take an entirely hands-off view of play (Almy, 1975). This happens when they allow play but do nothing to enhance or facilitate it. Practitioners who fail to provide a rich background of experiences as a foundation for play, who neglect to rotate props, ask questions, or provide information periodically to enlarge children's perceptions, are depriving children of valuable opportunities to develop and extend their play. Neither overcontrolling the play nor failing to support it altogether are consistent with developmentally appropriate practice.

Implications:

1. Early childhood professionals support children's play when they talk to parents and colleagues about the value of play and its relationship to children's development and learning.
2. One or more long blocks of time are devoted during the school day for children to become engaged in play. Some educators suggest no less than 60 minutes at a time (Cummings, 1991a, 1991b; Michigan Department of Education, 1986).
3. Classroom space and materials are organized to enable children to engage in both solitary and collaborative play.
4. Play is integrated into all curricular domains.
5. Educators can engage in operative, figurative, and connotative teaching within the context of children's play.
6. A variety of props and other materials are available with which to play.
7. Adults are joyful and playful as they work with children and stimulate children's play by modeling, taking roles, offering information, asking questions, playing with language, and

avoiding interrupting the play when they are not needed.

8. The sound and activity levels within the classroom reflect the quality of children's play—high quality play is often noisy and active.

Children's Learning Is Influenced by Early Dispositions and Perceptions

The whole time children are acquiring knowledge and skills, they are also developing dispositions toward learning. Dispositions are the typical reaction patterns people develop toward various life events. *Penchants, traits, tendencies,* or *attitudes* are other words that describe such reactions. For example, when confronted with a new idea, a child might have the disposition to be curious or apathetic, open-minded or rejecting. Whichever of these reactions the child habitually displays, one may infer that he or she has developed a disposition in that direction.

Dispositions have their foundations in early childhood and last a lifetime. As children see certain dispositions modeled by the people around them and as they are reinforced for displaying like behaviors, they adopt those dispositions as their own (Katz & Chard, 1989). Dispositions are not taught directly, nor do they come about as the result of a single incident. Instead, they emerge through accumulated experiences. Consequently, dispositions can be strengthened or weakened by the educational practices children encounter each day.

To illustrate, let us consider a classroom in which children's questions are treated as interruptions, the pursuit of one right answer is emphasized, and a strict timetable governs children's activities. These kinds of strategies detract from children's disposition for curiosity. On the other hand, to strengthen that disposition, the teacher could provide children with intriguing materials to examine, encourage questioning and other investigative behaviors, allow children to pursue self-determined projects, modify the classroom schedule in line with children's interests, and promote students' search for multiple solutions to problems. Likewise, the disposition to be cooperative is weakened when competition is used to spur children's performance but promoted when

teachers encourage group problem solving and implement group rewards.

In addition to dispositions, children form perceptions about themselves and about school. These perceptions are subjective, personal evaluations children make regarding their sense of competence, worth, and security. Interactions with others at school and the overall school climate are major contributors to the conclusions children make. Depending on whether such experiences are predominantly positive or negative, children may perceive themselves as

secure	or	insecure.
capable	or	incapable.
belonging	or	not belonging.

In addition, they may come to perceive school as

worthwhile	or	useless.
rewarding	or	punitive.
enjoyable	or	tedious, hateful.

Like dispositions, perceptions evolve gradually. Initially, they are difficult to discern from children's outward behaviors. For instance, youngsters required to master isolated skills prematurely may willingly perform as desired while simultaneously formulating a negative perception of school and themselves as learners. Only after such perceptions are well grounded do they become evident. By that time, they have become relatively enduring. Consequently, it can be surmised that the early childhood years are an optimal period for the development of dispositions and perceptions. This is why early childhood educators must exercise particular care to create school environments in which children's favorable dispositions and perceptions are enhanced.

Implications:

1. Teachers and administrators strengthen positive dispositions and perceptions among children when they consider carefully the dispositions and perceptions they hope children will develop in school (e.g., enthusiasm for learning, curiosity, absorption in tasks, deriving pleasure from effort and mastery,

friendliness, generosity, honesty, and cooperativeness, self-confidence, etc.).

2. Early childhood educators model the dispositions they wish to strengthen in children.
3. The school climate promotes children's feelings of competence, worth, and security.
4. Personnel consider to what extent school procedures and structures may undermine the dispositions and perceptions they hope children will develop. Such analyses take into account both direct and indirect strategies, intended and unintended outcomes. When incongruities are discovered, practices and routines are restructured to promote more favorable results.

THE OVERARCHING PRINCIPLE OF DEVELOPMENTAL DIRECTION

Both development and learning proceed in predictable directions. In other words, there is a beginning point from which development and learning progress. The principle of developmental direction defines that forward progress. For instance, in the body, maturation proceeds from top to bottom (head to tail) and midline to outer extremities, which is why infants are born with large heads and proportionately smaller lower bodies. The head region, containing the brain, on which all life depends, is more developed than the posterior region, which is not immediately necessary for survival. For the same reason, babies gain control of their head and neck muscles (lifting, turning, holding up the head) prior to mastering control of their legs and feet. Likewise, the heart and other internal organs are fully coordinated in the newborn, while coordination of the hands takes place much later. These outward manifestations of developmental direction are obvious to even the casual observer, but other, more subtle examples of internal change are equally important for educators to know about. Such changes influence child development and learning throughout the preschool and elementary years.

Development/learning proceeds from

simple	to	complex.
known	to	unknown.
self	to	other.

whole	to	part.
concrete	to	abstract.
enactive	to	symbolic.
exploratory	to	goal directed.
inaccurate	to	more accurate.
impulsive	to	self-controlled.

Simple to Complex

There are literally hundreds of examples of how this facet of developmental direction influences children's lives. To conserve space, let us consider just one—how children develop categories. At first, toddlers may categorize all fuzzy living creatures into one simple category, "doggies." Gradually as they gain experience and their cognitive powers expand, children differentiate among fuzzy creatures, thereby creating multiple categories, "doggies" and "kitties." Over time, these categorizations will become increasingly complex as children differentiate breeds of cats and dogs, friendly versus unfriendly characteristics of each, real and pretend examples.

Complexity increases as numbers of variables multiply and as the discriminations among those variables become less acute. Also, combining elements is more complex than dealing with them separately. This is why it is more complicated for a child to put together a puzzle containing eight large pieces than one containing four, and why it is easier to put together puzzles in which the color and shape of the pieces are extremely different as opposed to ones in which pieces are varied in color but shaped alike. Teachers have this principle in mind when they gradually introduce challenge to children by increasing numbers of elements, offer finer discriminations for children to consider, and ask children to group and regroup objects and events in different ways.

Known to Unknown

Children base what they learn and do on what is familiar. They build skills on previously learned behaviors. More sophisticated concepts grow out of those that already exist for them. When children can make connections between their prior knowledge and new experiences, those experiences become meaningful. When they cannot, the experiences are irrelevant. This is why it is necessary for teachers to discover what children know and can do prior to introducing brand-new material. It also provides the rationale for addressing concepts within a context that makes sense to the children. Thus, a teacher would introduce mammalian characteristics using as examples animals common in the children's environment, not ones they had only seen in pictures.

Self to Other

The young child's world revolves around him- or herself. All new experiences are considered within this sphere. It is not surprising then that among children's first words are *me* and *mine*. This preoccupation with the self is the child's way of learning about what is closest to him or her and of relating new experiences to familiar ones. At first, children's egocentric interpretations result from an erroneous assumption that all views of the world are identical and so must resemble their own. As experiences occur in which that perspective is challenged and as children develop greater cognitive sophistication, their interpretations expand. They eventually recognize that multiple perspectives are possible and those perspectives might differ. As this understanding takes hold, children become more adept at recognizing, valuing, and accommodating the needs, reactions, and experiences of others. This principle further underscores the importance of relating knowledge and skills to children in ways that have personal meaning. Explanations and experiences that make sense to adults but not to children do not enhance children's development and learning. This principle should also serve as a reminder that children's egocentric world view is a function of their development, not an aberration.

Whole to Part

Children perceive and experience the world in integrated, unified ways, moving from wholes to parts, general to specific understandings. Something like this happens to adults when they go to a movie for the first time. They usually come away with a basic understanding of the plot and sensory impressions of color, sound, and feelings. On seeing the same movie again, people often perceive things they missed initially because they are moving from the holistic sensation of the first experience to paying more attention to detail. A third or fourth trip could reveal even more specifics, contributing to better comprehension of subtle plot nuances as well as the mechanics of filmmaking.

Children take in experiences holistically in much the same way. Only after they have grasped the essentials of that experience do the details become meaningful to them. Hence, children might hear a song several times over before actually differentiating some of the words. Likewise, the value of paying attention to letter-sound associations only develops after children have formulated a concept of print and how it relates to their daily lives. Introducing the specifics prematurely or out of context renders them meaningless. Much the same result would occur were people shown a brief clip of movie dialogue, then asked to analyze it. This mechanical exercise would not lead to substantive gains in their understanding of the story or increase its personal relevance. In fact, if it happened often enough, it might promote a perception of films as boring or purposeless, thereby decreasing their appeal.

Teachers who think about the whole-to-part principle offer children a broad array of rich, multisensory experiences. They repeat activities often, giving children plenty of time to explore and formulate their own impressions and conceptualizations. As children express interest and understanding, teachers draw children's attention to relevant details that enlarge youngster's perceptions and challenge them to try alternatives or reconsider old ideas. Conversely, teachers are careful not to teach children skills or facts in isolation. They work from the general to the specific rather than the other way around.

Concrete to Abstract

The most concrete experiences are tangible ones that involve physical contact with real objects. They are ones in which children taste, touch, and smell as well as see and hear. The further removed an experience is from this tangible state and the fewer senses children are required to employ, the more abstract it becomes. Providing children with real leaves to look at, handle, take apart, smell, and taste are concrete ways to enhance children's interest in and knowledge about leaves. Giving children pictures to explore or having them cut leaves from magazines is a step removed from the real thing and so is more abstract. Even further removed is having children watch the teacher point to leaves in a book or on the bulletin board. The most distant and therefore most abstract activity involves having children think about leaves as the teacher talks about them.

Children throughout the preschool and elementary years benefit from concrete experiences in all developmental domains and across all subject areas. The more unfamiliar the object or phenomenon, the more this is true. Even adults who are learning something for the first time do better when given opportunities for real-life experiences rather than just seeing something modeled or having it explained. The danger in ignoring this principle is that children may parrot what the adult wants to hear but not truly understand essential concepts. It is for this reason that teachers provide children with many firsthand experiences and tangible objects on which to base their learning.

Enactive to Symbolic

Children begin representing the world enactively. They use their bodies to reconstruct or act out events and roles using objects, gestures, sounds, and words. This is a very tangible, concrete way to think through an experience and the most basic form of representation (Lawton, 1987). Teachers observe enactive representation when after taking a field trip to feed the ducks, the children return to the classroom imitating duck sounds, waddling, and making "quacking" gestures with their hands. Such representations duplicate and preserve many of the distinctive qualities one associates with the actual phenomenon, ducks.

A somewhat more abstract mode of representation involves children making pictures or constructing three-dimensional images of what they see and think about. These are iconic representations. Youngsters who reproduce or create their own interpretations of objects and events using art or construction materials, such as blocks, are demonstrating iconic representation. Thus, following the duck field trip, some youngsters might paint what they saw, and oth-

ers might sculpt ducklike shapes in clay. Although these pictorial representations share many of the same characteristics as real ducks (e.g., color and shape), other concrete cues such as sound and motion are less obvious.

The ultimate and most abstract means of representation is symbolic. In this mode, children manipulate words and symbols, such as letters and numerals, to interpret and represent particular objects and events. Youngsters coming back from a field trip could represent what occurred by dictating or writing descriptions of the trip. However, the symbols they use no longer bear any resemblance to real ducks, which makes this level of representation the most removed from the children's actual experience.

Enactive representation occurs in its most rudimentary form within the first year of life. Infants think in terms of actions and about objects by acting on them. Gradually, these enactive episodes become more elaborate, blossoming into pretend play in toddlerhood. Iconic representation first appears at about 18 months, with symbolic representation following soon after. As one form of representation emerges, children do *not* discard earlier forms. Rather, they build on and combine the different modes to enhance their conceptualizations and understandings.

The importance of these different modes of representation provides a rationale for including materials and experiences related to all three in early childhood classrooms. Children do not outgrow their need for pretend play, art, or construction materials when moving into the elementary grades. Nor is toddlerhood too early to encourage children to experiment with drawing or writing surfaces and related tools and implements. This continuum also suggests that the developmentally appropriate early childhood curriculum gives children ample opportunity to explore concepts through enactive representation prior to introducing children to the more abstract iconic and symbolic representations related to those concepts.

Exploratory to Goal Directed

There are many different notions of how children move along the continuum from randomly experimenting with objects and relationships to purposefully applying the knowledge and skills they gain. However, even theories that represent otherwise incompatible interpretations begin at the exploration phase. That is, children experiment and "play around" with objects and materials prior to using them in prescribed ways. Exploration is a time of self-discovery that occurs through the spontaneous manipulation of objects and informal social interactions with peers and adults. Knowledge grows as these interactions are mentally organized (Bergen, 1988). This is why children who had never seen a lotto game would have difficulty starting to play it right away. They need time to handle the pieces, look at the different pictures on the cards and boards, and experiment with making some matches. Prior to ever seeing that particular game, youngsters would need many previous chances to explore the whole notion of game playing, working with others in a group, and so forth. Were they to plunge into the game without that exploratory experience, chances are they would explore anyway, thereby missing some of the directions or not paying attention to the course of the action. The adult, trying to keep the children on task, would be fighting children's natural tendencies to explore. Neither adult nor children would benefit from the experience. For the adult, playing lotto might turn into a discipline-focused confrontation; for the children, the cognitive aspects of the game would not necessarily register.

The early childhood years mark a time when much of children's attention and energy is focused on exploring the world around them. As Hymes (1980) says, children are the aliens to the planet; they are the new beings for whom experiences are fresh and unfamiliar. We "old-timers" sometimes forget how novel it all is for children and how much there is to discover. Also, all the discovering is not over by ages 4 or 5, 7 or 8. The exploration phase is the threshold from which children gradually acquire knowledge and skills, practice their newfound understandings and behaviors, and eventually generalize what they have discovered across a variety of situations. It is the foundation of all understanding.

Once children have thoroughly explored a phenomenon, they display signs of being ready to move to the acquisition phase of learning. Children signal this when they ask, "How do you play this game?" "What comes next?" or "Why is the grass green?" Using a variety of indirect and direct instructional strategies, teachers respond to children's cues. In doing so, they help children refine their understanding, guide their attention, and make connections (Bredekamp, 1991). This form of inquiry is usually more goal oriented for both teachers and children than is characteristic of pure exploration. However, it is neither rigid nor unidirectional in nature. Children still have much latitude in how they proceed and in the paths they take.

Acquisition of new knowledge and skills is followed by a time during which children concentrate on practicing what they have learned. They use the new behavior or knowledge repeatedly and in a variety of circumstances. This is exemplified by the child who, having learned to play lotto, wants to play again and again, enjoying rather than tiring of the repetitions. Children who have just learned to wash the dishes beg to do them, at least for a while, and youngsters who have learned to dribble a basketball try it out in the hall, on the playground, in the gym, on the sidewalk. In every case, the child's practice is self-motivated and self-initiated. It represents the tangible way in which children gain mastery. Teachers facilitate children's practice when they allow them time to play out the same scenarios over and over again and when they follow children's lead in repeating activities more than once as well as varying the practice conditions.

Eventually, children have enough grounding to apply their newfound knowledge or skills to novel situations. When this happens, they enter the generalization or utilization phase of learning, which is the most advanced and goal-directed phase along the learning continuum. Within this phase children apply what they have learned in many ways and adjust their thinking to fit new circumstances or demands. They also formulate novel hypotheses, which may prompt them to initiate new explorations, thereby beginning the cycle again (Bredekamp, 1991). It is worth noting that the goal orientation so prominent in the generalization phase remains internally inspired. Therefore, the role of the teacher becomes that of creating vehicles for children to make applications to real-world situations and providing meaningful situations children can use for learning.

Children proceed from exploratory to goal-directed activity within all realms of learning: aesthetic, affective, cognitive, language, physical, and social. Where they are in the process depends on their backlog of experiences and understandings as well as the learning opportunities available to them. Therefore, each child's progress along the continuum will differ for various threads within each realm as well as from realm to realm. In other words, children are not in any one phase of learning for everything, simultaneously. Instead, youngsters may just be starting to explore some concepts or skills while acquiring, practicing, or generalizing others.

To accommodate such differences within and among children, teachers have to provide them with broad-based, open-ended activities. From these, children extrapolate experiences that correspond to the phase of learning most relevant to them. Thus, several children working with puzzles may use them for different purposes— exploration, practice, and so forth. Repeating activities is also a good idea, since children need many opportunities to progress along the learning continuum. Furthermore, teachers must support children in whatever phase of learning they are in for a given activity using different instructional strategies as necessary (e.g., providing many varied materials for exploration; offering feedback, information, or asking questions as appropriate; giving children chances to practice what they have learned under many different conditions; and encouraging children to apply what they have learned to new situations). Such adaptations are more easily made within individualized and small-group instructional formats than whole-group ones.

Inaccurate to More Accurate

Children develop hypotheses about the world in which they live according to internal processes of acquiring, structuring, and restructuring knowledge. Subsequently, young children's natural thinking and reasoning processes are filled with trial and error and incorrect conclusions. All of these come about as a result of children's continuous efforts to order the world into understandable patterns (McKee, 1991). These so called "mistakes" are *central* to children's men-

tal development. They serve as the means by which children refine their thinking and enlarge it. As children experience the mental conflict that arises through events that challenge their deductions, they resolve the dilemma through further mental activity and so gradually develop more accurate thinking.

Because of this principle, educators must be cautious about focusing on children producing "right" answers. A child who answers "correctly" may be responding from rote memorization or inaccurate conclusions rather than accurate reasoning processes. For this reason, it is better to emphasize how children derive answers. Activities that involve children developing predictions, evaluating their experiences, problem solving, and figuring out what they know as well as how they know should be featured throughout the day.

Impulsive to Controlled

Young children are active, noisy beings who come about these characteristics naturally. It is hard for them to control their impulses to touch, make sounds, move, or go after what they want. Waiting and holding back are acquired skills that develop in tandem with children's cognitive, physical, emotional, and social concepts and behaviors. Their acquisition is supported when teachers and administrators create classroom environments in which children have opportunities to move about freely, express themselves openly, learn alternate strategies for achieving their goals, and practice ways of delaying gratification that are in keeping with their comprehension and abilities. Forcing children into a passive, inactive state is unnatural and interferes with all other aspects of their development and learning.

The content of this chapter so far has focused on basic assumptions about how young children develop and learn. Potential implications for early childhood programming have also been explored. This information is provided to help define the concept of developmental appropriateness. Yet, to understand any concept, one must not only grasp what it is but also what it is not. What follows, then, are a few erroneous ideas people sometimes associate with developmentally appropriate programs.

MYTHS ASSOCIATED WITH DEVELOPMENTALLY APPROPRIATE PROGRAMS

It seems everywhere early childhood practitioners turn these days, people are talking about developmentally appropriate practice and programs. The term *developmentally appropriate* has become prominent in journal articles, books, the media, professional newsletters, conference presentations, publisher's materials, and manufacturer's advertising. Teachers and administrators, theoreticians and researchers, parents and politicians have all become involved in the developmentally appropriate programs discussion. The problem is, not everyone means the same thing when they use the term. In fact, *developmentally appropriate* is becoming a catchword people use to describe almost anything and everything associated with early childhood education. The same terminology may be used to justify such incompatible notions as "readiness" programs for children and programs that advocate giving children the "gift of time"—structuring children's learning experiences within narrowly defined parameters and not structuring them at all, grouping children by ability as well as by almost any criteria other than ability.

These inconsistencies have led to much confusion about what developmentally appropriate programs entail (Walsh, 1991). In the absence of true understanding, myths have sprung up representing collective opinions that are based on false assumptions or are derived from fallacious reasoning. Some have evolved from people's attempts to simplify complex phenomena, which results in oversimplification to the point of inaccuracy. Others have resulted from people's intuitive interpretations of child behavior or superficial understanding of child development and learning-related theories and research (Spodek, 1986). Still more myths have been created as a way for people to make finite and absolute a concept that is in fact open-ended and amenable to many variations. Unfortunately, these myths are widespread, which causes misunderstand-

ings and anxiety among practitioners and the public. What follows is a selection of the most common ones the authors have encountered both in this country and abroad.

Myth: There is one right way to implement a developmentally appropriate program.

When talking about developmentally appropriate practice with any group of educators, it is not unusual to hear statements like "You *always* use learning centers." "You *never* use whole-group instruction." "You *always* let children determine the content of the lesson." "You *never* correct children." "You *always* let children figure out their own spellings for words." "You *never* use lined paper." Likewise, teachers and administrators may ask, "Is it *ever* OK to show children how to hold a pencil?" "Is it *wrong* to spell words for children when they ask?" "Exactly *when* should we introduce cursive writing?" These kinds of pronouncements and queries represent efforts to establish single, correct approaches to instruction. They are based on the belief that one method of teaching suits all children and all situations.

Unfortunately, the reality is that teaching is complex; there is no one solution that fits every circumstance. On the contrary, individual teaching episodes can and should be qualified by "It depends" (Newman & Church, 1990). It depends on such variables as the child's current level of comprehension, experiences, and kinds of previous knowledge and skills. Contextual elements including time, human resources, the physical environment, material resources, and the values and expectations of the school and community must also be factored in. The goals, strategies, and standards school personnel finally choose are all affected by these constraints. Hence, every educational decision requires judgment, by teachers and administrators, made on the spot or over time, but always with certain children in mind.

This means practitioners must continually weigh out what they do in relation to their knowledge about how children develop and learn. To translate that knowledge into actual teaching strategies, they must be willing to explore a variety of practices in the classroom and to allow themselves to make mistakes. Moreover, teachers will have continually to examine their assumptions and learn from the children as they evaluate the effectiveness of their teaching. What meets the needs of several children in a group may not be appropriate for others. What was optimal for last year's class may not be so this year. One's search, then, is not simply for "right" answers but for the best answers to meet the needs of children representing a wide range of abilities, learning styles, interests, and backgrounds.

Finally, teachers also differ from one another and require flexibility to develop an approach to teaching that is compatible with their beliefs and comfortable for them as well as for their students. These variations in both children's and teacher's needs necessitate differences in the programs designed to meet them. Hence, there is no one model that is best for all.

Myth: Developmental appropriateness is just a fad, soon to be replaced by another, perhaps opposite trend.

One cannot blame practitioners for being skeptical about the potential longevity of any new idea in education. Teachers and administrators perceive that theirs is a profession in which instructional practices come and go with predictable regularity (Cummings, 1991a). Cyclic trends are also common, with ideas gaining notoriety for a time, then fading from the scene only to reappear years later in a newly packaged form. It is not surprising, therefore, that many practitioners figure developmental appropriateness is simply a "retread" of previous ideas or think, "This too shall pass." In either case, their motivation to embrace this philosophy is seriously reduced because they assume its influence will not be long lasting.

As with any myth, there is some truth yet also flaws in this reasoning. First, developmental appropriateness does share similarities with previous trends in early childhood education, but it also differs markedly from them. The concept represents an evolution in professional thinking that will continue to emerge over the coming decades. (For further information about how it has evolved to date, refer to chap. 1, "Early Childhood Education Today.") For now, suffice it to say that early childhood educators are not simply revisiting old ideas. Rather, they are integrating the truths of previously developed hypotheses with other, newer understandings. The result has been the creation of an enhanced concept that is uniquely suited to modern times.

Additionally, one reason why trends come and go is that old technologies are replaced by newer ones. This is a natural occurrence since people are constantly discovering better ways to do things. If developmental appropriateness is treated merely as a technology encompassing specific materials (e.g., unifix cubes or Big Books) and particular activities (e.g., choral reading or Math Their Way tubbing), it could suffer the same fate. For there is no reason to believe that we will not continue to find ways to improve instructional practices in the future. On the other hand, if developmental appropriateness is conceived of as a philosophy, it will not be technology bound. Certain basic assumptions and beliefs will prevail regardless of how we choose to operationalize them. In other words, the essence of developmental appropriateness is not simply what we do but how we think—how we think about children and programs, what we value children doing and learning, how we define effectiveness and success. If developmental appropriateness transcends technology and moves to this higher conceptual plane, then its influence is likely to endure.

Myth: Developmentally appropriate practice requires teachers to abandon all their prior knowledge and experience. Nothing they have learned or done in the past is acceptable in the new philosophy.

It is not only a daunting prospect but an affrontive one for seasoned practitioners to contemplate returning to novice status in their pursuit of developmentally appropriate practice. Those who approach the idea in this frame of mind are understandably discouraged and/or resistant. However, the fact of the matter is that few experienced teachers require a total makeover to become more developmentally appropriate in their practices. The knowledge of children and teaching they have gained over the years will serve as the foundation from which they can examine their pedagogical beliefs and instructional practices. In addition, since the concept of developmental appropriateness has evolved from past educational trends, most teachers are already implementing numerous philosophically compatible strategies and activities in their classrooms. Some practitioners simply need "permission" to continue. Others need help recognizing their own strengths. In either case, teachers are most successful making the transition to more developmentally appropriate practice when they build on what they know.

Myth: To be developmentally appropriate, elementary teachers and administrators will have to "water down" the traditional curriculum. Children will learn less than they have in the past.

This myth is based on two assumptions: that all learning is hierarchical in nature and that the curriculum offered in many elementary schools today is sufficient in scope. Neither is correct.

Learning can be characterized as occurring in two directions, vertically and horizontally. Vertical learning is hierarchical. It can be likened to climbing a ladder. A person starts at the base and gradually moves upward, pausing now and then or even vacillating between rungs, but with little veering off to the sides. This kind of learning piles one fact or skill on top of another. As the learner proceeds higher and higher, the result is an increase in the number and complexity of the facts and skills he or she has attained.

Horizontal learning, on the other hand, is conceptually based. An analogy that comes to mind is that of casting a net in all directions, then drawing it back in. Within this framework, experiences occur more or less simultaneously, and the role of the learner becomes that of making connections among them. It implies a deepening understanding of the world through the development of increasingly elaborate concepts.

Both vertical and horizontal learning are essential to human understanding. The former expands one's quantity of knowledge and skills; the latter contributes to their quality. Neither should be emphasized to the detriment of the other. Yet the lock-step nature of the curriculum in many primary schools promotes vertical learning to the exclusion of concept development. Curriculum guides delineate a vertical scope and sequence for every subject. Children are continually pushed upward, even when they show signs of inadequate comprehension. If

youngsters need more time to consolidate their understandings (an example of horizontal learning), they are identified as "falling behind" or "at risk" for potential failure. Conversely, when children complete the scope and sequence for a given subject in a particular grade, they are encouraged to continue their vertical climb into the next grade level rather than spending time on strengthening the linkages among the bits of knowledge they have acquired.

The fundamental flaw in all this is that children in the early years are establishing the conceptual base from which all future learning will proceed. Their need for a solid, broad foundation, and hence much horizontal learning, is great. The breadth of the conceptual base children form influences how well eventually they perform in school. The narrower the base, the fewer connections children are able to make among the pieces of knowledge they encounter over time. The broader the base, the more comprehensive their learning. More of a balance in the curriculum, with both kinds of learning being addressed and valued, is a fundamental tenet of developmentally appropriate programs. This would result not in children learning less but in children learning better.

The past decades have witnessed a narrowing of the elementary curriculum. Many schools have gone from a holistic approach to learning that included social, physical, cognitive, and aesthetic aims to one that focuses almost solely on isolated academic skills such as tracing letters and memorizing number facts (Peck et al., 1988). The beliefs underlying developmentally appropriate programs are that the curriculum needs to be expanded to include experiences related to all aspects of child development. Again, this is not a cry to limit children's learning but to broaden it. The result will not be a watered-down program but rather a richer, more comprehensive one.

Myth: Developmentally appropriate classrooms are unstructured classrooms.

Some people make this claim because they equate structure with rigidity and so shun the term. Others envision a classroom in which chaos reigns. Both interpretations are based on misinformation. Structure refers to the extent to which teachers develop an instructional plan, then organize the physical setting and social environment to support the achievement of educational goals (Spodek et al., 1991).

By this definition, developmentally appropriate classrooms are highly structured. Both teachers and children contribute to their organization. Teachers generate educational goals for students based on schoolwide expectations tempered by their understanding of individual children's needs, abilities, and interests. All of the activities and routines of the day are purposefully planned to promote these goals. Keeping their instructional plan in mind, teachers determine the arrangement of the furniture, which specific materials to offer children, the nature and flow of activity, the approximate time to allocate to various instructional segments, and the grouping of children throughout the session. As teachers interact with children, they observe, listen, instruct, guide, support, and encourage them. Consequently, while teachers carefully consider long-range objectives, their moment-to-moment decision making remains fluid in order to capitalize on input from the children (Newman & Church, 1990). Children ask questions, suggest alternatives, express interests, and develop plans that may lead the instruction in new directions. In this way, overall instructional goals are merged with more immediate ones, thereby creating a flexible, stimulating classroom structure.

Developmentally appropriate classrooms are active ones in which both teachers and students learn from one another. Such learning requires a constant interchange of thoughts and ideas. As a result, there are times during the day when many people are talking or moving about the room at one time. To the untrained eye these conditions may appear chaotic, but a closer look should reveal children on task, constructively involved in their own learning. If children are wandering aimlessly, screaming indiscriminately, or racing from place to place, the environment is not conducive to learning and so is developmentally inappropriate.

Myth: In developmentally appropriate classrooms, teachers do not teach.

This myth stems from the stereotypical idea that teachers are people who stand up in front of a group of students, telling them what they need to know, and that the teacher's most important duties consist of assigning work to children and checking for right and wrong answers. According to this scenario, teachers are always directive and on center stage. People who envision teachers this way may not recognize all the teaching that is going on in a developmentally appropriate classroom. For example, teachers create physical environments and daily schedules that enable children to engage in purposeful activity. Curricular goals are frequently addressed through pervasive classroom routines such as dressing to go outside, preparing for snack, and cleaning up. Although some whole-group instruction takes place, teachers spend much of their classroom time moving throughout the room working with children individually and in small informal groups. During these times, they influence children's learning indirectly through the provision of certain activities in which the focus is on children's self-discovery and exploration. They also teach children directly, using a variety of instructional strategies. Teachers initiate learning activities as well as respond to children's initiatives. They pose questions, offer procedural suggestions, suggest explorations, and provide information. As opportunities arise, teachers present children with challenges that help them move beyond their current understandings and strategies (Newman & Church, 1990). Additionally, teachers constantly reflect on what is happening in the classroom. They make judgments about children's progress and introduce variations or changes in focus as children's needs warrant. All of these activities are essential teaching behaviors.

Myth: Developmentally appropriate programs can be defined according to dichotomous positions, with one position always right, the other always wrong:

Process focused	versus	Product focused
Child initiated	versus	Adult initiated
Socially oriented	versus	Cognitively oriented

The dichotomies listed here are some of the ones people typically refer to when talking about developmentally appropriate programs. Such discussions tend to treat these variables as polar opposites. As a result, the items on the left are usually defined as "good," "desirable," and "appropriate"; those on the right as "bad," "undesirable," and "inappropriate." Furthermore, because the categories are mutually exclusive, they imply that developmentally appropriate programs are 100% process focused, with no thought given to products; that children initiate all learning episodes and adults initiate none; that social development is more important than cognition. None of these assertions are true.

Developmentally appropriate programming is not an all-or-nothing proposition. For example, process learning is very important to children and should be highly valued by teachers. The satisfaction a child gains from painting is more important than the degree to which his or her picture represents the adult's notion of reality. However, anyone who has watched young children proudly show off their work knows that products are sometimes important too. Likewise, many, many activities in the developmentally appropriate classroom come about through child exploration and initiation, whereas others are introduced by the teacher as a way to spark children's interest in something new. Furthermore, although social development cannot be ignored, neither can cognitive pursuits. To elevate one above the other denies the integrative nature of child development.

Consequently, it is more accurate to envision variables such as these along continuums. Rather than calling to mind issues of all or none, yes or no, good or bad, a continuum suggests that educational planning is really a matter of degrees and balance. Developmentally appropriate programs are both varied and comprehensive. They enable children to engage in the kinds of experiences they need at a given time. Such experiences will fall in different places along the continuum, depending on the child, and will differ from time to time.

Myth: All you need to create developmentally appropriate programs are the right materials.

If this myth were true, then the guidelines for developmentally appropriate practice would consist solely of an equipment list supplemented by the names of several early childhood materials catalogs. Although equipment does enrich the educational environment, research shows that the teacher is the essential ingredient in determining the quality of education received by children. In turn, program quality is directly linked to the teacher's knowledge of and ability to apply developmentally appropriate principles in his or her classroom (Bredekamp, 1988; Snider & Fu, 1990).

Myth: Academics have no place in developmentally appropriate programs.

Academics represent the traditional content of the schools. In most people's minds this encompasses reading, writing, and arithmetic. Proponents of this myth believe young children are not "ready" for academics. They proudly announce that students in their programs are not expected to read or use numbers or write. Opponents point to the myth as a sign that children who participate in developmentally appropriate programs are not "learning" the essentials. They worry that such children will lack critical skills necessary for achievement. Both claims are based on an overly narrow interpretation of academic learning. They equate academics with technical subskills (e.g., reciting the alphabet or writing out numerical equations) or with rote instruction (e.g., emphasizing worksheets and drills). Each of these definitions is too narrow in scope. They confuse concepts with methods and ignore how reading, writing, and number-related behaviors and understandings emerge in young children's lives.

Children do not wait for elementary school to demonstrate an interest in words and numbers. They manifest literacy-related interests as infants when they mouth a book or pat the bunny, and again as toddlers when they beg, "Read it again." Likewise, young children count: one cookie, two shoes, three candles on the birthday cake. They compare: "Which has more?" "Who still needs some?" Children calculate: "Will it fit?" "Now I have two; I need one more." These kinds of activities form the beginnings of literacy and mathematical thinking—the true essence of academics.

Children continue on in this manner as they mature, seeking new knowledge and skills as their capacities to know and do increase. Thus, there is no specific time when such learning is either appropriate or inappropriate. These evaluative labels are better applied to the parameters within which academics are defined and the strategies teachers use to address academic learning. Programs that focus on isolated skill development and rely on long periods of whole-group instruction or abstract paper-pencil activities do not meet the needs of young children. Those that emphasize concepts and processes and utilize small-group instruction, active manipulation of relevant, concrete materials, and interactive learning provide a solid foundation for academics within a context of meaningful activity.

Using children's interests and ways of learning as guides, early childhood teachers do four things to promote academic learning. First, they understand the broad nature of literacy and mathematics and are familiar with the concepts, processes, and content that comprise them. They recognize that reading is more than reciting the alphabet or making letter-sound associations out of context, that writing is not the same as penmanship, that mathematics goes beyond rote memorization of number facts. Second, they recognize manifestations of academic interest and exploratory behavior in the children they teach (e.g., "Teacher, what does this say?" "How many do we need?" "Look what I made!"). Third, teachers provide concrete materials and relevant experiences to enhance children's academic learning. They read to children often and invite children to respond and interpret the story. They sing songs, read poems, and play rhyming games in which sound associations are addressed. They give children materials to sort, sequence, count, combine, or divide and make estimations about. They offer children many ways to express themselves both orally and in writing. Fourth, teachers introduce new information, materials, and problems that stimulate children to make observations and comparisons, question, experiment, derive meaning, make predictions and draw their own conclusions. In this way academics become an integral part of classroom life.

Myth: Developmentally appropriate programs are suitable for only certain kinds of children.

Some people believe that the notion of developmental appropriateness only fits young children, or middle-class children, or Euro-American children, or children who have no special needs. This is a fallacy. While specific details of what is appropriate for children will vary from population to population and from child to child, the principles guiding developmentally appropriate programs are universally applicable.

To put it another way, one might ask, "For which children is it *appropriate* to ignore how they develop and learn? For which child is it *inappropriate* to treat him or her as an individual? Which children are *unworthy* of respect?" If the answer is none, then there is no group for whom the basic tenets of developmental appropriateness do not apply.

SUMMARY

This chapter has chronicled an evolving concept in education, that of developmental appropriateness. Developmentally appropriate programs match how children develop and learn with how they are taught. They are founded on faith in children's capacity to learn as well as respect for children as individuals. Educators working with youngsters between the ages of 3 and 8 recognize that their learning differs significantly from that of older children and adults. Consequently, practitioners and administrators approach early childhood education with that understanding in mind. Research supports the notion that developmentally appropriate programs represent positive educational experiences for young children. Not only do children perform well academically, but their attitudes toward school remain enthusiastic and optimistic. That is not the case for many youngsters enrolled in classes that ignore their unique educational needs.

Outlined in this chapter have been fundamental principles of childhood development and learning. Corresponding implications for program design and classroom practice have also been identified. The myths that sometimes arise out of people's efforts to understand what it means to be developmentally appropriate have been discussed, as well as the realities associated with each one. The entire focus of chapter 2, therefore, has been to establish the foundation on which developmentally appropriate programs are based. As readers explore the ramifications of this concept in the chapters that follow, the ideas expressed here will be revisited again and again. There is no element of early childhood education they do not touch. Activities and routines, materials, the physical environment, classroom management, methods of parental involvement, and assessment procedures are all influenced by these principles. With this understanding, it is time to turn our attention to the heart of every educational program—the curriculum.

PART II

The Curriculum

As a prospective parent is being shown around the center, she asks the director, "What kind of curriculum do you follow?"

The first-, second-, and third-grade teachers have been called together to reexamine the social studies curriculum for the lower elementary grades. There is much talk about how that curriculum should look in comparison to the one adopted by the upper elementary committee.

Mrs. Cohen, a new kindergarten teacher, asks whether she will be expected to teach children to "write on the lines." She is told, "Oh, no. We dropped that from the curriculum 2 years ago."

The program staff have spent an exciting day learning about children's self-esteem. The question they want answered is, How can we best address self-esteem within our curriculum?

As part of the accreditation process for their school, the early childhood coordinator is asked to submit a copy of the curriculum for review.

Curriculum is something everyone connected with education talks about, yet it can mean different things to different people. When some individuals discuss curriculum, they are simply referring to the goals and objectives of the program. Others have in mind a written plan for student learning or a syllabus that lists topics of study and how they will be taught (Brewer, 1992). Still others equate curriculum with certain materials or types of activities commonly associated with a particular center or school. The form the curriculum takes also can vary from detailed written descriptions to sets of beliefs and experiences that can only be grasped by observing the program in action (Schwartz & Robison, 1982). Because there are so many interpretations of what curriculum is, we will clarify how that term relates to the curriculum detailed in the next eight chapters.

THE CURRICULUM DEFINED

Curriculum is all of the organized educational experiences provided for children by the early childhood program. These experiences can take place inside the classroom or beyond, involving educators, family members, and other people in the community. In its written form, curriculum includes stated goals and objectives, strategies and activities aimed at supporting all aspects of children's development and learning, and methods of assessing children's progress and program effectiveness.

Formulated within a framework of developmental appropriateness, the curriculum described in the chapters that follow represents one interpretation of how to educate children from 3 through 8 years of age. Hereafter, it shall be referred to as the Children's Comprehensive Curriculum. The Children's Comprehensive Curriculum has a twofold purpose: (a) to help children develop the knowledge, skills, attitudes, and dispositions essential to becoming happy, contributing members of society and (b) to give educators the tools necessary to facilitate such learning. Developed in its original form by faculty in the Department of Family and Child Ecology at Michigan State University, the Children's Comprehensive Curriculum has been implemented and evaluated in the Child Development Laboratories on campus for the past 8 years. Variations of it have been adopted by nursery school, childcare, Head Start, Chapter I, and preprimary special education programs throughout Michigan. Numerous school districts have also used the curriculum as the basis for redesigning their goals, objectives, and methods for kindergarten through the fifth grade. The version offered in this book represents an amalgamation of these adaptations.

The Children's Comprehensive Curriculum

The Children's Comprehensive Curriculum is divided into eight domains:

Aesthetic

Affective

Cognitive

Language

Physical

Social

Pretend play

Construction

Looked at individually, the first six domains represent major facets of child development; the latter two, the processes by which these facets are integrated.

Although we realize that no one aspect of development can be isolated from the rest, we have found that purposeful planning for each domain results in a more comprehensive approach to instruction. Thus, taken altogether, the entire array represents a "whole child" approach to teaching. It unites an understanding of what is (e.g., how children develop and learn) with value statements of what ought to be (e.g., goals and objectives for children's development and learning now and in the future) and with methods for achieving these aims (e.g., teaching strategies and activities). A brief overview of each domain within the Children's Comprehensive Curriculum is presented in Table 1.

TABLE 1
Curricular Domains within the Children's Comprehensive Curriculum

Domain	Developmental Focus
Aesthetic	Appreciation of the arts and enjoyment of sensory experiences
Affective	Trust, autonomy, initiative, industry, self-awareness, self-esteem
Cognitive	Perception, physical knowledge, logical-mathematical knowledge, social-conventional knowledge, scientific understanding, critical thinking skills
Language	Receptive language, listening skills, expressive language, reading, and writing
Physical	Fine and gross motor skills, body awareness, physical health
Social	Social skills and socialization
Pretend play	Imitating, pretending, role-playing, dramatizing
Construction	Imitating, representing, creating

Why Emphasize Developmental Domains over Subjects?

Practitioners more accustomed to the traditional subject-matter designations of art, math, science, reading, social studies, physical education, and the like may question the child-oriented categories of developmental domains. They may wonder whether the material included within the following chapters will meet their needs and to what extent domains relate to their work with children.

While it is true that standard curriculum divisions are comfortable because they are familiar, subject matter alone is not a sufficient source of curriculum (Spodek, 1973). Too often it leads to fragmented, isolated skill development or the exclusion of other kinds of knowledge and skills essential to children's ultimate success in society. Consequently, a subject-matter orientation is not comprehensive enough to suit our purposes. We prefer to emphasize a broader range of perceptions, dispositions, knowledge, and skills. For instance, art and music are covered under aesthetics but so too are dance and other sensory experiences. The affective domain addresses learning processes related to self-awareness and self-esteem but also the development of independence and a sense of industry. Science and math are components of the cognitive domain but do not constitute the whole of it. This domain also includes problem solving, critical thinking, and perception. Reading is found within the language domain, and so are listening, speaking, and writing. The physical domain encompasses gross and fine motor skills, health, and body image. Incorporated within the social domain are social studies content along with processes and skills fundamental to children's increased social competence.

The curricular domains of pretend play and construction are unique in that they describe processes through which children integrate the knowledge, skills, talents, and abilities developed in the other six domains. As children engage in pretend play, they talk, listen, interact socially, express emotions, explore attitudes, manipulate objects, practice creative thinking, experiment with problem solving, use their imaginations, and assimilate a variety of role behaviors. When children create models or pictures that represent their internal vision of an object or event, they are involved in construction. Thus, in these domains children produce an event (pretend play) or a product (construction).

Both pretend play and construction require representational thought. Pretend play combines enactive representation (movement, gestures, and actions) with symbolic levels (language) as children perform a narrative that they create themselves. Construction combines the iconic (drawings or sculpted objects or events) with the symbolic (language) as children attempt to demonstrate their understandings of objects. This is frequently seen as children provide commentary and explanations to make their constructions more comprehensible to others. Ultimately, children combine pretend play and construction as they build objects necessary to make the narrative of make believe episodes understandable to a group of players. In this way both pretend play and construction function as linkages between the concrete and the real, the symbolic and the abstract. They also help children make sense of their experiences and reduce the incomprehensible to terms they understand.

As children participate in the eight developmental domains, they experience a comprehensive educational curriculum that goes beyond the subject-oriented programs characteristic of many primary schools. The domain-focused curriculum also transcends the traditional materials-based programs associated with numerous preprimary settings.

Why Emphasize Developmental Domains over Materials?

Several philosophers throughout the history of early childhood education have advocated the inclusion of certain materials to enhance particular learning goals for children. Froebel's gifts; Montessori's pink tower; and Hartley, Frank, and Goldenson's emphasis on blocks, water, and clay are typical examples. In each case the role of the teacher was closely tied to facilitating children's use of these items. However, with the advent of the 1940s and 1950s, many teachers began to take a more passive role, treating the curriculum as inherent in the materials. That notion stemmed from maturational and psychoanalytic perspectives that assumed development merely unfolded in a benign environment or children needed certain materials to use in cathartic ways (Hartley, Frank, & Goldenson, 1952; Read, 1966). That point of view has given way to the more interactive approach designated in chapters 1 and 2.

The idea that materials do the teaching is still prevalent today, however. Many practitioners assume that if they have the right equipment, the instructional aspects of the program will take care of themselves (Kostelnik, 1990). When teachers assume this posture, goals for children's learning are often unspecified or ambiguous, and teachers may neglect to challenge children sufficiently. Instead, their main focus becomes one of monitoring children for appropriate material use. Although having carefully selected materials and equipment is a necessary ingredient of quality children's programs, it is not a sufficient foundation for the early childhood curriculum (Bredekamp, 1987). Materials supplement the curriculum; they do not equal it. Moreover, the same material can be used to support learning across domains. It is this broader view that distinguishes a domain-focused curriculum from a materials-based approach.

THE STRUCTURE OF CHAPTERS 3 THROUGH 10

Each of the next eight chapters focuses on a single curricular domain. All of them include these segments:

I. Introduction—This part of the chapter describes the importance of the domain to children and its relevance to early childhood education.

II. Issues—A brief discussion of current educational issues related to the domain and how they might be addressed in early childhood programs is offered next.

III. Goals and Objectives—For each domain an ultimate goal and a list of mediating objectives are presented. The ultimate goal is a global statement referring to the idealized long-range educational purpose of the domain. Ultimate goals are lifelong in intent, spanning the entire period of an individual's educational experience. They are equally applicable to children in pre-primary programs, elementary school, and middle or high school and beyond. Knowing the ultimate goal for each domain helps educators keep sight of "the big picture," giving them a focus that goes beyond any one particular skill or bit of knowledge. Ultimate goals are guideposts educators can use to gauge how well their instructional practices support long-term aims as well as immediate outcomes.

Each ultimate goal is further broken down into several mediating objectives. Mediating objectives identify distinctive categories of behavior relative to children's development and learning within the domain. They help educators recognize domain-related skill patterns and concepts and outline the content and processes around which practitioners should plan classroom instruction. In this guide these are listed in sequence from most fundamental to most complex. Consequently, the mediating objectives can be used as a guide for sequencing learning experiences for each domain. Their purpose is to give teachers needed direction in planning while simultaneously allowing them the autonomy to decide how best to address each objective in light of children's interests and capabilities. Thus, teachers can use the mediating objectives as a source of activity ideas. Such activities could include classroom routines, children's explorations of objects and concepts using classroom materials, and teacher-initiated lessons. A diagram depicting the relationship between the ultimate goal, the mediating objectives, and activities for a sample domain is offered in Table 2.

Once teachers have settled on activities that address the mediating objectives they have chosen, it is possible for them to identify more specific instructional objectives (e.g., behavioral objectives) suited to the learning needs of children in their class. We believe these latter objectives are best created by individuals who actually know the

children. For that reason, we have not attempted to identify those in this guide.

IV. Teaching Strategies—This segment offers practical, pervasive strategies teachers can use to address the domain in their classrooms. The suggested techniques have been developed by practitioners in the field and represent concrete ways to operationalize the goals and objectives cited in the preceding section.

V. Activity Suggestions—Each of the curriculum-focused chapters ends with a selection of sample activities that support the domain. All activities include the following components:
A. The activity name
B. The mediating objective to which the activity relates
C. Recommended materials
D. A general procedure for carrying out the activity with children 5 to 6 years of age
E. Suggestions for simplifying the activity (for children 3 to 4 years of age)
F. Suggestions for extending the activity (for children 7 to 8 years of age)

These activity suggestions are illustrative, not exhaustive, examples of the types of activities and lessons teachers could plan for use inside and outside the classroom. However, we have strived to present a broad array of activities that cover the range of mediating objectives within the domain.

RECONCILING THE USE OF DOMAINS WITH OTHER CURRICULAR APPROACHES

Some practitioners work in programs in which the curricular focus is established on a programwide or even statewide basis. Teachers faced with having to reconcile a more traditional subject-based or materials-based curriculum with domains have two options. First, they can advocate for a domain-focused orientation within their organization. Suggestions for how this might be accomplished are offered in chapter 17, "Improving Programs For Young Children through Individual and Group Change." Second,

TABLE 2
The relationship between the ultimate goal, selected mediating objectives, and sample activities for the physical domain.

Ultimate Goal	Mediating Objectives	Sample Activities
	Children will:	
For children to achieve physical competence and to develop knowledge, attitudes, skills, and behaviors related to a healthy lifestyle	1. develop awareness of the location of their body parts. ⟶	a. sing and act out the "Head, Shoulders, Knees, and Toes" song. b. make body tracings, labeling external body parts. c. play the "Hokey Pokey" game emphasizing left and right. d. make body tracings, labeling internal body parts.
	2. engage in activities that require balance. ⟶	a. walk the balance beam. b. play the "statue" game. c. use stilts. d. ride a two-wheel bike.
	3. practice fine motor skills. ⟶	a. move small objects with kitchen tongs. b. string beads. c. make letters in sand on trays. d. cut out snowflakes.
	4. learn health and safety procedures. ⟶	a. brush their teeth each day. b. sing "This is the way we wash our face" to the tune of "Here we go 'round the mulberry bush." c. play the "red light, green light" game. d. read a story about "good touch and bad touch."

they can look for ways to integrate their current curricular approach with the one suggested here. Most often that involves subsuming subjects or materials under the broader construct of domains. For instance, some school districts have adopted the eight curricular domains along with the ultimate goals and mediating objectives for each one. Next, committees have examined current subject-related instructional objectives (often found in a district-adopted curriculum guide) to determine their appropriateness and to what extent they support a particular domain.

Based on the committees' recommendations, suitable revisions in objectives, classroom practices, and assessment tools are enacted. Individual practitioners can pursue a similar path, clustering subjects under domains, then evaluating their instructional practices in terms of the ultimate goals for each one.

Likewise, practitioners used to thinking of curriculum as materials have begun by taking equipment standard to their program and generating ideas for how that material might be used to support mediating objectives within various domains. Blocks, for instance, could be used to address objectives in any one of the eight curricular domains. This same process can then be repeated with other objects such as art materials, puzzles, small manipulative items, sand, and water. An illustrative example of this method of integration is provided in chapter 11, "Organizing Space, Materials, and Time."

In conclusion, we believe that as more and more programs consider adopting policies and procedures to support developmentally appropriate practice, the notion of curricular domains will become increasingly common. There are al-

ready numerous programs in which such designations are being used (Battle Creek Public Schools, 1990; Carman-Ainsworth Community Schools, 1986; Forest Hills Public Schools, 1988; Michigan Department of Education, 1985; Midland Public Schools, 1991; Ministry of Education, Province of British Columbia, 1989; Traverse City Public Schools, 1987). One purpose of this text is to help educators better understand this approach to curriculum planning and implementation. The best way to get started is to examine what each domain entails, beginning with the aesthetic domain.

CHAPTER 3

The Aesthetic Domain

*The teacher carefully uncovers a large print of
the painting* An Afternoon at La Grande Jatte,
*by George Seurat. "Here's another one to look
at. Tell me what you see in this painting."
The small group of 5-year-olds seated on the
floor kneel up to look more closely. Albert
announces, "This is good work. I like it." Gillian
says, "It's a happy earth." Bowa agrees, "I like
this. Lots of color and a cat." The teachers nods
and asks, "Where is this place?" Paul points to
the corner, "I see boats." Caitlin notices, "This
is a place with a lot of trees. There's a lady
trying to catch a fish." Kimberly leans in and
says, "I see a monkey and a dog. I think it's
South America or Africa." Their teacher smiles
and says, "You're all looking very carefully; I
wonder what you think the artist was trying to
tell us in this painting." Jill shouts, "It's about a
wedding — there's the wedding girl!"*

Watch the happy faces of the children surveying
a colorful painting; note the absorption of a
youngster carefully selecting a favorite rock from
the variety collected on a tray; notice the expressiveness of the child swaying slowly to a guitar
melody or moving rhythmically to the sound of a
marching band; see the intensity of a group of
children as they decide where to place the red
shapes on the collage, or the look of pride as a
child puts the finishing touches on a wood and
glue sculpture. Each of the youngsters described
is involved in an aesthetic activity appropriate for
early childhood educational settings. Activities
such as these "provide necessary opportunities
for children to develop creativity and perceptual
awareness, and also significant possibilities for
children to experience success in ways that
might not otherwise be available to them"
(Dixon & Chalmers,1990, p. 17).

AESTHETIC
DEVELOPMENT DEFINED

In the broadest sense, *aesthetics* is the awareness and appreciation of pleasant sensory expe-

riences (Feeney & Moravcik, 1987). Aesthetic
development deals with the child's capacity to
perceive, be sensitive to, and respond to human
creations and beauty in the natural environment.
In essence, it is the integration and organization
of thoughts, feelings, and perceptions involving
heightened awareness and increased intensity
of feelings — turning up the volume, so to speak,
on pleasurable discoveries. This process of integration may occur internally as insights or may
be expressed outwardly in a variety of personally meaningful ways.

Aesthetic development involves a combination
of both responsive and productive skill areas (see
Figure 3.1). The responsive component includes
(a) appreciation of beauty in nature, (b) appreciation of the arts, and (c) formation of judgments
and preferences; while the productive component
involves (d) creative expression. Creative expression provides opportunities for children to demonstrate or express their thoughts, feelings, and
perceptions in ways that can take nonverbal, verbal, or a blend of forms. Nonverbal expression
may be manifested through the visual arts (drawing, painting, sculpture, ceramics, and printmaking
are among those commonly introduced to young
children), instrumental music, movement, and
dance. Verbal expression can take the forms of
singing, composing poetry, telling stories, humor,
and so on. Other expressive modes are combinations of forms — for example, creative dramatics
and filmmaking, which may integrate both verbal
and pictorial elements. Young children frequently
combine their graphic representations with storytelling to achieve a more meaningful whole than
they are able to produce with either one alone.
Thus, teachers in preprimary and early primary
grades often see combinations of presentations
containing nonverbal symbols accompanied by
explanations, stories, gestures, sound effects,
and other expressions from youngsters.

THE SCOPE OF THIS CHAPTER

Aesthetic learning encompasses a broad spec-
trum of experiences related to many different art
forms: the performing arts, storytelling, poetry,
movement, dance, dramatics, visual arts, music,
and others. Although this chapter touches on

This chapter was written by Barbara Rohde, Department
of Family and Child Ecology, Michigan State University.

FIGURE 3.1
Components of Aesthetic
Development

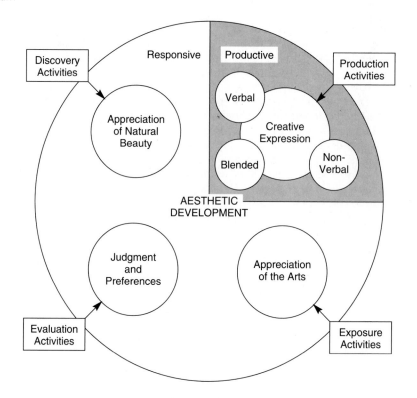

several of these, in order to be brief and utilize examples that are most helpful to early childhood professionals, the main focus is on the visual arts and music, two areas that tend to dominate planning in this domain for preprimary and early primary settings. However, it should be noted that activities involving the natural world, the performing arts, storytelling, poetry, movement, dance, and drama can be found in other chapters throughout the book. For example, nature discovery activities are found in the cognition chapter; storytelling activities are located in chapters dealing with pretend play and language; movement and dance activities are primarily found in the chapter devoted to the physical domain. Moreover, by selecting an aesthetic goal (such as to gain pleasure from a variety of sensory experiences or to contribute to the aesthetic environment of the school) and focusing on this purpose in carrying them out, many kinds of activities throughout other chapters can be transformed into purely aesthetic experiences for children.

THE AESTHETIC DOMAIN AND YOUNG CHILDREN

Because young children are naturally curious and exploratory, the aesthetic domain is particularly relevant to them. They love looking at nature, creating, looking at and talking about art. They express their feelings and ideas through succinct and picturesque language, improvised song, and expressive movements. They also have strong preferences for books, objects, and food. They are creative and inquisitive (Feeney & Moravcik, 1987). Very young children are often motivated to become involved simply by the art or musical materials presented, especially when variations of approach and media are introduced from time to time. Older youngsters often respond with interest to enthusiastic adults who show an interest in their work and teach them new techniques as they are ready.

Aesthetic development in young children follows predictable sequences or expected stages that are evident in both children's productive and responsive behaviors. Many aspects of aesthetic growth, including children's musical interests, art and musical evaluation behaviors, creative art production behaviors, listening skills development, and creative musical behaviors have been observed and recorded; aesthetic milestones in this developmental sequence are summarized here.

Expectations for Musical Interest

Studies have been designed to give educators a clearer idea of how musical interests develop in children (Dowling & Harwood, 1986; McDonald & Simons, 1989). In infancy the appeal is usually the quality of sound. Babies often show interest in adults singing to them, the sound of bells, and soft music. As children grow and are exposed to various musical experiences, their interests broaden to include the element of melody; they learn to prefer what they become familiar with, particularly enjoying songs with repetition in which the same melody is heard again and again. Later, children take a keener interest in pitch, recognizing when sounds go up or down and discriminating when sounds have changed. Older children eventually attempt to match pitches and correct mismatched pitches. Studies have also shown that many young children have difficulty attending to more than one musical dimension (such as pitch, volume, duration, rhythm, beat, or tempo) simultaneously and, when asked to make decisions about what they hear, do not respond with any degree of accuracy (Gordon, 1981). Though it is understood by educators that within any group of children of a given age a wide range of musical abilities will be found, it is also clear that musical interest and appreciation can be enhanced through a variety of regular musical experiences.

Sequence of Aesthetic Evaluation Behaviors

Children's early aesthetic responses begin with sensory exploration of objects. For example, a child may demonstrate preferences for a particular texture or smell, such as the soft edge on a blanket or a particular beloved toy. Many children as early as 3 or 4 years old begin to make choices from their environment, gathering and exploring collections of particular objects such as stones, shells, or buttons. At a later stage, these collections become more sophisticated and must be acquired by very deliberate searches. The treasured objects may be bottlecaps, coins, baseball cards, special dolls, or models of horses. In addition, children are likely to enjoy spontaneous conversations about these special objects and demonstrate beginning levels of adult aesthetic evaluative behaviors—describing, analyzing, interpreting, and judging—but often they need help organizing their comments and applying criteria.

Children learn evaluation skills (judging their own creative representations and the work of others) in predictable sequences as well. At first young children's experiences with art materials and musical instruments are purely sensory; often the process of manipulation is much more important to them than the product created. Frequently a youngster's early art or music is made without regard to the effect of their work on others. Later, a greater attempt to communicate ideas and meaning becomes important to children and they begin to evaluate their own work according to emerging aesthetic standards, based on their own developing taste and combined with messages they receive from their environment (Feeney & Moravcik, 1987).

Sequence of Visual Art Productive Behaviors

Creative art behaviors have been the subject of countless studies (Seefeldt, 1987). Children's drawings produced at various ages have been analyzed and grouped according to predictable stages. The classic work by Lowenfeld and Brittain (1965) describes these developmental stages in detail and is a good basic text about young children's art (summarized in Figure 3.2). Teachers who are looking for a simple summary of the stages of children's drawings can also find one in Jenkins's (1980) book, *Art for the Fun of It: A Guide for Teaching Young Children.*

Expected Musical Listening Behaviors

Before the age of 5 months, infants are generally passive receivers of music. Soon after, children begin to pay attention and respond to the dynamics and timbre of musical sounds. By as

Stage 1: Scribbling (approximate ages 2–4 years)

Early—Disordered scribbling (purely kinesthetic)
Middle—Controlled scribbling (child notices connection between motions and resulting marks; variety of motions)
Later—Naming scribbles (child connects marks to world around him or her; color designates different meanings)

Stage 2: First Representational Attempts—Preschematic (approximate ages 4–7 years)

The child controls scribbling motions to produce simple symbols (circle, vertical and horizontal lines) that relate to the visual world.
Early—Symbols change constantly; objects appear randomly placed; color choices not based on reality but emotional reactions; often produces a "person" using these symbols.
Later—Greater control allows experimentation with a variety of symbols; exaggeration of certain symbols indicates importance to the child.

Stage 3: Schematic (approximate ages 7–9 years)

The child arrives at highly individualized visual symbols (schema) that satisfy him or her and are repeatedly used. Schemas represent the child's active knowledge of objects; modifications of schemas result only when meaningful experiences influence their thinking. Spacial relationships are not random; inside-outsides are depicted simultaneously; colors are chosen according to perceptions of reality.

FIGURE 3.2
Developmental Stages of Self-Expression in Young Children

early as 1 year old, many can distinguish songs they hear often and are likely to notice pitch, melody, and rhythm. Much later they begin to take note of harmony. By 5 or 6 years of age many children can demonstrate an understanding of sound contrasts such as high/low, loud/soft, up/down. Six-year-olds are beginning to be able to identify pairs of chords as same or different (McDonald & Simons, 1989).

Expected Creative Musical Behaviors

Very young children (2 years old and younger) often explore musical instruments and singing using inaccurate rhythm with the focus on motor energy. Following a period of vocal play and experimentation, 2-year-olds may produce "phrase-songs" that consist of rhythmic repetition of a word or phrase with pitch inflection, close to that of speech. By 3 years of age many youngsters, if encouraged to express themselves musically, begin to impose structure on their improvisations by repeating selected patterns. As their vocal control is gained, they expand their range of usable pitches and can produce melodies more accurately. Later, they

are able to fit together diverse rhythm patterns and appear to sense the function of form. By age 5, many children can utilize a steady accurate beat and melody and rhythm repetitions (McDonald & Simons, 1989).

AESTHETIC LEARNING AND EDUCATION

While some theorists believe that acquisition of aesthetic competence develops over time with increasing age, many studies suggest there are sociological determinants of aesthetic perceptions such as family background, quality of education, occupation, and patterns of consumption of goods and services in the arts (Seefeldt, 1987). Teachers and educational programs greatly affect children's aesthetic development, influencing the extent they value the arts and providing a rich background of experiences that free them to become creative producers and tasteful consumers of the arts.

Aesthetic experiences in the classroom may involve children as participants, as observers, or a combination of both. Good educational pro-

The Scribble Stage

grams offer all three approaches, providing opportunities to make, see, and think about the arts and nature. Teachers that do this task well offer four sorts of activities:

1. *Discovery activities*—These encourage children to notice details, look and listen for similarities and differences, and point out the wonders of natural phenomena. They take advantage of outdoor settings where children are taught to watch, listen to, smell, and feel the natural environment with respect and appreciation.
2. *Productive activities*—Children are stimulated to use materials in expressive ways, explore new possibilities, and receive positive encouragement for their unique creations. They offer chances to sing, play instruments, dance, and move to music in self-expressive ways.

3. *Exposure activities*—Children are provided opportunities to see art exhibited, hear music played and sung, and watch performances of dance and theater. They give children a wide range of musical and art experiences that reach beyond what their daily life offers and broadens their repetoire of aesthetic understanding.
4. *Evaluation activities*—Children are encouraged to recognize and critique a variety of art and musical forms, select criteria for evaluation, and express preferences based on their criteria.

In addition to contributing to aesthetic development, art and musical experiences impact higher levels of thinking. They help develop the ability to visualize, stimulate use of the imagination, and offer opportunities for creative prob-

The Preschematic Stage

lem solving (Hitz, 1987) and decision making. The creative process "can be seen as a series of cognitive events for the child. It involves confrontation with obstacles and choices in a process of making and overcoming false starts, investigation, adaptation and transformation" (Dixon & Chalmers, 1990, p. 12).

An important role of aesthetic learning is to lay the groundwork for strong links to the achievements of the past. Teachers who successfully plan activities in this domain help nurture responsible citizens who value the arts as an essential part of everyone's life and who appreciate that the arts maintain and improve our collective existence. Additionally, aesthetic growth promotes a willingness to preserve that which they value for the generations still to come. Children who learn to love beauty in nature, music, and the arts are likely to want to support and protect these valuable resources.

Moreover, many educators feel music and art are essential for balancing the educational lives of children, to give them an avenue to find focus and achieve tranquility in an increasingly fast-moving world.

> For young children, experiences in music and art can compensate for the pervasiveness of verbal interaction and abstract symbolism in the classroom, at an age [stage] when words and written symbols may have insufficient relevance to their own expression of ideas. Plastic, visual, and aural media provide means for children to realize ideas that need not rely on verbal or numerical concepts stressed in other areas of the curriculum. (Dixon & Chalmers, 1990, p. 12)

In recent years, aesthetic learning has been valued as a tool for meeting other significant educational needs. As stated at the Mid-Atlantic Regional Forum on National Educational Goals

The Schematic Stage

(May 1991), the arts play a vital role in establishing a bond between the generations that technology sometimes drives apart. This important link is the glue that holds the generations together and adds to a shared affective experience for people of all ages.

All of the arts stimulate special qualities to the classroom social climate. Group activities that incorporate aesthetically enjoyable elements have been utilized by classes as cohesion facilitators and expressions of social solidarity. The group who sings together, creates puppets together, plays instruments together, and dances together is more likely to behave cooperatively in other circumstances.

Experiences with music, the visual arts, dance, and dramatics can serve as powerful symbols of cultural identity for children (Dowling & Harwood, 1986). Through exploring aesthetic examples of their own cultures, children's concept of their individual and collective heritages are enhanced, which thus adds to mutual respect

among cultures. In addition, carefully selected experiences with artifacts, music, fine crafts, and other meaningful artistic examples from other cultures can give children a broader understanding of diversity in the world.

Finally, research has shown positive links between the arts and learning in other areas. Several successful programs in various areas of the country have been taking advantage of the strong connection between basic academic learning and time spent in creative endeavors: *Arts Impact* (1973) is an example of a program that utilized the connection between the arts and learning to read. *All the Arts for Every Child* (1973) showed positive relationships among the arts, development of self-concept, and academic achievement. Other successful programs were established that linked the arts with language development and cognitive development (Seefeldt, 1987). A recently published study (Gunsberg, 1991) indicates the effectiveness of improvised musical play with young children to foster group cohesion, establish a play format, and elaborate on the play. It is easy to see why many educators are coming to realize the vital role this important domain plays in the education of the whole child.

CURRENT EDUCATIONAL ISSUES

Teachers and administrators are faced with many issues that affect their thinking, planning, and implementation of educational programs for young children. Some of the current concerns dealing with aesthetic development are discussed next.

Teaching the Arts without Special Training

"I am expected to teach art and music in my classroom. Isn't it best to leave those areas to the specialists?"

Classroom teachers need not be artists or musicians in order to teach children to appreciate the arts and be aware of beauty in their natural surroundings. Any personally productive experiences that teachers have had, whether writing a paper in college, decorating a home, or planting a vegetable garden, can help them identify with the act of creating. "Every teacher does not have to be practiced in all media in order to think creatively. It is rather the intense experience accompanying any creative occupation that is important for keeping alive the teacher's appreciation and understanding of creative experiences of their students" (Lowenfeld & Brittain, 1965, p. 81). Teachers who believe the arts and a love of natural beauty are important, who openly demonstrate these attitudes and encourage children to involve themselves in creative endeavors, do much to influence children's positive attitudes and aesthetic development regardless of the teacher's specialized background or training.

Schools with music and art instructors who are available to elementary classes are privileged to be able to take advantage of their expertise. Unfortunately, even districts with such resource people cannot meet the needs of individual elementary classrooms for frequent, meaningful, integrated aesthetic experiences for young children.

Teachers are wise to utilize specialists when possible, observe strategies of motivation and responding to children's work, and ask for advice concerning materials and techniques unfamiliar to them. However, teachers should avoid relying on specialists to provide the bulk of aesthetic experiences. Instead, their weekly planning should include aesthetic experiences designed for their particular group of youngsters, based on understanding individual and group interests and that unique knowledge of the children only classroom teachers can achieve. Moreover, children should have daily opportuntities for singing and making music with their classroom teacher in both planned and spontaneous activities, throughout each week.

Using Models with Young Children

"The parents love it when the kids bring home their paper turkey all decorated the way I do. What's the harm?"

Teachers sometimes fall into the trap of presenting art materials with a particular end product in mind (a model), one designed by either the teacher or a commercial firm, and believe they are encouraging aesthetic growth. Nothing could be further from the truth. Listen as the well-meaning teacher introduces the activity: "Today we're all going to make turkeys just like this one [holds up a completed brown paper tracing of a hand, with four fingers colored as feathers, and a head indicated with an eye colored on the thumb]. First you trace your hand on the paper I gave you, and then take your red crayon and...." When children are expected to follow step-by-step directions, severely limited to the teacher's idea, choice of materials, and techniques, they are forced to produce something that most likely holds no meaning for them and frequently causes feelings of frustration when they observe that their finished product does not meet the standard set by the teacher's model. The good intentions of the teacher for a fun activity result in students with negative attitudes about art materials, convinced they are incapable and can never be any good at art. Moreover, activities such as this are very destructive to whatever creative thinking children may bring to the activity, since all of the finished work is intended to look alike and children are not reinforced for imaginative approaches to the task set down by the teacher.

Consider how this same activity could be presented in a way that encourages more creative results: "Does anyone know the name of this bird? [teacher holds up a large photograph of a real turkey]. What do you notice about it? How many legs does it have? Look carefully at the neck, notice that reddish-orange piece of skin. Has anyone ever seen a turkey? Where do you think you'd find a turkey? Where else? What would that look like? OK, all of you had really good ideas. Today you can go to the art table and make your own kind of turkey if you want, any way you want. Remember, everyone's will be different because we all have our own ideas. There are some materials on the shelf nearby [points to baskets and small trays holding a variety of paper, crayons, scissors, glue sticks, markers, yarn, feathers, pipe cleaners, and scrap paper] to use. If you want to use anything that's not on the shelf, just ask me. I'll come by and see how you're doing in a while. Your turkey could be big or little, fat or thin, whatever you want. Now who will be the first four at the table?" Children who are interested and motivated readily move to the art table. Those who wish to make something different are also encouraged to take a turn. Finished works are hung or put aside to dry. The children produce a flock of unique creations that are personally satisfying. Children look at each other's work, notice new things, and learn from each other. The teacher has used a model (the photograph) that stimulated children's thinking instead of limited it.

Involving Children in Music

"I can't sing; how can I possibly get these children interested in music?"

All children sing; "they begin as soon as they gain sufficient control over their voice to talk. It is one unmistakeable universal that there is no human culture in which people do not sing" (Dowling & Harwood, 1986, p. 72). Even teachers with little musical training or who feel less than adequate singing can share the joy of music with youngsters. Some guidelines that will help are presented in Figure 3.3.

Choosing Appropriate Aesthetic Materials for Young Children

"There are lots of different materials out there. How do I choose what's best for my class?"

Art Materials.   Most young children enjoy open-ended materials (universals) that offer opportunities to explore, manipulate, and transform the medium into whatever their imaginations can think of. Lowenfeld and Brittain (1965) state, "Any art material used with children must fit their needs — should encourage free expression without the intrusion of technical difficulties" (p. 104). Tempera paints mixed to a good consistency — thick enough so they are not runny, but thin enough to flow off the brush (runny tempera and extra thick can be used for satisfying experiences occasionally) — large manila or newsprint paper, and a collection of various-size brushes are good basic art materials for any early elementary classroom. Other suggestions are crayons (various sizes), nonpermanent markers, colored chalk, a variety of construction paper colors, tissue paper, cheap white paper (computer or thin drawing paper), nontoxic glues, white paste, various kinds of tape, scissors, staplers, paper fasteners, hole punches, and collage materials (magazine pictures, string, yarn, fabric and paper scraps, cotton balls, glitter). For three-dimensional work teachers should have available cardboard of various thicknesses, potter's (ceramic) clay, Play-doh,® plaster of paris, liquid starch, and a good supply of old newspapers.

Materials that are *inappropriate* for young children include the following:

Oil-based paints

Inks that are not water soluble

Leaded paints of any kind

Turpentine

Paint thinners

Asbestos products

Chemically treated wood

Any products that are toxic or create toxic fumes

- Approach singing with a positive attitude. Think of singing as a valuable use of time that adds pleasure to everyone's day.
- Sing familiar tunes often. Children will achieve a sense of mastery and begin to create their own variations.
- Teach new songs occasionally to expand children's repertoire.
- Know the song well. Practice until you feel confident you can sing it without stumbling over the words or melody.
- Write the words to the song ahead of time on large paper. Have them available to use as a reference, help other adults sing along, and add a written language dimension to singing.
- Use your body and voice to show enthusiasm—smile, gesture, sing boldly, avoid apologizing for your voice, laugh with the children at funny parts or little mistakes.
- Tell children something you like about the song.
- Use songs from a variety of sources—songbooks, records, tapes, suggestions from children or parents, or your own childhood.
- Carefully select songs that are appropriate for the children in your class. Consider the following characteristics of songs:

  Content—Text subject and level of sophistication
  Range—Usually the notes that appear on the musical staff (not above it or below) are appropriate for young voices.
  Repetition—Younger children usually enjoy more repetition.
  Complexity—Simpler songs for the younger children, ones with a single melody that repeats. More complex forms may have various melody and/or rhythm changes and are appropriate for more experienced singers.

- Sing at various times during the session and in a variety of settings—at arrival, group time, outdoors, during free-choice times, on field trips, and at dismissal.
- Teach simple songs that, once learned in the original form, allow children to make up their own variations, such as the "Little Box Song" (sung to the tune of "Polly Wolly Doodle"):

  > Oh, I wish I had a little [red] box,
  > To put that [Peter] in.
  > I'd put him in and clap-clap-clap,
  > And take him out again.

  Invite children to substitute their name and a color they like.
- Challenge children to sing a familiar song in a new way—as fast, slow, quiet, or loud as they can; humming the tune; changing the rhythm; or inserting new words.
- Incorporate movement into singing. Use songs with hand motions such as "The Itsy Bitsy Spider," "Where Is Thumbkin," or ones that encourage whole-body movements such as "The Noble Duke of York" and "Head, Shoulders, Knees, and Toes."
- Play singing games such as "Here We Go 'Round the Mulberry Bush" or "Ring Around the Rosie" that involve everyone doing the same motions, or others that require leader/follower motions such as "Farmer in the Dell" or "Strut, Miss Mary."
- Play music that encourages children to dance or move spontaneously, alone or with a partner.
- Provide movement enhancers such as colorful scarves or streamers made from crepe paper attached to tongue depressor sticks or fabric strips to wave in response to music.
- Use speech-to-song instruction for helping the older nontuneful singer achieve greater pitch accuracy. Plan tone-matching experiences, then introduce short melodic patterns, pitched in the vocal range of the child, having him or her mimic you. Later gradually introduce melodies in a true singing range, having the child imitate them. (Roberts & Davies, 1975, p. 40)

FIGURE 3.3
Hints for Success in Teaching Music

Many early childhood educators favor use of a great variety of materials and are constantly searching for new and different ones to introduce to youngsters. As a result, some teachers are reluctant to repeat an activity or even to offer the same materials 2 days in a row, perhaps for fear children will get bored. Carol Seefeldt, professor of early childhood and child development at the University of Maryland, warns that "children continually faced with new media are never able to gain control over, or develop skill in the use of any one medium. Unless children have the opportunity to gain experience with a medium over time, they will find it difficult to achieve the skills required to use that medium as a means of artistic expression" (1987, p. 201). Teachers who agree that children should have many opportunities to use basic art materials to develop this sense of mastery make the same materials available several days in a row and repeat activities many times over the school year. After children have had repeated experiences with a medium such as clay or paint, their renewed interest can be stimulated if slight variations are presented along with the familiar materials. For example, a teacher who has provided poster paints with large newsprint paper and big brushes for several days might mix white paint into a set of the paint cups, thus making pastel colors available; other variations could be to suggest painting on black paper, large pieces of wallpaper, long paper on the floor, or wood.

Music Materials.   Materials for musical activities should follow the same criteria as those appropriate for art; that is, they should fit the needs of the children, encouraging free expression without the intrusion of technical difficulties. Rhythm instruments (drums, sticks, maracas, triangles, etc.) are appropriate for younger children. They can offer opportunities for musical expression and exploration of sounds, beats, and rhythms without concern for technique, except to use them in a safe manner. Older children who are becoming more interested in melody find pitched instruments (such as xylophones, pianos, bells, and recorders) to be satisfying for individual musical expression or for group playing. Accompanying chorded instruments (those able to play more than one pitch at a time) such as guitar, piano, keyboard, or Autoharp add interest and variety to children's singing but are not necessary for musical success in the classroom. Other musical materials appropriate for young children include a record player with a variety of records and a cassette tape recorder that can be used by children themselves, along with a collection of prerecorded and blank cassette tapes.

Avoiding Competition

"The best paintings will be hung in the hallway for everyone to see." "The one who tells the best story will win the contest." "Our daughter suddenly stopped singing after her experience in the vocal contest in elementary school."

Young children who are given opportunities for free creative expression in art and music are confused by practices that include competition. Children's musical and artistic expression are highly individual, with no two children entirely alike; indeed, an important goal of aesthetic development is to bring out this uniqueness, to show it is valuable, and encourage every child's involvement, assuming a broad range of talent, experience, and insights. To young children, there is no right or wrong way to create, and so to say there is a "best" product is meaningless to them. Imposing arbitrary adult standards of artistic excellence on their work is inappropriate and unacceptable for young children. "Particularly in the early years, children should be free from competitive and other imposed adult standards that can limit self-expression" (Dixon & Chalmers, 1990, p. 12–13). Teachers should be careful to encourage free creative expression and avoid using words that communicate competition or instill fear of failure such as *good, bad, best, worst, right, wrong, cheat,* and *mistake.* Likewise, all children should be encouraged to sing, dance, and participate in musical production without regard to the performance criteria. If music is seen as sharing and communicating rather than performing, the children are freer to explore their creative capacities.

Regular classroom or hall art displays, usually held for the children's sake, are a good way of showing what has been accomplished. Displaying children's art tells students that the teacher values their efforts, thinks the arts are important, and likes them as individuals. Therefore, it

Children enjoy creating a variety of musical sounds.

is important to show some of every student's work whenever possible; unfortunately, when space is limited, not all work can be exhibited and teachers are forced to make selections. In this event, the teacher could ask children to help choose what will be displayed and make selections based on what they feel they would like to have exhibited, having children take turns being the exhibitors. Using this strategy changes the focus to the children choosing what they feel best about, instead of the teacher imposing selection criteria from an adult point of view. It also involves them in an evaluation process that is personally meaningful.

While pattern work and copying can be important to meet other educational goals (see the chapters regarding cognitive and physical development), no work should be displayed as *art* that does not express the child's own experience. Therefore, teacher-designed patterns (such as the hand-tracing turkey described earlier), in which each student's product is identical to the next, do not reflect individual expression and should not be reinforced as successful artistic works.

Young children need not see their work displayed for long periods of time. Many youngsters quickly lose the intimate relationship to their own work when it is displayed too long; often very young children want to take things home as soon as possible. Teachers who change class displays frequently make more opportunities for children's work to be recognized and lend variety to the aesthetic environment of the school.

Another way teachers show they value creative aesthetic expression is by collecting samples of each student's artwork in individual "portfolios" kept as a record of progress over a period of time (e.g., 2 months), then sent home or given to parents at an evaluation conference. Such artifacts are extremely valuable in demonstrating the student's growth from one term to the next. In addition, other creative experiences can be recorded on audiocassette tapes. Children should be encouraged to record themselves singing songs, telling stories, playing musical instruments, and creating rhythms; they are more likely to do this if there is no pressure to be perfect. By preserving these creative endeavors, children may replay their own tape for themselves or for others, and recordings can also be available for conferences with parents.

Responding to Children's Aesthetic Products

"I'm not sure what to say to children when they show me what they've made. I don't want to say the wrong thing."

Traditionally, adults respond in various ways to children's artwork, and each approach can affect the child artist in different ways. Teachers who are sensitive to children's feelings and want to see them continue producing creatively should consider using strategies that encourage, not discourage children. Robert Schirrmacher, assistant professor of early childhood education and child development, Spring Hill College, has written an excellent article that analyzes the impact of six kinds of adult responses (Schirrmacher, 1986): complimentary, judgmental, valuing, questioning, probing, and correcting. Table 3.1 presents a short summary of the impact of each adult approach to a young student's art.

Effective Responses.   When a verbal response is needed, the educator should shift from looking for representation (adult realism) to a more effective approach, such as focusing on one or more of the elements of visual arts: line, color, form, texture, composition, balance, pattern, or contrast. For example, "You've used blue, yellow and orange in your picture today" or "You found a way to make this part look bumpy and that part look smooth." These kinds of comments encourage aesthetic awareness in the child and may establish the beginning of dialogue if the child is comfortable discussing his or her work further (Schirrmacher, 1986). Probing responses, used occasionally, encourage children to talk about their work from their own perspective. Listen to what the child says, and respond in terms of that, remaining nonjudgmental but interested. For example, if the child points out that all the bumpy part is the rough road that the tractor is driving on, the teacher can use that information for further responses, such as "You're interested in tractors" or "You wanted to show how rough that road is." Older children frequently use more realism in their artwork, and their pictures contain obviously recognizable symbols; it is still advisable for teachers to remain as objective as possible in their responses. Comments such as "That tree has lots of apples on it" or "You've made the cars all different colors" indicate understanding

TABLE 3.1
Impact of Various Responses to Children's Art

Response	Example	Impact on Child
Complimentary	"Very nice."	Cuts off discussion; lacks sincerity
Judgmental	"Great work, Joey."	Empty comment with overuse. Child thinks anything they do is terrific, no matter how little effort.
Valuing	"I like that a lot."	Puts emphasis on the product, not the process; too often rewards what is recognizable by adults, ignores personal expression that is not
Questioning	"What is it?"	Insists it be something; disregards nonrepresentational expression; disappoints the artist who thinks it is obvious
Probing	"Tell me all about it."	Encourages child to discuss; avoids passing judgment on child's work; assumes child will enjoy/learn from verbalizing ideas. Children may avoid adults that ask this every time. Use this method sparingly.
Correcting	"Very good, but the grass should be green."	Assumes child should copy reality; can discourage creative expression

of meaning but do not establish a preference for realism over nonrepresentational art. Teachers can bring closure to their comments by indicating progress the child is making and effort put in or simply acknowledging their feelings. Table 3.2 summarizes effective reactions to children's artwork.

Coping with Funding Cuts in the Arts

"My district is cutting back on money for things like art and music. I'm concerned about how this will affect the children."

When districts integrate the arts extensively into the curriculum, making the visual arts, music, dance, and drama part of the fabric of daily classroom experiences, they take advantage of the powerful positive influence that aesthetic growth can have on children's lives and community attitudes, judgments, and values. However, some districts experiencing financial problems see the arts as expendable.

Some schools that have their funds for the arts cut narrow the range of aesthetic opportunities for youngsters to a few public "end prod-

TABLE 3.2
Effective Responses to Children's Art

Response	Example	Impact on Child
Acknowledge effort.	"You worked a long time on that."	Effort is appreciated.
Comment on one of the aesthetic elements.	"You used lots of different shapes." "You found a way to make that part look bumpy and this part look smooth." "You made the bright yellow areas look even brighter next to the dark grey ones." "I see lots of zig-zags in that drawing."	Helps child organize thinking about various aspects of artistic expression
Indicate understanding of symbols used.	"Your tree has lots of fruit." "The people are standing in the rain."	Assures child his or her symbols are clear
Acknowledge feelings.	"You're disappointed in your painting." "You're pretty proud of your collage."	Lets child know it is OK to have various feelings about own work
Ask for information.	"Show me a part that you like." "Tell me one thing about your picture."	Encourages child to verbalize thoughts
Broaden their self-awareness.	"You really like animals." "That train was pretty scarey to you."	Expands child's concept of self
Indicate progress.	"This is the third painting you've made about the field trip." "You're pressing harder; I can see the leaf clearly under your paper."	Recognizes goal-directed behaviors in the arts

uct" goals such as an annual art display, a single dramatic production, or a concert. While these activities are valuable, educators are beginning to recognize the loss of the arts in the daily curriculum as a mistake. This limited approach to aesthetic learning cannot accommodate the broad range of individual interests and learning styles of all of the children. As a result, many young children only rarely participate in creative tasks, and some are not involved at all. The following list cites possible results of cutting school funds for the arts:

1. Fewer opportunities for creative experiences
2. A narrower range of chances for success for students
3. Decreased motivation among students
4. Limited recognition of talents
5. Less valuing and appreciation of cultural heritage
6. Less incentive to imagine, solve problems, and make decisions
7. Less cohesive bond in class groups
8. A widening gap between children and older generations
9. Aesthetic tastes more strongly influenced by mass media
10. Satisfying experiences sought elsewhere (streets, drugs, etc.)

Knowing the consequences of such cuts, teachers should do all they can to urge administrators and community leaders to speak out for maintaining strong programs that place high value on regular aesthetic experiences for young children.

GOALS AND OBJECTIVES

The ultimate goal is for children to integrate feelings, thoughts, and action within visual and performing arts and other sensory experiences to achieve pleasurable, personally meaningful ends.

Mediating Objectives

As children progress toward the ultimate goal, they will

1. gain pleasure from sensory experiences with no other goal in mind.

2. become more familiar with various forms of the arts.
3. become more familiar with various styles within a particular art form.
4. use tools, materials, and techniques to achieve a desired aesthetic effect.
5. become more familiar with basic elements of visual arts (line, color, form, texture, composition, balance, pattern, contrast).
6. become more familiar with basic elements of music (pitch, duration, rhythm, beat, tempo, timbre, simultaneity, tone color, dynamics, harmony, form).
7. actively engage in or respond to performing arts experiences.
8. recognize, reflect on, and discuss aesthetic experiences.
9. work collaboratively with others to create art and music.
10. appreciate art and music as means of nonverbal communication.
11. recognize the wide array of materials from which artists and musicians may choose to express themselves.
12. recognize their own strengths as creative and performing artists.
13. engage in art and music criticism (describe, analyze, interpret, judge).
14. develop their ability to imagine that which is not there (visualization) and to remember or create music in their minds (audiation).
15. contribute to the aesthetic environment of the school.
16. appreciate their own cultural heritage and cultures of others through the arts.
17. develop a concept of the arts as a lifelong pursuit.

TEACHING STRATEGIES

1. *Model aesthetic awareness.* Respond to the aesthetic qualities of the world around you. Talk about discoveries and enthusiasm you have about works of art or music you enjoy. Demonstrate a positive attitude about opportunities to be involved in the arts both in and out of school. Be a role model for how to be engaged in the arts; for example, tell children ways you are a participant (saw a theater performance, listened to music, played an instrument, or attended a

concert). Emphasize the enjoyment you and your family get from this kind of activity. Arrange for an artist or musician to visit your class, or take the class to visit an artist in his or her studio or at a rehearsal. A valuable school program that some districts have instituted is the artist-in-residence program. Children learn by watching the artist at work, seeing works in progress, and coming to realize that artists do this in real life.

2. *Take an active rather than passive role in this domain.* Some teachers treat aesthetic experiences passively; that is, they make basic materials available and provide time for creative endeavors but take a "watch and wait" attitude, assuming children who are interested will be productive. This kind of strategy can have negative effects on aesthetic growth since children may be getting the message "My teacher doesn't think those things are important." Instead, teachers should promote children's interests in experimenting with materials and tools, exploring new combinations, and suggesting ideas on which children can expand. Keep interest alive when offering repeated experiences with the same material, occasionally adding variations (such as various-size brushes, different wooden shapes for pressing into the Play-doh®), and suggesting individual or small-group projects from which children could choose. As children show interest in various topics, teachers should encourage children to participate in producing creative artifacts that relate to that topic. For example, a teacher may say, "That story was fun. Right now, those of you who would like to make birds like the ones in the story, or become a bird by making beaks, wings, and other things you can think of, may find paper, glue, scissors, crayons and staplers on shelf number two. This afternoon, we can act out the story and sing a bird song. The easel has yellow, green, and purple paint today with large paper for anyone who wishes to take a turn; perhaps someone would like to paint a bird picture."

3. *Talk to children about their art or music as they are ready.* Talking to children about their art enriches their immediate experience and expands their understanding of visual art and their own activity as artists (Thompson, 1990). It is usually a good idea for teachers to allow children to work undisturbed and to avoid injecting

themselves into the student's aesthetic discoveries until they indicate need for assistance, seek a reaction, or say they are finished. Occasional reflective statements to them (e.g., "You're working hard on that mask" or "I can tell you really enjoy playing the xylophone") help indicate the teacher's interest and support. If a student asks for help, the teacher should make suggestions and offer assistance but avoid drawing on, designing, or adding to children's artwork. Help with the mechanics of the art or musical experience without dictating or directing the activity. Often talking children through a problem or expanding their frame of reference will help children (e.g., "You're worried that elephant doesn't look right. Let's think about the parts of an elephant—the body, the legs, the trunk, the tail. Where can you put each part on your elephant? Try it. I'll come back and see how you're doing").

When children want an adult's reaction to their work, it is advisable at first simply to listen carefully or study the piece without saying anything. Then draw children's attention to appropriate elements (color, form, mood, tempo, beat, etc.). Guard against becoming the unquestioned authority in the conversation. Use simple ordinary language and appreciate children's insights, however unexpected (Dixon & Chalmers, 1990).

4. *Demonstrate materials and techniques that are new to children.* Teachers should spend a few minutes with art and musical materials before expecting children to use them, become familiar with what they can do, and recognize the problems children may encounter. For example, if the paint is too runny, powdered paint or detergent should be added beforehand, to avoid drips and disappointed artists. If the Autoharp is out of tune, take time to tune it to make the sounds more pleasant and appealing. Be sure to introduce the class to any new technique or material that may need explanation. For example, show children how to hold the buttons on the Autoharp down to create different chords while strumming lightly across the strings; show various ways to apply glue to styrofoam where it is most needed and appropriate amounts to use. A word of caution: when demonstrating art techniques, avoid actually making a recognizable picture as this will have

the tendency to establish a very strong model that children will most likely want to copy. Even very creative students have a difficult time thinking beyond what their teacher shows them in a demonstration of the "correct" way. Another way to focus on the technique, not the subject matter, is to make an imaginary picture; that is, talk about the steps of the process, for example, how to make cardboard prints (see Activity Suggestions) using gestures and tools, without really making anything or showing a finished product.

5. *Use a variety of methods to motivate children.* Teachers should help children choose subjects and expand their range of responses to their world by direct and indirect motivational experiences. Using one or more of the following motivational techniques can help excite children to be more creative and stimulate more imaginative responses.

a. *Provide direct hands-on time* with a special musical instrument or natural or man-made object. As children explore them, discuss the sensory aspects associated with the experi-ence (e.g., how it feels, what sounds can be made with it, how it smells, what different textures can be noticed, which colors can they see, etc.). Show examples of quality craftsmanship such as baskets, carvings, instruments, or quilts. Occasionally, show real paintings instead of reproductions so that children actually see and feel how paint was applied to the surface.

b. *Brainstorm ideas.* Follow up demonstrations or discussions with a quick brainstorming session in which children pool ideas that might work with that technique or material. For example, "Now that you know a good way to fasten pieces together, what can we make with our clay today? Who has an idea?" or "Now that you know how to use the tape player, what songs could you record onto your tape?"

c. *Role-play ideas.* One of the best ways young children learn about something is to experience the concept with their whole body. Research tells us that children's artwork increases in ingenuity and detail following role playing experiences (Eisner, 1970). Teachers

Interactive demonstrations help children explore new techniques.

can suggest children act like tall trees blowing in the wind, a wave crashing to the shore, or tiny mice crouching in the grass.

d. *Show pictures and discuss them.* This kind of motivation can help children notice more, enhance the appeal of expressing their own perceptions, and break down stereotypical ideas they may have developed through other experiences. For example, shown a picture of a thunderstorm, children use the rhythm instruments to create their own storm with great gusto; after viewing several pictures of homes (a log cabin, an apartment house, a two-bedroom ranch, and an igloo) and listening to a short discussion of homes, children are more likely to make pictures that are different from each other's and perhaps different from their own latest work.

e. *Encourage imagining.* Suggest that children close their eyes and imagine something that is very different from their immediate surroundings (e.g., looking down from a very tall tree, flying over the rooftops, or being an ant and looking up from an ant hole). Have them describe what they are picturing in their mind and encourage them to listen to each other's ideas.

f. *Use verbal and non-verbal reinforcement.* Rather than give praise directed at the work itself, respond positively to children's efforts, enthusiasm, and concentration. Smiles, pats on the back, or thumbs-up gestures as children work can be very reinforcing. Let children know you like it when they use their own ideas, even if they are different from others' or your own.

6. *Discover children's books as works of art.* Every year new and wonderful children's books are published that contain perfect examples of visual artistic expression. Teachers should share with their students at least one beautiful book each day. Help children discover the joy of art available to hold in your hand, explore and recognize techniques, and open doors to insights. Before or after reading the story, take time to introduce each picture as a painting, discussing the visual qualities. What child has ever read Sendak's (1963) *Where the Wild Things Are,* Keats's (1972) *The Pet Show,* or Rylant's (1985) *The Relatives Came* without pausing to look at

the incredible pictures? Teachers should treat books as priceless gifts, with each illustration a gem to be treasured. This demonstration of appreciation can influence children to develop a lifelong interest in collecting good art and owning beautiful books (Szekely, 1990). Other activities can be created using book illustrations to recognize various styles, artistic interpretation of similar subjects, or techniques such as collage (see works by Eric Carle or Ezra Jack Keats).

7. *Use questions to help children describe, analyze, interpret, and judge works of art and music.* Questions can extend children's ability to respond to the arts. Using various kinds of questions in discussions regarding visual arts, music, and performing arts elicits a variety of kinds of thinking from children:

a. *Cognitive memory questions* motivate thinking about facts — "What do you see [or hear]? What are some words you can use to describe this?"

b. *Convergent questions* have expected answers — "What is the largest [smallest] thing you see in this painting?" or "What was the fastest part of that song?"

c. *Divergent questions* have many answers — "Why do you think the artist painted this picture?" or "How does this music make you feel? Why?"

d. *Evaluative questions* ask for children's values — "What part of that dance did you like the best? Why?" or "Which statue is the one you like best? Why?" (Tauton, 1983).

8. *Avoid reinforcing only a realistic approach.* Children recognize when teachers truly value individual differences. Teachers who reward (verbally or nonverbally) only artwork that contains naturalistic symbols of real objects and who ignore more abstract and less pictorial works severely limit young children's creative expression of thoughts, feelings, and events. Young children often experiment with materials without intending to relate their finished product to reality, or even to their inner thoughts. They may be fascinated by how the colors change when they touch each other or how the sand sticks to the glue and not to the paper. Adults who insist they "see something" in children's pictures im-

pose the value of realism that can force children into this narrow mode of expression and the frustration of such limits. If the teacher focuses instead on the artistic elements of the work (such as color used, lines, arrangement of shapes, etc.) or the effort expended by the artist, students see that they are free to utilize whatever means of expression they want, without worry their work will be devalued.

9. *Enhance the aesthetic environment of the classroom.* Use the physical environment of the classroom as examples of aesthetic experiences. Mount and display artwork at children's eye level. Occasionally play music during free-choice activities for pure enjoyment. Encourage children to sing during various times of the day for pleasure. Remove clutter and use shelftops as places for displaying plants, sculpture, and items of natural beauty such as shells, flowers, or rocks. Display reproductions of the work of famous artists in the classroom as decorations or use them in planned activities. Reproductions are available from many sources; teachers can collect calendar reproductions, borrow them from libraries, or purchase postcard reproductions from galleries. A wonderful commercially offered collection of postcard-size reproductions is *Mommy, It's a Renoir!* (Wolf, 1984). The set includes sequenced activities for matching and comparing using various criteria, or it can be used as an exposure activity to acquaint children with various artists' works.

10. *Encourage musical exploration and creative improvisations.* The extent to which children's creativity in music develops is greatly influenced by their environment, the attitudes of significant adults around them, and their exposure to opportunity. Several studies devoted to observing and recording children's improvisational explorations led to the conclusion that four factors encourage musical creativity:

a. musical instruments that produce beautiful sounds,
b. supportive physical and emotional environments,
c. freedom of choice within structural limits, and
d. teachers who observe at times and at other times participate (McDonald & Simons, 1989).

ACTIVITY SUGGESTIONS

➥ Visit a Gallery

Objective: For children to become more familiar with various forms of the arts

Procedure: Take the class to an art gallery. Visit ahead of time, taking note of what pieces would interest the group. Purchase postcard prints of some of the artwork. Distribute these to small group leaders, along with suggestions for things to point out. Encourage the groups to move slowly through the exhibits, looking for the artwork depicted on the postcards. Move among the small groups, asking questions to motivate children to notice variety in use of materials, subject matter, and kinds of art (paintings, drawings, sculpture, carved designs, etc.).

To Simplify: Go for a very short time. Arrange for very small groups, or pairs of children assigned to each adult. Prepare adults to look at things in general, stopping to analyze those pieces children show interest in.

To Extend: Plan a longer visit; prepare children ahead for some particular art they will see. Analyze these carefully as they discover them. Plan follow-up activities of drawing or painting something they remember.

➥ Listen to This!

Objective: For children to become more familiar with various styles within a particular art form

Procedure: Arrange a tape recorder or record player and a collection of musical pieces in a quiet corner of the room. Encourage children to take turns listening to the musical selections alone or with a friend. To focus attention on appreciation of the range of styles, select music that varies greatly, such as folk, rock, classical piano, catchy tunes from commercials, TV theme songs, marching band music, part of a symphony, chamber music, and jazz. If making your own tape, organize the selections with blank spaces between them so that children can easily distinguish beginnings and endings.

To Simplify: Limit the number of music styles to a few.

To Extend: Ask children to bring in samples of various music they enjoy at home. Encourage parents to contribute to a collection of samples, especially requesting music from various cultures.

➡ Balancing Act

Objective: For children to become more familiar with basic elements of visual arts (e.g., balance)

Procedure: Introduce the idea of balance (and unbalance) by showing a balance scale. Using identical objects or a variety of objects, ask children to tell whether it is unbalanced or balanced. Show other examples of the concepts using groups of children, objects, and pictures of objects. Show children reproductions of famous paintings, and have them point out the objects and tell if they think each is balanced or not and why.

To Simplify: Leave the scale out for experimentation for several days with three-dimensional objects. Then apply the concepts to pictures.

To Extend: Providing construction paper (suggest they cut or tear shapes) and paste, have children make a picture or design and tell if it is balanced or unbalanced and why.

➡ Pitch Play

Objective: For children to become more familiar with basic elements of music (e.g., pitch)

Procedure: Teach children how to have musical conversations that involve matching pitches with one person leading and the other responding, like an echo. Demonstrate with another adult or a competent child. Suggest the children listen to what you sing, then repeat your words using the same sounds (matching pitches). For example, the leader says, "Hel-lo" using two pitches, one for each syllable. Response: "Hel-lo." Practice this using various words until it is easier. Next, have the child lead, and you reply with different words but matched pitches (leader, "Hel-lo"; response: "Hi-there"). Finally, switch roles again and have the students make

up their own response to your lead, still matching your pitches.

To Simplify: Start simple, using one-pitch conversations.

To Extend: Use two sets of pitched instruments (such as bells or xylophones), using the same procedure: one leads, the other echoes. Be sure to start with two pitches that are very different (high-low), and gradually utilize ones that are more difficult to distinguish (high-middle or middle-low).

➡ Oh Up! Oh Down!

Objective: For children to actively engage in or respond to performing arts experiences (e.g., creative dramatics)

Procedure: After reading or hearing a story they particularly enjoyed, the children stand up and form a circle (if possible) or stand facing each other. Tell them they are going to use their bodies to become people, animals, or objects in the story. Teach them signals to begin and end their dramatic interpretations: "Oh up" means to stand up and begin, "Oh down" means to stop and crouch down. Have everyone go down into a crouch; then say, "When we come up, we're all going to be [the papa bear tasting his porridge.] Oh up! [do it with them]…Oh down!" Verbally reinforce creative ideas children use. Repeat the procedure using other ideas. Encourage children to participate but do not force them. If a child insists on watching, select a place nearby where they may easily join in if they change their mind.

To Simplify: Select ideas that are obvious and easy to visualize (e.g., "Be the baby bear crying over his broken chair," or "be Goldilocks going to sleep in the bed"). Do this for a short time, and end before the children get tired.

To Extend: After the obvious ones, select ideas that are more subtle (e.g., "Be the chair that breaks when Goldilocks sit down" or "Be the door that opens when she knocks"). Let children take turns being the leader, suggesting ideas. Or use this as a warm-up exercise to actually acting out the whole story as a class.

➠ Let's Stick Together

Objective: For children to use tools, materials, and techniques to achieve a desired aesthetic effect

Procedure: Potter's clay offers opportunities for three-dimensional sculpture and ceramic design. However, occasionally in the drying process attached pieces fall off. Discuss this with the children and demonstrate a technique that attaches clay together so that this will not happen. Prepare two pieces of clay to attach. Using a tool (a table knife, fork, or wooden ceramic tool) that makes shallow cuts, score cross-hatching lines into the surfaces that are to be joined. Then apply plain water with a finger to wet both scored surfaces and produce a slippery film (called *slip*). Press the pieces together and blend the clay to completely cover the line of attachment. Give children clay, tools, and water and suggest they practice attaching pieces together.

To Simplify: Offer children large (fist-size) pieces to attach; set these aside to dry.

To Extend: Invite children to think of things that have parts (e.g., animals have legs, head, and tails) to attach. Brainstorm ideas. Encourage them to work on their own creations, using the technique demonstrated.

➠ Do You Want to Talk about It?

Objective: For children to recognize, reflect on, and discuss aesthetic experiences

Procedure: Plan an aesthetic experience for the class such as watching the cloud patterns change, experimenting with watercolor paints on wet paper, or listening to the music of *Fantasia* on tape. Afterward, gather children together to discuss what they remember, know, think, and value about the experience. Ask various questions such as "What did you see [or hear]? What do you remember about that?" (cognitive memory). "How high were the clouds in the sky? What colors of paint were we using today?" (convergent). "What shapes did you notice the clouds making? What are some words you could use to describe different parts of this

music?" (divergent). "How did you like this? What was the best part? Why?" (evaluative).

To Simplify: Ask only one or two questions. Keep the discussion short, but listen to everyone's reply.

To Extend: Follow up the discussion by having children write or dictate their feelings about the experience.

➠ Paint a Wonder

Objective: For children to work collaboratively with others to create art

Procedure: Organize a large place for groups of children to paint together on the same surface such as a long roll of paper, a large piece of cotton cloth, or burlap laid on the floor. Prepare 5 to 6 containers of poster paints of various colors. Suggest that children work together on one giant painting with each person making part of it. Encourage them to share the materials, decide where they will paint, and cooperate with each other; assist children in accepting different ideas.

To Simplify: Limit the number of children in the small groups to three or four, have one group at a time painting, and place one brush in each color.

To Extend: Have each small group choose an open-ended topic for their painting that would give children a direction, but still offer opportunities for expressing their individuality. Suggestions for topics could be happiness, winter, imaginary insects, the forest, or germs.

➠ What Does It Mean?

Objective: For children to appreciate art (or music) as means of nonverbal communication

Procedure: Show children a work of art (or music) that expresses an obvious message (e.g., a painting of a happy family or an obviously sad piano tune). Discuss the fact that many forms of art (music) are used to communicate ideas to an audience without using words. Ask children to look (or listen) carefully to your example, and tell what they think the message could be. Show other examples with an obvious message followed by examples of art (or music) in which the message may be open to interpretation such as more abstract paintings and drawings, abstract sculpture, nonrepresentational design, other instrumental music, and most modern or classical dance. Encourage children to offer opinions about what each one means. As children hear each other's interpretations, point out how theirs is different or similar to others' or your own. Let them know there are no right answers, that anyone's ideas can be valid, and that sometimes the same work has many messages, depending on who is experiencing it.

To Simplify: Relate the concept of artistic nonverbal messages to other nonverbal messages like gestures, facial expressions, and body language. Stay with the obvious messages, and use examples that communicate more obviously.

To Extend: Suggest children make something from clay, paper, or some other visual medium (or make up a tune on an instrument), and explain what their message is or try to interpret each other's.

➠ Print Spectacular

Objective: For children to recognize the wide array of materials from which artists may choose to express themselves

Procedure: Introduce object printing to the group by demonstrating the down-up motion to make prints on paper. Prepare several shallow pans of paint in a variety of colors. Pour the paint onto flat sponges or layers of paper towels, and offer a selection of interesting objects (wooden spools or other wooden shapes, small pieces of sponge, dowels, potato mashers, corrugated cardboard pieces, cotton swabs, forks, plastic cups, small pine tree bough, pine cones, etc.) with which to print. Provide large paper to print on, giving children a selection of colors. Encourage children to experiment with the various objects, and fill their paper with interesting printed shapes.

To Simplify: Limit the number of objects and/or the number of paint colors. Hammer a nail into wooden shapes to make them easier to manipulate.

To Extend: When the print is dry, have children try to recall what object they used to make individual shapes on the print. Another time, have children make their own collections of objects to print.

➠ Music That's Not There

Objective: For children to develop the ability to remember or create music in their minds (audiation)

Procedure: Sing a song with the class that involves words and hand motions (such as "The Itsy Bitsy Spider" or "She'll Be Comin' 'Round the Mountain"). After it has become familiar to the children, try humming it (not using the words) with the class, using the hand gestures when appropriate. Last, tell children they are going to "sing it in their head" but use the hand gestures when appropriate. Try it, using only the hand gestures, without humming.

To Simplify: Use very short simple songs that children know well.

To Extend: Teach the class a new song and try this exercise. Try it again the following day without singing it aloud first.

➠ That Was a Long Time Ago

Objective: For children to develop a concept of the arts as a lifelong pursuit

Procedure: Invite an artist or musician (one of the parents or a community person) to visit the class; ask him or her to bring a sample of some finished work and some in progress, or their instrument and some musical pieces they know well. Ask your guest to demonstrate or show some work that they did a very long time ago and to discuss when they first became interested in art or music. Have children tell about their own aesthetic interests and what they hope to do when they grow up. Follow this by suggesting children make a picture or write a story about when they grow up.

To Simplify: Keep the presentation short (10–15 minutes).

To Extend: Send home a note to parents requesting they help their child find someone they know who makes, collects, or enjoys art and/or music. Explain what your objectives are, and give examples so parents understand the purpose of the activity. Ask the children to talk to that person and find out the answers to some questions, such as "What kind of art [music] do you like?" "How did you get interested?" "How old were you when you started liking that?" Ask children to report to the class about people they found.

➡ Cardboard Prints

Objective: For children to use tools, materials, and techniques to achieve a desired aesthetic effect

Procedure: Remind children of their past experiences with printing (using stamps and stamp pads, footprints in the sand, or making handprints on the window). Help them see how they were able to make the same picture or shape over and over again, many times. Explain that artists sometimes need or want to do this with pictures they create. Demonstrate one method of doing this—cardboard printing. Using soft flexible cardboard (cut-up cereal boxes work well), cut some shapes and arrange them on another piece of cardboard. Glue them well and allow them to dry. Then apply water-soluble printing ink or poster paint thickened with liquid soap to the cardboard surface. (Ink can be applied easily using a roller or brayer, rolling it out on a hard slick surface, and then rolling it over the entire cardboard surface.) Work quickly so it does not dry. Lay a thin piece of newsprint over the inked design and press with your fingertips. Lift the paper and see the print.

To Simplify: Precut shapes and have children arrange and glue them as they wish. Avoid using letters or numbers because everything will print backward.

To Extend: Encourage children to print the same design many times, on the same paper, on different papers of various colors, or on burlap or other cloth. Another time, use corrugated cardboard to make the design for a more textured print. This is also called a *monoprint,* meaning one color is used to make the whole design. Another equally satisfying method for making monoprints is called styrofoam prints. Save flat foam meat trays, wash and cut off the edges, and have children make their designs with pencil lines. Print as above.

➡ Feel the Beat

Objective: For children to become more familiar with basic elements of music (beat and tempo)

Procedure: Play a series of instrumental numbers that have an obvious beat (the steady pulse under the music) using a piano, record, or tape. An audiotape of different kinds of music, each demonstrating a different tempo (the speed of the beat), can easily be made and works well when short segments of each musical piece are strung together. Stand and respond with your body to the beat (clap your hands, slap your thighs, etc.). Say, "Watch me [clapping on the beat]. When you're ready, do what I do." For those children who do not feel the beat, help them by placing their hands over yours as you clap; later, switch having yours cover theirs. A verbal cue on the beat will help some children become more aware as well; say, "Beat, beat, beat, beat, beat" or "Clap, clap, clap, clap." Younger children are better able to keep time with a moderate tempo than with a slower tempo. Next, suggest children move their hands in a different way to the beat (punch the air, point, slash, wave), then a different body part (foot, elbow, knee, hips), and finally their whole body to the beat (swaying or stepping in place). Model your own enthusiasm and enjoyment. In a large space, have children pick up their knees and march, walk, or run with the beat of the music. Last, offer children simple rhythm instruments to tap the beat of the music, such as sticks, tambourines, or maracas. Have children take turns using the instruments and responding to the beat and tempo of the music.

To Simplify: Play only instrumental music (without words). Begin by having the children move or play instruments to the beat, but not at the same time. Use only one kind of instrument, and provide one for every child to play.

To Extend: Explain the terms *beat* and *tempo;* play a game in which children take turns demonstrating a fast, slow, and medium tempo by hitting a tambourine as everyone else moves in time to that beat.

Elements of Visual Arts

1. Balance—the weight or force counteracting the effect of another (e.g., one large shape balances with five small shapes)
2. Color—the names and characteristics of hues used in the visual arts (e.g., red, orange, light, dark, bright, dull)
3. Composition—the organization of the parts; overall design of the piece
4. Contrast—use of opposites (e.g., dark and light colors, open and closed shapes, curved lines and straight lines)
5. Form—the shape of the whole or parts of a composition
6. Line—the characteristic of linear structures (e.g., thin, thick, wavy, straight, zigzag, bold, curved)
7. Pattern—a recurring series; repeated elements; the model to imitate
8. Texture—how a surface actually feels to the touch, or how it is made to look (e.g., rough, smooth, bumpy, shiny, slippery, grainy)

Elements of Music

1. Beat—the recurring pulse heard or sensed throughout the music
2. Duration—how long individual musical tones, phrases, or pieces last
3. Dynamics—the louder and quieter parts of the music; changes in volume
4. Form—the design of parts or phrases of a song or composition
5. Harmony—two or more tones sung or played at the same time
6. Pitch—how high or low the musical sound is
7. Rhythm—the organized patterns of sounds and silences in music
8. Simultaneity—occurring at the same time as something else, such as melody and harmony
9. Tempo—the speed of the music
10. Timbre—the tonal quality or characteristic of a voice or instrument
11. Tone color—the predominant feeling of the music; the mood

---

FIGURE 3.4
Glossary of Aesthetic Elements

CHAPTER 4

The Affective Domain

When we were one or two years old, we had what we might visualize as a 360 degree personality. Energy radiated out from all parts of our body and our psyche. A child running is a living globe of energy. We had a ball of energy, all right, but one day we noticed that [others] didn't like certain parts of that ball....Behind us we have an invisible bag, and the part of us [others] didn't like... we put in the bag....But why would we give away, or put into the bag, so much of ourselves? Why would we do it so young? And if we have put away so much of our anger, spontaneities, hungers, enthusiasms, our rowdy and unattractive parts, then how can we live? What holds us together? (Bly, 1988, pp. 17–24)

Learning appropriate ways to express every aspect of their personality is one of the toughest jobs young children have. They struggle daily with refining self-help and social skills, mastering unfamiliar tasks, and coping with their own emotions and tensions. Although to some extent adults also deal with these same challenges, most do so from a broad base of experiences and a great many more resources than are available to children.

A good share of the tools adults need in order to "navigate the troubled waters of society"—high self-esteem, self-respect, belief in themselves and in their future, and feelings of competency—are forged during childhood (C.A. Smith, 1988). An adolescent's or adult's mental health, relationships, ability to deal with disappointments, and general perceptions of the world will depend on how well the different aspects of intrapersonal strength were nurtured in the early years.

Obviously, cultural differences exist in the rearing of children that lead to variable conditions and values related to competence and interpersonal relations (Damon, 1989). While these must be understood and respected, Curry and Johnson (1990) underscore the need also to "recognize the larger conditions and values that are important for raising children in a modern, democratic, pluralistic, post-industrial society" (p. 30). It is on that premise that the ideas for helping children form strong intrapersonal and interpersonal structures are set forth in this chapter.

EMOTIONAL DEVELOPMENT FROM A PSYCHOSOCIAL PERSPECTIVE

Erik Erikson (1963) saw human development as the result of an individual's progressive resolution of conflicts between his or her own needs and social demands (Zigler & Finn-Stevenson, 1987). As was pointed out in chapter 1, Erikson theorized that development continues over the entire life cycle of an individual rather than being primarily set in infancy or early childhood (see Table 4.1). However, the ability to deal with later-stage problems was viewed as dependent on how well an individual dealt with and resolved crises in earlier stages.

Setting the stage for later trust or mistrust in social interaction is the primary caregivers' handling of a child in the 1st year of life. During this critical first stage, children learn that adults caring for them can be counted on to behave either affectionately and predictably most of the

TABLE 4.1
Erik Erikson's Psychosocial Theory of Personality Development

Stage	Approximate Age	Conflict Resolution Area
1	Infancy	Trust vs. mistrust
2	About 1–3 years of age	Autonomy vs. doubt
3	About 4–5 years of age	Initiative vs. guilt
4	About 6–11 years of age	Industry vs. inferiority
5	Adolescence	Identity vs. role confusion
6	Young adulthood	Intimacy vs. isolation
7	Middle age	Generativity vs. self-absorption
8	Old age	Integrity vs. despair

time or insensitively and neglectfully in response to their distress and needs.

As children move into the 2nd and 3rd year of life, the trust or mistrust they have developed impacts on achievement of subsequent developmental tasks. It is then that children begin to exercise increasing autonomy as physical, cognitive, and social abilities also develop. For those children experiencing day-to-day encouragement for active exploration in a safe and encouraging environment, increased confidence and competence are likely to be the outcome. On the other hand, children who live in chaotic environments with overly critical and controlling adults are more likely to develop a sense of shame and doubt about themselves and their capabilities for dealing with an enlarging life space.

Predictably, these children move less competently into the third stage outlined by Erikson—initiative versus guilt. During this period, 4- and 5-year-olds develop a sense of how others value their efforts to explore ideas, carry out plans, gain information, and master new skills. Children who develop a strong sense of initiative gain pleasure from increased competence. They seek ways to use their energy in appropriate and constructive ways and enjoy cooperating with others in activities that involve the use of real tools (woodworking materials, computers and tape recorders, magnifying glasses, magnets, kitchen utensils) in their building of skills (Kostelnik et al., in press). Conversely, children who have experienced less nurturing care in early stages of development are less likely to initiate activity on their own or be successful in ventures to do so. There may be problems related to task completion, and these children often demonstrate less ability in problem solving or decision making. They may hang back in play or act so aggressively that they fail to make meaningful friendships. For example, a 4-year-old boy who had grown bored watching his mother try on eyeglass frames in an optometrist's office began teasing a little girl standing by her mother, who was also trying on frames. Despite the fact that his behavior became highly inappropriate and annoying to others, his mother ignored what he was doing. At one point, the small girl said to him, "You're bad!" Surprisingly, the tone of her voice brought an abrupt stop to his teasing. He

looked confused for a minute and then went to his mother to report the affront.

"She said I'm bad," he complained.

"Well, you *are* bad," said his mother, not even looking at him.

The long-term effect of such labeling on the child's self-image is predictable, unfortunately, particularly when there is little or no effort to provide him with more appropriate behavior skills.

From the preschool years until preadolescence, all children struggle with developing responsibility and living up to reasonable expectations of those they come into contact with. They learn that doing so requires effort on their part and making choices between following through on such tasks as homework and household chores, or that failing to do so results in the disappointment and/or disdain of others. To the extent that children feel free to assert themselves in everyday interactions with peers, teachers, parents, and others and are also reinforced for efforts at skill building and successful accomplishments, they will develop an industrious approach to learning. When their efforts have been discouraged, ignored, or short-circuited by others, a sense of inferiority and low self-esteem results, which causes them to veer away from challenges and responsibilities or to behave in a hostile and socially inappropriate manner. These behaviors, while frustrating to professionals working with these children, are simply natural defensive mechanisms in youngsters who have experienced significant contact with others who are insensitive to and unsupportive of their developmental needs. While most educators empathically recognize the stimulus for such behavior, the conduct of poorly nurtured children is often disruptive and time-consuming. It impacts negatively on both their progress and that of other children. Character traits or dispositions such as the ability to be polite to others, honesty, observation of rules, self-discipline, responsibility, respectful use of materials, and helpfulness to others may be significantly weakened (Wynne, 1988). Professionals frequently find themselves with some ambivalence toward these children who are so difficult to manage on a day-to-day basis.

Of the eight stages of development delineated by Erikson, young children have already experienced two or three by the time they enter the primary grades. While children bring with them very different background experiences, strengths, and needs, it is likely that the school experience will also have much to do with the child's success in confronting conflicts experienced while in stages 3, 4, and 5. Children in the primary grades want to be competent and recognized by others as being competent. Educators can take advantage of this "optimal period" and natural motivation of children to guide them toward more fully integrated intrapersonal and interpersonal strengths. This calls for including in the early childhood program an adequate focus on the development of cooperative relationships, mutual respect, and a climate of fairness, caring, and participation (Lickona, 1988). Also, truly effective schools must work closely with families and the community before children ever enter the formal system. Those linkages with families must then be maintained and strengthened as children move through the developmental tasks of early childhood and into adolescence and young adulthood.

EMOTIONAL DEVELOPMENT FROM A COGNITIVE PERSPECTIVE

In terms of understanding their own emotions, children progress through a predictable sequence that is highly dependent on their emerging cognitive capabilities and language development. Young children with disabilities because of mental retardation, visual or hearing impairment, and physical or motor impairments may be handicapped in social-emotional development because of reduced capacity to interact with others (Curry & Johnson, 1990).

As primary children move toward the period of concrete operations (Piaget, 1952, 1954), developing more sophisticated intellectual capacity, they are better equipped to evaluate their own social skills and status in light of others' behavior and expectations. In developing a consolidated sense of themselves, children watch others' compliance and transgressions and the consequential approval or disapproval of that behavior. They listen to evaluations of their own and others' actions and begin to formulate a rudimentary understanding of the desires, beliefs, and emotions of others.

Here it should be noted that early psychosocial development also includes the construction of one's ethnic profile. Boyer (1990, p. 39) suggests that first graders, for example, who are involved with reading materials will naturally look for pictures of families like *their* families. When black, Native American, Latino, or Asian children fail to see people like themselves, there is no "confirmation of legitimate existence"; thus, the child receives a strong message that his or her ethnic category does not warrant endorsement. There may arise in the learner a reluctance to pursue tasks in an environment that fails to include people like themselves.

Children younger than 10 years of age, however, generally do not associate the source of their emotions with what happens in their own minds. Rather, there is a more simplistic and direct linking of their emotional state to their physical state of being. If they miss a parent or are hungry, tired, or injured, they perceive emotions such as sadness, irritability, anger, or fearfulness as directly resulting from the situation itself rather than from what they *think* about the situation or how they interpret it. They are also unaware that a person can feel certain emotions internally and mask them externally. Thus, they may not be alert for subtle cues in others' responses to them when their social behavior is inappropriate or "thoughtless."

Children younger than 5 years of age are generally unaware that people can experience more than one emotion at a time. For example, if they experience a parent expressing anger toward them, they believe the parent is completely angry and, therefore, not holding other emotions at the same time such as love, fear, sadness, disappointment. Five- and 6-year-olds, on the other hand, develop the recognition that people can feel more than one emotion at a time but still believe that contrasting emotions such as feeling angry and loving, smart and stupid, or happy and sad about the same event are not possible. It is not until middle elementary school that children begin to understand that such events as their parents' divorce or moving to another town can cause both positive and negative emotions and that people can hold contrasting feelings simultaneously about other persons, objects, or situations. Even with this understanding, however, there may be considerable confusion and a sense of anxiety over not having a clear-cut response (Kostelnik et al., in press).

SELF-ESTEEM IN THE EARLY LEARNING ENVIRONMENT

In a first-grade classroom, an educational consultant recently observed a group of children who had viewed a tape on space rockets and then had been invited by their teacher to draw a picture of a rocket. The teacher reminded the children to put their name on their pictures and also to date them so that the work could be entered into their writing portfolios. As the consultant drew near to watch Michael, who was drawing an especially creative rocket, he glanced up at her and then quickly covered the poorly scrawled name he had written in the upper left corner. When the adult smiled and complimented him on his beautiful rocket, he smiled back but kept his printing covered, covertly watching until she moved on and only then withdrawing his hand. Michael had already learned to be ashamed of his efforts to print.

In another classroom, a troubled child told his teacher, "I'm no good!" She responded emphatically, "No, no, no—you *are* good. We aren't going to talk like that. I don't want to hear anyone in this room putting himself down!" The child, who for some time had been experiencing alcoholic and abusive parents arguing and moving toward divorce, had trusted the teacher enough to bring his pain openly to her. He was being truthful about his feelings about himself. No matter how undeserved, he felt worthless. Wanting to help him think better of himself, the teacher had unwittingly (and unfortunately) denied both his emotions and his pain.

Each day of a child's life is filled with events and successful and unsuccessful interactions with others. Cumulatively, these become the "potent and orderly forces" that result in the child building an internal picture of him- or herself—as worthy, capable, lovable, and significant, or useless, inept, unlovable, and discounted (Elkins, 1979; Rogers, 1961).

Though an individual's "self" or concept of self, like everything else in an organism, develops

and changes over the life span, there is evidence that global self-concept (i.e., all the beliefs a person has about him- or herself) is structured fairly early in life and appears to be well developed by the time a child is 8 or 9 years old. Components of the self—perceptions about how competent one is intellectually, physically, emotionally, and so forth—are known as *self-esteem*. These perceptions are affected by how valued, lovable, and worthwhile a person feels in any particular situation. The resulting feelings of self-worth are reflected in a child's overt behavior in the classroom, in the peer group, and on the playground. Clues and patterns that suggest whether a child is experiencing low self-esteem can be found in the child's negative self-statements ("I'm rotten at this!" "I can never get anything right"); problematic behavior (unrealistic fear, unjustified anger, continued lying, conceit, overconcern with past or future); avoidance of play, projects, or working with others; or lack of interest in appearance, cleanliness, and care of possessions (Mental Health Association, 1982).

Because young children are still malleable, those who come with positive self-perceptions and those who come to school with somewhat damaged selves because of unsupportive situations will each continue to modify this most basic building block of emotional life. Poorly nurtured children will need a great deal of support from a patient, caring, and knowledgeable teacher to do so in a positive direction. This will call for a professional using constructive disciplinary strategies on a consistent basis in tandem with genuine reinforcement every time these children choose prosocial behavior. It calls for focusing daily attention on each of them, providing opportunities for them to work out their feelings through play, and teaching them to practice positive self-talk in difficult situations ("This is hard, but if I keep trying, I'll learn how to do it"). Positive behavioral changes can be facilitated by offering encouraging statements that verbalize positive aspects of a tough situation without denying children's feelings (Kostelnik et al., in press). For example, the teacher who responded to the child who said "I'm no good" by saying "No, no, no—you *are* good" might have said instead, "It sounds as if you're having a rough morning. In spite of that, you've managed to complete almost all of that project. Let's look at what you have left to do."

Ultimately, children's self-understanding is the result of the diverse and cumulative experiences with significant others in their world, both adults and peers. Urie Bronfenbrenner, professor of human development at Cornell University, maintains that not only do children need nurturing adults in their world who "are crazy about them"; there must also be times when those same adults are cool and capable of delivering authentic, corrective feedback to a child who has stepped outside of appropriate behavior boundaries. Curry and Johnson (1990) suggest that children "develop senses of resilience, power, competence, trust, and optimism from repeated experiences in which they transform negative states into positive ones" (p. 155). They add that children may be at risk when they experience persistently positive as well as persistently negative self-feelings, with the former resulting in narcissistic self-absorption and an inability to deal adequately with social challenges.

Because primary children are both "nicer and meaner than their preschool counterparts" (Curry & Johnson, 1990, pp. 82–83), they have no qualms about rejecting children who are self-absorbed, uncooperative, disruptive, and inappropriately hostile. Unless there is intervention in such cases to provide and reinforce more appropriate skills and behaviors, such children come to accept the negative identity ascribed to them by others. Later, they often tend to isolate themselves from others or gang up with other aggressive and hostile children who have also experienced rejection. Clearly, the fostering of effective social skills needed to work and play well with others is worth spending time on in the classroom. The constructed early childhood learning ethos that promotes in young children shared ownership, a sense of community, and responsible participation in turn motivates further positive development of cooperation, control, connectedness, and mastery.

VARIATIONS IN PERSONALITY DEVELOPMENT

Even when teachers and parents are fairly sensitive about factors influencing the self-esteem of growing children, negative interaction styles can develop when children are perceived to be difficult and consistently hard to manage (Soderman, 1985). It is important to understand that children exhibit very different personality attributes that may, in fact, be inherited characteristics that will then be further modified by the child's experiences and interactions with others (Brazelton, 1978; Buss & Plomin, 1975; McDevitt & Carey, 1978). Included are such traits as these:

- Activity level—motor activity and inactivity
- Rhythmicity—predictability in bodily function
- Approach/withdrawal—child's initial responses to new objects, people, foods, etc.
- Adaptability—response to change
- Intensity of reaction—energy level in response to stimuli and impulse control
- Responsiveness threshold—level of stimulation necessary to evoke a response
- Attention span and resistance—time spent in pursuit of activity
- Distractibility—vulnerability to interference when pursuing activity

These tendencies, by themselves, can influence the quality of children's interactions with significant adults in their world.

In a series of longitudinal studies to look at individual temperament in young children based on the traits just outlined (Thomas & Chess, 1977, 1980, 1984; Thomas, Chess, Birch, Hertzig, & Korn, 1963), three basic types have been documented: easy (40% of those children studied); difficult (10%); and slow to warm up (about 15%). About 35% of children studied could not be classified into one of these categories. It is, of course, the "difficult" and "slow-to-warm-up" children who react more negatively to change or seem to march to a slightly different drummer than most children. These are the children that often keep teachers awake at night thinking about more effective ways to deal with them. Often when adults look on these differences in personality as stubbornness on the part of the child, a power struggle can be set into motion. Altering a difficult child's behavior and still having both adult and child maintain a healthy sense of autonomy and power can be a very fragile undertaking (May, 1981). It calls for respecting such differences as legitimate but helping the child to see and appreciate how some changes might be personally advantageous, for example, in getting along better with others and forming friendships.

Adults wishing or attempting to modify children's interactive styles will need to examine what part their own personality is playing in the situation. It may be that the child's behavior is perfectly appropriate but simply irritating because of personality differences between child and adult. Legitimately, this may call for compromise. For example, perhaps the slow-to-warm-up child might not balk at schedule changes so much if the teacher took more care in warning the child ahead of time about them. It may be that the more active child is unable to sit still in large-group presentations but that they are also longer than necessary because they are a favorite part of the adult's teaching day. Shortening the session somewhat, at least for a period of time and having the child adapt to increasingly longer sessions, may be a workable compromise.

CHILDREN'S STRESS REACTIONS IN RESPONSE TO OVERWHELMING EMOTIONAL DEMAND

All of the aspects of affective development discussed thus far (i.e., emotional development, self-esteem, and personality), in combination with the quality of care giving the child experiences, result in a child's ability to cope with perceived demands in the environment. When the child's developed resources are unequal to the demands experienced, behavioral disorders and increased psychological vulnerability will result (Trad, 1988). Elkind (1981, p. 1) has cited the American Academy of Pediatricians' concern related to growing numbers of chronically unhappy, hyperactive, or lethargic and unmotivated children being seen by clinicians, in addition to others tending toward school failure, psychosomatic problems, and early involvement in delinquency and drugs. An inability to handle stressful situations increases a child's lifelong vulnerability in two areas: (a) eventual physical and/or mental disease, and (b) poorly developed stress responses that become ingrained behav-

ioral patterns, which impact negatively and continuously on relationships.

Children can experience overwhelming demand from any number of sources today. These range from individual stressors (handicapping conditions, inadequate or imbalanced diet, difficult personality) and intrafamilial stressors (birth of a sibling, death of a loved one or pet, marital transition of parents, poverty, abuse and/or neglect) to those outside the family. Extrafamilial sources include unsatisfactory child care, poor match between developmental levels and classroom expectations in the school setting, lack of appreciation of cultural differences, negative peer relationships in the neighborhood, and unsafe factors in the community. Other potential assaults include a fast-paced, high-geared, "McDonaldized" society (Pearsall, 1983, p. 2), "forced blooming" that usurps childhood in general (Elkind, 1981), high-fat diets and a lack of exercise to release tension, and heavy exposure to television (Soderman & Greenberg, 1986).

Children cope with these stressors with the same sorts of strategies that many adults use,

Just as stress can overwhelm adults, children are also vulnerable.

employing defense mechanisms that include denial, regression, withdrawal, and impulsive acting out. These behaviors in children are clear-cut signs that they need additional or different skills in perceiving or dealing adequately with a situation. Chandler (1985) has outlined the following questions that may be useful when adults must design some plan for intervention:

1. Is it possible to reduce stress through environmental manipulation?
2. Is it possible to reduce stress through changing the attitude and behavior of significant adults?
3. Is it possible to modify the child's extreme behavior so that it more closely approximates normal coping responses?
4. Is it possible to reduce stress by helping the child adopt a more realistic perception of himself and his life situation? (p. 184)

When stressful situations go on for long periods of time and the child is unable to experience relief, other symptoms may appear such as increased irritability, depression, anxiety, sleep disturbances, somatic problems, or a dramatic increase or decrease in appetite. Highly stressed children *look* stressed. Significant and long-standing tension may manifest itself in the quality of speech, as dark circles under the eyes, in the child's posture, and occasionally in compulsive behaviors.

Without additional help, children who are unable to cope effectively will hardly be able to benefit from what is going on in the classroom academically and socially. Nor do children necessarily benefit from the teacher offering quick fixes, dictating "appropriate" responses, or pushing them to talk when they are not ready to do so. Helping the child to replace ineffective strategies will again call for a patient and carefully planned approach from the teacher that utilizes many of the guidelines suggested in this chapter. When additional focused attention and support is not helpful, other professionals may need to be drawn in to help the child modify emotional upset and responses.

CURRENT EDUCATIONAL ISSUES

Although everyone agrees that good emotional health is necessary for effective functioning and a positive quality of life, not everyone agrees that educational professionals should be actively involved in guiding the development of young children in this arena. Several issues form the basis of that opposition. The first is the belief that academic achievement should be the primary and only concern in an educational context and that affective development should be left as the legitimate province of the family. This sort of attitude goes against a philosophical concern for the overall development of young children. Because the four major realms of development—physical, social, emotional, and intellectual—are highly interdependent (Gilligan & Bower, 1984; Starky, 1980), failing to provide spontaneous or planned experiences in the affective arena geared toward the development of positive affect would be obviously self-defeating (Currie, 1988). In addition, children are moving out of the family's care and into the extrafamilial arena earlier and earlier (National Council on Family Relations, 1990), with professionals in child care centers and educational settings assuming increasing responsibility for nurturing children as well as educating and keeping them safe. Moreover, increasing numbers of children come to the school setting with poorly formed attachments and in need of both emotional resources and a warm, trusting relationship with an adult to correct the direction of their affective development. A study by Erickson, Sroufe, and Egeland (1985) indicates that 4- and 5-year-old children who had formed weak affective ties predictably demonstrated poor school performance. They were less independent and more noncompliant, had poorer social interactional skills, and lacked confidence and assertiveness. Such children are more at risk for hostility, negative self-esteem, negative self-adequacy, emotional instability, emotional unresponsiveness, and a negative world view (Currie, 1988).

A second issue raised by those opposing teacher involvement with affective education is related to the perceived lack of training by professionals to be competent, sensitive, and effective in this area. It may be true that in the past and in particular institutions of higher learning, much of teacher training was focused on academic content and methods, with only cursory attention to the affective and social. More attention was given to structuring consequences for negative behavior than on developing children's self-esteem or establishing a positive classroom climate to nurture emotional development. As a result, many beginning teachers found themselves ill equipped to deal with children's affective and social problems and bought heavily into artificial methods for keeping children "under control."

Currently, in high-quality programs of study, preservice teachers are now equipped with training in understanding developmental sequences and the need to work with all children in a sensitive and supportive way. They also learn strategies for intervention when children lack emotional stability and social skills and are made aware of the need to design an atmosphere of trust and experiences for children that will actively enhance positive development. Similarly, effective public school systems are providing in-service aid to teachers to help children develop more positive self-esteem, find appropriate outlets for strong feelings, deal with natural and acquired fears, and learn conflict management. In short, affective development is not left purely to chance. It is considered as important as academic aspects in good early childhood programs, and well-trained and sensitive teachers are viewed as critical.

An issue frequently raised by educators in providing nurturance to children and satisfying their affective needs has been the increasing number of allegations of sexual abuse leveled against adults who interact with children. A number of wrongful accusations has resulted in many schools taking a defensive posture, which has led to taboos against any hugging, patting, or touching and thereby shortchanging children in the process. To get around cutting out this essential aspect of a school program and also to protect educators from precarious positions, it has been suggested that the need for a warm, caring relationship between the teacher and children be fully communicated to parents and the community; children should be instructed in "good touch, bad touch" presentations; and the hugs, touches, and short personal conversations that are so necessary in a nurturing climate be delivered only when others are visible (Currie, 1988, p. 90).

Measuring and evaluating affective development also seem to be problematic for many classroom teachers. This can be accomplished by using a variety of strategies. Criterion-referenced checklists can be developed directly from the curricular objectives that follow. Teachers can also use these checklists as a reminder about the need to structure a growth-producing environment and activities in the classroom. Other data sources might include a series of anecdotal records of particular behaviors such as offering assistance to another child, documentation through participation charts, notations about unstructured play and work partnerships formed, and structured and informal observations of the child's affective statements and behaviors. More specific strategies related to assessment and evaluation can be found in chap. 16.

GOALS AND OBJECTIVES

The ultimate goal of the affective domain is for children to regard themselves as valued and capable persons. For children to make progress toward this goal, they must perceive the classroom as a psychologically safe and supportive environment and have a variety of experiences that promote growth of emotional health and positive self-esteem.

Mediating Objectives

As children progress toward the ultimate goal, they will

1. learn that school is safe, supportive, predictable, interesting, and enjoyable.
2. demonstrate that they have a feeling of belonging in the school environment.
3. engage in affectionate relationships beyond the family.
4. identify the characteristics and qualities that make each of them unique.
5. identify their own emotions.
6. explore similarities and differences among people to gain personal insight.
7. demonstrate growing ability to care for themselves and meet their own needs.

8. independently begin and pursue a task and control their own behavior without external reminders.
9. make choices and experience the consequences of personal decisions.
10. gain experience and demonstrate independence in using age-appropriate materials and tools (writing implements, cutting tools, measuring instruments, the computer, tape recorder, record player, typewriter).
11. complete a task they have begun.
12. assume responsibility for caring for their personal belongings and classroom materials.
13. contribute to maintenance of the classroom (e.g., caring for classroom pets, watering plants).
14. demonstrate increasing awareness of and ability to evaluate their accomplishments, as well as to set new standards and goals.
15. voluntarily attempt experiences they are unsure of or that are new to them with reasonable confidence and enthusiasm.
16. learn satisfying and effective strategies to express and cope with personal emotions and tensions.
17. learn to accept both positive and negative emotions as a natural part of living.
18. become familiar with the situational circumstances that influence personal emotions.
19. learn how to act deliberately to affect their own emotions.
20. understand the concept of possession and ownership.
21. value their own gender, family, culture, and race.
22. engage in a full range of experiences, not limited to stereotypes related to gender or background.
23. increase their knowledge, understanding, and appreciation of their own cultural heritage.
24. develop cross-gender competencies of various kinds.
25. experience the pleasure of work.
26. recognize factors that contribute to quality work (e.g., time, care, effort, responsibility, etc.).
27. make reasonable attempts to master situations that are difficult for them.
28. become aware that criticism is about ideas, not persons, and learn how to recover from setbacks.
29. demonstrate reasonable self-confidence, and evaluate and describe themselves as valuable and capable.
30. imagine and speak of future potential for themselves.
31. feel free to give and accept opinions.

TEACHING STRATEGIES

1. *Set a positive classroom climate.* Structuring a positive classroom climate is essential in creating learning contexts in which children build a strong sense of feeling valued, confident, and competent. This requires that teachers are knowledgeable about and sensitive to variations in personality, as well as children's successes and failures in forming attachments to others. We need to assess and evaluate whether or not they are achieving competence or mastery, inner control and assertiveness, and prosocial behaviors to minimize developmental risk (Brendtro, Brokenleg, & Van Bockern, 1990).

Use a variety of strategies to promote children's development away from egocentrism and excessive individualism and toward cooperative relationships and mutual respect. Actively promote rapport and a sense of teamness. Impress on children that they need others in order to feel belonging, liked, valued, cared for, and in union with others. In order to develop a sense of community in the classroom, begin on the first day of school to develop social bonds and a sense of being a team among the children, using cooperative learning strategies. Encourage children to reinforce each other's efforts and to support one another in a respectful way. Provide activities that will sensitize them about the fact that we feel worthwhile not only when we achieve something but also when we display positive behaviors toward others and behave with kindness, courtesy, trustworthiness, and responsibility (Lickona, 1988).

2. *Establish a low-stress and emotionally supportive environment.* The classroom teacher is a key person in helping young children make a smooth and comfortable transition to school and also in developing and maintaining their enthusiasm for working and playing with others. Establish a predictable schedule, and provide daily an overview of the day's activities, including any changes in routine, notice of visitors,

and so forth. Monitor the pace at which the program moves and whether or not a distinction is being made that work is dull and play is the only thing to look forward to. Evaluate whether your sense of humor is alive and well, making the classroom a pleasurable place to spend time. Familiarize yourself with information about children's fears, and provide a safe and supportive context for children to gradually work through them. Teachers will want to examine their own self-esteem and how they model stress and conflict management to children when they are under pressure themselves.

3. *Assess the physical makeup of the room and use of space and materials.* Establish a stimulus-reduced area where children who are seeking quiet can work. Balance quiet and active experiences so that children are not emotionally or physically overloaded. Evaluate the room for visual and auditory overstimulation, as well as noise levels, lighting, and temperature. Make space available where children can store their individual belongings and where their work can be prominently displayed at their eye level. Make available some materials that children can select for themselves, and take time at the beginning of the year to make sure children understand how to use them. Follow through to see that they return materials to proper storage.

4. *Work collaboratively with parents, building effective, continuing home-school partnerships.* Handle the separation process from home to school with sensitivity and respect for children's individual needs. Provide, if possible, opportunities for a gradual introduction to the school setting. Comfort anxious children and parents, and provide information to parents about how to ease children's transitions from home to school. Develop a system with parents to share knowledge about events at home or school that may be emotionally upsetting to a child.

5. *Monitor school materials and routines to avoid reinforcing stereotypes, and create activities that challenge stereotypes and prejudice.* Continually evaluate the expectations you hold about what children can become. Also, survey the kinds of activities and materials used in the classroom. According to Boyer (1990, p. 63), educators should include at least 25% representation of minority groups in materials used, with particular attention to math materials, which are

particularly problematic. Portrayals should be positive. Provide children with opportunities to interact with adult members and other children of their own and of other cultures. Plan visits to a variety of work sites, and invite people to explain about a variety of occupations, including those that are nontraditional.

6. *Promote children's emotional development and sense of worth.* Talk with children about their emotions, and structure activities and experiences specifically to build awareness of situations and events that influence emotions. Praise children's accomplishments, and, in order to build self-esteem, use genuine praise and more reinforcement than negative criticism. Give children adequate time and encouragement to finish tasks for themselves.

Never shame or compare children with others or label them with derogatory words. Develop a ready bank of reinforcing and encouraging phrases, such as the following (C.A. Smith, 1982):

> You're on the right track now!
> I'm happy to see you working like that.
> Now you've figured it out.
> That's a kind thing you did.
> Fantastic! You really worked a long time on (remember to be specific so that praise does not become general and meaningless).
> You must have been practicing!
> One more time, and you'll have it.
> That's quite an improvement.
> You really make being a teacher fun.
> You've really got your brain in gear today!
> Now that's what I call a fine job.
> You remembered. I'm proud of you.
> That was a friendly thing to do.
> You're like a beautiful [name object], [name of child].
> Good remembering!

Accept and respect temperamental idiosyncrasies, providing support where it is needed for children who adapt more slowly to change. Avoid using children's names to mean "No," "Stop," or "Don't!"

Never ignore difficult behaviors or problems such as lying, stealing, or cruelty to self or others. When children demonstrate a pattern of difficult behaviors and are unresponsive to your attempts to modify them, seek help by working with other professionals who have more specific expertise.

Provide opportunities for children to describe their emotions.

Develop a sense of belonging and connectedness for each member of the class. Have the class send cards to children who are sick. Model and let children know that your motto is "We're a team; we respect and take care of one another."

7. *Promote children's competence.* Be patient in helping children modify their behavior. View children's inappropriate behavior as a gap in their knowledge or skills. Rather than expecting immediate change, identify steps in progress, giving children reinforcement when you see them trying to correct a particular behavior.

Use subtle cues to remind children that their behavior is close to exceeding limits. Whenever possible, allow children opportunities to assess the situation, figure out what should be done, experience consequences, and modify their own behavior in a positive direction.

Set effective limits with clearly defined expectations. Involve children in structuring classroom rules, and apply natural and logical consequences consistently when rules are not observed. (Refer to chap. 14, "Promoting Self-Discipline in Children," for further information regarding rules and consequences.)

Help children find satisfying ways to express their emotions to others. When an emotion has been expressed inappropriately, recognize a child's feelings about the situation before moving ahead with helping the child correct the situation or learn new skills. For children who have difficulty controlling impulsivity because of neurological disorders that manifest themselves behaviorally (e.g., attention deficit disorder, autistic-like disorders), use such approaches as nonpunitive separation to remove the child from an overstimulating situation. Use work completion strategies to help such children better organize their day (see chap. 14). Provide reinforcement for keeping on task as well as frequent goal-setting sessions and helpful, concrete suggestions for more appropriate behavior.

Protect children's growing sense of autonomy by giving them frequent choices. Offer these whenever you are willing to accept children's decisions. Be careful about providing too many choices or overloading children with decision-making "opportunities" that are meaningless or are better made by adults.

When children focus on the negative, accept their statements and then ask, "How do you wish it were different? What could you do to change it?" Help students set goals for what they can change and be more accepting of what they cannot.

Involve children in planning, implementing, and evaluating some class activities and decisions. Set aside a portion of each day for children to engage in free-choice, self-initiated activities. Design activities in which the primary purpose is to teach children to use various classroom tools. Give children opportunities to carry out classroom jobs. Encourage them to clean up after themselves whenever possible and also to assist others who need help. Encourage children to evaluate the decisions they have made by looking back at how well they defined the problem, whether or not they thought about all the alternatives, whether or not they persisted long enough, what turned out well, and what they might do differently the next time. Also, invite children to evaluate their accomplishments. Conference with them and provide task-specific feedback and questions to help them focus on what they have learned and next steps to enhance their learning. Guide them toward self-examination of their own growth and work rather than relying only on the teacher's or their parents' evaluation. Involve them in producing self-appraisal reports prior to parent conferences.

Support children in their efforts to try new or uncomfortable tasks. Verbally recognize their efforts, and praise courage and determination to try in the first place, not just the results. Include scaffolding strategies here; gauge the amount of support and challenge necessary for optimal growth, slowly decreasing support as the child moves toward increasing autonomy (Wood, Bruner, & Ross, 1976).

8. *In working with children with disabilities, avoid tendencies to overprotect them in order to develop their autonomy as much as possible.* Assist more able children only when needed. Encourage more able children to seek help from children with disabilities when it is possible for them to respond.

ACTIVITY SUGGESTIONS

➠ Toy Land Relaxation

Objective: For children to learn satisfying and effective strategies to express and cope with personal emotions and tensions

Materials: Toy soldier, limp Raggedy Ann and Andy dolls, taped musical selections for marching and relaxing, tape player

Procedure: In order to help children become familiar with and contrast feelings of bodily relaxation and tension, talk with them about how our bodies are hinged together. Help them discover where these "hinges" are located (neck, wrist, fingers, ankles, toes, waist) and how stiff and tight their bodies feel when the hinges are all "locked up." Contrast this with what happens when these same hinges are loose by having the children relax each locked body hinge, starting with the neck, then the waist, wrists, and so on, reminding them to sit down carefully as their body becomes increasingly limp.

To Simplify: Demonstrate the process of locking up and loosening up with toys, such as a stiff, inflexible toy solider and limp cloth Raggedy Ann and Andy dolls.

To Extend: To increase children's sense of contrast, use march music and practice being stiff wooden soldiers; then switch to some peaceful, relaxing music, and encourage children to slow everything down and become completely limp and relaxed. Discuss with children other states they have experienced and how their bodies felt at the time, what their facial expressions may have been, what they may have said, or how they may have behaved (e.g., being angry vs. being happy and relaxed). For a follow-up activity, have children choose pictures from magazines that depict faces of people who seem "tight," angry, and hurried and those in which people seem "loose," happy, and relaxed.

➠ A Special Self Award*

Objective: For children to evaluate and describe themselves positively

Materials: Precut "award" shapes, labels, glue, ribbons, mirrors, blank booklets, markers

Procedure: Discuss the ideas of valuing yourself and liking things that you do well. Explain

---

*Note: Adapted from Kostelnik et al. (1991, p. 22).

that awards are sometimes given to people to show what special things they do well. Ask the children to think of something they like about themselves and to design a special award for themselves. Provide a variety of precut shapes in colored and gold and silver paper, ribbons, glue, and labels that say "I'm Special Because I _____ ."

To Simplify: For children who have difficulty thinking of something, ask others in the group to help them by suggesting the things they do well.

To Extend: Have children develop individual "I Am Special" booklets where they either dictate or write a sentence at the top of each page about a skill they have developed in which they take pride. Have them illustrate the pages.

➡ **Who's in Your Family?***

Objective: For children to explore similarities and differences among people to gain personal insight

Materials: Photographs of household members, blank booklets, markers, children's literature about families including a children's story in Spanish or another language, persona dolls

Procedure: Borrow and/or take photographs of all the people who live with each child and staff member. Make a bulletin board of "The People in Our Homes." Label each photo with the names and family relationships of each person.

To Simplify: Talk with children about the similarities and differences in who lives together as a family.

To Extend: Make a class book about "Our Families" with a page for each child and staff member, telling who lives with each child and what work family members do in and outside the home. "This is Jamal's family. He lives with _____. His [mom, dad, grandma, grandpa, aunt, uncle] take care of him, work at...." Be aware that some children's primary family members are temporarily or chronically unemployed. Focus on what they do, not on where they work. Let chil-

_____

*Note: Adapted from Derman-Sparks (1991, pp. 59–60).

dren take these stories home to read to their families.

Read children's books about families reflective of the ethnic groups in your class. Always read more than one book about each group. Talk about the differences and similarities between the children's lives in the book and the children from that ethnic group in your class. Discuss the books: "Is this how you do it in your family?" Expand on this with books about families from ethnic groups not present in the classroom. Include books about interracial and intercultural families (see resources listed in Derman-Sparks, 1991, pp. 119–132).

Using persona dolls (those that represent a particular racial/ethnic group), tell stories about possible experiences or problems a child might have within the family, school, or neighborhood when belonging to that racial/ethnic group. For example, talk about a Spanish-speaking child's experience when beginning school, using a persona doll as a prop. Read a book in Spanish to the children, and talk about how they feel when they do not understand the words and how they think the doll felt. Tell a story where one of the dolls was teased for being Mexican; talk about how the doll felt and what the doll did to stand up for him- or herself.

➡ **I Can Can**

Objective: For children to demonstrate pride in their accomplishments

Materials: Large empty juice can, colored paper strips, markers, blank booklets

Procedure: Provide or have children bring in a large empty juice can that has been washed and checked for any sharp edges. Have them place a label around the can that says "I CAN!" and then decorate the can so that each is individual. As they learn and demonstrate a new skill, have them fill out a special colored paper strip, dictating or writing the skill and dating it.

To Simplify: Watch for the child who fails to recognize his or her accomplishments. Remind these children that small gains also need to be recorded, and help them identify some of these or set some goals that can be accomplished.

To Extend: At the end of each month, have the children transfer their "I CAN!" slips to an ongoing booklet, denoting the beginning of each month (e.g., "In November, I learned to do these things") and pasting in the strips following the heading. The pages could also be illustrated in some way. The booklets become a vehicle for children's self-assessment. They can also become one piece of a portfolio, shared with a portfolio buddy or the entire group, and shared with parents at conferences or open houses.

➟ I Can Get There All by Myself

Objective: To have children demonstrate pride in their accomplishments

Materials: Paper, markers, scissors, glue

Procedure: Demonstrate to children drawing a simple map from your home to the school. As you draw it, talk about several landmarks on the way. Draw them in also and label them. Draw a clock by the house noting the time (on the hour or half hour) that you usually leave for school. After drawing the school, add a clock by it indicating (again, on the hour or half hour) what time you usually arrive. Tell the children, "This is a map of the way I come to school every day. The clocks indicate the time I leave for school and the time I arrive. Each one of you gets to school each day by walking or riding in a car or bus. That means you have to get ready to leave by a certain time and then get to this classroom by the time school is ready to start." Invite each child to construct a simple map showing their home, the school, and a route in between.

To Simplify: Tell the children that you would like to construct a classroom map showing the school and the way to each one of their homes and that you need their help in drawing their houses. Have them make just a picture of their home on individual pieces of paper and cut around them. Construct a very simple mural showing just larger cross streets, and help the children paste their homes east, west, south, or north of the cross streets.

To Extend: Have the children also indicate the approximate time (half hour or hour) they leave their homes and arrive at school. Have them draw a more elaborate route between home and school on an individual basis. Have them take part in constructing the classroom mural that integrates all of their homes in relation to the school.

➟ We're Learning to Do So Many Things

Objective: For children to demonstrate pride in their accomplishments

Materials: Large precut hand on easel, markers, blank booklets

Procedure: Tell the children, "Just think of how many things each of you do every day from the time you get up in the morning until you go to bed." Place a large precut hand on the easel. Tell the children, "Sometimes when someone is able to do a lot of different things, we say they are 'pretty handy.' Ask them what they think the expression means, and discuss the many ways we use our hands in order to accomplish what we need to. Label the precut hand, "We Are Pretty Handy." Encourage the children to think of skills they have developed, print them on the hand, and then have the group decide where to place it in the classroom.

To Simplify: For children who have a difficult time thinking of things they do, have the group suggest something they probably can do.

To Extend: Have the children construct an individual booklet that contains about 10 pages titled "Learning to Be Handy." Have them work on completing the pages by drawing their hands on each page and then listing a separate skill they have learned on each of the fingers (e.g., "I brush my teeth," "I can count to 25," "I fix my own cereal," "I make my bed," "I feed my dog").

➟ Relaxing Our Bodies*

Objective: For children to learn satisfying strategies to express and cope with personal emotions

Materials: Tape of relaxing music, tape player

---

*Note: Adapted from Goth-Owens (n.d., pp. 39–41).

Procedure: One way to relax is through deep breathing. Even very young children can learn to do this with guidance. Have the children learn to assume a relaxed, comfortable position and be very quiet so that each of them can just listen to their breathing as they breathe in and out through their noses. As they relax, help them breathe more deeply and deepen their feeling of relaxation by having them try some of the following exercises:

- Imagine the air that comes to you is a cloud. The cloud comes to you, fills you, and then leaves you.
- Imagine your chest [or lungs] is a balloon. You may want to demonstrate this by putting your hand on your chest and then have them feel their own chests as they breathe in deeply. Tell them, "As you breathe in or inhale, your lungs expand like a balloon, don't they? As you exhale or breathe out, your lungs deflate like a balloon."
- As you inhale, say the word "in" to yourself. As you exhale, say the word "out."

To Simplify: Just have the children learn to assume a comfortable, relaxed position. Put on some very relaxing music, and have them stretch slowly to the music, and then just lie quietly and listen to it. Use the words "relax" and "relaxing" to acquaint them with relaxation terminology.

To Extend: Have the children experience tensing specific muscle groups and then relaxing them. First be sure that they are familiar with all of the body parts that follow, and demonstrate any unfamiliar terminology used such as "clench" and "shrug." Then talk them through the exercise as follows:

Muscle	Tensing Method
Forehead	Wrinkle your forehead. Try to make your eyebrows touch your hair. Count to five. Relax.
Eyes and nose	Close your eyes as tightly as you can. Keep them closed and count to five. Open your eyes and relax.
Lips, cheeks, and jaw	Keeping your mouth closed, make as big a smile as you can. Keep the smile on your face and count to five. Relax. Feel how warm your face is.
Hands	Hold your arms in front of you. Make a tight fist with your hands. Squeeze them as tightly as you can while you count to five. Relax. Feel the warmth and calmness in your hands.
Forearms	Extend your arms out. Pretend you are pushing against a wall. Push forward with your hands and keep them against the invisible wall. Hold them there and count to five. Relax.
Shoulders	Shrug your sholders up to your ears. Keep them there while you count to five. Relax.
Thighs	Tighten your thigh muscles by pressing your legs together as tightly as you can. Count to five. Relax your legs.
Feet	Bend your ankles toward your body as far as you can. Hold them there and count to five. Relax.
Toes	Curl your toes under as tightly as you can. Hold them there. Count to five. Relax.

Afterward, encourage the children to talk about how their bodies feel while they are doing the exercise. Tell them that some people like to relax their muscles when they go to bed by doing this exercise.

⟹ **We All Look Special***

Objective: For children to value their own gender, family, culture, and race

Materials: Paint chip samples, paper, markers, skin-colored crayons

---

*Note: Adapted from Derman-Sparks (1991, pp. 35–36).

Procedure: Get paint chips from a paint store. In small groups, identify the ones closest to each child's skin tone, hair color, and eye color.

To Simplify: Make a very simple graph using a range of colors and how many children have which color. Talk about how everyone has skin and the functions it serves for everyone. Provide skin-colored crayons that can be ordered from a number of companies such as Afro-Am Education Materials and Crayola. Help them choose the one closest to their skin color and then draw pictures of themselves. Mix paints so that each of the children has individualized color for painting pictures of themselves. Be creative in talking about the beauty of each shade.

To Extend: In an all-white class, help children identify more subtle differences in skin shades, including freckles, and emphasize that skin color differences are desirable. In a diverse interracial/interethnic class, emphasize the theme, "Beautiful children come in all colors" and that the classroom is a wonderful mixture of colors. Make a rainbow from skin shade colors, eye colors, or hair colors and label it "We All Make a Beautiful Rainbow."

➠ Angry Faces*

Objective: For children to identify their emotions and become more aware of facial expressions of anger

Materials: Paper plates with tongue depressor handles attached to them, yarn for hair, markers, crayons, glue, construction paper, facial features cut out of magazines (be sure to use magazines with pictures of many different races of children and adults)

Procedure: In the art center, spread out materials. Help the children use the materials to make puppets with angry faces, providing suggestions but not giving them a model to copy. Encourage them to talk about how they feel inside when they are wearing an angry face or how they feel when someone else looks at them with an angry face.

To Simplify: With extremely young children, provide already prepared puppets and encour-

age them to discuss feelings that go along with angry faces. Reassure children it is OK to feel angry.

To Extend: Have older children write and/or stage their own puppet show about the solution of an angry situation.

Extend children's ability to identify body language expressions of anger. Have them hold the stick puppets in front of their faces as they stomp up and down repeating this chant in an angry voice (to the tune of "Here We Go 'Round the Mulberry Bush"):

> This is my angry face, angry face, angry face,
> This is my angry face being worn at school today.
> This is my angry march, angry march, angry march,
> This is my angry march taking place at school today.

➠ We Get Angry When...†

Objective: For children to become more familiar with circumstances that influence emotions

Materials: Children's books about anger

Procedure: After you have discussed the feeling of anger with children in a large- or small-group situation and have read some books about anger (e.g., *Alexander and the Terrible, Horrible, No Good, Very Bad Day* by Judith Viorst; *Attila the Angry* by Marjorie Weinman Sharmat; *Let's Be Enemies* by Janice May Udry; *The Sorely Trying Day* by Russell Hoban; *The Hating Book* by Charlotte Zolotow), have the children share examples of moments when they feel or have felt angry. Discuss ways the characters deal with the situations that help them get rid of the angry feelings. Talk about positive and negative strategies people use in trying to get rid of angry feelings.

To Simplify: After reading the stories, talk about what made the main character angry or upset.

---

*Note: Adapted from C.A. Smith (1982, p. 114).
†Note: Adapted from C.A. Smith (1982, p. 111).

To Extend: Write the title "We Get Angry When..." at the top of a large sheet of paper on the easel. List examples or write a class experience story as the children share their ideas. Older children could write and illustrate individual "I Get Angry When..." booklets.

SUMMARY

Young children have so much to learn, about themselves and about the effect they have on others. And what they learn in the early years from significant others in their lives—particularly from parents, teachers, and peers—becomes vitally important in their later ability to form and maintain relationships, work and play well with others, and feel valued, confident, and competent in any number of situations.

The development of emotional strength and stability, a lifelong task, is interdependent with children's cognitive, physical, and social development. Because children spend major amounts of time in extrafamilial settings and because they are moving into these contexts earlier and earlier, good learning environments are those in which affective, physical, and social development are valued as highly as academic aspects of learning. Caring professionals who are able to structure positive learning climates, actively promote children's emotional development and sense of self-worth, and foster children's competence are key players in facilitating positive affective outcomes for young children. Also critical wll be the sensitivity of caring adults to differences in personality, gender, ethnicity, and race in the children and families with whom they work.

CHAPTER 5

The Cognitive Domain

Five-year-old Ervin looked thoughtful as he methodically munched his way through his peanut butter sandwich. He was wondering about Mrs. Stone, his teacher last year when he was in the 4-year-old group. She looked so different this year. "Mom," he asked, "What happened to Mrs. Stone?"

"What do you mean, 'What happened to Mrs.Stone'?" responded his mother.

"Well, she's not cushy anymore; all her pillows are gone!" Ervin answered.

"Oh," laughed his mother. "She went on a diet and lost a lot of weight this summer."

"Well," said Ervin, "maybe we could help her find it, so she would be cushy again!"

That young children's thinking is dramatically different than that of older children and adults is illustrated again and again by the "cute" but inaccurate statements they make. Quite literally, they see the world from an entirely different perspective, and their fascinating journey toward more mature thinking will be a combination of inherent capacities, accumulated experiences, and the quality of their relationships with others who will accompany them on that journey.

Development in the cognitive domain—that is, the maturation of processes and products of the human mind that lead to "knowing" (Berk, 1989, p. 219)—is a complex process that impacts significantly and continuously on all other domains of development. At the same time, growth and increasing competence in other domains influence the qualitative development of cognitive capacities. For example, a young child's ability to imagine or fantasize what it is like to be another member of the family—mommy, daddy, or baby—equips the child to take on such a role in a group of children playing "house." Interacting with other children as they play out their concept of "house" subsequently increases the child's knowledge and skill base in a variety of areas, for example, vocabulary, understanding of social do's and don'ts, one-to-one correspondence, and a sense of number as the children divide and combine materials. Also enhanced are conflict management as they sort out roles and goal-directed behaviors and a growing understanding of cause and effect as they operate on objects, challenge and cooperate with one an-

other, and figure out alternate ways to accomplish a variety of intended outcomes.

Because of the circuitous fashion in which the intellect evolves, promising new directions in early childhood education that support the integration of various learning domains through experiential learning have enormous potential. They are made even more effective when cognitive levels are matched carefully with classroom learning experiences and when professionals are sensitive to the negative effects of overchallenging or underchallenging the developing child.

COGNITIVE MATURATION

Piaget's Theoretical Contributions

Though the theoretical conclusions of the Swiss epistomologist Jean Piaget are being reexamined in light of current research in the field (Gardner, 1983; Steinberg & Belsky, 1991), his contributions continue to be highly useful in understanding the qualitative cognitive changes that take place in the young child. The aim of education, he maintained, "should be not to instruct, but to provide a formative milieu for the child's...intellectual, moral, and affective development—not just to furnish the mind, but to help form its reasoning power" (DeVries & Kohlberg, 1990, p. 14).

Piaget saw intellectual maturation as a progressive series of structurally defined stages. Maturation evolves out of the human organism's self-motivated efforts to adapt to and make sense of day-to-day experiences. In developing useful concepts, or *schemes,* children purposefully repeat certain acts again and again (e.g., dropping an object from the high chair, rhyming certain sounds or words, observing how someone ties shoelaces, drawing or scribbling, listening to a story, riding a trike, working a puzzle, or writing at school in a daily journal). These acts result in their "bumping into" new information that is either simply *assimilated* or produces a need for *accommodation* in terms of current functioning. When human beings cognitively assimilate experiential knowledge, they do so without feeling any need to adapt the way they think about a particular phenomenon or situation. However, there are other times when they become "disequilibrated," or thrown out of balance cognitively; this is because they have begun to notice something about a situation or phenomenon that no longer fits comfortably in their old way of thinking about it.

For example, a child may initially have only one concept for all vehicles and refer to them all as "cars." Later, as a result of new experiences with a number of wheeled phenomena and also structural maturation of the brain, it begins to dawn on the child that some vehicles *are* different from one another. As the child zeros in on how these newly noticed phenomena are different, the child also comes to understand that vehicles other than those initially catching his or her interest may also be different. If the child is then motivated to investigate these differences or pay more attention to them as encountered in everyday experiences, the child gains growing expertise related to vehicular phenomena, both in terms of vehicles in general and then in a horizontal fleshing out of vehicles in particular categories. The child comes to know that cars differ from buses and trucks but also that within the category of cars, there are Fords and Volvos, sedans and coupes, convertibles and hard tops, sports cars and family cars.

Thus, successful accommodation—a new sense of understanding or development of new strategies or schemes for interacting with and understanding the environment (Zigler & Stevenson, 1987)—results in the evolution of increasingly higher level thinking. Higher order schemes are an outcome of both genetic, biological unfolding and experiences that catch one's attention and produce a field of disequilibration, producing the motivation to try a task over and over in order to "figure something out." Teachers facilitate the development of children's internal structures when they construct enriched environments that include diverse and "interesting concrete materials for children to touch, see, hear, taste, feel, manipulate, arrange, rearrange, sort, resort, classify, etc." (Trepanier-Street, 1990, p. 182).

Mental operative power to make sense of events and phenomena differs depending on the evolved structures of the child. According to Piaget, there are four stages that build epigenetically on one another. Hamachek's (1990, p. 469) summary of the basic intellectual abilities associated with each of the stages appears in Table 5.1.

Ages connected to these stages are approximate, and children are continuously moving toward acquisition of higher level processes while still showing evidence of characteristic limitations identified with particular stages. Early childhood educators working with young children can benefit greatly by understanding and respecting the characteristic modes of thinking within certain stages so that activities and experiences match cognitive levels and do not exceed a child's ability to gain from them.

Characteristics of Preoperational and Concrete Operational Thought

Because this text focuses on constructing effective learning environments for children from 3 to 8 years of age, characteristics peculiar to children in the preoperational and concrete operational periods deserve a closer look.

Centration, children's tendency to center on only one aspect of a stimulus rather than processing all available information and holding changes in two dimensions at the same time, is an important aspect of preoperational thinking. As children move toward the end of the period, they are not as easily fooled and are more able to decenter in situations or with materials familiar to them. Although their thought is perhaps still not as logical as that of the average 8- to 11-year-old, they are relying less on intuition and the appearance of things when they explain why things happen. Their understanding of cause and effect becomes clearer, and more mature preoperational children are also beginning to move away from the *egocentrism* that limits them from seeing other people's points of view. Children who have moved into the concrete operational stage still benefit from using real objects when problem solving but are now better equipped to deal with symbolic forms. Their ability to decenter is more highly developed, which allows them to focus on details while keeping the whole in mind, a skill necessary for understanding part-whole relationships involved in place value in mathematics or phonics in literacy.

Closely related to centration is a lack of ability to think in more than one direction. *Reversibility,* the concept that objects can be structured, restructured, and then rearranged as originally structured, is limited in the preoperational child. Children under 5 years of age are influenced by perceptual salience; that is, their

TABLE 5.1
Overview of Piaget's Intellectual Stages

Stage	Age Range	Basic Characteristics
1. Sensorimotor	Birth–2	Infants learn that they are different from other objects and learn primarily through their senses and manipulations. There is a strong desire and need for as much stimulation as possible.
2. Preoperational thought	2–7	An essentially egocentric period insofar as children are unable to see things from others' point of view; they tend to classify in very simple ways (e.g., if a father is a man, then all men must be fathers).
a. Preoperational phase	2–4	
b. Intuitive phase	4–7	Children slowly begin to think in terms of classes, handle number concepts, and see simple relationships. Children are "intuitive"; that is, they are capable of making classifications even though they do not really understand why or how. They develop a gradual awareness of the conservation of mass, weight, and volume (e.g., they can see that the amount may remain the same even if transferred to a different size container).
3. Concrete operational thought	7–11	Children grow in ability to consciously use and understand logical operations such as reversibility (in arithmetic), classification (putting objects into hierarchies of classes), and seriation (organizing objects into a specified series, such as increasing size or weight).
4. Formal operational thought	11–15	Youngsters further develop the ability to comprehend abstract concepts (e.g., the ability to think about "ideals," understand cause-effect relationships, think about the future, and develop and test hypotheses).

Source: Adapted from Don Hamachek, *Psychology in Teaching, Learning, and Growth*, Fourth Edition. Copyright © 1990 by Allyn & Bacon. Reprinted with permission.

perceptions dominate their understandings, and seeing is believing. Thus, they do not automatically know what older children are coming to know—that number, mass, distance, volume, and area stay constant despite changes in appearance. Children in the concrete stage can be more reflective about such operations and also what it would require to undo an action. For example, at a summer camp craft class, 9-year-old Juana and her 3-year-old brother Carl had each created a sculpture from toothpicks and marshmallows. Each child had been given 20 marshmallows and 10 toothpicks to create whatever he or she wished. Carl, after completing a "spaceship" with his materials, began pestering Juana for more toothpicks and marshmallows to make a different one because he did not like the one he had created. "Just use the ones you have!" she responded testily. Carl looked down in a confused way at the unwanted creation, thought again about the other one he had in mind, and cried, "But they're all gone! I don't have no more!" Juana's point of view said it was possible to construct a new product from the materials available; Carl's said it was not.

It has been documented that, with coaching, children may be able to perform such operations somewhat earlier than Piaget believed they could and that early childhood educators and researchers need to be paying more attention to what preoperational children *can* do than what they cannot do, extending their learning

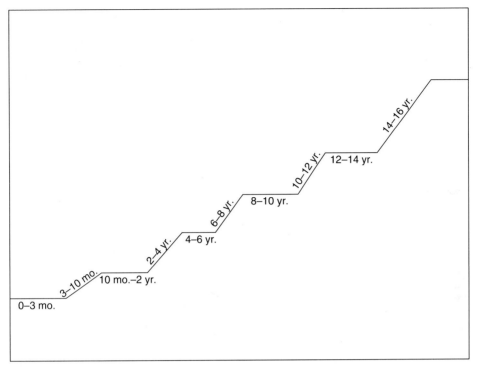

FIGURE 5.1
Plateau and Acceleration Periods of Brain Growth According to Epstein (1978)

from that point (Steinberg & Belsky, 1991). With the preoperational child, physical action and concrete materials are prerequisites to developing their understanding of particular phenomena. Also, they are often better able to express their feelings, thoughts, and conceptualizations through symbolic play than verbalizations. As they use varied strategies and trial and error to test out possibilities and problem solving, they become capable of more complex thinking and are able to use knowledge in increasingly sophisticated ways.

The Relationship between Cognitive Maturation and Brain Growth

Piaget's observations of young children's intellectual maturation have been supported by current research looking at neurophysiological age-related differences in children (Epstein, 1978; Thatcher, Walker, & Guidice, 1987). Five dominant brain growth periods have been docu-

mented, and there is evidence that they occur in plateau and acceleration periods corresponding very closely to those established earlier by Piaget (see Figure 5.1).

During acceleration periods (3–10 months and 2–4, 6–8, 10–12, and 14–16 years), myelinization (formation of the insulation around nerve fibers that allows the smooth passage of electrical and chemical impulses) and axon and dendrite growth in the brain is significant, which enables millions of new connections to form between billions of neurons (see Figure 5.2). From about the age of 2 until adolescence, neural "pruning" takes place, which leads to greater efficiency in thinking processes. As brain research becomes more sophisticated, we will continue to learn more about how early experiences may impact on optimal pruning of neural circuits, which contributes to the later quality of intellectual functioning.

Following each of the acceleration periods, children are able to attach to more complex lev-

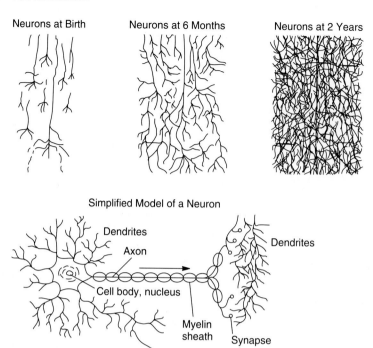

Neurons at Birth   Neurons at 6 Months   Neurons at 2 Years

Simplified Model of a Neuron

Dendrites
Axon
Cell body, nucleus
Myelin sheath
Dendrites
Synapse

FIGURE 5.2
Neuronal Growth

els of learning, and these, in turn, are enhanced during both plateau and acceleration periods by the quality, variety, and number of conceptual experiences that children have. When there is good fit between children's cognitive levels and classroom expectations, enhancement is optimal.

Although 85% of all children move through these stages in a predictable way, there is evidence that boys may enter acceleration periods 6 to 18 months behind girls. Poor recognition of this difference between boys and girls may be contributing to the significantly higher numbers of males in special education resource rooms for the emotionally impaired and learning disabled as well as larger numbers of males being retained in the early grades or recommended for developmental kindergartens and prefirst programs (Soderman & Phillips, 1986). Also, there may be critical periods for the acquisition of certain concepts, while others may be acquired at any time within a broader time span (Greenough, 1975). Trying to speed up learning or to produce "superchildren" through intensive instruction before children have forged neces-

sary mental connections has its consequences. One may be that inappropriate pushing distorts "the natural growth process" (Healy, 1989, p. 28), which perhaps may influence the strengthening or weakening of certain pathways in mental scaffolding.

INTELLIGENCE AS A SET OF INTEGRATED PROCESSES

Intelligence has often been mistakenly viewed as a single, fixed entity in human beings, something that can be "scored" on a standardized test. With what we now know about both biological structures of the brain and educational strategies for supporting development in the cognitive realm, such a narrow perspective is clearly outmoded. Rather, intelligence or cognition is more advantageously viewed as an integrated set of underlying processes that may be modified, for good or bad, by the quality of learning contexts surrounding the maturing individual. Gardner (1983) has addressed this in his seminal work that offers evidence for the existence of multiple "human intelligences" or domains that may be relatively independent of one another but work in harmony as individuals process incoming stimuli.

It is critical that educators recognize that knowledge cannot come in neatly packaged sets of understandings that can be passively laid on children. When this happens, we risk short-circuiting in-depth or true understanding of phenomena in children because we cut them off from the intriguing and engaging work of concept formation. According to Kamii and DeVries (1978), Piaget insisted that "all knowledge, including the ability to reason logically is constructed by the individual as he acts on objects and people and tries to make sense out of his experience....Piaget believes that knowledge is acquired not by internalization of some outside 'given' but by construction from within" (p. 16). This is accomplished as children acquire the components of a fundamental knowledge base.

Developing a Fundamental Knowledge Base

Up to this point, we have focused on *how* children come to know things; now we will concentrate on *what* they need to know. A necessary knowledge base is made up primarily of four subgroups (DeVries & Kohlberg, 1990; *Kindergarten Curriculum Guide and Resource Book,* 1985, pp. 25–34):

1. *Physical knowledge*—observable attributes of objects and physical phenomena: size, color, shape, weight, texture, tendencies under varying conditions (e.g., things roll downhill; snow is cold; sugar is sweet; spiders have eight legs)

2. *Logical-mathematical knowledge*—relationship between objects and phenomena growing out of observation; reasoning out a logical organization to deal more effectively with incoming knowledge, including classification, patterning, seriation, number (counting, one-to-one correspondence, equivalence of groups of numbers, invariance of number), space in relationship to their own bodies (vertical and horizontal coordinates; right and left, in front and behind coordinates; depth and distance coordinates; topological—closed or open shapes, inclusion/exclusion, proximity, order—

and Euclidian—geometrical perspectives, including lines, angles, equalities, parallelism, and distance) and time, including order of events and length of events. Development in this arena is critical in the child's ability to organize a very complex and confusing world. White and Siegel (1976) perceive the process of getting "unconfused" as the essence of cognition; that is, to begin to recognize distinct and recurrent patterns that emerge out of the stimulus flux surrounding the child.

3. *Representational knowledge*—imaginative expression of symbolic thought that represents the mental world of the child; manipulating images, art, symbols, language to stand for objects, events, and concepts (Steinberg & Belsky, 1991); competence in restructuring an experience in another way through symbolic representation (dramatic and creative play, rhythmic movement, imitation, construction of two- and three-dimensional models) and sign representation, which evolves through spoken language and then written language as follows:

- Using names for objects in the environment
- Using words to identify the properties and functions of objects
- Using words to denote location in space and location in time
- Using words that describe relationships (comparing, describing differences and similarities, enumerating, measuring, ordering)
- Using words to relate physical knowledge
- Using words to relate social knowledge
- Using words to tell events and stories
- Using words to relate personal feelings and thoughts

4. *Social-conventional knowledge*—cultural and societal conventions/rules/viewpoints transmitted to children by family, society, school, peers to guide behavior related to other individuals, institutions, and the use of goods and services (e.g., 911 is a number to call if in danger; some families have more than one mother and father; many Jewish families celebrate Hanukkah; most people finish high school; farmers produce some of our food)

Expanded discussion of two aspects of this knowledge base, representational knowledge and social/conventional knowledge, can be found in chapter 6, "The Language Domain," and chapter 13, "Theme Planning and Implementation." Two other aspects, physical knowledge and logical-mathematical knowledge, are considered in more depth in this chapter as we look at two major curricular vehicles for expanding children's conceptualization in these areas, science and mathematics.

The Young Child as Scientist

Children are full of questions and expend a great deal of their energy in figuring out how things work, what people do, and how they themselves can become more competent players in the general scheme of things. They have a driving need to investigate: how electric outlets work, how toilets flush, how things open and close, where bubbles go, how seashore waves "melt" sand castles.

Preschool children act on their intense curiosity through observation, trying out very simple operations, and questions to adults, over and over again. For these children, events simply happen or happen by magic. They turn on the TV and pictures appear. They ride with their family in the car at night, and the moon follows them—amazing! Later, as neural pathways mature and primary children gain additional experience and information, their still limited understanding of cause and effect is more often correct.

Because conceptualization in the early years is obviously unsystematic and intuitive, helpful adults want to guide the child toward more complex, integrated modes of thinking and capability in organizing knowledge. However, this will occur not from adults' merely providing information but from the child's many experiences in attempting to control and interpret events.

Obviously, the quality of a child's "sciencing" will depend on opportunities to collect a wide variety of information and support in making sense of and integrating that knowledge as they "mess around" with phenomena under varying conditions—acting, doing, and investigating the properties of objects and the relationships between and among objects (Bredderman, 1982; Brewer, 1992; Mechling & Oliver, 1983). Ideally, this calls for plenty of hands-on activity and sup-

Adults can help facilitate more complex conceptualization in young children.

portive adults who provide "pertinent information at strategic times" (Schickedanz, York et al., 1990, p. 237).

It is important to have children realize that science is more than a collection and organization of already known facts and that the solution to problems or new discoveries can sometimes spring from intuitive feelings about a particular phenomenon as well as already documented laws, theories, and principles. Thus, children should be encouraged to think divergently and creatively as well as convergently in their problem finding and problem solving. They must be made to feel safe to express and follow up on their own ideas as well as receive strategies for seeking information from established sources.

Scientific attitudes are as important as the subject itself, and children's curiosity is one of the most valuable. Others to be nurtured are skepticism, withholding judgment, objectivity, open-mindedness, integrity, and humility. Furthermore, children should be taught to avoid dogmatism, gullibility, and superstitions (Charlesworth & Lind, 1990, p. 52).

Meaningful content in the early years will most likely center around information related to life sciences, earth sciences, and physical sciences. Young children enjoy studying about plants and animals, the changing seasons, their own bodies, weather, space, machines, motion, energy, and the earth's ecology.

Although guided experience with the scientific processes will be most important, young children must also begin to develop strategies for making sense of, recording, and communicating their findings. These include graphs, pictures, and other representations such as dioramas, collections, checklists, oral reports, booklets and journals, gardens, cooked products, and even minidramas. Obviously, all curricular activity could spring from science; at the very least, good "sciencing" will require integration of activities and experiences from all other learning domains.

The Young Child as Mathematician

For the young child, mathematics is everywhere! It is a natural and integral part of their world. They see numerals everywhere—on their house, on the clock, on the cereal box, on the telephone, on the car, in books. They hear, "That will be six eighty, please." "Your change is two fifty-five." "It's four o'clock. One more hour until dinner." (Balough, 1990, p. 226)

Just as the entering kindergartener brings to school between 6,000 and 20,000 receptive words, young children also arrive with some logical-mathematical concepts somewhat developed. Many can count, identify objects to 10, recognize numerals, identify some coins and geometrical shapes, and solve simple addition and subtraction problems in their heads (Balough, 1990). However, as pointed out earlier, conceptualization is somewhat limited by thinking parameters common to the preoperational period: centration, egocentrism, and irreversibility. This means that children have a considerable amount of work to do before they will truly understand what "5" is all about, as well as other logical-mathematical concepts. While a child may be able to demonstrate "counting," there may be no true understanding of the hierarchical nature of counting. The child's logic may not yet be developed enough to know that a rearrangement of the same objects leaves the number or amount unchanged. For example, a child judging equality of two rolled tubes of clay may center on the ends of the tubes. Failing to notice that one roll is thicker than the other, the child says there is more in the longer tube simply because its length exceeds the other's. With this kind of understanding, the child has no anchor for making decisions in understanding the use of number.

Age is not necessarily the key in a child's mathematical ability; rather, advances are probably more related to experiences the child has—for example, being challenged to think about number relationships rather than simply being given an answer (Schickedanz, York et al., 1990). In this way, the child develops internal rules and principles to understand number and number relationships in our base 10 system of numbers. This internalized comprehension can then be used in other situations, such as those requiring understanding of multiple digits or place value. Children who are given the correct answer again and again do not necessarily *discover* why a fact is so. Thus, they are left with little ability to make use of the information without a helping adult continuing to do the "head" work. Teachers who encourage memorization of math facts, without teaching some simple but helpful rules or "tricks" to remember, produce children who "learn arithmetic at the expense of learning mathematics" (Baroody, 1987, p. 44).

Young children are eager to build on their basic concepts of logical-mathematical knowledge. Many of these, such as comparing, classifying, and measuring, are needed as the child grows conceptually in other developmental domains, including the affective, social, and aesthetic arenas. Similarly, concepts the child is developing in other areas such as science (observing, communicating, inferring, predicting, hypothesizing, defining, and controlling variables) and language (higher, slower, warm, hardest, longest, juicier) will be important for logical-mathematical extensions (Charlesworth & Lind, 1990). The K–4 curriculum, according to the National Council of Teachers of Mathematics (NCTM), should be conceptually oriented, actively involve children in doing mathematics, and emphasize development of mathematical thinking and reasoning abilities. In addition, it should emphasize applied aspects of mathematics, including a broad range of content, and make appropriate and ongoing use of calculators and computers (NCTM, 1989).

The bedrock of mathematics is problem solving—that is, identifying real problems, posing them, and finding solutions to them through mathematics. Centered around numbers and numeration, the various strands from which activities and experiences should be developed are (a) logical thinking/mathematical reasoning, (b) statistics and probability, (c) measurement, (d) geometry, and (e) patterns and functions (Brewer, 1992).

Preprimary and primary children need repeated and various experiences with hands-on, engaging materials in order to acquire the following fundamental concepts and skills:

- One-to-one correspondence—accurately coordinating number names or tags and objects in a set being counted
- Counting—developing a conventional list of tags

- Number sense—understanding our base 10 system, place value, and partitioning
- Matching—first by color, shape, and then size
- Sorting and classification
- Identifying and understanding sets (defined collections of objects, ideas, or symbols)
- Ordering or seriation (first by noting the way in which one item exceeds another, then 3 or more items, then by inserting an item)
- Comparing
- Geometrical experience—shape differentiation, concepts of flat figures and solids, open and closed, inside and outside
- Spatial awareness
- Money value
- Parts and wholes
- Ordering, patterning, and functions—patterns created as a result of particular operations on objects or numbers
- Measurement of length, width, and volume with standard and nonstandard units to describe something in terms of smaller parts of itself (Schickedanz, York, et al. 1990, p. 273)
- Measurement of analog and digital clock time, calendar time, class time, speed, temperature, nonconcrete quantities
- Graphing

To promote optimal development of these concepts, effective teachers equip their classrooms with a wide variety of interesting manipulative materials that invite exploring, sorting, combining, and experimenting. They structure many opportunities for children to *hear* the correct names for conventional tags again and again, especially those that tend to cause children problems (e.g., in 11, there is no "teen" sound; in 20, there is no "2" sound), thereby promoting understanding, proficiency, and the language needed to describe operations. They involve children in activities especially contrived to promote a framework for mathematical thinking and problem solving. They monitor and nurture that understanding by posing questions to help the child notice discrepancies and come closer and closer to the correct answer, encouraging children to think about relevant pieces of information needed to solve problems, and asking children to think of other ways to get an answer and defend their proposed solutions

(Brewer, 1992). Many of the experiences the children have are gamelike, including board games, dice, cards, bingo games, lotto, and measurement of real aspects of the near environment. Other experiences come naturally out of the everyday operation of the classroom, which helps children perceive mathematics as relevant and useful rather than something to memorize and repeat (Brewer, 1992). As with science, every aspect of the curriculum can and should be used to promote logical-mathematical conceptualization.

CURRENT EDUCATIONAL ISSUES

Making sense of all of the information we currently have about brain functioning and developmental considerations is a complex but critical task for early childhood educators to tackle if children are to become effective, lifelong learners. Barriers still exist in some early childhood programs that continue to get in the way of optimal cognitive development and learning. These include the following:

1. *Constructing early childhood programs in which all activity is teacher constructed and directed and little room is left for children to move around, talk with many people, calculate, explore interests, and work on real projects and problems (Mueller & Strahan, 1985).* — Children must be able to feel personally invested somehow in the activities and experiences presented to them in the educational setting. Sylwester (1986) reminds us that adults "who design educational activities must be sure the activities are as inviting to the students as they are to the adults, and must not confuse sheer activity (which is not necessarily stimulating) with meaningful stimulation" (p. 92).

Concept formation is better ensured when children experience both variety and repetition in learning experiences. According to Hart (1983), the brain requires a great deal of input in order to detect patterns. This means that effective teachers will develop classroom experiences that help children make meaningful connections through enriched, thematic, and real-life experiences, rather than cutting off connections by "bits and pieces" instruction that has no personal mean-

ing for the learner (Association for Supervision and Curriculum Development, 1991).

In addition, the learning climate must be appropriately stimulating rather than overwhelming. In highly stressful situations, children will tend to shut down cognitively and be less sensitive to environmental clues, less likely to encode information, and also less able to transfer information learned from one task to another. We can easily see this sort of shutting down in infants who have been overstimulated. They will tend to avert their eyes away from the stimulus (often, an overeager adult!). If that does not work, they are likely to begin crying. Young children also give us very clear messages that they have had enough of a situation or are having trouble making sense of something, but they do it by acting out behaviorally or by withdrawing in some way.

2. *Developing early childhood programs in which children do all the initiating of activity in the learning environment and specific strategies to support development of critical thinking are left to chance.* — Certain core thinking skills can, and should be, actively taught and reinforced in appropriate ways in the regular classroom. As adapted from British Columbia's *Primary Program* (1989, pp. 65–66), these include the following:

- *Focusing skills* — attending to selected pieces of information and ignoring others (defining problems and setting goals). Constructing and solving story problems in math develop these skills as well as such tasks as having children describe sequential events in a story they have read, looking at ways a character could have solved a problem in a different manner, or planning what needs to be gathered for a successful class outing.
- *Information-gathering skills* — bringing to consciousness the relevant data needed for cognitive processing (gaining information through the senses, observation, and inquiry). Teachers may use a number of real-life experiences, such as inviting children to keep track of types of lunches for the day. Children could observe the teacher taking roll and, as she calls each child's name, asking which children are planning to go home for lunch, have carried their lunch from home, or are

planning to eat hot lunch. The teacher might then ask, "Who can remember how many hot lunches in all?"

- *Remembering skills*—storing and retrieving information from long-term memory. Such skills, for example, are called on in the writing process as both inventive and conventional spelling are used.
- *Organizing skills*—arranging information so that it can be used more effectively through comparing, classifying, ordering, and representing (changing form but not substance of the information). For example, children who are involved in finding out which objects sink and which float might draw or list them on a graph.
- *Analyzing skills*—clarifying existing information by examining parts and relationships (identifying attributes and components, relationships and patterns, main ideas, and errors). Children might be asked to do story webbing after becoming familiar with a particular book, for example.
- *Generating skills*—producing new information, meaning, or ideas (inferring what might be true from available information, predicting, and elaborating). Children who have had experience with the elements necessary for healthy plant growth in the classroom might use the information to discuss what *all* living things need to be healthy.
- *Integrating skills*—connecting and combining information (summarizing information efficiently into a cohesive statement and restructuring to change existing knowledge structures to incorporate new information). Based on previous experiences and activities with real phenomena, children can make hypotheses about cause and effect and then draw conclusions relative to what they are presently learning. For example, previous to visiting a Michigan arboretum to look for winter birds, one of the children said, "I don't think there'll be any! They all fly away from here when it starts to get cold and then come back in the summer." Following the experience, he acknowledged to his teacher, "Maybe some of them changed their minds." This led to a discussion of and study about what kinds of birds usually stay (e.g., cardinals, blue jays) and which traditionally go farther south (e.g., robins, geese).

- *Evaluating skills*—assessing the reasonableness and quality of ideas by establishing criteria or standards for making judgments and verifying or confirming the accuracy of claims. Here, children develop strategies such as looking for patterns and relationships, discrepant events, sharing ideas with others, and practicing a variety of other problem-solving strategies daily.

Some children, because of personality traits or cultural differences, may be less apt to try new experiences without encouragement to do so. Others, because of negative past experiences with "failure," may avoid activity calling for higher order thinking and skills even when relatively ready. Instead, they persevere in areas where success is ensured. The teacher's role in moving such children along may include breaking more sophisticated tasks into manageable parts and helping children recognize how past success and experiences can be used to tackle new challenges. Although all children benefit from genuine reinforcement for efforts to attempt more demanding tasks, those who noticeably avoid learning challenges *must* receive such attention and support in order to modify their attitudes toward approaching more challenging learning experiences.

3. *Failing to provide a balance between activities that promote (a) children's acquisition of factual information (cognitive knowledge) and (b) qualitative change in conceptualization and process-based learning strategies (cognitive development)*—Though both are important, much heavier focus has been placed on knowledge acquisition and the "bottom-line" right answer. Concerned about this, Piaget once remarked, "If the aim of intellectual training is to form the intelligence rather than to stock the memory, and to produce intellectual explorers rather than mere erudition, then traditional education is manifestly guilty of a grave deficiency" (quoted in *Kindergarten Curriculum Guide and Resource Book*).

Teachers can facilitate expanded conceptual development by

- providing activities that involve grouping and manipulation of concrete objects.
- having children play games involving such objects as dice and cards.

■ using open-ended questions to direct and arouse interests toward discrepancy, cause dissonance, and promote active discovery. Examples include

Why do you think that happened?

What could you do...?

What would happen if...?

Is there something else you could try?

Is there another way you could do that?

What happened when you...?

■ Reflect and summarize actions and outcomes in order to provide verbal skill enhancement for children who have a receptive conceptualization but not enough language or labels to express their thoughts (Trepanier-Street, 1990, pp. 192–193).

4. *Continuing to group children in homogeneous settings rather than heterogeneous ones*—Children, like adults, are continuously scanning the environment to pick up information that will help them make sense of it. They watch what others do who are more or less skilled in accomplishing a task and then imitate, expand on, or modify what they see for use in their own problem solving, decision making, and leisure pursuit. Children on all points of a developmental continuum benefit from interacting with others who either need or can provide information or strategies for accomplishing a task. Research indicates that children who are grouped in homogeneous settings grow and develop, but not at the rate they would if placed in a supportive, heterogeneous setting.

5. *Failing to coordinate an authentic assessment and evaluation package (including the report card) with what actually goes on in a developmentally appropriate learning environment.*—When this happens, it is often the result of educators seeing standardized and basal text end-of-unit tests as the only acceptable and legitimate means for assessment and evaluation of children's progress. More often than not, this perspective creates test-driven curricula and learning environments, which severely and negatively affect the development of qualitative critical thinking skills in the young child. Because the young child's cognitive development is in process, teachers must assess a child's *approach* to a task and stages and quality of a child's thought processes as carefully as they assess outcomes and products. Strategies for assessing growth in conceptualization and skill building are outlined in chapter 16, "Testing, Assessment, and Evaluation."

Effective early childhood classrooms, then, are those in which children have many opportunities to express their thoughts, wishes, and ideas to one another as well as to adults. The best early childhood classroom exists in an active, well-prepared, workshoplike environment. It should contain familiar elements and also some that are slightly discrepant, which entice children to "actively explore, manipulate, transform, and discover. They need opportunities both to initiate action and imitate action, to reflect and summarize their own actions for themselves and to hear the reflection and summarizations of others, to represent their ideas and thoughts and to encounter the ideas and thoughts of others" (Trepanier-Street, 1990, p. 197). A truly effective early childhood classroom must be carefully constructed by a professional who understands that young children are eager to learn and will respond responsibly when given the freedom, resources, and guidance necessary to do so.

According to Teberosky (1982) and DeVries and Kohlberg (1990), educators must be cautioned against translating new knowledge about how children learn into narrowly prescribed classroom practices, formulas, recipes, or exercises. Rather, efforts should be undertaken to match what happens in the classroom as near as possible to what happens in the child's head. Moreover, in order to act effectively on a full range of later problems, children must maintain an appreciation for their own ability to think divergently, creatively, and imaginatively in addition to developing convergent modes of thinking. This kind of approach to information seeking and problem solving cannot result from learning a narrow set of learning strategies for information processing (Gardner, 1983).

GOALS AND OBJECTIVES

The ultimate goal of the cognitive component is for children to acquire, apply, adapt, integrate, and evaluate knowledge as they construct new or expanded concepts. There must be opportunities for children to develop physical knowledge, logical-mathematical knowledge, representational skills, common social knowledge, and critical thinking skills.

To help identify ways in which cognitive activities fit into the early childhood curriculum, selected mediating objectives for this domain have been divided into three areas: (a) general cognition, including problem solving, critical thinking, and perception processes; (b) mathematics, both emerging and extended skills; and (c) science. Because cognitive processes pervade all aspects of learning, there are universal mediating objectives that teachers should address each day. These are described in the general cognition section. More specific mediating objectives traditionally associated with the subject areas of mathematics and science are listed separately.

Mediating Objectives for General Cognition

As children progress toward the ultimate goal, they will

1. explore the observable properties of objects and the relationships among objects.
2. identify similarities and differences among objects.
3. organize objects and events via classfication (subclasses and supraclasses), sequencing, and patterning.
4. attach meaning to symbols in the environment (e.g., traffic signals, addition and subtraction, written words, etc.).
5. develop and refine their focusing skills by attending to selected pieces of information and ignoring nonrelevant information.
6. develop and practice strategies for remembering (e.g., recording, creating personal rules, making associations, etc.).
7. develop and refine their investigative skills by

   - posing questions or problems to solve that involve collecting and analyzing information.
   - using estimation, concepts of chance, and sampling to make better predictions.
   - gathering information (questioning, experimenting, observing, consulting).

   - analyzing objects and events.
   - applying prior knowledge.
   - making inferences.

8. develop organizational skills for arranging and using information more effectively by comparing, classifying, ordering, representing (changing form but not substance of information).
9. develop and refine their problem solving skills by

   - observing attentively.
   - exercising divergent as well as convergent thinking.
   - developing hypotheses.
   - making predictions.
   - developing plans.
   - testing their predictions.
   - experimenting with intuitive, imaginative ideas.
   - connecting and combining information in an integrative manner.
   - evaluating their predictions.
   - drawing conclusions.
   - reviewing/summarizing their experiences.
   - generating alternative ways to approach problems.
   - communicating their findings.

10. integrate knowledge and skills across subject areas and domains.
11. generalize knowledge and skills from one situation to another.
12. become aware of their own thought processes.
13. acquire factual information to support relevant concepts.
14. build more accurate, complete, complex concepts over time.
15. recognize and make use of diverse sources of knowledge.
16. recognize that data come in many forms and can be organized and displayed in diverse ways.

Mediating Objectives for Emerging Mathematical Skills

As children progress toward the ultimate goal, they will

17. connect mathematics with daily living and problem solving.
18. describe, discuss, and share mathematical ideas.
19. identify, reproduce, complete, extend, and utilize various formats of patterns, concretely, pictorially, and as they exist in the environment.
20. classify objects by common attributes (size, shape, color, pattern, position).
21. order objects by common attributes (length, size, texture, volume, etc.).
22. experiment with conservation of number, mass, volume, and weight.
23. compare lengths, masses, quantities, and volume.
24. estimate length, mass, quantity, and volume.
25. explore the concept of parts and wholes.
26. construct visual representations of given numbers using concrete materials (number sense).
27. explore the properties of a given number (number families).
28. participate in constructing and interpreting (predicting, comparing, drawing conclusions) graphs with real objects.
29. explore and practice adding and subtracting, using real objects.
30. explore and discover measurement relationships, using nonstandard and standard measuring tools (thermometer, clock, scale, ruler, cup measures).
31. associate the concept of quantity with the appropriate numeral.
32. expand their ability to count by rote.
33. identify numerals (0–10).
34. write numerals (0–10).
35. explore the concept of time as a sequence of events.
36. explore the duration of time within their daily routines.
37. associate numbers on the clock with the passage of time.
38. be introduced to the concept of calendar time (days of the week, months of the year) and calendar terminology (yesterday, today, tomorrow, before/after).
39. work with the ordinal concepts (1st, 2nd, 3rd).
40. extend geometrical sense through handling, identifying, describing, combining, subdividing, and changing real shapes (circle, square, rectangle, triangle, cone, cube, etc.).
41. grow in awareness of topological concepts (position, location) and the language of these concepts (between, behind, above, below, under, over, in, inside, outside, on top of, beside, close to, etc.).
42. grow in awareness of personal time as it relates to daily living.
43. understand how temperature affects daily living.
44. identify coins.
45. increase their mathematical vocabulary (estimate, graph, pattern, classify, sort, predict, more, less, same, different, large, larger, small, smaller, short, shorter, long, longer, near, far, equals, add, subtract, etc.).
46. expand their visual-spatial awareness of symmetry, balance, height, directionality by utilizing a variety of manipulative materials such as unifix cubes, blocks, and three-dimensional objects.
47. compose number stories orally.
48. create and transpose patterns.

Mediating Objectives for Extended Mathematical Skills

As children progress toward the ultimate goal, they will

49. count in sequence forward and backward.
50. extend their concept of parts of a whole to include fractions (halves, quarters, thirds).
51. extend their awareness of place value by identifying the number of 10s and 1s shown by a two-digit numeral.
52. measure with standard units.
53. name and correctly demonstrate the relative value of coins and how money is used in real-life situations.
54. develop their understanding of addition and subtraction using real objects and their ability to record number combinations operations (horizontally and vertically).
55. explore the concept of odd and even numbers.
56. write addition and subtraction facts symbolically.
57. develop ability to identify numbers (1st: 0–20; 2nd: 0–100).

58. write multidigit numbers (1st: 0–20; 2nd: 0–100).
59. practice skip counting (e.g., 2s, 5s, 10s).
60. begin adding and subtracting with trading (regrouping, renaming).
61. understand time concepts of before, earlier, now, after, later.
62. identify clock time on the hour and half hour.
63. increase their mathematical vocabulary (e.g., either, or, greater than, less than, if/then, therefore, corner, angle, rotate, flip side, side).
64. explain mathematical processes they have used.
65. compose number stories with words and writing.
66. solve word problems that require the correct operation in addition or subtraction.
67. grow in their familiarity with and ability to use tools, such as the calculator and computer, to explore mathematical concepts.

Mediating Objectives for Science

As children progress toward the ultimate goal, they will

68. examine natural objects and events using multiple sensory abilities.
69. gather information through collecting, classifying, ordering, measuring, sequencing, and so on.
70. predict what they think will happen based on a hypothesis.
71. guess why certain things happen.
72. carry out experiments.
73. talk about the result of their experiments.
74. formulate conclusions.
75. participate in recording scientific data.
76. explore firsthand a variety of cause-and-effect relationships.
77. learn terms, facts, and principles regarding the natural/physical world.
78. demonstrate an awareness of the interdependence of all things in the world.
79. investigate differences, similarities, and patterns in natural objects and events.
80. acquire scientific knowledge related to life sciences (characteristics of plants and animals, life cycles and basic needs, habitats, relationships).
81. acquire scientific knowledge related to physical sciences (change in matter; forces affecting motion, direction, speed; physical properties and characteristics of phenomena).
82. gain scientific knowledge related to earth sciences (weather, space, ecology, major features of the earth).
83. explore a variety of scientific equipment, such as simple machines, magnets, measuring instruments.
84. use scientific equipment appropriately and safely.

TEACHING STRATEGIES

The most important thing to keep in mind during the preprimary and primary years is that the "mind of the young child is qualitatively different from that of older children and adults" (DeVries & Kohlberg, 1990, p. 41). Teachers who fail to appreciate the young child's need to construct knowledge may, in fact, diminish potential development. On the other hand, teachers who go overboard in mimimizing their role in the child's developing intellect, morality, and personality also err. What is needed in the early years are professionals who are knowledgeable about constructing environments conducive to learning. Rather than imposing their own predetermined goals, these teachers provide materials, activities, and suggestions that encourage initiative and independent pursuit, allowing children adequate time to explore, investigate, reflect, and ask questions. They differentiate effectively between teaching strategies that promote logical-mathematical and physical knowledge and those needed to extend social-arbitrary/conventional knowledge in young children (Kamii & DeVries, 1977). This calls for, in the first case, refraining from giving the correct answer and challenging children to think about what it *might* be and having them follow through to investigate and evaluate their own ideas. When extending conventional knowledge, good teachers respond to children's inquiries with correct information; if they are not sure what the answer is, they are honest about not knowing and then work with the child to access the information needed.

1. *Encourage intellectual autonomy in expanding children's general cognitive skills.* The concept of hands-on experiences and activity in developing conceptual thinking on the part of the young child is important. Teachers will want to introduce every concept with real objects first and to plan several related experiences to reinforce a given concept rather than present isolated activities at random. There should be an emphasis on the process rather than solely the products of children's thinking.

Questioning used to stimulate their thinking or to find out why children have categorized, sequenced, or solved a problem in a certain way should be open-ended. Children should be allowed to reach their own conclusions regarding cause-and-effect relationships, and the answers they offer should be accepted. When children make errors, teachers will want to plan further experiences or suggest other approaches that might help the children discover the right answer or have more success with individual tasks. When children are having difficulty with a concept or demonstrating proficiency, teachers will want to help them break a task into more manageable parts and introduce them to the next step in the sequence when helpful. Particular skills and facts should be taught in contexts relevant to children.

2. *Use teaming and cooperative learning often.* Pairing children up and in small groups to solve problems or complete learning tasks has been recommended by the NCTM and other organizations. Doing so promotes the sharing of ideas, awareness of others, extension of conceptual understanding, and movement away from egocentric perspectives.

3. *Teach children mathematical concepts using real objects.* Provide a wide variety of manipulatives (real objects) to be used for sorting, classifying, comparing, estimating, predicting, patterning, graphing, measuring, counting, adding and subtracting, understanding parts and wholes, and gaining concepts of number, conservation of number, quantity, shapes, mass, and volume. When involving children in making

Pairing up children in cooperative learning situations enhances concept building.

mathematical equations, provide sets of real objects in addition to such materials as number stamps and number cards before paper-and-pencil tasks are introduced.

4. *Put more emphasis on children's understanding of concepts than on rote learning, and keep in mind that children's development of mathematical concepts follows a predictable pattern.* Always begin the teaching of new concepts with concrete experiences. After children have had numerous concrete experiences, introduce representational ones. Introduce abstract experiences last. Allow children ample opportunities to explore a given material prior to asking them to use it in a prescribed way. Present the same mathematical concepts and skills on many occasions and in many different ways (e.g., drawing numerals in the air, in sand, in salt, in fingerpaint, on the chalkboard, and on paper). Involve them in playing a variety of games utilizing cards and dice.

5. *Integrate mathematical concepts and skills throughout all areas of the early childhood curriculum.* Link math activities with social studies, science, language arts, as well as with pretend play, social, affective, aesthetic, physical, and construction activities as often as possible.

6. *Extend children's mathematical vocabulary.* Use a wide variety of mathematical vocabulary when talking with children about their day-to-day experiences (e.g., number, mass, size, shape, position of objects in space, relations among objects, change in the positions of objects).

7. *Extend geometrical understanding.* Give children experiences with geometrical shapes and properties throughout the early childhood years, preschool through third grade.

8. *Use everyday experiences in the classroom to help children connect mathematics to daily living and see it as useful and necessary.* Incorporate mathematical tools into classroom routines (e.g., calendars, clocks, rulers, coins, scales, measuring cups, graphs, etc.). Practice addition and subtraction in natural settings without symbols, encouraging children to use "head work" to solve problems. Draw children's attention to aspects of daily work and play in the classroom that utilize mathematical concepts (e.g., durations of time—5 minutes until cleanup; 15 minutes for recess; 2 weeks off for spring vacation).

9. *Develop positive scientific attitudes and practices in the classroom.* Model an interested, curious, enthusiastic attitude toward science, and encourage children's curiosity by providing them with numerous hands-on scientific experiences and relevant demonstrations. Carry out scientific demonstrations with groups small enough that children can become actively involved and will feel free to ask questions about what they are observing. Help children to observe more carefully by first directing their attention to a particular aspect of an object or phenomenon and then asking them to describe what they see (e.g., "Look up at the sky. Tell me what you see."). Encourage children to make predictions by asking them, "What will happen next?" and hypothesize and draw conclusions by asking them, "Why do you think that happened?" Convey only accurate scientific terms, facts, and principles to children, checking out any information about which you or the children are unsure. Help children recognize many sources of scientific information, such as their own experiences, books, and resource people.

10. *Help children connect science to everyday life.* Introduce scientific concepts by building on the everyday experiences in the lives of children in your class. Make available a wide array of natural materials through which children can explore the physical world. Examples of such items include collections of natural objects (shells, rocks, bird nests), live animals (fish, guinea pigs, insects), plants and scientific tools (scales, magnifiers, magnets).

Take advantage of spontaneous events to highlight scientific ideas. Emphasize children's discovery of principles of cause and effect by allowing them to draw conclusions based on their experiences with real objects. Select scientific themes that include firsthand experiences for children and those with which children are already familiar.

11. *Integrate science with other curricular activities.* Integrate scientific themes throughout all areas of the early childhood curriculum: within reading, math, social studies and language arts, as well as through pretend play, social, affective, aesthetic, physical, and construction activities. In order to reinforce certain scientific concepts, plan a number of spin-off and extension activities rather than isolated scientific activities or

random demonstrations. Help children see how knowledge of the physical sciences, life sciences, and earth sciences can be helpful in understanding other aspects of their world.

12. *Use collections as a way to extend and assess children's ability to categorize, classify, and display information.* Give children individual or group opportunities to create collections of natural objects. Offer them guidance about how to collect objects and what may be appropriate or inappropriate to collect. Provide opportunities for children to display and tell about their collections.

ACTIVITY SUGGESTIONS

⇒ Pictorial Story Problems

Objective: For children to develop number sense by constructing visual representations of given numbers using concrete materials

Materials: Pictorial scenes and sets of related objects, blank number strips, markers

Procedure: Give children individual pictorial scenes, such as an apple tree or field, a barn and corral, or a seashore. Invite children to place selected objects on a particular scene and to tell an arithmetic story problem about what they have just depicted (e.g., "There were 5 apples on the tree, and 3 fell on the ground. How many apples were there in all?").

To Simplify: Use only a few objects. Demonstrate a very simple addition problem.

To Extend: Use greater numbers of objects. Invite children to think of as many different combinations as possible. Have children develop written number strips for each combination after it is concretely constructed (e.g., $2 + 5 = 7$; $3 + 4 = 7$; $1 + 6 = 7$; $10 - 3 = 7$). Children may also work with partners, with one child thinking of and constructing the problem and the other child checking the work and developing a written number strip.

⇒ Caterpillar Hunt

Objective: For children to examine natural objects and events using multiple sensory abilities

Materials: One milk carton per child, string, punch; magnifying glass, *The Very Hungry*

Caterpillar (Carle, 1981); other classroom materials as needed

Procedure: Prior to going on a walk to find caterpillars, help each child prepare a milk carton as a container to carry back a caterpillar if found. String handles can be attached on each side of the carton. Using separate containers for each variety of caterpillar, bring them back into the classroom for observation over a period of time. If possible, try to capture a caterpillar attaching itself to a twig in preparation for pupation.

To Simplify: Have the children gather leaves over a period of time to feed caterpillars kept in the room. They can observe the insects eating the leaves provided and watch which parts of the leaves they eat. Children can also observe the caterpillar's locomotion and imitate how the caterpillar humps its body in order to get from place to place.

To Extend: Have children observe the caterpillars under a magnifying glass and examine and identify the various body structures, including simulated eyes and horns present for scaring enemies and the sharp spines on the true legs used for clinging and holding objects. Use the caterpillars as models for drawing, painting, clay modeling, and as subjects for fantasy stories. If one or more of the caterpillars goes into pupation, have the children observe the spinning of the cocoon. Because many butterflies and moths have a calendar-year life cycle, it may not be possible to follow all stages. However, with certain caterpillars/moths, children may observe the eventual emergence from the chrysalis and release of the butterfly or moth outside. Have them record over time the sequence of events in drawings and written journals. Read *The Very Hungry Caterpillar*. For more information on extended activities related to caterpillars and other nature activities for young children, refer to Nickelsburg (1976).

⇒ Problem-solving Activities

Objective: For children to develop and refine their problem-solving skills by observing attentively, exercising divergent as well as convergent thinking, developing hypotheses, making predictions, testing their predictions, experimenting with intuitive and imaginative ideas, evaluating their predictions, drawing conclusions, and generating alternative ways to approach problems

Materials: A variety of natural phenomena, such as objects that sink or float, magnets, ice, and so on; chart paper, markers

Procedure: Encourage children to explore and examine various materials and what happens to them under certain conditions. Emphasize the thinking process rather than aiming for "correct" answers.

To Simplify: Provide just a few materials and those in which differences are more readily apparent to children. After the children have had opportunities to examine them, ask them to "look" closely and tell you what they see or to "feel" carefully and tell you what they feel.

To Extend: Provide a greater number of objects. Have children develop a system to record outcomes—for example, a graph to illustrate the objects that fall into one category or another. A checklist could also be developed on which children could list the name of particular objects being used and how they function under certain conditions (e.g., sink/float; attracted/not attracted to magnet; melts/does not melt). Draw pictures and construct stories.

➡ More or Less

Objective: For children to seriate or order objects by common attributes

Materials: Sets of objects that may be seriated or ordered by size, shape, color, pattern, or position

Procedure: Have children work in pairs, and give them daily chances to order objects from the most to least or least to most of a particular property. Vary the properties so that children have opportunities to order textures, colors, tastes, sizes, widths, and lengths. Following exploration of the materials, guided instruction might occur as follows:

a. "Show me a way to put these _____ in a line from more to less of something."

b. "Good. You found a way to line up the _____."
c. "Tell me how you decided what went where." Teacher accepts child's answer.
d. "Show me a different way to put these in a line."
e. "Tell me why you decided to line them up that way."

To Simplify: Have fewer objects with one characteristic in common and obvious differences in gradation.

To Extend: Have a greater number of objects with one characteristic in common but differences in gradation that call for greater observation skills. Have a number of objects that can be seriated by more than one characteristic (e.g., sticks that range in color hues and also length and/or width).

➡ Soil Samples

Objective: To have children examine natural objects and events using multiple sensory abilities

Materials: Containers for gathering soil samples, trowels for digging, plastic wrap, magnifying glasses, pots and molds, water pitcher, paper and markers

Procedure: Help children gather a number of different kinds of soil samples, such as sand, gravel, clay, and loam, placing each sample in a different container and covering with plastic wrap to retain moisture. Before the soil samples have time to dry out, place them on separate sheets of paper for examination. (Note: It is better to work with small groups of children so that subtle changes can be easily observed.)

To Simplify: Invite the children to use magnifying glasses to observe any differences in the various samples. Have the children rub the samples between their thumb and forefinger to note differences in texture. Ask them to smell the samples to detect any differences in smell. Provide a number of pots and molds and suggest that they try to mold the samples. Discuss with them which samples seem to hold together better than others and why this might be so.

To Extend: Examine the various samples to see how much air they contain by filling separate glasses with each of the soil samples and leaving some room at the top to add water. Slowly pour in the water and watch as it soaks in and displaces any air, helping the children to note the size and frequency of bubbles. Assign teams of children to each of the soil samples to carefully examine the pile for organic increments, such as stones, insects, and leaves; have each team note what kinds of components are found, decide how to record their findings, and then report their findings to other teams. Place samples of each kind of soil in pots. Water to see if any weeds will sprout. Record findings. Place quickly sprouting seeds (one variety) in various samples to have children note which kinds of soil promotes the best growth. In another experiment, have children test different growing conditions by altering light, water, and heat (Nickelsburg, 1976).

➠ Grouping and Sorting

Objective: For children to classify objects by common attributes (size, shape, color, pattern, position)

Materials: Sets of objects that can be grouped on the basis of size, shape, color, pattern, or position

Procedure: Give children daily opportunities to classify a wide variety of objects. Remember that there are no right or wrong ways for children to classify. Instead, emphasize the process by which children reach their conclusions. Use the following script to guide your instruction:

a. "Show me a way to put these _____ into groups that are alike."
b. "Good. You found a way to sort the _____."
c. "Tell me why these things [point to one grouping] go together." Repeat for each grouping and accept the child's answer for each.
d. "Show another way to sort the _____ into piles."

To Simplify: Have fewer numbers of objects with more obvious grouping possibilities.

To Extend: Provide greater numbers of objects and ones with more than one common characteristic so that children will discover more sophisticated combinations (e.g., grouping all yellow objects that have something to do with transportation).

➠ Mystery Box

Objective: For children to develop and refine their focusing skills by attending to selected pieces of information and ignoring nonrelevant information

Materials: Box, set of objects that are related

Procedure: "Hide" one or more objects in a box. Provide verbal clues to the children about what they are. Invite them to ask you questions about the object(s) to discover what is in the box.

To Simplify: Place only one object in the box. Select one with which all the children are familiar.

To Extend: Place several objects in the box that are different from one another but have one characteristic in common (e.g., all are articles of clothing). Have one of the children take on the role of "clue giver."

➠ From Fiction to Fact

Objective: For children to build more accurate, complete, complex concepts over time

Materials: Children's books that contain the element of fantasy

Procedure: After children have been introduced to the "facts" related to a particular natural phenomenon such as insects, read a fantasy story on the subject (such as *The Very Hungry Caterpillar* by Eric Carle). Ask children to figure out what might be true about the story and what might be pretend.

To Simplify: Point out particular fantasy aspects of a story, and ask children why those things are only pretend.

To Extend: Have children develop and illustrate their own fantasy stories about a particular phenomenon, such as dinosaurs; have them share their stories with a partner, and have the partner tell which aspects of the story are pretend and which are true.

➡ **Count and Match**

Objective: For children to associate the concept of quantity with the appropriate numeral

Materials: Magazines, scissors, magnifying glasses, cards with numerals and representative symbols, blank cards, glue or paste

Procedure: Have the children gather pictures that clearly display a certain number of objects (e.g., number of teeth in a smiling face, number of birds flying in a flock, number of boats sailing on a river). Have children pair up and tell them to look at the picture, count the objects, and then match the picture to a card with the numeral identifying the number of objects. Magnifying glasses can be supplied to help children more clearly distinguish the numbers of objects.

To Simplify: Use cards displaying only the numerals 1 to 5 and also including matching round circles or other graphics to represent the number indicated.

To Extend: Provide materials for matching numbers of objects beyond five. Have children hunt through magazines for pictures that can be matched with particular numeral cards. These can be pasted on cards, mixed up, and then sorted by children into appropriate piles coordinated with the appropriate numeral cards.

➡ **Balloon Race**

Objective: For children to develop and refine their problem-solving skills by observing attentively, exercising divergent as well as convergent thinking, developing hypotheses, making predictions, testing their predictions, experimenting with intuitive and imaginative ideas, evaluating their predictions, drawing conclusions, generating alternative ways to solve problems

Materials: Balloons, straws, masking tape, easel paper, markers

Procedure: Provide a set of inflated balloons of five different colors and individual straws for a group of five children. Have other children observe, telling them they will also have a chance to do the activity. Establish a starting line that

has been marked off with masking tape. Tell the children that the object is to use their straws to blow the balloons as quickly as possible from the starting line to a designated wall.

To Simplify: Have the children participate in the activity and then discuss what they think made the balloons go faster. Accept their answers. Prompt them to think about any differences that may have contributed to speed or direction of movement.

To Extend: Prior to beginning the activity, explain the object and then invite the children to develop hypotheses and make predictions about directing the balloons. Invite the children who are observers to watch carefully to see if they will do something differently when they participate in the activity. Prior to each "team event," have children offer ideas about what they think contributes to speed and managing direction. Afterward, have them evaluate their ideas and generate new ones. After every child has had a chance to participate, ask the children to produce an "advice sheet" related to the activity, listing "tips" (conclusions) they would provide to other teams of children (e.g., blowing in the middle of the balloon, not blowing down on or on the side of the balloon, blowing steadily) who might want to try the activity in the future.

SUMMARY

Cognitive development in the young child is a complex process. Outcomes depend on the quality of children's experiences both inside and outside of the formal classroom as they move through a series of psychosocial and neurobiological changes.

Children's ability to acquire knowledge and then use it effectively to plan, monitor, and evaluate their own capabilities is better insured when they have developed and can maintain some measure of confidence in themselves and in others. This results when they are nurtured by adults who understand the critical interrelationship between cognition and all other areas of development.

Learning environments that stimulate optimal cognitive growth are those where curricular construction is guided by sensitivity to variations in development, where children are encouraged to be both independent and collaborative learners, and where high task involvement is motivated through the presentation of diverse and engaging activities that young thinkers and doers perceive to be personally useful.

CHAPTER 6

The Language Domain

Kathleen, 2½ years old, listened intently as her mother explained the child's familial relationships to both of her grandfathers.

"Grandpa Con is Mommy's daddy, and Grandpa Eugene is Daddy's daddy."

Kathleen looked puzzled.

Trying again, her mother said slowly, "My daddy is Grandpa Con, and Daddy's daddy is Grandpa Eugene."

Kathleen looked puzzled, then defiant. "No, Mommy, not Grandpa you—Gene! Grandpa my—Gene!" And she ran off to play.

Children's mastery of their native language is truly remarkable. From birth, babies are making noises that communicate their needs and satisfactions to their parents and caregivers. Gradually their sound patterns follow the intonation patterns of the language they hear around them, and in less than 2 years, sounds that approximate words in their family's native language become discernible. When children originate initial sentences, they tend to reconstruct some regularities of their native language but do not imitate their parents' speech patterns (Slobin, 1971, p. 40). Parents delight in the word and sentence approximations of their little ones, and they intuit the intentions of the children. The process is apparently so natural for nearly every child, so seemingly easy and regular, that adults tend to take language learning for granted and overlook the truly awe-inspiring complexity of the tasks each child accomplishes as he or she learns to speak. Parents and teachers also tend to overlook the beginning language-learning conditions required for the development of the listening, speaking, reading, and writing language skills of the preschooler and the primary-grade child. Among these conditions are settings where meaningful communication is expected, open opportunities are available for children to speak, and adults do not correct or punish when the children's speech is incorrect compared to adult form.

Kathleen's predicament about her grandfathers is indicative of children's struggle to make

sense of their world through the language they hear and speak. She knows that her mother is talking about some of the very important people in her life, but she is not ready to understand concepts of fathering and grandfathering. Undoubtedly, the meanings of the pronouns *me* and *you*, *my* and *your* are still confusing but greatly important to her at this time. When she hears her grandpa's full name, instead of the nickname "gene" that her grandma uses, she declares confidently that her relationship with her grandpa is unique to her; he is "my Gene."

It is very important that preschool and primary teachers, and their administrators, appreciate and understand the language growth of young children so that they can follow developmental principles of language learning after children enter school. Everything the child learns in school will be through verbal and nonverbal language; the verbal language can be oral or written. Language is the primary tool for all school teaching and learning in all subject areas. How preschool and school-age children experience language opportunities and expectations in classrooms rests heavily on the teacher's understanding of language development.

FUNCTIONS OF LANGUAGE

The British psychologist Michael Halliday (1975) studied babies from 9 months to 18 months of age to determine the functions of language the child attempts. The "functions in which the child first learns to mean" emerged in the following order:

- Instrumental, or "I want," which serves the child's material needs and wants
- Regulatory, or "do as I tell you," the child sensing he or she can use language to control the behavior of others
- Interactional, or "me and you," through which the child interacts with others using names, greetings, and so forth
- Personal, or "here I come," through which the child expresses awareness of self and feelings
- Heuristic, or "tell me why?," in which the child categorizes objects and explores the environment

---

This chapter was written by Sheila Fitzgerald, Department of Teacher Education, Michigan State University.

■ Imaginative, or "let's pretend," through which the child creates an environment first in pure sound but gradually in story and make-believe

Another function appears somewhat later, at about 2 years of age:

■ Informative, or "I've got something to tell you," when the child conveys information that the hearer does not already possess. (pp. 19–21)

These seven functions form the foundations for language use throughout life. They delineate the three broad functional components of language use: the *ideational* options, or content of what is said; the *interpersonal* component, by which the speaker participates in speech situations; and the *semantic* function, that which makes language operational in context and gives life to the other two components (1975, p. 17). As Halliday says:

> What is common to every use of language is that it is meaningful, contextualized and in the broadest

sense social; this is brought home very clearly to the child, in the course of his day-to-day experience. The child is surrounded by language, but not in the form of grammars and dictionaries, or of randomly chosen words and sentences, or of undirected monologue. What he encounters is "text" or language in use: sequences of language articulated each within itself and with the situation in which it occurs. Such sequences are purposive—though very varied in purpose—and have an evident social significance. The child's awareness of language cannot be isolated from his awareness of language function. (p. 20)

LANGUAGE AND THINKING

Noam Chomsky has argued that "language is a window on the mind." The noted Swiss psychologist Jean Piaget clearly demonstrated that children's development of concepts—thinking—depends on experiences that come to be understood through the senses (Inhelder & Piaget, 1964). Luria (1961), Vygotsky (1962), and Tough (1977), among others, have shown that talk that accompanies actions conveys certain values and introduces the child to different ways

Children need many opportunities to talk with peers as a way to increase their language abilities.

of thinking and communicating about experiences; the primary function of speech in children, as in adults, is social (Vygotsky, 1986, p. 35). While Piaget placed emphasis on the child's natural development of "spontaneous concepts," the other language theoreticians put more stress on the "nonspontaneous concepts" the child develops as he or she interacts with care givers at home or with other children and adults in learning contexts. Although they may disagree on how and when language and thought development intersect, theorists agree that oral language development is essential for learning.

When we expand the functions of language that Halliday identifies in the early development of young children's communication competence to specify the range of purposes for which children and adults use language throughout life, the interdependence of language and thought becomes even more evident. We use language, in both oral and written forms, to get what we want or need, develop individuality, learn, narrate, imagine, inform, think critically, discover, evaluate, clarify, criticize, control the behavior of others, entertain, reinforce what we believe, aesthetically fulfill ourselves, and develop social relationships. Because language and thinking develop together, school programs need to reflect the centrality of language for developing students' thought processes.

THE INTERRELATIONSHIPS OF LANGUAGE COMPETENCIES

Many authorities identify four major language competencies: listening/viewing, speaking, writing, and reading. As evident in a baby's first identifiable speech, listening to others plays one of the key roles in language development, yet it seems to be impossible to separate listening from nonverbal visual aspects of communication that intertwine in person-to-person communication. Listening/viewing forms the foundation for the development of the other lifelong language skills — speaking, reading, and writing. In fact, the listening skills are used much more than other language skills each day of our lives, on the average nearly 50% of our waking hours, yet education gives very little direct attention to

the development of listening skills and its related aspects of nonverbal communication.

Figure 6.1 is a simplified, two-dimensional expression of the complex interrelationships of the language skills. It shows the oral language competencies of listening/viewing and speaking in the larger circles; they are the most needed, the most used lifelong language skills. They form a very needed foundation for writing and reading as well. Of course, reading and writing are essential for education and for many aspects of life, so they receive particular attention once the child reaches school age. Yet, all of the language skills contribute to thinking throughout life, and thinking contributes to the development of all the language competencies. In Figure 6.1, the four language competencies are presented in broken-line circles to indicate that the skills are interdependent, that their development is often influenced by development of the companion skills. The diagram also shows that listening and speaking encircle the written language competencies, reading and writing. Preschool and kindergarten teachers tend to be well aware of the importance of oral language skills, and they plan their curricula to focus on listening/viewing and speaking in the group setting of the classroom. However, once children are introduced to formal reading and writing instruction, usually in kindergarten or first grade, the continuing need for instruction in the oral language competencies often is neglected even though all the language skills need attention throughout schooling.

Just as listening and speaking are interdependent oral skills, reading and writing are language in print. Contemporary teachers of young children not only recognize that instruction in reading and writing needs to be intertwined, they also know that when children listen to stories and study the illustrations, they are doing important work that contributes to learning to read. When children talk about the ideas of books or act them out, they are developing substantive comprehension skills. When children write down their ideas (see Figure 6.2), often using approximations in the shapes of letters or in the spelling of words ("invented" or "temporary" spelling), they are moving through levels of development similar to those they underwent when they learned to speak (D. Taylor, 1991).

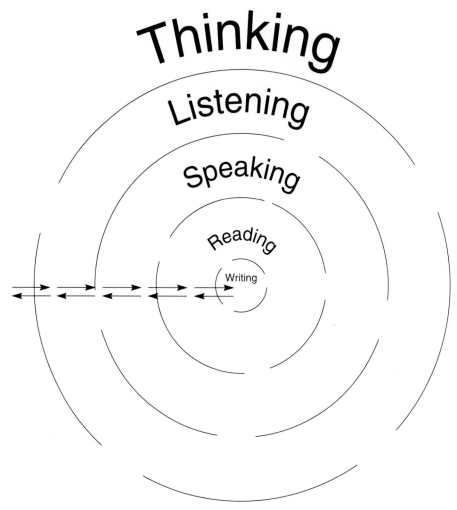

FIGURE 6.1
Lifelong Language Use

Holdaway (1979) reminds us that the speaking-like behavior of the baby is similar to the reading-like and writinglike behavior of the kindergarten and primary-grade child; he says that early reading and writing needs to be "self-regulated, self-corrected, and self-sustaining" (p. 61).

ADDRESSING LANGUAGE DIFFERENCES

It is particularly important that adults recognize the wide range of differences in the language development of children. There are so many distinctions in sounds, meanings, idioms, sentence patterns, and accepted usage patterns for each child to sort out. Perhaps 25% of children have difficulty untangling consonant sounds and blends in their native language until they are about age 7. They have problems understanding how to control the pitch and volume of their voices until they are between 5 and 7 years of age. "Stuttering," that is, having verbal rhythm problems, is found in nearly all 3- and 4-year-olds and often in older children, so it is only

I'm in the ballet class.

Susan

Kindergarten

FIGURE 6.2
Temporary Spelling—"I'm in the Ballet Class."—by a Kindergartner

when a child is exhibiting more than normal hesitation in speech that parents and teachers should seek professional speech and language evaluation. For all children, a relaxed and accepting environment for language experimentation is needed to support their confidence and risk taking (Curran & Cratty, 1978, pp. 34–38).

Many children come to school well versed in their home-based patterns of language, but they are unable to understand or express ideas comfortably in the standard English of the school.

A serious problem today, language diversity will soon become even more serious. Assuming that current population trends continue, over the next decade in many schools the number of children speaking foreign languages and nonstandard dialects will become the majority, challenging the ability of schools to educate them or their standard-English-speaking peers. (Bowman, 1991, p. 17)

Bowman provides five principles that can help teachers begin to bridge the gap between the home language of children and the goals of the school:

First, teachers need to learn to recognize developmental equivalences in patterns of behavior. All children have learned many of the same things—language, category systems, interpersonal communication styles—before they come to school. Although these accomplishments may look quite different, their developmental adequacy should not be questioned; there are a number of "equally good" ways to shape development....

Second, it is essential not to value some ways of achieving developmental milestones over others, since young children are particularly sensitive to how adults value them....

Third, teachers need to begin instruction with interactive styles and content that are familiar to the children. Whether this means speaking in the child's language, or using styles of address and patterns of management that are familiar and comfortable for children, the purpose is to establish a base line of shared knowledge....

Fourth, school learning is most likely to occur when family values reinforce school expectations....This means that interpretation of the school's agenda to parents is as important—perhaps more important—than many of the other tasks at which teachers spend their time....

Fifth, the same "contexts" do not have the same meanings to children from different groups, and the assessment of learning outcomes therefore presents a formidable problem as children misunderstand the meaning of a teacher's requests for information, knowledge, and skills....Formal assessment should be delayed until teachers and children have built a set of new meanings together so that the children understand the language and behavior called for in school. (pp. 26–28)

Creating conditions in classrooms that stimulate development of the language domain for diverse learners is not an easy task. Certain principles of curriculum planning can be gleaned,

however, from nearly a century of important research and classroom practice.

1. *Language is central to all learning.* No matter what is to be taught, teachers need to think through the children's involvement in language processes throughout the lesson.

2. *Talk is the primary manifestation of language learning and thought development.* Children need many different opportunities to express what they are attempting to understand. It is difficult but important to try to give each child enough time to speak to the teacher and to other children during each school day.

3. *Like most learning, language learning is more often "caught" than "taught."* Teachers need to be models for children in listening, speaking, reading, and writing. Time spent analyzing our own language competencies and perfecting them will often result in better learning of these skills by the children we teach.

4. *Speaking and listening are complex sets of skills and attitudes that can be taught and learned at increasingly higher levels of competence.* Direct instruction in listening/viewing and speaking skills, as well as indirect practice and reinforcement throughout the school day, will improve the children's competencies.

5. *Approximations in language use are appropriate and expected indicators of children's language development.* Children will not meet adult levels of correctness either in speaking or in writing, yet there is remarkable language proficiency even in the language of very young children.

6. *Central to learning to read and to write are daily, pleasant experiences with books and personal written expression.* Children should be helped to see that learning to read and write are natural, relatively easy extensions of their oral language abilities and that reading and writing habits are essential and desirable.

7. *Language learning takes a lifetime.* In spite of adults' efforts to push, test, and push again, real development in children's language takes time and is difficult to assess accurately.

ASSESSING LANGUAGE GROWTH

As the complexity of language learning is better understood, it becomes evident that current tests of language competence are woefully limited and often inaccurate. In place of tests, or at least in addition to them, teachers use a wide range of "kid-watching" techniques, observations of children using listening, speaking, reading, and writing for real purposes in a wide range of natural contexts. The learners themselves also take responsibility for judging and recording evidence of their progress in language skills. Records that teachers keep usually are not numerical scores but anecdotal notes, narratives, checklists, work samples, video- and audiotapes, and so forth. The teacher, often with the help of the child, develops a portfolio that profiles the child's performance, a file that may include test scores but includes much more. Each piece in the portfolio must be complete enough to give an accurate picture, but it needs to be simple enough for the teacher to fit the data collection into a busy school day. Figure 6.3 gives one example of such a form. Note that blanks are provided where the teacher can add other types of listening behaviors he or she deems to be important to observe. The checklist shows how a teacher filled out the form to record listening behaviors she observed one day for one child; later on in the year she will monitor Jamie's listening behaviors again and note any changes.

Name(s) *Jamie S.*

Date *11/3* Time of Day *9:15*

Setting *circle — total class*

Activity *critical listening to newspaper article on dinosaur bones*

Listens for information *yes* Example *answered a content question*

Retains what is heard *yes* Example *knowledgable about findings*

Follows oral directions *NA* Example *used Susan's response to*

Listens to peers *yes* Example *explain his idea*

Raises questions based on what is heard *yes*

Example *asked about age of the bones*

Is able to discount distractions

yes, (in high interest material)

Example *bothered by Susan but moved over*

Judges what is heard *yes* Example *asked about problems preserving bones*

__________ Example __________

extends learnings Example *chose a dinosaur book in free time*

__________ Example __________

__________ Example __________

FIGURE 6.3
Observation Checklist for Specified Listening Abilities

CURRENT EDUCATIONAL ISSUES

For some teachers, integrated language arts instruction, or what is currently called "whole language," is new and contrasts with the philosophy of language teaching that they were taught. Although there is new research, expert opinion, and teaching methods supporting integrated language learning, most of the ideas have been proposed for many decades, and the struggle to help educators understand their significance continues. In fact, in 1903 Percy Chubb, writing in his influential book for elementary and secondary teachers, *The Teaching of English,* stated:

> Our basic conception, be it remembered, is that the process of learning to use one's mother-tongue to good effect in speaking and writing it, and to appreciate and catch inspiration from its master-products, ought to be regarded as a single organic process, each stage of which must be seen in relation to those that precede and follow. The kindergarten teacher, therefore, must take account of the considerable progress already made by the child of four or five in its "mother-tongue," must know the extent and kind of its accomplishments, must understand the ways in which it has come by them, and so continue with greater skill and economy the methods by which these remarkable results have been achieved. (p. 19)

For the last half century, however, instruction has been dominated by behavioral psychology. Rather than viewing learning as holistic, integrated, and developmental, teachers have separated aspects of learning and instruction from each other, divided them into small increments, and taught them through drill and practice. Behavioral perspectives were particularly destructive to the language curriculum as teachers concentrated on the lesser aspects of language that were amenable to drill and testing, such as phonics, grammar, and spelling. For more than 50 years, the language curriculum has been disintegrating from the complex, beautiful, and challenging phenomenon that language experts know it to be. Fortunately, perspectives are changing, and as we enter the 21st century language teaching and learning seem new and exciting.

Most evident among the changes is the emphasis on student-to-student oral interaction in the classroom. No longer is a totally quiet classroom considered a "good" classroom. Of course,

there are times when the classroom is quiet—when children are listening intently to their teacher, a peer, a visitor, or a film—but many times during the day students are discussing, helping, or disagreeing with each other in pairs or in small groups. Teachers plan their lessons for interaction, recognizing that what children can talk about or question they come to understand. These teachers also know that good interaction skills are not learned easily, that they must be presented, practiced, and analyzed by the children in school if they are to develop the oral skills needed for people in a democracy.

Grade-level designations for curriculum hold far less significance in developmentally appropriate programs. Although younger children often speak and write in less sophisticated ways and they can comprehend less complex listening or reading materials, usually the differences depend more on the experiences of each child and his or her familiarity with the content than on age level. Teachers in integrated language arts classrooms soon learn to hold grade-level designations suspect, and they are very hesitant to label children as "competent" or "incompetent," "at grade level" or "remedial," "gifted" or "regular." To the extent that time and numbers of children in the class allow, teachers attempt to provide for a wide range of competencies, backgrounds, and interests, counting on the children's abilities to teach each other as well as the teacher's own ability to guide learning.

Following from this respect for the potential of all children, teachers in developmentally appropriate classrooms rarely group children in the traditional "ability groups" for reading and subject-matter instruction. They know that the background experiences of a child and his or her interest in learning are often more important than ability in determining what a child can learn at any given time. These teachers also respect the remarkable ability of children to teach each other, recognizing that participating in the instruction is often as much benefit for the child "teacher" as it is for child learners. Group memberships change frequently so that no child feels labeled as a "special needs learner," and all soon recognize that help is needed by everybody at times and available without stigma. Sometimes, of course, the teacher will call together children who are having difficulty with a concept or a skill or who need enrichment experiences in a unit under study, but the makeup of these groups will change because they are based on individual needs that vary among learning situations.

Without structured grouping designations and tight expectations for performance at a given age level, teachers are able to foster a climate of cooperation in the classroom. Competition consciously is diminished so that children feel satisfaction and responsibility for helping each other. Achievements are celebrated but not at the expense of other children who may need more instruction or more time. Children who speak easily and convincingly may not be the same children who read well; children who can perform dramatically may not be the same children who express themselves well in writing. The talents, interests, and learning styles of all children are recognized, but all are encouraged to continue developing the full range of listening, speaking, reading, and writing skills.

Language acquisition principles also guide teachers' perspectives on reading instruction. To traditionalists, it seems reasonable to begin reading with the smallest components of written language, the letters that form the sounds of words, and drill on isolated words to achieve sight recognition. Teachers now recognize that children do not learn language by pulling it apart and studying its phonetic elements. These concepts about language are very abstract; they have innumerable variations. Children never would have learned to speak if parents had thought that oral language was learned in such a piecemeal fashion! We now know that language is learned holistically in meaningful contexts, not in bits and pieces. This is nearly as true in learning written language as it is in learning oral language. In the context of a story, song, or poem that the children know and enjoy, the teacher will point out word and sound or spelling similarities that are of interest, but these pieces of information about language never lose their relationship to the content of the whole and the purposes for reading it.

Perhaps the most difficult change for teachers—and parents—as the curriculum moves from behaviorism into integrated language learning is the matter of "correctness." Schools have aimed at correct uses of language, and children have been rewarded when their reading, speaking, or writing was correctly produced. Yet the baby's learning of speech clearly demonstrates that language is learned developmentally, by making approximations and gradually reaching adult standards of correct form over a long period of time. Although this developmental progression is also true in listening, speaking, and reading, it is most obvious in writing. Rather than expecting children to spell words correctly or providing children with the correct way to spell words, teachers in developmentally appropriate programs encourage young children to spell words as they think they might be spelled, use what they know, and not worry about adult standards (see Figure 6.4). These teachers encourage independence and recognize that spelling, like all language learning, is learned developmentally as children take chances, make changes, and gradually work toward correct forms. They know that children are observing and using elements of all the standard spellings they see around them in their classroom and their world outside of school. Because English is especially irregular in spelling, children need many years before they take the responsibility for complete correctness. In the meantime, emphasis is placed on the more essential elements in what the child is trying to express in writing—the ideas. Removing fears of error in using language allows children to participate with confidence and enthusiasm in the listening, speaking, reading, and writing experiences the teacher has designed.

Integrated language arts classrooms are joyful places nearly all of the time. Although children sometimes feel frustrated reaching for a new goal, they know that their efforts will be respected. The joy of learning is especially important in reading and writing instruction. For many of today's children, reading is something that they only do in school; if school experiences limit their ideas about the values of reading, they are even less interested in reading outside of school. If writing is taught as only a set of skills to be mastered, or if writing is used to punish children for misbehavior, children who see little need for writing in the world outside of school give little enthusiasm or commitment to learning to write. Teachers in an integrated language arts classroom make concerted efforts to help children find satisfaction in their writing

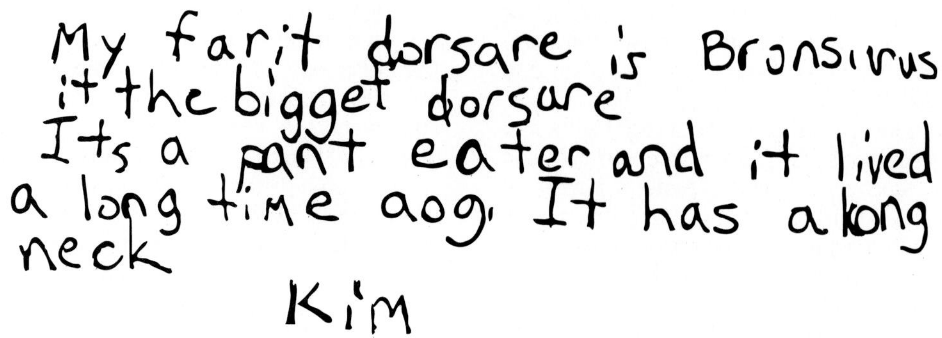
My farit dorsare is Bronsirus
it the bigget dorsare
Its a pant eater and it lived
a long time aog. It has a long
neck
Kim

My favorite dinosaur is brontosaurus.

It [is] the biggest dinosaur.

It's a plant eater and it lived

a long time ago. It has a long

neck.

Kim

Grade 1

FIGURE 6.4
Writing the Whole Language Way

efforts, and they use much of their reading instruction time for interesting children in books and giving them time to develop reading habits. Cooperation rather than competition among the children is the aim of the learning community in a developmentally appropriate classroom. Differences among children, including differences in cultural background, language, and dialect, become matters of interest and appreciation. Although teachers model standard English for children, the child's family dialect or language is respected. Children are encouraged, especially through role playing, to add a standard register to their familiar language patterns, but like all language learnings, this development will come slowly over a number of years.

Opening up language to all of its possibilities encourages teachers to look beyond the arts of the language itself to see how other arts can enhance language learning. Music, drama, and the visual arts are excellent language enhancers; they encourage children to improvise, discuss, investigate through reading, and react through writing:

> Education in the arts cultivates sensitive perception, develops insight, fosters imagination, and places a premium on well-crafted form. These skills and dispositions are of central importance in both writing and reading. Without them, children are unlikely to write—not because they cannot spell but because they have nothing to say. The writer starts with vision and ends with words. The reader begins with these words but ends with vision. The reader uses the writer's words in order to see. The interaction of the senses enriches meaning. The arts are not mere diversions from the important business of education; they are essential resources. (Eisner, 1981, p. 52)

The materials for language arts teaching, therefore, go far beyond the traditional textbook,

Developmentally appropriate classrooms are joyful places in which children commit their ideas to paper with confidence.

workbook, or kit; in fact, limiting language instruction to what these materials can provide impoverishes language participation. If textbooks and similar materials are used in language arts instruction, the National Council of Teachers of English (NCTE) asks teachers to scrutinize textbooks to ensure that they contribute to the following principles:

- Language arts instruction should center on children's own language.
- Language arts instruction should emphasize social uses of language.
- Language arts instruction should integrate reading, writing, speaking, and listening.
- Language arts instruction should recognize the developmental aspects of children's learning.
- Language arts instruction should help teachers to assess students' language learning.
- Language arts instruction should help children to think.
- Language arts instruction should respect cultural and other differences in our society.

- Language arts instruction should emphasize the centrality of listening, speaking, writing, and reading for learning in all subject areas. (NCTE Committee on Elementary Language Arts Textbooks, 1991, pp. 253–254)

GOALS AND OBJECTIVES

Language complements the thinking process. It is through language that children represent concepts, feelings, and understandings. Thus, all language, oral and written, is symbolic.

In the normal course of child development, listening precedes speaking, speaking precedes writing, and writing (the child's personal thoughts and language written down) precedes formal instruction in reading (study of the ideas and language of adults). The curriculum for preschool and primary-grade children, therefore, will have a strong oral basis, and it will accommodate the children's naturally emerging literacy by encouraging preconventional forms of writing and reading, gradually developing more conventional writing and reading behaviors.

Although listening, speaking, writing, and reading are often treated separately in instruction to focus on certain subskills, the integration and interdependence of the oral and written forms of language are undergirding principles of the language curriculum. Moreover, language activities are not limited to finite portions of the school day but are integrated into all subjects and lessons in the other content areas.

The ultimate goals of the language domain are designed to help children develop their innate capacities to share their thoughts and feelings with others and accurately interpret communications they receive. Although no language skill can or should be totally isolated from the others, to progress children must have opportunities to work on particular goals in particular activities. The curriculum should include the following experiences.

Mediating Objectives for Listening/Viewing

As children progress toward the ultimate goal, they will

1. participate in experiences that help them interpret nonverbal messages.

2. actively participate in activities or experiences aimed at enhancing and challenging listening skills (e.g., music, stories, conversations, audiotapes, films, etc.).
3. learn to demonstrate courteous listening behaviors by
   a. looking at the speaker,
   b. sitting relatively still,
   c. waiting for a turn to speak, and
   d. responding to oral cues.
4. increase their respective vocabulary.
5. identify and discriminate likenesses and differences among sounds (e.g., environmental sounds, words, etc.).
6. improve their ability to focus on relevant oral content and ignore distractions.
7. demonstrate auditory memory by repeating in correct detail and sequence the messages they hear.
8. develop some understandings of contemporary media, especially television, and their impact on their understandings and values.
9. demonstrate auditory comprehension by
   a. retelling in their own words the messages or stories they hear and films they see,
   b. responding to oral language with related comments or questions,
   c. verbally linking personal experience to what they have heard,
   d. responding accurately to single- and multistep directions, and
   e. laughing at the humor of what they hear.

Mediating Objectives for Speaking

As children progress toward the ultimate goal, they will

10. experiment with language sounds, rhythm, volume, pitch, and words.
11. expand their abilities
    a. to express intents, emotions, and desires;
    b. to describe single events from the past, present, or future;
    c. to describe a sequence of events or multiple events;
    d. to ask questions and demonstrate understanding of the answers they receive;
    e. to analyze situations and respond to them;
    f. to demonstrate their level of comprehension of concepts;
    g. to tell stories about pictures;
    h. to create and describe original imaginative situations;
    i. to persuade appropriately;
    j. to rephrase or add details to clarify their messages to others; and
    k. to become more fluent and coherent.
12. use appropriate body language (eye contact, body position, gestures) to alert a listener to their intent and convey emotion (remember: cultural differences in body language need to be respected).
13. notice how appropriate inflections, articulation, volume, intonation, and speed aid the listener in understanding their messages.
14. increase their expressive vocabulary in amount and precision.
15. participate in conversations with children and adults by responding with relevant comments when spoken to.
16. participate in group discussions, with and without teacher guidance.
17. participate in creative dramatics activities.

Mediating Objectives For Writing

As children progress toward the ultimate goal, they will

18. observe many examples of purposeful written language and thus extend their awareness that writing transforms thoughts, ideas, and feelings into print symbols that communicate meaning.
19. find satisfaction in trying to put their thoughts on paper.
20. observe adults and older children as they transcribe the children's oral dictation about personal experiences, pictures, and constructions.
21. produce written language for a variety of purposes (to list, inform, narrate, describe, persuade, etc.), increasing the amount of their writing over time.
22. confidently utilize their own versions of writing (drawing, scribbling, letterlike approximations, invented spelling, correct spelling, word spacing) as these are developmentally appropriate, working gradually toward conventional spelling, handwriting, punctuation,

and format, at least in some parts of what they have written.

23. expand their writing vocabulary without undue concern for spelling these new words correctly.
24. increase their ability to find topics to write about.
25. learn to organize their ideas in a logical sequence.
26. begin to use writing strategies for organizing and planning writing, such as mapping, webbing, and clustering.
27. improve their ability to evaluate their writing, revise as needs are perceived, and talk with peers and teachers about their goals and challenges in writing.
28. use references that will help them improve their writing.
29. begin to recognize and use correct formats for certain types of writing (e.g., personal letters, business letters, stories, scripts, etc.).

Mediating Objectives For Reading

As children progress toward the ultimate goal, they will

30. form habits of looking at, asking for, and enjoying literature (fiction and nonfiction, prose and poetry).
31. regularly use the classroom library, the school library, and the community library as interesting places to find books and other materials for entertainment and information.
32. practice readinglike behavior, moving from "pretend" reading to attempting to match the flow of their own language with book illustrations and with print.
33. respond to written symbols in the environment (signs, advertisements, labels, etc.).
34. make predictions about what will come next in stories that are being heard and that are being read independently, basing decisions on the information in the text and/or on personal life experiences.
35. read pictures and/or text for themselves (or listen to the teacher read), and discuss:
    a. story sequence (first, next, last; beginning, middle, end; before, after),
    b. main ideas both at literal and inferential levels,
    c. characters and character development,
    d. setting, and
    e. plot development and cause and effect.
36. tell or dramatize their own versions of stories to show comprehension of what they have read.
37. create new endings for stories, drawing on logical elements of the original stories.
38. read familiar or memorized nursery rhymes, songs, poems, plays, and finger plays from classroom charts and individual copies to get the flow and pacing of reading, as well as to develop sight vocabulary through favorite text materials.
39. distinguish between real and make-believe, fact and opinion, in written materials.
40. read their own and class-dictated stories.
41. learn to read independently for meaning (rather than for totally correct word identification), using context clues and initial letters to predict what makes sense; learn to reread for greater accuracy when the meaning breaks down.
42. identify upper- and lowercase letters, rhyming words, sight vocabulary; begin to develop concepts about letter-sound relationships and discrepancies.
43. identify the parts of a book—cover (title, author, illustrator), dedication page, table of contents, chapters, headings, index—only to the extent that this knowledge adds to the appreciation of the book.
44. use beginning reference books (e.g., dictionary, thesaurus) and library skills.
45. evaluate themselves as readers, identifying their strengths and needs.

TEACHING STRATEGIES

If the preceding list is the language domain goals for children, then it follows that certain principles will guide the actions of the teacher.

1. *Model appropriate, rich language usage.* Although you will not expect standard English usage from all children, you need to have a good command of standard English. In addition, your diction needs to be clear and your language understandable to the children, with interesting vocabulary that stretches the children's understanding and interest in language.

2. *Integrate language development activities and quality literature throughout all areas of the early childhood curriculum.* Because all subjects require language for learning, you will need to plan content around the language forms of listening, speaking, reading, and writing. High-quality literature uses language in its most crafted forms, and it is available at appropriate levels on nearly all topics of interest to children, so you will want to make a variety of literature central in your classroom. The literature will have important meanings for the children when you help them explore its relationships to, or its contrasts with, their lives.

3. *Listen to and talk with each child daily.* The school day is busy from beginning to end, and it is far too easy to neglect children who do not expect or demand attention. By making it a rule of thumb that every child will have a personal conversation with you each day, you are more apt to make individual attention a priority.

4. *Take advantage of spontaneous events to promote children's language development through discussion.* Some of the richest teaching moments occur unplanned. If you are too "scripted" by your teaching plans, you may not notice how something a child brings to the class, a change in the weather, or a chance happening can reach your immediate or long-range teaching goals beautifully. These serendipitous events often capture the minds and hearts of children, opening them to important learnings.

5. *When a child states something, extend his or her phrase by repeating it using a new term or by adding a clause appropriate for the meaning.* Often there is an opportunity to extend a child's vocabulary by repeating all or part of what a child says using an interesting synonym for a word or two or by adding a related idea.

6. *Plan the learning environment and the curriculum to provide opportunities for children to communicate informally with one another.* The activity-oriented classroom provides the natural environment for peer interaction. It is challenging for you to plan for children's purposeful conversations, but very important for their continuing language growth.

7. *Plan activities each day in which the primary goal is for children to use language to de-* scribe events, make predictions, or evaluate phenomena. All that you want to help happen in language development will not occur through activity centers. You need to plan particular small- and large-group experiences that stretch children's abilities to express themselves in particular ways. The challenge then is to see that each child in the group has enough opportunities to speak.

8. *Model good listening behavior by attending to the children and responding to the meanings of their verbalizations.* Modeling listening behaviors for children is often difficult to do because there are so many demands on your time. Stopping, looking at the child, and reacting probably will be the most important teaching of listening that you do.

9. *Give children appropriate cues to help them listen better.* Say "Look up here" or "Watch me"; use voice inflections; change your volume appropriately for the small- or large-group setting. You cannot expect children to know how to listen well, although they often are more attentive listeners than adults are! Clues to listening behavior will be useful for them and lessen your frustration over the children's listening behavior.

10. *Introduce sound discrimination by using common environmental sounds (e.g., telephone, doorbell), and gradually alert children to interesting sound-symbol relationships in written language.* Alerting children to the sounds in their environment calls attention to common experiences that are easily overlooked and creates understanding about hearing and sounds. When parents helped these children learn to speak, they did not focus their attention on the individual sounds that made up the words they were learning. Sounds and the letters that represent them on paper are more readily understood when they are examined in the context of a song, poem, or story the children enjoy. Brief, natural encounters with "phonics," usually on a class chart or on the blackboard, ensures that sound-symbol relationships will not be frightening or confusing.

11. *Maintain children's attention using props, gestures, proximity, and/or particular facial and vocal expressions, but also gradually help children maintain attention without extra el-*

ements. A book, puppet, picture, or your special action is a useful attention getter; often it visualizes for the children a concept that is difficult for them to conceive. But it is also important for the children to create their own mind pictures about the words they hear. You will need to plan listening experiences that develop the children's imaginations from verbal stimuli alone as well as with aids.

12. *Involve children in songs, chants, poems, finger plays, rhymes, choral readings, and dramatic play.* Dramatic activity is a natural learning mode for children. You will want to plan for the overt involvement of all of the children as much as possible. Combining speaking or singing with reading the lyrics of these favorite songs or poems leads children into intuitively learning about reading.

13. *Read to the children at least once every day, more whenever possible.* Most teachers know that reading to children is important, and they love to share quality books with their classes. As those who understand the interdependence of language learnings, they know that listening to well-written prose and poetry has significant effects on children's developing reading and writing abilities and interests. Remember that children who may come from literacy-impoverished homes are in even greater need of read-aloud opportunities.

14. *Utilize a variety of literary forms when reading to children (picture books, poetry, folk and fairy tales, factual books).* Most teachers give children a read-aloud diet rich in stories. You will want to plan your oral reading time carefully so that you "tune your children's ears" to the ideas presented in a variety of genres but also to the vocabulary and sentence structures typical of different forms of writing.

15. *Draw attention to story sequence, story development, characters, cause and effect, main ideas, and details, but only when these discussions will not interfere with the children's enjoyment of the story.* There are many opportunities when you are reading to children to teach them important concepts. You will want to do that on some occasions, but it is also important to preserve the continuity of what the children are listening to and the integrity of the overall meaning.

16. *Model real needs for reference books, and make the references available for children to use.* There are times when you will not have the information children need. It may be the answer to a question, the spelling of a word, or where a place is on the map. Use these opportunities to demonstrate to children that learning is a lifelong pursuit. Let them see you search for answers, and then offer children resources they can use.

17. *Consciously create an environment that is rich in print (e.g., charts, book-making materials, labels, names, directions, recipes, menus, children's writing, etc.).* The print that children see around them becomes their primary resource for their own writing and reading. You should make the environmental print serve real uses in your classroom. Put print materials at eye level for the children. Draw attention to print messages, pointing to letters or words and asking why the messages are important; refer back to them at appropriate times. Model print concepts by cueing left to right, top to bottom; page turning; and noting word and sentence formations (e.g., spaces between words, types of punctuation).

18. *Provide daily opportunities for children to "write" and to share their writing with peers and their teacher.* Writing is learned by doing it. The daily play-based experiences children have putting their ideas on paper—usually first in pictures, squiggles, and letterlike approximations, and later in letters, words spelled in invented ways, then in sentences—equate with the process they went through learning to speak. Just as in learning to speak, much improvement comes naturally as children "practice." Children need access to a variety of materials for making their own print. Place writing materials in all centers of the room: order blanks for the pretend restaurant, sticks for making words in the sandbox, and so on. Provide reference materials, such as a simplified dictionary, in some centers so that children can readily use them. Their enthusiasm for writing grows as they hear the responses of peers to their efforts. The children's writing can be shared through bulletin board displays or "published" books, or read by the child when he or she sits in the author's chair.

Danielle has taken advantage of the paper and markers available in the block area to let others know she wants her road to remain undisturbed.

19. *Have children dictate stories, experiences, or observations, and then let the children hear and see their own words in print.* You will also want to show children their own ideas and words written in "adult language" because, as they dictate, they will be able to concentrate on what they want to say without struggling with the way to write those ideas and words down. More often than not children are able to dictate longer, more complex pieces than they can get down on paper by themselves, and this convinces them that they can "compose." Be sure to write what the child says, whether or not it is said in standard English; the child needs to know that you value what is said and how it is said. Ensure that the child who is dictating is standing beside you so that he or she sees the words written right side up. At different times, you may want to take dictation using another type of tool (crayon, pen, marker) or writing surface (stationery, postcard, chart) to show the children other possibilities for recording their ideas.

20. *Recognize and accept the following developmental stages for writing words, yet know that the pattern will differ with each child and often with each word:*

- *Precommunicative spelling*—scribbles, letters randomly placed on the page, repetition of a few letters again and again, etc.

- *Semiphonetic spelling*—using some letters to represent sounds, using letter names to spell words, etc.
- *Phonetic spelling*—all essential sound features of a word spelled, letters chosen only on the basis of sound without regard for other English conventions, etc.
- *Transitional spelling*—adherence to basic English orthography, perhaps including all appropriate letters but reversing some, many words spelled correctly, etc.
- *Correct spelling*—growing accuracy, correct spelling of some irregular spelling patterns, most words spelled correctly (adapted from Gentry, cited in Tompkins, 1990, pp. 284–285)

Each child's level of performance in writing will depend on the opportunities he or she has had to write at home and in previous grades at school, understanding of the purposes of printed language, and the degree to which efforts have been accepted by others. Age-level designations for writing performance are not appropriate for most children. Expanding the vocabulary children are willing to try to use in their writing needs to be a higher priority than correctness in spelling.

21. *Avoid drawing attention to words and letters as the children write so that they can concentrate on the meanings they are trying to*

express. It has been a common school practice to spell words for children as they write or, before the writing session begins, to list on the blackboard words children think they might need, but these "helps" focus children's attention away from their thoughts toward correct form. At other, more appropriate times, point out similarities and differences in words, correct or unusual spellings, rhyming words, use of capital letters, and punctuation.

22. *Use games, songs, and other play-oriented activities to familiarize children with the alphabet.* Although knowledge of the alphabet and the sounds associated with letters is not as important for beginning readers and writers as many teachers and parents think, you will find that it is easier to talk with children about reading and writing when they have some knowledge of the alphabet. Call attention to letters individually and in words when reading charts of familiar poems, dictated writing, and so on. Model strategies for figuring out how to read unfamiliar words. Draw children's attention to various writing forms by providing examples (upper- and lowercase letters; manuscript, cursive, and italic forms; boldface, etc.) when they appear in contexts interesting to children.

23. *Provide opportunities for appropriate elements of the writing process: topic selection, drafting, and sharing drafts.* Children write best and write most about the topics they know and care about. They often find it difficult and unpleasing to change their writing after it is on paper or to edit for mechanical errors. Gradually young children will add additional words and sentences to their pieces or correct errors, and some young children may begin higher level revision strategies as they take increasing pride in what they have produced. You will want to take care not to push the children into revising or editing too soon for fear of diminishing their efforts in writing. Asking the child to read a piece to you or the other children often helps him or her see changes that need to be made.

24. *Accept children's risk taking in their listening, speaking, writing, and reading when their efforts may not result in correct or useful productions.* Teachers sometimes are so anxious to have learning occur that they "help" when they should wait. Children may perceive help as criticism of their efforts, and they become less willing to try and try again. You will want to observe, record children's needs in your head or on anecdotal records, and use correction judiciously.

ACTIVITY SUGGESTIONS

Following are activities that can be used to reach the goals of the language domain. They are only samples of lessons that can be used to involve as many children in the class as possible in sustained practice of a particular language skill. Often the activity involves children in practicing more than one of the language skills, but for teaching purposes, you may be focusing on only one. As you read these lesson ideas, other, perhaps better ways of meeting the language objective with your class may come to mind.

⇒ Creating the Learning Environment

Objective: To involve children in planning and preparing the classroom for the school year, a unit of study, or an activity

Procedure: Rather than preparing the classroom for the children and the work they will be doing, leave what can be left for the children as a group to discuss, organize, and set up. This problem-solving experience stretches the children's listening, speaking, negotiating, and thinking skills.

To Simplify: Limit the expectations, number of decisions, and complexity of the decisions the children will need to make.

To Extend: Children feel ownership and commitment when they have an important part in determining their curriculum; older children need increasing responsibility for these decisions and the consequences of them.

⇒ Simon Says

Objective: For children to listen for accurate information

Procedure: With the children lined up next to each other across the gym or the playground, demonstrate how to move forward as the directions of "Simon" dictates, but only when the caller also says "Simon Says." Give credit more for accurate listening than for reaching the finish line. The children then take turns as Simon and call out directions.

To Simplify: Have the children ensure success most of the time by limiting the number of steps, hops, or jumps that can be taken; emphasize that hearing the words "Simon Says" is the important factor.

To Extend: Encourage the child callers to increase the complexity of the directions given (e.g., hop forward three times on one foot).

➡ What about the Pictures?

Objective: For children to listen for appreciation

Procedure: Explain to the class that you are going to read to them a delightful story, *It Could Be Worse* by Margot Zemach (or any quality storybook), but that they will not see the pictures until later. After reading the story, ask individual children to tell about the pictures in their minds during highlights of the folk tale or to draw their favorite part; have the children put their pictures in the correct sequence of the story. Then show the author/illustrator's illustrations. Some class members may be able to tell how the author/illustrator's ideas were different from theirs, and perhaps why.

To Simplify: Select an easier, shorter story, perhaps one they are familiar with such as "The Three Little Pigs"; show the children illustrations for the story from a version that is new to them.

To Extend: Older children can discuss why they like the illustrator's interpretation of the story or why they do not. Listening to the story again may help them clarify their ideas.

➡ Friends and Strangers

Objective: For children to listen in order to make critical judgments

Procedure: Take a child aside and plan a short role-playing situation in which you act as an adult who meets the child at the school playground after school and offers him or her a ride home. Role-play the scene for the class and

have them discuss what was said and under what circumstances the child might accept the offer.

To Simplify: An older child in the school, perhaps a kindergartner or first grader, could act for the younger children; as the adult, the teacher may need to make appropriate decisions more obvious to the children.

To Extend: The situation can be more complex for the older children, requiring them to listen more carefully and think more critically about possible solutions to the problem; often child volunteers can role-play the adult as well as child's parts.

➡ I Have a Story to Tell!

Objective: For children to retell orally a favorite story

Procedure: When a story, such as *Cinderella*, is very familiar to the children, they enjoy retelling it in their own words, perhaps to the class with one child starting the story and others adding ideas in sequence until the whole story is completed. Comprehension of the main ideas, sequence of events, and fluency in oral expression are challenged in this activity. (Teachers need to model oral storytelling for children prior to the expectation that the children tell stories independently.)

To Simplify: Invite the children to retell shorter, less complex stories, such as *The Three Billy Goats Gruff*. Provide story props in a storytelling center, and pair children to retell the story taking turns.

To Extend: If you have modeled oral storytelling effectively, and if the class has had opportunities for total group retellings of favorite stories, the older children will be able to retell stories (or tell original stories or experiences) in groups of three. In small groups, more children have a chance to speak during the time frame of the lesson.

➡ Riddles around Us

Objective: For children to describe objects orally, withholding the most obvious identifying qualities

Procedure: As a demonstration, present oral riddles to the class, asking the children to guess objects or people in the room you are describing. Help the children identify the characteristics of a good riddle. Then some of the children, perhaps in small groups to involve more children, can create their own riddles about other objects in the room (a picture, a piece of furniture).

To Simplify: Place a limited number of objects directly in front of the class. After modeling some riddles, ask children to volunteer to make up their own riddles about the objects for the class.

To Extend: In addition to creating oral riddles about visible objects and people, encourage the children to create riddles about things that are not immediately visible (e.g., items on the playground, books you have read to the class, etc.).

➡ When Mommy and Daddy Were Young

Objective: For children to learn to ask a series of related questions

Procedure: Discuss with the class why we ask questions and how questions help us. Help the children ask you questions they might want to know about your childhood experiences. Then let the class use their new questioning skills on a parent visitor or another teacher. Analyze with the children which questions were on topic and elicited good information. Encourage the children to ask questions at home about their parents' childhood; bring that information to the class to share with peers, illustrate, or graph.

To Simplify: Younger children will be more comfortable asking questions about something they can see. Bring your pet or pictures of your family to class. After the children have had a chance to become acquainted with your pet, or after they have looked at your pictures, let them ask you questions.

To Extend: Older children can be helped to focus questions on particular categories of information, such as your hobbies, and to judge if a question is appropriate for the category. With guidance, they also can compare questions to

determine which are most effective in getting good information.

➡ Dramatic Storytelling

Objective: For children to retell a story using spontaneous oral language and expressive body movements

Procedure: Read and reread a favorite story to the class over a period of time. Follow by having the class retell the story in their own words. When the children have the plot line well in mind, ask for volunteers to act out the "play" with their own words and actions. Discuss possibilities for making the story become more alive, and give many children chances to perform. If interest is maintained, which it usually is, repeat the brief drama several times in the future until all of the children have had more than one part.

To Simplify: A classic story like *Caps for Sale* by Esphyr Slobodkina, *The Three Bears,* or *The Three Billy Goats Gruff* delights young children; *Caps for Sale* is a wonderfully humorous but simple story with parts as monkeys for many children. There is little dialogue, so the children are successful in their first play-acting experiences as a class. Colorful caps may be used as the only props, but the children will also enjoy using imaginative hats.

To Extend: The older children can stretch themselves to develop a play from a story that has more than one scene, such as *My Teacher Sleeps at School* by Leatie Weiss. They can identify the scenes and how the characters in each scene help them think more deeply about the story. The actors will then try to put the central ideas of the scene into the spontaneous dialogue they create, but they will not need to use any of the language that the author wrote. The children may decide to use some simple scenery, props, or costumes, but the teacher will want to stress the more important use of imagination and creative language.

➡ It's the Best!

Objective: For children to think about and produce language designed to persuade others

Procedure: Pick out three toys or games in the classroom that most class members enjoy. Encourage the children to describe the object, then ask the children to stand beside the toy or game that is the one they would pick first if they had a choice in playtime. Have the children gathered around each toy give the reasons for their choice, encouraging each group to think of as many reasons as possible. When the three groups have presented their ideas, ask if some now have changed their choices and what they heard that persuaded them.

To Simplify: Two objects may be the most little ones can compare. The objects, however, may be two objects that are similar in some ways, like two teddy bears or two puzzles. Small groups of children could do this at a time to keep the activity short.

To Extend: Have each group present its reasons to the class. Record on a chart the persuasive qualities suggested. Read these ideas back to the children, asking them to identify the ideas that are similar in meaning; ask them which ideas seem most persuasive to them. Help the children realize that some ideas will be persuasive to some children but not necessarily to others.

➡ Planning a Party

Objective: For children to learn to discuss in a small group without teacher direction and to come to consensus

Procedure: Use the occasion of a holiday celebration to involve the children in planning for the event. As a total class, discuss the decisions that must be made so that the party will be a happy event. Before sending the children in small groups of three or four to a specified place in the room for their discussion, be sure they understand which aspect of the party (food, games, etc.) they are to decide on and the brief amount of time they will have for the task. (Setting a timer for a few minutes helps children stay on task.) As the groups talk, the teacher moves from group to group to observe and occasionally to give help. A spokesperson for each group shares the discussion results with the class, and decisions are made about whether or not the suggestions are feasible.

To Simplify: The children probably will need more guidance than is possible when the total class is divided into small groups. While some children are involved in another activity, the teacher can have two small groups of three meet near him or her to do their discussing and planning. Again, however, the teacher will want to give the groups as much opportunity for independent thinking and interaction as possible.

To Extend: Older children will begin to experience the difficulties of making decisions in groups (e.g., the child who dominates the group, the child who does not contribute to discussion, the group's failure to reach consensus). Although the teacher does not want group discussion to be a continuing frustration for children, he or she also does not want to protect the children completely from the difficulties of this important life skill. Taking time to talk with the class about small problems often helps children become better participants in discussion groups as the year progresses.

➡ Read! Read!

Objective: For children to create habits of reading

Procedure: Encouraging young people to read voluntarily is the most challenging reading goal for teachers in today's world. Of course, reading to children is the best way to do this, and many parents have helped teachers by consistently reading to children since they were babies. At school, teachers continue developing reading habits by reading quality books aloud, scheduling daily independent reading times, providing attractive displays of books, taking children to libraries, encouraging talk and drama about books, and helping children learn to care for books as special materials.

To Simplify: Little ones can begin to develop reading habits. Encourage "reading" each day: help children select books, often ones they heard read, and sit quietly turning the pages, looking at the pictures, and perhaps retelling the story to a partner or to a favorite toy in the play area. You will want to read for at least part of the time when children are reading to model reading behaviors. Put reading books in the housekeeping center and in other places to help children see reading as connected to other life experiences.

To Extend: As children form reading habits, the teacher usually can expect them to stay at independent reading for increasing amounts of time. They can learn to replace a story they are not enjoying with another book without disturbing other readers, and they can learn to share quietly with a partner a special illustration or a passage they may be able to read aloud.

➨ Reading All around Us

Objective: For children to internalize concepts about the importance of reading in the world outside of the school

Procedure: Have the class brainstorm all of the places in the classroom where they see print language—names, labels, charts, books, writing samples, and so on. Discuss how these examples serve different purposes. If appropriate, brainstorm a list of places they remember seeing print language outside of school to see if there are other ways print is used to communicate.

To Simplify: Take a walk in the nearby neighborhood asking children to record the letters or numbers being used (e.g., stop signs, billboards, addresses, etc.). When the children get back to the classroom, discuss how the numbers and letters they saw help people.

To Extend: Names are very important for children this age. Often they can read their own names and the names of some of their classmates. Make simplified bingo cards using the names of children in the room and invite the children to play. This activity subtly introduces children to letter-sound relationships in words that have high interest for them. Also, ask the children to bring in the names of relatives on cards. The cards can then be used to make a family tree, order according to age, or alphabetize.

➨ Shared Reading

Objective: For children to gain individual help and encouragement in reading by working in pairs

Procedure: Because it is not possible for the teacher to give individual children all the help they need, and because children are often very good and patient in helping each other, a regular feature of the reading curriculum should be shared reading. During reading time, pairs of children sit together in a comfortable place in the room to read a favorite storybook, each child taking responsibility to tell about or read every other page.

To Simplify: Ask the children to read the pictures of a familiar story to each other, turning the pages one at a time, telling about the left-hand page before the right-hand page. Wordless picture books such as *Frog Goes to Dinner* by Mercer Mayer can be happy introductions to shared reading. The teacher demonstrates the procedures using a class-size "big book," then has a pair of children demonstrate the system before the partners are expected to work independently for a few minutes.

To Extend: In addition to retelling the pictures, thereby increasing their comprehension of the story, invite children to read to their partners some or most of the sentences. Highly repetitive picture books like *Brown Bear, Brown Bear* by Bill Martin give beginners successful oral reading experiences.

➨ Choral Reading

Objective: For children to develop pacing, eye movements, and the rhythmic patterns of language that are important for reading

Procedure: Nursery rhymes, songs, and poems that children have heard and enjoyed many times are important materials for introducing children to reading. The children read or sing the words at a pace that is natural to the poem or song as the teacher underscores the words with his or her hand or a pointer. Even very young children find that they are "successful readers" because they know the words from memory. The class will want to make a big book of rhymes they know and have it available to read independently or with a pal.

To Simplify: Common, brief nursery rhymes and folk songs are most useful for 3- to 4-year-olds. Make the printed lyrics available, but do not expect many of the children to attend to the charts for more than brief periods of time.

To Extend: In addition to the charts, older children enjoy having individual small booklets of each song or poem they are learning to read (8½ × 11 sheets folded, cut in half, and stapled into a four-page booklet).

➠ Sharing Who I Am

Objective: For children to realize that their young lives are full of ideas to write about

Procedure: When teachers accept that the first skill of writers is finding the topic they want to write about, they encourage children to write what they know and care about, not topics selected by the teacher. This means listening to what children want to say and reminding them that they may want to put those ideas on paper to keep (e.g., a new pair of shoes, a guest of the family, a hobby). The children need opportunities to talk with the teacher or a friend or to draw about what they are going to write so that the ideas and the words are more clearly in mind. Even when the class has a common experience they want to preserve, the different way each child chooses to write about the idea is celebrated by the class and the teacher.

To Simplify: Early writing experiences are important for developing both writing and reading concepts. Children of this age often are using writing instruments for the first time, and frequently they have few ideas about why people write or how to make letters. Teachers need to make writing instruments (markers, crayons, pencils) available during brief, supervised writing times. Any marks the child puts on paper (drawings, scribbles, letter approximations, etc.) need to be praised, and the child should be asked to tell the meaning of his or her writing.

To Extend: Children at this age need to continue to write about what is important to them. They also need opportunities to "read" their writing or tell about it to appreciative peers. Teachers find an "author's chair" a special place for the writer to sit as he or she shares writing with the class. By dating children's writing and preserving it in a folder, teachers have a good record of children's progress in the amount they can write and their ability to generate writing ideas, improve their letter approximations, and make more logical spellings of words.

➠ Dictating Ideas

Objective: For children to better understand how the ideas they can talk about look when they are put on paper

Procedure: Although dictation does not replace independent writing opportunities, it is another way teachers can use children's oral language to help them understand why people write and how speech sounds look on paper. Sometimes it will be a class dictation about a common experience (e.g., a field trip, a thank-you note the class wants to send, or a letter to a sick classmate). At other times the teacher may take dictation from an individual child about the pictures he or she has drawn, a block structure, and so on.

To Simplify: The dictation of a class of 3-year-olds or an individual 4-year-old will be short, perhaps only one sentence. The teacher will read it back and ask if that is what the child wanted to say. Then, if appropriate for the interests and developmental levels of the children, the teacher may point out one or two interesting things about the written language—that certain words look almost alike, that some words are short and some are long—or help children name the letters in a word. None of this attention to the details of the writing, however, should supersede concern for the meaning expressed in the writing.

To Extend: When children have developed good attitudes about participating in writing, their fascination with it and their eagerness grows for putting longer and more complex thought on paper. They also, without prompting, begin to try to use more standard conventions of written language (handwriting, spelling, punctuation, etc.), although often their choices are incorrect. They begin to observe more carefully teachers and parents as they write dictated pieces, and they attend to words on signs and labels and in books. A classroom climate that favors risk taking is essential for these writers.

➠ Re-created Writing

Objective: To relieve children of the need to create ideas and language for their writing as they are struggling to figure out how to represent those ideas and words on paper

Procedure: Occasionally, children may be encouraged to write a favorite short song or nursery rhyme from memory, particularly a song or poem they have been reading for some time from a classroom chart. Now the reading chart is put away. As they write, the children individually sing and resing pieces of the lyrics quietly to help them remember what they are trying to write.

To Simplify: Teachers will want to do this activity as a dictation experience with younger children. As the children sing and resing a line or two of a song, the children will watch the teacher put the words on a chart or a blackboard. A few children may want to re-create part of the song or nursery rhyme lyrics independently, but this needs to be a free-choice activity for very young children. What they write will probably be only a few squiggles or letters.

To Extend: Older children will be able to re-create more of a memorized song or poem and make somewhat more accurate representations, but there will be wide variations in what the same-aged children will be able to do. Teachers need to be careful not to compare the results of different children but to praise each child for effort. By analyzing the results of a child's re-created writing, teachers get a good picture of the writing problems he or she is trying to solve, what sound-symbol understandings are developing, and so forth. Later, when the children write the same song lyrics again, teachers can compare the early and later samples to get quite accurate indications of progress.

➠ Copying Writing

Objective: For children to experience good conditions for copying a piece of writing

Procedure: Copying writing from the blackboard has been a common practice in primary-grade classrooms. Young children's eyes, however, are not well developed, and the alternating of distant and close viewing required to copy a list, poem, or paragraph from a blackboard even a few feet away is stressful for young children. When individual children have a strong desire for a personal copy of a brief piece such as a rhyme or a song, it is appropriate, however, to put a copy of the original close at hand, on the child's table or desk, so that the child can make a copy. The child probably will need help when the piece is too long to sustain his or her interest.

To Simplify: Copying is rarely appropriate for very young children. Some children may show interest, however, particularly in writing letters of the alphabet, a task their older brothers and sisters know how to do. Paper, writing instruments, and an alphabet strip should be available for children to choose to use.

To Extend: Copying should not be a staple of the writing curriculum at any age. The limited time available for any part of the language curriculum needs to be used wisely; most of the time for writing needs to be used creating original thoughts, putting them on paper, and sharing them with friends. Copying should be a very occasional experience used only for a special purpose determined by the child's interest.

➠ Portfolios

Objective: For children to see their progress in language skills and to begin to take responsibility for judging their strengths and needs

Procedure: Provide each child with a folder with pockets inside. Encourage the children to stamp the date on pieces of writing and artwork they think are good enough to save (or to write the date) and store them neatly in their folders. These folders are also useful for parent conferences.

To Simplify: The young children will need help keeping their folders, but they will take pride in their collection. All but a few selected items may be taken home every week.

To Extend: Lists of favorite books that have been read also can be included. When possible, include a tape recording as a sample of the child's oral language during sharing time or discussion with peers. As time allows, meet with each child to review the contents of the folder, encouraging the child to discuss how and why his or her work shows growth.

SUMMARY

As you read this chapter on the language domain, you may have been saying to yourself, "I used to believe those things; how did I get so far off base?" or "I follow many of the suggestions I read; I feel pretty good about what I am doing for children." Many of the principles presented here have dominated the professional literature on language learning for nearly a century. Recent research has dramatically reconfirmed those principles and added to them. For three generations or more, however, the education of teachers, commercial materials, and the tests that have purported to measure language growth have followed the psychology of behaviorism; language learning and the learning in other fields have been viewed from a "bottom-up" perspec-

tive, a set of separate skills that accumulate into mastery. Now cognitive psychology, holistic or "top-down" perspectives, are better understood and accepted. Early knowledge of language learning, therefore, is new again, and it is better informed by important recent research, expert opinion, and classroom practice.

In some ways the contemporary classroom educator's job teaching language is easier in developmentally appropriate programs because more natural methods are used, the interests of children are followed, and the measures used to assess children's language growth accept the complexity of factors that affect language development. On the other hand, more is expected of teachers: more planning, more selection of appropriate materials, more observation of children in natural learning settings, more record keeping. Most teachers are willing to take on new responsibilities because they soon see happier, more involved children who are learning important life skills and attitudes. Teaching is back in the teacher's control and in the control of learners.

CHAPTER 7

The Physical Domain

Seven-year-old Jesse declared, "I'm not very good at games or sports." The teacher asked, "Why do you say that, Jesse?" Jesse replied, "Because all the children laugh at me when I run, and I'm always last in races."

Jesse then participated in an individualized, instructional program that was geared to matching the child's developmental level with appropriate levels of fundamental motor skills. Jesse's self-concept improved as success in motor skills was achieved. Eleven years later as a university freshman, Jesse volunteered to be an instructor in the program!

Knowledge of how children develop physically is vital to a complete understanding of their total development. Although the pattern of growth is similar for most children, the rate at which they mature biologically varies greatly among them. The development of the muscular, skeletal, nervous, and endocrine systems creates a dynamic and complex system within each individual child that is different from that of other children of the same as well as a different chronological age. It is imperative that teachers understand that these differences in biological development can affect how children perform on a variety of physical tasks.

For example, Haubenstricker and Ewing (1985) report that a combination of selected skeletal and body fat measures accounted for 17% to 40% of the variability in distance jumped on the standing horizontal jump of girls and boys ages 8 to 14 years. Body fat, skeletal size, or body type may affect the performance of younger children as well. These anthropometric factors, for the most part, are not under the control of the child, parents, or teacher; rather, they are controlled by a genetically determined "biological clock." Biological time does not necessarily advance in congruence with age since birth. Therefore, children of similar chronological ages can vary greatly in maturation of their skeletal or nervous systems. Some children (early maturers) will grow and develop sooner than their later maturing age-mates.

During the early and middle childhood years, children experience constant growth in their arms and legs. They typically gain about 2.5 inches per year in height and about 5 pounds in weight. However, the earlier maturing children will grow more, and the later maturing will grow less (see Tables 7.1 and 7.2). For this reason, the differences in body size and weight among children increases as they grow toward adolescence. The values in Tables 7.1 and 7.2 show that for females the range in inches between the short and tall girl is 8, 9, and 11 at ages 4, 8, and 14, respectively. For weight the ranges in pounds are 25 (age 4), 40 (age 8), and 87 (age 14). Likewise for boys, their range in heights is from 7, to 8.5, to 14 inches, while their weights vary by 23, 38, and 83 pounds during those same ages.

These variabilities in size and body mass offer teachers a multidimensional challenge when planning physical activities in a coeducational setting. One needs to accommodate safely for differences not only within gender but also across gender. When girls and boys are taught together, the ranges in physical development could increase over that of within gender (Tables 7.1, 7.2). For example, at age 8 the range of mean heights from the shortest girls to the tallest boys is 10 inches, as compared to the 9-inch and 8.5-inch variabilities within gender. Likewise, for weight at age 8 the range of mean values from the lightest girls to the heaviest boys is 46 pounds, as compared to the 40 pounds and 38 pounds of variability within gender. These height and weight differences among the children have implications for the types of activities that may be appropriate as well as the size and weight of equipment used. It is important for teachers to acknowledge and prepare for these normal size ranges.

Because their body proportions are changing, children often appear clumsy and uncoordinated in the classroom or on a playground. This awkwardness is normal and occurs because a change in body size or proportion can change the center of balance in the body and can affect the ease with which children move effectively. Teachers need to understand this growth variable in order to (a) offer appropriate encouragement to children, (b) help the girls and boys understand their physical self, (c) plan a wide

---

*This chapter was written by Crystal F. Branta, Department of Physical Education and Exercise Science, Michigan State University.

TABLE 7.1
Mean Height Values (inches) for Short, Average, and Tall Children*

	Short		Average		Tall	
	F	M	F	M	F	M
4	37.0	38.0	41.0	41.5	45.0	45.0
5	39.0	40.0	43.0	43.5	47.0	47.0
6	41.0	42.5	45.0	46.0	49.5	50.0
7	43.0	44.5	47.5	48.5	52.0	53.0
8	45.0	46.5	50.0	51.0	54.0	55.0
14	57.0	57.0	62.5	64.0	68.0	71.0

*Data obtained from the height/weight chart of the American Medical Association (1978).
F = female, M = male.

TABLE 7.2
Mean Weight Values (pounds) for Light, Average, and Heavy Children*

	Light		Average		Heavy	
	F	M	F	M	F	M
4	25	30	37	40	50	53
5	27	32	40	44	55	59
6	33	37	45	50	60	67
7	35	41	50	55	70	75
8	37	45	55	60	77	83
14	73	82	112	116	160	165

*Data obtained from the height/weight chart of the American Medical Association (1978).
F = female, M = male.

variety of activities to accommodate skill levels, (d) provide activities that allow all children the maximum amount of movement time, and (e) ensure successful motor experiences for all students. Children learn to control their movements through practice and with specific instruction.

Observed behavior (e.g., motor performance), as explained from the most current theoretical perspective (dynamic systems), is affected by multiple factors (Thelen, Kelso, & Fogel, 1987; Ulrich, 1989). The nature of these factors has not been fully examined in young children. Potential physical variables could include gender, body size, strength, maturation, and mechanical changes of the body segments (specifically arm and leg length). In combination with child interest, prior experience, perceived competence, and social stimulation, these physical variables impact how

children develop and, therefore, should become important to educators (Branta, 1992).

CONTRIBUTIONS OF THE PHYSICAL DOMAIN

Children who are physically active can accrue both physical and mental benefits from their participation. The contribution of physical activity to individual well-being has been researched and documented extensively. Evidence of the benefits of physical activity has been accumulated in a lengthy volume (Seefeldt, 1986) and condensed into shorter versions (Seefeldt & Vogel, 1986; Vogel & Seefeldt, 1988). Figure 7.1 provides a listing of the documented advantages of participation in the appropriate kinds and amounts of activity.

Regular, healthy activity:

1. promotes changes in brain structure and function in infants and young children. Sensory stimulation through physical activity is essential for the optimal growth and development of the young nervous system.
2. promotes early cognitive function through imitation, symbolic play, the development of language, and the use of symbols.
3. assists in the development and refinement of perceptual abilities involving vision, balance, and tactile sensations.
4. enhances the function of the central nervous system through the promotion of a healthier neural network.
5. aids the development of cognition through opportunities to develop learning strategies by decision making; acquiring, retrieving, and integrating information; and solving problems.
6. fortifies the mineralization of the skeleton and promotes the maintenance of lean body tissue, while simultaneously reducing the deposition of fat.
7. leads to proficiency in the neuromuscular skills that are the basis for successful participation in games, dances, sports, and leisure activities.
8. is an important regulator of obesity because it increases energy expenditure, suppresses appetite, increases metabolic rate, and increases lean body mass.
9. improves aerobic fitness, muscle endurance, muscle power, and muscle strength.
10. is an effective deterrent to coronary heart disease because of its effects on blood lipids, blood pressure, obesity, and capacity for physical work.
11. improves cardiac function as indicated by an increased stroke volume, cardiac output, blood volume, and total hemoglobin.
12. is associated with a reduction in atherosclerotic diseases.
13. promotes a more positive attitude toward physical activity and leads to a more active lifestyle during unscheduled leisure time.
14. enhances self-concept and self-esteem as indicated by increased confidence, assertiveness, emotional stability, independence, and self-control.
15. is a major force in the socializing of individuals during late childhood and adolescence.
16. is instrumental in the development and growth of moral reasoning, problem solving, creativity, and social competence.
17. is an effective deterrent to mental illness and the alleviation of mental stress.
18. improves the psychosocial and physiological functions of individuals with mental and physical disabilities.
19. deters the depletion of bone mineral and lean body tissue in elderly individuals.
20. prevents the onset of some diseases and postpones the debilitating effects of old age.

FIGURE 7.1

The Benefits of Participation in the Appropriate Kinds and Amounts of Physical Activity*

*Source: From *The Value of Physical Activity* (pp. 1–2) by V. Seefeldt and P. G. Vogel, 1986, Reston, VA: American Alliance For Health, Physical Education, Recreation, and Dance.

Clearly, the overall development of a child can be enhanced by regular physical activity. In order for children to obtain these benefits, though, they must (a) be able to perform a variety of basic motor skills and (b) be motivated to participate in vigorous, physical activity regularly. These two conditions, then, become im-

portant for teachers as they plan for the physical and motor development of the children under their tutelage.

Achievement in the motor domain can have long-lasting effects for individuals as adults and as senior citizens. Major health risk factors can be decreased through activity, while the cognitive and emotional functioning of individuals are improved. Development in the ability to perform motor skills contributes to the establishment of a stable, positive self-concept, especially for young children. Movement is the focus of their lives, and motor ability (or lack thereof) affects how children think of themselves as well as how they are perceived and treated by their peers, parents, and other adults. Success in the motor area will aid in the development of a conviction of personal worthiness for children that carries over into other aspects of their lives and into adulthood.

DEVELOPMENTAL SEQUENCES

During the preschool and early elementary years, children acquire and begin to refine a wide variety of fundamental motor skills. The development of such skills proceeds in a sequential order, from a most rudimentary attempt to a mature, efficient performance. Development of competence in skills such as balancing, throwing, catching, kicking, punting, striking, running, jumping, galloping, hopping, and skipping follows a predictable sequence of movement characteristics or stages. For example, throwing develops from the initial stage, characterized by a downward chopping motion of the arm with the hand beginning near the ear and a stationary base of support facing forward. The mature stage utilizes sequential rotation of the body, a sideward orientation, and a contralateral (right arm, left leg) step toward a target. The continuum of development from initial to mature provides several intermediate stages that reflect how children learn to throw.

Extraneous movements of the legs and using the chest to "hug" the ball are common characteristics of initial catching behavior.

The mature form of catching involves adjusting to the flights of the ball, reaching for the object, and securing with the hands only.

For example, in the skill of catching, children display different levels of ability to secure the ball. The first series of pictures depict a child at an intermediate level of performance. He has difficulty adjusting his body to the flight of the ball, must use his body to be successful in securing the ball, and must be provided with a larger object in order to catch it. The next series of pictures show an 8-year-old boy exhibiting a mature catch. He is able to position his body under the ball, reach toward the ball, and secure it with his hands only.

Progression through the developmental stages of each fundamental motor skill sequence takes time, instruction, and many practice opportunities. Exposure to a wide variety of manipulative,

locomotor, and stability movements should be the motor focus of the preschool years. Developing mature levels in these skills should be the goal of the early elementary years.

All children do not develop efficient movement patterns as a result of exposure to their normal environments, however (Miller, 1978). Learning occurs partially through imitation and exploration, but for some children these opportunities are not readily available or only available to a limited degree. Teachers can facilitate the motor learning of all children by planning a developmental program of motor skill activities that should provide opportunities for maximum involvement, encouragement, specific feedback on performance, and challenges appropriately geared to individual children. The ultimate goals of a developmental program for children would be (a) improvement of skill levels, (b) increase in health fitness, (c) attainment of success, and (d) development of a positive attitude toward active lifestyles.

CURRENT EDUCATIONAL ISSUES

In each domain there are issues important to that area's specialists with implications for teaching. The physical domain is no exception. Research has been conducted in numerous subdomains (e.g., motor behavior, exercise physiology, sport psychology, sport sociology, pedagogy) that provide information relevant for examination.

1. *Motor skills do* not *develop as a result of maturation alone.* Many parents and teachers believe that if an area is provided for free play or recess, children will acquire mature levels of motor skills automatically through their everyday play. While opportunities to explore movement and a stimulating activity environment are important factors in skill acquisition, the most critical variable in achieving proficiency in motor development is the quality of instruction provided to the children. Miller (1978) has found a significant difference between the motor skill development of preschool children taught by either a specialist or trained parents and those who were allowed free play with the same equipment for an equivalent amount of time. It is encouraging to note here that the parents who were trained by the specialist in specific aspects of skill development were as effective as the specialist in this short program of assisting their children's motor development. Possibly, the individual attention provided by the parents to their children offset the expertise of the specialist in a larger group.

One would not expect children to develop a proficiency in, for example, math by merely playing in a math center. Developmental instruction involving such concepts as patterns, grouping, adding, and subtracting would be needed. In addition, activities should be provided to enhance (a) each child's understanding of the concepts and (b) his or her proficiency in performing appropriate problems. Likewise, in the

motor domain developmental instruction and a variety of activities need to be offered for children to acquire mature levels in fundamental motor skills.

2. *Physical education should be taught by specialists and classroom teachers.* Motor development teachers and classroom teachers should work together to provide a coherent and meaningful activity program. Specialists should take the lead in developing goals and objectives for the program and should provide in-service workshops for classroom teachers.

These sessions should concentrate on reaching an understanding of the total physical education program and organizing appropriate activities that will complement the instruction by the specialist. Specific teaching cues and performance standards should be explained and practiced so that classroom teachers feel willing and competent in their vital instructional roles. The National Health Objectives for the year 2000 (U.S. Department of Health & Human Services, 1980) have set a standard for activity that could be met by quality, daily physical education of at least 30 minutes for every child in grades K through 12. The only realistic (i.e., financially feasible) way in which this objective will be met is for classroom teachers to become involved in direct instruction of physical activity as part of their planned day.

3. *Motor development is a "real" school subject.* Developed and taught correctly, motor development programs will improve a child's life immeasurably in several domains, as previously discussed. A good program will identify specific, attainable objectives based on the available research, direct the instruction toward those outcomes, and evaluate how well the objectives are being accomplished. When motor development is included as an important part of instruction, the goal of educating the whole child is more easily achieved.

4. *Specific skill learning is age related but not age dependent.* In general, as children age they can perform more complicated motor skills providing that the prerequisite skills have been mastered. However, the ability to perform high-level sport skills is not dependent on reaching certain chronological ages. There are numerous examples of young, coordinated individuals playing intense hockey or basketball or competing in

elite gymnastics, figure skating, or tennis. Sometimes changes need to be made in the size and weight of equipment (e.g., shorter hockey stick, junior basketball) or in how the skill is performed (e.g., two-handed backhand in tennis). But many young children have the neuromuscular development to perform these skills, while many adults do not. The chief differentiating factor between the two is the degree to which the necessary prerequisite skills have been mastered.

During the early childhood years, the focus of skill development should be on the acquisition of a wide variety of fundamental motor skills. These skills provide a large base repertoire on which to draw as children try the tasks involved in organized games, specific sports, and dances. Without the fundamental skills, children find it difficult to move efficiently and easily. They often experience failure, frustration, and criticism from their peers. It has been my experience as director of the Remedial Motor Clinic at Michigan State University that the children (ages 5–13) most often referred for clumsiness or lack of desire to be active are those children who never developed their fundamental motor skills fully. So, although the ability to perform skills is not age dependent, the necessity of mastering the basic skills should be directed toward the preschool and lower elementary years.

5. *Girls are often socialized away from vigorous physical activity at young ages.* Physical size differences between boys and girls are minimal from birth to adolescence and, therefore, should have little impact on ability to move. In fact, maturation favors girls in the ability to learn and perform complex movements, especially those involving eye-hand coordination (e.g., catching, striking, cutting). The central nervous system of females is usually more advanced than that of males at these ages. However, societal expectations favor motor skills for boys. Male infants often have Nerf footballs or baseball gloves placed in their cribs, while females receive stuffed animals or dolls. Boys are allowed and encouraged to be active; girls often are requested to be quiet and "ladylike." Garcia (1992) has found that girls ages 2 to 5 were reluctant to hit balls forcefully and preferred cooperative, interactive games with a partner or groups. Boys in her study were independent, forceful movers and dominated their equipment and the teacher's time. They enjoyed individual competition. Implications of the socialization research for teaching are that girls need to be monitored and encouraged in their physical capacities in order to be able to move forcefully and effectively when necessary. In addition, boys should be taught skills in cooperative play.

6. *Fine and gross motor skills are interrelated but not prerequisite to each other.* It is important for children to have instruction and practice opportunities in skills that require both fine motor and gross motor control. Difficulty in one area does not predict delayed development in the other. A few children are motorically delayed in fine and gross skills. They are usually the later maturing children whose central nervous system is not mature enough to help them handle the demands of the tasks. However, the vast majority of children who have problems in one area do not have difficulties in the other. Many of the clients enrolled in the Remedial Motor Clinic for gross motor delay had compensated for their lack of talent by developing their fine motor skills (e.g., reading, building with Legos®). It is important for parents and teachers to value the development of fine and gross motor skills without attaching significance to the order in which their children acquire these abilities.

7. *Handwriting is a fine motor skill that develops sequentially over time.* In the early stages of handwriting, children often use large sets of muscles for control. They will tense their entire arms and shoulders and lean over their work. Consequently, their muscles fatigue quickly, and performance deteriorates rapidly. It is important, then, to provide many practice opportunities of short duration to maximize success.

Children also must experiment with the various types of gripping behaviors. For example, in his classic study of infant grasping motions, Halverson (1931) showed developmental levels of grasps from a nonspecific reach toward a block, to a palmar grasp with thumb and fingers on the same side of the block, to a grasp where the thumb opposed the fingers, and finally to pincer prehension. Teacher observations as well as this developmental study suggest that preschool and early elementary children will experiment

Early attempts at writing involve using large muscle groups and result in the formation of large, skewed letters.

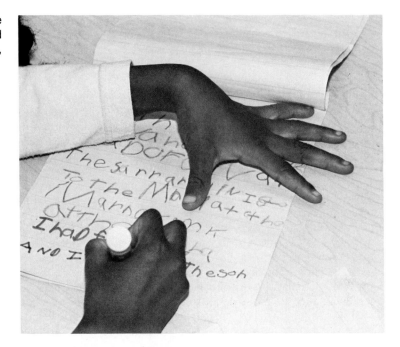

with these grasping forms in their attempts at forming letters and words.

Based on our knowledge of motor development, children should be provided with many varied opportunities to practice their handwriting skills. In the beginning, they should be given larger tools that are easy to grip, should be shown correct form, but should *not* be forced into a particular writing mode. As children mature and gain competence, they benefit from demonstrations of correct form and relaxed opportunities for practice. Children whose writing is legible should not be pressured to concentrate on handwriting mechanics since it may interfere with idea generation. Second or third graders who tire easily or whose writing is unreadable may require individualized strategies, including ones related to posture, trunk and shoulder stability, pencil grip, and correct form in order to improve (Oliver, 1990; Soderman, 1991).

8. *Health fitness is a relevant concern for the preschool and elementary school environment.* Children need to understand what constitutes healthful lifestyles, and their attitudes toward healthy activity patterns need to be established at young ages. Research on appropriate levels of fitness for young children and how these levels should be reliably measured is sparse. However, the concept of sustained activity (duration) is an important one to teach from preschool on (Branta, 1992). Results of a pilot study administered to twenty-two 4-year-old children provided evidence of the feasibility of assessing fitness via sustained activity levels (Branta, 1992). A "child-friendly" (posters, balloons, music, stickers, positive adult models) rectangular course was used to test the youngsters on their ability to complete a 9-minute walk-run test protocol (McSwegin, Pemberton, Petray, & Going, 1989). Twenty-one of the children finished the 9-minute activity, were happy, and showed pride in their accomplishments. Futhermore, their scores ranked around the 25th percentile rank of distances run by 5- to 6-year-olds. It is important for the initial strength and long-term health of young children that teachers appreciate the concept of sustained activity and incorporate it into their program plans.

GOALS AND OBJECTIVES

The ultimate goals of the physical domain are for children to achieve physical competence and for them to develop knowledge, attitudes, skills, and behaviors toward a healthy lifestyle. In order to accomplish these goals, intermediate curricular objectives will be utilized.

Mediating Objectives

As children progress toward the ultimate goal, they will

1. develop their abilities in a variety of fundamental motor skills. For example, they should become more adept in locomotor (walk, run, roll, gallop, slide, hop, skip, jump), manipulative (throw, catch, kick, punt, strike), and stability (swing, sway, twist, turn, bend, stretch) movements by having daily practice to use these large-muscle skills.
2. practice fine motor skills and increase small-muscle coordination through daily play activities with such items as pegboards, puzzles, paint, scissors, clay, sand, chalk, markers.
3. attain and maintain adequate levels of regular, sustained activity with activities such as walking, jogging, dancing, climbing, riding bikes, or completing obstacle courses.
4. learn about their bodies and how the various body segments move by identifying their five senses, describing the function of each, and matching a body part with each sense. They will gain confidence in their bodies by matching body segments with a variety of possible movements and executing skills that require coordination, flexibility, and agility.
5. describe and experience movement space, direction and laterality (e.g., personal space, general space, forward, backward, sideward, diagonally, and in various patterns).
6. increase their knowledge of factors important to health by (a) developing good nutritional habits (e.g., choosing nutritious foods over those with less nutritional value), (b) learning how to keep their bodies fit (e.g., getting proper sleep, exercising), (c) practicing appropriate personal hygiene (e.g., washing hands), and (d) learning safety procedures (e.g., identifying safety rules, recognizing safe practices and dangerous situations).
7. develop a positive body image and physical self concept by experiencing success in movement and health-related skills and in respecting and controlling their bodies.

TEACHING STRATEGIES

Teachers can employ many specific strategies to increase the chance of their students having success in the physical domain.

1. *Organize instruction for maximum on-task time.* Plan so that all children will be physically active for the greatest amount of time possible. Minimize logistical activities such as grouping, regrouping, taking attendance, or getting the initial attention of students. Provide activities that complement the objectives for the children to do as they enter the teaching station.
2. *Provide a piece of equipment for each child.* Children will have more specific practice time and develop skills quicker by continuing their practice without standing in lines or waiting turns. If there is not enough manipulative equipment (balls, bats, beanbags, etc.), then organize numerous other stations. These groups could be assigned to an area for climbing or practicing balance, a space for challenge activities such as tripods and tip-ups, an area to practice various locomotor skills, or an obstacle course to combine different movement activities.
3. *Use demonstrations.* A visual model is much more powerful than verbal instruction in helping children learn and perfect motor skills. Concentrate on the most salient parts of the movement that children need to acquire. Demonstrate from a variety of views and angles to improve the children's overall perceptions of the movement to be practiced.
4. *Emphasize qualitative movement over quantitative outcomes.* The key to developing effective, efficient movements is to concentrate on the form needed or pattern used to execute the skill. For example, in throwing, one should view the body orientation to the target, the step on the opposite foot to the throwing arm, the rotation used throughout the body, and the wind-up and follow-through of the arm. Product outcomes such as distance, velocity, or accuracy should not be attended to prior to the child's developing a mature throwing pattern. Likewise, in catching, the pathway of the arms and hands should be viewed rather than merely recording the number of successful catches.
5. *Plan for success of each child each day.* Activities should be provided so that children can practice skills appropriately at their own de-

Large, soft balls rolled along the floor help this preschool child learn to secure the ball using only his hands.

velopmental level. By conducting ongoing evaluation of the progress of children, teachers will be aware of the needs of specific students. Skill drills can then be modified or redesigned to offer appropriate challenges to the children. Or children can be grouped differently so that they get the proper stimulation for advancing their skills.

6. *Provide positive, specific feedback as soon as possible.* Specific feedback should be given students that is contingent on performance. For example, it is better to say "Step with your other foot the next time. You will have more power!" than "Good job of stepping." The feedback should also be congruent with the objective of the day. If the activities are designed to enhance weight transfer, then provide feedback on that point and not, for instance, arm positioning.

7. *Emphasize cooperative games and individual achievement.* Competition at young ages is not appropriate. The rewards should be designed so that they recognize individual improvement or group gains (e.g., everyone can kick a ball by using a backswing). Group games should be developed so that the orientation is

toward performance of the team rather than outcome of the game. Individual achievement can be recognized by providing points based on the day's focus. For example, if weight transfer prior to kicking is the objective, then children should be given points (or other rewards) for the number of times they used weight transfer while practicing the kick individually or in a group game.

8. *Develop extended learning opportunities.* Give students homework connected to the physical domain. This action indicates to children that the teacher considers motor skills, fitness, and health as important aspects of their development. It also serves as a tool to communicate with parents and get their involvement in the physical development of their children. For example, teachers could ask parents to walk or bike with their children for a specific number of minutes on the weekend. The homework assignment is more effective when it is accompanied by a rationale for the request, an explanation of how the activity fits into the curriculum, or a description of benefits to the child and family

9. *Set attainable goals.* Achievement is increased when teachers have high but realistic

Body Actions	Form and Shape
Alone-together	Big-little
Alternate	High-low
Freeze-relax	Long-short
Tense-collapse	Open-close
	Straight-crooked

Space and Direction	Time and Force
Above-below	Fast-slow
Around-through-	Heavy-light
between	Loud-soft
Away from–close to	Soft-hard
Forward-backward-	Strong-weak
sideward	
Front-back-behind-	
beside	
In-out	
Left-right	
Near-far	
Over-under	
Toward-away	
Up-down	

FIGURE 7.2
Concepts Easily Learned through Movements

expectations of their students' learning (Rutter, Maugham, Mortmore, & Ousten, 1979). Teachers should expect improvement and be committed to assisting students in achieving higher levels of skills. Instructors should communicate exactly what needs to be learned and should provide feedback so that the students understand their own progress.

10. *Teach cognitive concepts easily learned through movement.* Concepts such as space and direction (e.g., far-near, forward-backward), time and force (e.g., fast-slow, hard-soft), form and shape (e.g., circles, lines, weaves), and body actions (e.g., twist-turn, alone-together) are taught effectively via the physical domain (see Figure 7.2). When children move, the concepts are truly understood by them and can then be applied in other domains. In addition, this strategy helps integrate the physical and cognitive domains and provides for improved learning on the part of the child.

11. *Give children a variety of developmentally organized and developmentally appropriate activi-*

ties in each skill area. This strategy serves to increase interest on the part of the child and improves chances of success as there should be an activity available on the developmental continuum that is geared toward the level of the child. Provide a variety of experiences so that children may engage in fundamental skills, physical fitness activities, and movements requiring balance, flexibility, agility, muscular strength and endurance, and control. Certain enjoyable activities could serve as incentives or rewards as well.

12. *Emphasize a child's strengths.* Help children develop positive attitudes toward their bodies by stressing their abilities and assisting in improving their weaknesses. Let them know what they are capable of accomplishing in the physical domain, and assist them in using their strengths to their advantage. Discuss with children the importance of physical fitness and health. Help them identify ways to improve or maintain their physical state.

13. *Model physical activity.* Be an advocate for physical development by participating in physical activity. Describe to children your involvement in activity and help make it relevant to their lives. Keep them up-to-date on participatory events (e.g., "Crop Walk," "Magic Bike Ride") within the community that could benefit health. Bring in community leaders that are good role models. Be enthusiastic and active in class.

ACTIVITY SUGGESTIONS

Numerous activities, games, and skill drills exist to assist teachers in offering appropriate, developmental tasks and challenges for their students. The most effective activities are those teachers design themselves or modify from sourcebooks to accommodate individual school situations. This section provides a few activities to stimulate some ideas.

➠ Clean Up Your Yard

Objective: For children to become more adept at throwing or kicking with force

Procedure: Form two groups, one on each side of the room. Place a divider (such as balance beam, low table, cones) between groups. Give each group numerous soft objects such as yarn balls, foam shapes, pillow balls, or beanbags to throw into the other group's backyard. Both groups continue to throw simultaneously back and forth. If this activity is used for throwing, the objects used should be small enough to be gripped easily with one hand. If this is designed as a kicking activity, the objects need to be larger (approximately 8 in. in diameter or greater).

To Simplify: Have only one group (the whole class) perform at a time by throwing objects to the other side. Then, on cue, ask them to execute a specified locomotor skill to the other side where they will throw all balls back. One may also decrease time spent in the activity. For throwing, a lower barrier will make the task easier.

To Extend: Widen the barrier area (e.g., double rows of cones 15 ft apart). For throwing, increase the height of the barrier (e.g., use a volleyball net, or drape a sheet over a horizontal ladder).

➠ Kick the Can

Objective: For children to become more adept at kicking while moving

Procedure: Place light objects (plastic bowling pins, stacks of foam shapes, detergent bottles) around the area on the floor. On signal, all children run up to and kick over as many items as possible.

To Simplify: Give each child three objects and their own personal space in which to perform. Have them kick toward a wall or net to contain the objects.

To Extend: Place pictures or tape marks on the floor about a foot before the object. Have children leap over the mark prior to kicking. Have children try kicking with their nonpreferred foot.

➠ Walk, Jog, Run

Objective: For children to practice changing pace while using these locomotor skills

Procedure: Discuss the difference among walking, jogging, and running in terms of speed (slow, fast, very fast). Let children practice changing pace by using large letter cards (W, J, R) for signals as children move around the play area.

To Simplify: Have children move in rows in only one direction. Use only one card per trip across the area.

To Extend: Set up a course of cones, ropes, or other barriers. Have children walk, jog, and run through the course on instructor signal. Change signals frequently. Place directional cards throughout course and have children complete the appropriate movements.

➠ Jump the Brook

Objective: For children to practice their horizontal jump

Procedure: Place two ropes or lines on the floor in a horizontal, open-ended V pattern: ◁‾‾ Have children bend knees, then swing arms forward to jump over the brook. Pretend there are alligators in the "water." Let children decide to jump the narrow or wide parts of the brook.

To Simplify: Place two ropes parallel to each other 6 to 8 inches apart.

To Extend: Place a series of six colored lines about 12 inches apart on the floor. Encourage children to self-test for distance. Emphasize straight arms, overhead at take-off.

➠ Partner Catch

Objective: For children to increase their eye-hand coordination and improve their catching pattern.

Procedure: Partners stand approximately 5 feet from each other. They bounce the ball toward their partner who attempts a hands-only catch. Balls used for catching should be large, about 8 to 10 inches in diameter.

To Simplify: Partners should sit or kneel and roll ball back and forth. Emphasize reaching toward the oncoming ball.

To Extend: Partners should use an underhand toss and catch the ball in the air. Emphasize moving to the ball, reaching with the hands, and "giving" with the ball at contact. Gradually decrease the size of the ball down to a tennis ball. Gradually increase the distance between partners.

➠ Strike the Ball

Objective: For children to improve eye-hand coordination and striking ability

Procedure: Have children strike a stationary ball from a tee or a suspended Nerf ball. Emphasize a horizontal swing, and have them step forward onto a footprint to encourage the development of contralateral weight transfer.

To Simplify: Let children hit balloons across floor with their hands, a ping-pong paddle, or small homemade implements such as paper towel rolls or paddles made with coat hangers and nylon netting.

To Extend: Have children strike a moving ball by either swinging the suspended Nerf ball or tossing the ball. Gradually decrease the ball size and increase the distance between tosser and batter. Give reinforcement for use of a contralateral weight transfer.

➠ Skip-It

Objective: For children to become adept at skipping and maintaining beat

Procedure: Place a series of footprints and carpet squares to allow for a continuous step-hop pattern so that the children step onto a footprint and hop onto the carpet square with the same foot, then repeat using the other foot:

Step   Hop

To Simplify: Have children walk like a monster. Start each step from a slightly lowered body position and roll up onto the balls of feet. Gradually add a hop.

To Extend: Have children clap the rhythmical pattern of the skip while skipping to the beat of music, drum, or tambourine.

➠ Fun Run

Objective: For children to improve their levels of sustained activity

Procedure: Have children jog continuously by pretending to carry the Olympic torch (mail bag, apples) from one to the other. Play music and strive for 10 to 15 minutes of activity.

To Simplify: Pretend the group is going on a hike. Walk, jog, run, or swim as a story (e.g., running from a bear) is made up about what the group is experiencing. Maintain activity for a shorter time.

To Extend: Have children jog in place, around the area, backward, and forward. Increase the pace to a run. Increase continuous activity time.

➠ Dance Routine

Objective: For children to improve levels of endurance and agility

Procedure: Choose popular children's songs. Have children perform various movements (e.g., run, gallop, jump, hop, slide, skip) during the song. Add additional movements that utilize arms such as skating and skiing. Maintain movement throughout song.

To Simplify: Have children execute a repeating pattern of movements that has low-level activity (e.g., walking) placed between the patterns.

To Extend: Have children make up vigorous dance routines. Add calisthenic movements such as jumping jacks and knee lifts to the locomotor skills.

➠ Balance Blocks

Objective: For children to experience maintaining balance in a variety of positions

Procedure: Have children stand on a balance block (about 12 in. long and made out of 4 × 4, 2 × 2, or 2 × 4 boards). The blocks should be on a nonslippery surface. Have children stand on each foot and change body positions by placing the nonsupport leg and both arms in a variety of poses. Experiment with leaning the trunk forward, backward, and sideward.

To Simplify: Have children do the balance activities on a line on the floor.

To Extend: Execute the balances on a raised beam. Gradually increase the height of the beam.

Add locomotor movements such as walking or sliding and practice turning skills.

➠ Suspended Horizontal Ladder

Objective: For children to increase muscular strength in their upper arms and shoulder girdle

Procedure: Have children hang from one of the rungs of a suspended horizontal ladder and swing their bodies back and forth for 10 to 15 seconds. The height of the ladder should be 1 to 2 feet higher than the child's reach.

To Simplify: Let children simply jump up and hang suspended for 5 to 10 seconds. Some children may need to be assisted in the jump up or into the proper grip and body position.

To Extend: Have children travel from one end of the ladder to the other using a follow (or mark time) grasp. Work up to using an alternating grasp.

➠ Move and Listen

Objective: For children to enhance body awareness and improve listening skills and body control

Procedure: Have children perform different locomotor tasks around the area and freeze on signal. Have them stop on

- one foot.
- both feet.
- seat and both feet.
- back.
- hands and knees.
- feet and fingers.
- elbows and knees.
- head and feet.
- head, hands, and feet.
- one foot and one hand.
- head, two hands, one foot.
- seat and hands.
- seat and elbows.
- side.

To Simplify: Let children choose their own way of moving and freezing in different body positions.

To Extend: Permit children to problem solve by asking them to balance on five, four, three, two, and finally one body part. Let them work as one unit with partners and solve the problems again. See how many combinations partner groups can make.

➠ Geoboard Shapes

Objective: For children to have practice in fine motor manipulative activities

Procedure: Construct a geoboard by placing pegs in a 5-row by 5-column shape on a pegboard or by using nails in wood. Have children stretch rubber bands around the pegs or nails to make large, medium, and small shapes. Make triangles, squares, and rectangles.

To Simplify: Have children copy shapes that are traced on the geoboard.

To Extend: Encourage children to make their own designs by overlapping rubber bands and using different colors.

➠ Pattern Blocks

Objective: For children to increase fine motor skills in sorting and building

Procedure: Use blocks of various colors, shapes, and sizes. Have children construct a three-level design while using as many blocks as possible.

To Simplify: Ask children to sort the blocks by color, shapes, or size. Have them copy one- or two-level designs that have solid bases of support.

To Extend: Encourage children to extend their designs to five or more levels. Let them experiment with designs that have decreasing bases of support. Have them work in partners, taking turns placing a block chosen by the partner.

CHAPTER 8

The Social Domain

From one corner of the preschool room comes the following interchange:

"I want that truck."
"But I had it first."
"I still want it."
"You can have it when I'm done."
"Be fast."

Ms. Roth's kindergartners are on their way to visit the local fire station. Their mission is to find out how the fire fighters work and live and the ways in which they protect the community. The children have generated a list of questions they will try to answer through observations and discussion. One of their aims is to note diversity among the staff at the station. The children have brought paper, pencils, and markers in order to record, in any way they can, what they discover.

The first-grade class at the Greenleaf Elementary School embarks on a project to map the playground. Initially, they measure the space, choosing "footsteps" as their unit of measure. After much discussion, the children decide to create three-dimensional models of the playground equipment using boxes of various sizes and shapes. Small groups of children are taking responsibility for representing different areas of the schoolyard.

It is late October, and Mr. Hwang's second graders have been learning about the upcoming elections in their city, county, and state. The youngsters have demonstrated a great interest in voting, and lively discussions have arisen over issues of "fairness." When a guinea pig is offered as a class pet, the children ask if they can hold an election to choose a name for it.

While these scenarios depict children of different ages in a variety of school settings, they all represent a part of the social domain. The social domain encompasses four essential aspects of children's development and education. The first of these, social skill development, deals with the ways children learn to interact with others. So-

cialization is the process by which children learn to understand and adapt to rules. Children's social responsibility is a measure of their respect for individual differences, care of the environment, and their ability to function as good citizens (e.g., by resolving conflicts peacefully). Finally, social studies or social science is the curricular area that focuses on the whole of human behavior, now and in the past. Because of its roots in the traditional social science disciplines such as anthropology, economics, human ecology, geography, psychology, and the like, social studies provides us with an organizing principle around which to plan programs for children. Thus, although each facet of the social domain is not the same as any of the others, they are inextricably linked.

There are many possible approaches to addressing children's social development and teaching social studies in the early childhood curriculum (Brewer, 1992). One strategy is to treat social studies as a separate content area with a body of knowledge to be learned through formal experiences. Proponents believe that children could be learning more specific knowledge than is traditionally taught to them. A second view is that the most important concepts of both social studies and social skills are best learned through the naturally occurring interactions within the classroom and that it is inappropriate to focus on specific content. This chapter will present a means for combining the best of these two so that children learn content related to social studies in ways that are relevant to them, while developing the social competencies they need through productive interactions with others.

Teaching within the social domain provides children with opportunities to develop knowledge and skills regarding themselves in relationship to people in their near environment and to extend this information to understanding human relationships in the larger world. The family is the foundation of these learnings, while the classroom is often the place where children are confronted with ideas and people both similar to and different from themselves. During the early school years, children are figuring out how to establish and maintain relationships with members of their group. As time goes on, they explore their contribution to the well-being of the group. Throughout this period, they are continu-

This chapter was written by Laura C. Stein, Department of Family and Child Ecology, Michigan State University.

ally working out how to value others and how to understand and cope with the differences they encounter. Thus, the classroom functions as a "human relations laboratory" in which children explore social knowledge, concepts, and skills via daily interactions, routines, activities, and on-the-spot instructions (Reed, 1966). It is the place in which they assimilate values and attitudes about other people from listening and watching the adults around them. It is also the arena in which they practice citizenship in its most basic forms. Through their social encounters and activities, children build their understanding of history, sociology, economics, and culture. These are by no means the only issues they face, but they are so important that teachers have to know how to address them.

To derive an understanding of the social domain, it is necessary to look at its individual pieces. We will begin with a discussion of social skill development, including children's friendships and prosocial behavior, with an emphasis on the roles adults play.

SOCIAL SKILL DEVELOPMENT

Establishing relationships with others, learning to live within the bounds of societal expectations, and figuring out one's place in the group are all major tasks of early childhood and reflect aspects of children's social development. Indeed, as children mature, more of their time and energy becomes devoted to this area of their development. This is especially true as they move beyond their family and neighborhood and come into greater contact with community institutions, such as early childhood centers and elementary schools. In these circumstances, children encounter new sets of expectations to which they must adapt.

How well children perceive, interpret, and respond to the variety of social situations they meet is a measure of their social competence (Hendrick, 1990). A high level of social competence in our society means that a person exhibits responsible, independent, friendly, cooperative, purposeful, and self-controlled behavior. Youngsters with low levels of social competence, by contrast, act irresponsibly, timidly, hostilely, uncooperatively, or impulsively (Baumrind, 1970). Children who dis-

play socially competent behaviors are perceived in more positive ways by society, are therefore treated in a more positive manner, and the children thus experience more satisfying interpersonal interactions and are happier than their less successful counterparts. Furthermore, research demonstrates that children's social competence influences their academic as well as their social performance (Alexander & Entwisle, 1988). Finally, children who are socially competent experience high self-esteem, viewing themselves as worthwhile, capable people, which has positive effects on their social performance.

Children are not born knowing how to make friends and influence people, nor do they come into this world understanding the rules their society has established. It takes time as well as many varied experiences for them to master the skills that are necessary for successful functioning in society (Kostelnik & Stein, 1990). Children spend much of their early lives trying out a panoply of strategies in order to make sense of their social world. Through experimentation, they begin to figure out what works and what does not and under which circumstances. Once in school, their task becomes even more complex. Some of their actions may not lead to the same satisfactory outcomes as was true in former situations. For example, children may become bewildered when after having been taught to work together with others on projects in preschool, their "team" efforts suddenly are viewed as "cheating" in higher grades. Or youngsters accustomed to talking openly with adults about transgressions of their playmates may be labeled "tattle-tale" by their peers in school. Thus, children still have much to learn about the two major aspects of social development—socialization and social skills.

Children's social development can be looked at as the foundation upon which other types of learning takes place. Apart from nutrition and physical comfort, the need for human association is basic (Maslow, 1970). This further implies that until individuals' essential needs, including positive association with others, have been met, they are unable to move beyond those realms into other areas of learning (i.e., academic, cognitive). Thus, instructional time spent on social development that heretofore has been regarded as "icing on the cake" must, instead, be treated as an essential ingredient of that cake.

There are several critical issues of children's social development that impact directly on their lives at school that must be considered. The first of these primarily involves children's relationship with peers—that is, making and keeping friends and demonstrating prosocial behaviors, such as helping and cooperating. Another centers on children's interactions with adults, as they begin to figure out how to fit their behavior to adult expectations and rules. And, finally, learning to understand and appreciate differences in a diverse society and responding as a democratic citizen is a critical focus of youngsters' associations with both grown-ups and children as they develop.

Children's Friendships

Five-year-olds Bo and Casey are playing with dinosaur models in the dinosaur habitat. They are deeply engrossed in their activity, moving the figures from place to place and actively communicating with one another their ideas for the scenario. Jimmy walks over, picks up a dinosaur, and tosses it into the middle of the play area.

"Hey," says Bo, "you can't put it there. That's the water hole."

"Yeah," adds Casey. "Besides, you're not on our team!"

"I am so, if I wanna be," Jimmy asserts, angrily standing up with his hands on his hips.

"No, you can't," Bo responds.

"Teacher, they won't let me be on their team!" wails Jimmy.

Until fairly recently, most educators assumed that making and keeping friends were aspects of life that some children were better at than others but that there was nothing much that could or should be done about it at school. They reasoned that it was most appropriate for children to deal with this issue on the playground or before and after school rather than allow instructional time to be used. At most, the playground supervisor was expected to deal with children who were having school problems.

Those youngsters having persistent difficulty were referred to the school counselor or administrator. We now are more aware of the negative impact that disharmony in social relations has on children's abilities to concentrate on school subjects and, as a consequence, their school achievement. Furthermore, we know also that much can be accomplished by teachers and classroom aides in helping children become more successful in their friendship strategies (Asher, Oden, & Gottman, 1977; Combs & Slaby, 1978; Kostelnik et al., in press). To effectively assist children in improving their friendship skills, adults must understand the role that friendship plays in children's lives.

Why Friends Are Important.   As they mature, children become increasingly interested in establishing friendships (Hartup, 1983). In fact, it has been documented that by age 7, most children find it almost unthinkable not to have a friend (Hendrick, 1990). Among other benefits, friends provide stimulation, assistance, companionship, social comparison, and affection (Parker & Gottman, 1989). Furthermore, within a friendship children can experiment with a number of social roles, such as leader, follower, risk taker, or comforter. In essence, children develop a sense of belonging and security through the special relationship with a friend.

Life without friends can appear fairly bleak. While truly friendless children are few in number, there is evidence that poor peer relationships in childhood lead to difficulties later in life (Dodge, Petit, McClosky, & Brown, 1986; Hartup & Moore, 1990; Parker & Asher, 1987). For instance, adolescent delinquency and emotional instability have been linked to friendlessness in the early years. Naturally, just as in the case of adults, children vary in how many friends they want to have. Some are content with one "best" friend, while others seek a wide circle of friends. It is the quality of these relationships that counts more than the quantity (Stocking, Arrezzo, & Leavitt, 1980).

Children's Changing Ideas about Friendship.   Children's ideas of what constitutes a friend change as they grow older. Significantly, children at various stages of development view friends very differently from adults. It is valuable for adults to look at this developmental process in order to assess and facilitate children's relationships with one another more constructively.

In the early stages of friendship, children are preoccupied with their own emotions. They concentrate on youngsters who are available, as well as on their physical attractiveness or other outward characteristics and their material possessions (Selman & Selman, 1979). As part of their focus on the here and now, children between the ages of 3 and 7 are better at initiating relationships than sustaining them, and they may also inadvertently rebuff the advances of others because they are simply not very good at picking up friendship cues. They sometimes have difficulty entering an ongoing play situation or accepting others who wish to join, as illustrated in the example given earlier (Kostelnik et al., in press). Adults who observe these difficulties often view these children as being heartless and inconsiderate instead of recognizing that they are experiencing a cognitive dilemma, that of centering on one way to carry out the play episode.

Somewhat later in their understanding of friends, between the ages of 4 and 9, children begin to look for pleasing behaviors from others. This may entail giving one another turns, sharing toys, or deliberately choosing to sit together. Although children seem content with their choices, some of these relationships may not always appear equal in the eyes of an adult. They worry when children select friends that seem to be uncongenial companions, ones that are bossy or overly compliant, for instance. It is difficult for teachers and others to stand by when children persist in these types of friendships. Parents and educators are often tempted to separate these youngsters forcibly. It is important to remember that children are deriving benefits from these relationships that are not always apparent to adults. For example, they may use their companion as a model for their own future behavior. Thus, the shy child may observe the bossy child achieve his or her aims through assertiveness and may ultimately try out a few of those strategies. Similarly, the bossy child may admire the more modest approach of his or her peer. If, as the children as-

sume different behaviors within the friendship, their relationship flexes to accommodate these new variables, youngsters may continue to remain close companions. If it does not, they will lose interest in one another and try out new relationships. Adults must allow children themselves to decide when and if this change is to take place.

Children in this phase of friendship desire so much to have a friend that they often resort to bribery or threats. Furthermore, they still have difficulty having more than one close relationship at a time and are often heard to remark, "You can't be my friend—Jose is my friend." Adults are sometimes appalled at the tactics the children use toward one another. However, it is important to recognize that children are merely trying out strategies to get what they want and will soon learn from their peers how well they work; their aim is not to be deliberately mean or hurtful.

Because children at this stage actively seek friends that are like them, they are busy comparing themselves to others to determine likenesses and differences. They begin to choose same-sex and same-race playmates. This becomes even more pronounced at the next phase, which describes children between the ages of 6 and 12. Here, children are finally beginning to understand that their behavior must please another person, not simply the reverse. They are deeply involved in what is fair and not fair (as viewed from their special point of view). It is in this stage that children want to be most like their friends, and so conformity in dress, speech, and actions reaches a peak.

Furthermore, friendships at this stage tend to come in twos; girls especially form close-knit diads, while boys travel in looser packs (Hartup, 1983). Both boys and girls are extremely possessive of their relationships, and conflicts and hard feelings often result. Adults express concern over the extremes of self-segregation by sex, race, and differing physical abilities that frequently occur at this stage (Hartup, 1982; Shaw, 1973). While adults cannot mandate friendships, there is much they can do to help children recognize similarities between themselves and others in spite of certain obvious physical differences. Some common ground between children might include cognitive skills, degree of sociability, interests, and attitudes (Cavallaro & Porter, 1982). These issues are especially relevant when helping children develop nonprejudicial attitudes and behaviors. Adults must think of ways to take advantage of children's growing abilities to observe and reason in order to promote these values. (Strategies for helping children achieve a heightened awareness of similarity among people while recognizing and appreciating differences will be presented in the activity section of this chapter.)

How children look at interpersonal relationships with peers over time is an important aspect of their growing capacity for friendships. Other crucial factors in their ability to make and keep friends are the skills they bring to the process. These skills can be divided into three distinct categories: establishing contact, maintaining positive relationships, and resolving conflicts (Kostelnik et al., in press).

Friendship Skill: Establishing Contact. To start a potential friendship, one child must first make an approach to another. If the friendship has any chance of success, the second person must respond positively. How this contact is carried out influences each child's perception of the other. If they have a good impression, the interaction will continue; if they do not, it will terminate at that point. Children who are cordial—that is, who smile, speak pleasantly, offer greetings, and seek information—tend to elicit positive responses from others (Hazen & Black, 1989). These replies can be cast in the form of responding to others' greetings and questions, offering information, and inviting participation. Another successful strategy for breaking the ice is imitation. Very young children feel flattered when others mimic their actions by playing nearby or using the same materials, and they tend to welcome more direct involvement of the imitator (Hartup, 1978). Older children are more leery of this tactic and may become irritated at someone who is "copying." It may take some finesse on the part of the approaching youngster to recognize when he or she has breached the boundaries.

This kind of judgment may seem natural for all children to develop, yet there are many youngsters who fail to recognize that even the

seemingly simple strategy of acting friendly will gain friends. They may have the right idea, but their timing is off or their actions may be misapplied. These are children who benefit greatly from friendship coaching (Kostelnik et al., in press). This involves pointing out the child's own behavior and its effect on other youngsters using specific observable terms rather than generalizations. Then the adult should demonstrate the appropriate skill and include a rationale explaining why it will be effective. The next step is for the child to practice the skill and participate in an evaluation of how well it worked. Naturally, it takes a great deal of time and practice for children to learn to make themselves more appealing to others.

Friendship Skill: Maintaining Positive Relationships. The second level of friendship skills are used to maintain positive relationships once they have been initiated. Children who speak directly to one another, are attentive to others in particular interactions, respond in an interested fashion, and offer suggestions are popular with others (Hazen & Black, 1989). In addition, these youngsters demonstrate cooperation and helpfulness and are comfortable expressing emotions, such as affection, empathy, and joy in the accomplishments of their pals.

The children are able to sustain relationships because their behavior makes them fun and satisfying to be with. Children who lack these skills are far less successful in their abilities to sustain friendships over time. They annoy and antagonize their peers by showing off, being insensitive to people's reactions, becoming overly exuberant in their displays of affection, or taking over rather than being helpful or cooperative even though it is unintentional. In any event, their actions make it difficult for them to be viewed as potential friends.

Friendship Skill: Resolving Conflicts. The most complex aspect of peer relationships is handling conflicts. Children's ability to deal with disputes in democratic ways such as recognizing and taking account of differences in another's viewpoint, compromising, bargaining, or suggesting nonviolent solutions to the problem is highly indicative of the future success of a relationship

TABLE 8.1
Negotiating Conflicts

Strategy	Example
Expressing one's own rights, needs, or feelings	"It's my turn to use the stapler."
Listening to and acknowledging others' rights, opinions, and feelings	"Oh, you haven't finished yet."
Suggesting nonviolent solutions to conflict	"How about giving it to me in 2 minutes?"
Explaining the reasons behind the solution suggested	"That way we'll both get to use it before lunch."
Standing up against unreasonable demands	"No, it's not fair if you use it the whole time. I want it too."
Accepting reasonable disagreement	"OK, I hadn't thought of that."
Compromising on a solution	"I can use tape now, and you can use tape later when I'm using the stapler."

(Gottman, Gonzo, & Rasmussen, 1975). Children who forcibly demand that issues be decided their way or, conversely, who back down from establishing their legitimate rights lose the respect of their peers and tend to be rejected by them.

Thus, children who use constructive means of resolving disputes while at the same time satisfying their own needs are most successful in forming lasting relationships (Gottman, Gonzo, and Rasmussen, 1975). The facets of this process are illustrated in Table 8.1 (Stocking et al.,1980).

Educators play an important role in helping children learn how to use these strategies. One way they can do this is by modeling the role of a conflict mediator in disputes between children. This involves being a nonjudgmental facilitator so that children learn to find peaceful solutions that are mutually satisfying.

The conflict mediation process consists of seven steps, summarized in Table 8.2. How to present this process so that children can practice the specific skills is discussed later in the activity section of this chapter.

Children vary widely in their abilities to engage in this form of resolving conflicts. Success depends on their age, understanding of relationships, communication skills, and experiences. The technique has been used productively with children as young as 3 who could communicate their wants. As children mature, refine their abil-

ities to express themselves, and become more familiar with how it works, their capacity for staying with the process increases. They shift from the belief that disputes are caused by one person against another to a more balanced view of shared responsibility. The mediation model presented here helps children move in that direction. They have opportunities to observe problem solving firsthand and experience the results of nonviolent solutions.

In addition, as the negotiation process becomes more familiar, the number of participating onlookers grows, which thus increases the involvement of more children. There is also promising evidence that not only does aggression diminish, but positive prosocial behaviors increase in groups where mediation is commonly used (Kostelnik & Stein, 1986). Furthermore, when adults take on this role, the number and duration of children's conflicts declines over time and children take over the peaceful management of their disputes (Stein & Kostelnik, 1984).

As stated earlier, the give-and-take of children's relationships with their peers has a profound effect on their success at school. Also important is their understanding of how groups of people can live and work comfortably and productively together. Being kind toward each other by behaving helpfully and cooperatively

TABLE 8.2
Conflict Mediation

Steps in the Process	Role of the Adult
1. Initiating the mediation process	Assumes mediator role Stops aggressive behavior Neutralizes object or territory
2. Clarifying perspectives	Solicits statements from each party Paraphrases perspectives Establishes own neutrality
3. Summing up	Defines problem in mutual terms
4. Generating alternatives	Solicits ideas from combatants and bystanders Suggests possibilities, if necessary
5. Agreeing on a solution	Summarizes points of agreement Identifies resolution
6. Reenforcing the problem-solving process	Praises children for developing solution
7. Following through	Helps children carry out terms of agreement

makes group living a more positive experience for all.

Prosocial Behavior: Helping and Cooperating

Prosocial behavior represents the most positive attributes of society. Acts of kindness such as helping, sharing, sympathizing, rescuing, defending, cooperating, and comforting benefit all persons, the givers as well as the receivers. When children and adults cooperate with one another by working toward a common goal or help someone by alleviating their distress or facilitating work or play, they contribute to an environment in which friendly interactions and productive group efforts abound (Gazda et al., 1991). Furthermore, in such an atmosphere routine or uninteresting tasks are easily handled, since no one person is burdened with them. In essence, then, a classroom in which prosocial values and behaviors are transmitted and encouraged tends to produce participants with a positive self- and group image. Further, they are likely to view themselves and others as competent and congenial (Kostelnik et al., in press). Finally, children who learn to be kind tend not to be selfish or aggressive. It follows that providing instruction in prosocial behaviors within the classroom creates the kind of setting in which all learning is enhanced.

It was once believed that if people were taught to think prosocially, corresponding prosocial behaviors would follow automatically. Unfortunately, this correlation does not hold true. Good thoughts do not necessarily lead to good deeds (Bryan & Walbek, 1970). Although children can, on cue, proclaim, "We're supposed to share," all reason may go out the window in the midst of a race to get the red marker. Children must be helped to go beyond thinking and saying what is appropriate to doing what is right. To accomplish this, they must go through a series of steps. First, they need to recognize that help or cooperation is required, then they must decide whether or not to do something. Finally, they must perform a prosocial action that is appropriate to the situation at hand.

Prosocial Skills: Recognition, Decision, Action. Sensitivity to someone's cues for help or cooperation is the initial skill children must acquire to learn to be prosocial. The messages sent by others can be nonverbal (panting, crying, or sighing) or the more obvious verbal strategies of complaining or requesting assistance. Surprisingly, although these signals seem clear to most adults, some children appear to ignore them. Either these children misunderstand their meaning, or they do not think the signs are meant for them. Thus, it cannot be assumed that just because children are in the presence of such cues they necessarily recognize them.

Once they realize a person is in need, children must decide whether or not to act. Several factors play a role in their decision. Youngsters are most likely to respond to people they know, like, or admire (Staub, 1978). If they are in a positive mood, they will more likely act than if they are upset or in a neutral frame of mind (M. L. Hoffman, 1982; Strayer, 1980). In addition, they feel more responsible toward a person who has extended kindness to them in the past or from whom they hope to reap future rewards (Rosenhan, 1972). Older children and adults, in general, will respond independent of personal gain, as more generalized notions of justice play a role in their thinking.

Finally, a child must perform an action. How suitable the action is that they choose is influenced by their ability to take another person's perspective into account and by their instrumental know-how (Moore, 1982). At any stage of this process, children may experience difficulties. They may misinterpret cues or overlook them, they may miscalculate which behaviors would be appropriate, or they may act hastily or incompletely. As they mature and gain experience, their efforts will more likely meet with greater success.

Promoting Prosocial Behavior. As the primary conveyers of social values to children outside the family, educators play a key role in influencing prosocial behavior. Furthermore, educators have a profound effect on the degree to which children demonstrate prosocial behaviors in the classroom. They can increase children's kindness by creating an environment in which they themselves model the behaviors they expect of children, look for instances of prosocial behaviors and reward them, and teach children directly to think and act prosocially (Kostelnik et al., in press).

Additionally, children can be given many planned opportunities to participate in tasks and situations that allow them to rehearse prosocial skills. Children benefit greatly from these occa-

sions and demonstrate a greater frequency of such positive behaviors in similar circumstances after having practiced (Honig, 1982; Marcus & Leiserson, 1978). This occurs because children can better remember both the appropriate behavior and the cues that signal which conditions apply in a given circumstance when they have had a chance to practice. (Specific techniques that combine verbal descriptions and explanations with practice are illustrated in the activity section of this chapter.)

The educator's role is significant in influencing children's prosocial actions. In the same vein, how educators teach children about expectations for behavior impacts children's ability to understand and follow rules.

SOCIALIZATION: CHILDREN'S BEHAVIOR AND ADULT EXPECTATIONS

Much of children's interactions with teachers and other adults in school revolve around rules. Children are continually learning about what the rules are and how to act in accordance with them. This is not a simple process for children to master.

Educators often expect children to learn classroom and school rules within a few weeks and then be able to follow them consistently. Failure to do so has been viewed frequently as willfulness or resistance on the part of the child, and such youngsters develop reputations that follow them throughout their school career. Although teachers view it as important, they often resent having to take class time to teach children about the rules more than a few times. Furthermore, because following rules is an expected behavior, infractions are often noticed more than compliance. Learning rules and being able to follow them takes time. Just as in other areas, children vary in both the rates at which they acquire the knowledge and skills and also the extent of adult intervention they require.

A major goal of early childhood educators is for children to be able to understand and then follow the rules even when adults are not present, in other words, for children to achieve self-discipline. How this can be achieved is such a vital aspect of children's social development that chapter 14 has been devoted entirely to how children develop self-control and what the adult role is in the process.

SOCIAL RESPONSIBILITY

There have been many changes in the world during the past few decades, and more changes are to come. Families have become more mobile, special needs youngsters are being integrated in ever increasing numbers into classrooms, neighborhood boundaries are more permeable and so children are exposed to a wider variety of people, and the health of our planet has been brought into question. At the same time, educators have become aware that social attitudes are formed when children are young. Given these concerns, the question becomes how to prepare our young people to live in a pluralistic society in ways that uphold the democratic principles of fairness, equal opportunity, and justice. Thus we have come to understand that we must teach children about their responsibility to the world beyond their doorstep. This is the essence of encouraging children to become good citizens of their classroom, their neighborhood, and the larger society they will encounter as they mature. Through attention to social issues that are important to children's lives, we are teaching them what they will need to make reasoned decisions. Through instruction in peaceful conflict negotiation, strategies for confronting bias, and the promotion of prosocial behaviors, we are giving them the tools.

Respect for Diversity

religion	ethnicity	gender role
race	age	family composition
language	abilities	lifestyle
interests	values	skin color

This list represents only a small fraction of the variations children encounter among the people in the school setting. Some of these differences are immediately apparent to children, while others take longer for them to discover. Children's attitudes about issues of diversity have their roots in childhood. Even before they are 3, children notice others' physical attributes and begin to compare these with their own. As their experiences broaden and their cognitive and language abilities develop, young people also become aware of and comment on more subtle distinctions (Alejandro-Wright, 1985; P. Katz, 1982; Levitt & Cohen, 1966).

Once it was thought that simply bringing children into contact with others who were different from them would lead to understanding and tolerance. Unfortunately, this hope has proven to be naive. In some cases, already negative perceptions are strengthened rather than eliminated when diverse people are introduced into somewhat stable groups (Cohen, 1977). This occurs in part because adults neglect to take into account children's development and their own biases in teaching children positive responses to the differences.

The development of valid concepts of race, gender, and differing physical abilities appears to be age and stage specific, with older children displaying more accurate understandings than younger ones (Alejandro-Wright, 1985; P. Katz, 1982; Levitt & Cohen, 1966). As an example, children are not sure until about age 8 or older which physical attributes are constant and which will change with time. Furthermore, their rudimentary notions of causal relationships make it difficult for them to figure out what the process of change entails. They may conclude, for instance, that dark skin is dirty and, if washed, will turn white; that they may lose the function of their legs if they play with a child in a wheelchair; or that if a girl gets a short haircut she turns into a boy. Although there is some question as to the precise ages that children understand these questions, it is clear that it occurs during childhood.

Another developmental issue that comes into play here is children's continuing efforts to sort out likenesses and differences. In their attempts to figure out who is like them and who is not, their criteria may be based on obvious physical characteristics alone. At certain friendship stages, when children are seeking others who are like them, they may exclude children based on these external attributes unless other similarities are brought to their attention.

In addition to developmental considerations, how children evaluate differences and how they consequently behave are highly influenced by the adults around them, peers, and societal values as expressed in the media and other outside sources. Children's opinions of both their own and others' worth are affected by these forces, especially negative ones (Cross, 1985). Early childhood professionals must therefore pay attention to the messages they convey about diversity in the settings they create, the teaching materials they use, and the manner in which they respond to children's behavior and words.

Creating Inclusive School Environments.

Inclusive school environments and teaching practices are those in which all forms of diversity are fairly and consistently represented. By virtue of the interpersonal interactions and planned activities that take place, the physical structure of the space, and the materials on walls and shelves, communities are created in which all people, adults and children alike, feel acknowledged, accepted, and valued (Sapon-Shevin, 1983).

One strategy for ensuring that diversity is valued is to make sure that classroom activities and materials represent different cultures, lifestyles, people with differing abilities, and men and women in non-sex-stereotypical roles. Deliberate introduction and integration of diverse people into programs on an ongoing rather than special basis should be done. Furthermore, all materials that are used in the educational setting must be examined so that stereotypical portrayals of groups are not unconsciously displayed or categories of people are not left out. In addition to the obvious (e.g., Native Americans shown with feathers in their hair or only at Thanksgiving), more subtle cues should be explored. For instance, classrooms and school hallways that feature only Christmas trees in December send the message to non-Christians that their holidays and traditional practices are not important. Furthermore, cultural awareness should focus on how people live today in our country, not only on cultures and people in other nations. Thus the focus of teaching should be on Asian-Americans, African-Americans, and Hispanic-Americans rather than on people's countries of origin (Derman-Sparks & the ABC Task Force, 1989).

Adults have a responsibility to help children sort out valid conclusions from those based on incomplete or erroneous information. They can do this by providing accurate data for children to work with as well as deliberately setting up experiences that confound children's stereotypical assumptions. Answering children's questions honestly and carrying out frank and open discussions about the differences children observe is another way to help children gain important knowledge about others.

An additional strategy is to help children recognize the effects of their actions and words on others (Kostelnik et al., in press). Pointing out instances of kindness and explaining how that made another child feel encourage further prosocial behaviors. In addition, it is important to confront children directly when they show evidence of overtly biased behavior or opinions. Letting children know that insensitive remarks made that person feel hurt or angry is the first step in changing their behavior in a more socially responsible direction (Derman-Sparks & the ABC Task Force, 1989). The adult must be sure to indicate a positive alternative to the child as well as determine any appropriate acts of restitution.

Changing the Curriculum.

Several stages of curricular reform have been identified as teachers struggle with issues of inclusion in their programs (Banks, 1988). While these were originally designed to describe ethnic content, they can be generalized to encompass all areas of diversity. The first stage that teachers often go through is called the "contribution" approach. This focuses on heros, holidays, and discrete cultural elements. For example, teachers introduce heros into the program, treating their lives as exemplars with special abilities. They are not integrated into the curriculum, nor are the issues they confront as members of minority groups, such as discrimination, truly explored. Rather, their successes are promoted, and they are treated as exotic, exceptional human beings, not representative of their group.

The "ethnic added" approach is a second means teachers use to introduce content related to diversity into their programs. At this level, content, concepts, and themes are added without changing the curricular structure. That is, although important steps have been taken to integrate diversity, the curriculum is still based on a majority-centered view.

The third stage is called the "transformational" approach. At this level, teachers have infused various perspectives, frames of reference, and content into their curricula. The result is that students will come away with a greater understanding of the complexities of our society and how society itself is a result of a synthesis and interaction among the diverse elements that comprise it.

Banks's (1988) final stage is called the "decision-making and social action" approach. This is the most sophisticated of all. It includes all elements of the previous stage but requires children to make complex decisions related to their study and take some action.

The paradigm set forth by Banks (1988) offers much in the way of information for the teacher. A blending and mixing of the approaches just described seems a reasonable way to tackle the difficult task of changing one's own thinking and practice to be more inclusive. Professionals must examine their own attitudes and practices for evidence of prejudice. This is not an easy task, as bias may rear its head in numerous subtle ways and may emanate from sources that

relate to our own early life experiences and learnings. Thus, it is by monitoring their own behavior, as well as confronting children's stereotypical beliefs, reinforcing positive behaviors, and pro-actively teaching about the similarities and differences that make us all part of the human family, that educators can help children make strides toward a bias-free society.

Environmental Awareness

There is a popular saying used by individuals on almost every side of every issue: "Think globally; act locally." In no area is this more apt than when teaching children about their responsibility for the indoor as well as outdoor environments in which they live and play.

Environmental ecology deals with the complex interrelationships among all living things and their surroundings (Schickedanz, York et al., 1990). Like most areas of study, awareness of the environment spans more than one domain. It involves principles from science and the broad

The beginnings of social responsibility come about through such simple activities as planting flowers to beautify the neighborhood.

goals of the social domain. In addition, affective development is involved, since the problems of caring for the environment relate to how children's behavior impacts others. Thus, while it is true that pollution in its most overt forms is a concept difficult for children to understand, youngsters can, and should, be made aware of the effects of their own actions on their milieu. Attention to the environment has some far-reaching consequences in the lives of young children. Just as attitudes about differences are established at an early age, so, too, are one's attitudes toward the world. Adults, as we know, exert a powerful influence on children, and the behaviors they display are more significant in proclaiming their values than any words they profess. Thus, for children to become sensitive to the needs of the global community, adults must demonstrate their concern through their actions.

Specific planning within the classroom in terms of activities and routines are effective ways of conveying children's responsibility for their setting. Children can be taught to clean up their own mess, either individually or with help from others. They can be shown how to generate less waste in school and at home and find uses for scrap materials. A classroom recycling center is a way to prompt their excitement as well as create a hands-on, concrete demonstration project for other classes to emulate. An activity as simple as planting, caring for, and harvesting plants can make an important contribution to the classroom as well. Activities such as these reveal important causal relationships to children because they are able to experience directly the results of changes in their actions.

In addition, children can be made aware of the conflicting needs of human beings for resources and society's concerns about the untimely depletion of those resources. The classroom can be a microcosm for learning how these dilemmas are to be resolved in democratic ways, through negotiation and compromise.

SOCIAL STUDIES

Social studies has been defined as the study of people in society, past and present, and their relations with each other and the world around them, both near and far (National Council for the Social Studies, 1984). Its goals focus on expanding children's horizons and teaching the elements of democratic living. The ultimate goal is to produce individuals who feel good about themselves and develop the necessary concepts and skills to make worthwhile contributions to society. Social studies curricula take their perspectives from a variety of disciplines, such as anthropology, economics, geography, history, human ecology, political science, psychology, and sociology. All of these are similar in that they focus on the understanding of human behavior; however, each makes unique contributions to children's knowledge (Schickedanz, York et al., 1990; Seefeldt, 1987; Sunal, 1990).

Anthropology is the study of human beings and their diverse cultures and lifestyles. Children begin to understand that people represent many cultures as they come in contact with others in their school and community. Even people who look the same may have different beliefs, different ways of celebrating holidays and festivals, and different family structures. Children also learn that people who seem unlike them may share similar ideas and values.

Economics informs us about how people produce and consume goods and services. Children can be made aware of the diverse kinds of work adults engage in by talking with and observing persons who fight fires, care for people, buy and sell goods, grow produce and livestock, work in factories and build useful products, and perform services for pay. Money exchange and the value of money is a topic that can be introduced to children at a young age. Consumer education, such as learning how to evaluate advertising, is critical for children to understand. One component of this is for children to be able to distinguish their needs from their wants and to make informed decisions on the basis of the difference.

Geography illuminates the characteristics of the earth's environment and the relationship of that environment to the people who live in it. Where things are in children's near environment is important information to have as they move farther from their home. In addition, children develop a greater appreciation for the natural world and its resources when they learn to be responsible for the waste they generate and the ways in which they dispose of that waste. Geography also relates to how people get from one place to another and the reasons they choose to move.

History deals with the past, the concept of change, and the forces that influence it. Important to the lives of young children is their own personal history and that of their family. Every child has an ancestry, and becoming aware of one's forebears helps children develop a sense of belonging and pride. History also deals with the passage of time and the sequence of events. In the early childhood setting these elements are built into the structure of daily living. Bringing them to children's consciousness is the first step in their understanding of temporal relationships.

Human ecology is the study of the interplay between the individual and all systems with which that person comes in contact, both directly and indirectly. So, for example, the child is a member of both the home and the school setting and is also indirectly affected by his or her parents' place of work. Communication among these systems is also a part of the human ecological perspective and underscores the importance of regular contact between the child's home and school. When children bring items or information from home to the classroom, and when messages are sent home about possible visitors or field trips, children are active participants in their social groups.

Political science relates to the management and governance of social units. This very much relates to teaching children about living in a democracy. Children have opportunities to practice aspects of democratic living when they learn to understand the rules that govern the classroom and when they become involved in making some of those rules themselves. Within the social studies curriculum, children learn that everyone has rights and responsibilities and that it is sometimes necessary to negotiate and bargain for the things they need. Furthermore, they participate in group problem solving about issues that are important to them. All of these experiences teach them how societies function for the benefit of all members.

Psychology reveals the internal workings of the mind—how people think, feel, and respond. Every time children approach an interaction, they are dealing with their emotions. They are busy learning to recognize what these emotions are, the variety of ways they are expressing them, and what the impact of that expression is on other people. As they develop and extend their prosocial skills, children are finding out more about the emotions and the needs of others. Teaching children about the similar and different ways people respond to holidays, for instance, gives youngsters experience in understanding their own feelings and those of others.

Sociology helps us understand the social groups in which we live. Like adults, children belong to many social groups, such as their family, class, after-school activity group, and congregation. How people function within these different settings, as leaders or followers, initiators or passive observers, dependent or independent thinkers, provides a focus for discussion among children. Specific activities can be planned so that children will sharpen their awareness of the roles they and others play in their groups.

From its earliest inclusion in the early childhood curriculum, real experiences have been the vehicles for teaching social studies content and concepts (Banks, 1988). Children's active and direct participation in projects and activities is the necessary means of instruction, as it is congruent with what we know about children's development (Bredekamp, 1987). The classroom is an ideal arena within which children learn the social skills, values, and rules required for living in society. For young children, therefore, social studies is viewed as an extension of their social development. Understanding that children learn best that which is most important to them, educators can logically translate children's natural concerns about their relationships with others and the world around them into studies of the self, the family, the school, and the community (Ministry of Education, Province of British Columbia, 1989). Thus, the integrative nature of social studies promotes children's understanding of the society in which they live.

Goals of Social Studies

As with other curricular domains, the goals for social studies are grouped by knowledge goals, skill goals, and attitude goals (National Council of the Social Studies Task Force, 1989). *Knowledge goals* focus on concepts that reflect the content

TABLE 8.3
Implementing the Social Studies Curriculum in the Classroom

Social Science Discipline	Experiences for		
	3- to 5-Year-Olds	5- to 7-Year-Olds	6- to 8-Year-Olds
Anthropology	Children are provided with a wok, chopsticks, plastic models of sushi, and plastic plates with Asian designs as normal props in the Family Living Center.	Children are taught two versions of a similar singing game, one with African-American and one with Euro-American roots.	Children interview family members about their cultural heritage. They record on tape or paper a story that represents their heritage and share them with the class.
Economics	Children participate in a theme entitled "The Work People Do."	Children set up a store in the classroom. Classmates are allotted a limited amount of money with which to buy goods. They are encouraged to bargain or barter other goods and services to get what they want.	Children develop a plan for a class project to earn money for a special field trip.
Geography	After a walk in the neighborhood, children are encouraged to use blocks to reconstruct their experience.	After a walk through the neighborhood, children arrange photographs of features in the area in the order in which they observed them. At a later time, they make a return trip to check out their recollections.	After a walk in the neighborhood, children create a map representing the buildings and other landmarks in the school environs.
History	Children bring in pictures of themselves as babies and dictate stories.	Children bring in pictures of their parent(s) as youngsters. They write or dictate descriptions comparing how the people looked in the past and the present.	Children create their individual family trees. They get the information by interviewing family members.

of social studies, such as the uniqueness of all people, the interdependence of people, the influence of environment on people's choices of habitats and work, and the function and operation of social groups. Other knowledge goals deal with the structure of the social science disciplines, such as what and how we learn about human history and how decisions are made. Additional knowledge goals reflect the similarity and differences among individuals and groups and how people learn to live together. *Skill goals* are those that focus on children's mastery of techniques related to the gathering of information, improving their interpersonal interactions within their group, and problem solving, both in terms of content and social relations. *Attitude goals* relevant to social studies are those that, for example, emphasize respecting individuals both similar to and different from themselves, understanding and appreciating their own and

TABLE 8.3
continued

Social Science Discipline	Experiences for		
	3- to 5-Year-Olds	**5- to 7-Year-Olds**	**6- to 8-Year-Olds**
Human ecology	A local kindergarten teacher spends the day in the preschool classroom, while on another day, the preschool teacher teaches in the kindergarten room.	Children address envelopes to themselves, go to the post office to mail it, and trace its progress through the system by observing the sorting machines, seeing a mail deliverer in action, and so forth.	As a culmination to a study of the community, children create a diorama, depicting the interrelationships among all the community service agencies, such as the post office, fire department, police station, and the like.
Psychology	Each child wears a badge during the day that reads, "I'm special because I _____" (child decides what the special attribute or skill is).	Each child works on an "All about Me" book. In it are included favorite objects, favorite people, things they dislike, and other categories they choose.	On a table specially set aside for the purpose, children bring in favorite items from home. They display the items, along with guidelines that others must follow in examining them. Children describe the articles to each other and explain why they are special.
Political science	During interpersonal disputes, children participate in conflict negotiation, with the teacher assuming the role of mediator.	Children establish classroom rules for the safe use of a microscope on loan from the museum.	Children hold a mock election for a "town council seat." There is a period of campaigning so that children have the opportunity to influence their "constituency."
Sociology	Children take turns conducting a rhythm instrument band.	Children participate in a theme on "Friends and Friendships," during which they identify and practice friendship-making skills.	Small groups of children work on solving a designated classroom problem (e.g., figuring out how to make sure children's possessions remain undisturbed). The groups present their solutions to the class, where they are discussed and evaluated.

others' culture and traditions, and caring for the world around them. It is evident that these goals and their implementation across the early childhood age range encompass the entire range of the social domain.

Social Studies in the Classroom

It is instructive to examine how a social studies curriculum might look in practice for children of different ages. Table 8.3 includes sample experiences appropriate for the youngest children (4- to 5-year-olds), somewhat older children (5- to 7-year-olds), and the oldest children (6- to 8-year-olds). Children's maturity and prior access to the materials and activities will affect which are best suited to their needs. Therefore, the age range should be viewed as a guide.

It is evident that teachers have the responsibility to teach social studies directly, as well as help children learn to have positive interpersonal interactions. Clearly, this learning must take place in the context of the child's daily experience in the classroom. This is best accomplished when teachers carefully plan activities that relate to children's lives and take advantage of the spontaneous occurrences that are a natural part of group dynamics to teach important lessons. Active participation by children in the exploration of these issues ensures that they will derive the meaningful knowledge, skills, and attitudes that are the foundations of a social studies curriculum. As a result, these children will demonstrate good citizenship in their school, their communities, and, ultimately, their world.

CURRENT EDUCATIONAL ISSUES

Two questions teachers working with young children sometimes pose in relation to social development and social studies are (a) How does social development relate to the content traditionally associated with social studies? and (b) What is the best way to address the social domain within the school day? These questions represent key issues regarding the social domain and the early childhood curriculum.

The Relationship between Social Development and Social Studies

In order to live productively in the world, children must have satisfying relationships with the people in it. This means knowing about and following societal expectations, making and keeping friends, working out interpersonal conflicts, being kind to others and accepting kindness from them, and recognizing and valuing diversity among people. As they become aware of the impact of their ideas and behaviors on others, children gain an awareness of their own point of view and an understanding of the perspectives of people different from themselves. They also appreciate their own culture and family history. In addition, children become increasingly aware of the complex interrelationships among all things, living and nonliving, in the world. Through numerous experiences, children can be made cognizant of the necessary interdependence of people in any society and the need for responsible behavior toward the environment. Teachers can help children develop

the skills they need to live in a peaceful world and provide opportunities for them to practice democratic problem solving and decision making. This empowers children to affect the world they live in. As children's concepts broaden, they may introduce them to issues that go beyond their immediate concerns, through a focus on greater world issues, such as peace and war, homelessness and poverty, and vanishing species. Thus, the social realm requires children to look both within and outside themselves as they build their repertoire of social studies concepts.

How the Social Domain Fits in the School Day

Teachers have numerous demands on their time and resources during school. They are expected to plan for instruction in all the domains, as well as to fulfill many other responsibilities. Where, then, does teaching about the social domain fit?

One important factor to recognize is that social development is integral to every part of school life. It appears in both implicit and explicit forms. Fundamentally, teachers are conveying information and values related to social development in everything they do in the classroom. How they treat children both individually and in groups; how they interact with aides, volunteers, and parents; what disciplinary strategies they employ; and how they respond to diversity of all sorts within their school community directly impact children's social development. In addition, they influence children when they take advantage of spontaneous opportunities to make children aware of the effect of their behavior toward others and when they model, encourage, and promote helpful and cooperative behavior. Other ways in which implicit instruction is conveyed is when teachers set up routines and practices during which children are expected to care for their immediate as well as the school environment. In all of these areas, teachers are addressing important aspects of children's social development.

In addition to the subtle attention to social development, teachers can deliberately plan for the social domain's inclusion in their program. For example, it is not very effective to try to teach a social skill or improve children's proso-cial behaviors by using a predigested, 15-minute "kit." These are not very useful teaching tools, by themselves, since we now know that even when children can verbalize appropriate behaviors, they may not actually act in those ways without practice in real-life situations. A far better approach is to integrate social concepts throughout the day-to-day transactions of the classroom. They can also be highlighted within particular activities. Planning thematic units that revolve around social studies content, such as "Families," "People in Our Community," and "The Work People Do," is another way teachers can underscore these significant understandings and help children comprehend the relationship between what they are experiencing and the processes in the world outside themselves.

GOALS AND OBJECTIVES

The ultimate goals of the social domain are for children to develop successful patterns of interaction with peers and adults, gain internal control, acquire and practice prosocial values, demonstrate positive attitudes toward diversity, and build social studies concepts. For children to make progress toward these goals, they must have opportunities to attain interpersonal skills, learn the expectations of school and society, learn about and practice prosocial behaviors, gain respect and appreciation for the wide variety of people in the world, and achieve understandings and skills that relate to social studies.

Mediating Objectives

As children progress toward the ultimate goal, they will

1. develop play skills (e.g., initiate play, join a group at play, make suggestions, take suggestions, recognize ways to deal with unpleasant social situations and the emotions associated with them, learn to play productively alone).
2. develop peer friendship relationship skills (e.g., how to initiate, maintain, and terminate interactions and relationships constructively).
3. become aware of other people's opinions, points of view, and attitudes.
4. learn to negotiate conflicts in democratic ways (e.g., compromising, voting, bargaining).
5. develop empathy for others (recognize others' emotions, respect others' emotional responses).
6. perceive adults as sources of gratification, approval, and modeling.
7. learn how to conform to reasonable limits set on behavior, play space, use of materials, or the types of activities in which they are involved.
8. identify the reasons for classroom rules.
9. distinguish acceptable from unacceptable classroom behavior.
10. use their knowledge of appropriate behavior in one circumstance to determine appropriate conduct in another.
11. begin to develop skills related to self-control (e.g., impulse control, resistance, delay of gratification, and positive social actions).
12. learn approved behaviors related to social and ethnic customs (e.g., manners and other respectful behaviors).
13. learn how to cooperate (work with others toward a common goal).
14. learn how to be helpful (share information or materials, give physical assistance, offer emotional support).
15. develop awareness and concern for the rights and well-being of others.
16. develop positive attitudes about belonging to a group beyond the family.
17. become aware of similarities and differences among people.
18. develop positive attitudes toward people who are different from themselves.
19. develop an awareness and respect for the values, ethnic background, family traditions, culture, gender, differing abilities, and special needs of others.
20. become aware of how people live together in families, neighborhoods, and communities.
21. develop a sense of responsibility for the environment.
22. develop knowledge related to social studies content in the areas of

    ■ anthropology (e.g., culture),

- economics (e.g., money, consumerism, work),
- geography (e.g., home and school environs),
- history (e.g., personal history, family history),
- human ecology (e.g., child-school-home connection),
- psychology (e.g., understanding one's emotions and those of others),
- political science (e.g., democratic principles and practices, conflict resolution), and
- sociology (e.g., individuals and communities).

23. develop skills related to social studies content, such as collecting data, mapping, and decision-making.

TEACHING STRATEGIES

1. *Help children make friends at school by using their names.* Children feel most comfortable interacting with those whose names they know. Thus, acquainting children with each other's names is a basic strategy for facilitating children's friendships. To accomplish this, use children's names frequently. Identify by name youngsters that are sitting near one another, working together, and playing with each other. Unfamiliar or uncommon names will seem less strange with frequent repetition. Be sure you know how to pronounce every child's name correctly.

2. *Help children make friends at school by promoting social interactions.* To help children become more aware of others in their group, there are a number of successful strategies to try. For example, you can deliberately pair children to work on projects. Choose children whom you perceive to have something in common. Remember to point out these common attributes, attitudes, preferences, or shared experiences so that the youngsters will become more aware of them. Shy children, in particular, benefit from this technique, but it is effective with others as well. For the benefit of all children, remember to provide numerous opportunities during the school day for children to interact with each other informally. Another related idea is to plan activities that require more

than one child's participation. Observe how children behave with one another so that you can use that information in future planning.

3. *Provide activities that allow children to practice social skills.* Use the suggestions following this section to create activities that focus on specific social skills. For instance, teach children numerous ways to let others know that they want to play, by using skits. Carry out discussions during which children themselves generate alternatives and explore the effectiveness of different solutions. As a follow-up, create opportunities for children to practice the strategies in real-life situations. Then, provide them with on-the-spot information regarding their progress in applying their knowledge. This will help them figure out which techniques are successful and encourage them to eliminate those that are not. Other examples include deliberately setting out materials in such a way that children must ask, bargain, or trade in order to get what they want.

4. *Help children become more helpful and cooperative.* A necessary first step in this process is to recognize and acknowledge those times when children behave in positive or prosocial ways. Pointing out such instances increases the chances that children will repeat the acts of kindness. Another strategy is to plan activities in which children have opportunities to practice helping or cooperating. For instance, activities in which children must work together cooperatively to reach a common goal are far more supportive of children's prosocial behavior than those that pit child against child or group against group.

5. *Help children understand and follow expectations for behavior.* Use the guidelines outlined in chapter 14 to establish appropriate rules. Promote the development of children's internalization of rules through the use of the positive guidance strategies outlined there.

6. *Help children develop positive attitudes toward diversity.* As is well known, familiarity with a wide range of people helps children be more accepting of differences. Therefore, it is valuable to present children with opportunities to interact with adult members of their own and other cultural groups, individuals who display varying physical abilities, older people and younger people. Invite grandparents into the classroom, for example, to talk with children about what life was like

Indira's horizons have expanded through her relationship with Mrs. Anna, a classroom volunteer.

when they were growing up. Ask them to talk also about the activities that they engage in at present, to dispel stereotypical attitudes about old people being helpless. Have parents in the group come in to tell stories remembered from their childhood and, if possible, bring books in their language of origin. Send home a request to families to provide recipes from their culture. Finally, use neighborhood resources to acquaint children with people who are different from themselves. In sum, introduce and celebrate diversity by connecting it to children's common experience in the classroom.

7. *Provide children with classroom activities, materials, and discussions that address the wide range of diversity.* Ensure that diversity education and awareness is an ongoing part of your classroom by planning multicultural activities that are integrated into the daily routines

of the program rather than reserving them only for holidays or special occasions. Check the pictures, books, learning materials, and other classroom props for evidence of stereotypical portrayals of any group. In some cases, remove them; in others, use the biased depictions as springboards for discussions with the children. When appropriate, create new pictures that more justly represent the true diversity in the world. Finally, engage children in sending letters of criticism and concern to manufacturers who are producing and marketing toys and games that undermine a fair portrayal of an ethnic, racial, gender, or ability issue.

8. *Help children deal with stereotypical ideas.* The first part of this process is to provide accurate information about the differences and similarities that children perceive. This means that you should respond openly and honestly to

children's observations and to the questions they ask. Giving them chances to explore differences by providing direct experiences is an important component. For example, activities during which children compare and graph skin color or hair texture sharpens children's awareness while, at the same time, presents variety in a positive light. Another aspect of this strategy is to build children's critical thinking skills so that they will become more attuned to evidence of prejudice, within themselves, in others, and as portrayed in the media. Increasing their prosocial attitudes will make it possible for them to respond to these situations in positive ways. Furthermore, the more prosocial the child, the more likely it is that he or she can come to the aid of a friend. The final step is to assist children in defending themselves against bias directed toward them. School personnel are an important influence on how children view themselves and can therefore be effective in teaching children coping skills. Work with youngsters in designing verbal responses to name calling. Allow them time in the classroom to practice with their peers in the safe haven of the classroom. Give them opportunities to talk about their experiences within school time.

9. *Help children learn to care for their near and far environments.* Give children practical experiences in cleaning up the classroom, the school hallways, playground, and other areas in which they work. Use activities, such as those suggested in this chapter, to alert children to the uses of materials they would otherwise discard. When engaged in picking up litter, readying the classroom for the next day, and so on, use music to lighten the burden. Have children perform these tasks in groups so that they feel a sense of group participation and camaraderie and further develop their repertoire of shared experiences. Base themes around the issue of recycling. For example, prepare projects for children to ascertain the recycling efforts of their community, and invite local groups with interests in these matters to give presentations to the class. Assist children in assessing what actions they, as young people, can reasonably take.

10. *Help children build social studies concepts by practicing democracy in the classroom.* Plan activities in which children have opportunities to identify, generate solutions for, and carry out solutions for problems inherent in group liv-

ing. One way to do this is for children to create some of their own classroom rules and designate the appropriate consequences for infractions of those rules. When there is work to be done in caring for the classroom, let children decide on the means of handling them. In addition, promote children's abilities to evaluate the techniques they choose and to redesign the strategies as needed. Some school policies can also be decided by children and teachers working together. (An example of this in operation is described in chap. 14.) An additional way to practice democracy is for teachers to model strategies for helping children solve interpersonal conflict peacefully. Follow the steps outlined in "Activity Suggestions" as you take on the role of mediator in the conflicts that arise in the classroom or on school grounds. Peer coaches can also be trained to assume that role. In either case, with experience and feedback, children develop skill in managing their own disputes and the conflicts of others in nonaggressive ways.

11. *Help children build social studies concepts through theme choices.* When deciding on themes for teaching in the classroom, choose some that focus on social studies content. Such topics as the self, the family, the community, the interdependence of people, and caring for the environment are subjects in which children are naturally interested, since they are directly related to youngsters' lives and activities. Other aspects of social studies can be addressed, for example, when you teach children that people learn about the past from evidence left by others and that they, too, can leave records for others to study.

12. *Help children build social studies concepts and skills across the curriculum.* Social studies is truly an integrative area of focus. For example, teach historical understandings and literature comprehension through the use of modern and old versions of the same story. Another idea is to compare the ways of living of two families during different time periods in history, assessing both similarities and contrasts (e.g., *The Little House on the Prairie* books can be read alongside a modern story by Judy Blume). Assist children in relating mapping skills both to geography as well as to mathematics when they represent an area of their school in a diorama, after

having determined the unit of measure they will use. Combine political understandings with increased self-esteem as you aid children in expressing their needs and wants during a conflict negotiation session. These are only a small number of examples that illustrate the potentially pervasive nature of social studies.

ACTIVITY SUGGESTIONS

The following is a set of activities designed to encourage children to practice the social strategies outlined in this chapter. Each subarea of social development has been addressed by at least one activity. Thus, there are plans that touch on developing play and friendship skills, negotiating conflict, recognizing other points of view, establishing rules, cooperating, helping, recognizing similarities and differences between self and others, and solving problems of group living. These lesson plans are aimed initially at 5-year-old children, with suggestions for simplification and extension indicated so that they can be used successfully with children 3 to 8 years of age. Easily obtained materials are listed for each plan, where appropriate.

➠ Using Skits to Teach Social Skills*

Objective: To promote children's recognition and understanding of social skills

Materials: Two dolls, puppets or pictures of children, several small blocks or other objects

General Information: A very effective strategy for introducing and reinforcing particular social skills to children is to use skits or short scenarios. Children enjoy watching these presentations and can learn a great deal about effective and ineffective ways to interact with others. However, simply viewing them is not sufficient. Adults must point out the pertinent features of the interplay as well as pose questions that help children clarify their understandings. Older children benefit from opportunities to reenact the scenes as well as generate their

_____

*Many of these ideas are based on skits developed for *Teaching Young Children Using Themes*, M. J. Kostelnik (Ed.), Glenview, IL: Goodyear Books, 1991.

own. The following are some general guidelines for developing and presenting skits to children.

Procedure:

1. Select the social skill on which you wish to focus. This may be one of the friendship skills, such as initiating an interaction, maintaining contact, negotiating conflict, or an aspect of helping or cooperating. Be sure to concentrate on only one skill at a time so as not to confuse or overburden children with too much information.

2. Decide on the medium of presentation. Realistic props such as dolls and puppets or photographs that look like children are the most effective since youngsters can more easily identify with other humans than they can with animals or cartoon characters. Be sure the dolls or puppets represent both sexes (or are androgynous) and depict a variety of racial and ethnic groups and differing physical abilities. If you are using puppets, choose them with movable arms rather than mouths to make it possible to manipulate objects.

3. Outline a script that consists of five parts:
   a. Demonstration of skill
   b. Demonstration of lack of the skill
   c. Explanation by the adult
   d. Discussion by the children
   e. Opportunity for children to use the props

The best scripts are only a few lines long and make the point without too much elaboration.

4. Write out the statements and questions you will use to facilitate discussion. These discussions will revolve around which characters demonstrated the skill, which showed lack of skill, the reaction of each character, how viewers evaluated the behaviors and why, and what they think the characters could do to improve their situation. Be sure to include both effective and ineffective strategies. This is very important for helping children distinguish appropriate from inappropriate behaviors in a variety of different situations.

5. Rehearse the skit before introducing it to children. Using a mirror is a good technique for determining how well you are coming

across. Be expressive with your face and voice, and use different voices for each character. Manipulate the figures to correspond with the dialogue. Keep practicing until you feel confident. Write cue cards with the question you wish to ask, if needed.

6. Present the skit to all or part of the group. Seat children in a semicircle facing you. Make sure everyone can see your face and hands and the space directly in front of you. If you are sitting on the floor, kneel so that you are more easily visible to the children. If you are sitting in a chair, use a low bench or table to display the props.

7. Use the following as an introduction each time you do a skit. This prepares children to listen to what is coming next. Change the names and ages, as appropriate. Say, "Today we are going to talk about friends. Here are two dolls. We are going to pretend that these dolls are real children just like you. Their names are Sarvesh and Cathy. They are 5 years old and go to a school just like ours. Watch carefully and see what happens."

8. After you have presented the skit, ask the questions you have prepared, adapting them to situations that arise. As children suggest ideas, paraphrase them and possibly write them down where all the children can see them. Accept all ideas regardless of originality, correctness, or feasibility. If children have difficulty thinking of ideas, prompt them by providing information: "Sometimes, when people want to play, they can say, 'Hi. I want to play,' or they can ask a question like 'What are you building?' This lets the other person know they want to be friends. What do you think Cathy could do?"

9. Once children have suggested their ideas, replay the scene using each suggestion, one at a time. Ask the children to predict how Sarvesh will react in each case. Play out the scene as they suggest. Provide further information as appropriate. "John, you said Cathy could help Sarvesh build. Let's try that." (Maneuver the dolls and provide appropriate dialogue.) "Tell me what you think Sarvesh will do now."

10. Help children evaluate how well their solution worked. For example, "Sarvesh still

doesn't know that Cathy wants to be friends. Tell us another way that Sarvesh could ask Cathy to play." Continue trying out their ideas. As children find solutions, praise them for thinking of ways to help the friends figure out what to do. Summarize for them the ways that were tried and which ones proved more successful. As unfriendly solutions are suggested and role-played, point out that the results may be confusion, hurt feelings, sadness, and anger.

11. Later in the day, evaluate how well your skit got your point across. If it seemed children were interested and were able to generate relevant ideas, plan to present the skit another time. Make changes based on your assessment. Remember that children learn from repetition, so it is recommended that you present each social skill numerous times and in several different ways. Each time you do a new skit or repeat an old one, change the roles that the characters play so that particular behaviors will not be associated in children's minds with a specific figure.

To Simplify: Carry out the activity with a very small group of children. Keep the scenarios short and simple. As children suggest solutions, act them out and point out the results.

To Extend: Encourage the children to reenact on their own the scenario you demonstrated. Introduce open-ended scenarios in which a problem is posed but no solution (effective or ineffective) is modeled. Invite the children to create a solution and then evaluate it. Make dolls available to the children to role-play other scenarios of their own invention.

➠ Sample Skits

Skit 1. Sarvesh and Cathy in "Let's Play"

Here is a sample skit that illustrates initiating interactions. Set up one doll (Sarvesh) as if "playing" with several blocks. Place the second doll (Cathy) facing Sarvesh but at least a foot away.

Scene 1A: Say, "Here is Sarvesh. He is playing alone with the blocks and is having a good time. Cathy sees Sarvesh and would really like to play with him so she watches Sarvesh very carefully. Sarvesh keeps playing; he doesn't look up. Cathy feels sad. She thinks Sarvesh doesn't want to be friends."

Questions for Discussion:

1. Who was playing?
2. Who wanted to play?
3. Did Sarvesh know that Cathy wanted to play?

As children answer these questions, provide information to help in their deliberations: "Sarvesh was so busy playing, he didn't look up. That means he never even saw Cathy standing there. He didn't know Cathy wanted to play. Watch again and see what Cathy does differently this time."

Scene 1B: Say, "Here is Sarvesh. He is playing alone with the blocks and is having a good time. Cathy sees Sarvesh and would really like to play with him, so she watches Sarvesh very carefully. Sarvesh keeps playing; he doesn't look up. Cathy walks over to Sarvesh and says, 'Hi. I like your building. I'll help you get some more blocks.'"

Questions for Discussion:

1. Who was playing?
2. Who wanted to play?
3. Did Sarvesh know that Cathy wanted to play?
4. How could he tell?
5. What will Sarvesh do next?
6. Let's think of some other ways Cathy could let Sarvesh know she wants to play.

Skit 2. Aaron and Cindy in "I Want It"

Here is another sample skit. This time the skill addressed is resolving a conflict.

Scene 2A: Aaron and Cindy are each playing with separate toys by themselves. Aaron is playing happily with the boat; Cindy is using the puppets. After a short while, Cindy looks up from her play; she approaches Aaron.

C: Playing with that boat looks like fun. I want to play with it. Can I have it?

A: No.
C: But I like boats, too. I want it! [Cindy grabs for and pulls at the boat. Aaron clutches it tightly.]
A: You can't have it. Get away. [The dolls continue to tug at the boat. The scene ends with them tugging at the boat.]

Questions for Discussion:

1. Tell me what Aaron and Cindy did when they played.
2. Why did they play this way?
3. Were they having a good time? (You may want to talk about the differences in the way Aaron and Cindy felt; talk about the differences between good and bad times.)
4. How did Aaron feel about playing with the boat?
5. How did Cindy feel when Aaron did not give her the boat?
6. What other ways could they have played?

Scene 2B: Each doll is playing contentedly by itself. Aaron has the boat; Cindy has the puppets.

C: [Walks over to Aaron.] Playing with that boat looks like fun. I want to play with it. Can I have it?
A: If I give you the boat, then I won't have anything to play with. That would be a problem. Let's think of what we can do. [Pause.]
C: I know! If you give me the boat to play with, then I'll give you the puppets. We could trade!
A: OK, then we'll each have something to play with and we won't have a problem. [Dolls trade the toys; they each resume play, separately, with the exchanged toys.]

Questions for Discussion:

1. Tell me what Aaron and Cindy did this time when they played. Sometimes when children play this way it is called trading. Sometimes children trade or bargain with their toys when they play. When people bargain they each agree to do something to or for each other. For example, you might say, "If you'll let me play puppets with you now, then I'll let you play with the boat later."

2. What other ways could Aaron and Cindy bargain?
3. What would you do if you wanted to trade with someone and they don't want to?
4. What would you do if you don't want to trade your toy for what another child has?

➡ **Conflict Mediation***

Objective: For children to learn to negotiate conflicts in democratic ways

General Information: This activity is to be carried out during the course of a naturally occurring conflict between two children in the classroom or on the playground. The exact nature of the conflict will influence the specific words and phrases used by the adult. Be sure to follow exactly the steps of the mediation process.

Step 1: Initiating the Mediation Process

The adult in charge observes signs of a conflict taking place. He or she moves to the site and watches carefully. The adult takes action if children seem unable to resolve the dispute or if they behave aggressively toward one another. The teacher stops any aggressive behavior and separates the combatants, saying, for example, "Sookyong and Alonzo, you are both pulling the toy. It looks like you both want it. You've got different ideas about how to use it. I'll hold it while we're deciding what to do. I'll give it back when we've figured it out." The adult then removes the toy; if territory is at issue, he or she safeguards it from being taken over by other children by declaring it "out of bounds." This procedure stops the children from continuing to hit or grab, helps them to listen, and assists them in approaching a highly emotional situation more calmly and objectively.

Step 2: Clarifying Each Child's Point of View

Ascertaining and paraphrasing each child's perspective vis-a-vis the conflict is the second part of the process. The adult asks each one, in turn, to tell his or her side of the story, without inter-

---

*For a more detailed discussion of this strategy, see Kostelnik et al. (in press).

ruption: "Alonzo, you think...," "Sookyong, you wanted...." Then the adult paraphrases every statement as it is made. Demonstrate that children may need more than one chance to express their point of view. This step is critical. For the adult to be trusted not to make an arbitrary decision, he or she must establish neutrality. Thus, do not make any evaluation or comment on the merits of either position. This step in the process may take considerable time; do not expect inexperienced children to complete it quickly since they may require repeated chances to fully express their points of view.

Step 3: Summing Up

State the problem in mutual terms: "You each want....We have a problem. It is important that we figure out what to do so each of you will be satisfied and no one will get hurt." The problem thus defined implies that both youngsters have responsibility for the problem and its solution.

Step 4: Generating Alternatives

The focus of the fourth step is for children to think of a number of possible solutions to the problem. It is at this point that bystanders as well as the combatants can have their say. Every time a solution is offered, the mediator paraphrases it to the youngsters directly involved. Each is then asked for an opinion. It is typical for children initially to reject a solution they later find acceptable, so even repeat suggestions should be brought to the table. Make suggestions, such as "Sometimes when people have this problem they can decide to share or take turns," if children seem unable to come up with ideas on their own. However, in order truly to leave the solution up to the children, do not indicate by words or tone of voice that any one plan meets with your approval or disapproval.

Step 5: Agreeing on a Solution

The ultimate aim of step 5 is to agree on a plan of action that is mutually satisfying. Help children explore the possibilities and find one or a combination of ideas that is acceptable. Make sure that the final agreement generally involves some compromise on the part of the children and so may not represent anyone's ideal. The mediator states the result: "You've agreed that you can take turns. First Sookyong will have it for 2 minutes, then Alonzo. It sounds like you solved the problem!"

Step 6: Reenforcing the Problem-solving Process

Praise children for their hard work in reaching a solution. Your goal is to demonstrate that what the solution turned out to be is not as important as the process of reaching it. Thus, children's emotional investment in the problem and the compromises that were made should be acknowledged as well.

Step 7: Following Through

Help the children carry out the terms of the agreement. This is especially important so that children will learn to trust that the mediation process is worth the time and effort they have put into it.

To Simplify: Shorten some of the procedural steps if you see signs of boredom or fatigue, such as extreme restlessness, turning away, or yawning. Keep the dialogue short and simple.

To Extend: Present a skit using the conflict mediation process. Involve children in determining how each step is to be resolved. At first, focus on issues of rights, territory, and possessions. Write scripts that focus on children's feelings as well as on more concrete issues. For instance, use name calling as an example. Model how you would mediate this kind of disagreement. In this case, the appropriate intermediate objective is for children to develop empathy for others by recognizing and respecting their emotions.

➧ The People's Choice*

Objective: For children to have an opportunity to negotiate a conflict in a democratic way by voting

---

*Many of these ideas are based on skits developed for *Teaching Young Children Using Themes*, M. J. Kostelnik (Ed.), Glenview, IL: Goodyear Books, 1991.

Materials: Chalkboard and chalk or large writing paper, marking pen, and three to five 3-inch × 12-inch pieces of oak tag or sentence strips

Procedure:

1. Introduce the activity by explaining that the whole group will select a name for a class pet, their favorite story, or whatever. Tell them they are going to vote, which means that each person will have a chance to choose a favorite name or story, and at the end they will figure out which choice most people liked best. That one will be the most popular because the most people liked it best, and it will be the one that wins.

2. Begin the process of choosing the alternatives. Limit the number of possibilities to three to five, enough that children can have a real option, but not so many that the cluster of children for each group is too small. Explain the limit to the children. Solicit suggestions and write down the first ideas on the chalkboard or paper, reading each aloud. When the list is complete, read each entry, running your hand under the word as you say it so that children can "read" it.

3. Write each option on a piece of oak tag and place it in a corner of the group area, separate from each other. For younger children, place an adult with each tag.

4. Tell children they are going to vote. Explain that they will choose only one of the options and then stand by the corresponding name. Say that they may not change their minds once they are in place, but assure them that there will be many opportunities to vote throughout the year. Ask each child in turn to pick a favorite from the list. You should read the list before each child chooses to remind him or her of the options and to minimize the likelihood that children will simply repeat the last person's selection. Write the child's name on the chalkboard next to the choice, and send him or her to the appropriate station. Children may abstain from voting. In this case, direct the individual to remain seated and offer another chance when everyone is finished.

5. Once the group has divided into areas, instruct children to look at the groups and esti-

mate which has the most people (which choice is the most popular). Make sure everyone who wishes to has a chance to speak. Paraphrase and then summarize their ideas.

6. Tell children that there are several ways to find out which is most popular. Line up two groups and ask the children which line is longer.

7. Paraphrase children's responses. Compare another group's line with the longer line. Continue comparing until the longest line is determined. Then ask children which line has the most people.

8. With the children assisting, count the members of each group and record the number on the board or chart. Ask children which number is largest.

9. Explain again that the group having the largest number of members represents the most popular choice. Ask children to tell which entry "won the voting." Announce the result and mark it on the chart or board.

A child may insist that the name he or she has chosen is most popular (even if this is not the case). Differentiate what the child "wants" to be true from what he or she "thinks" is true. Carefully review the evidence (counting again if necessary) until the child can accept the answer. Be patient. This is evidence of egocentric thinking, not stubbornness.

To Simplify: Younger children may tire of the process before the final decision. If you detect signs of restlessness, move to the final step quickly (you may have to condense a few steps) so that the children experience closure to the activity. Limit the children's choices to two or three.

To Extend: In the step in which children "vote with their feet," substitute using their names on the chalkboard to represent them. Have youngsters count these and compare quantities. If this is your plan, print the names clearly enough for children to see easily. If children are having difficulty, quickly move to the original procedure. At a later time, ask children to recap the decision-making procedure that occurred and discuss the results. After a period of

days or weeks, revote and compare the results with the original outcome.

➡ **Rules of the Game**

Objective: To help children conform to reasonable limits set on behavior, play space, use of materials or the types of activities in which they are involved

Materials: Large paper and marking pen for recording children's ideas

Procedure:

1. Select an issue for children to make a set of rules about. These might include a play space that can comfortably hold a limited number of children, how to decide who should be first in line, problems involving safety, people's rights, or the preservation of property.

2. Assemble the whole group for a discussion. Pose the problem to them. Explain that when groups of people encounter such difficulties, they often make rules to help people live and work together more harmoniously.

3. Define a rule as "a guide for behavior," and be sure to highlight how the specific issue you have chosen impacts on one or another key element of safety, rights, and property.

4. Ask children to name some classroom or school rules and to give reasons why they think the rules were made. Find out what they think of the rule.

5. Elicit ideas from children about what rules could be made to solve the current problem. Write down all of their ideas on the paper. Urge them to state their rule in a positive rather than negative way. You may have to paraphrase to accomplish this. Repeat each idea as you write it. Acknowledge all ideas, even when they are repeats, by saying, "You also think...."

6. Next, go over the list with the children and refine it. If, for instance, someone thinks that 100 minutes is a good amount of time for a turn in the spacecraft, help children understand what that means (e.g., "That is as much time as we spend at group time, *and* free choice, *and* snack every day!"). Once the list has been pared down to a few items,

rewrite it and post it in an appropriate place for all to see.

7. At a later date, review the rules and assess with children how well they are working. Make changes, if children and adults agree it is necessary.

To Simplify: Choose very basic issues, such as how to carry blocks or scissors safely. Keep the rules simple.

To Extend: Have children generate consequences for rule infraction. Help them understand that these should be closely related to the rule itself. Focus on restitution wherever possible and on loss of access, when appropriate. Allow the group to make rules about an increasing number of issues in their school lives, as they become more experienced.

➡ **All Together, Now**

Objective: For children to learn to be cooperative

Materials: Boxes, cartons, and containers of various sizes and shapes (these could be provided by the adult, or children could be asked to bring one or more to contribute to the project), glue, masking tape, staple gun, stapler, poster paint, brushes, newspapers, towels, sponge buckets, scissors, markers, crayons, glitter, fabric swatches, wallpaper. There should be a wide variety of materials but a limited supply of each.

Procedure:

1. Establish small groups consisting of five to six children each. The groups will remain stable throughout the life of the project. Plan this project over several days.
2. Set up the activity prior to the children's arrival by placing all of the materials in the center of the project area—crayons in one bin, markers in another, scissors in another, and so on. This will encourage youngsters to share materials more than if each child had his or her own personal supply.
3. Introduce the activity by explaining that many people will work together to make a group sculpture; no one person will be in charge. Instead, everyone must work as a team. Ex-

plain that everyone will have jobs to do and that the finished project will belong to everyone. Tell children they will be planners as well as constructors. Point out the materials that are available, and say that children may use any of them they wish.

4. The first day is for planning. Help children as a group figure out if they want their constructions to represent something or simply to be a design. This step may take some time to complete. Mediate any conflicts that children are unable to resolve on their own. Point out instances of compromise, taking each other's ideas into account and other examples of prosocial behaviors that the children display. Make suggestions if they are needed to help children move toward closure. The theme children are studying is a good starting point. Allow children to take as much responsibility for their own project as they seem able to do.
5. The second day of the project is construction. Remind children again that this is a task in which everyone is to be involved. Children may choose to work individually or in pairs while contributing to the construction. Allow ample time so children do not feel hurried. Also, provide a safe spot for the project to be housed between work periods. Once you have set up the materials, step back and observe the children at work.
6. When the construction is completed to everyone's satisfaction, display it in the classroom or elsewhere in school. Let children report about the process to the rest of the class, highlighting who participated and how each person contributed to the whole.

To Simplify: Pair children to work on a short-range project. This may be as simple as painting on one paper at the easel. Set up a mural (e.g., of trees) and allow children to contribute parts (leaves, birds, etc.).

To Extend: Have children generate a list in advance of the tasks to be accomplished. Then let children volunteer for the various ones. Encourage children to evaluate the project once it is completed. They can also write or dictate guidelines for future similar endeavors.

➡ Helping Decisions

Objectives: To teach children to recognize situations in which people need help and to determine appropriate ways of helping

Materials: Eight to 10 pictures selected from magazines that show people or animals who need help in some way or people who are being helped in some way. These should be large enough for four or five children to be able to see them 2 or 3 feet away and mounted on cardboard. Pictures should depict a diverse population and different situations.

Procedure:

1. Select one picture at a time for discussion. Keep other pictures facedown.
2. Introduce the activity by saying, "I have several pictures here about helping. Look at this one: somebody needs help."
3. Prompt discussion with questions and statements such as "Tell me who needs help. How did you know? Is there anyone in the picture who could help? What could they do? Who has another idea? What do you think this person will do if someone tries to help? Why might the person in need of help not want the person offering it to help? What might you do if you had the same problem as the people in the picture?"
4. Paraphrase children's suggestions and ideas, and elicit reactions from other youngsters in the group.
5. Accept all the children's suggestions, and praise them for working so hard at figuring out who needs help, who could help, and what should be done.
6. Should the discussion falter, provide useful information by pointing out facial expressions or other salient features of the scene that might give children clues. Offer suggestions for possible helpful behaviors.

To Simplify: Focus on physical assistance and comfort as being the most easily discernible instances of need.

To Extend: Use pictures that depict people in situations in which the best way to help is to do nothing (e.g., a child with cerebral palsy struggling to feed him- or herself).

➡ A Fair Deal

Objective: For children to have an opportunity to learn to be helpful by sharing

Materials: Three crayons or markers and paper, or three animal models; table with five chairs—one for the teacher, the others for children

Procedure:

1. Place the markers (models) in the center of the table. Say, "I have three markers (models) and there are four children who want to use them. Tell me how everyone can have a chance."
2. Listen to children's ideas; elicit suggestions from everyone. Clarify each child's prospective by paraphrasing his or her ideas to the group. Follow up with "And what do you think of that?"
3. Remain impartial throughout this process. Do not show approval or disapproval of any child's idea, regardless of its content; what may seem "fair" to a child may not seem so to an adult. Remember, it is the children who are to determine the outcome.
4. Remind children as necessary that the first step in playing is deciding how that will take place. Point out areas of agreement as they occur. If children become bogged down, make suggestions, such as "Sometimes when people are trying to figure out how to share something, they decide that one person should use all the markers or that children should pass the markers around and everyone takes turns playing with them."
5. Acknowledge children's hard work and good ideas as they grapple with the problem. Remind them they are helping each other share.
6. Summarize the solution when it has been achieved, and help children carry out the terms of the agreement.
7. Repeat this activity another time using a different material but a similar central problem. Be sure every child in the group has an opportunity to take part eventually.

To Simplify: Limit the number of children involved to two. Watch for signs of frustration and condense steps if necessary to make sure children actually have a chance to use the materials.

To Extend: After children have been working for a while, have them evaluate their original solution. Allow them to make modifications as they choose. Ask children if they can think of other situations for which the same or a similar solution would be appropriate. Make arrangements so that they can implement their ideas.

⇒ Alike and Different

Objective: For children to become aware of similarities and differences among people

Materials: Standing mirror, paper and pencil for recording children's observations

Procedure:

1. Invite children two at a time to look into a mirror at themselves and each other. Help them discover characteristics they have in common and things that are different. This is an ideal opportunity to pair children who may be different in physical ableness, sex, and appearance in order to help them discover similarities beyond the obvious.
2. Make two lists, one in which likenesses are indicated ("We are alike") and the other that records differences ("We are different"). Urge them to begin with physical appearance and to move on to other attributes, such as interests, ideas, preferences, skills, handedness, number of siblings, letters in their names, and so on.
3. Tell the partners that as they observe more things about themselves and each other, they can add to the list throughout the day. At this point, allow the children to continue the activity without interference.
4. At the end of the day, suggest that children review the list and count up all the things they discovered. Let them find out if they came up with more similarities or differences.
5. Repeat this activity, mixing up pairs until all the children have had a chance to be paired with each other. If there is time, repeat the activity later in the year and compare with the original lists. See if the categories have increased as children learn more about each other over time.

To Simplify: Focus only on physical attributes, adding other dimensions as children mature.

To Extend: Without naming the children involved, read some lists to the class and have them guess the pairs in question.

⇒ We Are a Family

Objective: To help children develop a respect for the values, ethnic background, family traditions, culture, gender, differing abilities and special needs of others

Materials: Photographs of children and adults in the classroom and members of their families, a board on which to display these

General Guidelines: Request photographs from each child's family well in advance (2–3 weeks may be necessary). Assure the families that their photos will be returned. Label the pictures with names and relationships of each person. When you have secured the pictures, mount them temporarily on a bulletin board or oak tag, using care not to mar them. Label the pictures with names and relationships of each person. Numerous activities can then be planned using these family pictures.

Procedure:

1. Over a period of time, allow each person in the class an opportunity to talk about his or her family. Respond positively to children's comments about any similarities or differences they notice in family structures. Avoid using terms like *only* when describing a child's family, as in "Judith has only a grandma in her family." Talk with children about the range of possible family compositions.
2. Encourage children to write or dictate stories about their family, telling what they like to do together, how each person in the family works to help the family, how they celebrate special holidays or occasions, and so on. Tell children to read these to the other children. Elicit comments from children about these practices. Reinforce the idea that each family does things in ways that are meaningful to its members.
3. Instruct children to graph independently the various families in the group. These can be

compared with one another as children identify which families are composed of many people, which fewer; which families include pets, which do not; which family members look like other members, which do not.

4. Put the pictures in a book called "The Families in Our Class." Include stories and other descriptions that children have written or dictated. Make the book available for children to "read."

To Simplify: Focus on what children can see depicted in the photographs, such as family composition.

To Extend: Delve more deeply into family traditions by asking children to bring in and talk about important family artifacts. Elicit information from families about favorite stories, jokes, and so forth. Write these out for children to see. Compare them with other versions.

➡ Match-ups

Objective: For children to develop positive attitudes toward people who are different from themselves

Materials: One set of pictures portraying people of different ages, sexes, culture groups, races, and physical abilities; one set of pictures of commonly used tools, household implements, or office equipment; two boxes, one for each set of pictures

Procedure:

1. Mount the pictures on cards or tag board so they will stand up to repeated use.
2. Explain the procedure to children. Pair children or establish small groups. Say that they are to pick one picture from each container, decide whether that person could use the tools, and give a reason for their decision.
3. As they work, listen for indications of children's stereotypical thinking (e.g., that a person in a wheelchair could not work in an office or that a man could not, or should not, use a blender). Confront these erroneous notions directly, at a later time, by giving children accurate and relevant information. Ask other children who may be standing by for

their ideas. Facilitate discussions between children on these issues.

4. If children persist in their opinions, plan to introduce activities or visitors into your program that will confound their assumptions. For example, invite an individual in a wheelchair to demonstrate his or her abilities, or do a cooking activity with the boys as well as the girls.

To Simplify: Select pictures that depict a limited range of tools. Focus on one personal attribute at a time in your pictures.

To Extend: Write children's ideas on a sheet of paper. Discuss them with the group as a whole. Help children figure out how they could find actual answers to the questions that arise.

➡ Recycle-Ickles

Objective: For children to develop a sense of responsibility for the environment

Materials: Medium-sized plastic bags labeled with each child's name, safety pins to secure them to children's clothing

Procedure:

1. Carry out a discussion with children about trash—what it is, how it is generated, what the effect is on the environment, and what people can do to recycle materials that are no longer wanted. Explain that each child will collect the trash he or she produces during a day and place it in the plastic bag. Tell children that at the end of the day they will examine their trash and make determinations about how to reuse it. Then allow children to proceed on their own.
2. Plan a time at the end of the day for children to examine the things they have collected in their bags. Ask each individual to state one way he or she can recycle the materials (include the collection bag, as well). Tell children that they are now "Recycle-Ickles." Provide each child with a badge that says, "I am a Recycle-Ickle. I reuse my trash."
3. Set aside a recycling center in which to store the materials they have collected and encourage children to reuse it on the following day.

To Simplify: Use a classroom collection bag rather than individual bags.

To Extend: Carry out the activity over an extended period of time. Evaluate whether children are able to generate less trash as time goes on. Set this as a goal for the school year. Extend the activity to include a collection of schoolwide trash. Follow a similar procedure and acknowledge the efforts of each classroom as they cut down on the trash they generate over time.

CHAPTER 9

The Pretend Play Domain

Four first graders were talking intently in the bushes near the corner of the playground.
"Let's pretend that we are lost and all alone and have to build our house," commented Alice.

"Yeah, we'll have to build it here. This could be a place to sleep," contributed Diane.

"And nobody knows where we are. No grown-ups. And no boys can come in here. Right?" Joan queried. "Shari, you get started on the kitchen. We gotta have a kitchen. Tomorrow we can bring some food."

"You say these children are learning! What are they learning? Does this kind of activity really belong in school?"

Teachers, along with much of the general public, take children's pretend play for granted and either do not think of it at all or assume that its place is in the home or playground.

Pretend play is the hallmark of the early childhood period. In fact, Piaget (1962) used simple pretend as one of the criteria for differentiating between the sensorimotor period and the preoperational period that encompass children from 3 to 8. Adults recognize it immediately, frequently dismissing it as a trivial pursuit of young children. More recently scholars have recognized that pretend play has a *formative* function that enables the child to adapt to the social and physical environment as well as an *expressive* function that facilitates children's communication with others about their thinking and feelings related to their understandings of the world as they experience it (Bergen, 1988; Frost, 1991). Early childhood educators have long perceived pretend play as a vehicle for integrating various developmental capacities, allowing for practice of skills, and the mastery of new challenges as children's pretend play grows increasingly complex during this period.

CHARACTERISTICS OF PRETEND PLAY

In chapter 2, the nature of all play is described. Play is fun, carried out for the pleasure of doing it, free of externally imposed rules, spontaneous, and voluntary. It also requires the active involvement of the player, as well as the suspension of

reality. It is symbolic behavior that allows the player to treat objects as though they were something else. The spoon becomes the musician's baton or the block structure becomes a spaceship. Players take on roles as though they were performers or explorers and sometimes as though they were machines. Players establish rules consistent with the play theme and roles requiring each other to perform in patterns that fit the narrative. For example, any contribution to the establishment of a household, the protection of the group, or other survival topics would be appropriate to the scenario described at the start of the chapter. Extraneous events, comments, or behavior either would be rejected or ignored by the players or would cause the play to disintegrate. Reality is suspended, but the play is governed by rules so that the play event itself has internal coherence. Children function in the enactive mode as they do simple make-believe, shifting to the iconic mode when they need to construct an object to further their play and utilize the symbolic mode in complex play scenarios. Thus, imaginative, abstract thinking, set within the play frame and composed of sequences of action events, is typical.

The play frame describes the scope of the pretend play event. Inside the play frame are all of the people and objects that the children are using to enact their imaginative episode. The people, objects, and pretend narrative are all relevant to each other and the progress of the play event. If a photograph were taken of the pretend play episode described at the beginning of the chapter, the photographer would automatically move back to include all the players and relevant objects, even though other persons might be in either the foreground or the background of the photo. Players within the frame are those who have a communication link, who are engaged in the play. All of the other persons and objects without a relationship to the pretend narrative in progress are not in the play frame.

The frames of play may be established by a variety of modes (Sutton-Smith, 1986). Establishing the frame of the play allows children to communicate the theme, roles, and specific story to be enacted. Children might establish the frame by announcing it—"This is the house"—or by announcing a play role—"I'm the policeman"—or simply by acting on objects such as putting the train track together and running the train on it. Sometimes a smile and a gesture is sufficient between familiar players revisiting a common action sequence.

Recognition of play frames is important to educators because, though pretend play has its own internal logic with a unique imaginative quality, the player's behavior must be understood from that frame of reference. Usually, however, the "reality" described in the pretend play does reflect the level of understanding shared by the children. For example, if children are pretending to be firepersons and they assign one of the players to set fires, they lack information about the causes of fires and the true functions of firefighters. Although everyone agrees that play within the play frame is not "for real," adults may get insight into children's thinking by the content and skill with which they play.

ELEMENTS OF PRETEND PLAY

Pretend play is composed of a set of skills or elements that may be used singly (in less skilled players) or in combination (with players of greater skill). All players must be able to participate in *make-believe;* that is, they must be able to suspend reality, even momentarily, to engage in the simplest form of pretend play, which is pretending with an object. When children pretend with objects, they act as though the stuffed animal were a baby, or as though bits of Play-doh® were food, or as though the toy cars were real vehicles. Often the characteristics of the object itself suggest the pretend to the child. For example, a classroom computer might suggest to the child to play airport controller, mission control for a space launch, or a worker with computers. Stuffed animals might suggest the pretend notion of zoo, farm, or veterinarian in much the same way.

When the object needed is not at hand, children engage in *object substitution.* This is straightforward representational thinking in which the child represents one object with another closer at hand (Raines, 1990). Whereas one child might get a pencil and paper to take an order in a restaurant, another might substitute a hand for the paper and a finger for the

pencil to represent the needed tools. Object substitutions are signaled by either actions or narrative. Three-year-olds can readily substitute one object in their play, and older children are capable of using more when playing alone. In addition, younger children are more likely to substitute objects that perceptually suggest the needed device. For example, a shell or a can is more likely to be substituted for a cup than is a string or a stick.

Primary-age youngsters may not need an object for the substitution. Instead, they use *object invention* and represent the objects needed solely through pantomime. A 7-year-old may open the door of a cupboard (that does not exist), remove a bowl (that is not there), place it on a real table, and begin to stir with an imaginary spoon. Measuring cups and ingredients may be represented either through the narrative or through actions alone. Three- to 5-year-olds find it very difficult to play with a variety of object inventions, although older children do it more easily. Additionally, all children have difficulty when playing in groups with more than one imaginary person or object. They appear to need something as a placeholder to engage in shared imaginary objects. For example, three 6-year-olds who were engaged in playing out small-town life together drew streets in the dirt with their fingers and used leaves for community buildings and small mounds for houses. One child had designated an empty area as the vacant lot early in the play, and later another started to construct a house on it. After much discussion, the children agreed to draw a ring around the vacant lot to designate it so that others would not forget what it was. The ring defined the vacant lot and became the placeholder for empty space. Frequently iconic representations of objects are used as placeholders with several players, just to avoid the confusion these children experienced.

Children throughout the early childhood period play like someone or something. They take on *roles.* These roles may be based on TV or movies (*Teenage Mutant Ninja Turtles*); functional roles (one who eats or uses a computer); familial or relational roles (husband/father, wife/mother); or occupational roles (nurse, robber). Obviously, children must be familiar with the roles that they

"...3, 2, 1, blast-off!" Charlotte has transformed the computer station into mission control.

assume. Pretending to be oneself in another setting occurs between ages 2 and 3. *Family roles* predominate during the preschool period, with presentations of primary caregivers portrayed with emotional meanings (Garvey & Berndt, 1977). *Nurturing roles* may become very elaborate over time as children incorporate greater complexity into the action sequences that they represent. *Occupational roles* emerge slowly in older preschool children as they become aware of the larger community. These roles are heavily influenced by the experience children have and their school curriculum. School-age children elaborate on earlier roles and include frightening fantasies and themes of victim and aggressor. *Fictional roles,* those developed in television, movies, or literature, generate high-action, powerful roles particularly attractive to boys. Though these roles are fun, they may be somewhat flat, having limited dimensions of character. The sarcastic humor and the use of phrases having more than one meaning that are common in cartoons are not fully understood by young children, so they depend predominantly on the action to interpret the character. Sometimes these portrayals lack the personal creativity that the children are otherwise capable of demonstrating.

Children learn to transform *time, place,* and *setting.* These transformations enable them to pretend to be pioneers or space adventurers. The beach, stores, circus, or market might be places visited in the classroom play space. Time and place simply have no restrictions except those of information available to the players. For example, a 3-year-old who remains at home while family business is transacted would not have sufficient information to pretend banking or stores, whereas a second grader who had both a school social studies background and more community experience would be prepared to engage in these play themes with considerable elaboration.

When children play together, they must engage in complex communications called *metacommunication,* which means a communication about a communication (Bateson, 1971). These communications tend to describe what is "play" and what is not. They may serve to construct the play frame ("Let's pretend to be hunters") or define roles ("We can be neighbors who don't like each other").

Metacommunication statements transform objects and settings. "This [puppet stage] is the post office window" or "I'm in a dark forest and lost" typically set the stage for continuing the play and provide the beginning narrative and context for continuing communication.

Additionally, children use metacommunications to extend their play and elaborate on characters' feelings or actions. In each case, cues for the content of continuing communication are provided: "This is a very dark forest, and I hope there are no monsters here" or "Pretend that you are a really mean bad guy."

Metacommunications also end the framed sequence. Children may deny the role ("I'm not the bad guy any more"), change the meaning of the props ("This window [puppet theater] is really a window out of a spaceship"), or redefine the setting ("Why don't we pretend we were rescued and put in the hospital?").

Metacommunications serve to combine the basic elements of pretend play and the framing process so that all players in a cooperative play venture can participate knowledgeably. All of the preceding elements of pretend play may be engaged in alone; however, once more players are involved, metacommunications are necessary for the pretend sequence to have any coherence.

ACCOUNTING FOR DIFFERENCES

Maturity, family life experiences, and cultural background are factors that influence the content of pretend play as well as the skills players possess. First of all, maturity is a factor. Three-year-olds do not possess the vocabulary, life experience, or level of abstract thinking that older children demonstrate. Their pretend play is usually solitary, beside another player who is playing similarly, or in short episodes of cooperative pretend play. Frequently they are unable to express the metacommunication messages necessary for more elaborate play. They usually select content based on familiar roles, such as those of the family, rather than fiction.

The general life experience varies considerably as well. Children from rural areas know more about farming than urban children and can pretend appropriate roles much earlier than their city counterparts of similar maturity. Some children have experienced police raids in the neighborhoods and have a working knowledge of street gangs by the time they are 5 years old, whereas other children of similar ages are completely ignorant of such occurrences. Children tend to play out the scenes and scenarios with which they are most familiar. Therefore, for most teachers, variety in content and leadership is typical.

Smilansky (1968) was the first to note that skill development in the elements of pretend play was limited or absent in lower socioeconomic groups in Israel. This finding was later verified in studies in the United States (Fein & Stork, 1981) and modified by Eiferman (1971) to indicate that the deficiency was one of developmental delay rather than inability. This means that some children may not possess even the rudimentary pretend skills at age 5 or 6 that other children exhibit at age 3. Children can and do learn the elements of pretend play with appropriate adult instruction in educational settings (Christie, 1986).

Many classrooms are composed of families from a variety of cultural backgrounds. The way families play out the role of mother is different in different families. This is true of the individual family culture as well as nationality such as Arabic, Japanese, or Spanish. Players of different backgrounds often need help in negotiating their play. Younger children generally do not realize that different people may come to the play with perspectives vastly dissimilar from their own.

Finally, there are differences in the quality of pretend play. These differences tend to center on the ability to maintain a group play theme over time and the inclusion of problems to be solved by the players in the theme (Roskos, 1990). Typical themes might be bakery, flea market, beach, school, or library. Children enact roles relevant to these settings. When they include a problem within the play, such as a fire starting in the library basement or an emergency patient entering the hospital, the narrative and enactment of the pretend play has more storylike qualities. There is (a) a beginning, (b) problem identification, (c) the development of the plot, (d) resolution of the problem, and (e) an ending. Increased complexity of play is possible for 4- and 5-year-olds in environments that support their play and if they are skilled in all the play elements. Maturity is necessary but not sufficient to enable children to engage in high-quality play. Skill, supportive environments, and practice are essential ingredients to achieve the most advanced levels of pretend play.

PLAY AND OTHER ASPECTS OF DEVELOPMENT AND LEARNING

Cognitive Development

Theorists have not always agreed about the role of play in cognitive development. Piaget (1962) assigned a consolidative role to pretend play, stating that play reflected the child's cognitive constructs and allowed for assimilating new feelings and experiences. Pretend play is a clear example of representational thought (Yawkey, 1987) in which the child transforms objects, situations, and events using make-believe (Piaget, 1962). On the other hand, Vygotsky (1967) viewed pretend play as being responsible for the emergence of abstract thought. Whether pretend play mirrors children's cognitive processes or causes them is yet unclear. There is still ample evidence that pretend play is a significant factor in children's intellectual functioning.

Pretend play experiences result in improved problem solving (Dansky, 1980). Children are able to create new strategies applicable to novel situations (Bruner, Jolly, & Sylva, 1976). In pretend play children must invent as well as consider "what if" propositions in the normal course of the episode (Wolf, 1991). They try on new roles and engage in experiences not otherwise available to them. Opportunities for problem identification and the generation of varieties of solutions to ordinary situations created in make-believe situations abound. Children simply can practice and consolidate their skills.

Children also construct cognitive prototypes or models for thinking about something in their play (Sutton-Smith, 1977). What is most remarkable is that children as young as 3 are able to think about a role at all. Although they cannot explain or define a role, they have little difficulty in observing, abstracting out the outstanding characteristics of a particular role, and then portraying them. All the while, they are perfectly aware of what they are doing. Similar strategies are developed for other aspects of the pretend play process. Pretend play also results in improved creative thinking during which children can develop increasing numbers of divergent uses for objects (Pepler, 1982). This appears to be a byproduct of the ability to transform one object to be used as another.

Children may also acquire new information, although that is not the primary function of pretend play. It is most likely to occur when children of differing background and experience confront one another in the play setting. Players tend to require their peers to play consistently within the theme and behave appropriately to the role. To that end they may inform, coach, or direct other players and teach one another.

Emotional Development

Pretend play has long been recognized as a vehicle for children to express their innermost thoughts and feelings. Although most play episodes are based either on immediate past observations and experiences or in response to cues from the physical environment of the school, children can and do enact play sequences that express their concerns. Children achieve mastery of their feelings when they rework a scene to a happier conclusion, can express repressed feelings, and can try out solutions to normal daily crisis. All children experience fears about being accepted, may actually be temporarily rejected by their peers, or may have concerns about family members. For example, two 8-year-olds played out marriage, separation, divorce, courtship, and remarriage over a period of several weeks. One child came from a stable two-parent family, and her best friend had already lived through the divorce process, with her father remarrying and a mother contemplating a second marriage. Through multiple play sequences the inevitable uncertainties that this child was experiencing were portrayed. Pretend play is a normal process by which healthy children learn to cope with the problems of daily life.

Social Development

Social competence, or the ability to function effectively in society appropriate to one's age, is composed of several aspects (Eisenberg & Harris, 1984). Perspective taking, conceptions of friendship, interpersonal strategies, problem solving, moral judgment, and communication skills are all components of social behavior. Participation in sociodramatic play requires a high level of both social and cognitive abilities, including sharing and cooperation, appreciation of role reciprocity, and self-regulation of affect (Frost, 1991). Generally, increases in pretend play skills are associated with corresponding increases in all three aspects of social cognition:

- Visual or perceptual perspective taking—How does another person see the world?
- Cognitive perspective taking—What are other people thinking? What are other people like?
- Affective perspective taking—What kind of emotional experiences is another person having? (Johnsen & Christie, 1984, p. 109)

The spontaneous play of pretend scripts provides the context and the practice for children to learn negotiation skills and achieve social acceptance (Doyle & Connolly, 1989). Children, via the metacommunications that structure and direct their play, continually engage in social comparison and check out with one another their perceptions of what is going forward. These checks are frequently in the form of tag questions ("You're not going to her house, right?") as a request for information. Correspondingly, they make requests for agreement ("Let's not play house today, OK?"), permission ("I need to make this street longer, right?" [moving into another's play space]), compliance ("You can put those babies to bed now, huh?"), verbal response ("You like to play cars, right?"), and attention ("This is a bridge, see?") (Chafel, 1986). As children initiate and respond to verbalizations that are essential to social play, they develop leadership skills (Trawick-Smith, 1988). In early childhood, the children high in leadership are also high in following. They can contribute to the direction of play but do not dominate it.

Language Development

The research on the role of pretend play on language development is extensive with most studies finding positive relationships (Frost, 1991). In a detailed review of the literature, play was found to have the following specific effects (Levy, 1984, p. 167). Play

- stimulates innovation in language (Bruner, 1983; Garvey, 1977),
- introduces and clarifies new words and concepts (Chukovsky, 1968; Smilansky, 1968),
- motivates language use and practice (Bruner, 1983; Garvey, 1977; Garvey & Hagan, 1973; Smilansky, 1968; Vygotsky, 1962), and
- encourages verbal thinking (Vygotsky, 1962).

Apparently the relationship between symbolic play and language increases with age as the play becomes more abstract and independent of real objects as a source of shared meaning. Good players are more verbal during play. In fact, in kindergartners, observations of children's language at play were found to be better indicators of language ability than formal assessments such as the Illinois Test of Psycholinguistic Abilities (Levy, 1984).

Recently, there has been a marked increase in the research relating emergent literacy to pretend play of children between 4 and 6 (Christie, 1990). When pretend play is enhanced with appropriate materials, children incorporate literacy acts such as looking at a cookbook while preparing a pretend meal or writing an address on an envelope to be mailed from the pretend post office into their play. When appropriate teacher guidance is added, the variety and frequency of such acts is increased (L. Morrow, 1990). Children also produce a variety of written language that is functional in nature. They write to (a) serve instrumental purposes (making a list of things to get), (b) regulate the behavior of others (preparing a "Keep Out" sign), (c) meet interactional needs (writing a phone number for a friend), (d) fill personal needs (own name on paper), and (e) relay information (making a "Telephone Broken" sign) (Schrader, 1989). Children also engage in conversations about literacy within the play context, which might include using literacy conventions, naming literacy-related objects, or even coaching one another in some literacy task in order to achieve a play goal (Neuman & Roskos, 1990). In addition, it has been suggested that children use similar representational mental processes in both symbolic play and literate behavior (Schrader, 1990) so that the enhancement and practice of pretend play is likely to facilitate the acquisition of reading competence.

TYPICAL TYPES OF PRETEND PLAY

Usually adults conceive of pretend play as being unidimensional. Selected forms of pretend play will be described here, but this listing is not intended to be definitive. The quality and complexity of the play as well as the setting are important variables among the types of play. Probably the outcomes described in the previous section are limited to the more complex sociodramatic play sequences, although skill in play can be developed in any form.

Make-Believe

Simple pretend is when the child takes on the characteristics of an object or person and acts out a sequence. For example, 3-year-olds might pretend to be balloons who are being blown up by another child. Five-year-olds might walk down the hallway connected to each other to form a train and "chug, chug, chug" as they move. Eight-year-olds might pretend to be an airplane or a cloud moving over the mountains. Such episodes may be interspersed deliberately by the teacher or developed spontaneously by the children.

Pretend with Objects

Exploration of an object or any new material always precedes well-developed play sequences regardless of the children's age, skills, or familiarity with the material. In exploration the child discovers "What is the nature of this object?" whereas in pretend the child wonders, "What can I do with this?" Unskilled players may vacillate between pretend play and exploration while they are learning how to pretend with an object. For example, Rico, age 4, picked up a stethoscope and correctly identified it as a "doctor thing." He swung it around, talked into it, hung it

on his neck, and used it to hit at Maria. Mark told him to put the earplugs in his ears and listen to the heart. Rico tried this. He listened to tables, the window, and the radiator before attempting to listen to another child. Then he engaged in a brief doctor episode while listening to a doll's chest. Alternating between listening to dolls and children and other objects in the environment, Rico's play vacillated between pretend with an object and exploration. Older children may also pretend by themselves and focus on the object that they are using. Children who have few playmates may be very skilled in developing a variety of pretend scenarios based on a single object. Over several play episodes, Allison used an old-fashioned wash basin as an ocean for stick boats, a wash basin for a doll, a helmet, and a cooking pot. Even in the most traditional classrooms, teachers are familiar with children's tendency to use anything for play: bits of paper, pencils, articles of clothing, science equipment, and so on.

Pretend with Art Materials

Some 3- to 5-year-olds are primarily concerned about the pattern, color, or form of their visual art experiences, while others typically have a story that the graphic portion represents. Children may express verbally the pretend story component as the child produces the graphic: "And the scary spider dropped down...to the ground. And he moved around. He went up and the wind blew him. Almost hit the boy." Thus, they use the "movements of play, the lines of drawing, and the sounds of language to represent the people, objects, and events that comprise their world" (Dyson, 1990, p. 50). Children may even share a pretend play sequence, talking and drawing at the same time. Five- to 8-year-olds may contribute the pretend portion of this creative experience but are more successful in doing so without speech than are the younger ones. Drawings incorporate more of the movement and more details of the pretend as children mature.

Pretend with Construction Materials

Probably the most complex of all play episodes are ones in which children construct the necessary play props to support their pretend theme or action sequence. In this case, the play shifts back and forth from construction to pretend play. In younger children, this is most frequently seen in the blocks with which a child might build a house or a barn and then use cars and small dolls to enact a scene. Older children may continue the same play action sequence for several days, building additional components as they go along. In one Indiana kindergarten, children reconstructed their own small town over a period of several weeks using clay, small cardboard boxes, and other discards. Throughout the elementary school period, children build snow forts, treehouses, stores, and homes in which to engage in increasingly elaborate pretend play sequences.

Pretend with Miniature Buildings and People

Dollhouses, barns and animals, vehicles with passengers, and other miniature pretend settings are available to stimulate pretend play. Children provide the story and manipulate the characters that are suggested by the manufacturer. The big difference in this play is that children do not engage in the movement and cannot use facial expression or body action to convey ideas and feelings. They become the narrator; although they might portray many parts, they are not an actor with their own bodies. Children from 5 to 8 usually have the capacity to use their voices to portray a variety of affect. Younger children are likely to find some way to include larger movements, such as transporting the farm animals in a truck.

Dramatic Play

During dramatic play the child carries out a sequence of events or actions that are related to one another. Pretend with object, place, time, and setting may all be utilized by the child in a particular episode. With younger children, the sequences are likely to be based on routines familiar to the child such as feeding the doll, bathing the doll, putting the doll to bed, with other care-giving activities included as called for by the player. In older children, the child might

play a more distant role and pretend to be a bus driver or even a worker at mission control guiding spaceships (that are being constructed out of clay) in takeoff or landing sequences. The play may be solitary or in the company of other children but not necessarily interacting with them except through observation or shared space. Seven- and 8-year-olds are able to pick up the play theme from day to day and continue where 3- to 5-year-olds are more likely to start over. Such differences in skill and maturity influence the selection of the play topic and the duration and complexity of the play enactment.

Sociodramatic Play

This kind of play involves several children playing together for at least 10 minutes and engaging in the same thematic sequence. The narrative is negotiated, the roles established with various directives on how to forward the play plan. Usually pretend with time, setting, and place are agreed on by the players as the play progresses and may be completely embedded in the script. "Gee, it's getting dark now" automatically calls for an evening sequence of actions by other players. A second child might respond, "Where will we sleep?" which draws the play into a housing or furnishing problem. The story line is shared by all the players, with any individual child both following others' leads as well as contributing new ideas. Children frequently prompt each other when factual errors are made in the play, such as one child whispering loudly, "The store man collects the money for the stuff. Doesn't pay someone to take it." This play is very goal directed and may center around a number of themes: beauty shop, school, camping, hospital, restaurant, family, or fire station. Children of 4 to 5 rarely have more than one intangible object, if any, when playing in groups. It is difficult for several children to keep in mind objects that do not exist in reality.

Detail and accuracy of portrayal increase with practice and maturity. In addition, children add problems that must be solved within the play. These frequently are reasonable for the setting, such as having a fire drill while playing school, or running out of permanents in a beauty shop, or having a fire in a garage. Primary-age children may successfully incorporate themes from television, video stories, or literature within their sociodramatic play. Preschool children are able to play their most complex sociodramatic scenarios based on settings with which they are most familiar, such as babies, families, and neighbors, although they sometimes also attempt fantasy characters.

Story Reenactments

This type of play has been called *creative dramatics* and also *thematic-fantasy play*. It involves children developing the skills of taking on a role and re-creating a plot. Through story reenactment children are able to take on a variety of roles that they otherwise would have no way of experiencing. The scope of mood, setting, and plot structures in literature far exceeds what a small group of children can imagine without any additional sources.

Write and Play

In this type of play children dictate or write a story and then play it out. Sometimes the story is started by the pretend play episode, sometimes by the story dictation. This form of pretend play builds on the skills of 6- and 7-year-olds for pretend play story plots and characterization. The additional transformation to word stories connects this form of play to learnings in the language domain. When children convert from the literary form to the enactment form, they are faced with complex problems that lead to staging events creatively, creating props, and representing characters cooperatively (Nourot & Van Hoorn, 1991).

Fundamentally, children's story writing and their pretend play are blended so that the strength of one can be used to foster the other. For example, a simple story written by a 6-year-old was only two sentences: "My baby brother got in my room. He made a mess." Several first graders were asked to think about this basic plot and pretend-play it out. The author was in the group and watched as various children played roles of baby, older brother, and parents. More than one pretend sequence was tried, and several solutions to the problem were explored as children acted out their roles. The author had the choice to incorporate some of the details, problems, and solutions in the story or leave it alone

as he saw fit. The advantage of this play form is that the connection between the familiar play and the new tasks of writing are clear, meaningful, and obvious.

CURRENT EDUCATIONAL ISSUES

1. *What will the parents think if children are playing in school?* Parents are very supportive of children playing in child-centered programs for 3- and 4-year-olds and generally believe that the time spent in play should decrease as children get older (Rothlein & Brett, 1987). However, parents do not indicate that play should be eliminated for 6-year-olds, merely that the amount of time should be less than for 3- and 4-year-olds. Parents, therefore, are likely to express their concerns and will have particular interest in how much school time is devoted to play. The value of play to the development of the competent child has considerable support in research and can be presented understandably to parents (Bergen 1988; Nourot & Van Hoorn, 1991).

The research on the importance of play to development has been accumulating for the past two decades yet still receives limited acknowledgment by professional educators. Therefore, it is unreasonable to suppose that the general public would be better informed. As with any educational practice change, parents need basic information about the total program and how pretend play is likely to benefit their children.

2. *How does pretend play relate to the real learning that is supposed to occur in the primary grades?* If the play is integrated into the curriculum, it becomes a meaningful part of it. For example, if birds are being studied, young children might pretend to be birds in the nest and older children, scientists studying birds. Pretend play uses the information that children have to solve problems. In addition, teachers are able to assess the level of understanding children possess about the topic based on their play. If children are unable to incorporate information into pretend play sequences, they do not really understand it very well.

Furthermore, if properly structured, pretend play may incorporate numerous literacy experiences and require children to use mathematical skills and ideas to further their own play goals.

These second graders are combining mathematics, language, and social skills as they pretend "store."

3. *Should second and third graders really spend school time in pretend play?* If children have had appropriate early experiences, 7-year-olds will be skilled players. They are in the strongest position to do creative problem solving, to explore in depth the possibilities in any situation. They add detail and substance to their play, which may continue, even though interrupted, over several weeks. Pretend play is a strength of children that may be utilized to help them understand science, the humanities, and the world around them. Story reenactment is particularly useful in developing reading comprehension skills as well as in motivating children with more limited reading skills.

Integrating curriculum requires that a topic or focus be selected, and then content brought together in a meaningful way. For example, the scientific topic of physics can be brought to children as a unit on machines. Children read about machines, observe simple machines in action, making graphs and written recordings of their observations, and discuss the use of machines in society. They might construct simple machines such as wheels or levers to make a task easier. They may also pretend-play a variety of themes, depending on their maturity, experience, and knowledge, such as hardware store, gas station, repair store, machine shop, or factory. Within the pretend play theme, children must use their knowledge and demonstrate their understanding. In addition, other players provide feedback and correction if necessary. A variety of pretend play theme kits are suggested, with the corresponding teaching units that might be present in many early childhood programs, in Figure 9.1.

4. *Don't children get enough pretend play at home or on the playground?* For children who come from less advantaged backgrounds and enter school without pretend play skills, the school is the only source of such information. If the parents of these children knew how to support pretend play, the children would have some of the skills when they entered school. In addition, few homes have the materials, information, and guidance techniques for developing a variety of play opportunities such as archeologist, scientist, or space explorer. Families may supplement what schools do, if they receive information and suggestions.

Recess in most schools is usually 15 minutes outdoors morning and afternoon. Some pretend play may occur in this setting, but it will not have the scope possible in a prepared environment or sufficient time to accrue the full benefits. In addition, children need time to run and climb. In many settings recess is the primary vehicle for meeting physical exercise needs.

However, the outdoor environment can be an excellent setting for planned pretend play. Building pretend play opportunities outside makes a great deal of sense, especially in those climates that have access to the outdoors during a good portion of the year. Even in colder climates, opportunities for pretend play can be managed. One group of second-grade children played weather forecaster as a part of a sequence of units during the year. They collected information on wind direction, temperature, cloud formation; used weather maps, graphs, and other documents; and even researched previous years' weather conditions for their make-believe weather reports on television.

5. *How can I incorporate pretend play in my classroom when I have neither the time nor the space?* Preschool teachers and kindergarten teachers should plan for pretend play first and for other activities thereafter. (Various suggestions for the management of space are provided in chap. 11.) For these youngest children, the development of play skills is critical for the emergence of abstract thinking and problem-

solving abilities. Therefore, pretend play should be a priority. Teachers should ensure that all children in the earliest years have opportunities for extended time for pretend.

The space in primary classrooms is frequently inadequate. However, teachers of older children have been successful in incorporating pretend in the following ways: using miniature materials and pretending in a small space, planning for pretend play twice a week for a longer period of time, involving children in moving equipment and setting up the play space, and including simple make-believe in a variety of other activities. One building with particularly small classrooms set up a separate classroom

FIGURE 9.1
Pretend Play Kits with Associated Teaching Themes
Source: Adapted from material in *Teaching Young Children Using Themes* (Kostelnik et al., 1991).

Unit Theme: Living in Homes

Pretend Play Theme: Real Estate

Props: Pictures of many kinds of homes magazines, real estate brochures, desk, telephone, paper, pencil, chairs, "contract forms," "Real Estate" and "For Sale" signs

Moving Houses

Props: Wagons, small moving dollies, boxes with ropes, rags for wrapping goods, telephone, work order forms, pencils, child furniture, clothing, stuffed animals, dolls, "Moving Day" sign

Unit Theme: Clothing

Pretend Play Theme: Washing Clothes

Props: Doll clothes, a tub or water table with soap, clothesline and pins, plastic aprons

Dress Up

Props: Scarves, hats, curtains, coats and capes, shoes, mirror, dresses, ties, shirts

Unit Theme: Vehicles

Pretend Play Theme: Gas Station

Props: Gas pumps with hoses, windshield wash equipment, tires, tire pump, wrenches, fan belts, screwdrivers, cash register

Vehicle Show Room

Props: Many vehicles arranged, car sales brochures, ads, calculators, pencils, forms, price stickers, balloons

Unit Theme: Insects

Pretend Play Theme: Entomologist's Laboratory

Props: Insect pictures, specimens, tripod, magnifying glass, white coats, paper, pencil, insect books, dried insects, wasp nests or other real things

Picnic Partners

Props: Dishes, pretend food, tablecloth, plastic or paper insects

FIGURE 9.1
Continued

Unit Theme: The Sky

Pretend Play Theme: It's Raining, It's Pouring

Props: Sand table village or miniature houses; rocks; seashells; twigs; miniature people for the houses; squirt cans; small drum for thunder; "Cirrus," "Stratus," "Cumulus," and "Nimbus" signs

Outdoor Slumber Party

Props: Sleeping bags or blankets, alarm clock, different phases of the moon to hang, stars, large pajamas (worn over clothes), stuffed animals

Unit Theme: Machines

Pretend Play Theme: Repair Shop

Props: Wrenches, screwdrivers, pliers, old clocks, radios, toasters, pencil, paper, do-it-yourself books, "Repair Anything" sign

Bike Repair

Props: Wrenches, loose spokes, cogs and sprockets (donations from local bike shop, cleaned), rags, telephone, pencil, paper, bikes or tricycles

Unit Theme: Storytelling

Pretend Play Theme: Storytelling Theater

Props: Chairs for seating, a "stage" marked off with blocks or tape, tickets, playbill, cash register, dolls for audience, dress-up clothes, hats, child-constructed costumes if desired, child-painted backdrops for older children

Measuring

Shoe Store

Props: Ruler or bannock device, shoes of various sizes, stickers to indicate size and price, "Shoes for Sale" sign, cash register, receipt book, pictures and advertisements

---

for all of the first-grade children to use for pretend play and established a schedule for use. Each day, children were allowed to go down to this room, which was supervised predominantly by volunteers.

Pretend play needs at least 20 minutes for full development and even longer for older children. If the time for pretend play is less than this, children usually do not even start. Therefore, it is better to have pretend play once or twice a week for a longer time, such as 25 to 40 minutes, than to try to have four 10-minute periods.

6. *What can I do if I do not have the proper equipment and materials?* Because pretend play for 3- to 5-year-olds is a priority, programs should allocate resources to this domain first. (A practical plan for the gradual addition of materials is suggested in chap. 11.)

Many of the materials for pretend play are found rather than purchased. For example, teachers can gradually develop pretend play kits

as illustrated in Figure 9.1. The task of adding to and replacing materials in the pretend play kits may be shared among teachers. Parents, garage sales, flea markets, and discards from industry are sources for pretend play props. File boxes are often useful for storage, and schools may install near-ceiling shelving to hold them.

7. *How do I maintain control? I'm concerned that the children will just go wild.* Pretend play is treated seriously by children. They become involved and focus their energies on what they are doing. They do have conflicts about roles, story direction, and use of materials, which they negotiate among themselves. Teachers may need to assist them in the mediation process, but learning interpersonal skills is one of the chief goals in early education.

Loss of self-control, destructive behavior, or disruption of classroom processes will occur from some individuals regardless of the curricular design. In some ways, pretend play may alleviate the frequency of the outbursts as children gain control of a medium for expressing their feelings acceptably.

A more practical problem is the misuse of materials by children who do not know how to play. If a child does not know how to make-believe, that child may have no idea how to function in a housekeeping area. Dishes may be crammed into purses, dolls undressed and thrown around. This is symptomatic of children who need educational intervention. Once teachers recognize that the problem is one of knowledge, then teaching should follow. Pretend play is the outcome of learning and is not guaranteed by development alone. Most youngsters learn to pretend-play from their parents and siblings between 1 and 3 years of age; other children who have the developmental capacity to pretend-play but lack adult guidance and/or playmates may learn later in the school setting from teachers and classmates. Rarely does a classroom exist without some of the children knowing how to pretend. Children learn readily from each other, and the teacher may have to supervise the pretend play carefully so that maximum advantages of this process can be accrued. Children's behaviors offer cues that they do not know what to do. Certain behaviors, then, may indicate that the child does not have the skill rather than that the child is being disruptive, disobedient, or uncooperative. Although the techniques for teaching pretend play skills are discussed later in this chapter, some common behaviors of children that concern teachers are listed, with possible strategies for intervention, in Table 9.1.

However, there are occasions when teachers need to use guidance techniques to promote social responsibility and order. Procedures for setting and maintaining limits for children in groups are presented in other books as well as in chapter 14 of this volume (Kostelnik et al., in press). All areas of the classroom and all functions of curriculum require quality classroom management skills. Reasonable limits should be set for the dramatic play, story reenactment, or other forms of pretend so that all children can profit from their learning experiences. Certain behaviors may indicate when a child is beyond these reasonable limits. Such a child may demonstrate

play skills on other occasions but need adult guidance when she or he

- engages in silly, unfocused, or irrelevant behavior;
- grabs materials obviously to prevent other's access to them;
- pushes, hits with a fist, or grabs and runs; or
- makes excessive noise that is unrelated to a role (e.g., there is a difference between being a fire engine and just shrieking).

Just because children are playing does not mean that "anything goes."

8. *What is the teacher's role when the children are playing?* Pretend play usually occurs while other activities are also in progress. The teacher is responsible for setting the stage for play, providing sufficient information to support the play activities, supervising the quality of play, and extending it as needed. Younger children are likely to need more support than older children because they have less information about the world and may be less skilled in negotiating differences. Older inexperienced children profit from direct instruction in how to play (Christie, 1986). In addition to teaching pretend play, the adult may be called upon to provide instruction related to the cognitive domain, as is illustrated in the following experience.

A student teacher planned a unit on seeds and established a seed store as a sociodramatic play opportunity. Shelves, envelopes, pencils and paper, scales, a variety of seeds, money, and a cash register were available for the children to use. The 4-year-olds entered the play area and mixed up the seeds, throwing them around and otherwise demolishing the area. Intervening in this activity, the young teacher began to ask what the children knew about a seed store only to discover that these urban children simply had no ideas they could easily apply to this activity. For the next few days the pretend play area became the scene of considerable instruction. The teacher addressed questions such as "What are stores for? What do store clerks do? What do customers do?" On the second day, the only players allowed in the store were employees. They sorted seeds, weighed and placed them in envelopes, labeled

TABLE 9.1
Common Child Behaviors Indicating Lack of Pretend Play Skills and Selected Teacher Intervention
Strategies

Behavior	Teacher Intervention Strategy
Avoiding the pretend play area	Encouarge participation directly. Assist the child in entering the area before others arrive.
Continuing a pattern of exploring materials without using them for play	Use open-ended questions: "What else do you think you can do with that?" "Show me how you might use that if you were a [role] policeman."
Manipulating play materials and discarding them	Engage the child in thinking about the materials: "Tell me about the _____." "How could that be used to _____?"
Misusing materials	Assess whether the material is appropriate for the age of child. If it has either too little or too much challenge, it may be misused. Ask children to tell you about an object. Some very young children may not "recognize" a common play prop. Suggest appropriate object substitutions: "Pretend that the _____ is a _____."
Focusing on the reality aspects only; insisting that the stove will not cook something, for example	Explain that pretend play props are not supposed to work. Demonstrate pretend play with the object.
Regarding other players with amazement; watching, staring, and appearing confused (common among 3- and 4-year-olds)	Move close to this child and provide comments of what they are doing. "George and Alfie are pretending to be truckers. They are...." Engage in pretend play with this child. Select another child with slightly better pretend play skills, and encourage them to play together.
Either coercing others or participating very passively; not engaging in mutual theme or shared goal	Often 3- and 4-year-olds will work out patterns of leadership on their own, but if this goes on with older children or is persistent, play with the children and demonstrate mutual play. Discuss the play theme in a group, and explore possible ideas before children begin play. Ensure that most of the children have the knowledge they need to play out the theme. In some instances intervene directly in the play and use the mediation strategies suggested in chap. 9.

the envelopes, and wrote down prices. Flower seeds were in one display and vegetable seeds in another. Again the teacher provided direction, assistance, and instruction as needed. On the third day signs were placed and advertisements prepared. More discussion was held about what the customers would do with the seeds once purchased. Finally, the children were able to have their grand opening. Customers purchased seeds, some of which were later planted in peat cups. The seed store play continued for another week successfully. Children provided new players with information as they joined the activity.

Clearly, science and social studies concepts were taught within the structure or place usually set aside for pretend. Children needed more information to use, which was quickly apparent in the first day of play. Once children had the information, the teacher focused her attention more on other activities and allowed them to proceed with adult observation, support, and supervision as needed.

9. *What do I do about superhero play and other play themes that make me uncomfortable? Sometimes it's violent.* Teachers are legitimately concerned about the level of violence in children's play. There are several sources of violence that might appear in pretend play, and each should be treated independently. First, there is violence that is simply the imitation of observed adult behavior at home and in the community. Second, there is violence portrayed as a result of events such as earthquakes, war, car accidents, and other catastrophes. Third, there is play that is related to children's inner needs to handle their feelings of aggression and helplessness. Fourth, children use pretend play toys and scripts from television, generally selecting only the action sequences and violent scenes for reenactment. Last, there is masked play in which the child engages in play for the purposes of behaving aggressively against others without having to be responsible for the consequences of the aggressive act. Each source of violent play will be considered briefly here, one at a time.

Teachers of preschool children are likely to see youngsters play out sequences of events that they have observed or have participated in. Adults in some families have very little privacy so that children are likely to incorporate behaviors such as parental arguments, physical fights, and sexual intercourse into play sequences. Young children simply have no understanding of what should remain private and what is appropriate for play in school. Teachers who observe inappropriate play have found simple redirection to be most useful. Focusing on other activities that adult men and women engage in is usually sufficient. Effort should be made to keep this redirection low keyed as children tend to imitate each others' outstanding play sequences. By first grade,

youngsters generally can distinguish between public and private family information and are less likely to enact the latter. Frequent, repetitive, or excessively detailed play sequences of violent or sexual behavior may be an indicator that the child is living in an unwholesome situation that requires additional attention.

Children who experience a natural disaster such as an earthquake or flood and those who witness serious accidents or violence on the street experience feelings of great fear and helplessness. A 7-year-old whose mother has just left to fight in a war on the other side of the world simply may be terrified. Children must have opportunities to express such feelings through their pretend play. In the process of enactment, the child can work out a variety of situations and solutions so that mastery of these feelings might be achieved. Such play may take many repetitions for the child to feel safe. In fact, the parent may return home from the military service commitment before the child has completely worked out the fears associated with this dangerous situation. The role of teachers to provide accurate information and reassurance as children play out violent scenes facilitates this process. The content of the play is the violence itself and the fear, and other players often take on the roles of nurturer, rescuer, or comforter.

Five- to 7-year-olds frequently are concerned with social position. Competent students and skillful players are accorded high status among peers. In some schools toughness or skill in fighting is another avenue to social position. This type of fighting has nothing to do with pretend play and should be handled by adults as inappropriate behavior. However, children also are concerned about aggressor and victim roles in a more general sense, as can be seen from cops and robbers, good guys and bad guys. The roles of the players are designed to be oppositional. Opposing-force pretend play may occur during children's recess or noninstructional time without real violence occurring. Frequently the bad guys are imaginary. If there are no injuries and no real violence, dealing with the forces of good and evil as a play theme may allow children to work out their ideas of right and wrong in an acceptable framework. Play around issues of justice, right and wrong, and fairness are important concepts for children to explore.

Television has increased in the level of violence portrayed over the past decade. Considering that young children are exposed to as much television as they are to schooling, it is not surprising that children reenact media episodes. These reenactments rarely are more than the sequenced-action scenes. With roles selected from commercial characters, children incorporate rough-and-tumble play into their pretend play. When children are forbidden to play these superhero roles, they do not have opportunities to explore the full range of roles involved: hero and villain, protector and victim, leader and follower. Although it is difficult, teachers may guide children in fruitful ways of playing superhero (Kostelnik & Stein, 1986).

Rough-and-tumble play, consisting of laughing, running, smiling, jumping, open-hand beating, wrestling, play fighting, chasing, and fleeing, looks aggressive to many adults. However, children engaging in this play do not get hurt or cry. Frequently rough-and-tumble play is a transitional activity leading to games with rules, especially for popular boys (Pellegrini & Perlmutter, 1988). Aggression, which includes fixation, frowning, hitting, pushing, taking, and grabbing, is more likely to occur in relation to possessions than in the fast-moving superhero play.

10. *Wouldn't the time spent in play at school be better used in teaching the basic skills and academics?* The practice of separating tasks down to skills and drilling them separately has not been a spectacular success (Peck et al., 1988). Skill instruction embedded in meaningful activity makes more sense to the children, and they are more likely to learn and use the skills. Thus, we might try strategies that make sense to children, building on what they already are able to do and then providing the skills instruction to expand their capacities. Including opportunities for pretend play does *not* in any way preclude skills instruction. For example, when children play post office, they must make change, weigh parcels, compute postage, read addresses to deliver the mail, and engage in a variety of academically based tasks that make

Shashank and Julie practice counting, weighing, sorting, and reading in the pretend world of the post office.

sense to them. Opportunities for integrating science, social studies, reading, writing, and mathematics abound.

Now that the reasons for incorporating pretend play into the curriculum have been examined, specifics of implementation are presented in the next sections.

GOALS AND OBJECTIVES

The ultimate goal is for children to integrate meaning derived from their experience with knowledge and skills from all developmental domains as they create roles or scenarios.

Mediating Objectives

As children progress toward the ultimate goal, they will

1. mimic in their play behaviors that they have seen or experienced.
2. use their bodies to represent real or imaginary objects or events.
3. assign symbolic meaning to real or imaginary objects using language or gestures.
4. take on the role attributes of beings or objects and act out interpretations of those roles.
5. create play themes.
6. experiment with a variety of objects, roles (leader, follower, mediator), and characterizations (animal, mother, astronaut, etc.).
7. react to and interact with other children in make-believe situations.
8. dramatize familiar stories, songs, poems, and past events.
9. integrate construction into pretend play episodes.

TEACHING STRATEGIES

1. *Set the stage for children's play.* The teacher is responsible for establishing a general climate in which play is accepted and encouraged. Some of the ways in which this can be accomplished follow:

- Incorporate make-believe into transitional times such as cleanup, dressing, or moving from one room to another as a group.
- Encourage pretend in other aspects of the curriculum.

- Coordinate the theme of the dramatic play center to match other ongoing themes in your room.
- Provide adequate space for play. This may occasionally mean moving furniture or making room for miniature play sets.
- Provide materials that will enhance pretend play (see Figure 9.1). Add additional materials to the pretend play setup to expand the play as needed.
- Provide enough time in any one segment for play to get under way.
- Pay attention to what children say and do during play. Watch carefully, concentrate. Listen for children's appropriate application of concepts or misinformation.

2. *Actively engage in helping children improve their level of performance in pretend play.* Table 9.2 cites procedures that increase in the level of intrusion and power exercised by the teacher. Usually, the teacher selects the least intrusive strategy that will accomplish the change. For example, either active onlooking or nondirective statements may facilitate the children's becoming more focused or starting to develop the theme for skilled children. Inexperienced youngsters may need stronger measures such as modeling and physical intervention (Wolfgang & Sanders, 1986).

Modeling is always done inside the play frame. The teacher becomes a player and assumes the role. Physical intervention during the play usually requires that the teacher enter the space of the play frame, if only briefly, to provide or take away materials. Removing materials is usually more effective if the adult assumes a role ("I'm the plumber and I have come to get the sink [full of water] for repair. You will get it back in a day or two."). This would be done only if there were sufficient reason to intervene—say, if children began adding real water to pasta the teacher had provided for pretend cooking. The water would ruin the pasta and make a sticky mess.

Nondirective statements, questions, and directive statements might be made to offer suggestions or assistance quickly from outside the play frame. Usually the teacher would watch, make the verbalization, and listen to the children's response but would not move into the

TABLE 9.2
Methods of Instruction From Least to Most Intrusive

Methods of Instruction	Example
Active onlooking	The teacher watches intently what children are doing and saying while they play.
Nondirective statements	"It looks like you're going to the beach." or, "You're a cloud floating in the air."
Questions	"What do heros really do?" or, "When you go to the store, does the customer pay the storekeeper, or the other way around?"
Directive statements	"Tell me about the family that lives in the dollhouse." or, "Think about the middle Billy Goat Gruff and show me how he crossed the bridge."
Modeling	"I'm your new next-door neighbor. [Knocking at the pretend door.]" or, The teacher picks up a stethoscope and says, "Is your baby sick?"
Physical intervention	The teacher adds or removes props during the play.

play directly. These strategies are effective before and after a play sequence for assisting in the planning and evaluation process.

3. *Whenever possible, allow children to create their own sociodramatic play independently.* Prepare the environment, provide information and resources, and then allow the children to create their own scripts. If intervention is necessary, do it and withdraw promptly. Most 5-year-olds have all the basic skills and are able to elaborate them within an appropriate setting; therefore, this is one center that may run rather smoothly for 5- to 8-year-olds with limited adult intervention. Encourage experimentation and creative problem solving whenever possible.

4. *Provide information relevant to the play theme.* Use picture books, field trips, videotapes, photos, and other sources of information so that children know what is supposed to occur in the pretend situation. For children with extremely limited skills, Lois Lenski's *Let's Play House* is effective in stimulating homemaking play. Although dated and illustrating traditional sex roles, this black-and-white picture book helps the least skilled child get some ideas of roles. Themes and topics from social studies, science, and literature support older children's knowledge needs and can be most easily incorporated into related pretend play themes.

5. *Evaluate the level of skill development.* Observe all the children and determine if each child is able to pretend-play. If a child is able

to pretend-play, then check such qualitative aspects as posing problems to be solved, generating ideas, initiating play, following play, negotiating, allowing new players to enter the play, and creating objects to be used in the play.

Some of the activities listed next are teacher initiated. They have been included so that a variety of play skills such as taking on a role or using movement to convey meaning are clearly included. The most common activity, theme play, is used most extensively with 3- to 5-year-olds, with the theme being varied from time to time. Its popularity will continue with older children who can incorporate more ideas into the roles and demonstrate their knowledge and competencies in a variety of ways. Three- to 5-year-olds can do simple versions of creative dramatics such as "Jack and Jill," but older youngsters can use most folk tales and patterned stories in story reenactments more successfully.

ACTIVITY SUGGESTIONS

⬛➡ Animal Movements

Objective: For children to mimic in their play behaviors that they have seen or experienced

Procedure: Set up a space where children can move without colliding into each other or furnishings. A gym or outdoor space is excellent, but a group space or between tables is acceptable if furnishings are pushed aside. If space is very constrained, half the children at a time may be asked to participate.

1. Select animals to imitate that are most likely to be familiar to the children (e.g., a cat, dog, butterfly, caterpillar, sparrow, ant).
2. Ask the children to stretch out their arms so that they know where their personal space is. Remind them to stay in that space and not get into the space of another child. At first the animals will be still, then they move.
3. The teacher describes the animal and its typical behavior, and the children attempt to imitate it: "Listen carefully as I describe the cat. You think of yourself as a cat and try to do what the cat does. All my cats will be quiet at first."
4. Describe the behavior of the animal in detail. It is important to be accurate. A household pet cat is not a jaguar and the children know it. Neither does the sparrow soar like the hawk. "The cat is sitting on the floor where the sunshine strikes the carpet. She pulls her body up and stretches her back. She begins to lick her paw and rub it behind her ear. She does it again...and again...then she cleans the other ear. Licking her paw and rubbing it....She stops and looks out the window."
5. The teacher should prepare a sequence such as sitting, cleaning, looking, hearing and turning, eating, sleeping, prancing, and so on. The pace of the teacher's narrative should be appropriate to that of the animal. Movements of cats are usually indolent, whereas mice either are alert and still or scurry.
6. End the sequence of motion so that the children are at rest. If they have done much stretching and slow motion, ask them to shake out their muscles like children. This signals the end of the pretend sequence.

To Simplify:

■ Use fewer action sequences, or select the most familiar animals. Consider using insects, as they are in all environments, whereas cows and horses are rarely seen by urban children.
■ Younger children who do not know the vocabulary may need to imitate the playing adult.

Adults may demonstrate selected words such as *pounce* before the play begins.

To Extend:

■ Actions sequences may be composed of up to 10 or 12 items. Vary the pace of the presentations so that some are slow and some are faster.
■ Combine the sequences to include two animals such as a cat and a spider. Help children select a partner and decide who will be which animal.
■ Encourage children to pretend to be animals in other play settings such as outdoors or in the housekeeping area.

➡ **Machines**

Objective: For children to use their bodies to represent real or imaginary objects or events

Procedure: The space needed is similar to that for the previous activity. Prepare a list of machines that the children are likely to be familiar with, both simple ones (screwdriver, hammer, pencil and paper, scissors, rolling pin, knife, clothespin, bowl, spoon) and more complex ones (wheelbarrow, mixer, washing machine, vacuum cleaner, automobile, bus).

1. Ask the children to sit in the group and indicate their willingness to answer or demonstrate by raising a hand. Present the problem: "If you wanted to show someone how to turn a screwdriver and you did not have one, what could you do?"
2. Accept any verbal answer and then ask the child to demonstrate: "Show us how to do it." Encourage variation and creativity by asking, "Is there another way?" for more complex tasks.
3. Repeat your problem statements with some variations to cover a variety of situations and objects: "A little boy wanted to pretend to cook outdoors, but he had no bowl or spoon. What could he do?"

To Simplify:

■ Shift to imitation if the children cannot do it at all and demonstrate. This changes the objective to an easier one.

- Select tools that the children have used during the day.
- Apply the strategy across the play frame when children are experiencing the problem in a one-to-one instructional mode. For example, if a child is unable to "cook" because he has no bowl, help the child recognize the problem on the spot and either guide the child to the solution or demonstrate it yourself. Encourage other children to contribute alternatives within the play setting: "What can Phillip do about this?"

To Extend:

- Select more complex machines. Many of them will take two children to demonstrate. Encourage sound effects.
- Develop the task into charades with one child becoming the object and others guessing it. This is easiest when children know the selections of objects from which to guess. It is harder when there are no preconceived limitations.

➡ Role Playing

Objective: For children to take on the role attributes of beings or objects, and act out interpretations of those roles

Materials: Select one or two props for each situation, keeping it simple. A man's hat for the father, a purse for the mother, a bib for the baby, or a menu for a restaurant worker would be typical. Older primary children may have signs with their role printed on them like name tags.

Procedure: This activity may be done in a large group or in a center. A few props may be needed for inexperienced players so that the roles are clearly defined for participants. The adult selects the content of the situation and the characters.

1. Explain that role playing is a way of pretending in order to figure out how people might think and feel.
2. Set the scene by describing the characters and the problem that they have to figure out. For very inexperienced players the teacher may have to take on the role.

3. Watch the playing and give hints for moving the scene along.
4. At the conclusion, elicit comments from the players and audience, if there is one. Ask children to recommend alternative solutions to the problem.
5. Play it again. Role reversal is very helpful to some children; they get the feel from both perspectives.

To Simplify:

- Pretend to be yourself as you do a daily task (washing, dressing, eating, etc.). This is as easy as it gets.
- Pretend to be a child in a normal problem experienced by children in the age group: (a) walking to school alone while other kids are on their way to school, when you would rather be walking with someone; (b) a mother trying to get a sleepy child out of bed and off to school; or (c) a younger sibling being delighted at getting into the older child's room and making a mess, followed by discovery.

To Extend:

- Increase the number of characters or give the children a problem in cooperation to solve: (a) A family of four members suddenly has to take care of the sick grandmother. The mother no longer has the time for the children; the father cannot afford eating at McDonald's any more. (b) The class is going to have a new student who is blind, and they have to pretend to alter the room, play together, and so on.
- Select a problem and characters from a historical event, such as Europeans coming to America. Limit the space, called "America," and have a few children play the Native Americans within the space. At first only a few Europeans come and are welcomed by the Native Americans, and the space is shared. Then more and more Europeans come until the Native Americans are all crowded into a corner. Discuss how both groups felt. (Note: Five- and 6-year-olds who have done the activity sometimes shift from pretend to real anger at being crowded out of their space. Because of its analogous nature, this activity is best suited to children 7 years or older.)

➠ Theme Play

Objective: For children to create play themes

Materials: See Figure 9.1 for pretend play kits. Materials change from theme to theme.

Procedure: Arrange the props related to the theme where children can see them. Create an enclosed space so that the limits for the number of players are clear. Add props as a part of the daily setup to maintain interest.

1. Provide experiences for children so that they know what should go on in the setting. Housekeeping is the only theme for which instruction might not be necessary. However, other themes such as camping, bakery, grocery store, and doctor office are not necessarily familiar to all children. These activities do not occur at the time of pretend play but during other periods.
2. Discuss with the children some of the props and how they are used, if necessary (e.g., ounce scales for postage). Explore possible things people could do in the pretend play area. Generate several possible action sequences with the children. This may be done in the group briefly just before children move into centers or in the play center itself.
3. Allow children to choose pretend play or other activities. Guide children as indicated in the guidelines section in this chapter.
4. Change the props to other play themes as appropriate for those themes. Usually 2 to 3 weeks is plenty of time for a number of children to have an opportunity to play out the theme. Do not leave one set up without variation for the entire school year.

To Simplify:

■ Keep thematic content familiar to the daily lives of children. In the beginning, this means variations of home life such as caring for babies, preparing food, washing clothing and ironing, doing dishes.
■ Maintain the basic theme and vary it slowly by adding and removing props. Inexperienced players may do nothing but housekeeping play for a month or more at the beginning of

the year. Then add elements such as "flower arranging in the home."

To Extend:

■ The selection of topic may become one based on the past (pioneers), the remote present (astronauts or ornithologists), or a fantasy or fiction (lost children who have to survive in the winter). Children must seek information and use it in their play in order for this to work well.
■ Involve the children in the planning of pretend play. Guide them in thinking of what they might play and which props if any they would need to gather and/or construct. Then let them play it out. Seven-year-old experienced players may spend much happy play time in the getting-organized process. A great deal of planning, problem solving, negotiating, compromising, and organizing occurs during this period that may seem excessive to the uninformed adult but are the desired outcomes of the process.

➠ Write and Play

Objective: For children to react to and interact with other children in make-believe situations (With modifications this activity could be directed to many different objectives.)

Materials: Materials depend on the story. They may emerge from the play theme activity, or children may collect or make the props themselves as a part of the plan. Often there are no props.

Procedure: Five- to 7-year-olds are usually very good at pretend play, but their skills at writing stories are just emerging. This activity uses the competence that children already possess to enhance their story-writing abilities.

1. Bring together several children who have written a story. Ask one child to share a story. Discuss the setting and the situation of each story carefully.
2. Ask the other children if they would be willing to play out the story based on the setting and situation established by the author. Let

children determine the role and the detail of action.

3. Once the pretend play sequence related to the composition is played out, discuss the setting, situation, plot, and dialogue. Repeat the play sequence as necessary.

4. Allow each author to revise his or her story, including ideas from the pretend play if desired. Some children will incorporate more detail, and others will reject the entire pretend play ideas. Accept each child's effort.

To Simplify:

■ Use an experience story based on the pretend play theme that the children have enacted several times and are very familiar with. All players will be able to contribute to the story line and to detail.

To Extend:

■ Select another aspect of the story to develop, such as plot, mood, and even dialogue. Sometimes, teachers write the dialogue as the children are playing. It helps children to comprehend the relationships between the spoken and written language.

■ Carry out this activity over a series of days on the same story plot, and revise and expand. Children usually do not have an ending in their pretend play as decisive as in a story. Discuss this and try out several different possible conclusions. Prepare the final draft for the children's library of stories for reading.

➠ Puppets*

Objective: For children to assign symbolic meaning to real or imaginary objects using language or gestures

Materials: Several puppets. Usually hand puppets are easiest to use. Stick puppets and finger puppets also may be used if they are sturdy.

Procedure:

1. Begin by explaining to the children that today you will show them how to create a story

---

*Adapted from Kostelnik et al. (1991).

character using a puppet. Emphasize that it will be important for them to listen to your directions throughout the activity.

2. In front of the children, spread out an array of as many puppets as there are children plus two.

3. Invite each child to pick a puppet. Give them several minutes to examine and handle the puppets prior to making a final choice. Select a puppet to use yourself.

4. Ask the children to put their puppets on their hands and try moving their fingers around in a variety of ways. Demonstrate as you talk. Tell them, "Make your puppet move toward you, away from you." Offer the mirror so that children can see what their puppets look like when they move them.

5. Once the children have experimented with a variety of methods of maneuvering their puppets, ask them to give their puppets names. Invite each to announce the name to you and the other children.

6. Build on the preceding steps by giving the following directions:

■ "Give your puppet a voice."
■ "Have your puppet tell its name to the group using the voice you have given it."
■ "Show the group how your puppet walks, sits, runs, sleeps, and so on."
■ "Show the group how your puppet would express feelings such as happiness, sadness, fear, or excitement."
■ "Tell the group if your puppet is friendly, shy, bouncy, lazy, and so on."
■ "Show how your puppet demonstrates the characteristic you have chosen."
■ "Tell the group one way your puppet is like [not like] the puppets you have met here today."

7. Show children how to use their puppets to act out a simple sequence of actions, such as "The boy walks down the street, sees a flower, then smells it" or "The cat is sleeping, hears a loud crash, and scampers away." Demonstrate first, then have the children mimic your actions. Eventually, describe a short vignette for them to enact without a demonstration. Continue to use the mirror to

help children see their puppets' actions from another perspective.

8. Praise children throughout the activity for listening to your directions. Point out to them that they are creating characters for their puppets.

To Simplify:

- Conduct this activity with only a few children at a time.
- Limit the activity to steps through the third instruction in step 6.

To Extend:

- Introduce the final parts of step 6 through step 8.
- Proceed to teach children how to use their puppets to act out simple conversations or interactions. In this way, children begin to learn how to use their puppets in conjunction with one another.
- Invite children to reenact familiar folktales such as *The Three Little Pigs* or *The Tortoise and the Hare* using puppets. Introduce this phase of puppetry only *after* children have been through all the preceding steps.
- Give children opportunities to go through the process outlined here using various kinds of puppets such as finger, stick, paper-bag, or sock puppets.

➠ Story Reenactment

Objective: For children to dramatize familiar stories, songs, poems and past events

Materials: Appropriate book, selected props. Use only enough props to identify roles or engage in actions adequately.

Procedure:

1. Select a nursery rhyme, poem, or folktale and read it several times to the children. Stories such as *The Three Billy Goats Gruff* or *The Gingerbread Man* work well, as would *Jack Be Nimble, Little Miss Muffet,* or *Humpty Dumpty.* Modern folk-type stories such as *Ask Mr. Bear* or *Caps for Sale* are excellent

alternatives. Repetition, a simple plot, and clear action sequences are necessary.

2. Discuss the plot and characters. Examine relevant elements of selected roles and try them out briefly before the story run-through.

3. Few props are used and no costumes. Younger children may need a picture to keep track of their part in *Ask Mr. Bear* or a goat-horn headband to indicate which goat they are in *The Three Billy Goats Gruff.*

4. Read or tell the story as the children go through the parts, providing their own dialogue. The speaking parts are not to be memorized. The point is to keep to the plot and scene. The teacher does the narrative until the children understand the story and process well. Repeat, with children taking on a variety of roles.

5. Place the book and whatever props are used in an area for children to enact the story on their own. The teacher will note that variations in the story are tried. At this point the children may return to the book for detail or may revise the story in some way of their own.

6. Once children know how to do story reenactments, supplement teacher readings with a tape of the story in the listening area and provide props. Children may initiate dramatization of literature on their own with merely pointing out the possibilities during the daily planning session.

To Simplify:

- Select poetry and very short stories or stories that everyone can do together such as *Caps for Sale.*
- Try key action components together such as being the small, the middle, and then the large Billy Goat Gruff.

To Extend:

- Select from a wide array of folk stories from all over the world. As children are more experienced, they are able to incorporate more roles and more complex motives for characters.
- Challenge children to exhibit an array of emotions and use gesture effectively. Help them

become more sensitive to mood, motives, feelings, and other nuances in the stories.

■ Encourage creativity as children remake these stories on their own. Support innovative interpretations.

At no time is the pretend play of young children to be performed for an adult audience.

Children's play is spontaneous, creative, but often very personal. Many children simply stop playing in the presence of adult strangers. Play does not have the characteristics of an impersonal performance that theater does. *Children's theater is generally for children of age 10 and up.*

C H A P T E R 10

The Construction Domain

Four-year-old Kate spent several minutes studying a spiderweb in the fence of the play yard. When she returned to the classroom, she used Sticky Wickets, which are flexible, colored strips of plastic that stick to many surfaces, to reconstruct the spider web in a three-dimensional form. Then she drew the spider web on paper with crayons, and announced, "I can make a spider web, too!" She was completely engrossed in her activity.

Aida was playing store with other kindergarten children. She seemed dissatisfied with simply pretending to offer money to the clerk and said, "I gotta get some real money to buy this stuff." Looking around the room, Aida walked to the paper supply shelf, selected a few sheets of green paper, carefully tore it into rectangles, wrote numerals on each piece, and returned to complete her purchases in the pretend store.

Mark, who had been participating in a unit on trees in his third-grade classroom, spent several days accumulating leaves from the trees in his neighborhood on his own. Each leaf was mounted on a sheet of paper and labeled with its name. He carefully drew several trees with some details of the surrounding environment and labeled them "Tree in front," "Mr. McDirmid's tree," and "On the corner." Then he arranged them into a book of leaves in his neighborhood.

Each of these children have demonstrated their ability to represent objects, events, or groups of objects that are meaningful to them in a concrete, physical way. All three children were able to bring together a variety of skills and concepts to be successful in their projects. For example, Kate demonstrated memory skills, imagination, perseverance, planning, and fine motor skills. She used her knowledge of materials, whole-part relationships, and concepts of line, direction, and space in addition to her obvious understandings about the spiderweb itself. Her emotional satisfaction was expressed in her comment. Aida, who could not pretend-play comfortably with no "placeholder" for the symbolic money that she needed, used her knowledge about money and good problem-solving skills in "making" the money so that the play

could continue smoothly. Mark, who is much older, was able to represent a group of trees, their location and environment, and their relationship to people and places familiar to him. He incorporated information that he had learned at school and used skills of observing, recording, and communicating his experience.

Construction is the transformation of an experience or object into a concrete representation of that experience or object. Children use materials to make a product. "Often these are symbolic products, such as drawings, paintings and three-dimensional creations that represent objects (e.g., house), ideas (e.g., friendship), or processes (e.g., war). Constructive and symbolic play can also be combined to create a poem, a dramatic production, a tape recording, or other visual or technological products" (Bergen, 1988, p. 247).

Children may use sound effects, vocalize, or speak to explain or activate a construction. Most physical products are accompanied by children's commentaries as they are building. These comments "complete" the representation. For example, a child might name a particular block a "car" although it does not differ obviously from the block next to it. When children build machines, the adult may be able to identify them because of the associated sound effects. Thus, auditory information may supplement the physical to represent the child's idea more adequately.

TYPES OF CONSTRUCTION PROJECTS

New (1990) has identified three broadly defined types of construction projects: "those resulting from a child's natural encounter with the environment, those reflecting mutual interests on the part of the teacher and children, and those based on teacher concerns regarding specific cognitive and/or social concepts" (p. 7). In all three types of constructions, the products emerge out of an intense interest, an acute investigation, or a hands-on exploration of some object or event that appeals to the children. Constructions are children's attempts to solidify their own ideas or communicate ideas to others through imagery.

Projects Stemming from Natural Encounters

All young children are in the process of trying to understand their world. Often an ordinary object or some aspect of nature will capture a young child's interest. Drawings of people, houses, and animals are typical, as are modeling-dough constructions of cakes, cookies, snakes, and bowls. Some constructions may be extremely simple, as when Sasha, age 3, watched the raindrops flow down the pane and then painted the irregular vertical lines at the easel. Other times children's constructions are more elaborate. For example, when three children noticed the movement and seemingly purposeful activity of ants on the playground, their teacher suggested that they make something to help them remember what they saw. Other children joined the discussion about the ants' behavior and were encouraged to elaborate on their comments by making something with clay or illustrating their understanding of the ants using paper and chalk. This group of children continued to observe the ants and document what they saw with the encouragement of their teacher.

Projects Stemming from Mutual Interests of the Teacher and Children

This type of construction requires more advanced planning by the teacher, who often stimulates it by designing experiences based on common events in children's lives. For example, many young children are concerned about having a friend. Discussions of friendship enhanced with constructions of modeling dough or collages of magazine pictures representing children's ideas about friendship further mutual communication and understanding. Sometimes current events discussed at home or on television may stimulate both children and adults to read, discuss, and construct images related to the topic. For example, during the disintegration of the Soviet Union, one youngster illustrated the break-up by soaking Manilla paper in water and distributing bits of it over a blue piece of construction paper; another drew lines of people; still another painted the tanks in the street during the coup. The teacher provides accurate information, ignites the children's creative thinking, questions, and supports the further examination of ideas. Often children's constructions provide cues that children have misinformation and misconceptions to which the teacher then responds.

Projects Stemming from Teacher Concerns Regarding Specific Concepts

The third type of construction focuses on ideas or concepts initially unfamiliar to children but that adults perceive as valuable for children to explore. They may be the subject of expressed interest or the outcome of the children's current experience. Such construction activities are embedded in a theme or unit in which children learn about other aspects of the social and natural world using a variety of the strategies described in previous chapters. For instance, children living in the forested areas of the country are exposed to ideas related to the oceans and deserts. Children living in a homogeneous community may explore ideas about people of various ethnic and racial backgrounds. Children may generate construction activities that emerge from topics in science, social studies, mathematics, health, literature, or music. Children listen or read, discuss, and then construct a representation of their understanding. Both children and the teacher have opportunities to share insights into the thinking of others as the projects are examined and classmates communicate their interpretations (Gardini & Edwards, 1988). Constructions of this type are more typical of the primary child, although some 4- and 5-year-olds may attempt them.

COMPARISONS OF CONSTRUCTION AND OTHER RELATED ACTIVITIES

Object exploration, practice in fine motor skills, and craft projects are related to children's construction activities but are not quite the same. Each of these three activities involves knowledge or skills children use when constructing, but they do not require the level of representational thought and creativity associated with construction.

Construction Is Not Simply Object Play

Object play is exploration and investigation. The child attempts to discover the properties of the object itself or answers the questions "What is this object like? How does it work?" The novelty of the object attracts the child's attention, and its complexity sustains interest. Behaviors such as repetitive actions, systematic examination, and attempts to use the object in a variety of ways are typical of object play. Thus, exploration and object play usually occur before construction becomes possible (Tribe, 1982).

When children stop investigating the nature of objects and begin using them to build something, they shift into construction. The contrast between object play and construction can be seen in the behaviors of two 3-year-olds. Jerry John arranged several blocks in front of him and engaged in snapping them together in various combinations. He seemed most interested in determining whether any combination could be snapped and unsnapped readily and answering the question "How does this work?" In contrast, Alexi selected only the units that could be fastened in a linear pattern and commented, "See my snake." He then arranged the snap blocks to represent the snake.

Three- and 4-year-old children may spend substantial time exploring a material, creating a combination that reminds them of a familiar object, and naming it, as Billy did in one of his re-arrangements of the blocks: "Look here, I got this house." Sometimes youngsters are aware of this, as Dimitri was when he told an inquiring adult, "I'll know what this painting is when I've finished it." Regardless of age, all children move between object play and construction when they encounter new media or materials or ones they have not used in a long time. In general, however, as children mature, they spend less time exploring and more time using the materials to construct.

Construction Is Not Simply Fine Motor Practice

The imitation and practice of hand skills such as holding a writing implement, cutting with scissors, sewing, weaving, and using various tools are addressed in chapter 7, "The Physical Do-main." Something may be produced, but it is a byproduct of the process and not intended to represent an idea or concept of the child. Instead, it is the natural outcome of the process such as fringe produced while snipping paper or the cut-out of a pattern given to the child to practice cutting. Occasionally, preschoolers will name their byproducts at the end of practice experiences if they resemble a familiar object, such as labeling a spiral-cut paper "snake" when they pull the ends apart. Primary children may have the basic skills and refine them during the construction process as the need arises. Clearly, children must control the materials and tools used for construction and apply their knowledge to tasks skillfully.

Construction requires that the child have an image in mind that she or he then represents using familiar processes. For example, Rebecca carefully cut along the lines of a pattern drawn for her. She focused her entire attention on the process of producing a smooth curve and turning corners neatly. In contrast, Marietta left a group of children looking at the visiting cat, walked to the center where materials were stored, and created a cat face by cutting into a paper plate to form eyes and ears and adding whiskers with a marker. Rebecca and Marietta both produced products, but only Marietta had a specific idea in mind when she engaged in the activity. The child's imagination is central to the reasoning process, and no activity is undertaken without some image of the result, whether his or her conception is accurate or not (J. Smith, 1990). As with object play, the skills with which to control the processes of construction are necessary but insufficient by themselves.

Construction Is Not Simply the Demonstration of Technique

Children must also learn techniques (N. Smith, 1982). For example, a child who wishes to adhere two pieces of paper together must learn where to put the paste. Children also learn when to use which adhesive such as white liquid glue, school paste, rubber cement, or the mixture of white glue and paste that will adhere pieces of wood or cardboard. Skill in the use of tools and techniques generally precedes construction activities or is learned in the context of a construction project as the need arises.

Construction Is Not Simply Following Directions for a Project

In her kindergarten class, Diedra listened carefully as the teacher gave directions and demonstrated how to make a rabbit. Each piece had been reproduced on paper, and the rabbit would have movable legs. She cut, colored, and assembled the rabbit as directed, even though it did not quite look the same as her teacher's. Diedra used her language, memory, and motor skills to perform this task. In the kindergarten at another school, Fredrico had listened to the story of Peter Rabbit and studied several photographs of real rabbits. He constructed a rabbit from materials that he selected from those on the shelves. Fredrico also used language, memory, and motor skills to produce a rabbit. In addition, he made decisions about materials and used imagination and representational thinking to form his image of the rabbit. Both children created products, but only Fredrico was involved in the representational thought necessary for construction. However, Diedra might have produced a rabbit more appealing to adults by copying her teacher's image rather than creating her own.

Knowledge of necessary processes or step-by-step operations necessary to achieve a specific end is useful to the construction process but not a substitute for it. Does the child-drawn image of the human figure with a very large mouth and exaggerated hands mean that the child is unable to perceive the difference in length between fingers and arms and legs? Of course not! The specific proportions of the human body are not necessary to convey the idea, and children between 3 and 8 have no difficulty in perceiving such contrasting lengths readily. Yet adults sometimes behave as though children are functioning without sufficient information. The copyist theory of knowledge is that children learn by closely attending and that if the child were sufficiently skilled in perception, then he or she could accurately duplicate the idea (Forman & Kuschner, 1983). If children only followed the directions with care, the product, and incidentally the idea, would be replicated.

Unfortunately, imitation is not sufficient to develop a concept (Piaget, 1962). Children during the preoperational period do increasingly develop their abilities to perceive with accuracy. They also learn to use step-by-step procedures to achieve a specific outcome. Following directions, imitating, and copying enable children to acquire the techniques that provide them with the skills and procedures for carrying out their construction projects. For example, two 5-year-olds re-created their experiences with vehicles in the snow, using different media. One child drew a rectangle with circles on the side with a red crayon on blue paper, then neatly glued cotton balls around it. The second child used two paintbrushes held side by side and made parallel wavy lines across white paper to illustrate car tracks in the snow. Both youngsters demonstrated their abilities to use materials and fashion a concrete representation of an idea. Both used appropriate techniques for the medium selected and worked with care and deliberation. Imitation of the technique might be important, but once the technique is mastered, children construct the product according to their own ideas and interpretation. In fact, providing children with patterns to color in specific ways and expecting youngsters to replicate the teachers' models are likely to limit childrens' own abilities to make constructions of their own (Moyer, 1990). They may lose confidence in themselves if they must meet adult standards prematurely.

A second-grade teacher who had provided models and detailed directions for products in the past commented about a marked change in children's behavior when she altered her approach. "I have been really surprised. The children used to be concerned that their pictures looked just like their friends'; now they are trying to be unique in what they do."

Arts and crafts are favorites of young children and their teachers. When children make holiday ornaments from printed fabric and canning lids, decorate orange juice cans with macaroni and paint, or weave pot holders, they are participating in activities that have become traditional in some communities. These activities are legitimate exercises in fine motor control and may be useful in promoting perceptual development or listening skills. They have a place in the curriculum but do not substitute for genuine opportunities for children to construct something on their own. They have independent value but do not require the transformation of an idea into a product.

CONSTRUCTIVE PLAY AND OTHER ASPECTS OF DEVELOPMENT

Constructive play allows children to integrate and apply concepts and skills to a task. Cognitive skills of creative thinking, concept development, planning, and evaluating are important components of the construction process, as are social and affective components.

Construction and Creative Thinking

Construction activities provide opportunities for children to apply creative thinking skills. All creative efforts require two familiar elements of the active imagination: the generation of alternatives and a selection among these alternatives (J. Smith, 1990, p. 83). Children must choose among a variety of materials that may be suit-able for their project. In addition, materials themselves may provide ideas for constructions. Given encouragement and time to think, children will propose many uses beyond the obvious for common materials such as paper (Tegano, Sawyers, & Moran, 1989). Even properly identifying the problem is a challenge for the very young, and the support and guidance of teachers even for older children may be necessary (Tegano et al., 1989).

Construction and Planning and Evaluating

Children also plan what they are doing (Casey & Lippman, 1991). They may do so briefly and casually at first, beginning with an idea or a goal. Once materials are assembled and implementation begins, children often start over or add and delete materials as they alter the direction of their work. Sometimes, they comment on the criteria with which to judge their products. When Janet and Lanna, age 4, were building a house of blocks, Janet said, "We gotta get the bigger ones. These won't fit [across the roof]."

Anne Janette created this iconic construction to represent the snowman she had built the evening before.

Lanna replied, "Yeah, and get some little red and blue ones from the table to be flowers."

More mature creative efforts are never haphazard. Older primary children may plan a "fort" or "clubhouse" for several days before beginning construction. If allowed to continue, such constructions may be transformed repeatedly as children think of new alternatives.

Construction, Social-Conventional Knowledge, and Physical Knowledge

In the process of construction, children use the concepts they already have as well as learn from others (Cartwright, 1987). Children need information about texture, size, shape, weight, flexibility, and translucency of materials to carry out their projects. They also learn about part-whole relationships as they construct complex forms having many components (Reifel & Greenfield, 1983). Position in space and the placement of objects in relation to one another are typical learnings of children during the construction process. Children may use their drawing constructions to facilitate memory of an important experience (Raines, 1990). The picture at left is the painting of an 8-year-old child with disabilities shortly after she and her father built a snowman. The most complex construction that the child produced during the early years, this painting provided a source of many good memories as she grew.

Construction and Affective Development

Children gain self-confidence and demonstrate pride in their creations: "I did it!" "Look at mine!" "This, here, is my house!" Children have a sense of mastery as they work hard, solve problems, test their skills, and demonstrate patience and perseverance in the construction process. Such concentrated efforts lead to satisfaction (Cartwright, 1988).

Construction and Social Development

Children may construct with other children. This is particularly true when blocks are used, group murals are produced, or a cooperative project is deliberately planned. Group work enables children to negotiate ideas, share information, cooperate, share space and materials, and compare their performance with others (Chafel,

1987). For example, large hollow blocks challenge 3- to 5-year-old children physically, being difficult to handle alone. Such blocks also give them opportunities for immediate holistic experiences requiring social organization and cooperation as they build and later engage in pretend play (Cartwright, 1990).

Thus, constructive play is integrative in nature. Children must synthesize in this experience and utilize a variety of skills and abilities. In this process, the child is a meaning maker, the embodiment of knowledge rather than a passive recipient of it (Jalongo, 1990). Like pretend play, constructive play challenges children to use all that they know and can do to be successful.

Accounting for Differences

Maturity, experience, and style preference are factors contributing to the outcome of children's construction activities. Experience with materials is essential for learning techniques. Children who have limited access to a variety of materials will not be as skillful as those who do, regardless of age. For example, although many 3-year-olds can cut simple straight lines, 5-year-olds who have just acquired access to scissors may still be figuring out how they work and so use them with less skill.

Maturity. A few children will begin true construction with regular materials as early as 3. If the construction is not named by the child, it is difficult to tell if the child is involved in object play or simple construction. As children mature, their structures become more complex and have more parts (Reifel & Greenfield, 1983). Details of interest become elaborated and are often the subject of conversation among children. In addition, the intent of the child is much clearer, being either announced in advance or obvious from the context of the ongoing play. Four- and 5-year-olds regularly engage in pretend play during the construction process. Six- and 7-year-olds may discuss in detail what they plan to construct and even determine the relationship among the structures before they begin. At any point in time children produce constructions that are more recognizable (drawing of a person) or abstract (whirling leaves in the wind). They may do this independently or as part of a larger, more complex play frame. The

TABLE 10.1
Developmental Stages of Block Play

Stage	Description
1: Object exploration	*Carrying blocks*—Children move blocks around and discover the properties of the material.
2: Learning techniques	*Piling blocks and laying on the floor*—Children arrange both horizontal and vertical sets of blocks. Sometimes completed arrangements suggest a use, such as a "road."
3: Construction	*Connecting blocks to create structures*—Children make enclosures, build bridges, and design decorative patterns and layouts.
4: Advanced construction	*Making elaborate constructions*—Children create complex buildings, often with many parts, using curved as well as straight lines, building around or over obstacles. This stage is frequently associated with pretend play.

developmental stages of block play are pre-sented in Table 10.1 because this is a very familiar and typical construction material. A more elaborate and complete description of block play can be found in *The Block Book* (Hirsch, 1984).

Play style. Children seem to prefer one of two play styles: patterners and dramatists. Patterners tend to focus on form, line, color, design, and the general aesthetics of the construction. A 5-year-old with this style will build a more elaborate block structure, with turrets, corners,

The "house" built by these 3-year-olds is a typical Stage 2 block play construction.

Stage 3 constructions like this "skyscraper" are common in the kindergarten.

These second graders have constructed an elaborate Stage 4 movie theater, complete with screen, seating, concession stand, and parking.

arches, and generally more blocks and space needed than a 5-year-old who does not predominantly prefer this style. The form, line, or design is important. Patterners may be very interested in maintaining the structure for several days. In contrast, dramatists tend to focus on the narrative of the pretend play and might use only a few blocks as long as it represents the idea they have in mind. For this child, the form is much less important than the function. As soon as the pretend sequence is complete, this child is "finished" with the materials and more readily returns them to the shelf. A youngster's characteristic style applies to all materials. Children can and should be encouraged to extend their constructions beyond the limits of the preferred so that dramatists pay more attention to form and patterners become more involved in the pretend play possibilities. More than a third of all children use either style with equal ease (Shotwell, Wolf, & Gardner, 1979).

CONSTRUCTION AND MATERIALS OF CHOICE

Construction opportunities are facilitated when children have access to a large array of materials. For example, one 4-year-old wanted a "cape." He examined butcher paper that was stiff but could be wrapped around and taped. He tried some lightweight tissue paper. Then he discovered some yarn and a piece of fabric. The texture of the latter made this his best choice for the purpose. Children can engage in this scope of problem solving to make successful constructions only in an environment where there is access to a supply of materials.

Various Blocks

Blocks abound in sizes, colors, and textures. Some fasten together and have pieces designed for wheels and axles. Others such as unit blocks are cut in regular, predictable intervals. Some sets have a color for each shape and provide a variety of angles in wedge-shaped pieces.

Commercial Sets

There are numerous commercial construction sets with sections that children can fasten to-gether using nuts and bolts or pieces that fit together when laid in place. These sets often have extender sets that include more complicated pieces and may even come with electric motors so that children can make more complex machines that run. Products that have many units and can be assembled in different ways provide for more diversity of construction than those with fewer units or those limited to some predetermined structures (Whiren, 1979). Older children frequently want their constructions "to work."

Carpentry Supplies and Tools

Woodworking benches with real hammers, nails, saws, drills, screws, screwdrivers, and other tools to enable the child to construct with real wood are an alternative in many programs for young children. Tools should be of home-use quality. Most toy tools are impractical because they do not work. Some programs allow children to build with wood and later take the structures apart to reuse the wood for new projects. Soft woods are easier for children to use than hard woods. They are also less expensive and can be obtained as discards from local businesses.

Art Materials, Paper, and Common Discards

The scope of art materials was discussed in "The Aesthetics Domain," chapter 3. Children use these materials to represent their ideas graphically. A multitude of papers that differ in color, texture, and size are available for purchase and as discards from businesses or families such as old wrapping paper, commercial sacks, forms, used computer printouts, and even trim cuttings from printers. The numbers and colors available in paint and writing implements are considerable as well. In addition, a variety of three-dimensional materials such as egg cartons, packing material, meat trays, and other throw-away objects with interesting patterns, colors, or textures can be obtained for children to use.

Open-ended Materials

Flexible materials such as sand, clay, plasticine, and Play-doh® can be used to represent a variety of ideas. Once children understand the properties of the materials and if they have supporting tools, children can create a wide array of representations. The advantage of these materials is that they are three-dimensional, with an undetermined shape in the beginning. With sand, children can try out their ideas and erase them without fear of making mistakes (Barbour, Webster, & Drosdek, 1987). Children can exert greater control over the medium at younger ages.

Natural Materials

Sticks, leaves, stones, mud, and other plant materials have long been used by children to create little worlds where pretend people carry out their lives. Snow is another excellent building material. These natural resources may be used outdoors or brought into the classroom as the occasion demands.

Materials Assembled with Specific Teacher Goals in Mind

Older children can create board games from file folders, poster board, or shirt boxes with assorted stickers, markers, and pieces to move (Castle, 1991). The child is required not only to construct a product but also to establish the rules of the game. The problems they encounter, such as how to have moving pieces that can be distinguished from one another or how to make the game challenging and fun, engage their creative interest as well as require access to an array of materials.

INDEPENDENCE OF MATERIALS FROM THE IDEAS THEY REPRESENT

At times, children use the same materials to represent a variety of ideas. Painting and dough are particularly versatile. In one small group, children used dough to make nests and eggs, dishes, cups with handles, a ring, a long snake, and a cake. The diversity of ideas that individual children expressed expanded the vision of the entire group. Children see more and more possibilities as they practice with the material and as they modify them by using tools. In another group, children used paint to represent abstract

ideas like friends, conflicts, or feelings in more concrete terms. On the other hand, some of the first identifiable drawings of people, vehicles, and houses are also made with paints (Kellogg, 1969). Whether or not children depict their ideas in realistic or abstract constructions, they tend to become more versatile when they are thoroughly familiar with the material and are in control of the process. Yet, each material also limits the content of expression and approach used to some extent (N. Smith, 1982). For example, it would be easier to represent the ocean using paints and paper or a paper collage than blocks.

Children often depict the same idea using a variety of materials. Children must use problem solving when they have a choice of materials for representing the same general idea. Different materials give different results, so the character or mood may vary from one depiction to another. Children also must solve a variety of problems relating to technique when materials are varied. Developing a theme of "Houses," the same child made houses using sticks, straw, and string; sugar cubes; blocks; crayons and paper; and paints and small boxes. The gravest technical difficulties were experienced when the child tried to use the straw, finally tying it at the top and sticking a finger in to make an interior. Various adhesives were tried, and the sizes of the houses differed considerably. The block house had an interior and an exterior. When given crayons, the child drew only the face of the house. These activities, extended over several days, involved much peer cooperation and prosocial behavior. Children also compared their own work on the same idea from one medium to the next.

As children increase in their ability to represent objects and events, they also correspondingly are better able to select the appropriate material to achieve their desired end. With practice, they become more confident, more skillful, and often more creative.

CURRENT EDUCATIONAL ISSUES

1. *What can I expect from 3-year-olds? I don't think the children in this classroom can do the activities suggested here.* Three-year-olds

engage predominantly in object play and the exploration of construction materials. They are learning techniques and expanding their conception of how to use a variety of materials. A few 3-year-olds will make a representative object, but not all. Five-year-olds attempt many symbolic representations, and 7-year-olds are generally quite skillful. Children continue to increase in construction skills throughout the elementary years (Hirsch, 1984).

2. *What do I say to a child who wants the symbolic representation to work like the real thing?* Remind younger children that they can pretend to make their construction work. The constructed object "stands for" the object but is not the same thing. A discussion of what the differences are between the real thing and the play one will help children accept the limitations of their projects. Often older children are able to construct something that will "go," such as using a twisted rubberband to power a Tinker Toy® car.

3. *Won't children make a big mess?* Sometimes they will, but then they can clean it up. The key to successful management is to have accessible storage that is labeled in a way children understand. In addition, children value their construction opportunities and tend to manage their time and materials to control the mess. Giving children advanced warning of when they must clean up enables them to achieve some closure on their project and then begin to put away materials themselves. Cleaning up must be planned for in the schedule and be allotted enough time for completion. Some primary teachers have managed this problem by having a substantial period of time one day a week for construction activities.

4. *The things children make themselves are not as nice as the ones they do when they follow directions.* Of course, it is infinitely easier to copy another's idea than to produce an idea oneself and figure out how to implement it, which is more challenging and complicated intellectual work. The craft may appear to be more attractive to adults, but it is not a product of the child's thinking processes. When the learning and problem-solving process is explained to parents, they too value the children's own work.

Crafts that are undertaken for their benefits to children's motor coordination and social skills or that are related to other domains serve these functions, but they do not replace the need for opportunities for children to represent their own ideas concretely.

5. *What do you do if the child has worked with blocks or wet sand and has nothing to carry home?* An instant photograph taken periodically to represent the child's construction is very useful. Although it is too expensive to do this frequently, the child might select one or two constructions that are to be preserved in this way. Occasionally, dough products can be taken home by youngsters when the dough needs to be replaced anyway. Children who produce music as a creative effort might be willing to tape it if the teacher is unable to write the notation. Older children are often less concerned with carrying something home than they are with saving it from one day to the next. Block or box structures may be saved for a short period of time to maximize all the opportunities for elaboration and expansion typical of these activities. Often these problems can be discussed with the class so that the group itself can establish its own ground rules and propose potential solutions.

GOALS AND OBJECTIVES

The ultimate goal is for children to translate mental images into tangible products that represent their own interpretation of an object or event.

Mediating Objectives

As children progress toward the ultimate goal, they will

1. engage in a wide range of experiences from which to draw their interpretations.
2. interpret events and reconstruct them in tangible ways.
3. use diverse approaches and materials to represent objects or events by

   ■ representing a single object or event using different materials or techniques and
   ■ representing different objects and events using one material or technique.

4. collaborate with classmates to construct a representative object.

TEACHING STRATEGIES

Many of the guidelines listed in "The Pretend Play Domain" are applicable to construction because so much of construction activity, particularly of older children, is integrated into pretend play sequences. Therefore, only additional guidelines are suggested here.

1. *Provide a psychologically safe environment.* Children must feel comfortable and acceptable to their peers and to the adults in order to wander into unknown territory. Children then are able to risk being wrong or having a project not work out as they hoped. Creativity is the outcome of challenge and risk taking. Guidelines for promoting such an environment are available in chapter 5, "The Affective Domain," but here are some specifics related to construction:

- Ask about a project (Cassidy, 1989); do not assume you know what it is. You might be wrong. "Tell me about your drawing" or "I don't quite understand what you are trying to do here" are general statements letting the child know that you are not able to interpret his or her construction. "Did you have something specific in mind?" is more direct and is responsive to questions or comments from the child when the teacher is unable to respond because the representation is not clear.
- Describe what you observe about the materials or technique being used or other specific characteristics of the project. Such statements should not be judgmental but might be comparative, such as "I see Harry has used all bright primary colors and George chose the pastels." Describing specifically what the child has done provides modeling for language as well as conveying a respect for the unique characteristics of each child's work. Below are some examples about using blocks from Dodge (1991, p. 91):

  - What blocks were used: "You found out that two of these make one long block."
  - Where the blocks were placed: "You used four blocks to make a big square."
  - How many blocks were used: "You used all the blocks to make the road."

  - Whether the blocks are all the same: "All the blocks in your road are exactly the same size."
  - How the blocks are connected: "All your blocks are touching."
  - How the blocks are balanced: "Those long blocks are holding up the shorter ones."

Similar statements can be made about constructions of many different materials. Such observations may assist children in opening conversations about their constructions so that both adults and children increase their understanding.

- Provide opportunities for children to share their products with others. Display drawings, paintings, and sculpture regularly. Ask the child who made the construction to talk about his or her ideas at group time. Encourage peer questions and comments that are relevant and useful. Color, line, mass or volume, pattern, shape or form, space and texture are appropriate topics for discussion (Moyer, 1990). Demonstrate how to give feedback or ask questions about the construction. "You selected interesting colors for the [purple] cow" or "The size of this drawing is very small; tell us why you chose to do it that way" are statements based on observations of the construction as well as openings for explanation if the child wishes to provide it. Never use sarcasm; the child's feelings will be hurt and no educational goal can be reached. Do not allow children to provide gratuitous negative comments without making them accountable. For example, if a child says, "That's ugly!" respond by saying, "You think that drawing is not attractive; tell us why you think that." If the child responds with detail, then discuss how the same characteristics that appeal to one person may not be attractive to another.
- Help other children focus on the play potential of the construction. If a child has made a particularly effective supplement to pretend play, then recognize his or her contributions to the play. When children are working together on a construction, encourage children to discuss what they plan to do and how the construction will fit into their continuing play plans.

- Support children who are feeling frustrated and angry when their work appears unsuccessful to them. Help them define the problem ("Tell me why you think this isn't going to work. What is wrong? What do you think you can do about it? Is there anyone else in the class that might be able to assist you?"). Children should be able to achieve their goal with their own actions when they work together (Tudge & Caruso, 1988). Occasionally offer assistance, but allow the child to maintain control of the decision making.
- Provide display opportunities to everyone. Keep the displays up a few days and then dismantle them. Avoid selecting the "best" construction for display. Sometimes the most appealing product does not indicate the most creative thinking.
- Teach children to respect the work of one another. Help them to understand that it is because of respect that they do not kick down someone's blocks, make noise while someone shares a song, or jeer when someone hangs up a drawing (Kostelnik et al., in press).

2. *Provide a solid base of information and experience from which children develop their constructions.* Projects of investigation should be a regular part of the curriculum, not an add-on or an extra (Webster, 1990). Build on children's interest, and use the surrounding community as a source of information and assistance (Borden, 1987). Both field trips and visitors to the classroom enhance the information base. Some suggestions about how to do this follow (Borden, 1987):

- Keep it simple. A field trip may be one block away to the shoe repair store. The exploration and information sought should be easily accessible to the children once they encounter it.
- Discuss, read, and play in advance. Children who have some information are better prepared to ask appropriate questions and understand what they see. Children who have no background information find it difficult to process the new experience rapidly and do not benefit as much as those who are better prepared.
- Encourage detailed observations. Photographs and videotaped segments by the children or

teacher might contribute. Even planning what to look for will enable children to attend to relevant attributes. One teacher of 4-year-olds gave children a three-by-five card and a pencil and suggested that they make a mark on the card to help them remember what they saw. When they returned to the classroom, they met in a circle, showed their mark, and reported on what it reminded them of.

- When safe, encourage the children to touch, smell, manipulate, and examine closely and from multiple perspectives the environment and the relevant objects within it.
- Ask questions to encourage children's thinking. Simply announcing what the questions will be in advance helps children attend to particular information. Point out salient features of the experience.
- Give small amounts of information if children are interested. This is not the ideal time for extensive information sharing except from people not otherwise available.
- Provide time, materials, and enthusiasm for extensive follow-up discussions, pretend play, and construction activities.
- Repeat the excursion with small groups of children if needed, and encourage parents to take their children to the places visited and share in the learning experience.
- Incorporate construction experiences into units and other activities that are discussed in the other domain chapters. The concrete depiction of ideas is appropriate for all content and all aspects of development.

3. *Prepare the physical environment.* A clean, orderly classroom is an asset when children use many materials in creative ways. Several suggestions are in chapter 11, but, again, there are a few specifics related primarily to construction:

- Store unit blocks on open shelves, and tape silhouettes of the shapes on the back of the cupboard so that children can easily find and take care of the materials.
- Provide sufficient floor space for unit blocks and table or floor space for construction materials. Place construction activity spaces, which tend to be noisy, on a carpet and near each other, away from the quiet areas of the room.

- Provide the materials for cleaning up messes and preventing them. For example, children who have access to newspaper will cover tables to keep them clean when their work is likely to be messy if supplies are available. Small brooms and dustpans are easy to use in sweeping the floor.
- Keep basic supplies of scissors, papers, writing instruments, and paints accessible. Permit children to request materials that cannot be stored in open shelves.
- Keep an inventory and check out materials that are limited, expensive, or frequently misplaced. Children can learn to be responsible for these. On the other hand, there is no virtue in saving materials indefinitely and not letting the children learn from them.
- If problems occur related to the physical environment, involve the children in exploring alternative solutions. Children involved in planning and decision making are more likely to comply with the rules and plans.

4. *Support children in their problem solving, and encourage them to expand the number and diversity of potential solutions* (Casey & Lippman, 1991). (The corollary is that teachers should not arbitrarily announce "That won't work!" before the child has had a chance to think about it.) The following strategies will be useful:

- Attempt to grasp the child's intent. Direct observation sometimes works, but it may be necessary to check it out ("It seems that you are trying to..."). Honestly inquire if necessary, "I don't understand...."
- Ask about alternatives children considered ("Tell me what you thought about doing. Anything else?").
- Inquire about the possible sources of information ("Has anyone done anything like this before? Might he or she help?"). Encourage the use of reference materials ("Where might you get a picture of the...?" or "Is there anything else that you might use to help you figure this out?"). In one instance a 4-year-old was attempting to build a pair of walkie-talkies. She had already nailed long spikes into the ends of two blocks of wood and was worried that "they won't work just like that." She had

never seen a walkie-talkie up close but knew they had more than an antenna to make them go. The teacher could have just handed her a walkie-talkie. Instead, she carefully engaged the child in a conversation until the child herself recognized the scope of the problem and then could quickly identify a potential solution to it.
- Encourage children to participate in the general planning and decision-making process. When a child enthusiastically asks, "Can we build a...?" respond, "Yes, and what materials [space, time] will you need?" or "Yes, and how will you do this?" Avoid "Yes, but...." Children cannot do everything just when they might like to. Older children are particularly sensitive to the competing needs for time and space. Involve them in making the opportunities for carrying out projects as well as in building projects.
- Actively involve children who are less likely to initiate construction projects (Tudge & Curuso, 1988). Some children have more confidence in themselves than others. Often the more timid child is left out of group constructions or does not initiate construction activities independently. Good ideas may be lost to the group and the timid child's abilities not acknowledged or recognized, even by the individuals involved. Watch for opportunities to suggest that the timid child participate in the group endeavor. Interact with the less forceful students, and encourage them to share their ideas with you and one or two others. Avoid telling them what to do or giving them solutions to problems. Standing by them (literally) when they approach other children is more likely to give them confidence and practice as well as helping them with the task at hand.
- Allow time for children to think and develop their ideas. Very few problems are solved spontaneously. Very little creative work happens on the spur of the moment. It sometimes takes more time to think about and plan a project than it does to carry it out. Rather than urging a child who is sitting quietly or abstractedly to "Get started on...," offer a listening ear: "Would you like to share what you are thinking about? Maybe that will help."

Learning how to use a variety of tools expands children's construction skills.

5. *Teach children the technical skills needed to use materials.* Creativity is not impeded by the child's being shown how to use materials appropriately. On the contrary, lack of skill inhibits children's ability to do construction at all. For example, show children how much paste to use and where to place it; show them how to cut; demonstrate sewing; model the use of a wire cutter on potter's clay; deliberately mix paints so that they can see the effect. Then let them use the skills to implement their own goals (Cole, 1990).

6. *Encourage the flow among play, construction, and information acquisition.* Given the appropriate circumstances, experiences that are intended as basic information generate construction. Equally often the desire of children to construct something for their play motivates them to seek out the information. Topical reference materials are essential to every classroom, even for the youngest children. Older children may look up information for themselves, and younger children can watch teachers who "don't know, but I'll find out."

ACTIVITY SUGGESTIONS

➠ Flower Garden

Objective: For children to engage in a wide range of experiences from which to draw their interpretations

Materials: Tissue paper, construction paper, egg cartons, watercolors, paper, selected scented oils, toothpicks, paste, scissors, a few cut blossoms of common plants, green pipe cleaners

Procedure: Take the children on a walk near the school during a time when neighbors have flowers in bloom. Point out the scent, color, relative size, and other characteristics of the flowers. Include blooming weeds in your examination. Encourage children to share their thinking about the flowers when you get back. Ask the children to record what they saw, heard, smelled, and felt about the flowers using the materials. Listen to their comments as they construct. Demonstrate how to put the tiniest amount of scented oil on paper with a toothpick. This is very potent! Provide display space for the flower garden.

To Simplify: Younger children may, with permission, pick some of the flowering plants, especially dandelions and Queen Anne's lace to return to the classroom and arrange the flowers in jars.

To Extend: Select a fairly large bloom and dissect the flower to examine the pollen, stamen, pistil, interior of the stem, and veins of the leaf. A tulip works well. Suggest that the older children might want to construct the "inside" as well as the outside. Encourage discussion about how to accomplish this. Provide plenty of time as this is quite difficult to do.

➠ Growing Frogs

Objective: For children to engage in a wide range of experiences from which to draw their interpretations

Materials: Drawing paper, green and black felt-tip pens, clipboards, child's old swimming pool with a log or large rock in it and filled 3 to 4 inches

Procedure: Collect a few tadpoles in a nearby pond, and put them in the outdoor pool during early spring. Label the pool and place signs so that other people will not disturb it on weekends or when school is not in session. Examine the tadpoles periodically, and encourage children to draw them. Point out details but do not expect to get anatomical drawings. Children might record the wiggling motion, length, or some characteristic adults might not consider. Date each drawing and keep them in a file to record the changes in the tadpoles and in the way children represent them for several weeks. Then have each child review his or her own products and comment on them. (Do not forget to feed the tadpoles/frogs if you do not live in an area where sufficient bugs will breed in the pool.)

To Simplify: Ask children to represent the movement of the tadpoles using their own bodies instead of recording with drawing.

To Extend: Provide Play-doh® or clay for children to represent the tadpole or frog when they do not have it in front of them. Encourage them to reflect on its shape, size, and movement before they begin and to verbalize what they plan to do. Also, other living creatures might be brought into the classroom periodically such as a puppy that grows bigger. Red leaf worms live on garbage and paper, readily reproduce in a box or jar, and can be repeatedly examined.

➡ Cloud Watch

Objective: For children to engage in a wide range of experiences from which to draw their interpretations

Materials: Whipped liquid soap, cotton balls or stuffing, milkweed seed, white packing materials or other white fluffy substance, firm paper, glue

Procedure: Over several days, take the children outside to watch the clouds. Name the cloud types and help them discriminate among them. Encourage the children to describe what they see. Deliberately extend their descriptive vocabulary. Read poetry about the clouds; most of the Romantic poets have appropriate selections. You may also want to read *It Looked like Spilled*

Milk by Charles G. Shaw. Use photographs of clouds in climates where cloud variations are limited. If possible, expand their sensory awareness using music. The "Thunderstorm" section of *The Grand Canyon Suite* by Ferde Grafe is one effective, provocative piece. With several ways of experiencing clouds, encourage children to represent them using the materials.

To Simplify: Reduce the number of alternative materials that children can use to construct clouds, or suggest that children construct the clouds they see on a daily basis rather than after several observations.

To Extend: Older children might be able to make a cloud record representing the daytime sky over the period of a month as associated weather. Also, videotape daily broadcasts of the satellite pictures of the cloud cover over the United States. Share these with the children and encourage them to construct a cloud map over the outline of the United States, which must be provided for them.

To Combine Construction and Pretend Play Experiences: Following the experiences in which children acquire information about clouds and attempt constructions that represent their ideas, add the following pretend play objective: to integrate construction into pretend play episodes.

Procedure: Suggest that the children make a representation of the cloud they want to be. This may be a symbol on a headband, a picture tied around the neck, or a construction pinned to clothing. Provide the children with cotton garden gloves, and let some of them pretend to be clouds moving into and over other areas of the room. If all the children know this is going forward, they will respond appropriately to being blown, rained on, and so forth.

Variations: Follow up these experiences with the following pretend play objective: for children to use their bodies to represent real or imaginary objects or events.

Procedure: Encourage simple make-believe and ask children to move like various clouds. The cumulus tend to roll and lumber across the sky, depending on wind velocity. The cirrus are slower, stretched out, thinner, and higher. Children particularly enjoy being thunderstorms and rain clouds.

⯈ Field Reports

Objective: For children to interpret events and reconstruct them in tangible ways

Materials: Variety of paper, markers, crayons, scissors, collage items, magazine pictures, paste or glue, clay or Play-doh®

Procedure: Whenever children engage in a field trip or school assembly or when a visitor comes into the classroom to expand their connections to the community, ask children to record what they thought about it. Allow them to select the material they will use to record their impressions, feelings, or ideas. Ask them to tell you about their project ("Tell me what you plan to record" or "How will you be able to get that across?"). The constructions then can be used later in the learning episodes as children explain the ideas they had when they made them. This activity is most suitable for 6- and 7-year-olds.

To Simplify: The teacher may take dictation about the idea that the younger child is trying to represent so that it is not forgotten. Young children's representations are much less realistic or pictorial and they may forget.

To Extend: Add the following construction objective: for children to interact with classmates to construct collaboratively a representative object. Ask children to work in groups and represent the event in one construction. They must make group plans and cooperate to achieve the result. A large piece of paper inspires cooperative planning, separate sheets encourage sequences, and graphing triggers counting. By careful selection of materials and discussing possibilities for their use, the teacher can promote particular learning objectives.

⯈ Daily Life

Objective: For children to interpret events and reconstruct them in tangible ways

Materials: Unit blocks

Procedure: Encourage children to build with blocks. Listen to their comments and help them solve structural problems such as multiple bridging by assisting with locating the source of the difficulty ("Why do you think this isn't working?"), encouraging them to try solutions ("Try it out and see if it will work"), and evaluating and going on ("Do you think that is the way you want it, or would you like to try something else?"). The purpose is to enhance their problem-solving abilities. The meaning of the construction should be determined by the children.

To Simplify: Allow the children to explore with minimal intervention. They may be just investigating the properties of the materials. Three-year-olds may need to be shown how to use blocks and stack them safely.

To Extend: Add new materials such as small dolls, cars, trucks, road signs. Encourage the extension of the construction to include the pretend play component. You may also add signs and art materials for children to make their own signs. Or add this objective: to interact with classmates to construct collaboratively a representative object. Help the children who are building with blocks to coordinate their structures. They might be connected with roads. The full structure system might represent a neighborhood. Facilitate planning by helping the children as a group work toward a unified goal.

⯈ Books

Objective: For children to use diverse approaches to represent objects or events

Materials: Stickers, markers, glue-on stars, toothpicks, pebbles, twigs, leaves (and other small, relatively flat consumable items for larger numbers), crayons, scissors, markers, stapler, glue or paste, and construction paper cut in half

Procedure: Place the materials in separate containers. Encourage children to construct books representing their knowledge of the thematic units being taught.

To Simplify: Take dictation from younger children and then print it on the constructions or the facing page.

To Extend: Encourage older children to write captions or explanations for their constructions themselves. You may wish to make a list of key words available that children are likely to use. For example, in a unit on cats such words as *paw, claws, whiskers, fur, tail, purr, hiss,* and *prance* might be appropriate.

➠ Houses

Objective: For children to represent a single object or event using different materials or techniques and engage in a wide range of experiences from which to draw their interpretations (Note: Since the first objective is in the use of diverse materials, several specific constructions will be suggested with their appropriate materials.)

Procedure: Provide experiences for children in which they explore the diversity in housing. Houses vary in construction materials and size, and they may be attached, as in duplexes, single, or in apartments. They also vary by climate, culture, and the degree to which family living is mostly indoors or mixed between indoor and outdoor environments. Some housing is temporary such as tents, RVs, or trailer campers. A variety of photos, picture books, advertisements, or reference materials can be used to stimulate children's thinking.

1. Materials: Blocks, small furnishings, and dolls

Procedure: Encourage children to construct homes. Prompt children to use enclosures and construct apartments or other housing forms.

2. Materials: Sand, twigs, rakes or spoons and shovels, cans or containers of various sizes, water (sprinkling can)

Procedure: Suggest that the children make houses of sand. They can mold it with their hands or use containers to construct three-dimensional shapes. Homes can be elaborated with the other materials to vary the texture and size of the house. Young children rarely make complex castles. Damp sand works best for this.

3. Materials: Magazines and real estate brochures, scissors, and paste

Procedure: Suggest that children make a collage of many homes. They may use exteriors or interiors. You may extend to the affective domain and ask children to select only the items they like best.

4. Materials: Small boxes, shoe boxes, thread spools and other small objects, fabric, wallpaper, tissue paper, markers

Procedure: Ask the children to make a house for someone very tiny. A variation is that several children make rooms for a house and fasten them together with masking tape.

5. Materials: Blanket or sheet, rope, stakes, and strong string. Or, blanket or sheet and a small table

Procedure: Help the children tie a sturdy rope up about 2.5 to 3 feet off the ground. They can stake out the sheet to make a tent. Other materials may be added to make bed rolls and a floor during outdoor play. Or, provide the children with the sheet near a table. They are likely to make a tent with it.

6. Materials: A large refrigerator box, markers, wallpaper paste, wallpaper, fabric, and other materials suggested or gathered by the children, plus a sharp knife to be used by the teacher

Procedure: Cut windows as directed by the children; otherwise, let them construct the interior and exterior of the house themselves. Encourage cooperation and communication so that a unified plan may be implemented. As changes are made from day to day, help them check out these changes with players who have worked previously before they start to implement them. Discuss the rules for making this larger house with the group so that children cooperate effectively.

PART III

Implementation

CHAPTER 11

Organizing Space, Materials, and Time

"Is it possible to utilize developmentally appropriate practices in our current program with the materials we already have?"

"How can we implement a more developmentally appropriate curriculum without spending more money this year?"

"Just what do I do to get started on this? I have always had three reading groups, whole-group instruction, and workbooks for math."

"Can you really do centers with one adult in the classroom?"

Each of these questions addresses resource use and allocation. The most typical resources that programs have are time, space, equipment, and materials. Developmentally appropriate curricula use all of these resources, but in very specific ways. Usually, school districts have to reallocate resources rather than generate new resources. For example, when workbooks are no longer purchased for math, the dollars saved could be made available to purchase manipulatives that support math and science learning. Over the years, the variety and scope of the equipment and materials purchased in lieu of these workbooks provides sufficient resources for more child-centered approaches (Cummings, 1991b). Sometimes child care centers fail to plan for equipment replacement and renovation in their efforts to maintain minimal fees and consequently suffer from inadequate, incomplete, or inappropriate equipment and materials.

The role of the teacher in organizing the classroom is essential for the effective implementation of the developmental approach. The use of the physical facility, the daily schedule, and the type and quantities of materials and equipment are fundamentally interactive. For example, the amount of space influences the number of learning centers that can usefully be developed; if there are fewer learning centers, more children are likely to be at each one, which necessitates larger quantities of materials per center. Similarly, if children must share equipment and materials, then time allocated to the activity must be adjusted to reflect that need. For the purposes of clarity, general principles related to the physical environment will be presented with suggestions for structuring the environment. We then suggest typical materials for each of the domains of learning described in this volume and sample daily schedules.

ORGANIZING THE PHYSICAL ENVIRONMENT

Safety

Teachers are responsible for overseeing the building and room safety and training children to use materials safely. The children's safety is always the top priority. Three- to 5-year-olds need much more careful supervision for all safety practices than children aged 6 to 8 because they are less likely to have learned safe practices well. However, all children during the early childhood period should be monitored by adults, as they have yet to develop the judgment as to what is safe and what is dangerous. This supervision can be simplified by adjusting the physical environment itself to minimize potential hazards. Consider these guidelines:

1. Cover electrical outlets except when in use.
2. Use extension cords of adequate size only when necessary. Never string them together for long distances or across pathways.
3. Remain with any electrical appliance or heat source if children are present.
4. Remove (and repair if possible) any materials or pieces of equipment that appear unsafe, including those on the playground.
5. Use barriers such as placing tools on high shelves or moving tables near equipment that may be unsafe without supervision when attending to other things. For example, prevent 4-year-old children from touching a cooling iron after a project in which crayon shreds were melted between sheets of wax paper by putting the iron in an inaccessible spot.
6. Place all chemicals (plant fertilizer, cleaning compounds, medicines, etc.) out of reach of children.
7. Scan the environment regularly for safety hazards such as water or sand on pathways, clutter near exits, and improper use of equipment.
8. Include teaching children the safe use of materials as a normal part of instruction.

9. Teach children to recognize the common symbols indicating a dangerous situation or object, such as the symbols for poison or stop.

Comfortable Climate

Teachers are responsible for ensuring that children can use work and play places easily and comfortably enough to engage in meaningful activities. Children work best when the temperature is comfortable, the air is fresh, and light is adequate. Most practitioners are accustomed to adjusting these dimensions regularly; however, if the school does not have windows that open and close, a round cushion fan is useful even in winter to move air. Lighting in most schools is usually full-intensity, with on and off switches. A dimmer switch is inexpensive and can be installed with any lighting system. Children tend to be quieter and more socially interactive in less than full-intensity light, but they need the latter for close work.

Children are also most comfortable when the size of the furniture is correct for their heights. As public schools move into serving children under 5 years of age, they will have to purchase chairs and tables that are adjusted for the height of younger children.

Space

Teachers are responsible for planning the effective use of classroom space. Facilities are not within the control of classroom personnel, but the use of space within the room can be modified to support curricular goals. Ideally the floor space will be at least 35 square feet per child, not counting closets or immovable storage, hallways, and so on, although some experts recommend up to 100 square feet per child (Spodek et al., 1991). With greater densities (more children or less space), teachers can expect more disruptive behavior (Polloway, 1974). The probability of children physically bumping into each other increases at the same time that space to spread out the work is reduced. Sometimes facilities that might at first glance appear very limited can be adapted. For example, in high-ceiling classrooms, a loft can be built with a ladder to increase the total space available. Activity centers that are fairly stable, such as the listening center,

could be placed on the top level, with another center, such as pretend play, underneath, which would make better use of the vertical space.

The organization of physical space is an effective predictor of program quality as it impacts what children can do, determines the ease with which they are able to carry out their plans, and affects the ways in which they use materials (Kritchevsky & Prescott, 1977; Schickedanz, York, et al., 1990).

When teachers arrange space in the classroom, they must consider how that arrangement will influence children's behavior. Children need *private space* where they can work independently or gain control of their own thoughts and feelings. A study carrel, secluded chair, or pile of pillows can meet this need. The coat storage area, cubby, or children's school bags are other private places that children might store their work and private possessions.

A learning center of two to six children requires a *small group space.* Children are able to interact quietly with one another, talking at conversational levels. They are likely to exhibit cooperative and helping behaviors when they are in close personal space (2–4 ft) and when the task set for the group in noncompetitive. Small group spaces should vary in size, with secluded spaces for a pair of children as well as spaces for four to six children. Often a small table with the appropriate number of chairs may meet this need. Other small-group activities abound when the curriculum is organized into learning centers of various sizes (see chap. 12). When learning centers are designed for small groups rather than only for individuals or large groups, behaviors such as wandering, running, fighting over materials, repeating the same activity over and over again, crawling under tables, and consistently depending on adults for the things children need can be minimized (Dodge, 1989).

The third kind of space is for a *large group* in which children listen to stories, sing, engage in games or other movement activities, and share whole-group instruction. Although it is possible to carry out some common activities while children are seated at desks or tables, it is often preferable to have a separate area where children can sit on the floor. They are closer together, can see pictures or demonstrations better, and often feel more like a cohesive group.

To structure all three types of space, separate them by boundaries that are clear, physical entities. Imaginary boundaries, such as a pretend line between two children sitting side by side at a table, are not effective. Children naturally expect to interact with neighbors. Children can determine the appropriate number of participants for a specific space by the number of chairs or the amount of floor space within the boundaries. Teachers have also effectively used signs indicating the number of children for a given area. Storage units, pathways, equipment, low dividers, and even the arrangement of materials on a table can delineate boundaries. As one second-grade teacher indicated, "I painted an old bathtub red, filled it with pillows and placed it near the window. When a child wishes to be alone he or she gets a book and sits in the tub. The other children do not bother them and neither do I. When ready, the child returns to the ongoing activity." Another second-grade teacher put an area rug in the classroom because "whenever we are working together on the rug, children know that they must work quietly and that cooperation is expected."

Noise

Sound control is an ongoing challenge in programs that encourage independent work, cooperative work, and center work. Hard surfaces in the classroom are easy to keep clean but tend to increase noise, and softer surfaces that absorb noise give a warmer, more resilient surface to touch but are more difficult to maintain. Hard-surface floors are best where there are messy activities or children are likely to track in dirt from outdoors. Carpeted floors are best in areas children will be sitting and playing actively. Many facilities have sound control in the ceilings, and a few have installed sound-absorbent units on cement walls to reduce noise.

Although teachers cannot control most of the surfaces built into the facility, they can and should give some thought to noise control. A generally noisy environment from which children cannot get relief is not conducive to overall cognitive development or academic achievement (G. T. Moore, 1987). Teachers have little

control from external noise but may adjust the classroom environment to modify the amount of noise and plan for quiet and active participation of children. With soft, sound-absorbing materials in the classroom, normal noise is diminished. For example, large pillows instead of chairs can be used in the independent reading area placed on a small carpet so that children can read aloud without disturbing others nearby. Draperies, carpet, pillows, stuffed animals, and upholstered furniture are all sound absorbent. Rooms with large expanses of bulletin boards are quieter than those with plain hard wall surfaces.

A second strategy to control sound environmentally is to increase the secluded spaces for one or two children and decrease the number of spaces for six or more children. This can be done by using furniture or mobile screens for barriers between activity areas or decreasing the floor area of some of the centers.

Noisy activities should be arranged in close proximity to each other and away from the quieter activities. For example, block play and pretend play tend to be noisier, naturally. These should be in a different area of the room than the book corner or listening center.

Some children are noisier in highly complex environments. If a particular center seems to be noisy, unproductive, congested, or disruptive, observe carefully what is going on. Sometimes the activity needs to be redesigned or reorganized, separated into two activities, or possibly eliminated. Sometimes simply adjusting the amount of table space or floor space will correct the difficulty.

Mobility

Teachers are responsible for planning programs that encourage the active involvement of children and allow children to move from place to place in an orderly manner during the session. Pathways should be wide enough for children to move from one place to another without bumping into other children or interfering with the work and play of others. Avoid long corridors as they tend to invite running or hurrying. Instead, break up the space by carefully arranging the centers. When children must move around a diagonally placed table or walk around a pair of easels, they slow down. Some teachers use the center of the room as open space, with learning areas arranged on large tables or clusters of small tables placed so that traffic must move around them.

Attractiveness

Teachers are responsible for providing children with a clean and orderly environment. When teachers demonstrate their own respect for cleanliness and attractiveness, children are more likely to imitate this desirable behavior. Organize the classroom so that it is uncluttered, clean, and visually appealing. An orderly environment is more interesting, and children can see the materials that are intended to attract their attention. Adults who sit down on the floor and look around have a keener perspective of the room from the child's point of view. Sometimes a room that appears attractive at an adult level may give a different impression when seen from the child's height.

Teachers are responsible for helping children care for their learning and living environment. As a part of the learning responsibility, children should be encouraged to put materials back where they belong. This is also an opportunity for children to learn classifying, matching, and reading skills if the storage areas are adequately labeled. Keeping working surfaces clean is also a reasonable expectation of children. Before children leave an area that is messy, encourage them to wipe the surfaces and clean up for the next child's use. Pictographs or written instructions for cleaning and storage also contribute to children's emerging literacy skills because the information is practical, useful, and meaningful to them.

Ultimately, adults must arrange the physical environment to contribute to the ongoing instructional program. Materials, bulletin boards, and pictures should be rotated to reflect the theme being taught. Bright touches attract children to centers where the teacher intends them to become engaged. Both elements added to attract children and the substance of the learning centers should be changed regularly and should reflect the changing needs and interests of the children. Overall, simplicity is the key to the entire physical setting. Remove materials that are extraneous. Each object visible in the room should have a purpose and meaning for the children. When you ask yourself, "Is this contributing the goal I had in mind?" or "What am I trying to accomplish with this?" you should have a clear immediate answer. Avoid leaving children's work displayed longer than 1 week; take it down and display other, newer work.

A pleasant learning environment is a comfortable, beautiful place that looks and smells good (Greenman, 1988). The elements of the physical environment fit together in a comprehensible way and are designed to make life a rich experience. Light, color, texture, art from around the world, children's art displays, and living things add to the beauty and the livability of the classroom. A classroom that is more homelike and less institutional helps children feel secure and ready to learn (Silvern, 1988).

Storage

Teachers are responsible for the selection, storage, and display of materials. Objects should be stored near the area of use. Ideally, materials will be in open shelving if children are to have ready access to them and in closed cupboards or on high selves if the teacher needs to maintain control of the materials. For example, pencils, paper, scissors, and paste are frequently used and should be readily accessible each day near the tables at which they are used. On the other hand, fingerpaint or a microscope might be put away and retrieved as needed. Materials that are small and have many pieces such as counters, small plastic building blocks, or fabric scraps should be stored in plastic containers. Usually the cardboard boxes in which the materials are sold do not hold up well in long-term use. Plastic transparent boxes are a good alternative. Teachers should also consider safety in storage, especially when stacking containers or placing heavy items on high shelves.

Breaking with Tradition

Professionals must sometimes question the patterns of the past in order to create effective child-centered classrooms. Most elementary schools have a desk for each child. In a classroom that uses center-based instruction or in-

Children have ready access to materials that are stored near the area where they will use them.

dividualized instruction, the use of individual desks for kindergarten and first grade should be evaluated. If group instruction is provided with children sitting on the floor near the teacher and small-group instruction occurs at tables or clusters of desks, extra desks may be put into storage to prevent overcrowding. For teachers who are wary of this approach, they may want to move the extra furniture into temporary storage in their own building for several weeks before transporting it to permanent storage. A kindergarten teacher commented, "Well, I had to do something. With a large number of children in my group, there wasn't room for all those tables, the equipment and materials needed for instruction, and the children too. So, instead of having two children per table, I kept only enough tables so that four children could work face to face and what I needed to set up the centers. The group functions well, now that the crowding is diminished." In another classroom, the Head Start teacher was confronted with the problem of stored mats at one end of the room that were pulled out everyday after school for gymnastics practice. She improved the classroom environment by hanging these mats on the walls of the classroom, which reduced the noise level and increased the space at the same time. Second graders may have greater needs for the personal space that a desk supplies. A few desks could be left for individual but not exclusive use, along with the group-oriented activity areas just described (Clayton, 1989). Regardless of the age of the children and the nature of the program, professionals would do well to ask themselves if there is an alternative way to use the space and equipment.

Another space saver has really worked well for a group of primary teachers in Traverse City, Michigan. They have substituted a child-height kidney-shaped table, additional shelving, and two filing cabinets for the teacher's desk. The teacher has the necessary storage space for personal things, records, and supplies that are not available to children. The table is large enough for an adult to spread out if needed or to move papers to one end while children may approach and work at the other end. This is where teachers deliver many guided experiences with reading skills and math concepts. Furnishings that can be used in more than one way provide increased flexibility for the teacher.

Few Room Arrangements Are Ideal

Consider the following setups. The preschool classroom (Figure 11.1) is long and rectangular but has a sizable segment of space cut out of the middle that diminishes visual supervision from some segments of the classroom. The kindergarten classroom (Figure 11.2) has the advantage of a large adjacent storage area, but again the classroom has numerous corners. In both instances the teachers have carefully selected the size of the centers located in hard-to-see spots and the nature of the activities going on in them when setting up the classroom. The

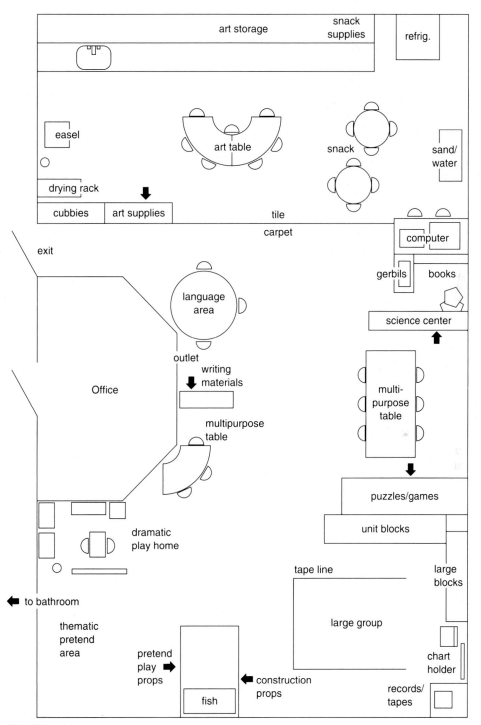

FIGURE 11.1
Preschool Classroom

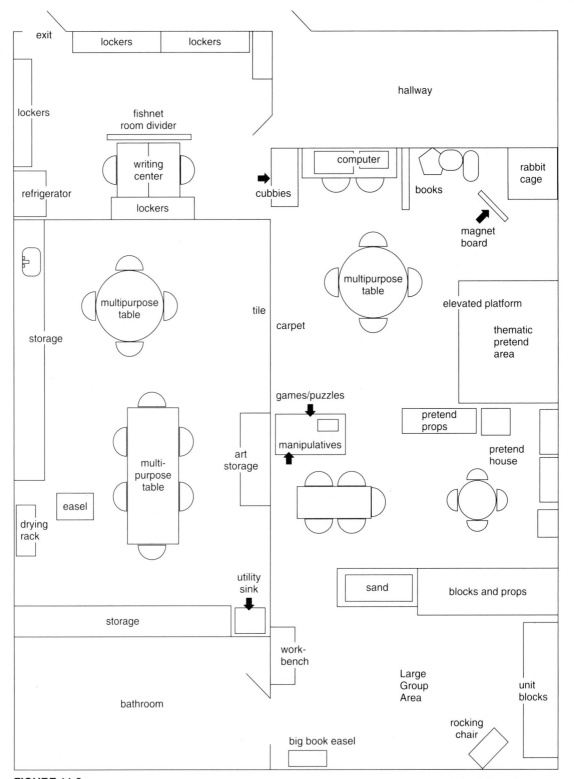

FIGURE 11.2
Kindergarten Classroom

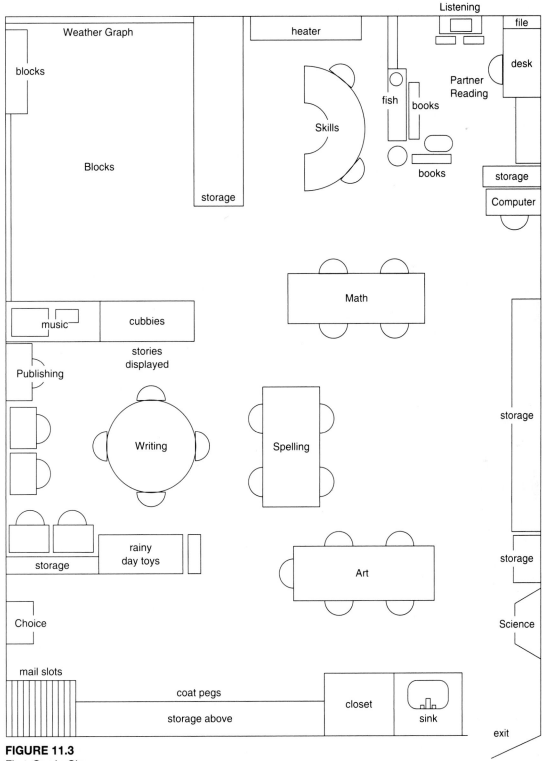

FIGURE 11.3
First-Grade Classroom

first-grade classroom (Figure 11.3) is a more traditional shape and has been arranged to accommodate center-based instruction for most of the day. Whole-group instruction occurs in the block area with the children sitting on the floor. Subject-matter labels are used to denote the activities that are usually located in the various areas of the room, but these are not rigid. For example, social studies activities are often located at the center labeled "Spelling" and many science activities are moved to the art table when more space is needed or when more children are at work in the center.

Outdoor Environments

The principles of using the indoor environment to influence development in desired directions apply to outdoor environments as well. The level of planning for learning outdoors should be similar to the level of planning inside. The outdoor environment is particularly useful in supporting children's scientific investigation of living things and earth science in the immediate vicinity. Social and physical skills may be practiced in a properly supervised environment. In addition, activities often delivered indoors may be moved to outdoor environments when the weather permits.

ADJUSTING THE PHYSICAL ENVIRONMENT

When the physical environment is managed so that children are receiving clear cues as to their expected behavior with materials or in a specific place, the teacher is providing an indirect approach to guidance (Eliason & Jenkins, 1990; Hildebrand, 1990). Children respond in predictable ways to changes in the environment. There are three fundamental ways for adjusting the environment: the teacher adds something to the environment, the teacher removes something from the environment, or the teacher alters something to make it more childproof (safer and easier to use correctly for the age of child).

Adding to the Environment

To improve children's abilities to maintain a clean and orderly classroom, several things might be done. Putting a colored cube in a plastic bag outside the bin where the inch cubes should be stored helps children locate the bin easily. Adding drawings and labels to shelves work well for 5- to 8-year-olds. Adding a cloth covering to the front of the block shelf forms an effective barrier so that children do not manipulate them when that center is not open.

If the teacher wants children to record their findings in an activity in which objects are weighed, then pencils and paper (or graph paper) should be added to the learning center. Adding reference books to various learning centers in the room supports the goals of children understanding their utility. For example, one teacher placed a telephone book in the housekeeping pretend play area and a children's encyclopedia with the section on hamsters marked and displayed near the hamster cage. Children are basically curious and will use these reference materials, given appropriate support and instruction.

Guidance by manipulating the physical environment is the least intrusive and sometimes the most effective approach to an orderly classroom. In one classroom where the teacher was continuously admonishing a group of 6-year-olds to play cooperatively with the blocks, she introduced a sign that said "6 Children." Once children's attention was focused on the sign, they agreed to monitor the overcrowding in the center themselves. In a second-grade classroom where children were having difficulty with story reenactment when the teacher was not in the center, the teacher added a few distinctive props and a name tag for each character. These materials were sufficient to help the children keep track of the story line and the identity of each of the story characters.

Removing Something from the Environment

Occasionally, simply removing chairs from an area is sufficient to let children know that fewer than the usual number of children can work in that center at the same time. In the Head Start classroom, the teacher removed 10 pairs of scissors from the basket because she was unable to assist more than six inexperienced children at the same time. When several youngsters persistently became unruly as they drove their large wheeled trucks through a kindergarten classroom, the teacher simply placed the trucks in storage at the end of the day for the time being. In a suburban school, a first-grade teacher removed toys from home that appeared in the centers because they distracted the children from their work. When materials distract children from engaging in profitable experiences, when they pose hazards, or when teachers need to provide cues for children's appropriate behavior, these materials should be removed or reduced so that appropriate behavior is most likely to occur.

Altering the Environment

Indirect child guidance through managing the physical environment sometimes takes more ingenuity. A first-grade teacher substituted an electric pencil sharpener for the traditional variety so that children would not grind their pencils to nubs and she would not have to remind them repeatedly. A kindergarten teacher provided a simple wooden boot jack so that children would no longer use the edge of their lockers to pull off their boots. A teacher of 4-year-olds used a baby cupboard safety device to ensure that the cabinet where plant fertilizers were kept remained closed. One third-grade teacher obtained one taller table and higher chair for a youngster who was exceptionally tall and appeared to fidget uncomfortably in the furnishings that were suitable for his classmates.

Teachers must also make accommodations for children with special needs. Children in wheelchairs or walkers need wider pathways than children who walk unaided. Some of them may need trays on their chairs to work, while others can work successfully at a table with a cut-out portion. Teachers who have vision-impaired children must examine the environment very carefully so that pathways are kept clear and the arrangements of the room remain stable over time. Children with hearing aids often experience excessive background noise, so teachers may need to adjust the location of centers or the amount of "soft" things in the environment. Children who are emotionally impaired may profit from having a private place where they may go when under stress. Teachers can also assist more able children to become aware

of potential hazards to the less able and make the appropriate accommodations.

Teachers must observe their children carefully in the environments they have created and adjust the physical environment first if children are failing to engage in productive activities as desired. Play and work can be facilitated in this way without complete reliance on admonitions and verbal directions, which if overused can be wearing on children and adults alike.

SELECTING MATERIALS FOR EACH CURRICULAR DOMAIN

Since hands-on learning is a fundamental premise of developmentally appropriate learning, a variety of materials are necessary to provide a balanced program. Many school districts have found that it takes from 3 to 5 years to supply classrooms adequately, since most of them begin to add equipment and materials a little at a time. However, if the resources previously used to purchase workbooks and series textbooks are shifted to materials acquisition, the cost of the programs is eventually less than the cost of more traditional approaches. This is because workbooks are used up every year, but the materials purchased to replace them tend to last 2 to 3 years longer. Eventually, all materials should be added to or replaced as they become lost or broken. In addition, nearly all elementary classrooms have insufficient storage space for these materials, so mobile storage, additional shelving high in the room for long-term storage, and plastic containers, bins, or baskets to contain multipiece manipulatives should be obtained early in the acquisition plan.

Programs for 3- to 5-year-olds often begin with appropriate equipment but must plan for replacement and expansion of choices. Child care centers have the particularly challenging task of providing interesting materials for the morning and different but appropriate materials for the late afternoon so that children's interest is maintained while their learning progresses. Fortunately, many excellent alternatives are available that address similar competencies. For example, the seriation tasks of stacking containers can be met with stacking circular cups, hexagon cups, octagon cups, kitty in the keg, square boxes, and

Russian nesting dolls. For the preschool child, the perceptually new material is treated as a different task, and children approach and use such playthings with interest and enjoyment.

GENERAL GUIDES TO MATERIAL SELECTION AND USE

Provide materials that are developmentally and age appropriate (Bredekamp, 1991). Young children require materials that support hands-on experiences. Indeed, if children are unable to have some form of hands-on experience, then, most likely, the topic is being introduced prematurely. For example, children learn about plants by growing seeds. They learn about culture by sharing family traditions within the class. They learn about geography by finding something in the classroom using a map. They learn about reading and writing by participating in functional written communications. The greater the number of manipulative materials and firsthand experiences with real things, the better. When a book such as this one is directed to programs serving a wide range of ages, 3 to 8 years, the specific selections are important at each age level. For example, simple balance scales are adequate for 4-year-olds to understand heavy and light, but a more accurate scale with weights or a spring scale that is calibrated is more appropriate for 7- or 8-year-olds who must learn to add and subtract accurately using them. Both scales provide direct experience with the concepts of mass, volume, and weight.

Individual children vary greatly in their abilities to handle abstract concepts. All programs should have opportunities for them to begin instruction using concrete materials first and later reconstruct their experiences using increasingly abstract materials. Children gain exposure to more abstract experiences as they mature and are more capable of understanding symbolic representations. Many children learn to comply with requests by adults to use more abstract materials prematurely. They go through the activity but do not emerge with increased understanding or comprehension. Children construct their own concepts as a result of guided use of real things. Generally, selecting materials or designing activities that are either too easy or too difficult results in wasted time and misused materials. In either case, children are not profitably involved in learning. The presentation in Table 11.1 illustrates concrete materials, bridging materials, and more abstract materials. Three- to 5-year-olds need the predominance of the concrete materials, whereas 7- and 8-year-olds may use a mixture of concrete and a few more abstract materials as a basis for learning. All children throughout schooling profit from hands-on learning regardless of age.

Provide materials that are complete, safe, and usable. Puzzles with missing pieces, dull scissors, unstable climbing equipment, and any

TABLE 11.1
Examples of Materials Varying from Concrete to Abstract

Concrete	Increasingly Abstract	Abstract
Bulb planted in soil for observation	Photographs of bulb growth	Discussion or graph of plant growth
Parquetry blocks and corresponding colored pattern cards outlining each shape	Parquetry blocks and black-and-white pattern cards outlining each shape	Parquetry blocks and pattern cards outlining a general shape rather than individual shapes
Unit blocks	Graph paper	Numerals
Field trip	Film or pictures	Letters or words
Cooking activity	Pretend play kitchen	Picture book recipe

broken tools or equipment should be repaired or replaced. Materials that do not work do not contribute to the learning experience but rather tend to engender frustration and distress. This is as true of teacher-made materials as for old purchased materials. For instance, if a set of materials is constructed by the teacher, the items should be sturdy and usable so that many children can interact with them. This may mean laminating hardboard items rather than making them from construction paper or thin cardboard.

Demonstrate the proper use of materials and equipment. Teachers sometimes assume that children "ought to know" how to use materials properly. Some children come from home environments where play equipment is nonexistent and material possessions are scarce. Other children may have an ample supply of some equipment but may encounter new things in the school. A simple direct demonstration of materials and equipment at the time of use increases the probability of safety as well as conserving the materials. For example, the 5-year-old who may know how to use cellophane tape may have no idea as to the use and function of paste and may have never seen glue. Rarely do young children know how to conserve these products appropriately.

Purchase sturdy, high-quality equipment. A set of hardwood blocks is expensive as an initial purchase, but since they are almost indestructible, they can be in use for 40 years or more. Housekeeping furnishings made of hardwood and carefully crafted last over a decade, in contrast to products designed for home use, which last 3 or 4 years. High-quality materials are also necessary for effective instruction. For example, a toy xylophone in comparison to a quality instrument is lacking in tone and often off pitch. Administrators and teachers who make long-range plans and purchase high-quality equipment find that durability offsets the initial cost.

Demonstrate the proper care and storage of materials, and supervise children as they take on organizational tasks. Show them how to handle the materials correctly. Label shelves or containers with words, symbols, or pictures depending on the age of the children. Storage, of course, should be near the place of use and accessible for children.

Give reasons for the standards you set for children's use of materials. In one first-grade classroom, the teacher indicated, "If I see someone being careless with materials once, I demonstrate again and remind them what they are supposed to be doing. I explain that everyone wants a turn to use the materials, and if they are destroyed, no one else can use them. The children in my group know that continued misuse of materials leads to the lost privilege of using them" (Whiren, 1990). Giving children reasons for the standards helps them understand the principles involved.

In the following section, specific materials are suggested for each of the eight learning domains. These suggestions are not intended to be exhaustive, but only illustrative. In addition, materials suitable for the entire range of early childhood have been included so that items must be assessed for safety and value for any particular group. In each category, numerous kits, equipment, and materials are available from commercial suppliers. Only generic items are listed here. An excellent resource for a listing of suppliers with suggestions for materials and equipment is *Selecting Educational Equipment for School and Home* (Moyer, 1986).

Aesthetic Domain

Equipment: Record player, tape recorder-player (a separate children's tape player may be desirable for 3- to five-year-olds), easel, woodworking bench or table with vice, table and chairs, open storage for art materials and supplies, camera, camcorder, sewing machine

Paper of Various Textures: Construction paper, tissue, glossy fingerpaint paper, newsprint, cardboard, wallpaper, cellophane, standard reprocessed paper, sandpaper of different grains, waxed, contact paper, plates, small bags, tag board, plastic wrap, paper plates, Kleenex, papier-mâché strips, paper cups

Paints: Watercolors, tempera, crayons, fingerpaint, ink, laundry starch to extend and thicken tempera, stamp pad and ink, food coloring

Applicators: Flat and round brushes, tiny watercolor brushes, sponges, string, Q-tips, feathers, pipe cleaners, adult-type brushes, paste brushes, stamps with various designs, empty deodorant roll-on bottles, cotton balls

Drawing Instruments: Pencils, colored pencils, colored chalk, crayons, felt-tip pens, markers

Tools: Scissors, knives, flatware, kitchen tools, crewel needles, embroidery hoops, weaving frames, drinking straws, pails, water containers of various sizes, lidded paint containers, muffin tin, source for heating, hole punch, grater, stapler, clay-working tools, toothbrushes, screening, rulers, pinking shears, rollers, cookie cutters, pie plates, cake tins

Sculpting Materials: Boxes, newspaper, papier-mâché strips, wire, wood pieces, potters' clay and storage container, Play-doh®, flour, alum, salt, cornstarch

Found Objects: Fabric scraps, netting, wood scraps, spools, paper tubes, small boxes, flat-surfaced stones, Popsicle sticks, meat trays, egg or milk cartons, baby food jars, plastic bottles, styrofoam pieces, feathers, eggshells, bottle caps

Adhesives: School paste, white glue, rubber cement, cellophane tape, masking tape, wallpaper paste, flour/water, egg white, gummed shapes or stickers

Cloth: Fabric scraps, net for embroidery, thread, yarn, felt, Pellon or other bonded inner lining (for story boards), lace, ribbon, rickrack

Prints: Paintings and reproductions of sculpture from around the world, well-illustrated children's books, photographs of nature, artwork, musical instruments

Recordings: Music of all types, children's songs from around the world, excerpts from classical music for movement experiences, poetry

Instruments: Quality hand drum for the teacher; rhythm instruments such as triangles, rhythm sticks, wood blocks, temple blocks, tambourines, cymbals, small and large drums, maracas, cleaves; piano, Autoharp, guitar, or ukulele; melody bells, step bells, resonator bells, or tuning forks so that singing can start on

pitch; real musical instruments borrowed or demonstrated as a part of the learning program

Literacy Support Materials: Easel or experience story stand and paper, heavy marker, music staff paper, children's books about art and artists and those involving music such as *Hush, Little Baby* (Zemach, 1976) or *The Fox Went Out on a Chilly Night* (Spier, 1961), paper and pencils

Teacher Resources: Several songbooks for children including culturally diverse selections, one or more music series books, books on making instruments, musical games and movement activity books, books and recordings about instruments

Affective Domain

Equipment: Low room dividers (some with corkboard, some with holes and hooks), large pillows, child-sized easy chair, area rugs, cleaning equipment (child-sized broom, dustpan, carpet sweeper), lamp for private space, child-sized rocker, easy-access shelving and storage units

Cleaning Supplies: Dustcloths, sponges, pail, mop, spray bottles, pans, cleaning compounds (only for oldest children)

Children's Literature: Illustrated and nonillustrated books focusing on the emotional challenges of childhood such as new siblings, handling anger, accepting people who look or function differently, death, divorce, remarriage

Photographs: Depicting various emotions; people at work; ordinary people doing everyday tasks; people of various ages, races, ethnic origins as they are functioning in the United States today; cultural events or celebrations of historical or traditional nature

Literacy Materials: Empty books for personal messages, personal telephone directories, personal calendars or schedules, tapes and tape recorders, drawing materials, paper, pencils

Cognitive Domain

Measuring Tools: Ruler, tape measure, scales and weights, measuring cups and spoons, large liquid measuring units, calipers, thermometer, clock, stopwatch, calendar, hourglass or egg timer, Cuisinaire rods

Equipment: Sand table, water table, computer and software, calculators, oven or hot plate, rock tumbler, aquarium and related equipment

Tools: Eye droppers, mortar and pestle, siphons, prisms, flashlight, compass, garden tools, screw, lamp, birdhouse, hoses, tongs, tweezers, locks and keys, stethoscope, weather vane

Simple Machines: Screws, screwdriver, wheels, knives, pulleys, hammer, dowels, wheelbarrow, simple motors, battery with electric circuit setup, saw, windmill, waterwheel

Counters: Multiple small objects that may be counted or grouped and that vary in size, shape, color, and type; abacus; Cuisinaire rods; poker chips; Unifix cubes

Signs and Symbols: Numerals in sandpaper and written on other surfaces, traffic signals and signs, safety signs, labels as appropriate, math signs, pictographs of events or observations

Children's Literature: Information books that support units, dictionary, encyclopedia, Time-Life-type books

Literacy Materials: 1- and ½-inch graph paper, notebooks, recipes, frame and large paper for recording events, drawing materials, clipboard

Games: Board games, picture card games, standard playing cards, dominoes, picture dominoes, lotto games, checkers, Chinese checkers, bingo type games, pattern cards, colored inch cubes

Problem Solving: Objects of various attributes that sink and float; magnets and objects that are or are not attracted to magnets; sorting boxes and materials that vary systematically by size, shape, texture, color, or function; pegboards and pegs; peg pattern card; magnets and prisms; color chips from paint stores; nuts and bolts; puzzles; sieves; funnels; containers of irregular size and shape; Montessori graduated cylinders; attribute blocks; nesting dolls or barrels

Living Things: Dish garden, plants, watering cans and fertilizer, plant containers, seeds of various sorts, potting soil, an animal (iguana, hamster, fish, snake, rabbit, turtle), appropriate cage(s) and food, litter and cleaning supplies, ant farm, worm farm

Transportation Toys: Cars, trucks, boats, airplanes, trains and tracks, farm equipment, construction equipment

Materials from the Natural Environment: Leaves, stones, sticks or bark, grasses, grains, flowers, root systems, foods in the unprocessed state, insects

Models: Globe, maps, skeleton(s), plastic farm or wild animals, dinosaurs, insects, snakes, flowers, airplanes (realistic toys)

Pictures: Photographs or drawings of objects or events that represent the physical or social environment related to units taught, films, filmstrips, videotapes

Blocks: Unit blocks, bristle blocks, inch cubes, snap blocks, various other blocks needed for math and science instruction

Teacher Resources: Manuals for the use of science equipment; reference books on science, social studies, and other topics; reference books on math learning and teaching based on materials

Language Domain

Equipment: Listening center with headphones, tape recorder-player, audiofilmstrip projector, videocassette recorder and television, laminator, duplicator, computer and software, flannel board and easel, chalkboard, bulletin boards, book display shelving, storage units for equipment, big-book easel, chart holder, adult-sized chair, phones

Paper: Lined and unlined, bound in empty books, small pads around the room, notebooks, tagboard strips, file cards, tagboard for charts, laminating material, paper and holder for experience stories, chart paper, receipt or order pads, computer paper, newsprint, Post-it notes, all kinds of recording materials, tracing paper, flip chart

Writing Implements: Thick and standard pencils, felt-tip pens, drawing or painting tools

Office Supplies: Stapler and staples, paper clips, gum erasers, adult- and child-sized scissors, tape dispenser, tape, stamps, envelopes

Charts and Pictures: Maps, graphs, charts illustrating instructional content and labeled, photographs, prints of paintings, charts displaying alphabet at child's eyeview (wherever they are needed or children are writing), word charts or classroom dictionaries related to topics of instruction, labels, written directions

Children's Books: Picture books, illustrated and standard dictionaries, illustrated encyclopedias, other reference books, information books, pattern books, poetry, songbooks, cookbooks, joke books, telephone books, books illustrating the cultural diversity of the United States, books illustrating other cultures, easy-to-read books and chapter books, big books, individual books, children's magazines

Audiovisual Materials: Commercially prepared tapes of children's books, films or videotapes of children's literature, filmstrips and tapes of content and literature, teacher-made audiotapes of classroom books, flannel board stories

Literacy Support Materials: Word-based games, story sequence puzzles and games, selected software, finger puppets, child-sized puppets, large puppet flannel board, flannel letters and numerals, letter templates

Textbooks: Selections to support content instruction, optional reading texts, children's magazines and newspapers, array of children's reference materials

Teacher Reference Books: Reference books on the instruction and evaluation of the developmentally appropriate approach, reference books on content, poetry collections, read-aloud books, story collections

Physical Domain

Balls: Sports, large rubber, Nerf, small soft, marbles, beanbags, yarn

Tools: Bats, mallets, ping-pong paddles, Nerf paddles, bowling pins, nets, baseball gloves, hoops, badminton set

Climbing and Balance: Balance beam, parallel bars, jungle gym, hung ropes, net climber, slide, planks and triangles, ladders, jump ropes

Wheeled Toys: Trikes, pedal wheel toys and wagons, roller/ice skates, skateboards, scooters

Containers: Basketball hoop, laundry basket, hoola hoop, pails of various sizes

Manipulatives: Poultry baster, tongs of various types, tweezers, plastic or metal plumbing joints, beads, strings, plastic tubing, lacing boards, lacing shoe, button and zipper frame, computer mouse, Marble Run or Plex-a Plax (or other more complicated "fit-together" materials with various commercial names), buttons with needles and thread

Models, Pictures, and Charts: Models of internal body; pictures of good health and safety practices; charts enumerating safety with bikes, fire, automobiles; pictures of foods, charts of the food groups, fire and tornado drill signs, models of teeth

Food: Samples of foods from the basic food groups for children to learn to taste wide ranges of foods, foods prepared from various cultural groups, plastic models of foods

Health-related Supplies: Human thermometer, toothbrushes, toothpaste, paper cups, antiseptic soap, first aid kit, room thermometer, facial tissue, cleaning supplies

Music and Tapes: Aerobic dance audiotapes for children, music excerpts for free dance, musical game books and recordings, large drum, fitness videotapes for children

Literacy Support Materials: Sample menus from various cultures, children's recipes for healthy snacks, children's cookbooks, standard cookbooks, forms for recording foods eaten, chart paper for safety guides at school, sports magazines depicting men and women, sports biographies and autobiographies, pencils, score pads, materials to make signs

Teacher Resources: Game collections including those requiring cooperation, games from various cultures and ethnic groups, charts of the fundamental motor skills depicting increasing levels of maturity

Social Domain

Materials Requiring Cooperation: Long jump rope, games requiring two or more players, pretend telephones, hose- or string-and-can phones, miniature transportation toys and signs

Play Props Supporting Social Study Themes: Small family dolls, community helper dolls, sets of small stores and houses on a street system, dollhouse with furnishings

Pictures: Photos and paintings of various social studies themes such as sharing, helping, families, neighborhoods, clothing, occupations, historical events, heros and heroines, stores of various kinds, workers of diverse ethnic groups

Literacy Support Materials: Books selected to support social studies content, children's literature about common social experiences, camera and film for recording local community and school events, children's literature about family life in the United States and abroad and about families across the life cycle, paper supplies suitable for invitations and thank-you notes, pencils

Teacher Resources: Reference books on social development and guidance

Pretend Play Domain

Furniture: Doll bed, refrigerator, stove, sink, washer, drawers, small coatrack, small table and chairs, rocking chair, child-sized sofa if room exists, cabinets, mirror, clock radio, toaster, rug

Clothing: Dress-up clothes, hats for family, hats for community workers, aprons, laundry basket, clothesline, bedding for dolls, scarves, ribbons, shoes, vests, work boots, cloth strips for multiple purposes, curtains threaded with elastic or cloth tape

Dolls: Several dolls of various sizes and races, doll clothes, washable stuffed animals, bottles, cradle, high chair, baby toys

Tools: Dishes, flatware, pots and pans, telephones, clothes baskets, ironing board and iron, cleaning equipment, suitcases, dishwashing supplies and equipment

Large Toys: Child-sized traffic signs; riding wheeled trucks; steering wheel mounted on a board, box, or tree stump

Story Reenactment: Picture books and tapes, character labels, props essential to the story, simple costume props (such as three sizes of horns made of tag board for *The Three Billy Goats Gruff*)

Literacy Support Materials: Paper, pencil, phone book, wrapping paper, old greeting cards, newspapers, various print ads, magazines

Other Materials: Props appropriate to specific themes such as camping, space flight

Construction Domain

Equipment: Wheeled storage for large blocks, large storage shelves for unit blocks, rug or carpet, crates, planks

Blocks: Lots of unit blocks, large hollow blocks, foam and plastic blocks, card board or milk carton, unit cubes, small table blocks, Legos

Support Supplies: Carpet squares, tiles, and cloth pieces for rivers and roads, pulleys

Pictures Depicting: Other block structures, objects and events related to themes

Construction Sets: Erector, Lincoln Logs, various commercial sets

Art Supplies: See the list under "Aesthetic Domain."

Raw Materials: Water, sand, clay, and dough (flour, salt, alum)

Woodworking: Workbench and vice, saw, hammer, nails, screws, sandpaper, bit and brace, screwdriver, level, carpenter's square, other woodworking equipment

Literacy Support Materials: Paper and pens for writing directions, sample directions for constructing something, pictographs for construction by children and teachers, music score paper, tapes and tape recorders, tape, materials to make signs

Using the Same Materials for Many Purposes

Some materials (blocks, sand, water, clay) are extremely flexible in their use. The same items may be used to meet goals across the curriculum. In the developmentally appropriate classroom, children are often free to use such

materials to meet their own needs, which may be related to any domain. On other occasions, the teacher guides children's material use to address particular curricular goals. For example, collage materials, which have traditionally been associated with aesthetics, can be adapted for use in other domains as well because the material is content-free. This is illustrated in the sample activities cited in Figure 11.4.

Each of the activities in Figure 11.4 is designed for center use in which children may choose to engage in the activity and for how

---

Affective

Activity: 1-2-3-4-5 Collage
Purpose: For children to work through a task from beginning to completion
Procedure: Select several items for a collage. Make your collage, show it to a friend, and talk about it. Put your extra materials away, and announce "the end."

Aesthetic

Activity: Color Collage
Purpose: For children to contribute to the aesthetic environment of the school
Procedure: Make a collage in colors that you like best. When you are finished, hang up your work for everyone to see and enjoy.

Physical

Activity: Snip or Tear Collage
Purpose: For children to practice fine motor skills
Procedure: Choose some large paper. Either cut or tear it into little pieces to make your collage.

Language

Activity: Texture Collage
Purpose: For children to increase their descriptive vocabulary
Procedure: Choose some materials from the box that feel different. Create a collage of many varied textures. Tell someone else as many words as you can think of to describe the textures.

Social

Activity: Buddy-up Collage
Purpose: For children to practice negotiation skills
Procedure: Each of you will receive a bag containing different collage materials. If you need or want something from someone else's bag, find a way to ask, trade, or share to get what you want.

Cognitive

Activity: Number Collage
Purpose: For children to practice number skills
Procedure: There are four pans of materials for you to choose from. Select four items from each pan and glue them onto your paper. You will then have four sets of four.

FIGURE 11.4
Collage Materials in Several Domains

long. Naturally, when the collage materials are being used for one domain, other activities with other materials are planned for the remaining ones. Notice that the difference in domains is apparent in the strategies and guidance provided by the teacher. This demonstrates the potential for adults to consider materials flexibly and broadly.

DEVELOPING AN ACQUISITION PLAN

Teachers rarely have the level of equipment and supplies that they desire or that fully facilitates the curriculum. The following guidelines are proposed as processes that will lead a very poorly equipped school into a more effective operation.

1. Take stock of all materials, books, and equipment available at the classroom and school levels. For example, if the classroom has very few picture books but the school library has many, evaluate the scope of the library holdings. Some picture books used in the first grade during the fall might be desirable for some children in the kindergarten in the spring. Many materials selected to support curriculum in the past are still of great importance in fundamental learning using a hands-on approach. Examples would be decks of cards, checkers, and board games. Include them in the inventory if they are in usable condition.

2. Determine whether some equipment is available for each of the eight domains. A developmentally appropriate curriculum is balanced. If a developmental domain has little or no materials to support it, then this area should receive priority attention. Using the materials, supplies, and equipment lists, select materials from different categories for each of the domains. For example, if you have no pretend play equipment, you might choose a small table and chairs, a rocking chair, two dolls, doll clothes, and props for story reenactment for two different stories. The following year, additional equipment to complete a house, some small toy cars or other vehicles, and additional props for stories might be added.

3. Evaluate the capacity to store materials and equipment. Some districts have built above-the-chalkboard storage; others have purchased mobile shelving. Sturdy containers to store small manipulatives should be purchased at the same time as the manipulatives so that materials can be conserved. Adjustable metal shelving of varying widths is durable and worth the expense.

4. Assess the cost of commercial and homemade supplies. For example, modeling dough can be made from flour, water, salt, alum, and starch very inexpensively in comparison to purchasing ready-made dough. However, the supplies should be purchased by the school, not the individual teacher, if this option is chosen. Frequently, when commercially produced products are compared with teacher-made learning aides, the homemade product is more expensive when the cost of construction is estimated. The general rule is to make only those learning aides for which there is no commercial option that is as well designed as teachers can do themselves.

5. Plan on what equipment might be shared and what should be purchased for each room. For example, two or three accurate scales might be adequate for several classrooms, but each teacher might require his or her own set of magnets or sifters. Some teachers have found that if each of two adults chooses a set of construction materials such as Legos, there is not enough to operate a center, but if the two sets are combined and shared between two classrooms, the center functions smoothly as children are not in competition for the materials. This works satisfactorily while the classrooms are becoming better equipped. For long-term, shared-use plans, a locked classroom-size room with floor-to-ceiling shelving is needed to store materials. Teachers then must agree on a plan to check out materials and rules for the maintenance of storage area.

6. Identify equipment and supplies that will support more than one developmental domain. For example, unit blocks, sand and water tables, and various collage materials can be used in all of the domains, depending on the activity design and the direction given to children. The best choices are those materials that are multipurpose.

7. Initiate the practice of identifying domains and relevant intermediate objectives that will be addressed by certain materials during the selection process. Allow enough time for careful consideration. This will take longer the

first time than later. In the long run, the utility of each item in the inventory is likely to be greater.

8. Consider acquiring materials by concentrating on one curricular domain at a time over a 5-year period. This approach provides depth to your acquisition plan. For example, some schools have chosen to focus on the language domain first and purchase puppets, listening posts, taped stories, tape recorders, empty tapes, big and individual books, a large array of children's literature, and assorted writing supplies all in one year. During the second year, they add to the variety in the language area and select equipment and supplies in the cognitive area, focusing on science and mathematics concepts. In the third year they add to the first two domains, select program materials to enhance health concepts, and purchase basic equipment for construction and pretend play. In the fourth year, additional attention is given to supplies for math and science, and substantial investment is made in social studies equipment, including children's literature, floor maps and appropriate toys to construct a village, transportation toys, a dollhouse, and doll furnishings. In the fifth year, additions are made to the playground, the classroom supplies for motor development are supplemented, and major investment is given for classroom-based music and art equipment and supplies. At the same time, new selections in all other areas, particularly in manipulative toys that support cognitive skills, are selected. In the sixth year, major equipment that has been shared is duplicated as needed, and replacements are selected for worn or damaged language supplies.

9. Once the basics are provided for each of the eight domains, selections should be made for each domain annually. A variety of materials in the domain allows for a "new" activity that provides practice of skills presented earlier. Replacements must be planned as objects are broken or wear out.

10. Remember that a developmentally appropriate curriculum does not cost either more or less over the long run than other alternatives. Resources should be allocated for young children's programs based on the regular average rate of allocations to other grade levels in the school budget. A major pitfall some school districts experience is to "save" dollars from reduced spending on workbooks, then reallocating the funds outside of the early childhood program after the first year or so.

ORGANIZING THE SCHEDULE OF THE DAY

The ultimate goal in preparing a schedule for the day is to provide a social context in which children feel comfortable and secure. Such a schedule would allow time for children to begin a task, engage in it, and complete it without hurry or interruption. Routines represented by the schedule are predictable so that children feel continuity from one day to the next, from one week to the next. In developing the fundamental plan or routines of the day, teachers must consider the pace at which children work, the variety that children need in mode of instruction and in the groupings of children that work together, and the overall balance of the program.

Pace

The pace or speed of activities within the day is something often determined by the overall schedule of events. Teachers must decide who is to set the pace. When adults set the pace, children change activities when told to do so. Some children may be finished well ahead of schedule, and others may be just beginning an activity. Adults generally set the times in the schedule when children must be in a specific place at a specific time. Therefore, times for recess, lunch, special teachers, and special events must be established by adults.

There are other times when it is appropriate for children to set their own pace. For example, when some tasks are required and others are optional within a long time segment, children may set their own speed of moving through the planned experiences. One child may complete only the assigned tasks, another child may complete one or two additional activities without feeling any pressure or hurry, and a third child may not be able to complete the assigned tasks on a specific day and may need more than one day to accomplish the educational goals successfully. Children vary considerably in the pace of learning, task completion, their needs for repetition, and the attention and intensity they bring to each learning experience. Such individual differences in style or pace can best be managed by encouraging self-regulation. Teachers, of course, have the responsibility to guide and encourage children who appear to be disengaged, distracted, or otherwise uninvolved in the program.

Usually 3- to 5-year-olds thrive in an open setting where most of their program day has child-paced activities. Many youngsters of this age are just beginning to attain the self-control necessary to pursue a task in depth. Older children respond well to a balanced program of child- and adult-directed activities.

Variety

Provide learning experiences in a variety of group compositions. The size of the group of children engaging in a learning experience impacts the nature of children's and adult's interpersonal interaction as well as the methods of instruction that can be used. *Whole-group* instruction is planned and directed by the teacher toward all children. Listening to music, reading aloud to children, and making plans for the day are generally done with the whole class. The *small-group* period is often a time when children are working toward very specific skills. Usually the groups are pulled together based either on the observed needs of the children or a balance between more and less skillful children. Teachers may have each group rotate the tasks daily or work on the same skill using different materials during the week. Once the children have been shown how to do the task and all groups are started, then the teacher may focus on one or more groups for more intensive instruction. The teacher must monitor the ongoing work of all the groups when this strategy is being used. During *free-choice* time both the task and the group of children are selected by the child. *Individual* activities may be initiated by either child or the adult but are carried out by one child working alone. Developmentally appropriate classrooms have daily opportunities for children to work alone, with small groups, and with the whole group.

Variety may also be achieved by changing the purpose, size, composition, and duration of the group. The purpose that a group of children may have for working in a small group may vary, with some groups working together to clean an area of the room, another group working on a common mural, and a third group meeting with the teacher for reading instruction. Children work in pairs, groups of three or four, or casual groupings at centers where the group size varies as children move in and out of the specific center.

The actual composition of groups may be determined by the teacher, common interests of the children, friendships, or chance. Knowing that some children share a common interest, such as baseball, may provide the perfect vehicle for learning about players, reading scores, or figuring averages. Other small groups may be based on a common skill they have or need to practice. Of course, teachers are very familiar with friendship groups as they form and reform throughout the year. Chance groupings are usually the outgrowth of other factors such as the speed with which children finish a task. Another format is small coaching groups of children in which their abilities are deliberately mixed so that the more capable may assist their peers in learning. Each type has specific strengths that make it contribute to the total program. For example, friendship groupings take advantage of the children's knowledge of each other. Little time is lost in negotiating for leadership or learning to share ideas. Usually friendship groups already have mechanisms for establishing leadership. In addition, children are more likely to continue the learning activity beyond the classroom. The formation and utilization of all these groups vary throughout the year as the needs of the class change.

Variety of activities and materials used within the program is also important in maintaining interest and enthusiasm in the program. For example, in child care settings, table toys used during the morning may be put away during nap time, and toys designed to meet similar needs put out for children to use after naps are more likely to be used than if the same materials were in place all day.

Balance

A balance between self-selected activities and small-group, teacher-led activities must also be maintained (Hendricks, 1986). Children have opportunities to make decisions and develop their unique interests and competencies when they are allowed choices within the curriculum. If all of the alternatives are well-planned, wholesome choices consistent with the overall curricular goals, teachers can feel confident that children are learning from materials and each other when the teacher is otherwise engaged.

The schedule also must take into account the balance between physically active and passive tasks. Usually children function best when vigorous and quiet activities are alternated. For example, outdoor play or gym should follow or precede periods of whole-group instruction. Most young children cannot be physically passive in prolonged time periods. Movement that is embedded within a longer time period, such as moving to another center, or substantial handling of materials allows for moderate physical involvement.

Children also need balance in the amount of time indoors and outdoors. Frequently recess is not seen as an integral part of the educational program, but children are learning all the time, not just when they are indoors. Therefore, some consideration should be made as to the opportunities for learning desired habits and skills outdoors. For example, teachers may take children outside as a component of instruction related to the natural environment. In addition, outdoor play equipment and space should be evaluated for its safety and educational value. If teacher aides or parent volunteers supervise children during periods outdoors, they must become involved in the strategies being used in other parts of the program to promote the children's development.

In a recent workshop, a group of kindergarten, first-, and second-grade teachers representing a variety of communities identified the following guidelines for achieving a balanced schedule (Kostelnik, 1990). A balance of short and long time segments, active and quiet periods, and self- and teacher-directed activities are needed. Within time periods, children should have opportunities to explore, acquire skills and information, and practice emerging competencies. Variety in the focus of activity is important as well. Children need chances to focus on materials, interact with their peers, and engage in teacher-child interactions. The balance of these many dimensions varies across grade levels as well as throughout the school year.

Coordination of Efforts

Many school districts have programs in which children leave the classroom for special instruction. This special instruction may be for the whole group, such as for art, music, and physical education. On the other hand, specific children may be removed from the ongoing class for specialized instruction, such as for gifted students or children with disabilities, computer instruction, or special reading activities. Comprehensive planning among classroom teachers, specialty teachers, and administrators is required if the schedule is to remain coherent. In some primary grades, the general teacher may have the whole group present for a complete half day only one or two half days per week. In addition, the time the children are gone and the number of children gone is not consistent across the week. Not surprisingly, teachers and children see this as constant interruption. Such fragmented schedules should be carefully evaluated and redesigned. Consideration should be given to specialty teachers moving into the group rather than children moving out of it. Such approaches are more common in programs for 3- to 5-year-olds.

Interesting alternatives are being explored. For example, in one school district, where the criteria for "special reading instruction" eliminated some children who really needed the support, the district defined one teaching position as half-time regular teacher and half-time specialty teacher. The teacher in this position moved from classroom to classroom, monitoring her own training center within free-choice time. Each classroom teacher, then, planned to have his or her free-choice period correspond to the time this visiting specialist was available.

Another approach is based on cooperation and communication between the specialty teachers and the general classroom teacher. The music teacher would select some pieces that related to themes of instruction as well as to the music concepts being taught. The classroom teacher used the same pieces when children sang together in the classroom. Although the overlap was not large, the program was more cohesive than the previous pattern of each teacher doing his or her own, separate curriculum.

Adapting the Schedule

Schedules will vary depending upon the specific characteristics of the individuals within the group. Some children have less self-control and fewer skills in regulating their own behavior than others. Groups of children are thus likely to vary considerably in their ability to engage in a responsive learning environment. Therefore, even within schools, schedules are likely to vary from room to room. Also, the time allotments within the daily schedule will change over the course of the year. The amount of time outdoors is related to climate and weather. Variations are appropriate by season and from one climate to another. Schedules also change as children mature. As children grow in their capacity to do independent work, and as the level of their involvement in learning center activities increases, greater amounts of time should be devoted to those tasks that require these capacities.

Integration

In a developmentally appropriate classroom the teacher attempts to integrate topics in science, health, social studies, and other important segments of information by providing reading experiences from information books, setting up centers with related activities, and developing full units of study that incorporate all of the developmental domains on specific topics such as trees, families, or dental health. Therefore, separate segments of time with those labels generally do not appear in the daily schedule.

Incorporating Whole-Group Instruction

To demonstrate how one aspect of a routine may be more fully developed, whole-group instruction is described next in greater detail, with particular emphasis on its organization.

All whole-group instruction activities have three parts: (a) the *beginning* when children are gathering and starting to pay attention, (b) the *body* when the teacher and children are engaged in a learning endeavor, and (c) the *closing* when the teacher summarizes what is to be done and guides children into the next segment of the schedule.

Planning is the key to success. Schedule whole-group instruction to eliminate distractions. It usually works best between activities that are more active or based on individual action. Select high-interest, appropriate activities. All children in the group should be able to participate in the learning. If the activity is appropriate only for part of the group, do it during small-group activities. Plan carefully how you will begin and end whole-group instruction so that the pace varies and related activities are presented. Anticipate problems and think through alternatives in advance (McAfee, 1985).

Begin the group as soon as two children are ready. Finger plays, songs, riddles, and humorous poetry bring children into the group. Once children are gathered, tell them what the activity is about. Share the planned purpose of the activity. Invite their participation by asking open-ended questions or posing a problem.

During the body of the presentation, monitor the group and alter the pace of presentation accordingly. Maintain eye contact with the children. Vary the pitch, speed of speech, or voice volume to maintain interest. Let children know what is expected, and acknowledge appropriate behavior. Give clear, specific directions to children. Keeping the group moving is important so avoid interruptions and delays. Use a variety of strategies to focus children's attention such as the use of props, demonstrations, pictures, humor, mime, and so on.

At the close of the group, summarize the key idea that was the purpose of the instruction and direct individual children into other learning activities. Never simply send children away from a group; instead, direct them toward a different activity.

For example, in a whole-group planning activity, the teacher would begin by conversing with one or two children while the others are entering. This might be followed by a favorite greeting such as "Hello, everybody, how are you?" Once the alternatives for free choice are described and appropriate demonstrations of materials conducted, the teacher would briefly list the alternatives and then ask each child to state what activity he or she prefers to start with and then dismiss them to begin.

Finally, as with all instruction, evaluate what happened and use what you know about yourself and your children to plan more effectively the next time.

How to Prepare a Schedule

1. Prepare a form that designates space in 15-minute intervals beginning a half hour before the start of the session and ending a half hour after the session and divided by the days of the week.

2. Block in time segments that are established for your group at the school level, including such things as outdoor play time, lunch, specialty teachers, and pullout schedules for specific individuals.

3. Place whole-group instruction in time segments so that this approach may be used for group planning, giving directions on the use of centers, or shared experiences with music, literature, and games. Be sure to indicate if the specialty teachers are providing instruction to the whole group or if they also structure for small groups. A short whole-group activity before center time is very useful to help children focus on alternatives and remind them of their learning goals and responsibilities.

Whole-group activities should not exceed 15 minutes of sedentary time or 20 minutes of active time for 3-year-olds. Whole-group, teacher-directed instruction for 7-year-olds should not exceed 20 to 30 minutes. When an activity alternates between hands-on activity and teacher direction, it may be longer and still successful. Fifteen-minute intervals are very successful for giving directions for centers.

4. Schedule center time so that children have a minimum of 1 hour of uninterrupted time. Three- and 4-year-olds may need less time at the beginning of the year, and 8-year-olds may be profitably engaged for 2 hours or more. Some teachers have independent work by pairs of children at one time of the day and more openly flowing small groups in centers at another time. The opportunity for self-pacing work is important here.

5. Indicate where teacher-directed, small-group instruction will occur. If this is embedded into the center time, carefully consider how to bring children into the small group and supervise the centers. Several sets of small groups working cooperatively on projects may also be planned. Teacher-directed small groups are usually 10 to 15 minutes for the youngest children and 15 to 20 minutes for older children.

6. Minimize transitions of the whole group. Plan curriculum changes to occur either midway between school-set times or at these times. On all occasions children must know which activity occurs next and know where to go and what to do. Schedules should be discussed with the children and clear communication signals given. Signal 5 minutes before center or independent work is to be set aside so that children have an opportunity to bring their work to a close.

7. Indicate clearly times of cleaning up, putting on and taking off outdoor clothing, doing classroom chores and maintenance tasks, collecting lunch money, taking attendance, and tending to other responsibilities that the teacher and children share. Although these activities are seldom seen as part of the curriculum, many of them can become important opportunities for children to develop in the affective and social domains.

8. Allow for flexibility. If children are to respect their work and the learning of others, they must have an opportunity to complete their tasks. Some small groups will become so interested in their learning activity that they will pursue it much longer if allowed to do so. In general, child-generated learning about topics that truly interest the children lasts much longer than the guides suggested here. Teacher-controlled learning in which children have less interest may be much shorter in duration.

9. Prepare children for changes in routines. The daily schedule is a source of predictability and security for children. If the schedule must be altered to respond to the children's needs, follow these steps:

- Identify the goal to be met by the change in the schedule.
- Consider more than one alternative change. Can the change be accommodated without

altering the whole schedule? Can an addition be made within free-choice or center time and not change the duration or sequence of events?

■ Discuss the changes with the children. Usually telling them briefly the day before and reminding them early on the day of the change are sufficient. Write the change on a poster or on the chalkboard for older children, posting the new schedule. An alternative would be to write the current schedule on sentence strips and then rearrange them with the children.

■ If new or more independent behavior will be required of the children, discuss this with them. Changes in schedule are opportunities for addressing affective and social learning goals.

■ Allow time for children to accommodate to the alterations. Three- and 4-year-olds usually take 3 weeks to be comfortable with a new schedule; 6- and 7-year-olds may adapt in half that time.

■ If possible, plan major schedule changes after holidays or school vacations. Every time children are out of school longer than the weekend, they are experiencing a schedule change. Three- and 4-year-olds may repeat their separation behaviors; 5- and 6-year-olds will take several days to readapt to school. If teachers adapt their schedules when children must go through an adjustment period anyway, the number of adjustment times are reduced.

10. Schedule a closure with the children at the end of each day.

SAMPLE SCHEDULES

Preprimary Schedule

Presented next are two schedules that are fairly typical for children of 3 to 4 years. Most noticeable are the long time segments within the schedule. Many activities would occur within each of the long time sequences, some of which are self-selected and others teacher initiated or directed. All choices are planned according to the curricular goals in this book, and the equipment to support appropriate activities is assumed available.

What follows are suggested processes designed to help teachers develop an effective classroom schedule. In addition, several sample schedules are provided, each coming from a different district. Note that some variations occur. These plans were in use at varying times of the year and in both rural and urban schools. The teachers using them necessarily adapted their program to fit the needs of the children, the school schedule, and the curriculum of the district.

Schedule A:

5–10 minutes	Arrival, greeting, and personal sharing with the teacher. As children enter the room, the teacher greets each child by name and listens to the comments that child has to make. The purpose is to affirm each child and let each one know their importance. On any particular day, the greeting time may be the only time of one-on-one conversation.
45–60 minutes	Free choice of indoor activities
10 minutes	Cleanup, reminder to use the bathroom, washing hands
10–15 minutes	Snack (everyone sits down and eats together)
15–20 minutes	Group time: poetry, story, music
30–45 minutes	Outdoor play or gym
5–10 minutes	Review of the day and departure

Schedule B:

5–10 minutes	Arrival and personal sharing time with the teacher
10–15 minutes	Group planning
45–60 minutes	Free choice of indoor activities
	Open snack (snack is treated as an activity center, children are free to come and go as they choose)
10 minutes	Cleanup

15–30 minutes	Group time: poetry, story, music, or dance. Children rest quietly while they listen to a story or sing together. If they dance or engage in vigorous physical activity, this group time is longer and the outdoor or gym time shorter.
15–30 minutes	Outdoor play or gym
5–10 minutes	Personal sharing with the teacher and departure

In Schedule B, the first whole-group activity is for children to deliberately choose where they will begin their participation. The group planning time is also an opportunity for the teacher to present a general focus of the day, demonstrate new equipment, or give directions on the use of a new center. Many 3- and 4-year-old children simply need careful direction if they are to function independently.

Schedule A has a group snack and Schedule B an open snack. The former structure is useful when the experience of sitting together, talking, and eating is desirable. For some children, communal conversation and eating are a new experience. On the other hand, the open snack makes food available to young children in one of the learning centers. Children may eat or not, may spend 5 minutes or 15.

Both schedules have a midmorning, whole-group instructional activity during which children sit quietly together or participate in fingerplays and musical activities. This period usually has poetry, story, music, or other literary activities. In Schedule B the quiet time may be followed with whole-group physical movement activities.

A modification of both these schedules for cold climates is to have outdoor time near midday for each group. It would then be last in the morning and first for the afternoon children. Wind chill and frostbite risk is much lower at midday.

In this classroom, regular instructional time outdoors is an important part of the daily schedule.

Kindergarten Schedule

Each schedule here was designed in response to the children's behavioral skills and needs. The literacy skill development and mathematical thinking activities are incorporated in the open-choice time. All centers have materials for recording by drawing, writing, graphing, or using other materials to represent an idea, such as a hardboard thermometer whose given temperature could be adjusted via string. Schedule C is from an all-day, alternate-day program. Schedule D is from a classroom in which children had very limited entry skills. It is described in greater detail because it has more components.

Schedule A:

10–15 minutes	Morning exercises
60–80 minutes	Free-choice time
10 minutes	Cleanup
10–15 minutes	Small-group time
10 minutes	Snack
30 minutes	Outdoor play or gym, or special instruction
5–10 minutes	Closing exercises

Schedule B:

60–80 minutes	Free-choice time
10–15 minutes	Cleanup, Snack
20–25 minutes	Whole-group activity: story, music, discussion
20–30 minutes	Outdoor or vigorous physical activity
5–10 minutes	Attendance, announcements, preparation to leave

Schedule C:

20 minutes	Free choice of manipulative materials, lunch count, and attendance
15 minutes	Opening and planning the day
150 minutes	Center time. During this time, the children have the opportunity for free choice as well as small-group activity time with the teacher. Centers are set up that offer experiences in all of the domains. Some of the choices will be theme-related activities.
25 minutes	Stories, music, creative movement
60 minutes	Lunch
30 minutes	Films, stories, restful activities
25 minutes	Materials-based math experiences
30 minutes	Gym
15 minutes	Large-group evaluation and sharing, closing
20 minutes	Recess and dismissal

Schedule D:

15 minutes	Morning exercises: group greetings and a presentation of various centers for the first activity period. These were briefly described, and children chose where they would go first. One major goal was to work toward planning and decision making for the children in addition to the rituals of the morning opening.
30–45 minutes	Limited free-choice time. The teacher had previously determined what goals were to be implemented and developed several centers that use different materials but are structured to meet the same goal. One teacher used all activities related to the "Math Their Way Program," for example. Some teachers who use this approach rotate the focus regularly to include *all* areas of programming so that limited choice may be set up to enhance basic motor skills, social cooperation games, or problem-solving experiences. Children chose

	among alternatives that were all excellent and appropriate for the needs and interests of the group.
5–10 minutes	Cleanup and preparation to go outdoors for recess
15–25 minutes	Outdoor play, weather permitting, return inside, taking care of clothing
20–30 minutes	Morning discussion: music, story, alphabet exposure, or some topic related to a theme. The selection of the topics to be covered should be related to content areas in which the teacher must tell children new information. For example, safety in the streets is typical for an autumn group discussion. Other topics related to content such as machines, health, the life of animals, and so on are of great interest to kindergarten children.
45–60 minutes	Open free-choice time. More activities are available than in the previous session. These activities should be related to a broad selection of goals. At least one activity should be a follow-up to the theme or topic presented earlier. For example, if the topic were machines, using nails, hammers, screws, and screwdrivers with wood would provide children with the firsthand information about the efficiency of machines and tools.
10–15 minutes	Evaluation. The teacher and children discuss together what they have done that day and how they feel about their accomplishments and their interactions with others. Such evaluations include discussions of what

children chose to do (journal writing, Play-doh,® painting, pretend play), the reasons they chose them, or perhaps what fun they had in a particular experience. This may be done in a large or small group, or it may be done as children finish cleaning up and move to speak to the teacher in smaller groups or a combination of both. Usually kindergarten children find a summary of the events and ideas of the day helpful for remembering, and parents are pleased and supportive of efforts when children are able to report what they did or learned on a particular day. Sometimes this time is used for handing out notes to go home or planning for the next day.

Other structures and schedules are equally useful, such as the one developed by Weikart and his associates (1971). Schedules with longer open-choice periods and no limited-choice activity are very successful and commonly used. Many kindergarten schedules resemble the preschool schedules.

First-Grade Schedule

Considerable variation in schedules is common. The one given here incorporates a number of special, once-a-week activities common for all first grades in the district. It uses a materials-based math program and the whole-language approach (Sharpe, 1990).

Schedule

8:25–8:50	Arrival and opening exercises, attendance, lunch count, collecting folders (on Monday only), and journal writing. Timing should minimize any interruptions during journal

writing. Journals are kept by each child and gradually move from drawing and dictation to written messages. The content of the journal is confidential unless the child wishes to share it, although children may share ideas of what they are writing about in a round-robin to help others get started. Children may read their entry to another child or the teacher. The teacher responds to the meaning of the journal entry, not the technical aspects of written communication. When children are finished, they move to the common area and engage in quiet book sharing. These books may be brought from home or the classroom.

8:50–9:15 Large-group discussion, songs, movement, or common writing experiences. Concepts related to a unit may be presented. At the end of this period, the teacher explains small-group activities, demonstrating as necessary and writing appropriate directions on the board.

9:20–10:25 Children rotate among three groups as follows:
1. *Reading group.* Children meet with the teacher for small-group reading experiences. Children bring their poetry folders. Reading poetry together is the warm-up to all other reading instruction.
2. *Reading and writing activities.* Each child works with a "study buddy" on an assigned activity. The children rotate through a variety of activities during the week. A "Reading and Writing" activity chart is

kept so that both the children and teacher can monitor the progress.
3. *Free choice.* Children may choose activities from a variety of centers, including the art table, math/science center, sandbox, easel, blocks, pretend play, or computer. Other choices may be available on a given day.

10:25–10:40 Recess

10:40–11:00 Snack and story. Once the children have removed outer clothing and have drinks and snacks, they are asked to recall the events from previous chapters of a book being read to them. They may move quietly about the room to throw their trash away while the teacher is reading.

11:00–11:20 MWF Spelling. Children recite rules and engage in finger spelling and arm spelling (the latter is used only for words that do not fit the rule). Children have individual chalkboards to practice writing words and sentences.

11:00–11:20 TTh Gym with the physical education teacher

11:20–11:40 Sharing. Three types of activities occur during this time. The reader's chair provides opportunities for a child who has written and published something to read the work aloud, or a child may read another child's book to the class that they have practiced reading. In the author's circle, children gather and read their unpublished writings. Listeners may say what they liked about the piece they heard or ask questions about the story. The author may incorporate suggestions in the finished

9:05–9:15	Daily business: attendance, pledge				
9:15–9:30	Large group: explain schedule for morning and directions on how to do independent work				
9:30–10:00	Small group: focus on any content or skill that the teacher deems appropriate				
10:00–10:30	Large group: motor skills in the gym				
10:30–11:45	Children are divided into groups of 4–7				

Language Art Centers

Start:	9:35	10:35	11:00	11:25	
Group:	1	2	3	4	Creative writing
	2	3	4	1	Listening
	3	4	1	2	Reading
	4	1	2	3	Independent work

11:45–12:40	Recess and lunch
12:40–12:45	Attendance; go over schedule for afternoon
12:45–1:05	Large group: calendar (skills: counting, days of week, months, time, etc.), story time
1:05–1:45	Math Their Way: individual or small-group instruction with activities
1:45–2:00	Music (large group): always involves movement

Free-choice learning centers or separate time periods, depending on the project, from 2:00–3:20

2:00–2:20	Science or social studies: varies in form depending on the project
2:20–2:45	"Author's chair": children share their stories in large group
2:45–3:20	Free-choice activity: often based on some type of theme
3:20–3:30	Cleanup and dismissal

FIGURE 11.5
Sample Schedule for Full-Day Kindergarten and First Grade

piece. Lastly, one child each day has an opportunity to put something in the mystery box and write three clues about it. Children try to guess what it is. Usually these activities are in small groups but may be a part of the whole group.

11:40–12:30	Lunch/recess
12:35–1:15 M	Whole-group instruction in mathematics. Children are introduced to concepts and materials. This instruction is designed so that children may use the learning centers effectively later in the afternoon.
12:35–12:50 TWTF	DEAR (drop everything and read). Teacher and children read books, magazines, and

journals quietly. Children may select their own reading material, or the teachers may assist them. Many children read "published books" of their classmates as well as commercial literature. Children may read anyplace they want to, including under the tables and among the coats. Everyone reads, however.

12:50–1:15	Process writing. This creative writing period incorporates a peer conference and/or a teacher conference. Children indicate a willingness to peer conference by putting a sign ("Stop/Go") on the corner of their desks. Children sign up for a teacher conference after

they had a peer conference. Once the child has edited the work based on conferences, it may be published or set aside for a new piece.

12:50–1:15 Th	Library
1:15–2:00 MTWF	Free choice. Centers are designed to promote children's thinking. Some centers are new each week, and some are "must do," with children being expected to complete them during the week. The teacher circulates among the centers. Children may complete morning tasks if necessary.
1:15–2:00 Th	Music with a specialty teacher
2:00–2:15	Recess
2:25–2:55	M: Music T: Projects: Small-group activities related to units in health, social studies, or science W: Math activities Th: Math and spelling review F: Science or social studies
2:55–3:00	Cleanup and dismissal

The last schedule in Figure 11.5 demonstrates the combination of group reading instruction and center-based instruction. Centers are set up by goal area such as math or social studies or by projects. Children have many hands-on learning activities yet also have the opportunity for directed instruction in language. Notice that other activities are used in lieu of the previously used workbook and ditto exercises.

Second-Grade Schedule

In this classroom schedule, many similar activities occur as they did in the first grade. Where they are similar, no additional explanation is provided. This teacher has greater similarity in schedule across the week than did the previous teacher. She also reports that throughout the year, she operates on longer time segments than is represented in this schedule, which was used in the autumn (MacLean, 1990). A sample direction/record sheet is presented in Figure 11.6 that illustrates some of the activities children do on their own.

Schedule:

8:50	Opening exercises: student jobs, attendance, lunch count, pledge, current events, calendar history of the day, Constitution tidbits, WEB (Wonderfully Exciting Books, an at-home reading program)
9:15	Big Book: a whole-group reading activity with the teacher modeling reading
9:40	Aerobics for children
9:45	Reading groups I. The reading groups have heterogeneous grouping. They start by reading a chapter in a book, then move to reading entire storybooks, then to individualized selections. Daily informal observations and evaluations are done by the teacher. Both VCR and audiocassettes are used to assess skill development. There are three groups during each of these periods. One group meets with the teacher, the second group reads silently or with a partner, and the third is engaged in a variety of language arts activities.
10:15	Free-choice A. A variety of centers (health, social studies, science, etc.) are available, with the students participating in planning some of them. The activities are chosen by the children.
10:45	Recess
11:00	Media/story time. The teacher presents a film or filmstrip related to the unit and reads a book aloud, or the children engage in a choral reading. Efforts are made to present a variety of styles.
11:15	Reading groups II

Centers

* means *write* about it.   _____Name

_____ Scale—measure 56 each of 2 things.

*_____ Water table—measure and compare foam to measuring bird seed to water.

_____ Find these places on the pull-down world map *and* globe:

Antarctica   New Zealand   Australia   South Africa
Falkland Islands   Galapagos Islands

_____ Tell the 4 directions on a compass and where the needle points.

_____ Measure the height of the penguins on the penguin cards and arrange little to big.

*_____ Read "Penguins" quietly to yourself.

_____ Basic "Bear Facts": M _____ T _____ W _____ Th _____ F _____

_____ Fill in the overlapping shapes.

*_____ Put a note on your TV at home to watch the "Trans-Antarctica Expedition" Dec. 17 (Sunday) on ABC.

*_____ Write the names of *all* Mr. Popper's penguins.

_____ Make a "Super Dad Penguin Poem" poster.

_____ Walk like a penguin (*carefully!*) across room.

*_____ Tell Fred why penguins like to "toboggan"!

*_____ Compare how you stay warm in cold weather to penguins.

*_____ Write real facts from "Mr. Popper's Penguins."

*_____ "Mr. Popper's Penguins" activities 1 _____ 2 _____ 3 _____ 4 _____ 5 _____
6 _____ Penguin Book _____ Popper's Worksheet _____

_____ Color the "Follow the Directions" paper.

_____ Read and color "The Anxious Snowman."

_____ Spelling M _____ T _____ W _____ Th _____ F _____

Sunday   Monday   Tuesday   Wednesday   month
Thursday   Friday   Saturday   week   year

FIGURE 11.6
Center Selections from a "Penguin" Unit over a Week

11:45	Aerobics/movement activity
11:50	Math. Whole-group instruction, with the teacher demonstrating materials and center work
12:00	Chapter books. The teacher reads aloud.
12:20	Lunch
1:05	Drop everything and read: silent reading
1:15	Reading group III
1:45	Journal writing. The teacher writes too!
2:00	Physical education, art, music specialty teachers. This is the classroom teacher's planning time.
2:45	Free-choice B
3:15	Closing exercises: author's chair, evaluation of the day's activities, music, writing the day's events on the class calendar, sharing
3:38	Dismissal

SUMMARY

The organizational responsibilities of the teacher using developmentally appropriate practices are considerable. Classrooms must be arranged to facilitate quiet movement and help children maintain the focus of their work. Equipment must be chosen to meet the specific goals of the curriculum. The schedule of the day is generally divided into longer time periods than in more traditional classrooms, with children moving among carefully selected centers. The purpose of all organizational work is to prepare the physical, cognitive, aesthetic, and social environment so that there are opportunities for learning and growth-producing interaction among the people in that context. Fortunately, once the basic plans are made and implemented, teachers can concentrate on fine-tuning them to suit particular children and meet individual needs.

CHAPTER 12

Implementing Learning
Centers in the Classroom

Don't you know that in every task the most important thing is the beginning and especially when you have to deal with anything young and tender? Plato, *The Republic*

How human beings function in any particular setting depends a great deal on the physical and psychological climate they perceive to exist: factors in the environment that promote or discourage curiosity, exploration, engagement, and calculated risk taking, and the resulting extent to which they feel free or constrained to behave and to act. Most young children readily adapt to contexts that adults prepare for them, even when those contexts are not optimal in promoting growth and development. For example, current legislation and research related to special education placement, retention of children, placement of children in homogeneous settings, and teacher-dominated classrooms have caused us lately to rethink early childhood educational practices that had become rather entrenched. We have learned that, although it could be documented that children were growing in these more narrowly defined settings, they were not growing *as much* as when they were provided opportunity to function with same-age peers in more heterogeneous settings and with additional support.

As a group, young children share a number of characteristics and needs. Their growth is very uneven and rapid, which makes it more difficult to predict their future successes on the basis of their present skills and abilities. They have a need to move about and be active, exploring and responding to their world through their senses. Boys and girls may vary significantly in the way they approach learning tasks (Soderman & Phillips, 1986), and young children will vary within gender groups as well, calling for the presentation of conceptual ideas in multiple and diverse ways and embedded in what they already know. L. Katz (1987) indicates that "it is reasonable to assume that when a single teaching method is used for a diverse group of children, a significant proportion of these children are likely to fail" (p. 3).

Preprimary and primary children love developmentally appropriate language experiences—familiar songs, books, finger plays, poems, rhymes, and stories. Many enjoy the "magic" of being someone else as they act out roles of more powerful figures in their world—mothers, fathers, teachers, doctors, firefighters, truckers, and fairy godmothers. They are intrigued with age-appropriate science experiments, although they often do not understand causal relationships, and they are easily engaged in logicomathematical activity that helps them "sort out" a very big world. They are drawn naturally to two- and three-dimensional creative art and construction materials and can demonstrate significant concentration in drawing and writing activity.

While they can function well for increasingly longer periods of time in large and small group settings, they have a visible need to select activities of personal interest and be involved in them for uninterrupted periods. Play, quiet observation and imitation of others, experimentation, and error making that brings them closer and closer to skillful functioning are their primary modes of learning.

They seek adults who are supportive and contribute to feelings of security and comfort. They are eager to please, and most of them trust that adults surely must appreciate how wonderful it is to have time to explore and investigate all the interesting and unfamiliar aspects of any particular environment in which they find themselves, including the early childhood classroom.

WHY USE LEARNING CENTERS?

Learning centers in early childhood settings have proven to be an apt and responsive vehicle for meeting such needs in children. Centers are "carefully designed areas that contain a variety of learning activities and materials drawn from the classroom's basic skills programs and from the themes and units being pursued" (Day, 1988a, p. 91). Because they offer choices to children, the difficulties usually connected to developmental and experiential differences are minimized.

Centers allow active and purposeful construction of the learning environment by adults in order to promote the development of useful skills and abilities in children. When well constructed and carefully thought out, learning centers resemble an effective blend between a workshop and library setting.

Since children are free to move about the room, centers allow for differing attention spans and need for movement, as well as the wide range of developmental differences usually found in young children. Used in collaboration with thematic planning, they provide opportunities for children to explore concepts in an indepth and integrated manner. Since children are able to experience extended time blocks rather than brief periods during which they move from one workbook/worksheet exercise to another, task perseverence and concentration are fostered. As related ideas and concepts are presented in a number of ways that become readily apparent to the young learner, divergent as well as convergent thought is promoted. Cooperative learning, which teaches both leadership and following skills to children, is implemented easily in a center-based classroom.

Benefits to teachers are as numerous. Their responsibilities in the early childhood context—to prepare and monitor the environment, evaluate both children and programming in the setting, and bring about responsive and needed changes to support optimal development in the children (McKee, 1990b)—are made easier through the use of learning centers. Very simply, they are free to be up and about the room and involved in spontaneously evaluating the children's use of materials and learning experiences. They find opportunities for effective "chats" with children, to ask probing questions and provide academic and emotional feedback when most advantageous to do so. Teachers can watch to see which kinds of activities actively engage individual children and which pro-

mote only cursory interest. They can note where children are able to integrate and transfer concepts developed in one area to their work and play in other areas with different materials. A first-grade teacher who had successfully made the transition from workbooks and worksheets to center-based activity said, "I was afraid to put the texts away and rely on the enrichment activities the children seemed to love so much—worried I wouldn't be 'teaching them enough' or 'the right thing.' When I looked more closely at the difference in children's reactions to one teaching method and the other, I realized the workbook exercises were pretty grim—and also pretty narrow. I gave myself permission to get rid of them for good!"

Because children in learning centers are active and busy, the teacher is also able to use brief periods of the time to work with selected individuals or small groups of children on various aspects of knowledge and skill building. Evaluation of children's progress, which should take place in the natural setting by the teacher, is more easily accomplished. Finally, disciplinary problems, which frequently result when children are disinterested or lacking in a skill required of the whole group, are minimized.

The many advantages resulting from implementing a center approach may not be readily apparent to parents, board members, or administrators, who may need reassurance and information about what children are actually doing and learning. Strategies to share information about the learning taking place include a listing of developing concepts and skills posted in a particular center area, guided tours conducted by trained parents or older students, newsletters, or letters sent directly to parents and other interested persons.

CHARACTERISTICS OF EFFECTIVE EARLY CHILDHOOD LEARNING CENTERS

Establishing learning centers in the early childhood classroom is not a guarantee, of course, that optimal knowledge and skill building will take place. Much thought has to go into the use of the physical space available; number and kind of centers; materials, supplies, and resources;

quality of thematic units; interest levels, talents, and abilities of the children; and the overseeing of activity, evaluation, and feedback to children by knowledgeable and capable adults. Children must be equipped with the "necessary skills and prerequisite knowledge for effective use of the centers," including the purposes of the centers, ways to exercise self-discipline, and strategies for self-appraisal related to what they are learning from participating in center activity (Day, 1988a, p. 75). In general however, well-constructed centers are built with attention to the following:

1. *They are organized and implemented on the basis of knowledge the teacher has about the children and their abilities and well-grounded information about early childhood development and early childhood education.* This point must be underscored, for it is the rockbed of effective planning. For every activity and experience that goes on in a classroom, teachers must ask themselves the following questions:

- How does each one contribute to long-range outcome goals?
- What domain-related objectives serve as the basis for this activity/experience?
- What do I hope to have children get out of this?
- How does it build on past knowledge of most of the children?
- Is it the best possible way to present such an idea/concept?
- Is it the best possible use of the children's time?
- Are the activities, experiences, and materials showcased matched well to the developmental levels and interests of the children or simply "cute" ideas picked up somewhere?
- How can I evaluate effectiveness of the activity/experience?

2. *Activities presented within the centers are flexible and adaptable rather than rigid and static* (Ministry of Education, Victoria, Province of British Columbia, 1988). While we may have in mind a particular outcome following children's use of materials in a center, we will want to be alert for paths children wish to take in their own exploration and use of the materials. Children often have pretty good ideas about creative and divergent ways to use available materials! In a well-designed learning center, it is possible for children to work on domain-related goals established by the teacher while still fulfilling their own needs in that or another domain. This can be accomplished by using open-ended materials and by making available an array of materials in each area.

3. *The array of learning centers provided to children in a day, and over time, are well diversified and provide for a balance of cognitive, affective, and psychomotor development* (Cummings, 1990b; Day, 1988a). Activities represent a cross-section of domains and varying modes of child development. A classroom in which this principle is evident, for instance, would not have several learning centers emphasizing cognitive goals to the exclusion of other domains, nor would arts and crafts projects dominate the kinds of experiences offered to children.

4. *Children understand how to use the learning centers properly* (McKee, 1990b). Center-based activity can be much more successful when teachers take time to introduce children to new activities and materials in centers *before* children encounter them. Some teachers prefer to give children "previews of coming attractions" by letting them know what to expect for the next day just before they prepare to leave. Others plan an "opening" or "greeting time" in their schedules. Before children move to center activity in the morning, they are brought together in a large group to talk with the teacher about what they will find in the room that may be new or unusual, any safety information they need to have in working with certain materials, and any limits on numbers of children who can be involved on a particular day. This is also a time when demonstrations of how to use particular materials or work with unfamiliar equipment can take place.

After children have had opportunities to explore the materials, teachers may wish to assign certain tasks to be completed with the materials. For example, as part of a thematic unit on clothing, one teacher set up a center as a "shoe shop." One of the tasks the children had was to weigh one of their own shoes with nonstandard weights, record the number on a paper shoe the teacher had provided, and place their work in a shoe box positioned in the area. The teacher

FIGURE 12.1
Painting at the Easel Pictograph
Source: Drawing by Barbara Rohde. Used with permission.

demonstrated the activity from start to finish by weighing one of *her* shoes and having the children count the numbers of weights used. She then recorded the number on one of the paper shoes and placed it in the designated shoe box. The teacher reminded the children that, in this particular activity, it would be important to keep the container of nonstandard weights in the shoe shop area and limit use of them on that particular day to the children who were involved in weighing, although children "might be interested in using the weights to weigh other objects in the shoe shop area." Besides serving the purpose of knowledge and skill building about use of the materials, such introductions also activate children's curiosity and encourage them to visit a particular center.

In addition to these kinds of introductions, the focus of a learning center may be made evident to children by the placement of materials within it. For instance, after children have had previous experience with rubbings of objects, the teacher may highlight a leaf-rubbing activity by putting all the relevant materials in the middle of the art table. This would draw children's attention to the leaves, crayons, and paper, which would make the activity appear inviting. Yet children could still have access to other art supplies stored on shelves nearby.

Written directions in the form of pictographs or words (see Figure 12.1) as well as periodic participation by the teacher are other ways the goals and procedures of an activity can be made clear to children.

5. *The same learning center, at different times, can be used to address different domains.* Materials are not bound to any one domain. Depending on how teachers structure a learning center and how they set goals, the same materials (e.g., art materials, blocks) could be used to address the cognitive domain one day, the language domain on another, and the social domain on yet another. This principle was illustrated in chapter 11 in relation to collage materials. The same can be said for all the core centers described here.

6. *Teachers use learning center time as a period to interact spontaneously with children rather than time to grade students' work or prepare other materials and activities.* They are available to children and able to take advantage of appropriate opportunities to enhance, extend, and evaluate cognitive, social, affective, and physical learning experiences and developmental outcomes. They are able to hold brief conferences with children about processes and products as children act on the materials in the room. Teachers who choose to be active with the children during this time are also able to

ward off potential difficulties as children work and play together in the context.

EXAMPLES OF CENTERS

The kinds of centers found in any early childhood setting vary dramatically in terms of number, materials and equipment available, and creative ideas generated by both teachers and children. Included here will be descriptions of centers that are often found in many early childhood settings, that is, "core" centers (McKee, 1990b), and also several examples of "special interest" centers.

Core centers may change slightly in the materials that are added or subtracted but not in their particular focus. Included here may be a language arts center, creative arts and construction center (two- and three-dimensional art/ modeling), science/exploration/collections center, math/manipulative materials and table games, a dramatic play area, gross motor, music, blocks and wheeled toys, and a large group area. Some of these centers may be broken down further into subcenter areas. For example, a book corner and listening center may be established separately from a writing center, although some content areas such as these naturally lend themselves to integration so that children will have easier access to equipment and materials needed to carry out their ideas.

Special interest centers may be set up for shorter periods of time (1 day to 4 weeks), based on the interests of the children and teacher. For example, large motor equipment such as a climber or balance beam may be added, particularly when weather or space would limit outdoor use of such equipment. Music, woodworking, cooking centers, and special collections of one kind or another are introduced, removed, and then reintroduced periodically. Such centers may require the use of additional adults to monitor and/or support children's use of materials or space. Teachers who work on a day-to-day basis with the help of a full-time aide or parent volunteers often elect to add one or more of these centers to their repertoire of core centers, making them available to children on a more consistent basis.

Following are descriptions of some core centers that are often included in early childhood learning environments, preschool through second grade, and the benefits derived by including them. (Suggested listings of materials, supplies, and equipment helpful for implementing particular activities in the center may be found in chap. 11.)

Language Arts Center

The most important rationale for providing language experiences to children via a center-based approach is that it supports children's emerging language skills and abilities from a constructivist approach. This means that the development of a child's knowledge and reality evolves primarily through an internal psychological core in interaction with the physical and social environment rather than through simple biological maturation or direct instruction (DeVries & Kohlberg, 1987). A special part of the classroom becomes an arena for children's active discovery of language through quality, age-appropriate experiences in listening, reading, writing, drawing, and story reenactment. Activities and resources are geared toward progressive conceptualization on the part of children rather than the more traditional drilling of me-

chanics by adults, skill-based grouping, use of abstract worksheets, and teaching of isolated letters and sounds. Children are able to collaborate and compare their products, both with one another and against the rich and diverse literature sources introduced into the environment.

Research indicates that literacy difficulties in young children are more often cognitive, rather than perceptual or motor, and that only the most conceptually advanced young children profit from more traditional approaches (Ferreiro & Teberosky, 1982). Thus, children "search for coherence" in coming to an internalized understanding of what reading and writing are all about. When children are given opportunities to make predictions about what they think is correct, practice, seek verification, and correct errors based on their changing operatory levels, they eventually arrive at "more and more adequate hypotheses" (DeVries & Kohlberg, 1987, pp. 244–245), which thereby extends and enhances a useful and broad bank of language-related skills. Consequently, effectively constructed language arts centers become ideal environments for supporting many of the intermediate objectives and activities cited in chap-

Concentration is focused when language centers are placed in a quiet area of the room.

ter 6, "The Language Domain," and chapter 5, "The Cognitive Domain."

The language arts center area should be located in a quiet area of the room to facilitate concentration. It should also be a place where children can go to rest, reflect quietly, or become involved in using a rich variety of literacy materials, including such resources as sand trays for drawing, printing, and writing.

Some teachers interact personally with each child on a daily basis in this center through the use of brief "mailbox" messages. Students eagerly look forward to checking each day to see what special messages the teacher has left and frequently respond by writing one to the teacher. At first, it may be only a word or their name and a picture. Eventually, as children's skills grow, the messages do also (Routman, 1987). Children also begin to write notes to one another and answer messages received. Mailbox "messaging" in the language arts center is a highly motivating activity; children enjoy the surprise element of finding and leaving messages and are writing for real purposes. This is a powerful factor in their *wanting* to develop literacy skills.

A couple of attractive, inviting cushions positioned in near proximity to a well-displayed collection of age-related books and other reading materials will draw children to use them. Book selections should be displayed with the covers showing and should also be regularly replaced, except for some that are children's favorites (Hildebrand, 1991). Ample table space and supplies that are easily accessible will also make this important center a popular one with the children and one that will support the overall goals of the entire curriculum.

Creative Arts and Construction Center

Young children are naturally drawn to creative arts and construction materials with which they can produce two- and three-dimensional products representing their perceptions, feelings, and ideas about their world. One can often hear children egocentrically expressing those thoughts aloud as they tactilely manipulate a variety of textures, patterns, shapes, and products in this area. It is here that children's inner cognitive perceptions are revealed as they move developmentally from simple to more complex views of their

world. Cows can be any color, not just brown or black and white; the sky is something over their heads, not coming down in a distance to meet a horizon; adults tower over children, and suns are reserved only for happy, warm pictures, not for every picture. In construction activity, children develop increasingly sophisticated skills in manipulating materials, arranging and rearranging them to represent aspects of their world. Models should be discouraged in this area so that children feel free to explore and construct materials on their own terms (see chaps. 3 and 10).

Teachers will want to offer a selected array of resources that catch children's interests, perhaps offering suggestions about how the materials could be used but encouraging children to think of divergent ways they can be used. There should be explicit valuing and reinforcement of children's personal expression and private interpretations.

Science/Exploration/Collections Center

> Basically, children who are engaged in sciencing are given a chance to observe and manipulate a variety of man-made and natural objects in ways that help them to recognize similarities, differences, and relationships among the objects and phenomena. They sniff, look at, listen to, feel, pinch, and if possible taste a variety of materials in order to develop and extend their ability to make careful and accurate observations. (Neumann, 1972, pp. 137–138)

Encouraging children's investigation of natural and man-made phenomena in their world is the primary focus of this center. Teachers guide children toward an understanding of scientific processes as they have them scan, explore, discover, attend, observe, sort, classify, vary conditions, compare, predict, describe, label, and evaluate outcomes. In addition to learning the "scientific method," children come also to value the role their own sensory perceptions, imaginations, and intuition play in understanding these phenomena.

To prepare the science/exploration/collections center adequately, teachers must become efficient in gathering, taking inventory, and replacing science resources, protecting children's safety, organizing interesting indoor and outdoor experiences, arranging the environment, and making themselves available to children for spontaneous discussions. They also need to be alert about the quality of science experiences they are providing for children and make certain that these contribute to conceptual growth rather than fostering magical thinking (C. Seefeldt, 1980).

While young scientists benefit most from exploring and working with real materials, many good videotapes are now accessible and can be stocked near a VCR and monitor for the children's independent use. Exciting full-color, realistic photographs can be gathered and displayed selectively in the center. Holt (1988) suggests that teachers who want to attract children, rather than dust, to a science center will work hard at setting up attractive, attention-getting displays, using novelty, humor, simplicity, and suspense to draw children. While many "sciencing" materials will be offered selectively to children, basic supplies should be consistently available on low shelves or in drawers marked with pictures and labels of contents. (A listing of these materials can be found in chap. 11.)

Manipulative Materials/Table Games Center

In order for children to acquire mathematical concepts, attach language and symbols to these concepts, and grow in their ability to learn new concepts, they need a great deal of hands-on experience with diverse logicomathematical materials. The activities and gaming experiences children encounter in a math/manipulative materials/table games center guide them toward increasingly complex organization of motor behavior, perceptual development, and mathematical concepts.

The teacher's role is to provide stimulating materials and structure sequential experiences that will move the children from a concrete, intuitive level of thinking to higher, reflective, and autonomous thought (Cruikshank, Fitzgerald, & Jensen, 1980). Although children will eventually *not* be so reliant on concrete materials, they are extremely important beginning tools to facilitate children's conceptualization. In the beginnings of concept development, abstract symbolization interferes with children's understanding (Baratta-Lorton, 1976, p. xiv). No matter how carefully we design or simplify the presentation

of abstract symbols to young children, they "cannot involve the child's senses the way real materials can. Symbols are not the concept, they are only a representation of the concept, and as such are abstractions describing something that is not visible to the child. Real materials, on the other hand, can be manipulated to illustrate the concept completely, and can be experienced visually by the child" (Baratta-Lorton, 1976, p. xiv). The most viable arena in which to give children time for such exploration and application of logicomathematical materials and games is in a center that highlights activity revolving around patterning, sorting, classification, invariance of number, comparisons, graphing, and number/symbolization connections. The objectives and activities outlined in the mathematics section of chapter 6, "The Cognitive Domain," can be carried out most successfully through organized center activity. In addition, this center might focus on fine motor skills, problem-solving activities, or enhancement of memory skills.

Blocks Center

Many skills and abilities are fostered in the blocks center. Besides fine and gross motor coordination that develop out of children's bending, lifting, stacking, balancing, pushing, pulling, and reaching, there is also increased understanding of directionality, manual dexterity, eye-hand coordination, configuration, problem solving, socialization, and conceptualization of patterns, symmetry, and balance (McKee, 1990b).

Obviously, block play is a powerful medium for promoting growth and development skills and abilities in every curricular domain. Hildebrand (1991) notes that parents may sometimes question the skill-building benefits of block play and why it should be found in classrooms after the kindergarten year; after all, blocks are among the earliest playthings valued by children. Professionals will want to share with parents the many positive attributes of children's block play. When considered with other props such as those in the following list, this center holds superior potential for child development in all domains addressed within the curriculum. The following materials, supplies, and equipment are suggested:

Unit blocks

Hollow blocks

Blocks of various sizes, colors, weights

Assortment of miniature wooden, rubber, plastic people, animals, trees, houses

Traffic and safety signs

Cars, trucks, boats, planes, trains, school and city buses, taxis, car carriers, cranes, steam-shovels, firetrucks, wagons

Steering wheel

Large empty boxes

Highway maps

Train tracks

Wheelbarrow

Shelves to store blocks and other equipment

Cloth and plastic street layouts, rivers

Colored masking tape

Hats (police, fire, ambulance driver, construction, etc.)

Photographs of construction sites, forms of transportation, people in building occupations, truck drivers, and so forth

Fire and gas station "hoses"

Pretend Play Center

In the pretend play center, children interact with one another to reenact their own life experiences and play out any number of imagined roles. Here is where they have a chance to be in charge! They can pretend to be an authority figure (doctor, teacher, big brother, policeman, mother, father), someone who does dangerous, risky things (soldier, boxer, race car driver), or even someone who does *bad* things (robber, monster). They can experiment with cause and effect with only pretend consequences. Since peers are relative equals, they can debate and hope to win their share of victories. They can integrate and extend their understanding about what happens in particular settings (pizza place, beauty shop, post office) and build varying perspectives about social, family, and gender roles. In addition to benefits already cited, children gain in the areas of self-expression, vocabulary development, sense of belonging and cooperating, and various modes of social exchanges that require the development of physical, logico-mathematical, and social knowledge.

Age and developmental level of the children being served, and individual needs and interests will be important considerations in promoting certain activities and experiences in the pretend play center. For example, younger children, 3 to 5 years of age, may have a real need to use the center for housekeeping. They will want relevant props, such as dolls, doll furniture, and dress-up clothes. Children who may be upset because of unstable family situations benefit by having the "family living" section of pretend play readily available to them for playing out internal thoughts and feelings. This is true for older children as well as for preschoolers.

Most 6- to 8-year-olds will also enjoy using housekeeping materials occasionally. However, they may be more interested in using the center when it is equipped to simulate other contexts they are coming to know about in their ever-widening world: stores, a space command center, TV station, auto repair clinic, restaurant, formal school setting, post office, or hospital. This will be especially true in encouraging boys to use the center. Also, the activities and experiences will be played out in very different ways by younger and older children. As children mature, their play may become more realistic. Instead of merely *playing* at pizza making, they will want to make the real thing and "sell" it to classmates who come in, sit down, order, eat, and pay before leaving.

As in most of the other centers, the resources available to children will vary. Suggestions for materials that might be used in a pretend play center and further information about how to promote children's learning may be found in chapter 9, "The Pretend Play Domain," and chapter 11, "Organizing Space, Materials, and Time."

Cooperative Project Learning Center

The cooperative project area is one in which children work together toward a common goal. The activities offered there involve tasks too big or too complex for any one child to complete alone. Thus, the emphasis is on children collaborating, generating ideas, developing plans, giving suggestions, listening to one another's opinions, negotiating, and evaluating their work.

Such a center could make use of any of the materials described in chapter 11. Some teachers plan a cooperative project each week; others make sure to offer one once a month and then let it continue at a pace determined by the children's interests.

For instance, in a classroom in which dinosaurs constituted the theme, the kindergarten children created a "Boxosaurus."

■ Day 1: The children planned how to make a large dinosaur out of boxes (a Boxosaurus). The group generated ideas regarding the parts of the dinosaur that should be made, tools and materials that were needed, and who would help with each stage of production: assembly, painting, and decorating. The teacher wrote out their plan for all to see.
■ Day 2: The children gathered materials and began the assembly stage of production.
■ Day 3: The painting phase of the project was introduced.
■ Day 4: The children added various decorations to the Boxosaurus.
■ Day 5: The children measured all the parts of the Boxosaurus and recorded the vital statistics on a graph.

■ Day 6: The children evaluated their work. They responded to such questions as these:

1. Could the job have been done as well by one person?
2. How satisfied were the children with the results?
3. How might the children change their plan in the future?
4. What kinds of decisions were necessary throughout the project, and how did they turn out?

Other projects children have carried out include making a meal over a period of several days and then eating it on the last day, creating a replica of their "town" using small boxes and other "beautiful junk," scripting and producing a class dramatization, and building a museum through which children eventually conducted tours for another class.

Large Group Center

Perhaps this center is one that most develops a spirit of unity within the classroom. It is where children come together with the teacher as a group for a number of purposes: singing, listen-

In the large group center, children gain a sense of community in the classroom.

ing to a story, discussions about what is to occur or has happened during the day, writing a group letter to someone, choral reading, musical activity, entertainment or information from visitors, finger plays, or story reenactment. It is a place where a lot of enjoyable experiences happen and where safe learning occurs: it is not even noticeable when a child does not know every word in the song or in the story being read. And, because lots of stories, songs, poems, and rhymes are shared over and over, eventually children *do* know every word—and are proud of it!

Large group is a place where young children begin to lose some of the egocentrism that is so characteristic of them. This happens when good discussion goes on following shared experiences, and children begin to understand that other people have different points of view and different ideas, thoughts, and feelings about things that are shared. They learn to trust that these various points of view are acceptable to the teacher and other children and that it is safe to express their own viewpoints.

In general, activities experienced in large group are more teacher directed and are more easily facilitated with the following resources:

Carpeted space or individual carpet squares for each child

Chalkboard, chalk in different colors, sizes

Big book easel

Big books

Newsprint for easel

Flip chart

Song charts

Poetry charts

Flannel board

Flannel board story and information sets

Adult chair or stool

Record player, tape recorder, records, and cassette tapes

Guitar

Piano

Bookcase

Collections of song and rhythm books

Rhythm instruments (drums, triangles, bells, cymbals, rhythm sticks [set for each child], maracas, castanets, tone blocks, tambourines, xylophone, sand blocks, waxed paper and combs, kazoos)

Multicolored scarves

Streamers on sticks

Pom-poms

Fans

DEALING WITH IMPLEMENTATION ISSUES

Parents, teachers, and administrators often have a number of questions about classrooms that include large segments of time devoted to center activity:

"How can you tell what they're learning?"

"How do you know what children are participating in, since they're all over the room?"

"What if a child *never* visits the language arts center and spends all his time playing with blocks? Will he ever learn to read?"

"Can I still use reading groups?"

"There are so many materials needed— where can I get them all?"

"I'm uncomfortable not having *any* structured time. Do I have to use centers all day long?"

How to Get Started

Construction of learning centers depends on the philosophy of the professional staff; resources such as numbers of staff available, funding, materials, and space; and any constraints such as a program's established curricular and evaluation requirements. Preplanning involves deciding on room arrangement, organization of materials, number of centers to be used, time to be allotted to center participation, and introduction of the process to children. The "comfort level" of each teacher involved needs to be addressed, and teachers beginning to use centers for the first time should set up the number and kind of centers they feel they can manage and keep in order—those that need the least direction and contact from the teacher, utilize materials familiar to the children, and have a clear and direct purpose. Later, teachers can add or expand already established centers to be more responsive to the interests and needs of the children (Day, 1988a).

For example, staff at Sandy Oaks preschool begin each year by introducing children to the core centers using simple materials that are generally self-directing and self-explanatory. Examples of these include housekeeping in pretend play, small vehicles in the blocks center, modeling dough and markers in the art area, and puzzles with only a few pieces and easily manipulated building bricks in the manipulative center. Gradually, as children become familiar with the daily routine and how to use these basic items, the teachers introduce more complex materials such as fingerpaint, a make-believe restaurant, more demanding puzzles and construction materials, as well as an increased variety of unit block props.

In another example, one group of kindergarten through third-grade teachers who had never used a center-based approach to teaching decided on an "additive" means of easing into center use. They began to introduce centers to the children for a short period of the day, usually just half an hour, and providing only two or three center options. Children were individually assigned to sample the materials and activities in one of the centers and then, before the period was over, were rotated to one of the other centers to briefly experience planned experiences there. Gradually, the number of centers was increased, as well as the freedom the children had in both choosing a center and the time they wanted to be involved in particular activities.

Alternately, teachers and principals in the Battle Creek, Michigan, schools who were reflecting on their initial efforts to begin using centers described the tentative steps taken by teachers wanting to get started and also some of the pitfalls in their attempts:

1. At first, centers were established on the edges of the room, with children's desks remaining in the middle. Time to work in the centers and time to work at desks was established, and these times were mutually exclusive. Two problems quickly emerged: space allocation and also the extensive planning involved in designing activities for both centers and seatwork. Essentially, the teachers found they were running two classrooms in one, and it was wearing them out!

2. To cope with space problems, several teachers then decided to eliminate their own desks. Centers were constructed more prominently in the middle of the room, and more time was allotted to center activity. However, while children investigated activities in the centers, the teacher was usually stationed in one particular area, working with a small group of children. This type of arrangement spawned new feelings of frustration: the teachers felt they were not interacting enough with the children working in centers and unable to observe what they were doing. The children were virtually on their own.

3. In an effort to modify the situation further, teachers decided to divide their attention between stationing themselves in only one point in the classroom with small groups and moving more freely about the room. Although they felt somewhat freer to interact with children, resolve conflicts that arose, and replace needed materials and supplies, they continued to feel limited about the quality of instructional guidance they were able to provide for children working in the centers. Largely, they felt they were simply managing the classroom situation.

4. As they became more confident about what children were able to learn in a well-constructed center and also more confident about children's ability to function independently and successfully, teachers became more actively involved in facilitating center activity, instructional guidance, and assessment and evaluation of children's developmental growth during center-based activity.

Structuring Self-sustaining Centers. Although the presence of aides and volunteers in an early childhood classroom certainly can enhance learning center activity potential, additional adult support is not always possible. Many classroom teachers find themselves the only adult overseeing everything that goes on in the classroom. When this is the case, teachers must become skillful in setting up centers that are self-sustaining and need less direct guidance. Following are guidelines for enhancing learning center activity that requires initial guidance only

Some classroom centers should be self-sustaining, requiring only initial guidance on the part of the teacher.

or allows completely independent action on the part of the children.

1. Introduce the activity during large group, explaining its purpose and demonstrating actual use of materials. This provides opportunity for children to ask questions. Children are told where and for how long materials will be available and given necessary reminders about using them cooperatively with others, such as keeping resources only in the learning center so that others can find them.

2. Introduce new centers and more complex activities only after general center activity has begun. Work closely with an initial, smaller group of children who can then provide assistance to other children subsequently wanting to participate. Polaroid pictures of children going through each of the steps in an activity can be taken, with sequential steps numbered and labeled. This contributes not only to children's autonomy in the classroom but also to their understanding of sequence involved in various processes of product development.

3. Use a variety of direction-giving strategies, such as pictographs for very young children and written instructions or verbal instructions on the tape recorder for older children.

4. Structure activities in which children can complete a project independently. One teacher had planned to make fruit salad with her preschoolers and considered eliminating the activity altogether when she learned that a parent volunteer was ill and would not be coming in to help. Instead, she slightly altered her original plans. She brought in only soft fruit, put it all in the water table, and provided plastic knives. She put footprints on the floor around the sides of the water table to indicate how many children were allowed to participate at any given time and explained these guidelines to the children in large group before learning center activities were made available. Thus, she was able to move ahead with the activity, which went very well with only periodic guidance on her part.

Deciding Which Centers to Make Available

How many centers to operate at any particular time will depend on physical space and the teacher's wish to limit or expand learning options for children. In general, at least 1½ center activity "slots" should be made available per child; for example, 20 children would require at least 30 activity spaces. In order to focus their attention more specifically on particular "projects," a teacher may wish to close down a more popular center temporarily. A useful way to decide which centers to include is to consider "generative possibilities: that is, which centers have the greatest potential to generate the greatest number of individual and group learnings and to produce the most developmental progress?" (McKee, 1990b, p. 34). These are activity centers that

- generate multiple and integrated learnings, such as physical, emotional, social, intellectual, linguistic, and aesthetic;
- invite enthusiastic participation in using materials and media;
- produce sustained interest and perseverance to a play task;
- whet and extend children's curiosities and appetites for continued learning;

- permit the expression and expansion of different intelligences (inherent talent) of individual children;
- permit use of convergent learning, or one approach and answer;
- permit use of divergent learning, or several approaches and answers;
- provide for multiple ways to solve problems in the physical, social, intellectual, and aesthetic realms;
- promote opportunities for positive feelings about one's abilities as a solitary player;
- promote opportunities for positive feelings about one's abilities as a group player, linking the self in interaction with others; and
- develop positive motivation toward school, teachers, and adult rules and expectations.

Planning Specific Lessons within a Center

The individual activities and experiences structured in each of the centers become important

---

Cognitive Activity

Step 1: *Intermediate objective.*	For children to develop finer degrees of sensory acuity.
Step 2: *Specific objectives.*	The children will (a) examine the paint chips and (b) practice seriating colors of varying intensity.
Step 3: *Materials.*	Two to four identical sets of paint color samples cut so that only one color shows on each segment. For younger children, select samples not much alike; for older children, select more samples and those closest in hue. Place each color group in an envelope.
Step 4: *Selected space.*	Place the materials in the table games center near a window to facilitate the most accurate sensory discrimination.
Step 5: *Directions.*	Show the children the contents in one of the envelopes. Invite them to seriate the colored chips, using a "problem-solving story" to stimulate their interest in the activity. Tell the children there will be other envelopes with chips they can work with and where these will be located. Plan to stop by the center during free choice.
Step 6: *Evaluation.*	Suggest that children work together to check the paint chips and determine whether any seem "out of order."
Step 7: *Adaptation.*	On a nearby shelf, place other materials that may be seriated on the basis of color, texture, or size, such as fabric swatches or attribute blocks. Add pencils and paper to the area so that children may make a record of their choices.

FIGURE 12.2
Constructing a Learning Center Activity

vehicles for cognitive, social-emotional, and affective development in children participating in centers. A step-by-step process for developing individual learning center activities might look something like this:

Step 1: Select an intermediate objective from one of the eight curricular domains.

Step 2: Identify three or four specific objectives to be addressed within the activity.

Step 3: Select the materials best suited to facilitate meeting the objectives.

Step 4: Select the learning center that is most suitable, taking into consideration electric outlets, tables, water access, storage, noise levels, and traffic patterns.

Step 5: Prepare directions for the children. Consider pictographs, written and oral directions.

Step 6: Plan how you will evaluate the children's use of the center, as well as the outcomes they achieve.

Step 7: Provide for more sophisticated adaptation of the activity.

An example of implementing this process in the cognitive domain can be seen in Figure 12.2.

The cognitive activity described in Figure 12.2 would complement the broad array of materials typically available in the table games center. The "paint chip" activity could be prominently displayed in one part of the center to pique children's interest. However, youngsters would also have access to additional games and manipulatives. After 2 or 3 days of being the featured activity, the paint chips might be made available on a shelf in the area, and another material could take center stage. In this way, teachers can draw children's attention to certain materials and tasks, while simultaneously giving them access to self-selected materials. Opportunities to revisit activities over time and combine materials into activities of their own creation are also provided.

Monitoring Children's Use of Centers

When moving to a center-based approach, good record keeping and evaluation will be important if the teacher is to have a clear idea of the accomplishments of each child within the group. Useful evaluation can take place through observation when children have complete freedom of choice, which is most often the case with very young children. Participation by older children may include teacher-assigned tasks to complete or choices from a few options so that specific processes or skills can be observed and documented.

There are several approaches that have been useful to professionals using the developmental approach. The first is to keep careful records of the activities available to children on a daily basis. The teacher first must have a clear idea of the overall goals and program objectives. Once these have been clearly developed and listed, activities planned to support them are briefly described and dated. Some teachers leave space for comments on how the activity worked out. This becomes a record of program presentations, but it does not provide information about individual involvement and performance.

Two approaches that can determine which activities children are selecting work fairly well. Participation charts can be developed that provide a systematic basis for recording such information. A list of children's names going down a page and a list of centers going across the page form a checklist that can be used quickly several times a week at different times during center activity to give a reasonable sample of children's involvement (see chap. 16, "Testing, Assessment, and Evaluation," for a more explicit example of this). Another strategy used is to provide a set of "tickets" for each child with his or her name written on them. These tickets are then deposited in a box or envelope in each of the centers as children enter the activity. The teacher determines the number of tickets that each child has available on a given day. The number of tickets is related to the amount of time for choice of activities and the time teachers think children will need in particular activities. This approach was highly successful for a group of children who had difficulty making choices and sticking to the choices they made. The teacher then recorded which children had been in which centers after they went home by checking them off as she picked up the tickets.

This approach is sometimes modified for older children by having two colors of tickets. One color represents the center or centers where the teacher expects *all* the children to participate during the day or week, and the other color may be used anywhere. The centers are clearly labeled with the color of tickets that may be used there. The teacher distributes a few of the color-coded tickets each day, and children are asked to use them only in specific centers. Although children may choose the teacher-indicated center at other times, they *must* choose it at least once during the period indicated by the teacher. In one first-grade classroom in Fort Wayne, Indiana, the first thing children do when they arrive each morning is to check the "learning center guide" written on the blackboard. This guide lets them know what centers will be available during the day. It also identifies the centers in which each child *must* participate, which vary from child to child. A sample of the learning center guide is provided in Table 12.1.

Children are free to choose any of the available centers. However, they must be sure to visit and complete the task in the center under which their names appear. When they have completed an activity that was listed as a "have-to," the children cross out their name on the board. In another class, with a similar schedule, children keep track of their have-to centers on a form that includes the week's activities (see Figures 12.3 and 12.4). These are then kept by each child in a folder from which he or she will select portfolio materials at the end of the week. The teacher determines have-to centers based on children's interests and learning needs. She changes the children's names daily so that youngsters have different have-to assignments each day.

Another technique used by some first-grade teachers who wanted to be sure language arts were highlighted was to have all of the alternative centers relate to reading skills during a 60- to 80-minute period of the day. Children were given pictographs (strips of paper with drawings in 1-inch segments) representing specific activities. The children colored in their pictographs as they completed each task. Less advanced children had shorter pictographs with three or four designated centers, and more advanced students had up to 10 segments. Teachers also placed a checkmark on the pictograph for some children, which indicated they needed to check with the teacher before coloring in the segment. Children later recorded their progress on a master pictograph of all children in the class.

Evaluating Skill Development.   To check on children's development of basic skills, some teachers select small groups of children and provide key activities that are instructional and provide information on child performance. These small-group activities are in operation during center activity, and the group of children selected will vary, depending on the teacher's objective and children's need for information. For example, one teacher noticed that four children were having difficulty leaving spaces between words in their journal writing. During center activity, she asked the four of them to come together to discuss the need for a strategy to help them remember and asked them what could be done. It was interesting that the children offered different "solutions." One suggested putting periods

TABLE 12.1
"Have-To" Centers

Painting	Listening	Computer	Reading	Games	Math	Journals	Cooperative Project
Tara	Megan	David	Leroy	Anne	Jerry	Carol	Beth
Lisa	Tom N.	Barry	Leslie	Sam	Ian	Cal	Sarah
Viola	Mark	Tom W.	Mara	Andy	Tara	Leroy	Ian
	Barry	Sarah	Cal	Carol	Beth	Sam	Lisa
	Jerry	Beth	Anne	Tom N.	Barry	Leslie	David
	Lisa		Megan	Viola	Andy	Mara	
			Mark			Sarah	

Activity Report	Week of _____
ART TABLE	**PRETEND PLAY**
BLOCKS/CONSTRUCTION	**PUZZLES**
BOOKS	**SNACK**
COMPUTER	**WOODWORKING**
EASEL	**WRITING**
MATH	

This is how I felt about the day:	Terrible	Sad	O.K.	Good	Terrific!
Monday	1	2	3	4	5
Tuesday	1	2	3	4	5
Wednesday	1	2	3	4	5
Thursday	1	2	3	4	5
Friday	1	2	3	4	5

FIGURE 12.3 Sample Activity Report

Source: From Donna Howe, Child Development Laboratories, Department of Family and Child Ecology, College of Human Ecology, Michigan State University. Adapted with permission.

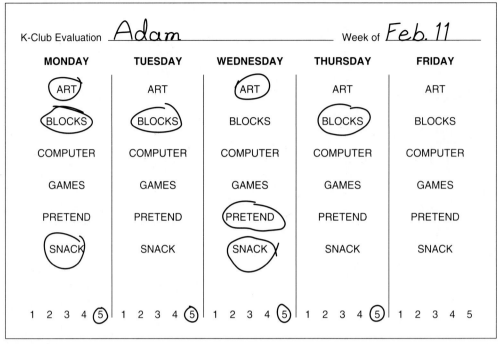

FIGURE 12.4
Sample Evaluation Form
Source: From Donna Howe, Child Development Laboratories, Department of Family and Child Ecology, College of Human Ecology, Michigan State University. Adapted with permission.

between each word to indicate a space. Another thought that hyphens would be helpful until she remembered simply to leave a space. The important thing here is that the children were involved in solving the problem rather than relying on the teacher to do so or being told the "correct" way to improve their writing. It did not take long for the four children to begin leaving spaces between their words, and the temporary aids they had devised—periods and hyphens—soon disappeared.

While teachers *could* include traditional reading groups during learning center activities, the technique of selective small-group structuring is more effective than the traditional maintenance of static groups (e.g., established reading groups such as the Bluebirds, Cardinals, and Orioles). Small groups of children are brought together for specific purposes and problem solving. These groups are as variable as the problems children are likely to encounter while growing in their conceptualization and competence in working with objects and people. Children are less apt to see themselves as "slow" or "only average" across an entire subject such as reading or math, as can happen when placement is based on ability grouping or tracking. Instead, they have opportunities to participate in diverse kinds of meetings with other children who are simply working on similar aspects of problem solving.

Teacher-made checklists are helpful in looking at individual and general class progress in any domain of interest. For example, a preschool teacher wanting to document evidence of social interaction listed each of the children's names across the top of an observation form and variables down the left-hand side such as "developing friendship skills," "initiating play/work with others," "cooperating with others," "helpful to others," and so forth. A clipboard containing the developed checklist was kept readily available over the next week, and when certain behaviors were observed, they were dated and documented. A second-grade teacher interested in whether or not children were picking up phonics skills made a listing of those he had been introducing to children in large and small groups through a variety of literature experiences. From this, he developed a checklist with spaces to record when a child had been introduced to the particular skill, when the child had participated in activities that supported development of the skills, and when the child demonstrated mastery of the skill.

As pointed out in chapter 16, "Testing, Assessment, and Evaluation," in which we have taken a more in-depth look at evaluation, there are a variety of strategies to look across children's developmental progress as they work independently and together in the learning centers. Teachers who elect to use center-based activity will find themselves free to hold many brief conferences with children to determine particular aspects of children's growth in knowledge and skill building.

Problems Related to Scheduling and Equipping Centers. Center-based activity is rarely implemented for the duration of a class day. Instead, preprimary and kindergarten teachers usually structure *at least* 45 to 60 minutes for centers. Breaking this up into more than one period (e.g., two 25-minute periods) is problematic; it tends to fracture children's concentration and ability to sustain involvement and interest. First- and second-grade teachers who work for an entire day with children often elect to have a 90-minute block of center time in both morning and afternoon or a 2-hour morning or afternoon block. Some elect to call it "project" time rather than center time and may give children certain tasks to accomplish during the time, although children are more free to work at their own levels and with other children in completion of the tasks.

As noted in chapter 11, there are no set rules about implementing centers in the early childhood setting. L. Katz (1987) suggests that a good rule of thumb about deciding how much class time is spent on direct or large-group instruction, small-group work, and individual activity is to divide the allotted time into thirds. When one considers how difficult it is to sit still

even for adults (remember the last conference you attended?), this is probably a reasonable guideline for structuring time allotments in *any* learning environment if we want good learner involvement and outcomes.

Effectively equipping a classroom with necessary materials, supplies, and equipment in order to carry out center-based activity will be critical for successful implementation. In some school districts where thousands of dollars had been allocated previously for workbooks and basal texts, teachers have often found themselves suddenly resource poor when they elected to replace more traditional learning activity with children's literature, logicomathematical materials and games, and hands-on science and cooking. "I'm being nickeled and dimed to death!" said one second-grade teacher. "I was told the money that had been originally slotted to second grade for curricular material is now being shifted to later elementary staff who will use it, since it *must* go for textbook purchases. They [administrators] have no idea how much it is costing me to get my classroom up to speed in order to use centers." This teacher's morale was at a low point. She felt she was making a supreme effort to program more effectively for children but was not getting the kind of support she needed from those who allocated resources for programming. She added that she and three of her second-grade colleagues are planning to do a little "attitude adjustment" on the part of their school principal and curriculum resource committee. They have made a list of activities they want to implement with the children for the following school year, comments about the particular skills and abilities each of the activities support, and a complete list of the supplies and equipment they will need for reasonable implementation.

SUMMARY

The benefits of carefully constructed learning centers in the early childhood setting are numerous, for both children and teachers. These specially designed learning arenas include core centers that children can experience on an ongoing basis and also special interest centers that are set up for shorter periods of time, based on children's interests and the purposes the teacher has in mind.

Implementation issues center on strategies for getting started, structuring self-sustaining centers, deciding which centers to make available at any particular time, and carefully planning specific activities for each center. Other issues to consider are monitoring children's use of the centers, evaluating the skill development that is taking place, and equipping the centers.

There is no doubt that center-based programming requires a great deal of planning on the part of the classroom teacher, and particularly creative planning. However, once a repertoire of activities have been designed, implemented, and evaluated, teachers may draw spontaneously from it to meet the interests and needs of the children they have in future sessions. This mode of programming allows professionals to form the most perfect match possible between the young learner's developmental abilities and curricular objectives. Center-based, thematic learning has great potential for providing solid beginnings for young children, beginnings that better ensure a lifelong zest for learning and optimal growth and development.

CHAPTER **13**

Theme Planning
and Implementation

Having gathered many kinds of rocks to make a classroom collection, the children and their teacher create a graph depicting color, size, and shape differences.

The children employ smooth, round rocks as tools to grind corn into meal. Later, they use the cornmeal to make fried mush.

The teacher reads a story about an artist who makes rock sculptures, then assists the children in recalling the sequence in which the sculpture was created. Next, children are given props to act out the events as they remember them.

A lively discussion takes place when the teacher asks the children to predict what they think will happen to two large rocks when one is placed in the shade and the other in the sunshine. She records the group's predictions, and after the experiments are carried out, children compare their ideas with the actual results.

The children create a classroom book in which they draw, dictate, or write descriptions of rocks found on a recent rock hunt.

These are typical activities one might see in any early childhood classroom from preschool through the early primary grades. All entail hands-on experiences for children and provide them with data or insights about rocks. They also give children opportunities to further develop such skills as observing, comparing, counting, predicting, remembering, role playing, expressing ideas, and developing fine motor control.

In one classroom such activities might be dispersed throughout the year; in another, offered within the framework of a multiweek theme focusing on rocks. Children experiencing either approach would profit from the activities and would probably increase their knowledge of rocks. However, youngsters involved in several rock-related activities within a short period would have the added advantage of being able to make connections among those activities that would be harder to make were the lessons more spread out over time. It is the creation of such linkages that is the essence of theme teaching (Kostelnik, Howe, et al., 1991).

THEME TEACHING DEFINED

Theme Teaching involves offering children an array of activities built around a central idea. Teachers select such ideas, keeping in mind children's interests, their developmental capacities, and the ecological context in which they live and learn. Related activities are integrated into all aspects of the curriculum and take place within a concentrated time frame. This creates a common thread among activities that facilitates children's generalization of knowledge and skills from one experience to another (Eliason & Jenkins, 1990; Machado & Meyer, 1984). Early childhood educators who implement themes well also incorporate into their teaching principles of developmentally appropriate programs as described throughout this volume. Such principles are the foundation on which effective theme teaching builds.

THE CONTRIBUTION OF THEMES TO CHILDREN'S CONCEPT DEVELOPMENT

Using themes to organize young children's school instruction is not a new idea. It is a method popular since Dewey first proposed that curriculum be related to children's real-life experiences. Since then, educators have looked to themes as a way to help children gain an overall sense of direction and consolidation in their learning (Hendrick, 1990). Through participation in a theme, children form linkages among individual bits of information. These relationships contribute to children's concept development and are the most important reason for advocating a theme-oriented approach to teaching (Bredekamp, 1991). *Concepts* are the fundamental ideas children form about objects and events in the world. They serve as the cognitive categories that allow children to group together perceptually distinct information, events, or objects (Welman, 1988). As such, concepts serve as the building blocks of knowing, thinking, and reasoning.

How Concepts Are Developed

Children form concepts through firsthand experiences (Lawton, 1987). Each time they act on objects or interact with other people, they extract relevant bits of meaning. These data fragments are stored in the mind to be combined with previously acquired knowledge and perceptions, clarify or modify current understandings, and, later, be used in assimilating new ideas (Hunt, 1961). By mentally cataloguing a growing number of experiences and making finer discriminations as well as more abstract connections among them, children build, adjust, and expand their concepts over time.

The Link between Concepts and Themes

The natural process of mentally connecting bits of information into more unified ideas is enhanced through children's engagement in theme-based instruction. Classrooms in which this kind of teaching goes on provide children with opportunities to integrate learning across several curricular areas simultaneously (Cummings, 1989). As they participate in math, science, language arts, or social studies activities permeated by the theme, children go beyond the bounds of traditional subject matter to form more holistic, comprehensive understandings (Hendrick, 1990). These understandings represent increasingly elaborate concepts. Because young children are continually striving to make sense of their environment, the early childhood years are ones of rapid concept development (Eliason & Jenkins, 1990). Consequently, educators are increasingly interested in helping young children make conceptual connections via an integrated school curriculum that also provides concept organizers such as themes, units, or projects (Bredekamp, 1991; Katz & Chard, 1989; Kovalik, 1986).

FURTHER ADVANTAGES TO CHILDREN

In addition to contributing to children's concept development, themes provide other advantages to young learners in early childhood programs. First, they offer children a means for exploring a central pool of information via many different routes. Regardless of whether children prefer small- or whole-group activities, active or passive modes of interaction, auditory, kinesthetic, visual, interpersonal, or intrapersonal experiences, they can gain access to a topic in ways attuned to their individual needs. If one activity is unappealing, if it does not match their learning style, or if it fails to suit their capacities, it is not the only chance children have to learn about the concept. They may pursue alternate activities instead, gaining similar insight. Such is not the case when ideas are presented only once or through a singular means.

Themes also allow children to immerse themselves in a topic. As youngsters become interested in an idea, they often want to know all about it. Exploring a theme-based concept satisfies this desire. It also enhances children's disposition to become mentally absorbed in pursuing ideas (Katz & Chard, 1989).

Keeping the early childhood curriculum varied and interesting is another value of theme teaching. Both children and teachers experience a sense of novelty with each new topic. As themes change, so too do props, activities, and room decorations, which reinvigorates daily routines. Not only do new themes spawn original activities, but the same or similar activities are afforded a fresh emphasis as they are used to support different topics.

Additionally, group cohesiveness is promoted when children focus on a particular topic simultaneously. Children who have experiences and knowledge in common develop a nucleus of mutual interests that provides a natural context for cooperative learning. As children discover classmates whose interests match their own, their social circles widen. Their perceptions of one another broaden also because with each theme change, different children act as novices and experts; youngsters who are leaders for one topic may be followers for another. Thus, their patterns of interaction vary, which allows each youngster an opportunity to experience varying social roles.

Finally, children's changing interests are accommodated throughout the year via theme teaching. As children become excited about new ideas, those ideas can be highlighted throughout the curriculum. This gives children the message that their ideas are valuable and worth exploring. Also, themes developed in response to the expressed interests of some children in the class may spark the curiosity of their peers; children's notions of what is worth investigating are thus enlarged.

TEACHER BENEFITS

Themes give practitioners a focus around which to plan. This helps them organize their thinking, encourages them to choose relevant activities to support theme-related goals, and enables them to seek out resources prior to unit implementation. All of these factors tend to increase teachers' confidence in planning an integrated array of educational activities for young children (Cummings, 1989).

Another advantage is that theme teaching enables educators to address topics in sufficient breadth and depth to feel assured that each child has had a chance to learn something new. Both of these dimensions are enhanced by having multiple theme-related activities in a variety of curricular domains. Such cross coverage allows teachers to structure the presentation of concepts more coherently and devise sequential plans that gradually challenge children's thinking (Eliason & Jenkins, 1990).

Along with stimulating children's cognitive powers, a traditional component of the instructor's role is continually to assess how well children grasp concepts addressed within the curriculum (Whiren, 1990). Early childhood teachers are expected to carry out this responsibility whether or not they use theme teaching. They do so by observing children and interacting with them individually and in groups. Attempting to evaluate children's concept development on a child-by-child basis, with no unifying framework within which to make judgments, is very difficult because it is so fragmented. On the other hand, such assessments are more easily accomplished when the practitioner has a unifying concept on which to focus. Seeing and hearing many children within the group demonstrate varying understandings of the same concept provides a context for the teacher's judgments. For instance, the adult is better able to determine whether children's incomplete or erroneous ideas are universal or particular to an individual. He or she can also gauge which of several activities enhances or detracts from children's grasp of a particular idea. This is harder to accomplish within a totally unrelated set of activities.

Additionally, teachers who approach theme planning appropriately research each topic, generating a pool of factual information on which to build instruction. This increases the adult's knowledge base as well as the accuracy of the information provided to children. Further, it allows practitioners to consider in advance how to handle sensitive issues associated with the theme and prompts them to think of original activity ideas. Practitioners find this process intellectually stimulating. The collegiality that sometimes arises when educators collaborate on developing thematic units is also pleasing. Brainstorming theme-related activities, problem solving in relation to the theme, sharing props, and swapping written plans are time-saving, invigorating activities that teachers find rewarding. For these reasons, practitioners report that theme teaching is very self-satisfying (Kostelnik, Palmer, & Hannon, 1987).

PROGRAM EFFECTS

We have seen that theme teaching can enhance both children's and practitioners' educational experiences, but there are also some benefits with programwide ramifications.

First, it is useful to note that theme teaching can be implemented across diverse program structures, among children of all ages, with youngsters whose needs differ greatly, and by teachers whose philosophies and styles vary too (Bredekamp, 1991). This universal applicability provides a common bond between programs and increases the potential for collaboration among professionals. Conversely, because educators create themes with a specific group of children in mind, such instruction is very individualized and meets the autonomy needs of both children and teachers.

Second, family members who are kept informed of upcoming themes are better able to contribute their knowledge, expertise, and resources to children's educational experiences. It is often easier for them to envision how to participate in children's schooling with a particular topic in mind than to do so in terms of the more generalized instruction that takes place from day to day (Kostelnik, Howe, et al., 1991). Consequently, family support for the program may go beyond the traditional donations of discarded meat trays and toilet paper rolls. For instance, knowing the class is studying birds, a family may send in a bird's nest they found, a photograph of a bird taken at their feeder, or a magazine article about birds. An older sibling may help the children build bird feeders, or a grandparent may show the children how to care for a baby bird fallen from its nest. This kind of family involvement promotes constructive home-school relationships and helps parents and other family members feel more involved in the educational process.

The third and perhaps most important programwide impact of theme teaching is that it provides a tool by which content learning and process learning can be integrated within the curriculum. Often treated as mutually exclusive categories of knowledge, theme teaching is a means by which the two can be synthesized without violating the integrity of either one.

Focusing on Content

Content learning consists of the social-conventional knowledge around which each theme is planned. As such, it encompasses all of the factual information relevant to the theme. Learning content requires such mental abilities as attending, listening, observing, remembering, and recounting (Hendrick, 1990). Thus, a group of first graders studying wild birds might engage in a variety of experiences to learn the following facts:

- Birds live in a variety of places—woods, meadows, plains, deserts—near ponds, lakes, and oceans; or in cities.
- Each species of bird builds a nest characteristic of the species.
- Birds build nests to protect their eggs, which contain baby birds.
- Birds build nests of varying complexities.
- Different bird species build their nests in different places—on the ground, above the ground, in the open, or hidden.

Simple exposure to factual content such as this does not teach in and of itself. It is only when children become motorically involved in, talk about, and reflect on their experiences that they learn from them (Elkind, 1988a; Short, 1991). Thus, children might gain access to factual knowledge about wild birds through hands-on activities such as going outdoors to watch

birds nest and fly, recording the numbers and kinds of birds they see, or examining several different abandoned bird's nests. Teachers might also give children make-believe wings and straw to use in acting like birds caring for their young, or they could work with children to construct a replica of a bird's nest. Throughout these activities, teachers and children also would talk and exchange ideas about which type of bird might build which type of nest, which would thereby promote children's content learning further.

Focusing on Process

All of the aesthetic, affective, cognitive, language, social, and physical operations and skills that form the infrastructure for children's experiences within the early childhood classroom comprise process learning. Because they encompass the "whole" child, such processes range from imagining, creating, and performing, to grouping, differentiating, inferring, and concluding, to pretending and constructing. Just as with content learning, children gain proficiency in process learning through hands-on activities. In fact, the same activities cited earlier could provide the means for increased competence and understanding in any domain.

Integrating Content and Process

Content (expressed via factual information related to the theme) and process (expressed by the goals associated with each domain) come together in the activities teachers plan. These activities form the basis for instruction and offer children an applied means for experiencing the curriculum. Thus, two children engaged in acting out the roles of wild birds not only gain factual insight into bird life but also have opportunities to practice processes such as offering ideas ("You be the baby bird, I'll be the mommy"), reaching compromises ("OK, I'm the mommy bird first, then you"), and drawing conclusions ("If we have two mommy birds, we'll need two nests"). Likewise, we know that during the early childhood period, often the content included in each activity is simply the medium through which children explore other, more process-oriented operations and skills (Hendrick, 1990). Consequently, even when children are involved in theme-related activities, it is not always the thematic content that captures their attention. They may be much more involved in the process learning represented within that experience.

Furthermore, although teachers usually have a domain-specific set of goals for each activity they plan, children frequently proceed from that original aim to explore processes within the activity related to other domains. Moving from content to process or from one process to another are both natural, appropriate ways for children to expand their knowledge and skills. Yet, such adaptations do not mean teachers should simply provide generic activities with no real content learning or process learning goals in mind. Rather, practitioners must be purposeful in their planning. This assists children in exploring facts and processes they might not otherwise experience and ensures a coherent, comprehensive set of activities from which children may choose. The integrative nature of such activities is well suited to the integrative manner in which children learn.

THE NEGATIVE SIDE OF THEME TEACHING

In view of all the pluses cited thus far, it may appear that theme teaching is automatically an appropriate educational practice. Unfortunately, that is not always true. Themes can be enacted poorly (Goetz, 1985; Hendrick, 1990). For instance, some teachers may violate the tenets of developmentally appropriate practice by failing to accommodate children's needs for movement and physical activity, social interaction, and independence. They may ignore certain domains or assume that theme teaching involves simply coordinating their ditto sheets around a single idea. Another pitfall arises when teachers, determined to get across the "facts," rely on reciting them to children rather than providing opportunities for children to engage in content learning through hands-on activities.

A second problem occurs when teachers select themes that fail to support children's concept development. That happens when topics are too narrow or when the linkages between the topic and the activities are contrived. This causes the theme to lack the depth and substance necessary to stimulate children's thinking. One such instance is exemplified by weekly plans centered around a letter of the alphabet, such as G. As children paint with green tempera at the easel, eat grapes for snack, and growl like lions, the teacher may confidently believe that youngsters are learning all about the letter G. In reality, the children may be focusing on the subject of their paintings rather than on the color, they may be thinking of grapes as fruit rather than a G word, and they may be more aware of the loudness or mock ferocity of their growling than the consonant sound they are making. Since G is not a concept and does not directly relate to children's real-life experiences, these are poor attempts at theme teaching.

Misdirected attempts at dealing with content are a third source of poor theme use. Some teachers so value content over process that the integrated, child-centered nature of appropriate themes is negated. Others take the opposite position, ignoring content learning altogether. This happens when practitioners thoughtlessly create a theme based on conventional wisdom but with no real data to support it. A similar outcome occurs when teachers assume that a few decorations and craft projects equal theme teaching. In both cases not enough attention is paid to conveying accurate, meaningful information to children. As a result, children are not exposed to valuable content that could be relevant to them. Worse, they may even obtain inaccurate facts from teachers whose general store of knowledge is inadequate to support the theme.

Finally, some teachers assume they are theme teaching well when they relate several activities to a central prop, such as pockets (Cummings, 1989). Children may sing about having a smile in their pocket, hear a story about pockets, eat "pocket bread," for snack, and decorate paper pockets. Yet, there is little relevant factual knowledge for them to extract from these experiences, and the process learning involved is perfunctory. Although the activities may keep children busy or entertained, they fail to engage their minds in the challenge of real learning. Since this type of theme planning addresses neither content learning nor process learning, its educational value is limited.

PRINCIPLES THAT GUIDE EFFECTIVE THEME TEACHING

Effective theme teaching is much more complex and comprehensive than any of the misdirected approaches just described (Cummings, 1989). It can be achieved without undesirable side effects when the following principles are incorporated into teacher's planning and implementation with children (Deardon, 1984; Goetz, 1985; Katz & Chard, 1989; Kostelnik, Howe, et al., 1991).

1. The theme is directly tied to children's real-life experiences, building on what they know and what they want to know more about.
2. Each theme represents a concept for children to investigate. Throughout its implementation, the teacher helps children build theme-related concepts rather than expecting children to memorize isolated bits of information.
3. Every theme is supported by factual content that has been adequately researched.
4. All themes integrate content learning and process learning.
5. Theme-related information is conveyed to children through hands-on activities and active inquiry.
6. Theme-related activities represent a variety of curricular domains and differing modes of child involvement.
7. Children have access to the same content more than once and in more than one way.
8. The theme allows for the integration of several curricular areas within the program.
9. Each theme is expanded or revised in accordance with children's demonstrated interests and understandings.

When these principles are kept in mind, the negative outcomes associated with theme teaching are eliminated while the benefits are maintained.

HOW TO CREATE THEMATIC UNITS

Sources of Ideas

Ideas for potential classroom themes have many sources: the children themselves, special events, unexpected happenings, school-mandated content, and teachers and parents.

Children's Interests.   The best source of thematic ideas are the children themselves. The things children frequently enact, discuss, or wonder about offer the most appropriate source of theme selection. Teachers discover what interests children by talking with them informally, observing them, and listening as they talk with one another. Practitioners may also engage in more formal means of assessing children's interests, such as interviewing them or initiating brainstorming sessions in which children generate ideas regarding topics they would like to investigate. In addition, information from parents regarding upcoming events in children's lives or events at home provide clues about which concepts will be important to children throughout the year.

By considering these kinds of issues, teachers might introduce the theme "Machines" based on children's interest in the heavy equipment they observed at a nearby construction site. The birth of new siblings to one or more families in the class might precipitate a unit on babies. The children's frequent discussions about who can play with whom could serve as the impetus for developing a theme on friends. It is ordinary events like these that are important to young children and so provide the strongest foundation for planning and implementing themes in the classroom.

Special Events.   Occasionally, out-of-the-ordinary occurrences such as the school's annual farm trip, an assembly featuring leader dogs for the blind, or the celebration of Arbor Day could also serve as the impetus for theme development. Occasions like these, which teachers know about in advance, may be integrated into or serve as the cornerstone for related units of study such as "Farm Products," "Working Dogs," or "Trees."

Unexpected Happenings.   At other times, unanticipated events stimulate children's thinking in new directions. Such was the case for kindergartners intrigued by the habits of a grackle whose nest was in the eavestrough above their classroom window. The teacher responded to their curiosity by introducing a unit on wild birds, using the grackle as a firsthand example. Along similar lines, a sudden hailstorm

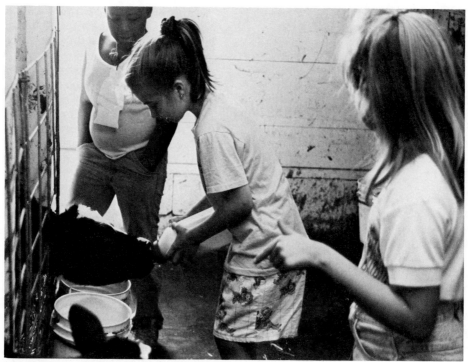

This field trip resulted from the children's interest in animals and gave them a firsthand experience with the "real" thing.

prompted so many questions from children that a unit on weather followed naturally.

School-mandated Content.   In addition to child-instigated content, most school districts require particular subject matter to be addressed at given grade levels. Such required content can also serve as the basis for thematic teaching. Social studies, science, health, math, or language arts concepts can be used as the core around which a variety of theme-related activities are created and integrated throughout the school day. This approach has the advantage of ensuring that important but sometimes neglected subjects like science, social studies, and health receive adequate attention. Moreover, teachers gain the satisfaction of covering prescribed material in ways that are meaningful to children.

Teacher/Parent Interests.   Theme ideas may also have their source in concepts important to teachers and parents. A teacher en-

thralled by the stars may seek to share his enthusiasm via a unit on the nighttime sky. The teacher's desire to teach children constructive ways of working together could be the motivation behind the theme "Cooperation." Apprehension expressed by parents regarding child sexual abuse might stimulate the development of a unit on personal safety.

Obviously, themes originate from many different sources. Furthermore, the number of potential topics usually exceeds the time available to teach them. Thus, certain additional criteria must be considered when narrowing down one's choices to the actual units children will experience throughout the year.

Criteria for Unit Selection

When finalizing an idea for a theme, teachers should consider four factors:

- relevance to children,
- hands-on activities,

- diversity and balance across the curriculum, and
- the availability of theme-related props (Deardon, 1984; Kostelnik, Howe, et al., 1991).

Relevance. Of these criteria, the most important is relevance. Themes are relevant when the concepts they represent are directly tied to children's real-life experiences and build on their interests. Such thematic units usually highlight concepts with which children are familiar and provide new insights into their daily experiences. Therefore, themes like "Self," "Home," "Family," "Foods," "Plants," or "Night and Day," are relevant because they help children make sense of their own lives and expand their understanding of life around them. On the other hand, for most children in the United States, themes centering on life in ancient Rome or children in Sweden are too far removed from their day-to-day living to be relevant. Thus, the early childhood period would not be the time to introduce these kinds of themes.

Naturally, themes become even more meaningful when their content is adapted to the needs of particular groups of children. Locale as well as family and community resources or traditions will influence which aspects of the concept are most pertinent. For instance, the theme "Plants" has relevance for most children no matter where they live. Yet, children growing up close to a marsh would find it most comprehensible to focus on cattails, marsh grass, and milkweed as examples of plant life, while youngsters living in an arid region would find it more relevant to study desert vegetation such as cacti, sagebrush, and yucca plants. Likewise, it is the principle of relevance that makes backyard birds more relevant for most children than exotic varieties with which they have had no experience. Moreover, entire topics, relevant to one group of young children, may be irrelevant to others. For example, studying tidal pools could be a significant learning experience for children living in Kennebunk, Maine, but not so for those in Lansing, Michigan. Having never seen a tidal pool, the latter group would benefit from studying a more familiar water habitat, such as the pond.

In each of the preceding examples, thematic relevance is determined by suitability of subject matter. Another attribute of relevance is timeliness. Timely themes build on children's current interests. Thus, rather than planning a year of themes in advance, teachers create units, a few at a time, in response to children's expressed curiosity or concerns. Additionally, timeliness prompts some teachers to substitute one theme for another in order to take advantage of an opportune event or deal with shifts in children's needs.

Such was the case in the following situation. A group of first graders attending the International School in Hong Kong were deeply engrossed in a unit on folktales. During that same time they learned that a dinosaur skeleton had been found in the Gobi Desert of China. While discussing these events, several children wondered whether the dragons they heard about in Chinese stories were based on real dinosaurs. This notion elicited much interest among the group. Capitalizing on their excitement, the teacher substituted a dinosaur theme for the poetry unit she had originally planned to come next. Delaying attention to dinosaurs or ignoring children's hypotheses would have resulted in missed learning opportunities. It was the timeliness of the dinosaur theme in relation to the children's expressed interest that made it so relevant to these youngsters.

Hands-On Activities. A second criterion for theme selection is how well the content lends itself to the creation of related hands-on activities. Only units whose content children can experience through the direct manipulation of objects are suitable for children in the early childhood period. Hands-on activities come in three varieties: firsthand experiences, simulations, and projects.

Firsthand experiences are ones in which children become directly involved with the actual objects or phenomena under study. These are real, not analogous or imaginary experiences. Consequently, they afford children opportunities to derive relevant bits of information from the original source of the concept. For instance, youngsters engaged in the theme "Pets" would gain firsthand insights into the life and activities of pets by observing and caring for pets in the classroom. A visit to a pet shop to see the variety of pets available or a trip to a veterinarian to see how pet health is maintained are other examples of these real-life experiences. Simply looking at pictures or hearing about these things could not replicate the richness or stimulation provided via firsthand involvement. Firsthand activities are so essential to children's concept development that teachers should avoid themes for which few such lessons are possible. In other words, when teachers know children have had no direct experience with the theme and they themselves are unable to provide related firsthand activities at school, the theme is not appropriate for that group. All themes should include several real examples of the concept for children to explore at school.

Simulations are another hands-on activity type. They approximate but do not exactly duplicate firsthand experiences. Providing make-believe ears and tails so children could enact life as a pet or working with children to construct a replica of a veterinarian's office using toy animals are examples of simulations. In each case children act directly on objects or carry out activities that resemble the real thing. Although one step removed from the original concept, simulations give children access to data that, for safety or logistical reasons, they have no other means to discover.

Projects are a third way to provide hands-on experiences with the theme. These are open-ended activities in which youngsters undertake, over a period of days, the in-depth study of some facet of the theme (Katz & Chard, 1989). Ideas for which projects to pursue emerge from the children as they gain experience with the concept and become curious about particular aspects of it. Projects are not predetermined by the adult. Rather, as children's interests evolve, individual or small groups of children, in consultation with the teacher, plan then carry out a relevant project. For example, children involved in the pet theme might decide to create a catalog of all the different pets owned by children in the class then use it to create graphs, stories, and displays related to their investigation. Building a model of an animal hospital following a visit to one in the community is another project possibility. Small groups of children might choose to examine different aspects of the real setting then take responsibility for re-creating it back in the classroom. Project work requires sustained

effort and involves such learning processes as exploring, investigating, hypothesizing, reading, recording, discussing, and evaluating. Not only are they child initiated, but projects also give children many chances to plan, select manageable tasks for themselves, apply skills, and monitor their own progress. More structured than spontaneous play and more self-determined than teacher-planned instruction, projects provide a bridge between the two modes. They offer children strategies for exploring the theme in ways that are individualized and, therefore, personally meaningful.

Finally, in addition to making sure that each theme incorporates the three hands-on activity types described here, it is also important to consider the degree to which potential activities represent varying instructional modes. For example, themes that prompt many craft ideas but that are not well suited to pretend play, games, or problem-solving activities should be rejected as too limited. Teachers are advised to select instead themes conducive to activities representing several of the curricular domains presented in this text.

Diversity and Balance within the Curriculum. During the course of the school year it is desirable for children to experience a broad array of themes. As teachers contemplate potential themes, diversity across the curriculum and balance within it become another criteria for consideration.

For example, some themes are primarily scientific in nature (e.g., seasons, machines, leaves, insects, fish), others reflect a social studies emphasis (e.g., families, friends, occupations, the neighborhood), still others highlight language arts content (e.g., storytelling, poetry, writers), some focus primarily on mathematical ideas (e.g., stores, measuring), and some are more health oriented (e.g., foods, dental hygiene, fitness). Furthermore, many topics can be adapted to fit one or more of these foci depending on what intrigues the children and what the teacher chooses to emphasize. A unit on stores, for example, could stress the mathematical content of money and counting, the more social aspects of employees working together toward a common goal, or the health-related focus of safety in the store. It would be possible to deal with these ideas separately, sequentially, or in combination.

In selecting themes, teachers should choose a cross section of topics in which all of the preceding content areas are eventually addressed. Over time, this gives children opportunities to expand their concepts and skills across a wide range of subjects, with no one predominating. It is both diversity and balance the teacher has in mind when in response to children's fascination with the space shuttle, she plans a natural science unit on the sky to be followed by a theme on space exploration in which social cooperation is the primary focus. In this case children initiated the original idea for the themes, but the teacher influenced their direction.

Resources. Availability of props and other support materials is a fourth consideration in determining what themes to carry out (Kovalik, 1986). Since children need objects to act on, it is best to choose themes for which several such items are obtainable. Relevant materials might be accumulated over time as well as solicited from parents, libraries, museums, and so forth. Also, when fellow teachers pool or trade props, the number and variety of materials at their disposal greatly increases.

Themes for which no real objects are available for children to use are best dropped from consideration. This is also true for units that depend on one spectacular prop, such as a hang glider or spinning wheel, which, if suddenly unavailable, would spell ruin for the entire theme. Better themes to develop are those for which a variety of props can be made easily accessible to the children.

Creating an Information Base

The core of every theme is the factual information on which it is founded. This information is embodied in a comprehensive list of terms, facts, and principles (TFPs) relevant to the theme. *Terms* are vocabulary used to describe theme-related objects and events (e.g., a *lamb* is a baby sheep, or *piglet* is the name given to a baby pig). Something known to exist or to have happened is a *fact* (e.g., sheep give birth to lambs; pigs give birth to piglets). *Principles* refer to combinations of facts and the relationships among them (e.g., animals only give birth to

their own kind). Although the TFPs embody the theme, adults do not recite them to children. Children learn TFP-related content by participating in the hands-on activities through which it is conveyed. As youngsters engage in such experiences they gain meaningful insights that enlarge their concepts.

To be useful, TFPs must be accurate and thorough. Five steps are suggested for creating a suitable listing.

Step 1: Select a theme. Keep in mind relevance to children, hands-on activities, the issues of diversity and balance in the curriculum, and the potential availability of theme-related props.

Step 2: Use reference books, trade books, program-adopted textbooks, children's books, or other people as resources. From these, generate a master list of TFPs. Begin by writing down every item that seems cogent to the theme. At this point, do not worry about differentiating terms, facts, or principles. Simply list relevant bits of information.

Step 3: As the list grows, if subtopics become obvious, group the TFPs accordingly. For instance, a unit on clothing might include the following subtopics: (a) the functions of clothing, (b) the origins of clothing, (c) how people select clothing, (d) types of clothing, and (e) where clothing can be obtained.

An alternative approach to steps 2 and 3 is to create a topic web (see Figure 13.1). Create the web by brainstorming logical subtopics for the theme first, then look up TFPs to support each one.

Step 4: Based on your understanding of the children's interests and abilities, decide whether a general overview or a more in-depth study of one of the subtopics is best suited to your class. If the former is true, choose a few TFPs from each of the subcategories; if the latter is your choice, focus primarily on one subset of TFPs.

Step 5: Pick 10 to 15 TFPs on which to focus directly. Use the others simply as background information or as a guide in

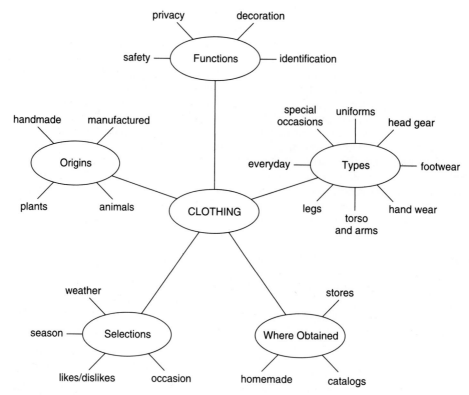

FIGURE 13.1
Initial Topic Web for "Clothing" Theme

responding to children's queries regarding the topic.

Once these five steps have been accomplished, it is time to create activities to address the TFPs.

Developing Activity Ideas

The steps for developing appropriate theme-related activities are straightforward and not nearly as time-consuming as those required to create TFPs.

Step 6: Focusing on the 10 to 15 TFPs selected for a particular unit, brainstorm activities that could be used to convey each one. Go through the TFPs one at a time, generating two or three activities per item before going on to the

next. Carry out this exercise with a colleague or in a small group to enhance the richness and variety of the activities generated.

Step 7: Assign each activity to one of the eight curricular domains described in this text, making sure to put at least one activity under each domain. Use the theme-planning worksheet provided in Figure 13.2 as a tool for organizing your ideas.

Notice that depending on how you structure it, the same activity could be adapted to more than one domain. Thus a clothing collage, designed to help children become familiar with clothing that protects the body, could take on a social focus if children were asked to cooperate as a group to create one large collage. On the other hand,

---

Name of Theme: _____

Content Areas:

1. *Aesthetic*—Focus on stimulating children's appreciation of the arts and nature.

2. *Affective*—Focus on promoting self-awareness and positive self-esteem.

3. *Cognitive*—Focus on expanding children's perceptual, conceptual, and problem-solving skills.

4. *Language*—Focus on increasing children's ability to represent thoughts, ideas, feelings, and perceptions via language.

5. *Social*—Focus on teaching children to develop more successful patterns of interaction and gain greater self-understanding.

6. *Physical*—Focus on improving children's gross motor and fine motor skills as well as contributing to a positive body image.

7. *Pretend Play*—Focus on providing opportunities for children to engage in role playing, make-believe, and dramatization.

8. *Construction*—Focus on enabling children to create a tangible product that represents their own interpretation of an object or event.

FIGURE 13.2
Theme-planning Worksheet

giving each child his or her own collage to work on, along with several different cutting tools, would place a greater emphasis on the fine motor aspects of the activity, making it more physical in nature. Alternately, if the structure of the collage activity emphasized children following step-by-step verbal directions, the focus would shift to listening skills and therefore the language domain.

Step 8: After all the activities have been assigned to domains, make certain that they represent varying modes of presentation such as firsthand experiences, simulations, projects, demonstrations, discussions, and small- and whole-group activities. If you become aware that the activities are dominated by passive means of participation such as watching or listening, reconstruct some of them to include more hands-on involvement for children.

Making a Plan

Once the TFPs and activities have been fully developed, it is time to put them altogether into a thematic plan. Such a plan typically covers no less than 1 week's instruction and may be extended for several weeks after that. Ways to determine how long a unit should last will be described later in this chapter. The following steps outline the actual planning process.

Step 9: Commit your ideas to paper, incorporating several theme-related activities into your lesson plans. It is easiest to review plans when the entire week is represented on a single page. Consider what time of the day certain activities will take place and whether each will be presented once or over several days. Design additional non-theme-related activities to fill in the rest of the instructional time and give children some respite from the theme. Remember, it is better to have fewer well-developed theme-related activities than to contrive to make every activity fit the theme.

Step 10: Check your plan to be sure there are at least two theme-related activities every day and that by week's end all of the domains have been included.

Step 11: Tell specialists such as the physical education instructor and the art and music teachers the content of your theme. Explore with them ways they might support or complement children's concept development in their designated time with the class.

Step 12: Consider classroom management issues such as availability of materials, numbers of adults available to help, and special events. Make adjustments in your plan if necessary. For instance, if you have scheduled easel painting and tie-dying for the same day and time but have only three smocks in your room, move one of these activities to another time in the day or to another day altogether so you will have enough smocks for children at both areas.

Step 13: Plan a portion of a circle time to focus on the theme each day. Such whole-group activities allow children to become aware of certain concept-related information simultaneously, which provides a common foundation for explo-

ration. Carried out at the beginning of class time, circle activities serve as an introduction to the day's experiences. Conducted at the end, they give children a chance to review and summarize their current understandings of the theme. Teachers whose daily schedules do not include circle times should consider adding them to their routines as another valuable means for acquainting children with particular facets of the concepts being emphasized (McAfee, 1985).

Step 14: Make a final check of your written plan, focusing on how well you have addressed the TFPs. Tally how often you have used each one. Refer back to your original brainstorming list if you need a reminder of which activities relate to which TFPs. Verify that each TFP has received attention at least three or four times during the week. Also make sure that individual TFPs have been addressed within different domains across the plan. If you notice that some domains are seldom theme related or that certain TFPs are always addressed within the same domain, revise your plan to achieve better integration. In ad-

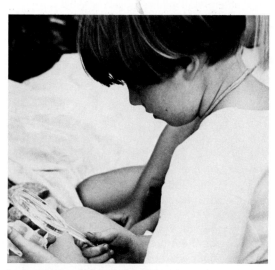

The children's interest in a theme on tools has led them to examine rocks found near their school.

dition, if you realize that some TFPs have been left out or are underrepresented, either add a few related activities or extend the theme another week, focusing on these TFPs as well as some additional ones to give the children more time to explore the concept. In this way you can build 2-, 3-, and 4-week units.

Step 15: After your plan is complete, gather your materials. Create any props you will need. Make an effort to use some props for more than one activity as a way to minimize preparation time.

Step 16: Create a thematic atmosphere in your classroom. Post theme-associated pictures at children's eye level. Choose records, books, finger plays, and songs related to the topic.

Implementing the Theme

Once you have a sound plan, implement the theme with children. Use the following steps to guide your actions.

Step 17: Carry out your plan. Also, take advantage of spontaneous events that may further children's understanding of the concept they are exploring.

Step 18: Assess children's understanding and interest in the theme through observations, interviews, and group discussions. Make note (either mentally and/or through brief written anecdotes) of times when children talk about the theme, when they exhibit theme-related behaviors and knowledge, and when parents mention incidents illustrating children's awareness of and reactions to the topic. If a free-choice or learning center period is part of your day, keep track of the activities children choose and the amount of time they spend there. A participation chart is a good tool for maintaining this type of record (described in chap. 16).

Step 19: Talk with children about what they want to know more about. Help them develop projects to address their questions and areas of curiosity.

Step 20: Consider extending the theme if children's interest remains high. As children demonstrate understanding and curiosity about the subject matter, introduce additional TFPs in subsequent weeks.

Step 21: Establish two-way communication with parents about the theme. Provide theme-related information to them via newsletters. Invite parents to contribute materials or their talents to the classroom. Suggest ways in which parents might support the theme at home.

Step 22: Evaluate your implementation of the theme using the theme teaching checklist presented in Figure 13.3. Write down the changes you made in your plan and what you might do differently were you to repeat it in the future.

The entire process of developing a theme, from the initial steps of creating the TFPs to evaluating its implementation, is summarized in Figure 13.4.

COMMON QUESTIONS TEACHERS ASK ABOUT THEME TEACHING

Teachers, newly involved in theme teaching, often have questions regarding this process. What follows are their most common queries.

Does every activity have to relate to the theme?

No. In fact, it is preferable to create a mix of theme-based and non-theme-related activities each week. If the classroom is overly saturated by a given topic, the subject matter loses its appeal for children and teachers alike. Moreover, the link between activities and the concept becomes contrived rather than obvious and real. Finally, children are deprived of additional content or process-learning experiences, from which they would benefit but which are not theme oriented.

To avoid these pitfalls, intersperse several non-theme-related activities throughout your weekly plan. Reprising children's favorites, reviewing past experiences, and including subject-based activities whose content is mandated by

Purpose: To help teachers assess the effectiveness of theme implementation in their classrooms

Directions: Put a *1* by each item that accurately depicts the classroom being observed. Total the items to achieve a final score.

Score	Level of Effectiveness
23–25	Excellent use of themes
20–22	Good use of themes; minor additions could make it better
17–19	OK start; gradually address missing items in order to improve
16 and below	Poor use of themes; major revisions necessary

Theme-related Activities

☐ 1. The theme planner can articulate the relevance of the theme to the children with whom it is being carried out.

☐ 2. The theme-related information conveyed to children is accurate.

☐ 3. The theme-related information conveyed to children is meaningful (of interest to them and age appropriate in terms of vocabulary and detail).

☐ 4. Two or more theme-related *firsthand* experiences are made available to children each week.

☐ 5. At least two theme-related activities are made available to children everyday.

☐ 6. Theme-related activities take place at different times throughout the day.

☐ 7. Every week at least one theme-related activity has been included for each of the eight domains.

☐ 8. Opportunities for children to apply, synthesize, and summarize what they have learned about the theme are made available throughout the week.

Child Involvement

☐ 9. Children are talking about the theme (offering information, asking questions, conversing with peers and adults).

☐ 10. Children are pretending in relation to the theme.

☐ 11. Children are creating theme-related products of their own invention.

☐ 12. Children report discussing or playing the theme at home.

☐ 13. Children demonstrate linking the theme to their past or current experiences either motorically or verbally.

☐ 14. Parents report that children have discussed or played out the theme at home.

☐ 15. Children continue to refer to the theme or demonstrate knowledge of its content after the unit is over.

Classroom Environment

☐ 16. TFPs are posted or otherwise available for adult reference.

☐ 17. Children's own theme-related creations (projects, writings, etc.) are hanging up or otherwise displayed in the room.

☐ 18. Theme-related props are available to the children each day.

☐ 19. Theme-related pictures, songs, poems, books, and other such items are used to create a thematic atmosphere.

☐ 20. One circle time each day is theme related.

☐ 21. The theme-related purpose of the circle time is made clear to the children.

☐ 22. Theme-related circle time activities include active child participation.

Parent Involvement

☐ 23. Parents are provided with information about the theme.

☐ 24. Parents are invited to contribute to the theme.

☐ 25. Parents receive feedback regarding children's interest and participation in the theme.

FIGURE 13.3
Theme Teaching Checklist

Selecting a Theme

1. Observe children, talk with them informally, interview children, or engage in group discussions to gauge children's interest and needs. Based on your understanding of children's capacities and preferences, choose a theme.

Creating the TFPs

2. Generate a master list of TFPs.
3. Cluster the TFPs with subtopics or create a topic web, then generate the relevant TFPs.
4. Based on your knowledge of the children, choose a general overview of several subtopics or an in-depth study of one.
5. Pick 10 to 15 TFPs on which to focus.

Developing Activity Ideas

6. Brainstorm activities related to the TFPs.
7. Assign each activity to one of the following curricular domains: aesthetic, affective, cognitive, language, physical, social, pretend play, or construction.
8. Check activities for balance and diversity.

Planning the Unit

9. Incorporate the theme-related activities above into a written lesson plan for the week.
10. Check to see that there are two theme-related activities each day and that all the domains are addressed at least once within the week.
11. Inform relevant colleagues about the theme.
12. Consider classroom management issues.
13. Plan one large group activity each day that addresses the theme.
14. Check your written lesson plan to determine how well the TFPs are covered and addressed throughout the week.
15. Gather relevant materials.
16. Create a thematic classroom atmosphere.
17. Carry out the plan developed.
18. Observe children and talk to them to assess their understanding of the theme. Take advantage of spontaneous events.
19. Help children develop projects to address aspects of the theme they want to explore further.
20. Consider expanding the theme as children's interests warrant.
21. Establish two-way communication with parents about the theme.
22. Evaluate theme implementation using the theme teaching checklist.

FIGURE 13.4
Theme Teaching Summary

the school curriculum are appropriate alternatives to consider.

When I get an idea for a theme, I immediately think of related activities. Later I try to match them to the TFPs. Is that OK?

As soon as you settle on a topic, it is natural to envision activities that might fit into a thematic unit on that subject. Although it is a common initial reaction to create an entire theme this way, it neglects the essential step of linking activities to the specific bits of information you want to convey to the children. Moreover, you may generate a lot of activities that all impart the same narrow range of content while inadvertently overlooking other aspects of the theme, useful for children to explore. The result may be an array of activities that lack substance, balance, or cohesion. Thus, it is better to work from the TFPs to the activities than to try it the other way around.

How do I fit in teaching a theme when I have so much other required content to cover?

Theme teaching is not an add-on. It is not another strand to be incorporated into the day's instruction, nor is it an additional layer to be added to an already bursting curriculum. Rather, teaching from a thematic perspective is a strategy for breaking away from rigid compartmentalization of subject matter and the traditional use of designated time blocks for each of these.

Because time is limited in early childhood classrooms, it is not efficient to confine subjects only to certain slots in the day. Teachers, who attempt this, find they run out of time without having adequately addressed all areas of the curriculum. In particular, we know that over the past decade, it is the knowledge, processes, and skills related to science, social studies, health, and the arts that most suffer in this regard (Jalongo, 1990; Malecki, 1990). Yet the concepts associated with these areas are essential to children's understanding of their experiences and the world around them. In response to this dilemma, professionals in a variety of disciplines are advocating a more holistic, interdisciplinary approach to educating children at all grade levels and across all subjects (Heibert & Fisher, 1990; Hurd, 1990; Kovalik, 1986; J. M. Palmer, 1990). Consequently, it is a good idea to create some themes each year focusing on concepts generally associated with underrepresented portions of the curriculum. Also, by using required content as a source for themes and the development of related TFPs, teachers can combine what were previously isolated subjects or skills, such as science and writing; social studies and math; health and reading; speaking, reading and writing; or art and critical thinking. This makes the day less fragmented, which allows children and teachers more time to explore topics in depth.

How do I incorporate theme-related activities into my daily schedule?

Are learning centers the only way to get across the theme?

Do I have to set aside a certain portion of each day to offer children theme-related experiences?

Theme-related activities can be incorporated into any classroom routine: whole-group instruction (all or most of the children are expected to do the same thing at the same time), small-group activities (a few children, assigned to one of several groups, carry out certain tasks during a particular time of the day), and free-choice options (children move among a variety of learning centers at will). The most effective approach is to cover thematic content using a combination of these strategies throughout the week. Moreover, within a particular routine on a given day, such as small groups or learning centers, some activities will center on the theme while others do not. Themes may also provide a unifying structure for only certain portions of a day or all of it. Thus the time frame and format taken by theme-oriented activities may vary from day to day as well as from classroom to classroom.

Although there is no one right way to fit themes into your schedule, remember to address the theme more than once every day. Vary the materials, instructional modes, and the domains through which children have access to theme-related content. Give the students in your classroom enough time each day to explore the theme adequately as well as apply and extend their conceptualizations in personally meaningful ways. This means providing children some uninterrupted blocks of time in which to pursue these aims (Michigan Department of Education, 1986).

How can I ease into theme teaching?

At first, follow these tips:

■ Plan one theme (lasting 2 or 3 weeks) every 3 months or so. The rest of the time, teach as you always have. This means the first year you will only teach a total of three or four themes, which will give you enough time to develop each one thoroughly.

- Choose familiar topics for themes or ones that particularly interest you.
- Plan theme-related activities only in those domains about which you feel most confident.
- Plan two theme-related activities each day.
- Incorporate theme-related materials during those portions of the day easiest for you to plan.

As the year progresses, consider these suggestions:

- Branch out; select themes less well known to you.
- Gradually increase the domains in which you plan theme-related activities until all eight are included.
- Increase over time the number of theme-related activities you plan each day, working toward a goal of three or four.
- Expand the modes through which you offer children theme-related activities; eventually incorporate the theme throughout all parts of the school day.

Aren't themes just too time-consuming for most teachers to prepare?

Theme planning does take time. However, as with any skill, practice leads to greater speed and proficiency. The most time-consuming element in developing any theme is generating an accurate list of TFPs. Once that is accomplished, the rest of the planning steps take only an hour or two. One shortcut that saves time is to use commercially prepared thematic units as a base for creating your own. A few that include TFPs or similar factual content to get you started are listed here:

- *Teaching Young Children Using Themes* edited by Marjorie J. Kostelnik (Scott-Foresman, 1991)
- *A Practical Guide to Early Childhood Curriculum* by Claudia F. Eliason and Loa T. Jenkins (Merrill-Macmillan, 1990)
- *Resources for Creative Teaching in Early Childhood Education* by Darlene S. Hamilton

and Bonnie M. Flemming (Harcourt Brace Jovanovich, 1990)
- *Creative Resources for the Early Childhood Classroom* by Judith Herr and Yvonne Libby (Delmar, 1990)

In addition, practitioners report that working with colleagues is more efficient than working alone, especially in the beginning. Start by collaborating with one or more teachers on the same theme. Brainstorm ideas and create props you all can use. Later, move to an arrangement in which you each plan different themes. Generate TFPs, activity ideas, and props to switch and share. This reduces the number of themes you have to create from scratch. In subsequent years, revise already developed themes, but continue to add some new units to your collection to better address the needs of differing groups of children.

How long does a typical unit last?

Coverage of a theme may consume a week or a month depending on the children's needs and interests as well as on how the teacher structures the topic. Assume that the less experience children have with a concept, the more time they will need to explore it. Youngsters who have had many prior opportunities to go to their local library or bookmobile may find that 2 weeks is enough time to study more about them. On the other hand, children who have few books at home and have never visited a library may enjoy and profit from several weeks focusing on these related ideas.

In addition, concepts can expand or be explored in greater depth when carried out over several weeks. For instance, a unit on space might begin with a week-long overview of the nighttime sky, followed by a second week focusing on astronomers and the tools they use in their work. A third week in which astronauts and actual space travel are featured could come next. The unit might end with a week during which children consider potentially intelligent life in space—how such creatures might look and act, how to develop communication systems with them, and how to live peacefully with alien beings.

Educators find working together on theme ideas satisfying and stimulating.

For some groups of children, this calendar would be well suited to the degree of their desire to learn about space. Other youngsters might benefit from even more time spent on the topic, while still other groups would find less time better suited to their needs. Teachers must exercise judgment in determining what approach is most fitting for their class. However, many report that planning units to last 2 to 3 weeks with an optional follow-up week available if needed, is a good rule of thumb.

Is there a difference between planning themes for 3- and 4-year-olds and planning ones for children 6 to 8 years of age?

The *process* involved in planning and implementing themes is the same regardless of children's ages. Selecting a topic, creating the TFPs, generating activity ideas, planning the unit, and carrying it out are steps required for every theme. However, themes may vary in terms of TFPs selected and in terms of the con-

cepts chosen for study based on the ages of the children and their prior experience with the theme. To make these kinds of differentiations, it is necessary to divide the TFPs into two categories: simple and advanced.

Simple TFPs consist of terms or facts that can be directly observed or experienced by the children. They are ones children comprehend directly through their own activity (although they might not be able to put them into actual words). Existing in the here and now rather than the future or past, simple TFPs do not require teacher explanations for children to understand them. Adult talk may reinforce children's self-discoveries, but it is never a substitute for direct experience. Principles, because they often involve abstractions, are not identified as simple. For example, the theme "Clothing" could be supported by the following simple TFPs:

Terms: 1. *Dressing* is when people put on their clothes; *undressing* is when people take off their clothes.

Facts:
2. People wear clothes.
3. Certain articles of clothing go on certain parts of the body.
4. Clothes have different fasteners: buckles, buttons, snaps, zippers, ties, and Velcro®.
5. Clothing comes in a variety of sizes, shapes, colors, patterns, and textures.
6. People wear clothing for different reasons.

All of these TFPs are ones that children, engaged in activities and routines in the classroom, could incorporate into their concept of clothing based on actual experience.

Advanced TFPs, on the other hand, are ones children often learn about through representational experiences such as pictures or models. Advanced TFPs may refer to past or future events or events that take place beyond the immediate classroom. These TFPs may also require children to envision something mentally in order to comprehend it. That cows have four legs is a simple fact because it is readily observable both in real cows and in toy cows one might have in the classroom. The fact that cows have multiple stomachs is advanced because it can only be represented in a picture, diagram, or discussion and requires children to envision the internal workings of a cow without experiencing them directly. Advanced TFPs consist of more elaborate or enigmatic vocabulary, more complicated facts, and principles. Because of these TFPs' complexity or abstractness, children generally need more opportunities and time to grasp them than is usually true for simple TFPs. Advanced TFPs related to the theme "Clothing" are offered as examples below:

Terms:
1. When two pieces of fabric are sewn together, the joining point is called a *seam.*
2. *Natural fibers* are made from animals or plants.
3. *Synthetic fibers* are made from chemicals.

Facts:
4. People make leather from the skins of various animals.

5. People created synthetic fibers for many reasons: strength, durability, ease of care.

Principle:
6. People sometimes change their minds about the kinds of clothes they like. They may be influenced by what others think or what they have seen or read about.

The designation of simple and advanced TFPs enables teachers to identify which category of TFPs to emphasize when working with a particular group of children. Simple TFPs should be used with 3-, 4- and 5-year-olds and older children who have little experience with the theme. Advanced TFPs are more appropriate for kindergartners who know the theme well and for children in the early primary grades as well as youngsters beyond the early childhood period. This stratification makes it possible to choose a subset of TFPs that best corresponds to the needs of children in your class. Depending on the concept to be addressed, the subset may be composed of TFPs representing either or both levels of difficulty.

The criteria that differentiate simple TFPs from advanced ones can also be applied to concepts overall, which thereby influences your theme choice. Concepts that deal with the here and now and that youngsters can explore through numerous, direct hands-on experiences are most suitable for younger children. Examples are clothing, water, plants, textures, books, and people at school. All of these topics are ones children can explore right in the classroom. They do not rely on field trips or visitors as the children's *only* firsthand experience with the concept. Neither must children try to remember or project in order to think about the concept meaningfully. Concepts dependent on these latter forms of experience are more abstract and would be considered advanced. Samples are the circus (dependent on children remembering or envisioning a circus experience), storytelling (focuses on actions rather than tangible objects), and the eye (focuses on representations such as models and diagrams to illustrate how the eye functions). Advanced concepts are better used with children toward the latter phases of the early childhood period and beyond.

Is it ever appropriate to repeat a theme during the year?

Yes. First, it must be remembered that concept learning does not stop simply because a particular unit ends. Children will continue to explore and apply related knowledge and skills within subsequent themes. Although they will do this spontaneously, it is also useful for teachers to plan some activities throughout the year that call for children to retrieve content and processes explored in previous units.

Second, some concepts are greatly enriched when they receive formal instructional attention for several days, at different times during the year. A unit on leaves is one such example. A leaf theme could be introduced in the fall, then repeated in the spring, building on what children learned earlier in the year as well as contrasting leaves and leaf growth during two different seasons. Likewise, some teachers choose to begin the year with a unit on friends, the primary aims of which are to help children "discover" one another and create a sense of cohesiveness within the class. Later in the year they return to the concept "Friends" as a means of reinforcing social harmony and addressing more advanced TFPs that the children, now more thoroughly acquainted, are ready to explore.

What about repeating themes from one program level to the next?

Sometimes teachers and parents worry about children revisiting certain themes as they move from the 3-year old room to the 4-year old class, from kindergarten to first grade. They think children may get bored or that they will not learn anything new. When these issues surface, it helps to remember that children learn through repetition. Having opportunities to explore familiar concepts further is not only worthwhile, it is the best way for children to expand their understanding by building on what they already know. Each different time children participate in a given theme, they glean new insights and skills from the experience. No one period of investigation is ever complete or offers children all they want or need to know about any topic. Consequently, re-peating some themes from one year to the next is an effective instructional strategy.

On the other hand, simply rehashing the exact same material year after year may not provide enough stimulation to hold children's interest or enhance their concept development. To avoid this problem, teachers within the same program can plan similar themes to draw children's attention to different facets of it. They can also use multiyear themes to help children move from focusing on simple TFPs to more advanced ones. For instance, dinosaurs, a topic beloved by children throughout the early childhood period, is one they often request. It may be covered 2 or 3 years in a row, which makes it an ideal vehicle for collaborative planning among teachers at different levels of the program. Such a plan could be formulated keeping in mind that 4- and 5-year-olds are fascinated by the terms associated with dinosaurs, especially their names. Simple facts regarding dinosaurs' physical characteristics are also appealing to them. First graders, already familiar with dinosaur names, continue to be intrigued with the physical attributes of dinosaurs as well as where they lived and how they protected themselves. By second grade, children who have experienced the theme twice before tend to be no less enthusiastic about dinosaurs, but they may have moved into exploring more advanced facts (e.g., why dinosaurs became extinct) as well as considering principles (e.g., attributes of the jaw and teeth are what distinguish meat eaters from plant eaters). Creating a programwide plan that incorporates this developmental progression from simple to complex and from concrete to more abstract supports children's interest in the theme. It also gives each teacher a chance to offer children opportunities for new insights. Obviously, the more often teachers within the same program talk to and collaborate with one another regarding theme planning, the more likely it is that they will complement rather than duplicate one another's efforts.

Is there one *best* way to cover particular concepts?

Every theme can be approached from a variety of angles with potentially beneficial results for children. To illustrate this point, a unit on pets could be carried out in any of the following ways.

Option 1:

Week	Content
1	General introduction about what pets are and why people keep pets
2	Pet selection
3	What pets need and how to care for them

Option 2:

Week	Content
1	General overview of pets and the role they play in humans' lives
2	Mammals
3	Reptiles and amphibians
4	Fish
5	Birds

Option 3:

Week	Content
1	Pets that live on land (cats, dogs, horses, rabbits)
2	Pets that fly (parakeets, ducks, geese)
3	Pets that live in or on the water (turtles, frogs, fish)

Option 4:

Week	Content
1	People and their pets
2	People who help others select pets (pet store owners and/or animal shelter employees)
3	People who help others care for pets (veterinarians, groomers, trainers)

Obviously each of the previous options emphasizes different facets of the concept "Pets." Which one the teacher selects will depend on children's expressed interests, their prior knowledge, availability of props, other support materials, and resource people.

What about having all my themes revolve around holidays?

A common preprimary and elementary practice is to formulate themes that highlight the holiday of the month. Weeks at a time center around Halloween, Christmas, St. Patrick's Day, Washington's Birthday, Groundhog Day, and so forth. For some programs, holidays are the core of the curriculum. A number of potential problems are associated with this approach.

First, such themes run the risk of being little more than a convenient backdrop for children's participation in numerous craft projects, with minimal attention paid either to content or process learning (Kostelnik, Howe, et al., 1991). Youngsters usually come away from these units without having increased their skills or expanded their conceptualizations.

Second, when children spend an entire month focusing on Halloween or St. Patrick's Day, those times come to dominate children's lives. They take on a disproportionate importance in comparison to the more common and relevant phenomena that constitute children's real-life experiences.

A third risk is the inadvertent teaching of cultural or religious stereotypes. For instance, in many schools across the country, November marks the time when children hear about pilgrims and Native Americans. All too often the Native Americans are depicted as wearing feathers in their hair, dancing, and war whooping while their real contributions toward helping the pilgrims are overlooked (Hendrick, 1990). Moreover, Thanksgiving is presented as a time of universal celebration and feasting. While true for many people, there are some Native Americans who fast at this time and view the day as one of mourning in remembrance of the many tragedies suffered by native people following the arrival of the first white settlers (Heinrich, 1977; Little-Soldier, 1990; Ramsey, 1979). Equitable treatment of the subject demands a balanced point of view that would be too abstract for most young children to understand. Yet, promoting the traditional stereotypes, assuming they will be altered or undone when children are older, is risky and unwarranted.

Similarly, units that promote children's creation of Easter baskets, Easter rabbits, parading in Easter finery, and playing Easter Bunny math games presuppose that every family celebrates this particular holiday or that such items and activities are nonreligious symbols of spring. Both notions are erroneous. Such practices violate the principle of respect for cultural and religious differences and make them inappropriate.

Finally, because there is so little time in school to cover every important topic, it is best to omit ones that focus on social-conventional knowledge that children get heavy exposure to outside the classroom. Holidays, which children learn so much about at home and through other sources, fall into this category. Consequently, they are not the most *worthy* topics on which to spend large chunks of school time. Having fewer holiday themes allows more attention to be paid to concepts for which school support adds richness, variety, and a dimension not so easily obtained elsewhere (Deardon, 1984).

Not using holidays as the sole basis for unit planning does not mean ignoring them altogether. Instead, it is most relevant to incorporate these special times into the context of a larger concept such as "Celebrations" or "Family Traditions." Both of these themes, for example, could support a wide array of TFPs, as illustrated in Figure 13.5. Moreover, such concepts tend to be inclusive rather than exclusive in nature. They support children's growing awareness and appreciation of the similarities as well as the differences among people.

Additionally, integrating Valentine's Day into the more global theme "Friends," using Halloween as an impetus for piquing children's interest in "Costumes and Masks," or exploring and comparing rituals in the home associated with Christmas, Hanukkah, and Kwanza via a unit on "Families" or "Homes" are all ways to

---

1. A family tradition is an activity families repeat in much the same way time after time.
2. Traditions are an important part of family life.
3. All families have traditions, such as special songs, celebrations, foods, activities, stories, recollections, routines, rules, beliefs, and values.
4. Family celebrations are often influenced by tradition:
   - Particular foods may be prepared.
   *- A certain sequence of events may be followed.
   - Special clothing may be worn.
   - Special songs may be sung.
   - Special stories may be told.
   *- People may have special roles within the celebration.
   - Special activities may be carried out.
5. Families vary in the traditions they observe.
*6. A family's religious and/or cultural heritage influences the traditions they adopt.
7. Traditions help family members feel close to one another.
*8. Some family traditions have been carried out for many years, and some are relatively new.
9. Some traditions are very elaborate; others are quite simple.
10. Sometimes outsiders are invited to participate in a family tradition, and sometimes only the family participates.
11. Every family has stories or anecdotes about how certain traditions developed or how certain family members were involved in family traditions.
12. Photographs, home videos, or cassette recordings are often used to record traditional family events.

FIGURE 13.5
Terms, Facts, and Principles: "Family Traditions"
Source: These TFPs were developed by Laura C. Stein, M.S., Instructor, Department of Family and Child Ecology, Michigan State University. Those marked with an asterisk are advanced.

acknowledge and enjoy holidays as they occur, while making more relevant connections to children's lives.

Finally, holiday customs need not be confined only to holiday times. Instead, a variety of observances could be addressed within such seemingly generic themes as "Clothing," "Seasons," "Storytelling," or "Healthy Foods." These could be carried out at any time of the year, incorporating rituals, games, props, and foods associated with a variety of holidays.

When is it appropriate to introduce more abstract content to children, and how should it be done?

The younger the children, the more important it is for themes to relate directly to their own first-hand experiences and immediate environment. This applies to preprimary children as well as primary children whose participation within the community has been extremely limited. As children gain maturity and experience, thematic content can be broadened to include the environments and activities of others, those at a distance, and some from the past (Katz & Chard, 1989). Yet even when children seem ready for the latter content, it is best to broach it within a familiar context. An illustration of this point is how one might assist children in exploring the concept of "Bears."

By 5 or 6 years of age, most youngsters are well acquainted with bears of the make-believe kind. They encounter fictional bears via oral storytelling, picture books, songs, and film. Throughout the early years, too, children frequently play with their own toy bear or know another child who has one. It is also not unusual for children to see live bears on television, at the zoo, or in a circus. Thus, in one form or another, bears are familiar creatures to young children.

Yet, real bears are somewhat distant from children's immediate environment, so you might choose to create a bear unit by building on the children's knowledge of the more common pretend varieties.

Week 1: Introduce one or more fictional bears as they appear in favorite children's storybooks. Highlight one story each day and create activities that revolve around such tales as *Goldilocks and the Three Bears, Blueberries for Sal,* or *Ask Mr. Bear.*

Week 2: Promote children's observation and investigative skills via a study of teddy bears.

Week 3: Concentrate on real bears as they exist in nature.

To make the last week more real for children, take the class to see a live bear, if possible. If that is not feasible, use pictures to help children contrast bears in nature with the ones they focused on in previous weeks. Also, since bears are fellow mammals, aid children in drawing parallels between human behaviors and those of bears such as playfulness, locomotion, and care for the young.

In these ways the more abstract concept (real bears) has been developed by focusing first on more immediately available, familiar phenomena (story bears, toy bears, and human characteristics).

How do I know children are developing more sophisticated, complex concepts?

Children reveal their conceptual understandings through their play, conversations with peers and adults, questions, errors, and methods to investigate objects and events. To find out what children know, take time to observe them and talk with them about the concept. Give children opportunities to talk and interact with their peers and provide open-ended activities through which they can explore the concept in their own way. Make notes about what you see and hear using the assessment techniques described in chapter 16.

Should I expect every child to demonstrate the same or equal levels of understanding the theme?

First, presume that children come to your class already possessing rudimentary concepts about themselves and the world in which they live. Assume, too, that because each child's cadre of prior experience is unique to him or her, the exact makeup of these concepts will differ from child to child. Youngsters may have some conceptual understandings in common, but they will also exhibit gaps in their knowledge that do not exactly match one another's. Moreover, as children participate in various theme-related activities, they will take away meaning that is relevant to them. Again, the insights children glean will vary.

Consequently, your role will be to help children expand or alter their concepts in ways that are personally meaningful to them. Encouraging children to create their own extensions of the concept is a more appropriate aim than attempting to have them all derive a uniform understanding.

SUMMARY

Coordinating activities around a central theme has long been a tradition in early childhood education. The benefits to youngsters, practitioners, and programs are many. Yet, surely the greatest value of theme teaching lies in its use as a concept organizer. As young children engage in activities permeated by the same basic idea, they make connections among individual bits of knowledge and perceptions to form more comprehensive, accurate concepts. Such positive outcomes, however, only result when practitioners keep in mind principles of developmentally appropriate practice as well as the principles of effective theme teaching. The latter principles include relying on children's interests and capacities to influence theme selection and direction; focusing on the conceptual nature of thematic teaching; using an accurate, thorough body of factual information to support the theme; emphasizing the use of firsthand learning as well as real objects in carrying out the theme; and integrating thematic activities across domains, subject areas, and parts of the day.

Creating thematic units involves several steps. The first is to select a topic. Ideas for themes most often come from the children but may also be initiated by special events or unexpected happenings in the program, school-mandated content, or teacher/parent interests. In addition, potential topics must be screened so that they are relevant to children and conducive to many hands-on experiences in the classroom. How well each theme contributes to diversity and balance across the curriculum and the availability of theme-oriented resources are other factors that have to be considered when choosing themes.

Once an idea has been settled on, the next step in theme planning is to create an accurate information base to support the concept under study. To do this, practitioners research relevant terms, facts, and principles (TFPs). These TFPs serve as the basis for activity development. Thus, each theme-related activity has its source within the factual base for that theme. This linkage between content and experience increases the accuracy of the information provided to children and elevates theme teaching beyond mere entertainment. To increase their educational value further, activities related to the theme also represent a variety of domains and learning modes.

Making a plan is the third phase of theme teaching. It involves distributing theme-related activities throughout one's weekly lessons and across all parts of the day. Although it is important to have several theme-related activities included in the plan so that the linkages among them are easier for children to grasp, not every activity in a day or week must focus on the theme. In fact, children and adults benefit when some theme-independent activities are offered. Such experiences give participants a break from the theme, help ensure that activities are not contrived simply to fit, and enable teachers to address important knowledge and skills that do not match the central topic under investigation.

The last phase of theme teaching involves implementing the theme, evaluating and revising it as children become engaged in the topic. Within this chapter, a theme teaching checklist has been offered as a tool to help practitioners assess theme implementation in their classrooms as well as children's theme-related learning. Potential questions educators might have regarding theme teaching have also been posed and answered.

In sum, it can be said that theme teaching is a valuable instructional tool when used properly. Practitioners who have never engaged in this kind of teaching may find it time-consuming at first. Nevertheless, as their familiarity with the process increases, so will their speed and efficiency in carrying it out. Collaboration among colleagues is another way to make the process easier and richer. Moreover, as children come to the program eager to know "what we're talking about this week," and making obvious connections between the information and processes they experience, educators will sense the re- wards this kind of teaching can bring. Helping to make sense of what could otherwise be frag- mented educational events is a plus both chil- dren and teachers will enjoy.

CHAPTER 14

Promoting Self-Discipline in Children

The children are sitting in a circle. Having spent much of the morning creating a spacecraft from a refrigerator box, they are now talking about what rules should govern its use. Their discussion was prompted by some children's concern that the vehicle "not get wrecked" and others' desire that "kids play fair." Aided by the teacher, the conversation lasts several minutes.

After much consideration, three rules are agreed on: No pulling off the knobs; tell the astronauts when you want a turn; three people inside at a time. As the group is about to disperse, Adam says, "We need a sign." Noah asks, "Why?" Adam responds, "So's the afternoon kids knows how they's supposed to do it."

NO PULLING OFF THE NOBS

These youngsters have been engaged in a fundamental aspect of community living—deciding on rules to regulate human behavior. Such rules are really guides to assist people in getting along safely and harmoniously. And, because Adam knew that not everyone entering the classroom would automatically know what rules applied, he recognized the need to communicate the agreed-on standards to others.

In this classroom community, the children's actions have mirrored those of society at large. Since the earliest times, people have created rules to make living in groups both possible and worthwhile. Although no code of behavior is universal, all cultures and settings devise rules participants must obey if they are to remain in good standing (Hendrick, 1992). Traditionally, it is the job of adults to transmit this code to the next generation.

"Wait your turn."
"Keep your hands to yourself."
"Put your materials away when you're through."

These are some of the rules children encounter early in life. Such behavioral guides are aimed at maintaining safety, order, justice, and efficiency—conditions necessary for constructive learning to take place (Kostelnik & Stein, 1990). From birth, children begin learning rules from parents and other family members. Once children arrive at school, adults there also figure prominently in the socialization process. Since children spend most of their school time in the classroom, it is teachers who play the dominant role on the school scene. However, administrators, specialists, lunchroom aides, playground monitors, and bus drivers are also influential. Collectively, these adults, with parents, help children learn to carry out socially desirable acts like sharing, answering politely, and working cooperatively with their peers. Additionally, they teach children to forego inappropriate behaviors, such as shoving, tattling, or interrupting. Their efforts are focused on getting children to know the difference between acceptable and unacceptable behavior. Initially, adults spend much time monitoring how well children conform to these standards. However, their hope is that in time children will behave appropriately without constant reminders and an authority figure always present. Their ultimate goal, then, is for children to become self-disciplined.

CHARACTERISTICS OF SELF-DISCIPLINE

When we say people are self-disciplined, we mean they can regulate their behavior in ways that consider other people's needs and feelings, while simultaneously conforming to socially accepted standards (Mussen et al., 1990). Self-disciplined children initiate positive social interactions and undertake constructive social plans without having to be told. Such youngsters also resist temptation, inhibit negative impulses, and delay gratification independent of supervision (Bukatko & Daehler, 1992; Fabes, 1984; Mischel, 1978). Examples of these kinds of behaviors are offered in Table 14.1, all of which involve children knowing when and how to distinguish

appropriate from inappropriate behaviors and acting accordingly. As children mature, they vary in how well they can do this, with skill levels ranging from no control to much self-control. Many scientists have tried to explain these variations (Gilligan, 1982; Hoffman, 1970; Kohlberg, 1976). Although there are differences among their points of view, they generally agree that people progress through different phases of behavioral control. Each phase is distinguished by the factors that motivate a person to behave in socially acceptable ways.

The Amoral Phase

At birth, children are *amoral;* that is, they have no sense of right or wrong and are incapable of making ethical judgments about their behavior. Thus, infant Cassandra, reaching for her mom's earring as it dangles tantalizingly near, is not thinking of the pain she will inflict when she pulls on it. Neither can she stop her exploration simply by seeing her mother frown or by hearing "No." She has not yet learned to understand such cues or to

TABLE 14.1

Components of Self-Discipline as Exhibited by Young Children

Behavior	Examples
Initiating positive social acts	Shannon comforts Latosha, who is sad about a ruined project. Jason shares his glue with a newcomer to the art center.
Making and carrying out social plans	Vinny wants a turn with the magnifying glass. He figures out a strategy for getting one, such as trading, and then tries bargaining with another child.
	Ashley recognizes that Marcus is having difficulty carrying several balls out to the playground. She helps him by holding the door open.
Resisting temptation	Jerome walks all the way over to the trash bin to deposit his gum wrapper, although he is tempted simply to drop the crumpled paper on the playground.
Inhibiting negative impulses	Anthony suppresses the urge to strike out in anger when someone accidentally trips him. Hessa keeps herself from laughing aloud when Anthony falls down.
Delaying gratification	Rachel waits for Marla to finish telling her story before blurting out her own exciting news.
	Steven postpones taking another fruit kabob until everyone else gets one.

interrupt her action because of seeing or hearing them. Her mother must exercise sole control of the situation by either repositioning the child away from the earring or taking it off. Despite which strategy the mother chooses, it is she, not the child, who regulates Cassandra's behavior. Gradually, through experience and maturation, this complete lack of self-monitoring, so common in infancy and toddlerhood, begins to change. Young children learn to respond to external cues to guide their actions. The most basic way in which this occurs is adherence.

Adherence

Children motivated by *adherence* obey rules simply to gain external rewards or avoid negative outcomes expected from authority figures (Bukatko & Daehler, 1992). Adrian exemplifies this when she waits her turn in line solely to get a smiley sticker or avoid a scolding by the teacher. Her reason for waiting is self-serving; it has nothing to do with concern for the rights or welfare of others (Stengel, 1982). Besides, Adrian may stay in line only when the teacher is present. Because she has no internal basis for following the rule, she may resort to pushing or cutting in front of others as soon as the adult focuses his or her attention elsewhere.

When children follow rules because of adherence, adults must constantly monitor behavior because they cannot rely on the children to exercise any self-control. The longer these circumstances persist, the more dependent children become on having adult rewards and punishments guide their actions. They develop few other strategies for determining right or wrong and have no means of figuring out how to conduct themselves properly in unfamiliar situations. Also, children may behave in the presence of certain authority figures but fail to obey other adults, respect the rights of their peers, or comply with rules if the threat of a punishment or the promise of a reward is not evident.

Identification

A more advanced degree of compliance occurs when children follow a rule in imitation of someone they admire. Children's compliance becomes their way of emulating the conduct and values of an important person in their lives (M. L. Hoffman,

1970; Sroufe & Cooper, 1988). This phenomenon is called *identification.* Although children consider another person's opinion, they still have little understanding of the real reasons behind the rules they follow. Influenced by identification, Jacob may wait his turn in line because a teacher he especially likes advocates such conduct, not because he grasps the ideas of justice or fairness that waiting represents. In addition, identification requires children to second-guess how another person might behave under certain conditions. If Jacob comes across a situation to which he has never seen the teacher respond, he may be at a loss for what to do himself.

Because children tend to identify with the nurturant, powerful figures in their lives, teachers are often the focus of their admiration. However, children's imitative behavior may only last throughout the time they have contact with a particular teacher, then fade once they move on to other grades.

Internalization

When children treat certain rules as a logical extension of their beliefs and personal values, we say they have *internalized* those rules (Hoffman, 1970; Kelman, 1958; Shaffer, 1989). Internalization is the ultimate form of self-discipline because it involves attainment of an internal code of ethics. It is this code to which children refer in deciding what action to take. The course they choose is aimed at avoiding self-condemnation rather than gaining the approval of others or external rewards.

This form of reasoning is often referred to as *conscience,* which means that the child feels a moral commitment to behaving a certain way. Internalization, therefore, implies comprehension of such concepts as justice, honor, and truth. People who reason according to internalized beliefs consider how their compliance with a rule will affect not only themselves but others as well. Thus, Mariah demonstrates internalization when she waits her turn in line because pushing ahead would interfere with the rights of her classmates, which would thereby violate her sense of right and wrong.

Internalization benefits children because they understand the reasons behind the rules they follow. This gives them a reference for figuring

TABLE 14.2
Four Types of Compliance

Type of Compliance	Definition	Source of Motivation
Amoral	Children have no sense of right or wrong.	External to the child
Adherence	Children respond to rewards and punishments; they often anticipate these and behave accordingly.	Shared between others and the child
Identification	Children attempt to adopt behavioral codes of admired others; they second-guess how that person might behave in varying situations and act likewise.	Shared between others and the child
Internalization	Children govern their behavior using an internal code of ethics created from their own values and judgments.	Internal to the child

out how to behave appropriately in all kinds of situations, even unfamiliar ones. Children motivated by identification or adherence do not generalize in this manner.

The benefit to society is that children who have internalized rules do not require constant supervision; instead, they can be depended on to regulate their own behavior. Moreover, internalized behaviors are long-lasting. Children who internalize notions of fair play or honesty will abide by those ideals long after their contacts with certain adults are over. Table 14.2 provides a summary of the four phases of compliance just described.

ARE YOUNG CHILDREN CAPABLE OF INTERNALIZATION?

There is strong evidence that children within the early childhood period are not yet capable of regulating their behavior according to internal principles of ethical behavior (Walker, 1989; Walker, deVries, & Trevarthen, 1989). However, this is the time when they can develop fundamental skills and understandings that lead to the higher order reasoning characteristic of internalization. For instance, given appropriate adult support, children in the early childhood period can begin to

consider a variety of factors (e.g., motives and intentions) in response to social dilemmas (Moran & McCullers, 1984; Surber, 1982). Also, during the early school years children broaden their experiential base, gleaning more clues as to what constitutes appropriate versus inappropriate conduct and why.

In addition, children do not move from an amoral orientation to higher levels of conduct strictly according to age. Research supports the notion of a developmental progression, but it also indicates that children achieve self-regulation at rates and in degrees that vary from child to child (Bukatko & Daehler, 1992). For instance, one child may require several experiences to learn to raise her hand before speaking at circle time, while another child grasps this notion much sooner. Furthermore, the same child may at different times act out of adherence or identification or internalization. The reasons why children follow the rule at one level or another are often situation bound (Burton, 1963, 1984). That is, Juanita may keep out of mud to avoid a reprimand. She may adopt a similar attitude toward cheating as that held by an admired teacher, and she may return too many milk tokens inadvertently received because it would not feel "right" to keep them. In the behavior of young children, these patterns typically vacillate a great deal.

DEGREES OF SELF-CONTROL EXHIBITED BY YOUNG CHILDREN

Teachers should expect to see variations in the degree to which individual children, and their class as a whole, demonstrate self-discipline. At the beginning of the year, many youngsters will be motivated by adherence. Uncertain about classroom rules, they will rely on constant adult reminders and monitoring to achieve compliance. Some children will soon figure out which behaviors are rewarded and which are not and use that knowledge to guide their actions. Others will take longer to recognize and use this kind of information. Gradually, as the school year progresses and teachers build relationships with their students, many children will begin to identify with the adults' rules. When this happens, children will try to follow teachers' codes of conduct and behave in ways aimed at pleasing them. By year's end, as children come to understand the rationale for certain teacher expectations, a few may demonstrate internalization of common rules, such as walking in the classroom or raising their hand before speaking.

With each new teacher and each new year, the process begins anew. However, as children work their way through the grades, their time at adherence may lessen, especially for rules that are upheld from one year to the next.

There is no way to predict how many youngsters eventually will achieve the highest form of self-discipline. Still, it can be said with complete certainty that children's degrees of compliance will vary widely. Some will still be at adherence for almost every rule; others will rely on rewards and punishments in some situations, identification for others, and internalization for still others. These differences are a normal result of children's development and experience.

DEVELOPMENTAL INFLUENCES ON SELF-DISCIPLINE

Children's capacity for self-discipline increases with maturity. Although 4- and 5-year-olds may have internalized some familiar rules, they are not capable of the same degree of self-control as children in the upper elementary grades. Several developmental factors contribute to these differences, most notably variations in emotional development, cognitive development, language development, and memory skills.

Emotional Development

Two emotions that strongly contribute to self-discipline are guilt and empathy (Eisenberg, 1986; Erikson, 1963; L. W. Hoffman, 1984). Guilt serves as a brake, warning children that current, past, or planned actions are undesirable. Empathy conveys the opposite message, prompting children to initiate positive actions in response to emotional situations.

Children as young as 3 are capable of both guilt and empathy (Zigler & Finn-Stevenson, 1987), but these emotions are prompted by different events for preschoolers than those to which fifth or sixth graders respond. At first, children experience guilt when they violate a known rule. For instance, 5-year-old Carl slaps Selma in an argument. She begins to cry. He does not feel guilty until the teacher reminds him that the rule is "Keep your hands to yourself." Carl's guilt stems from discovering a discrepancy between his behavior and the rule, not the distress he caused Selma. Were he 7 or 8, Carl might empathize with Selma's unhappy response and feel remorse and guilt at being the source of it (M. L. Hoffman, 1967). This combination of both empathy and guilt could even prompt him to do something to make up. Eventually, during middle childhood, children feel these emotions even when they are not the perpetrator but perceive that they could have done something to prevent the problem (Kostelnik et al., in press). Hence, a third youngster seeing the fight between Carl and Selma might intercede out of empathy toward two persons in distress and to avoid feeling guilty over not helping. In this way, children gradually respond to guilt or empathy out of a need to support their personal notions of right and wrong. However, this more complex and "other-oriented" motivation does not come about until adolescence.

What this means for early childhood educators is that they will witness some occasions

Children need adult support as they develop the emotional and cognitive skills necessary to follow rules on their own.

when children offer help or comfort to their peers and others when the same children are oblivious to people's reactions or concerns. In either case, children's emotional development is enhanced when adults point out how their actions impact those around them. Children benefit from hearing how other people feel and having either the positive or the problematic aspects of situations described to them. Likewise, children follow rules better when they are taught how those rules protect people's rights and feelings. Finally, when children demonstrate that they have reacted out of empathy or guilt, their efforts need to be noticed and reinforced.

Cognitive Development

Children's notions of what constitutes "good" and "bad" behavior evolve in conjunction with changes in their cognitive powers (Kohlberg, 1964; Piaget, 1965; Tisak & Block, 1990). Whether they judge that an action is right or wrong is influenced by their *reasoning abilities* and the extent to which they comprehend the *perspective of another person*. How well they

conduct themselves from one situation to another is further affected by the cognitive operations of *centration* and *irreversibility*.

Children's Reasoning Abilities. Four- to 6-year-olds make judgments about right and wrong based mainly on whether behaviors are immediately rewarded or punished. Children interpret actions that result in social rewards as good and those that incur social costs as negative. This is true even if the behavior is viewed differently by society. For instance, children may conclude that putting materials away neatly is good because teachers praise them or that writing in picture books is bad because parents correct them. Conversely, children who observe a classmate gain attention by clowning around may interpret silliness as "good" because it is reinforced. They might also surmise that comforting a peer is "bad" if it results in rejection.

Another way children of this age decide that actions are "bad" is if they result in physical harm to people or property or if they violate people's rights (Tisak & Block, 1990). Those that do, such as hitting, breaking, or calling names, are readily identified by children as unacceptable. However, behaviors that disrupt the social order of the group, such as not putting toys away, and those that violate interpersonal trust, like telling a secret, are not construed as inappropriate until later childhood.

Older children (3rd, 4th, 5th graders) use more sophisticated reasoning in thinking about rules. They take into account a wide range of variables, such as people's intentions and the effects of behaviors on others. For this reason, they know that a person's thoughtless words may unintentionally hurt the feelings of another. Also, children in the upper elementary grades think more abstractly about relationships between actions and their eventual aftermath. Unlike the younger child, they see beyond immediate results and project long-term outcomes. Thus, fifth graders figure out that although making fun of a classmate could result in attainment of a short-term positive goal (i.e., attention), the long-term negative effect could be rejection by their peers. At this age, too, children value interpersonal trust and recognize the need for maintaining some form of social order to protect the rights of the group as well as individuals.

Because the moral reasoning of younger children is still immature, they need much help in knowing what is expected and why. Adults who offer clear guidelines for children's behavior along with reasons for program rules help children progress toward self-discipline. The reasons that make the most sense to children during the early childhood phase of development are those that focus on harmful effects to people, property, and human rights. Children's confusion about rules is reduced when inconsistencies are minimized and when discrepancies are explained.

Children's Perspective-taking Abilities.
To interact effectively with others and make accurate judgments about what actions would be right or wrong in particular situations, children must understand what other people think, feel, or know. Termed *perspective taking,* this capacity is not fully developed in young children. Youngsters 8 years of age and younger often have difficulty putting themselves in another person's shoes. That dilemma is a result of

being unable, rather than unwilling, to comprehend or predict other people's thoughts (Vasta, Haith, & Miller, 1992; Weston & Turiel, 1980). Thus, children have trouble recognizing other people's viewpoints, especially when those views conflict with their own. They erroneously assume that their interpretation of events is universal. Frequently, such differences must be brought to children's attention before they begin to recognize that their perspective is not shared. Sometime between their 6th and 8th year, children start realizing on their own that their interpretation of a situation and that of another person might not match (Bukatko & Daehler, 1992; Selman, 1976). Still, they do not always know what the differences are, or they may conclude that variations are a result of the other person having access to incorrect or incomplete information. As a result, these youngsters may go to great lengths trying to convince others of the validity of their view. Their seemingly endless arguments and rationales are an outgrowth of their immature reasoning, not tactics deliberately aimed at frustrating the persons whom they are trying to persuade. On these occasions, children need adults to listen carefully, without interruption, and acknowledge their perspective. They also need to hear the "facts" of the situation repeated, more than once, and in varying ways.

Nine- and- 10-year-olds realize that their views and those of another person may be different, and even contradictory. They comprehend that two individuals may have access to the same information yet react to it in opposite ways (Forbes, 1978). Such comprehension increases upper elementary school children's ability to internalize rules because they can understand the reasoning behind certain actions as well as consider how their behavior might affect another person. Younger children have not yet achieved this degree of understanding and so require adult assistance in recognizing the perspectives of those with whom they interact.

The Impact of Centration.
Throughout the early childhood period, children tend to direct their attention to only one attribute of a situation, ignoring all others (Peterson & Felton-Collins, 1991). This phenomenon, known as *centration,* restricts children's ability to see the "big picture"

and generate alternate solutions to problems they encounter. Thus, throughout the early childhood period youngsters have a limited rather than comprehensive perception of events. Centration causes them to overlook important details relevant to their actions as well as the behavior of others and persist in using a singular approach to achieve their aims. This explains why youngsters may try the same unsuccessful strategy repeatedly and why they have difficulty shifting their attention from one facet of an interaction (e.g., "She pushed me") to another, ("She was trying to get my attention"). Even when youngsters recognize that their actions are inappropriate, they may be unable to generate suitable alternate behaviors. The younger the child, the more this is so. Decentering occurs only gradually, as children are confronted with multiple perceptions and methods of resolution. Adults enhance the process when they point out options to children and when they help youngsters brainstorm suitable alternatives as relevant circumstances arise.

In addition, younger children tend to view individual social acts as separate entities, with no real connection to past or future events. They frequently fail to comprehend how one behavior or episode (e.g., hitting) is like another one (e.g., pushing) or how a current incident (e.g., calling a child names) may influence those that follow (e.g., rejection in a game by that child). Adults who offer children reasons for rules and prohibitions help children make the connection from one circumstance to another. With maturity and experience youngsters do become more proficient at making such generalizations. Also, they become better able mentally to categorize like behaviors and comprehend the similarities among varying circumstances. However, these processes are still forming well into adolescence, and it is not until then that children can be expected to make accurate connections entirely on their own.

Finally, it is worth noting that as children's thinking becomes more complex, they must continually readjust their notions of desirable and undesirable categories of behavior. For instance, throughout the preschool years children learn to seek help from adults when they see trouble and work cooperatively to get things done. Many children learn these lessons well. But, as they move

into first and second grade, such formerly desirable behaviors take on negative connotations. Labeled tattling and cheating by adults, such actions are discouraged. At first, these new interpretations are confusing to children, causing them either to persist in relying on old concepts or become immobilized by uncertainty. Through trial and error, they eventually incorporate new definitions into their thinking and act accordingly. This reprocessing of information occurs repeatedly throughout the grade school years. It is enhanced when adults provide concrete rationales to children for classroom expectations and when they exercise patience as children work toward more comprehensive, sophisticated understandings.

The Effects of Irreversibility. Besides the constraints posed by centration, children do not routinely mentally reverse actions they initiate physically (Flavell, 1977; Tribe, 1982). In other words, their thinking is often irreversible. This means they are not adept at contemplating opposite actions and they have difficulty interrupting ongoing behaviors. For instance, when Kyley pushes on the door of the toy stove to open it, the words "Don't push" called out by the parent volunteer hold little meaning for her. She is unable mentally to transpose the physical act of pushing into its opposite action pulling or stopping. Neither can she interrupt her pushing simply by "thinking" about what to do. She needs assistance to reverse her behavior. This could be supplied through a verbal direction from the adult to pull on the door or through adult modeling of the desired behavior. With maturation, children do improve in their ability to reverse physical actions, but the influence of this cognitive characteristic remains evident throughout the preschool and elementary years. It explains why children often ignore negative directions (e.g., "Don't run," "Don't hit," "Don't push at the top of the slide."). Conversely, it provides a rationale for stating directions and rules in positive terms and modeling desired behaviors.

Language Development

As children acquire greater and more complex language skills, their capacity for self-control also becomes greater. This is because language contributes to their understanding of why rules are made and gives them more tools for attaining their goals in socially acceptable ways. Most children first come to school with command of a well-developed receptive vocabulary (8,000 to 14,000 words) and the ability to express their basic needs (Schiamberg, 1988). Yet, they are not always successful at telling others what they want or responding to verbal directions. As a result, it is not unusual for 4- and 5-year-old children to resort to physical actions in these circumstances. They may grab, jerk away, fail to respond, push, or hit rather than use words to express themselves. At such times, these children need teacher assistance in figuring out what to say.

As the elementary years progress, children become more proficient in both receiving and giving verbal messages (Maccoby, 1984; Marion, 1991). Consequently, they find words a more satisfactory and precise way to communicate. When this occurs, their physical demonstrations become less frequent and intense. Eventually, children learn to use self-talk as another strategy for exercising self-control (Wertsch, 1985). That is, they reduce frustration, postpone rewards, or remind themselves of rules by talking aloud to themselves. We hear this when older grade schoolers go over the directions for an assignment in a mumbled tone or when a child who is losing patience putting a model together quietly repeats to him- or herself, "Slow down, take your time. You'll get it." Since younger children do not automatically know how to do this, adults can give them scripts and help them practice such phrases as a way to increase their self-control.

Memory Skills

Closely related to language skills are those associated with memory. As children grow older, their memory does not necessarily increase—they just become better able to use stored data as a resource for determining future behavior (Maccoby, 1984). Whereas preschool children and children in the lower elementary grades are still very dependent on having others show or tell them how to behave in new situations, their more mature peers draw on remembered information to guide their actions (Boneau, 1974). This means educators working with children throughout the early childhood period should expect children to periodically "forget" the

rules. Also, they may be unsure of how to respond in unfamiliar circumstances. Children this age will need frequent reminders about rules and procedures and clear explanations about what to expect when routines change or new activities are introduced.

EXPERIENTIAL INFLUENCES ON SELF-DISCIPLINE

From the preceding discussion, we can conclude that development plays a vital role in how adept children are at regulating their own behavior. Children's day-to-day experiences with peers and adults are another influential factor. The only source children have for learning the specific societal expectations that apply to them are other human beings. Although age-mates become increasingly important socializers over time, throughout the early childhood period children look primarily to parents and teachers for guidance about how to behave (C. A. Smith, 1982). Grown-ups provide this guidance in several ways. They teach children the do's and don'ts of group living through modeling, attribution, instruction, and consequences (Bandura, 1989; S. G. Moore, 1986).

Modeling

One way children learn how to behave is by imitating the actions of powerful adults with whom they have strong, affectionate associations (Bandura, 1989; S. G. Moore, 1986). Teachers serve as such models who, through their behavior, demonstrate compliance or lack of compliance with a given code of ethics. Young children learn potent lessons regarding desirable attitudes and behaviors as well as how to enact them when they observe their teachers treat others with kindness, tell the truth, use reasoning as a way to solve problems, or assist someone in need. Alternately, because youngsters also follow negative models, they imitate the aggressive or thoughtless acts they observe in those around them.

Attribution

Attribution is a verbal strategy adults use to influence children's images of themselves and therefore their behavior (Grusec & Mill, 1982;

S. G. Moore, 1986). Teachers use attributions unconsciously or deliberately to direct children's attention to positive traits (brave, smart, kind) or negative ones (stupid, lazy, good for nothing). For instance, teachers may characterize children as "patient" or "good at waiting." When this occurs, children gradually become even more patient and better able to delay gratification. On the other hand, when adults tell children they are naughty or irresponsible, children not only incorporate these negative labels into their self-image but adapt in greater measure the corresponding behaviors to support them (Dreikurs & Soltz, 1964; Schiamberg, 1988). Attribution induces children to think of themselves in the terms described and behave accordingly to live up to the teacher's image of them.

Instruction

Instruction comes in two forms, indirect and direct. Indirect instruction involves all the behind-the-scenes work and planning that ultimately influences the behavior of young children (Hildebrand, 1990). These teaching methods tend to be aimed not at any one child but at creating a classroom atmosphere in which self-control is either promoted or ignored, enhanced or impeded. Thus, how adults manage space, equipment, materials, and time in the classroom affects the degree to which children do or do not develop the skills they need to be self-regulating.

Direct instruction, on the other hand, involves on-the-spot physical or verbal intervention aimed at influencing the behavior of particular children at a particular time. Physical assistance, demonstrations, redirection, distraction, substitution, removal, and physical restraint are all examples of direct instruction techniques (Hildebrand, 1990; Marion, 1991). Moreover, what is right, what is wrong, which behaviors are expected, which are restricted, how behavior standards are to be met, and how children's behavior appears to others is information conveyed directly to children via words. Grown-ups try to teach children how to behave using verbal strategies such as informing, suggesting, advising, explaining, reasoning, encouraging, and clarifying (Maccoby, 1984; C. A. Smith, 1988). Typical remarks include "Cover your mouth when you cough," "Maybe you could take turns," "Tell him you're angry—don't hit,"

"Mr. Ramirez really appreciated when you helped him carry those boxes," or "When you didn't say 'Hi' back, she thought you didn't like her."

Consequences

Teachers also use consequences to reward desirable acts and penalize negative ones. For example, they reinforce children for following rules using praise ("Good job" or "You remembered your pictures from home; now you're ready for today's work on animals") and tangible rewards ("Here's a star sticker for remembering to return your library book" or "You did such a good job cleaning up, you can have 10 more minutes of recess"). These strategies are aimed at increasing the likelihood that children will repeat their positive acts in the future (Marion, 1991; Mendler & Curwin, 1988). Conversely, teachers use negative consequences to reduce the probability that undesirable behaviors will be repeated (Dinkmeyer & McKay, 1988; Vasta et al., 1992). Such consequences range from dispassionate corrections to harsh actions dependent on force and power. The way in which consequences are enacted influences their effectiveness. Some implementation methods achieve the aims adults have in mind when they enact them; other approaches actually undermine those aims. More about how such results come about is presented in the next section.

How Teaching Style Influences Children's Self-Discipline

Instruction, modeling, attribution, and consequences are socialization strategies all adults use. Yet, how they are combined and the ways in which adults implement them differ. Such variations have been the subject of research for the past 25 years. It has been found that the blend of socialization strategies parents and teachers adopt has a major influence on children's personality development and whether children follow rules because of adherence, identification, or internalization. Both short- and long-term effects have been noted (Franz, McClelland, & Weinberger, 1991; M. L. Hoffman, 1970, 1983).

In a series of landmark, longitudinal studies, Baumrind (1967, 1977) identified three common adult socialization styles: permissive, authoritarian, and authoritative. These three styles continue to be the standard for comparison today (Bukatko & Daehler, 1992; Marion, 1991; Vasta et al., 1992). Each is characterized by certain adult attitudes and strategies related to the socialization dimensions of control, communication, maturity demands, and nurturance.

The way and extent to which parents and teachers enforce compliance with their expectations is termed *control*. *Communication* involves how much information they provide children throughout the socialization process. *Maturity demands* is a term used to describe the level at which adults set their expectations for children's behavior and compliance. How much caring and concern is expressed toward children constitutes *nurturance*. Differences among the permissive, authoritarian, and authoritative styles occur because of varying combinations of these dimensions.

Permissive adults are low in control, make few maturity demands, and use little communication, but they rank high in nurturance. Those employing an *authoritarian* style are high on control and maturity demands, low in communication and nurturance. Adults high along all four dimensions demonstrate an *authoritative* style (see Figure 14.1).

Few people personify a "pure" style regardless of which one they adopt. Instead, adults demonstrate behaviors characteristic of all three from time to time. Yet, most socialization practices used by any adult tend to be dominated by one style over the others. Although most studies have examined parent-child relationships, teacher-child interactions also have been considered with much the same results. Understanding the characteristics of each style and their impact on children is important knowledge for teachers to have. It enables them to assess their use of discipline in the classroom and provides insight as to why children respond as they do.

The Permissive Teaching Style. In classrooms supervised by permissive teachers, children are treated with warmth and affection. Such teachers sees themselves as resources to children but not as active agents responsible for shaping children's present or future behavior. They accept a wide range of children's actions either based on the conviction that external controls stifle children's development or out of uncertainty about how to achieve compliance. Consequently, permissive teachers provide little instruction to children about how to behave. They establish few rules, ignore children's transgressions, provide few explanations, and seldom

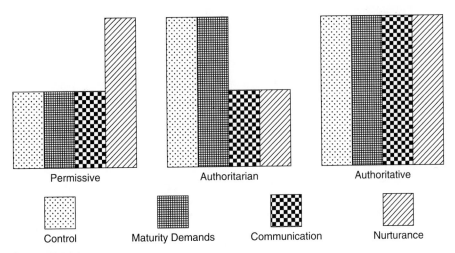

FIGURE 14.1
Differences in Attitudes and Practices among the Permissive, Authoritarian, and Authoritative Discipline Styles

give children opportunities to assume responsibility. At those infrequent times when they feel compelled to administer a penalty for gross misconduct, the favored technique is temporary love withdrawal ("I don't like children who hit") (Baumrind, 1978; Schiamberg, 1988).

Unfortunately, children subjected to this approach show few signs of internalization. In fact, they exhibit the lowest levels of independence and internal control of all three teaching styles (Baumrind, 1967). Since youngsters receive almost no cues about which behaviors are socially appropriate and which are not, they fail to develop mental guidelines or strategies to refer to in various social encounters. Moreover, they have little chance to develop feelings of empathy for others because the impact of their behavior on those around them is not pointed out. Their unrestrained behavior is often viewed as immature, inconsiderate, and unacceptable by peers and adults. The general negative reception such behaviors receive contributes to children's feelings of anxiety and low self-esteem. As a rule, children whose world is dominated by permissive adults tend to be withdrawn, unproductive, and unhappy. In adolescence, this style is frequently associated with delinquency and poor academic performance (Patterson & Stouthamer-Loeber, 1984; Pulkkinen, 1982).

The Authoritarian Style. Unlike permissive educators, authoritarian teachers have high standards for children's behavior. To achieve those standards, they act as autocrats who value children's unquestioning obedience above all else. Theirs is the philosophy of "Do what I tell you" and "Do it because I said so!" Failure to meet their expectations is dealt with swiftly and forcefully, most often through shaming techniques or physical punishment. In either case, their chief aim is to show children who's boss as opposed to helping children consider how their behavior affects others or how to figure out what better strategies to use in the future. Not too surprisingly, authoritarian teachers have cold, distant relationships with the children in their classes. Youngsters view them as harsh taskmasters who focus more on finding mistakes than on recognizing their attempts to comply (Schiamberg, 1988). Children whose primary experiences are with authoritarian adults

generally become unfriendly, suspicious, resentful, and unhappy in the classroom. They tend to be underachievers and exhibit increased incidents of misconduct as well as more extreme acting-out behaviors (Baumrind, 1983; Maccoby & Martin, 1983; Sroufe & Cooper, 1988).

In addition, the coercive disciplinary strategies characteristic of the authoritarian style cause children to remain dependent on adults to dictate behavioral standards. Youngsters follow rules out of fear or blind obedience, not out of empathy or concern for others (Raffini, 1980). This impedes their ability to develop the reasoning and caring necessary for internalization; therefore, children maintain an external orientation and remain at adherence.

The Authoritative Teaching Style. Authoritative teachers combine the positive attributes of the other styles just described and avoid the negative ones. They respond to children's needs with warmth and nurturance while establishing clear behavioral expectations (Bukatko & Daehler, 1992). Authoritative teachers also rely on additional strategies both permissive and authoritarian adults fail to use altogether. Thus, teachers who exemplify an authoritative style treat students in a friendly, affectionate manner. They make children feel important by allowing them to assume appropriate responsibility as well as by acknowledging their accomplishments. They also teach children relevant social skills to help them meet their needs in socially acceptable ways. Simultaneously, authoritative teachers establish high standards for children's behavior and are quick to take action to teach them how to behave. Explanations, demonstrations, suggestions, and other-oriented reasoning are the primary socialization strategies they use (LeFrancois, 1992; C. A. Smith, 1988). These adults use discipline encounters as opportunities for discussions related to guilt and empathy and as a means for teaching lessons about which behaviors to choose, which to avoid, and which to try instead. This nonpunitive form of behavior regulation is sometimes called *inductive discipline* because adults induce children to regulate their behavior based on the impact their actions will have on themselves and others.

It is the authoritative socialization style that has been most strongly correlated to the development of internal behavior controls in children (Franz, et al., 1991; Vasta et al., 1992). Children know what is expected of them and how to comply. Moreover, they tend to be sensitive to the needs of others, happy, cooperative, resistant to temptation, and socially responsible. They are also better able to initiate and maintain tasks on their own (Baumrind, 1983). Their behavior is the most socially competent of the three patterns described here. For these reasons, young children benefit when their teachers display an authoritative teaching style.

Adopting an Authoritative Teaching Style

Once it was thought teachers were instinctively authoritarian, permissive, or authoritative (Lewin, Lippitt, & White, 1939). We now know that although teachers do have personality traits and abilities that seem more compatible with one style or another, through training and practice any teacher can learn to be more authoritative (Kostelnik et al., in press; Peters & Kostelnik, 1981). The following strategies are ones that in combination exemplify an authoritative approach. They are listed sequentially so that in-

direct, preventative strategies precede more direct, remedial ones.

1. *Authoritative teachers make a special effort to build positive relationships with their pupils* (T. Gordon, 1989). In the classrooms of authoritative teachers, children are treated with warmth, caring, and respect. Teachers assume *all* children are worthy of such consideration despite their grades, behavior, appearance, or ethnic or socioeconomic background. This positive attitude is manifested in the following ways:

- Greet children by name.
- Get down to the children's level when talking with them.
- Smile at children often.
- Listen carefully to what children have to say.
- Speak politely to children.
- Invite children to elaborate on what they are saying.
- Wait for children to finish talking before introducing your own ideas.
- Comfort children who are unhappy or afraid.
- Laugh with children at their jokes.
- Acknowledge children's emotions.

Authoritative teaching begins with positive teacher/child relationships.

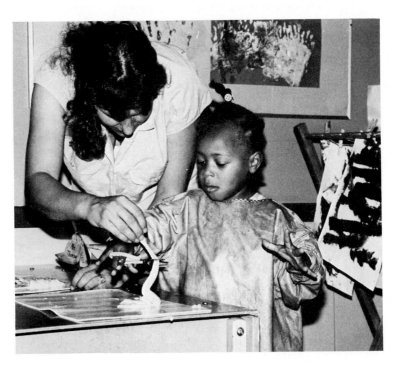

- Help children sort through their emotions.
- Assist children in finding constructive ways to express their emotions.

Authoritative teachers never coerce, shame, taunt, or physically hurt children for any reason.

2. *Authoritative teachers model the behaviors they hope children will imitate* (Bandura, 1989; Meichenbaum, 1977). Setting a good example is an effective way of teaching children right from wrong because it proves to them that the behavior is really desirable. But, simply observing appropriate actions does not necessarily teach children how to enact it themselves. To move to that level of learning, children's attention must be drawn to the specifics of the model's behavior. Teachers provide such guidance when they point out the model's actions and talk children through what they are seeing. This helps youngsters identify critical facets of an interaction that they might otherwise miss. Therefore, if a teacher wants children to copy his gentle handling of the class gerbil, it would be useful to say, "Watch how I pick up the gerbil. First, I'll put both hands under her tummy so I don't drop her. See how I'm holding my fingers? This way I don't squeeze her too hard." Showing children the procedure without direct explanation or hoping that they will figure it out themselves simply by watching is less likely to result in accurate imitation. Moreover, modeling is most potent when the teacher behaves in ways consistent with his or her words. Mrs. Lopez, who emphasizes the value of polite behaviors and who remembers to say "please," "thank you," and "excuse me" when talking to the children, illustrates such congruence. She is more likely to achieve compliance with her expectations than will Mrs. Kelly, who preaches good manners but frequently interrupts children or orders them to do things without the customary social graces.

3. *Authoritative teachers use positive attribution to support children's favorable self-perceptions* (S. G. Moore,1986; Ritchie & Toner, 1985). Teachers help children become tidier, less impulsive, more generous, or more cooperative by referring to them in these terms and espousing their belief that the child in question can act in these ways. For instance, when the children are standing at the door, Mrs. Martine notices their efforts to wait and makes remarks

such as "Corey, you're waiting very patiently," "Janice, you really know how to wait—you're standing with your arms down and your feet still," and "Keiko, you're showing a lot of patience standing there." Children hear remarks such as these frequently. The teacher does not wait for full compliance but recognizes approximations toward the desired end. In this way, children gradually perceive themselves as capable of exercising patience and become more patient over time. Likewise, before starting a small-group activity, Mr. Noor prefaces his directions by stating, "This project is going to require a lot of cooperation, and I know you can do it." In both examples, teachers have deliberately used positive attribution to promote children's positive self-image and increase their repertoire of socially acceptable behavior.

4. *Authoritative teachers emphasize cooperation rather than competition to promote empathy among children and increase children's social skills.* They encourage all children to do their best, but never at one another's expense (Marion, 1991). Thus, they avoid pitting one child or group of children against another (e.g., "Let's see who will get the most problems right, the boys or the girls") and refrain from using competition to motivate children to get things done (e.g., "Let's see who can put the most blocks away" or "Whoever gets the most problems right can pick the game for recess"). Similarly, they do not reinforce one child at the expense of another (e.g., "Cathleen, your paper is so very neat, I wish the rest of the class would try hard like you"). Such competitive strategies cause children to conclude there can only be one winner and that helping or cooperating with others will sabotage their chances to come out on top. To counteract self-centered thinking, teachers focus on individual progress and group accomplishments instead (e.g., "You got more problems right today than you did yesterday" or "Let's see how quickly we can all put the blocks away"). Remarks like these clear the way for students to come to one another's aid and work together as appropriate. In addition, group rewards encourage children to work as a team to accomplish common aims. Putting up a star for each book read by the class or each act of kindness shown is one way to help children keep track of their progress as a whole and di-

rect their attention to the positive outcomes an entire group can achieve.

5. *Authoritative teachers help children learn prosocial skills as a way to extend other-oriented understanding* (Eisenberg, 1986). Teachers plan activities such as inviting children to create a mural cooperatively or assigning "buddies" to help one another with a project as a way to accomplish this aim (C. A. Smith, 1982). They also carry out spontaneous instruction in naturally occurring circumstances. Inviting children to comfort an injured classmate or giving children information about how their teasing hurt another child's feelings are typical situations in which such on-the-spot teaching could occur. Through these means children learn the basics of kindness—what it looks like, how it feels. They also explore its applications to real-life situations and have opportunities to rehearse related skills. It is prosocial teaching that teachers have in mind when they use the following techniques (Kostelnik et al., in press):

- Model prosocial behaviors themselves.
- Watch children for signs of prosocial behavior, and highlight instances of kindness as they occur.
- Help children become aware that someone needs help or cooperation. Give children relevant information such as "Look at Veronica. She's struggling to carry all those books. She could use some help."
- Teach children various scripts or words they might use to elicit help and cooperation from other people. For instance, "Tell Mona, 'This board's too big for me to carry all by myself. Please help me'" or "I need your help."
- Point out situations in which people could help or cooperate.
- Assist children in figuring out what kind of help or cooperation best fits different situations.
- Work with children to evaluate the results of their actions.
- Help children recognize kindness directed at them.
- Help children accept kindness from others.
- Support children when their attempts at kindness fail.
- Create classroom activities (at learning centers, in small or large groups) in which children practice prosocial skills such as asking for help, working together, or evaluating their combined efforts.

6. *Authoritative teachers help children learn the skills of compromise as a means for achieving goals nonaggressively* (Reynolds, 1990). Teachers do this in three ways. One is to create natural opportunities for children to practice interpersonal skills. For instance, rather than putting the same color of paint on two easels to avoid arguments, the teacher makes available different colors at each. He or she then urges the children to find ways to share their resources. Children are allowed to work things out for themselves with on-the-spot coaching provided by peers or the adult as needed.

A second approach is for teachers to use puppets, flannel board stories, storybooks, or skits to illustrate relevant skills such as sharing, taking turns, and bargaining (Crary, 1984). Children have chances to see both appropriate and inappropriate skill use, evaluate the tactics chosen, and generate ideas for alternate resolutions.

A third strategy is to turn children's everyday arguments into opportunities for them to learn conflict resolution techniques in real-life situations. This latter method is particularly important, since even youngsters who can rationally discuss the value of compromise within the context of a planned activity may forget and resort to aggressive strategies in the heat of actual confrontations. At times like these, children benefit from having a third party such as a mediator assist them through the steps necessary for reconciliation to occur. Mediators are often adults, but they may also be other children at school (J. Gordon, 1990; Kostelnik & Stein, 1984). (Refer to chap. 8, "The Social Domain," for an account of what conflict mediation entails and how to teach children effective mediation skills.)

7. *Authoritative teachers manage time, space, and materials to maximize children's self-regulating behavior* (Hildebrand, 1990; Schickedanz, Hansen, & Forsyth, 1990). They understand the link among timing, the physical setting, and children's behavior, which allows them to use classroom management as a tool to achieve social goals. Authoritative teachers develop daily schedules that reflect children's attention span and needs for activity and social interaction. Quiet times are followed by active

ones; teacher-led instruction is balanced by long periods of child-directed activity. Teachers signal changes in routine well in advance and minimize the time children spend waiting.

When they arrange classroom furniture and equipment, teachers strive to give children easy access to functional work spaces. The physical environment also provides children clear signals about how particular spaces are to be used and how many students can be accommodated in each place. Enough activity spaces are available so that all children can be occupied constructively while still having choices about what they might do.

Materials are organized, complete, and in good repair. Those meant for children are placed where students can find and use them safely, with minimum supervision. Forbidden or dangerous objects are stored out of sight and out of reach.

Indirect instructional techniques such as these reduce conflict and frustration among the children. They also allow youngsters to function independently and practice making choices. As a

result, positive social interactions increase, and fewer rules are necessary to guide children's behavior. This makes it easier for both children and adults to concentrate on those rules that are truly essential to the group.

8. *Authoritative teachers encourage children to participate in the rule-making process* (Schickedanz, Hansen, et al., 1990). In open-ended discussions about rule-related situations, they invite children to generate personal ideas for rules. These are duly noted, recorded, then posted for all to see. Such discussions are carried on throughout the year so that youngsters may consider the value of their rules over time and revise them as necessary.

9. *Authoritative teachers establish only a few well-chosen rules at a time* (Hildebrand, 1990). To decide what rules to make, they consider the following questions: (a) Is the child's behavior potentially or currently unsafe for the child or others? (b) Does the child's behavior threaten to damage property? (c) Does the child's behavior interfere with the rights of others? If the

Even very young children can help create meaningful rules for the classroom.

answer to any of these questions is yes, the teacher intervenes by making a rule (Kostelnik et al., in press). While individual teachers vary in their interpretation of what makes a situation potentially dangerous or threatening, considering these three questions is a consistent, dependable means for deciding when to set limits on children's behavior.

In addition, authoritative teachers only make rules that are important enough to enforce every time they are broken. In other words, they determine whether the problem behavior deserves attention each time it happens. If this is the case, a rule is set; if not, no rule is created (Gootman, 1988). For instance, when Ms. Williams sees a child deliberately ruin another child's artwork, she intervenes immediately, reminding children of the rule about respecting people's property. Also, she continues to enforce the rule, day after day, no matter how tired or otherwise occupied she might be. On the other hand, although she sometimes finds it irritating for children to smack their lips loudly while they eat, there are many days when she does not want to be bothered with restricting that behavior. Since "on again, off again" rules do not provide the consistent enforcement children need to learn them, Ms. Williams tolerates this minor annoyance in order to address more important issues for the time being. Later, if she determines that children's lip smacking truly interferes with their ability to eat safely, she would then make "quiet lips" a rule and enforce it each day. Thus, the issue of importance helps authoritative teachers figure out their priorities and focus on only a few rules at a time. This makes it more likely that children will be able to follow them successfully.

10. *Authoritative teachers offer children reasons for why certain behaviors are acceptable or unacceptable* (Brody & Shaffer, 1982; Marion, 1991). Why are some teachers upset when children push others off the swing? Because they fear someone might get hurt. Why do they become irritated when pupils interrupt the story, time and again? Because interrupting interferes with their train of thought and makes it difficult for other children to concentrate. Although these are obvious conclusions to grown-ups, they are less apparent to children. Reasons clarify the situation and help children recognize the

logic of rules they might not discover on their own. Furthermore, reasons offer information to children regarding the effect of their behavior on others. This increases their understanding of interpersonal dynamics, that is, the relationship between their acts and the physical and psychological well-being of others.

Also, because children do not always make the connection from one interaction to another, reasons provide a link that may otherwise be missing. For instance, a child who has been told that pinching is taboo because it hurts may not conclude that hair pulling and scratching are likewise inappropriate until the teacher points out their similar negative effects. As children hear such explanations repeated over and over again, they eventually use them as guidelines for determining right from wrong on their own. Thus, reasoning is essential in helping children achieve self-control.

Teacher's reasons are most effective when they are specific. Mr. Ramirez is being specific when he tells Dana, "Read silently so that other people can concentrate on their work." In this way he has linked the desired action to a rationale based on the rights of others in the class. In other situations, he might refer to safety issues or the protection of property. It would be too general, and therefore inappropriate to require silent reading "because I said so" or "because that's the rule in our room." Moreover, the way he stated his reason was in a short, simple sentence that focused on one behavior at a time rather than telling Dana to do several things at once. Under the latter conditions, the child might be confused and so unable to comply.

11. *Authoritative teachers make rules that are reasonable, definable, and positive* (Clarizio, 1980; Hildebrand, 1990). Reasonable means children can actually do the required behavior; that is, youngsters have both the knowledge and ability to follow the rule. For instance, if children are expected to work on their journals independently, the teacher must first determine if they already possess the necessary skills—knowledge of where the journals are kept, previous practice with paper and writing tools, the ability to determine their property from that of others, and the skills to write in a focused way for a period of time. If children lack know-how about any of these things, the teacher might re-

vise the rule to match their abilities or spend time teaching them the required actions.

Definable rules are ones in which both the adult and child have the same understanding of what the rule is. Effective rules identify the exact behaviors the adult wants the child to perform. Specific rules such as "Walk, don't run" or "Knock over only your own blocks" are easier for children to follow than are vague statements, such as "Act nice" or "Behave yourself."

Finally, children are more successful at following rules that tell them what to do, instead of what not to do. "Put your hands in your pockets" is less difficult for children to respond to than "Don't fidget" or "No pushing." Likewise, "Sing softly—don't shout" is more apt to lead to compliance than the statement "Don't shout" all by itself. Therefore, how rules are set has much to do with how well children can follow them (Marion, 1991; Raffini, 1980). Teachers who keep these characteristics in mind are more likely to help children move toward internalization than those who do not.

12. *Authoritative teachers remind children of the rules often.* They know children may forget what constitutes appropriate behavior from one day to the next or from one situation to another. They also realize that although children may understand that certain behaviors, such as running in the classroom, are not allowed, youngsters may not remember what to do instead. Teacher efforts to help children in this regard take two forms. One is to talk with children about desirable behaviors at times when infractions are not an issue. Such discussions allow children to explore calmly the value and reasons for certain expectations without the added pressure of conflict between their needs or desires and those of others. A second strategy is to remind children of the rules right before those rules are needed. For example, teachers say, "Remember to walk in the classroom" when children are caught running. They avoid accusatory statements such as "How many times have I told you about running inside?" or "You know better than to run inside." These latter phrases fail to teach children the appropriate alternate behavior and do not help them remember what to do the next time. The former reminder serves as a minilesson from which children can extract meaningful information for the future.

13. *Authoritative teachers use positive consequences to maintain children's desirable behaviors.* They recognize the effort it takes for children to display proactive behaviors or compliance, and they take the time to acknowledge those productive outcomes. One way they do this is by using effective praise (Goode & Brophy, 1984; Hitz & Driscoll, 1988). This means giving children specific feedback about the appropriate behaviors they display and why such actions are desirable. Thus, Ms. Tanimoto reinforces Bert's efforts to remember to raise his hand by saying, "Bert, you remembered to raise your hand. That shows you have something to tell us." She does not simply say, "Good job, Bert." The former comment highlights Bert's appropriate behavior in a way that makes sense to him and acknowledges that he has followed a classroom rule. Conversely, the perfunctory "Good job" gives Bert little information and may lose its meaning over time.

Sometimes positive consequences are implemented in the form of earned privileges. For instance, if the rule is "Push the keys on the computer one at a time," children might be told that when they demonstrate this skill that they can use the computer on their own. By granting increased independence, the teacher rewards children for carrying out the desired action.

14. *Authoritative teachers treat lapses in children's compliance as opportunities to teach them constructive alternate behaviors.* They realize that children are just learning how to behave in the childhood setting and that mistakes are a natural part of the process. Subsequently, teachers pay careful attention to the dynamics of problem situations and look for cues that may point to real, underlying issues related to children's negative behaviors. It is these issues that serve as the basis for instruction (Hendrick, 1992). For instance, when Mr. Krushka sees Hallie hit Lucy, he immediately stops the unacceptable behavior. He also conducts a brief discussion with the girls to find out what caused the argument. He may discover that Hallie is angry because Lucy pushed her on the way out the door. His response would be to forbid hitting because it hurts and help Hallie figure out a way to tell Lucy of her anger rather than hitting. Hence, the rule would be "Talk, don't hit." On the other hand, if Hallie's hitting was an attempt

to gain Lucy's attention, the rule might become "Call Lucy by name or tap her gently on the arm. Hitting is not allowed."

15. *Authoritative teachers stop children's unsafe behavior first, then work on resolving the problem that prompted it* (Reynolds, 1990). When children's actions are potentially harmful to themselves or to others, teachers step in immediately to halt the dangerous actions. At times that requires physical intervention such as positioning oneself between two combatants or using mild physical restraint. Once the dangerous situation has been neutralized and children can focus on what is being said, the adult begins to help children work through the difficulty. This may be accomplished through holding a conversation, redirecting, offering children choices, removing the child from the situation for a brief time, or modifying the environment in some way to make it easier for children to meet their needs and get along.

16. *Authoritative teachers use logical consequences to help children learn acceptable conduct from the experience of being corrected.* Logical consequences are carried out with the long-term goal of teaching children self-discipline. Properly applied, they teach children alternate behaviors to replace the inappropriate strategies they may be using to satisfy their needs and desires. As these substitute means are strengthened through practice and positive consequences, children gradually incorporate them into their behavioral repertoire, which makes it easier for them to act appropriately in the future.

Logical consequences make an obvious connection between the child's behavior and the resulting disciplinary action (Gootman, 1988; Marion, 1991). Consequences of this type help children either rehearse the desired behavior or, in some way, restore a problem situation to a more positive state. For example, if the rule is "Walk, don't run" and Louise runs down the hall, a logical consequence would be to have her retrace her steps and walk. The act of walking actually approximates the rule and allows Louise to enact it physically. This provides her with a better reminder of it than simply scolding her. Children who practice rules in this way increase their chances for future compliance (Dinkmeyer & McKay, 1988).

At times, such approximations are not feasible, and so restitution is an alternate choice. For instance, if Julie draws on the classroom wall, it would be logical to insist that she wash off the marks. This action returns the wall to a more acceptable state and shows Julie that the unacceptable act of defacing the classroom will not be tolerated. This type of teacher intervention is a better solution than simply forbidding her to participate in a favorite activity or making her sit away from the group for awhile. Although the latter acts demonstrate adult displeasure, they do not teach Julie responsibility toward school property. Used too often, such unrelated consequences keep children at the adherence level of compliance rather than providing them with the tools needed for internalization.

17. *Authoritative teachers warn children of the logical consequences for breaking rules before applying them.* This is accomplished through an "either-or" statement that repeats the rule and describes to the child what will happen if the rule is broken (Kostelnik et al., in press). For example, if the rule is "Push your sleeves up before you paint," the warning could be "Either push your sleeves up yourself, or I will help you." If the rule is "Wait your turn in line," the warning might be "Either wait your turn, or go back to the end of the line." In both cases, the warning gives children the opportunity and incentive to change their behavior themselves. It also serves as a signal that if they do not comply of their own accord, the adult will take steps to ensure their compliance. Maintaining a calm demeanor is essential so that the warning becomes a plain statement of fact rather than a threat. Its purpose is to provide maximum guidance to children before adult enforcement.

18. *Authoritative teachers follow through on their warnings when children fail to comply.* Following through is essential because it helps children make a connection between the broken rule and a more desirable alternate behavior. Since logical consequences are educational in nature, following through gives children valuable information about how to redirect their behavior (Rich, 1985). It also shows children that adults mean what they say, which makes the classroom a more predictable place in which to learn.

The follow-through procedure consists of first acknowledging the child's desire within the situation. This is a nonevaluative summary of the event from the child's point of view. The next step is to repeat the warning briefly and then declare that the consequence will take place. A sample script follows: "Ralph, you're eager to get a drink. Remember I said either wait your turn or go to the end of the line. Now go to the end of the line." The teacher waits a moment to see if Ralph can do it himself. If not, the teacher might have to escort Ralph to the designated spot as a way to maintain enforcement.

Following through in this way must be consistent: every time the rule is broken the consequence must be enforced. Rules enforced erratically, varying from situation to situation or from child to child, are ones that children ignore. So, authoritative teachers insist on only a few rules as a way to maintain consistency.

The timeliness of the follow-through is another important factor in its success. Rule enforcement must be immediate. Once the teacher gives the warning and a short time for the child to comply, he or she must follow through if compliance does not occur. Long delays between when the child breaks the rule and when the follow-through takes place diminish the educational impact of the consequence.

Finally, it should be noted that when warnings are consistently followed by enactment of logical consequences, teachers' actions become predictable to children. Youngsters learn that if they do not comply at the warning stage, a follow-through will take place. This encourages them to respond to the warning without having to experience a consequence directly. Behavioral change at this point shows some self-regulation by children, although at the adherence level. Gradually, children learn to use rules and their accompanying reasons as a behavioral guide. In this way, they begin to exercise greater control over their behavior while the teacher exerts less. A strong foundation for eventual internalization is thus formed.

Practitioner Reactions to Authoritative Teaching

All the authoritative teaching strategies outlined here can be adopted by individual teachers with positive results (Gootman, 1988; Peters & Kostelnik, 1981; Stein & Kostelnik, 1984). Those who use such techniques report greater self-satisfaction and confidence in their disciplinary actions, increased harmony in the classroom, and more frequent incidents of positive behaviors among children (Richberg, 1991). These productive outcomes can be enhanced even further when authoritative methods are used throughout an entire building. That is, self-discipline among pupils is more likely to develop and flourish when all school personnel (full-time, part-time, paid, and volunteer) collectively and consciously set out to adopt an authoritative style (Hyman & D'Alessandro, 1984). The following section is an abbreviated summary of how one school went about accomplishing this aim, and Figure 14.2 presents its final discipline plan.

PLANNING AND ORGANIZING A PROGRAMWIDE DISCIPLINE POLICY

Teachers and administrators as well as parents whose children were enrolled at Adams Elementary expressed concern over worsening disciplinary problems at the school. They noted that incidents of students fighting, disruptive behavior, and children defying teachers seemed on the rise. Such difficulties were especially prevalent in the halls and on the playground. Moreover, they were not confined to any particular classroom or grade level but seemed to pervade the whole school. Problems were just as likely to occur in the Chapter I class or in the kindergarten as they were in the fifth grade. Both adults and children lamented the unhappy atmosphere that resulted.

The Process

February 1989: Following a series of informal discussions, the issue of discipline was brought up at an after-school staff meeting. It was agreed that something had to be done to improve the learning environment at Adams School. Individual teachers volunteered to solicit disciplinary procedures from other area schools for the Adams staff to review.

March 1989: At an after-school meeting the Adams staff read through materials gathered from other schools. After much discussion, they agreed that a buildingwide disciplinary policy was desirable. However, they were not comfortable with the penalty-oriented procedures that characterized most of the materials they had read. The principal was asked to contact a child development expert at a nearby university, to help the staff sort through the issues and provide guidance about what to do next.

April 1989:   At a breakfast meeting with the university consultant, the principal and several staff members discussed various disciplinary concerns. At its conclusion, it was agreed that solving the disciplinary problems at Adams School would be the focus of staff training for the entire 1989–90 school year. A later analysis of that discussion revealed the following problems:

- School rules were vague ("Share your smile"; "Respect others") or negative ("Don't run in school").
- Rule enforcement lacked immediacy. Staff were hesitant to correct other teachers' children; playground and lunchroom infractions were referred by monitors to classroom teachers to deal with long after they occurred.
- Rule enforcement was inconsistent from adult to adult, child to child, and situation to situation. Staff varied in the rules they enforced, in the kinds of consequences they used, when consequences were applied, and what prompted a trip to the office. They also differed in their ideas of what should happen "at the office" and if and when children should be suspended from school.
- Little time was spent teaching children the rules. It was assumed that students should know what to do and why.
- Children spent a lot of time in situations with adults with whom they had no close ties (on the bus, in the lunchroom, on the playground). The primary adult role during these times was to watch for infractions.

May–June 1989:   The principal, the university consultant, and three teachers representing the staff met and developed a training proposal. It was submitted to the total staff and approved with suggested revisions.

July–August 1989:   The training proposal was next submitted to the district office as a professional development project. Funds were granted to support two half days of in-service training, pay for refreshments for eight working sessions, provide written materials for each participant, and cover the costs of the consultant. School staff agreed to devote six after-school staff meetings to the project.

October 1989:   Session 1 entailed a group discussion of self-discipline and principles of authoritative rule making. Session 2 was a group discussion of appropriate consequences.

November 1989:   Session 3 involved a group discussion of how to promote children's prosocial behavior.

January 1990:   Teachers began practicing some of the skills they had learned in sessions 1, 2, and 3. Teachers conducted discussions with children about rights/rules and recorded their ideas. Specialists, lunchroom aides, playground volunteers, and bus drivers also visited classrooms to discuss children's notions of desirable behavior. The children generated 280 rules. These were turned over to the consultant to consolidate for staff review. At a Parent Teacher Organization (PTO) meeting, parents were invited to make suggestions about children's school conduct and their own role in a schoolwide discipline plan.

February 1990:   Session 4 was a half-day in-service program devoted to further consolidating rules and linking them to authoritative principles. Teachers engaged in mutual problem solving regarding their use of the authoritative skills they had been practicing since January.

March 1990:   Session 5 was another half-day in-service meeting devoted to developing logical consequences to support each rule and determining appropriate unrelated consequences.

April 1990:   Session 6 was a workshop for volunteers and bus drivers to review the Discipline Plan and to practice authoritative strategies. Session 7 was also a workshop for teachers and administrators to review the Discipline Plan and practice authoritative strategies.

May 1990:   An open meeting was held with parents to elicit reactions, review the Discipline Plan, and demonstrate authoritative strategies.

June 1990: Session 8 involved an after-school meeting to revise the written plan in accordance with feedback received from all groups concerned. It was agreed that future rule changes must be discussed and approved by the staff and children. Procedural changes would require adult approval only.

July and August 1990: Volunteers from the staff met to clarify details of the Discipline Plan and develop a fall orientation for children and parents. The plan was sent to all families and staff with a cover letter prior to the first day of school.

September 1990: First-day assembly for parents and children was held. The Adams School Discipline Plan was introduced by the principal and the guidance counselor, with children and parents having an opportunity to ask questions. The next day, classroom orientations were conducted, emphasizing the children's contributions. Later in the month, lunchroom, playground, and schoolbus orientations were also carried out classroom by classroom. The guidance counselor assumed responsibility for the latter orientations in conjunction with the relevant supervising adults. These latter adults also spent time in classrooms getting to know children.

October 1990: A newsletter was sent home from school to parents describing initial results of the plan. A PTO meeting was held highlighting the plan and giving parents opportunities to brainstorm related problem-solving strategies for use at home.

November 1990: Meetings were held with all paid and volunteer school personnel to discuss successes, concerns, and possible revisions.

January 1991: The guidance counselor began to train fourth and fifth graders who had volunteered to be playground mediators.

February 1991: Peer mediation on the playground began. Playground monitors participated in a workshop on cooperative games (at their own request) to gain strategies for promoting prosocial behavior on the playground.

March and April 1991: Meetings were held with parents, children, staff, and volunteers to discuss successes, concerns, and possible revisions.

May 1991: Plans were made for maintaining the Adams School Discipline Plan the next year.

The Results

Following 1 year of implementation, initial results of the Adams School Discipline Plan are positive. Surveys and interviews with teachers, administrators, volunteers, children, and parents indicate a widely held perception among all groups that the school atmosphere has greatly improved. On-site observations clearly show that the adults' emphasis is on teaching children the rules and acknowledging children's positive behaviors rather than simply penalizing inappropriate actions. Most infractions are dealt with on the spot. During the first 3 months of school, the penalty room was used almost every week. However, no child moved beyond a second visit within a given week. By January, the penalty room received less use. This trend continued throughout the rest of the year, with entire weeks of disuse occurring by May (Preston, 1991; Richberg, 1991). Adults and children identified the following strengths as contributing to the plan's success:

- It was based on a team effort that included everyone who might potentially be affected by it.
- The plan set forth only a few rules that children helped to define.
- It emphasized teaching alternative behaviors to replace inappropriate ones.
- It established a link between beliefs (rights) and actions (rules).
- It provided a consistent guide for appropriate school behavior known to everyone, adults and children alike.
- The plan included opportunities for home and school input over time.
- It also included opportunities for staff, children and parents to discuss ideas and work together to find solutions.
- The plan endowed all participants with a sense of competence, accomplishment, and hope.

The Adams School Discipline Plan is simply an example of one school's approach to adopting authoritative strategies aimed at enhancing children's development of self-discipline. The product it created was uniquely suited to its own

FIGURE 14.2
The Adams School Discipline Plan

Preamble

The ultimate aim of the Adams School Discipline Plan is to create a happy, predictable learning environment in which both children and adults flourish. School staff, volunteers, children, and parents all contributed to this document. It was created with the following beliefs in mind.

- People learn best in an environment in which they are safe and in which they are treated with kindness and respect.
- Everyone at Adams School has certain rights. These rights form the basis for school rules.
- Rules are guides for behavior. They tell people what to do versus what not to do.
- People learn best when they know what the rules are and why those rules exist.
- When people behave in ways consistent with school expectations, their efforts should be acknowledged.
- When people's behaviors are inconsistent with school rules, consequences aimed at teaching more appropriate behaviors should be used. The first consequences of choice are logical ones, that is, consequences directly related to the broken rule. If such consequences are used to no avail, appropriate unrelated consequences (involving loss of certain school privileges) will be carried out.

Rights and Rules at Adams School

People have the right to play and work in a clean school.

Rule 1: Keep the school building clean.
Examples of this rule as suggested by the children:
   a. Pick up all litter and gum and dispose of it in trash containers.
   b. Preserve hall and room bulletin boards.
   c. Mark, paint, write, or draw on paper only, not directly on walls, floors, desks, tables, or chairs.
Rule 2: Keep the classrooms clean.
Examples of this rule as suggested by the children:
   a. Clean up your own mess.
   b. Return materials to their proper place.
   c. Pick up what you drop.
Rule 3: Keep the bathrooms clean.
Examples of this rule as suggested by the children:
   a. Put litter and paper towels in trash containers only, not in sinks or toilets.
   b. Urinate only in the toilet or urinal.
   c. Flush toilets after using.
Rule 4: Keep the lunchroom clean.
Examples of this rule as suggested by the children:
   a. Keep food on trays, in lunchboxes, or in your mouth.
   b. No food fights.
   c. No putting food on people.
   d. Put trash in trash containers.

People have the right to feel and be safe at school and on school grounds.

Rule 5: Play safely outdoors.
Examples of this rule as suggested by the children:
   a. Stay on the playground.

FIGURE 14.2
continued

    b. Use equipment and materials (e.g., balls, bats, etc.) as they were intended.

    c. Don't push people off equipment.

    d. Keep sticks, stones, ice, and sand on the ground or in your pocket.

    e. Keep from hurting others. Do not push, hit, jump on, kick, trip, scratch, punch, spit at, bite, tackle, pull at, grab, or snatch things from people.

    f. Stop chasing, wrestling, or play fighting when children or adults tell you to stop.

Rule 6: Behave safely inside the school building.

Examples of this rule as suggested by the children:

    a. Walk in school.

    b. Use materials as they were intended.

    c. Leave things that might hurt or frighten yourself or others at home, including hardballs, wooden or steel bats, any kinds of guns or knives.

    d. Leave classrooms only with permission and return there when you have finished.

    e. When leaving your classroom, go directly to your destination.

    f. Follow all drill procedures.

Rule 7: Behave safely to and from school.

Examples of this rule as suggested by the children:

    a. Stay seated on the bus.

    b. Obey safeties at the crossings.

People have the right to feel good about how they are treated at school.

Rule 8: Respect the personal property of others.

Examples of this rule as suggested by the children:

    a. Touch other people's personal property only with their permission.

    b. Stay out of other people's desks, backpacks, cubbies, and lunch space.

    c. Take only what belongs to you.

Rule 9: Treat people with respect.

Examples of this rule as suggested by the children:

    a. Touch other people only with their permission. Do not push, hit, kick, trip, bite, tackle, spit at, kiss, fight or chase.

    b. Stop (e.g., chasing or teasing) when children say "stop."

    c. Do not peek at others in the bathroom.

    d. Wait your turn.

    e. Address people by their appropriate name.

Rule 10: Be kind to others.

Examples of this rule as suggested by the children:

    a. Be patient with others.

    b. Comfort, sympathize, reassure.

    c. Offer encouraging words rather than laughing at the mistakes of others.

    d. Offer put-ups, not put-downs.

    e. Use polite language—"Please," "Thank you."

Rule 11: Be helpful to others.

Examples of this rule as suggested by the children:

    a. Speak quietly while inside.

    b. Look for ways to help.

    c. Decide to help.

    d. Offer to help one another by carrying things, picking up something dropped and giving it back, or opening doors.

 e. Offer to share materials, give information, provide assistance.
 f. Help children in conflict. If children are arguing without striking one another, stand by to offer ideas, if asked, but do not interfere. If children are arguing and physically hurting one another, tell an adult.

Rule 12: Use nonhurtful ways to express yourself and to get what you want.
Examples of this rule as suggested by the children:
 a. Speak politely to others (no teasing, bugging, swearing, putting down, name calling).
 b. Resolve conflicts in a peaceful manner by discussing, persuading, negotiating, compromising.

Rule Enforcement

All adults working with children at Adams School will proceed through the following steps in teaching and enforcing school rules.

Step 1: If a child's behavior violates a school rule, the child will be reminded of the rule and the reason behind it, in a serious, firm tone. If the child complies, he or she will be praised. If the behavior continues, the adult will proceed to Step 2.

Step 2: The adult will issue a verbal warning to the child. The warning will include a repetition of the rule and identification of what logical consequence will occur if the child continues the unacceptable behavior. The warning will be stated matter-of-factly.

Step 3: The child will be given a few moments to comply. If this should happen, the child will be praised. If compliance is not forthcoming, the adult will proceed to Step 4.

Step 4: The adult will follow through with the stated consequence.

If the rule violation involves the destruction of property, a logical consequence would be to have the child repair, replace, or clean up the damaged item or area.

If the rule violation involves unsafe use of objects or equipment or dangerous actions within the school building or on the playground, a logical consequence would be to have the child rehearse the appropriate alternate behavior with adult assistance if necessary.

If the rule violation involves dangerous or unkind acts toward peers (verbal and/or physical abuse), the logical consequences in the case of physical injury would be for the perpetrator to assist with first aid needs and accompany the victim to the nurse if necessary. In the case of emotional injury, the students involved will be expected to work toward reaching a mutually agreeable solution through dialogue. This may be supported through the efforts of an adult or peer mediator.

Step 5: If children fail to comply with the preceding consequences, they will be reminded that further noncompliance will result in the unrelated consequence of losing recess privileges.

Step 6: The child will be given a few moments to carry out the logical consequence. If the child complies, the episode is over and the child may resume his or her normal activities.

If the child continues the problem behavior or refuses to carry out the logical consequence, he or she will be told to report to the "penalty" room either immediately (if the incident occurs during the noon hour or recess) or at the soonest recess time. He or she will be given a paper identifying which rule was broken to give to the adult in charge. (The penalty room will be supervised by different staff members on a rotating basis.) The adult in charge will fill out a behavior report form, identifying the child by name, the broken rule, the name of the adult who sent the child, and the name of the child's teacher.

- First visit within a week—The child remains in the penalty room for the rest of the noon hour or recess (maximum of 15 minutes). The child works with the penalty room supervisor to develop a prevention plan for how to avoid this problem behavior in the future. Library books are available for children to read for the rest of the time. The behavior report and a copy of the child's prevention plan is sent to the child's teacher and to the principal.

FIGURE 14.2
continued

- Second visit within a week (for the same infraction)—The child remains in penalty room for the rest of the noon hour or recess. Revisions are made to the prevention plan as needed. The behavior report and prevention plan are sent to the child's teacher, the principal, and the child's parents for a signature. Recess privileges will not be reinstated until the signed form is returned.

- Third visit within a week (for the same infraction)—The child will call his or her parent or write/dictate a letter explaining the problem. The principal or a designate will cover for teachers who are supervising children throughout this phase. The parent will be informed that the next infraction for the week will result in a school conference between the family and school personnel. A signed form must be returned to the school in which the parent acknowledges receipt of this information.

- Fourth visit within a week (for the same broken rule)—Parents will confer with student and school personnel before recess privileges are reinstated.

- Fifth visit within a week (for the same broken rule)—A 1-day out-of-school suspension will be invoked.

Students begin with a clean slate the first school day of each week.

circumstances and would not match exactly those of another program. However, the process the school went through is illustrative of what any program might do in creating its own buildingwide discipline plan.

QUESTIONS ADULTS ASK ABOUT DISCIPLINE

The subject of discipline prompts many questions from teachers, administrators, and parents regarding philosophy and implementation. The following are some of the most common issues they think about.

Shouldn't children already know how to follow rules by the time they get to school?

Children are not born socially competent. Rather, social learning evolves slowly over many years. Thus, children ages 3 through 8 are still novices at knowing the rules of society and how to comply with them. Also, they are just beginning to comprehend the complexities of interpersonal relationships and still have much to learn about human interactions. Although such learning begins at home, school entry (whether it be nursery school, Head Start, kindergarten, or first grade) marks a transitional period during which children must redefine

themselves within the context of an institution more formal than the family, neighborhood, or child care center (Alexander & Entwistle, 1988). Throughout this time children are figuring out the parameters of the student role and how to function successfully within it. As a result, children in early childhood programs continually experiment with assorted social strategies, discovering what works and what does not, what is allowed and what is not.

Not only does this kind of learning take time, but it cannot be hurried. Children are not simply memorizing rules—they are having to construct an understanding of what each rule means as well as apply that conception to their own behavior. Consequently, knowing school rules and being able to follow them independently are two important but very different tasks, with the latter being much more challenging than the first. It is unrealistic for school personnel or parents to expect children to have achieved self-discipline before they enter school or soon thereafter. It takes years, not days or weeks, for such mastery to develop. For these reasons, child socialization deserves special consideration in the early childhood curriculum. Adults cannot simply demand that children engage in socially acceptable behaviors; instead, their focus must be on teaching children how to do so.

Why can't I just tell children "No"?

I've heard of an approach to discipline that involves simply informing children of the rules, then marking their names on the board with a series of checkmarks for each violation. This sounds like a real time saver. What's wrong with that?

When children break rules, adults sometimes find it quicker and easier simply to say "Stop" or "We don't do that here." Occasionally these shortcuts have the desired effect: children quit what they are doing. Unfortunately, such success is usually short-lived and children repeat the same infractions later on. Moreover, youngsters tend to comply only under direct supervision. The moment the adult's back is turned or the child is in a new circumstance, the problem behavior resumes. Such lapses occur because admonitions alone do not lead to children's internalization of the rules but to adherence instead (Reynolds, 1990). The same is true for any disciplinary procedure that emphasizes rewards and consequences to the exclusion of reasoning, rehearsal, restitution, and cooperation. The former methods promote children's reliance on external controls; the latter enhance self-discipline.

Don't authoritative strategies take up a lot of teacher time?

The disciplinary strategies teachers use when children are young influence the attitudes and dispositions youngsters carry with them into later life (Katz & Chard, 1989). Likewise, the strategies they use early in the year affect how well children behave as the year goes on. If self-discipline is our ultimate aim, then we must consciously use the authoritative strategies that fit that goal, right from the start. Initially, such strategies will be more time-consuming than authoritarian or permissive techniques. However, as the weeks and months go by, children will gradually grow in their ability to monitor their own behavior. Moreover, as children's skills increase, not only will they refrain from inappropriate actions, but they will also initiate greater numbers of positive ones as well. As these conditions prevail, time spent on corrective action becomes less and less, making the initial investment of teacher time well worthwhile.

What about sending rule violators to the principal's office?

The old standby of sending children to the see the principal when they are disruptive in class actually undermines the teacher's authority and makes subsequent confrontations between adult and child more likely. Although teachers may wish to impress on children the seriousness of their misdeeds by banishing them from the classroom, the message actually conveyed is "I give up" or "I don't know how to handle your behavior." A better alternative is to use logical consequences consistently within the classroom each time children break rules. This familiarizes them with appropriate alternate behaviors and shows them that teachers mean what they say. Early on, teachers may have to sacrifice instructional time with the group in order to follow through on stated consequences with an individual child. The story may be set aside for the day or the math activity shortened. However, these immediate liabilities will be offset in the future because fewer such incidents will occur (Stein & Kostelnik, 1984). Children will come to recognize the predictability of the teacher's response and discover that corrective action is always taken without the adult losing patience or giving in. Trips to the office will happen rarely and only in the most serious circumstances. When they do, it will be in the company of the teacher, who with the principal will participate in a team-oriented approach to problem solving with the child.

How can we achieve consistency among all the adults in the program?

The essential element in achieving long-term consistency is communication. Communication is enhanced when

- disciplinary policies are written down and known to all;
- orientations are conducted for newcomers;
- periodic staff meetings are held in which staff members brainstorm solutions to typical behavior problems, discuss ways to promote positive child behaviors, and reach a consensus about how certain rules will be interpreted and enforced; and
- school policies are reviewed and revised annually or as needed.

Communication is also essential day to day. This is especially true when some children push the limits with one adult, only to move on to someone else when a follow-through is in the offing. That is, the same child may engage in a series of inappropriate actions without experiencing any real consequences. Adults minimize such problems when they advise one another of the warnings they have given certain children. This is best done within the child's hearing so that he or she becomes aware that a particular rule is still in effect regardless of location. For instance, if Leona has been warned that pushing again on the playground will result in her having to sit on the side for 5 minutes, other playground monitors should be alerted that this is the case. Anyone seeing her push once more can enforce the consequence regardless of whether it takes place near the swings or on the slide. Such communication creates a consistent environment in which the child soon learns that pushing is truly unacceptable.

How can we promote consistency between the way discipline is handled in the program and how it is addressed in the home?

The key to achieving some measure of consistency between home and program is to establish open channels of communication in which all parties feel valued and respected. The first step is for each group to share basic information. Parents need to know how children will be socialized at school and the rationale for particular goals and strategies. It is also necessary for them to receive accurate information about their own role in the process. Teachers in turn need to know about parents' aspirations for their children and measures they use at home to promote these aims. This kind of data could be exchanged during a home visit, at a school orientation, or through written materials.

Consistency is further enhanced when parents, teachers, and administrators get together to explore values and philosophies. Workshops, parent-teacher conferences, and informal discussions at the classroom or program level are effective ways for school staff and parents to share ideas and problem-solving techniques related to child socialization (National Association of Elementary School Principals, 1990). These times are most productive when the emphasis is on mutual understanding and collaboration.

What can be done when conflicts exist between the teacher's and parents' approaches to discipline?

There are many times when the influential people in children's lives have different ideas about how children should behave. Consequently, they may advocate conflicting codes of conduct (R. D. Morrow, 1989; Shanab & Yahya, 1977). For instance, in the interest of group harmony, program personnel may require children to respond to bullying from peers using nonviolent strategies. Family members, more focused on children's self-defense skills, may encourage them to "fight it out" when threatened. Both ideas—harmonious living and personal safety—have merit, but they are different and seem to call for incompatible responses from children. This puts children in a dilemma: to obey one set of expectations, they have to violate another.

Whenever contradictory situations such as these arise, there are three ways they might be handled. The first is for teachers and parents to discuss their differences honestly and directly, searching for common ground. In the preceding situation, it is likely that both teachers and parents want children to be safe. They agree on the goal, but their means for achieving it differ. If they recognize their mutual aim, they will have a compatible base from which to explore potential resolutions to the child's predicament.

On other occasions, conflicts arise from differences in style. Teachers sometimes believe they have little in common with parents who hold nonauthoritative attitudes toward discipline. Likewise, parents who espouse more authoritarian or permissive philosophies may question the authoritative techniques used in the program. Under these circumstances, the most effective approach is to emphasize the similarities between philosophies rather than concentrating on the discrepancies (Bollin, 1989). Authoritarian and authoritative styles both advocate firm control and high standards; laissez-faire and authoritative styles promote warm, accepting relationships between children and adults. Discussing authoritative strategies in terms of how they support these overarching principles provides some common ground between philosophies.

For instance, parents with more authoritarian attitudes may believe that offering children choices is unnecessary or undesirable because youngsters should simply do as they are told. To help such parents feel more comfortable with choices for children, the teacher could point out that the adult *first* establishes boundaries on the child's behavior (such as getting dressed now) and *then* offers the child a choice (what color shirt to wear). This explanation combines an authoritative value (helping children achieve independence) with an authoritarian one (achieving compliance) and builds a bridge between the two.

A third strategy for reducing children's confusion over contradictory home-program expectations is to help children realize that adults have differing reactions to their behavior. This enables teachers to stress that certain standards may be situation-specific: "You're upset. At home you don't have to pick up. That may be, but it bothers me when the puzzles are all over the floor. Pieces could be lost. Here at the center everybody is expected to help. Find a puzzle to put away."

On those rare occasions when no mutually satisfactory resolution seems possible, it is best to acknowledge that differences exist and make clear to parents how and why authoritative strategies will be used at school. Children benefit from exposure to authoritative models, even when other adults in their lives are more authoritarian or permissive. Teachers and administrators who reason with children provide alternate models of interaction and problem solving for children to evaluate and try out themselves.

The authoritative style precludes physical punishment. Doesn't that lead to undisciplined classrooms and chaotic programs?

Shouldn't programs hang on to corporal punishment as a last resort for use with children with whom nothing else works?

Corporal punishment has been used since colonial times as a response to the need for discipline in our nation's schools (Van Dyke, 1984). Paddling has been declared constitutional by the U.S. Supreme Court, and 29 out of the 50 states permit school personnel to use "reasonable force" against children as a way to maintain discipline (Keeshan, 1989). The majority of reported incidents involve young children and youngsters of small physical stature attending middle school (Ball, 1989). In fact, in 1991 more than 1 million such cases were recorded. Moreover, in those states in which spanking is prohibited in public programs, there are child care directors who are nostalgic for the "good old days." "I believe spanking would be ever so much more effective for us! IF ONLY WE COULD USE IT" (Coburn, p. 11).

Such lamentations are based on the assumption that physical punishment improves student behavior and contributes to a more effective learning environment. Yet, *no research has ever indicated that corporal punishment yields any positive outcomes*. On the contrary, studies by such groups as the National Education Association (NEA), the Association for Childhood Education International (ACEI), and the National Parent Teacher Association (PTA) have shown that rather than curbing disciplinary problems, corporal punishment exacerbates them.

For instance, children subjected to corporal punishment in centers and schools become more aggressive, destructive, and coercive over time (Bongiovanni, 1977). Incidents of vandalism, attacks against teachers, and more disruptive student behavior in the classroom, in the halls and lunchrooms and on the playground, have also been reported (Ball, 1989). Possible explanations for such trends include the obvious fact that no matter how it is structured, the adult administering the paddling is modeling aggressive behavior as an acceptable way to solve problems and deal with other human beings. Thus, the essence of corporal punishment is inflicting pain and humiliation. It is teaching by fear and has several likely outcomes, none of which are developmentally enhancing:

1. Physical punishment keeps children at the adherence level of compliance and gives them no tools with which to progress toward internalization.

2. Children whose own behavior is aggressive do not learn alternatives to such strategies when subjected to methods so closely resembling their own. The lesson they learn is that might makes right, and so they continue to apply that principle in their own lives.

3. Children can become so accustomed to physical pain that the pain is no longer a deterrent to them. In fact, habitual offenders may interpret their ability to withstand a paddling without flinching as a badge of honor. This may prompt them to repeat their provocative behavior as a means to gain status with peers.

4. The use of physical punishment often serves as the stimulus for vengeful counterattacks by children in the future. These may be directed at either adults or peers.

Findings such as these indicate that corporal punishment benefits neither children nor the adults who carry it out (Vasta et al., 1992). As a result, one might question why it is still common practice. Surveys of practitioners suggest that physical punishment is used by default. Exasperated and at their wit's end, some teachers and administrators resort to spanking because they are at a loss for what else to do (Gootman, 1988). However, nonviolent alternatives do exist, and there are many schools and centers that effectively use the authoritative strategies described in this chapter. Such programs operate in urban, rural, and suburban communities; high-crime and low-crime areas; wealthy and poor neighborhoods. Although each of these programs has its own approach to positive discipline, there are certain tenets to which all subscribe (Gootman, 1988; Hyman & D'Allasandro, 1984). Many of these were evident in the Adams School Discipline Plan described earlier in this chapter.

1. Educators make the assumption that teachers, children, administrators, and parents have the capacity to solve problems and make decisions.

2. Time is allocated for program staff, children, and parents to plan and organize the alternative discipline system.

3. The system that is ultimately devised is consistent throughout the school. Everyone is involved in a unified approach.

4. All rules are based on the principles of safety and protection of property and rights. Those listed are kept at a minimum and are clearly and positively stated.

5. Rules are enforced firmly, fairly, and matter-of-factly.

6. The consequences for breaking the rules are logical and realistic.

7. Teachers, administrators, and volunteers are trained in authoritative strategies.

8. Parents are welcome in the program and encouraged to become involved in program activities.

9. Methods for examining children's extreme behaviors are put in place, and appropriate referrals are available to children, parents, and staff.

From this discussion it can be concluded that corporal punishment has no place in a developmentally appropriate early childhood program. Spanking hurts children, and it negates the development of self-discipline. As professional early childhood educators, it is our ethical responsibility to seek alternatives that demonstrate respect and compassion toward children while at the same time offering effective behavioral guidance. The authoritative strategies presented throughout this chapter have been put forward with that idea in mind.

SUMMARY

Although children are born social beings, they do not come into the world socialized. How to achieve goals within a social context, how to get along with others, and how to adjust personal behavior within the bounds of societal expectations are things children have to *learn* how to do. This learning begins at birth and continues throughout the school years. Parents, teachers, other significant adults in children's lives, and peers all contribute to the lessons children experience during this time. Initially, young children depend on others to make social decisions for them and to direct their behavior in appropriate ways. However, in time, they learn to respond to rewards and punishments or the moral codes of admired adults as clues for how to behave when. These guides are useful and necessary but do not represent the most self-reliant form of social behavior; that only occurs if children treat rules as logical extensions of their beliefs and personal values. Whenever children think about rules in that way, they are said to have internalized them. Internalization of rules equals self-discipline, which has benefits both for the individual and society. It is the hallmark of social maturity.

The extent to which children exhibit self-discipline is affected in large measure by developmental factors such as emotional maturity, social skills, cognition, memory, and language. Another major influence involves children's daily experiences with people. Throughout the early childhood period, parents and teachers in particular have a tremendous impact on what social behaviors and motivations children adopt. These grown-ups use a variety of socialization strategies such as modeling, attribution, instruction, and consequences to help children learn acceptable codes of behavior. However, not all adults use or combine these strategies in the same way. Three of the most common variations — permissive, authoritarian, and authoritative — have been the subject of much research. All three styles have some positive outcomes. But, the permissive and authoritarian styles yield negative results that undermine self-regulation and positive social adjustment in children. It is the authoritative style that has been most strongly linked to the development of self-discipline. Consequently, much of this chapter has been devoted to describing techniques associated with authoritative teaching. Such strategies can be applied in a single classroom or on a programwide basis. Typical questions practitioners might pose about school discipline also have been addressed.

The preceding discussion covers much ground but is permeated by a common theme: *Adults cannot simply demand that children behave; they must teach them how to do so.* Youngsters need sustained adult guidance to become socialized. Thus, teaching children how to behave is a critical aspect of the educator's role and one that cannot be ignored. However, socialization of the young is also a shared responsibility between home and program, which makes teachers and parents partners in the process. Some ideas for how to work with parents in this regard have been touched on here. Additional suggestions for how to establish effective home-program partnerships are described in the next chapter, "Parent Involvement in Children's Early Education."

CHAPTER 15

Parent Involvement in Children's Early Education

In talking with the preschool teacher at their fall conference, Mrs. Gonzales mentions that Jorge seems uninterested in the phonics flashcards she has purchased. "He just doesn't care about learning to read," she laments. "What can I do?"

Kathy Hale inquires why the first-grade teacher still has games in the classroom. She's eager for her daughter to begin doing "real" schoolwork.

Mrs. Salari wonders whether or not her 7-year-old son is showing signs of a learning disability. Her best friend says yes, her mother-in-law says no, and now she is asking the teacher's opinion.

Patrick's father suggests eliminating the children's outdoor recess period so that teachers can have more time for classroom instruction.

Although each of these parents has different concerns, they also share certain characteristics:

- All are parents of young children enrolled in early childhood education programs.
- Every one of them has an emotional investment in his or her own child.
- All have perceptions and opinions regarding their children's early education.
- Each parent has the potential to become more actively involved in the early childhood program in which his or her child participates.

THE CHANGING NATURE OF PARENT INVOLVEMENT

The notion of involving parents in their children's early education is not new. For years, connecting home and school* has been a fundamental aim of parent cooperative nursery schools, Head Start, and other early intervention programs (Johnston, 1982). Those efforts have had such promising outcomes that now when we talk about creating or maintaining appropriate educational programs, invariably parent involvement is cited as an essential quality indi-

---

*Throughout this chapter the word *school* will be used to refer to all types of early childhood programs for children ages 3 to 8, including child care, nursery and primary school programs, and programs for children with special needs.

cator (Bredekamp, 1987; Day, 1988b; National Association of Elementary School Principals, 1990). In fact, the National Association of State Boards of Education ([NASBE], 1988) recommends that *all* educational programs serving children ages 3 through 8 should do the following things:

- Promote an environment in which parents are valued as primary influences in their children's lives and are essential partners in the education of their children.
- Recognize that the self-esteem of parents is integral to the development of the child and should be enhanced by the parents' positive interaction with the school.
- Include parents in decision making about their own child and the overall early childhood program.
- Assure opportunities and access for parents to observe and volunteer in the classrooms.
- Promote exchange of information and ideas between parents and teachers which will benefit the child.
- Provide a gradual and supportive transition process from home to school for those young children entering school for the first time. (p. 19)

The nature of parent involvement as referred to here contradicts long-standing stereotypes. The traditional role of parents simply providing refreshments for school parties or attending the once-a-year "Parents Night at the Center" has been expanded. The role of the school or center has also been enlarged to encompass more than merely sponsoring a fall open house or periodically rounding up experts to speak to parents about current issues in education. That old vision relegated parent involvement to a few obligatory events dominated by one-way communication from the school to home. It assumed that educators knew best and parents knew little, and it assigned program professionals leadership positions, with parents serving as followers.

The concept of parent involvement within a developmentally appropriate framework is much more comprehensive, interactive, and collaborative than the stereotypic model described. Within this newer interpretation, involving parents in their children's education is a continuous process that incorporates parents in various phases of the total educational program, including planning, implementation, and assessment (O. Seefeldt, 1985; Johnston, 1982). Parents and teachers form an alliance in which they develop a common understanding of what children are like—how they develop, how they behave, the challenges they face, and how they can be helped to meet these challenges. The adults also come to a shared conception of what "good" education is—what it looks like, how it operates, what it strives to achieve, what it requires, and what it precludes (Hymes, 1974). When such alliances occur, parents and teachers actually learn together, providing mutual support to one another in their efforts to make life more meaningful for children and themselves (Swick & Duff, 1978).

This coalition between parents and teachers can take place in several different ways and with varying degrees of participation by both groups. Joyce Epstein, a leading researcher on the subject, has identified five categories of parent involvement that range from lesser to greater ties between children's homes and early education programs (see Table 15.1).

The desirability of all five types of parent involvement is currently so well accepted that the federal government now mandates inclusion of parents as participants, advisors, and knowledgeable consumers of services in all phases of Project Head Start, the education of children with disabilities (Public Laws 94-142 and 99-457), and agency-administered child care (Kostelnik et al., in press). State governments have followed suit as exemplified by the "California

TABLE 15.1
Five Major Types of Parent Involvement

Type 1: Parenting	Type 2: Communicating	Type 3: Volunteering	Type 4: Learning at Home	Type 5: Representing Other Parents
Parents become involved in the basic obligations of ensuring children's health and safety. They acquire the parenting and child-rearing skills needed to prepare children for school, supervise them, teach and guide children at each level, and create positive home conditions that support learning.	Parents receive and respond to communications from the center or school regarding educational programs and children's progress.	Parents become directly involved on site—they assist teachers, administrators, and children in classrooms or other areas of the program. Parents also come to the school or center to support student performances or other events and attend workshops or other programs for their own education or training.	Parents respond to child-initiated requests for help as well as ideas or instructions from teachers. Parents monitor or assist their children at home in learning activities that are coordinated with children's experiences at the school or center.	Parents take decision-making roles on advisory councils or on other committees or groups at the program, district, or state level. Parents may become involved in community activities or independent advocacy groups that monitor the program and work for educational improvement.

Source: From "Five Types of Parent Involvement: Linking Practices and Outcomes" by J. L. Epstein, Forthcoming, in *School and Family Connection: Preparing Education to Involve Families.* Adapted with permission.

School Improvement Plan" and the "Michigan Standards of Quality for Preschool Programs for Four Year Olds." As a result, in early childhood programs across the United States, parents today are involved in their children's education at all levels—from tutors at home to classroom participants, from volunteers to paid employees, from advisors to program decision makers. Those involved include first-time parents, teenage parents, older parents, single parents, dual-career parents, stepparents, parents of children with disabilities, and grandparents (Powell, 1989). Moreover, while originally targeted at programs for very young children, parent participation efforts have expanded beyond these, into elementary, middle, and high schools (Galen, 1991). All of this has come about because we have discovered that children, parents, and programs benefit greatly when parents take an active part in their offspring's educational experiences.

CHILD BENEFITS

Most of what each child learns has its beginnings in the home. It is there that children first develop emotions and values, and it is there that they learn to walk, talk, and make sense of their everyday surroundings. Parents teach not only directly but also indirectly by approving or disapproving, supporting or negating what children learn elsewhere (Bobbitt & Paolucci, 1986). For these reasons, including parents in early childhood programs provides continuity between home and school and enhances children's learning in both environments. For instance, parent participation has been linked to greater awareness and responsiveness in children, more complex child language skills, greater problem-solving abilities in children, increased academic performance, and significant gains in cognitive as well as physical skill development (Eastman, 1988; Meier, 1978; Miller, 1978; Powell, 1989).

PARENT BENEFITS

Although parent outcomes have been studied less often than child effects, the results of parent involvement on parents is also encouraging. Parent participants are known to gain greater understanding of their children's development and needs, exhibit greater acceptance of children's individual differences, find more enjoyment in their children, and develop more flexible child-rearing attitudes (Meier, 1978). Increased feelings of competence and self-worth also have been reported (Powell, 1989).

PROGRAM BENEFITS

Active participation by parents has been found to provide them with more accurate and timely information regarding program aims and strategies. Closer contact between home and school gives both parents and teachers a more complete picture of children's abilities and improves their consistency in working toward desired goals (Umansky, 1983). This in turn seems to promote parent identification with the program, which heightens parents' satisfaction and increases children's success (Bronfenbrenner, 1977; Revicki, 1982). Additionally, as parents become more influential in program decision making and increasingly active in school or center activities, they are more likely to communicate to children the importance of the programs in which both they and their children are involved (Nedler & McAfee, 1979; U.S. Department of Education, 1986).

Involved parents also serve as additional human resources to early childhood programs, extending the reach of the program, making it possible for children to receive more individual attention, and making available additional knowledge and skills to teachers and administrators (Gilmar & Nelson, 1975; J. A. Harris, 1978; Institute for Responsive Education, 1990). Finally, we know that highly involved parents are more likely to support program policies, offer financial assistance, and rally community efforts to promote or maintain the early childhood programs with which they are affiliated.

BARRIERS TO PARENT INVOLVEMENT

With all the benefits that come from parent involvement, it would seem that both teachers and parents should be eager to engage in the process. Yet, frequently misunderstandings exist that impede the development of effective home-school relations.

One pervasive problem is that parents and teachers may hold images of one another that are not conducive to cooperation. For instance, both may feel unwelcome—the parent at school, the teacher in the home—or ill suited to function in a collegial capacity—the parent as teacher, the teacher as peer. The teacher may be viewed as less helpful and less interested in the family than he or she really is, and teachers are likely to underestimate parents' strong desire to be included in their children's education (Hess, Block, Costello, Knowles, & Largey, 1971). For example, researchers affiliated with the Carnegie Foundation for the Advancement of Teaching (CFAT) report that of the 21,000 teachers they contacted, 90% considered the level of parent involvement in their classrooms inadequate (CFAT, 1988). Yet, less than half the teachers responding to a subsequent survey made parent involvement a high priority in their classrooms. They believed that such efforts would prove fruitless (Brandt & Epstein, 1989). Convinced that today's parents (especially low-income, single-parent, and dual-career families) would be unwilling or unable to participate in program-related activities, most teachers chose not to involve them at all. However, the results of several parent questionnaires throughout the past decade run counter to this perception. Large numbers of parents (as many as 90%) report caring a great deal about their children's performance in school and being interested in learning effective ways to support children's learning on the home front (Epstein, 1986; Lightfoot, 1980; Snow, 1982). Approximately 20% of the parents surveyed were already successfully involved, but another 70% wanted to become more active in their child's schooling (Brandt & Epstein, 1989). In particular, it was inner-city parents, single parents who worked outside the home, and parents of children beyond the preschool years who felt they had the

Parents need to feel welcome at school to become involved in their children's education.

least opportunities for contact with teachers and other school personnel (Berger, 1991).

This huge discrepancy, between parents' stated desires and the degree to which they actually participate, stems from several sources. Some parents believe that because they lack professional teaching skills, they are unsuitable partners in the educational process (Moles, 1982). Others hold back because they are unsure of what to do—how to offer support at home or what strategies to use. Still others are put off because, at their child's school or center, parent involvement is confined to menial tasks or is so ill timed (last-minute, inconvenient hours) or so ill conceived (disorganized, irrelevant, uninteresting) that only a few parents have the means or desire to come forward. In other cases, parents answer requests for volunteering but receive no follow-up contact or acknowledgment of their interest. Also, it is not uncommon for parents to be treated as intruders at school (Greenberg, 1989). Rebuffed, ignored, or patronized, many parents conclude they have little to contribute.

These obstacles to parent involvement are exacerbated among the poor. Many low-income parents have a history of unfavorable school experiences dating from their own childhood. They may relive those unhappy times when their offspring enter programs outside the home. Moreover, because it is not unusual for program personnel to focus on what they perceive to be low-income or minority family deficits, parents' initial negative perceptions are often reinforced. Matters become worse over time because low-income parents are usually contacted by teachers or administrators only when their children are having problems (Institute for Responsive Education, 1990). These kinds of encounters contribute to parents feeling shame, anger, distrust, or hopelessness, all of which detract from their motivation to become involved in the educational process.

Additional stumbling blocks develop when policymakers think that simply mandating parent involvement makes it happen or when they presume involvement by parents comes about spontaneously. Our national experience over the past 20 years underscores the fallacy of both these assumptions (McLaughlin & Shields, 1987). One does not have to travel far to find teachers, administrators, and/or parents lamenting a lack of parent volunteers in the classroom or on program advisory boards.

The truth is that to succeed, both parents and teachers must sincerely believe that parents can contribute in important ways to the education of young children. In addition, the most successful outcomes occur as the result of hard work, deliberate planning, and persistent efforts by teachers and parents alike. Unfortunately, many parents lack the skills to negotiate the educational bureaucracy successfully, and few teachers have adequate preparation for working with parents (Greenberg, 1989).

A readjustment of attitudes in schools and at home, as well as more concerted efforts to emphasize the partnership aspects of parent involvement, are needed if these misunderstandings are to be corrected. Some programs have risen to the challenge by instituting written policies that make parent participation more visible and more clearly understood. These policies ensure that parents are central to the early childhood program and help staff and parents better understand how parents can become involved. Workshops in which parents and practitioners learn how to improve their skills for working together as well as for working with the children have also helped to alleviate erroneous conceptions (Williams & Chavkin, 1989).

Overcoming barriers to parent involvement is essential if parents are to recognize the significance of their role in enhancing children's learning. Facilitating parent involvement in children's *early* education can be a productive means for achieving this aim.

CHARACTERISTICS OF EFFECTIVE PARENT INVOLVEMENT

As educators have become increasingly aware of the benefits of parent involvement and the obstacles that sometimes hinder its development, their attention has shifted from answering the query "Why?" to exploring the question "How?" Consequently, much of the research of the past decade has focused on discovering those variables that characterize effective parent involvement efforts. From these studies, four key elements have been identified: *collaboration, variety, intensity,* and *individuation*. A brief overview of each of these follows.

Collaboration

Collaborative relations between early childhood personnel and parents yield fruitful results for both parties as well as for children. Such relations are most apt to develop when parents and teachers recognize each other's importance in the life of the child. Since neither school nor family have the resources to take on the entire job of educating the young, it is not in their best interests to attempt to duplicate one another's efforts. Rather, children's education is enhanced when home and school see themselves as distinct entities, performing complementary, interconnected functions (Griffore & Bubolz, 1986). One interpretation of how parents and teachers might function in a mutually supportive relationship is offered in Table 15.2.

Establishing a working alliance between home and school entails forging open, reciprocal channels of communication as well as affirming the authority of parents and teachers within their respective domains (Power & Bartholomew, 1987). Collaborative relations are also fostered when there is shared decision making regarding programmatic goals for children and the nature of parent participation (Powell, 1989).

Viewed in this light, parent involvement represents a balance of power between parents and teachers. It is a partnership in which each member is valued and contributes breadth of understanding and depth of knowledge to their deliberations concerning children (Balaban, 1985; Kostelnik, 1989a). Parents bring breadth to the partnership by understanding their own child within the context of many different settings—home, neighborhood, church, park, laundromat, Grandma's house, and so forth. Teachers provide breadth by understanding many different children within the school context. Knowing their own child thoroughly comprises the depth offered by parents; depth for teachers comes from their knowledge of child development, program content, and educational strategies. When parents and teachers combine knowledge and understanding along these two dimensions, collaboration becomes a reality.

Variety

Parents differ in the extent to which they are willing or able to take part in educational programs and in how they wish to be included. Consequently, effective parent involvement en-

TABLE 15.2
The Home-School Alliance

10 Things Parents Wish Teachers Would Do	10 Things Teachers Wish Parents Would Do
Help build children's self-esteem.	Provide the resources at home for reading and learning.
Get to know each child.	Set a good example.
Communicate often and openly with parents.	Encourage children to try to do their best in school.
Give parents direction for how to work with their children at home.	Emphasize academics.
Maintain high academic and behavioral standards.	Support the program's rules and goals.
Welcome and encourage parent involvement.	Use pressure positively.
Be active in and support parent council or PTA activities and/or projects.	Call teachers more often and earlier if there is a problem.
Provide enrichment activities.	Take responsibility as parents.
Expect and encourage respect for other children, classroom visitors, and yourself.	View drinking alcoholic beverages by underage youth and excessive partying as a serious matter, not a joke.
Remember that parents are allies and want to help.	Be aware of what is going on in the school and become more involved in school activities.

Source: From *PTA Today*, November 1984. Complete article available from the National PTA, 700 N. Rush St., Chicago, IL 60611-2571. ©1988 National PTA School Is What WE Make It! planning kit. Adapted with permission.

compasses a variety of means for parents to participate and does not require all parents to be involved in the same ways, at the same time, or to the same degree (Becher, 1984). Variety can be considered in terms of the *kinds* of contacts that occur between home and school, the *format* they take, who *initiates* them, for what *purpose* exchanges are made, *where* they occur, how *frequently* they take place, the *resources* required for participation, and the *level of response* necessary for success to be achieved. These variations are outlined in Figure 15.1.

The more variety, the better. This is true both within a single home-school interchange and across the whole array of contacts that transpire throughout the child's life at the center or school. When a broad mixture of parent involvement opportunities take place, programs demonstrate their interest in and acceptance of many different kinds of families. Also, parents receive visible proof that they may contribute according to their own preferences, talents, resources, and degree of comfort with the interface between home and school (Berger, 1991).

Intensity

There are strong indications in the literature that the greater the number of contacts between parents and the early childhood program and the

---

FIGURE 15.1
Variable Characteristics of Parent Involvement

Kind of Contact
Predetermined agenda/Informal structure
Scheduled/Spontaneous
Face to face/Indirect

Format
Written/Verbal
Goal directed/Open-ended
Presentation or discussion/Hands-on experience
Large group/Small group/Individual

Purpose
Provide input/Elicit input/Collaborate
Build/Establish/Maintain/Change relationships, goals, strategies

Initiator
Child/Family member/School personnel

Location
Home/School/Community

Frequency
One-time event/Several times/Continuous

Role of Parent
Receiver of information/Program supporter/Audience/Home tutor/Classroom participant/Colearner/Decision maker/Advocate

Resources Required
Time and energy (ranges from little to much)/Skills (ranges from few to many, general to specialized)

It is possible to combine variables within each characteristic as well as create combinations among them.

more frequently they occur, the more likely it is that parent participation outcomes will be positive (Lazar, 1981; Powell, 1989). Thus, the notion "more is better" would seem to apply. This may suggest that there is a certain duration of contact necessary to promote the development of trusting relationships between parents and practitioners (Powell, 1989). Also, when opportunities for involvement are numerous, families can more easily find entrees to programs that better suit their needs and interests. In addition, it has been found that parents generally do not feel a part of their child's education unless the school or center places particular emphasis on involving them (Gotts & Purnell, 1986). Frequent, varied contact over time conveys the message that parents are valued by the program and that their inclusion is not simply tolerated but actually welcomed and expected.

Individuation

Existing research suggests that educational programs are most likely to elicit a positive response from parents when opportunities for participation are tailored to meet family's particular needs and perceptions (Eastman, 1988). There is no one formula for parent involvement and no single program that can be generalized successfully to every population. Instead, the best outcomes emerge when there is a match between what programs set out to do and what parents want, when there is congruence between the strategies implemented and those to which parents feel receptive, and when program designers take into account parent constraints such as child care and transportation needs or employment obligations (Berger, 1991; Powell, 1989). Once this process is under way, the chances for collaboration improve; and as collaboration becomes greater, so do opportunities for individuation.

Clearly, educators can facilitate parent involvement when they design programs that take into account collaboration, variety, intensity, and individuation. These broad concepts can be operationalized in a single classroom and on a programwide basis. The rest of this chapter is devoted to outlining sample techniques educators can use to involve parents at both levels.

EFFECTIVE PARENT INVOLVEMENT TECHNIQUES

For ease of reference, the guidelines for parent involvement that follow are divided among seven categories:

> Building a Firm Foundation for Parent Involvement
>
> Providing Information to Parents
>
> Gathering Information from Parents
>
> Establishing Two-Way Communication between Parents and the Program
>
> Integrating Parents into the Program
>
> Providing Parent Education
>
> Facilitating Parent-to-Parent Support

All of the strategies are written for use by individual practitioners but could easily be generalized to whole programs. They are illustrative, not exhaustive, and they provide a wide array of options for practitioners to consider. On the one hand, these guidelines are by no means the only ones to consider. On the other hand, no single person or program would institute all of them at once. Instead, readers might review the suggestions offered here, then adapt one or two from each of several categories to create a comprehensive plan to meet the needs of the people in their own program.

Building a Firm Foundation for Parent Involvement

1. *Make frequent attempts to include parents in children's early education.* Begin by planning several simple forms of contact throughout the year rather than focusing on a single colossal event. Choose to offer some one-time involvement opportunities as well as a few that permit sustained participation over time.

2. *Create many different ways for parents to become involved in the early childhood program.* Remember to diversify the kind of contacts that are made, the format they take, their purpose, and location. Also, vary what role parents assume as well as the time, energy, and physical resources required to participate. Make sure to create involvement opportunities related to all five types of parent involvement. Exam-

ples of practices to support each type are presented in Table 15.3.

3. *Treat parents as individuals.* Communicate with them on a one-to-one basis as well as in groups. Find out something about each parent's aspirations, concerns, special interests, skills, and hobbies. This might be accomplished through informal contacts as well as by having parents fill out a personal interest survey for you to keep and refer to throughout the year.

4. *Tailor the involvement strategies you select to meet the needs of the actual families with whom you are working.* Avoid using the same approaches time after time, without considering how parents' needs might differ from one year to the next. Likewise, be cautious of commercially prepared "parent involvement" programs. These do not always match the interests and requirements of a particular group of parents. If your school or center has adapted such a program, review it carefully. Carry out only those segments that are suitable for your group.

5. *Reflect on your potential to be a full-fledged partner in the home-school alliance.* Use the assessment tool offered in Figure 15.2 to measure this dimension of your work.

Gathering Information from Parents

1. *Early in the year, solicit information from parents to help you better understand children's ecological contexts.* Be sure to explain to parents that the family information they provide will be used to individualize the program to meet their children's specific needs. Such data could be elicited through enrollment forms or an initial intake interview. Sample questions are presented in Figure 15.3.

2. *Throughout the year, ask parents to provide anecdotes and information about their child.* These can be used as the basis for classroom activities and to increase your knowledge of the child and his or her family. Word such requests as invitations to share information, not as commands to meet your expectations. Two examples are offered in Figures 15.4 and 15.5.

3. *Elicit input from parents about learning goals for their children.* Talk with parents about their children's activities at home as well as what skills or behaviors they would like to see

further developed. Give parents a short list of program-related goals for children such as those depicted in Figure 15.6. Ask them to rank these goals in relation to their own child and according to their own perceptions of which are least important and which are most important. Collect the information and use it in designing activities for the classroom. Refer to the parents' lists periodically, and use them as the basis for some of your communications with parents throughout the year.

4. *Ask for evaluative feedback from parents throughout the year.* Let parents know that their opinions count by providing numerous opportunities for them to evaluate your performance as well as the early childhood program. Suggestion boxes near the school entrance, short questionnaires sent home that can be returned anonymously in a postage-paid envelope, written or verbal evaluations administered at the end of workshops or other school events, and telephone surveys conducted by teachers or administrators are some methods that have prompted parent input. Another effective strategy is to hold parent-teacher forums once or twice a year at school. These regularly scheduled, informal gatherings are designed to give parents and teachers a chance to evaluate the program together. Loosely structured around a broad topic, such as children's personal safety issues or promoting children's problem-solving skills, they provide a vehicle for mutual exploration of educational ideas and strategies. Moreover, parents can ask questions and make suggestions for changes or additions to school programs in an atmosphere where such communication is clearly welcome.

As a follow-up to these evaluation efforts, let parents know you intend to act on some of their suggestions. Later, inform parents (via the school newsletter and/or at a group meeting) of the changes that have come about as a result of input received from them.

Providing Information to Parents

1. *Develop written policies for your classroom that clearly emphasize the importance of parent involvement.* Identify benefits to children, parents, and the program as a whole. Pro-

TABLE 15.3
Examples of Practices to Promote the Five Types of Parent Involvement

Type 1: Parenting	Type 2: Communicating	Type 3: Volunteering	Type 4: Learning at Home	Type 5: Representing Other Parents
Provide suggestions for home conditions that support children's learning.	Conduct conferences with every parent at least once a year, with follow-up as needed.	Develop a school volunteer program whose focus is on supporting early learning activities.	Provide information to parents on concept and skill development in young children.	Encourage parent participation and leadership on center or school advisory councils or committees such as curriculum or playground improvement.
Provide workshops, videotapes, computerized phone messages on parenting and school issues.	Make available translators for families who speak languages other than your own.	Create a parent club for school volunteers.	Provide calendars that describe simple daily or weekly learning activities that parents can try at home with their children.	Support parents as they become involved in independent advocacy groups.
	Send home anecdotes regarding children's progress and participation in school activities for parents to review and comment on.	Conduct an annual survey to identify all available talents, times, and interests of parent volunteers.	Make available a toy-lending library for parent use that includes a variety of appropriate educational materials.	
	Provide opportunities for families to communicate information, knowledge, needs, and opinions to people in the program.	Invite parents to participate in the classroom on a one-time or ongoing basis.	Conduct workshops in which parents learn how to teach specific early learning skills via home activities.	
	Create opportunities for informal conversations between parents and program personnel: coffee klatches, one-a-month breakfasts or lunches with the children at the center, forums, open houses, interactive workshops, and program-initiated outings are typical social events that can bring the people from home and program closer together.			
	Make available a parent library containing books about children's development and learning. Include books that contain games, activity ideas, and toys to be made from simple household materials.			

Source: From "Five Types of Parent Involvement: Linking Practices and Outcomes" by J. L. Epstein, forthcoming, in *School and Family Connection: Preparing Education to Involve Families.* Adapted with permission.

vide specific guidelines for the form such involvement could take and how home-school contacts might evolve. After clearing them with your supervisor, send these policies home to parents and go over them on a home visit or during a program orientation at the school or center.

2. *Acquaint parents with the assumptions, goals, and expectations of your classroom and/or early childhood program.* Integrate such content into a beginning-of-the-year parent orientation as well as in any written materials (e.g., handbook, program brochure, written bulletins, videotape of program activities) sent home describing the curriculum. Discuss child development and program-oriented goals for children, offering examples of related classroom activities parents might see or hear about. Use some hands-on activities to help parents better understand the materials in the classroom and their relationship to children's learning.

3. *Familiarize parents with a typical day for children in the program.* It helps parents to feel more comfortable with the program if they can envision how their child spends his or her time there. Acquainting families with school or center routines can be accomplished in one of sev-

eral ways. At the very least parents should receive a copy of your daily schedule in which the timing of classroom events is outlined and the general purpose of each segment is explained. Some teachers further reiterate the day through a slide presentation, held early in the year, that illustrates how children in their class move through the day. Motivated to attend by seeing pictures of their own child, parents leave having learned more about the early childhood program and its philosophy. A similar outcome occurs when programs put on a "miniday" in the evening or on the weekend, when parents proceed through an abbreviated but total schedule in the company of their child. Children are proud to "lead" their mom or dad through the routine, and parents gain insights into their child's classroom participation.

4. *On the spur of the moment, write one- or two-line notes regarding children's positive program experiences.* Send these "happy notes" home with the child to demonstrate your interest in both the child and the parent (Berger, 1991; Bundy, 1991). A child's first journey to the top of the climber, or an enthusiastic creative writing experience, or the child's pride in knowing many new facts about insects are all good

Provide parents with the information they need to become partners in the education process.

Circle the appropriate letter (A = always; B = sometimes; C = never). See what your answers mean at the bottom.

Are You a Practitioner Who...

1. Has a sense of humor?	A	B	C
2. Treats all students fairly?	A	B	C
3. Isn't afraid to say "I don't know, but I'll find out" to parents?	A	B	C
4. Enjoys parent-teacher conferences?	A	B	C
5. Has examples of children's work to show parents when they visit?	A	B	C
6. Finds ways to praise rather than criticize children?	A	B	C
7. Refuses to be intimidated by parents or students?	A	B	C
8. Provides a wide variety of ways to involve parents in planning for their children?	A	B	C
9. Is honest with parents?	A	B	C
10. Listens to both students and parents?	A	B	C

What your score means: If you checked mostly A answers, you're one of those teachers administrators dream about and parents and children never forget! Mostly B answers? You try hard to be fair to children and honest with yourself and, most of the time, you're successful at it. Mostly Cs? Perhaps teaching is no longer enjoyable for you, or you're getting "burned out." Consider asking your administrator or colleagues for new ways to enliven your classroom.

FIGURE 15.2

Assessing the Educator's Role in the Home-School Alliance

Source: From 1988 National PTA School Is What WE Make It! planning kit, available from the National PTA, 700 N. Rush St., Chicago, IL 60611-2571. Copyright © 1988 National PTA. Adapted with permission.

occasions for a short handwritten note from you. If you write one note every other day, the parents in a class of 30 children could receive three or four such contacts in a year. Once or twice include an instant snapshot of the child happily engaged in a classroom activity as a keepsake for parents of the child's early school experience.

5. *Create a weekly or monthly newsletter to inform parents about the program and children's experiences away from home.* This simple form of communication can be used to familiarize parents with what is happening in the classroom, give parents ideas for things to talk about with their youngsters at home, and stimulate parents to engage in home-based learning with their children.

Newsletters produced at the preschool level are written by the practitioner. Those designed for the early elementary grades may include contributions from the children (Berger, 1991). In either case, make newsletters short and visually interesting by using subheadings and graphics. Avoid overcrowding. Divide the content into sections in which items are highlighted by outlining, indenting, underlining, capitalizing, or changing typeface.

The content of the newsletter may include one or more of the following items:

- A review of the children's experiences at the center or school since the last newsletter
- A description of activities children will take part in throughout the next several days or weeks
- Specific, practical examples of how parents could address or reinforce children's learning at home
- A brief discussion of the theme (if you engage in theme teaching) and what facets of it children will be exploring

Family Structure

- How many children are in your family?
- Who lives in your household?
- Who else takes care of your child during the day or on weekends?
- How are decisions made in your family?

Parenting

- What words does your child use for urination? Bowel movement? Private body parts?
- Describe your child's eating schedule.
- What foods does your child like or dislike? Are there any foods to which your child is allergic?
- Describe your child's sleeping schedule.
- How do you put your child to sleep?
- How does your child react when he or she is angry or unhappy? Excited or confused?
- How does your child relax or comfort himself or herself?
- What are your child's favorite activities?
- How do you handle the following situations?

  Toilet training
  Sharing
  Messy play (paints, sand, water)
  Sex roles
  Racial concerns

- Who does your child play with at home?
- What rules do you have for your child at home?
- What do you do to teach your child to behave?
- What are your child's responsibilities at home?
- Are there other things you think we should know about your child?

Family Culture

- What is your ethnic or cultural background?
- What languages are spoken in your home?
- What traditions, objects, or foods symbolize your family?

FIGURE 15.3

Family Information of Interest to Educators

Source: Adapted from *Parents as Partners in Education* by E. H. Berger, 1991, New York: Macmillan; *The Anti-Bias Curriculum: Tools for Empowering Children* by L. Derman-Sparks and the ABC Task Force, 1989, Washington, DC: National Education of Young Children; *Roots and Wings: Affirming Culture in Early Childhood Settings* by S. York, 1991, St. Paul, MN: Toys n' Things Press; and Michigan State University Child Development Laboratories enrollment forms.

- Relevant classroom, family, or community news

In addition, invite parents to participate in the classroom, donate materials, or suggest upcoming classroom events.

6. *Stay in touch with parents who seem unresponsive.* Avoid stereotyping them as uncaring or impossible to work with. Remain pleasant when you see them. Periodically, send notes home letting parents know about their children's positive participation in program-based activities. Continue to offer simple, easy-to-do suggestions for home-based participation. Keep the input from the program as positive as possible, and make few demands. You might not see

Dear Parents:

Soon we will begin a unit on how people are born and grow. We need some pictures and information about your child as a baby. Please fill out this form and use this plastic bag to send in one or two baby pictures of your child or your child's "baby book" if you have one. We will be sure to keep things clean and safe and will return them by the end of next week.

My Child as an Infant

My child, _____, was _____ inches long at birth and weighed _____ pounds. My child liked to eat _____ when he/she was a baby. He/she didn't like _____. His/her first word was _____. His/her hair was _____. (Please share any other information that would tell us about your child as a baby such as habits, sleeping patterns, favorite toys, etc.)

FIGURE 15.4

Request for Information about Child: Example 1

Source: Adapted from *Teaching Young Children Using Themes,* M. J. Kostelnik (Ed.), 1991, Glenview, IL: Scott-Foresman.

immediate results; however, you could be contributing to a more favorable impression of the educational process for that parent. This in turn could serve as the foundation for greater participation later in the child's school career.

Establishing Two-Way Communication between Parents and the Program

1. *Vary the communication strategies you use rather than relying on one method alone.* Make sure to exchange information with families regarding the program in general and their own children in particular. Both kinds of communication are necessary if parents and practitioners are to know and understand one another (Bundy, 1991). A summary of communication strategies by type (general vs. specific) is provided in Table 15.4.

2. *Establish telephone hours during which you and parents may call each other.* Set aside 2 or 3 hours each week for this purpose, varying and dividing the time between 2 or more days. In a note home to parents notify them of your availability as well as the telephone number where you can be reached (at home or at

TABLE 15.4

Home-School Communication

Ways to Convey General School Information	Ways to Convey Specific Information about Individual Children
A program handbook	Enrollment forms
A videotape of program activities	Telephone calls
Orientation meetings	Home visits
Home visits	Greeting and pickup routines
Newsletters	"Happy notes"
Bulletin boards	Photos of children engaged in activities
Program visits/observations by parents	Parent-teacher notebooks kept for individual children
Educational programs for parents	Regular and special conferences
Social events for parents and families	
Articles sent home to parents	
Parent-teacher forums	

The Family Name Game

Purpose: To record some of your family names and expressions for things to help your child discover your family's unique language

You'll need: Pen or pencil

Time: Varies

How to do it: Write the names or expressions your family has used (when you were younger) or uses now for these categories. *Warning:* You may need extra sheets of paper. One family who did this activity came up with over 40 names they call their cat.

People (nicknames)	Pets (nicknames)	Places (rooms, community places)
_____	_____	_____
_____	_____	_____
_____	_____	_____

Food (meals, snacks, dishes)	Activities/Actions (eating, working, playing)	Things (tools, toys, clothes)
_____	_____	_____
_____	_____	_____
_____	_____	_____

Other Situations/Occasions

_____	_____	_____
_____	_____	_____
_____	_____	_____

What else?

1. Write a family dictionary or your family's unique language.
2. Make a list of expressions you associate with particular family members.

FIGURE 15.5

Request for Information about Child: Example 2

Source: Adapted from the 4-H Folkpatterns project, Cooperative Extension Service, Michigan State University, East Lansing.

the program). Also ask parents to indicate which time slot might be the most convenient for a call from you.

Early in the year establish a positive basis for communication by calling each family very briefly to introduce yourself and share a short happy anecdote about the child. This practice does much to dispel the dread some parents have that a call from a teacher always means trouble. It also makes it easier for parents to contact you as needs arise. Make it a goal to touch base in this way with each child's parents two or three times a year. It is this type of open communication that parents report as least stressful and most rewarding (Metropolitan Life Survey of the American Teacher, 1987).

3. *Create a notebook for an individual child through which parents and staff communicate*

Below are listed 21 goals preschool teachers commonly have for the children in their class. All of them are important. However, as a parent, some goals will probably seem more relevant for your child than others. This year we would like to use information you provide to personalize your child's experience in our program. For this reason we would like you to prioritize these goals in the following way:

1. Read the entire list of goals once through.
2. Cross out any goal to which you are opposed altogether.
3. Add any goal you particularly value that is not included on the list.
4. Select the *three* goals you consider *most* important and assign them a value of 7.
5. Assign a value of 6 to the *three* goals you consider to be next in importance.
6. Continue this process by assigning a value of 5 to three goals, a value of 4 to three goals, a value of 3 to three goals, a value of 2 to three goals, and a value of 1 to the remaining goals which you consider least important for your child.

Please Note: Teachers work on all of the listed goals sometime during the year. The information you provide helps them know which particular areas to emphasize when working with your child.

Child's name:_____Child's age:____

____ A. Develop an appreciation of art, music, movement, drama, and poetry
____ B. Learn how to make choices and decisions
____ C. Learn how to get along with other children
____ D. Become more aware of personal feelings and the feelings of others
____ E. Learn to appreciate people of varying races and cultures
____ F. Learn how to work independently
____ G. Learn how to persist at a task
____ H. Develop effective problem-solving skills
____ I. Learn scientific or historical facts
____ J. Increase his or her vocabulary
____ K. Develop good listening skills
____ L. Develop confidence in using his or her body
____ M. Develop a positive attitude toward school
____ N. Learn appropriate manners
____ O. Learn how to express him- or herself using words rather than physical force
____ P. Make a successful separation from home to school
____ Q. Develop basic perceptual skills such as recognizing patterns or sequences in objects and events
____ R. Develop basic prereading skills such as grouping objects and events
____ S. Develop basic premath skills such as arranging objects in order, grouping objects into sets, recognizing the concept of "oneness"
____ T. Learn the alphabet
____ U. Learn how to dress him- or herself
____ V. Learn how to count
____ W. Other_____

FIGURE 15.6
Personalized Goals for Children

Source: Adapted from materials developed by the Child Development Laboratories, Family and Child Ecology Department, College of Human Ecology, Michigan State University, East Lansing.

as it is sent back and forth between the child's home and the program. This notebook can serve as an alternative to the "happy notes" described earlier. Write brief anecdotes to the parent regarding the child's school experience. Encourage parents to write about home events (e.g., visitors, changes in routine, illness, disruptions, accomplishments, interests) that might influence the child's performance in the program. A line or two conveyed once or twice a week between the home and school settings can do much to expand parents' and teacher's knowledge about the child and each other. This strategy is particularly effective when children participate in multiple educational settings outside the home, such as after-school child care or a special education program, in addition to his or her daily preschool or early primary classes. Passing the notebook among all these settings increases communication and makes it more likely that the child will receive a better coordinated program. Sample entries are provided in Figure 15.7 for Sarah, a 5-year-old child with cerebral palsy who attends a special education class in the morning and an after-school child care program in the afternoon.

4. *Structure parent conferences so that collaboration between parents and teachers is emphasized.* Consider the following points as you plan each conference (Berger, 1991).

■ Create a cordial written invitation in which parents have options for scheduling times and you indicate a real desire to meet them.
■ Provide parents with sample questions they might ask of you as well as examples of some questions you might ask them (see Figure 15.8). When providing these, assure parents that they are just samples and do not preclude any other inquiries parents may have.
■ Confirm each appointment with a brief personal call to clarify parents' questions or a short note to let them know you are looking forward to meeting with them.
■ Allow enough time for each conference so that a genuine exchange of ideas and information can take place.
■ Secure a private, comfortable place in which to conduct the conference.

■ Greet parents and thank them for coming.
■ Begin on a positive note, conveying a pleasant anecdote about the child.
■ Briefly outline the major areas you hope to cover. Ask parents if they have additional items they would like to add. Mention that the purpose of this conference is to exchange ideas. Urge parents to ask questions or interject their own comments as you go along.
■ Throughout the conference, refer back to the goals the parents signified as most important on the personalized goal sheet (see Figure 15.6) they filled out at the beginning of the year. Provide evidence of the child's progress in these areas. Add other goals you may also be focusing on.
■ Keep the conference as conversational as possible, eliciting comments from parents as you go along.
■ Answer parent questions directly, honestly, and tactfully. Avoid using jargon and judgmental terms to describe the child. Deal in specifics rather than generalities, and base your discussion on objective observations and concrete examples of work.
■ End with a positive item.
■ Collaborate on future goals and strategies.
■ Clarify and summarize the discussion.
■ Make plans to continue talking in the future.

5. *Carry out home visits as a way to get to know children and parents in surroundings that are familiar to them.* Although time-consuming, such contacts are a powerful means to demonstrate interest in the child and his or her family as well as your willingness to move out of the formal educational setting into a setting in which parents are in charge (Kostelnik et al., in press). Additionally, visiting children at home enables you to meet other family members or persons living there and observe the child in context.

Home visits also benefit parents by giving them a chance to talk to the teacher privately and exclusively. Parents may feel more comfortable voicing certain concerns in the confines of their home than they would at school. When conducted early in the child's participation in the program, children have the advantage of meeting their teacher in the setting in which they are most confident. Moreover, when they arrive at

Jan. 8, 1991

Sarah had a wonderful Christmas vacation. We spent the last week in Miami—temps 80–84 degrees, sunny, swimming every day. She is *not* eager to be back, I'm afraid. We tried to tell her that kids who live in Florida have to go to school and don't get to swim all day and go out every night to dinner with Grandma & Grandpa. She's not convinced.

Mrs. G. (Mom)

1-8-91

Hi. Welcome back. Sarah is "stacking" in her wheelchair—is there a change in seating? Just curious. She ate a good lunch.

Leslie (special ed. teacher)

1-8-91

I hate to be out of it—please define *stacking*. Sarah spent today at a tea party with Michelle and Kelly and Lara. They discussed vacations, served "milkshakes" and muffins. Ryan asked Sarah several times to come and see his block structure. She finally agreed.

Dana (child care teacher)

1-9-91

Dana, "stacking" is a postural problem where the head is tilted back and her shoulders flopped forward. Sarah will sit up if we say "Can you pick your shoulders up better?" or anything similar, and she's very proud that she's able to do so.

Leslie

1-10-91

Sarah is bringing dinosaur stickers for sharing—the other kids can have one to take home.

Mrs. G.

1-10-91

Stickers were a hit! Sarah would like to also share with her Adams School friends.

Sarah enjoyed reaching for and grasping scarves in the gym. She chose pink ones (we didn't have purple). She elected to "supervise" the art area where Michelle and Kyle asked her for choices for the Boxosaurus decorations.

Dana

1-13-91

Sarah was very rigid in PT today. She relaxed during "rolling inside the barrel!"—her favorite activity—but tightened up when she attempted any play activities or position changes. I asked her if she was upset, "no," unhappy, "no," So, I'm not sure what the problem was.

Leslie

1-14-91

Sarah was able to say "yes" or "no" (with her eyes) to answer "Mother, may I?" She seemed to like this. We measured things in the room, including her chair with cubes at small group.

Dana

FIGURE 15.7
An Example of Parent-Teacher Communication Using Notebook Entries

Sample Teacher Questions

1. How does your child seem to feel about school?
2. Which activities or parts of the day does your child talk about at home?
3. Which children does your child talk about at home?
4. How does your child spend his or her free time?
5. Is there anything that your child dreads?
6. What are your child's interests and favorite activities outside of school?

Sample Parent Questions

1. How has my child adjusted to school routines?
2. How well does my child get along with other children? Who seem to be his or her best friends?
3. How does my child react to discipline? What methods do you use to promote self-discipline and cooperation?
4. Are there any skills you are working on at school that I/we might reinforce at home?
5. Are there any areas in which my child needs special help?
6. Does my child display any special interests or talents at school that we might support at home?
7. Does my child seem to be self-confident, happy, and secure? If not, what do you think the home or school can do to increase his or her feelings of self-worth?

FIGURE 15.8
Potential Parent Conference Questions

the center or school, the teacher is already familiar to them.

Despite all of these potentially favorable outcomes, some parents are uneasy with home visits. They may be ashamed of where they live, or fear their child will misbehave, or suspect that the teacher is merely prying into their private affairs. To avoid aggravating such negative perceptions, give parents the option of holding the visit at another place (e.g., coffee shop, playground, church, community center) or postpone your visit until you have established a relationship in other ways and the family is more receptive to your coming (Berger, 1991).

Teachers, too, may have qualms about going to children's homes. They may feel unsafe in certain neighborhoods or believe that the hours invested will prove too great. Additionally, some programs discourage home visits because of liability concerns or unavailable compensation. Yet, home visit programs can and do occur in many early childhood programs. Once confined mostly to preschool settings, some schools now schedule K–2 home visits during "record days" for the district or when the upper grades are having conference days. For instance, K–2

teachers at the Mary Harrison school in Toledo, Oregon, requested a small remuneration per family for home visits equal to that allowed for middle and high school teacher participation in extracurricular activities. Altogether they visited at home or in other public locations, in the evenings and on Saturdays, 97% of the families enrolled. Both teachers and parents were enthusiastic in their response to the visits and agreed to continue the practice in coming years. Parents felt genuine interest from teachers, and teachers found the insights and relationship enhancement that occurred well worth their time and energy (Cummings, 1991b).

Suggestions for how to conduct successful home visits are offered in Figure 15.9.

6. *Make contact with noncustodial parents.* Provide opportunities for them to participate in home visits, open houses, and other school activities whenever possible. Mail newsletters to those who live elsewhere.

Integrating Parents into the Program

1. *Institute an open-door policy in which parents are welcome to come to the program*

Before contacting families determine the purpose of your visit. Some teachers choose to focus primarily on meeting and working with the child; others prefer to make the parents their major concern. Still others decide to split their attention somewhat evenly between the two.

Create a format for your time in the home that supports your purpose in going there. A sample agenda for the third option cited above might be as follows:

1. Arrive.
2. Greet parent and child.
3. Chat with parent a few moments. Give him or her program forms to fill out and a short description of how children spend the day at the center or school. Usually these are written materials, but some programs offer information on audiocassette for parents who cannot read.
4. Explain that next you'd like to get acquainted with the child and that you'll have a chance to talk to the parent in about 15 minutes.
5. Play and talk with the child while parent is writing, reading, or listening. Use modeling dough you have brought with you as a play material.
6. Give the child markers and paper brought with you and ask him or her to draw a picture that you can take back to school to hang up in the room.
7. While the child draws, talk with parent(s) about concerns, interests, questions.
8. Close by taking a photograph of the child and parent(s) to put in the child's cubby or in a school album.

Supplies needed:

Map with directions to child's residence
Markers
Paper
Modeling dough
Camera
Film
Audiocassette tape player

Inform parents of your intention to carry out home visits in a letter. Explain the purpose of the visit, how long it will last (not more than an hour), and potential dates from which they might choose for one to take place.

Follow up on the letter with a phone call a few days later to arrange a mutually convenient time for your visit and to obtain directions.

Carry out each home visit at the appointed time.

Follow the visit with a short note of thanks to the family for allowing you to come, and include a positive comment regarding the time you spent together.

FIGURE 15.9
Home Visit Hints

unannounced. Invite parents to watch or to participate in some aspect of the children's day. Provide simple guidelines so that parent guests will know what to expect from you and the children while they are on site. For instance, let them know if there is a place from which they can observe unobtrusively. Make clear times when you are available to chat and times when your attention must be focused on the children. Offer suggestions of typical times during the day when parents might drop in for a short while to interact with the children without ar-

Children enjoy having their parents serve as "teachers" in the classroom.

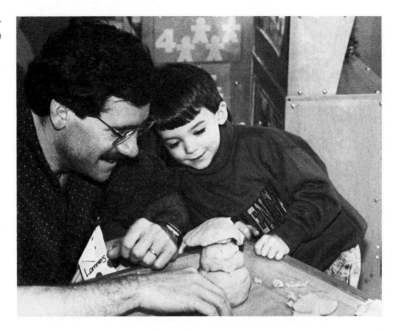

ranging in advance to do so. Snack time, the story time before recess or nap, and outdoor times are periods of the day when parent visitors might easily be accommodated.

2. *Invite parents to visit the classroom for particular occasions.* These times might be incorporated into a whole-group social affair such as a parent-child breakfast or a Sunday afternoon open house. Parents might also be invited to share in a certain classroom activity such as making applesauce or planting seeds. Consider asking individual parents to become involved in a specific project (e.g., making bread, supervising the children's creation of a "Boxosaurus," or listening to children read). Likewise, suggest that parents share their interests or experience with children via free-choice activities or at a circle time. In every case, let parents know they are welcome and how their presence will enrich the program. Issue your invitations long enough in advance for parents to arrange time to be there. Follow up each visit by asking parents to fill out a reaction sheet. Provide a simple form on which they can briefly record their impressions, suggestions, and questions. This evaluation lets parents know that their opinions are valued. It also tells them they can influence their child's educational experience through di-

rect contact with the children and with feedback to the teacher.

3. *Encourage parents to participate in the classroom as volunteer teachers for part or all of a day.* Issue an invitation in which you describe the volunteer role. Make it clear that parents, by virtue of their life experiences, have the skills necessary to do the job. Follow up by speaking to individual parents about how they might become involved. Support your volunteers using the suggestions outlined in Figure 15.10.

4. *Involve parents in making classroom collections either for their own use or for children to use at school.* Ask parents to donate a song, story, or recipe that is a favorite in their family. Collect these from parents individually (in writing or in person), or plan a school event in which such items are shared. A potluck dinner or family songfest in which children also participate may pave the way for beginning such a collection. Likewise, stories can be obtained by inviting parents one at a time to spend a portion of their day in the classroom telling their child's favorite bedtime story. During the telling the teacher could note the book used or tape-record the parent's rendition so that it could be transcribed later and added to a class anthology. An evening story hour in which children come

☐ *Establish clear guidelines for parent volunteers regarding their responsibilities in the classroom.* Offer specific suggestions for what volunteers are to do and a rationale for delegated responsibilities. An activity card with this information could be prepared then handed to a different parent day after day. Read the card aloud, or prepare an illustrated chart if the parent is an uncertain reader. An example of such a card is offered below.

> Welcome! Today please:
> 1. greet children and help them find name tags. Goal: to make them feel welcome and to learn how their name looks.
> 2. supervise matching game. Goal: for children to notice similarities and differences.
> 3. join the children at lunch. Encourage them to pour and serve themselves. Goal: to model trying new foods (Payne, 1991).

☐ *Take time to demonstrate some activities parents are to supervise that day.*

☐ *Help parents feel welcome in the classroom.* Introduce them to the children, and provide youngsters with name tags so that parents can interact with them more comfortably.

☐ *Inform parents that when they volunteer in the classroom, all children in the group will view them as a teacher.* Remind the parent's child that the parent will be helping many children and will have special responsibilities throughout the day. This helps clarify the parent's role for both Mom or Dad and for the child (Payne, 1991).

☐ *Talk with parents about how to handle some potentially disruptive situations in the classroom.* Also discuss what to do if their own child is involved. When this latter issue is ignored until it happens, some parents may fail to act or may overreact out of embarrassment. Neither response is conducive to the parent's feeling comfortable at school.

☐ *Give parent volunteers in the classroom meaningful tasks to carry out,* helping children in the pretend area, engaging children in conversation, assisting children at the snack table. Avoid requesting them only to do "busy work" like washing the easel and brushes or cutting straws for a future fine motor activity. If parents are to become partners in the educational process, they must be given real responsibilities from which they can derive genuine satisfaction.

☐ *Notice parents' successes in the classroom and comment on their helpfulness and effectiveness.* Describe their work in terms of better class functioning and individual child learning. This will underscore their value to the educational process.

FIGURE 15.10
Guidelines for Working with Parents as Teachers in the Classroom

dressed for bed, are served a light snack, and hear three or four short selections by parents and teachers has also proven popular in some programs (Zimmer, 1990). In each case, collections such as these are tangible evidence of parents' contributions to the program. They can be assembled over time with minimum hardship to either families or staff. Moreover, they signal to parents that their family traditions are valued by the program and are worth sharing with others.

In a similar vein, some early childhood programs have invited parents and children to contribute their talents and ideas to a decorative collage or patchwork quilt for display at school. Offering workshops in which parents along with their children are given materials and guidance in how to create fabric squares or pieces of the collage, for example, encourages participation. When the emphasis is placed on participation by many families rather than perfection of the final product, even adults who believe they lack arts and crafts talent can be enticed into the project. Decorations such as these, exhibited throughout the program or in the classroom, add warmth to the environment and convey visible proof of parent involvement. The contributors feel pride in their accomplishment, and families in subsequent years get the message that parents are important to the program.

5. *Create home-based alternatives to on-site volunteering.* For instance, ask parents to volunteer to prepare materials at home, make arrangements for field trips and resource people, coordinate parent discussion groups, find resource materials at the library, compare prices of certain types of materials or equipment at local stores, or react to activity plans that eventually will be used in the classroom.

6. *Provide home-based learning activities for parents and children to do together.* This strategy is appropriate for all parents, but most especially for ones whose time is limited because of income, employment, and family constraints (Walberg, 1985). In fact, the evidence suggests that for these families, home-based learning is the single most effective means of parent involvement (Epstein, 1984).

To achieve positive outcomes, however, parents require clear expectations and guidelines for what to do. With this in mind, let parents know early in the program that home-based activities are essential to helping children learn. Ask them to carry out activities at home for which you provide specific, yet brief, written or audiotaped directions. Provide these on a regular (e.g., weekly) basis. For each activity, invite parents also to critique how easy it was to do and how much they and their children enjoyed it. Offer feedback to parents about how their assistance at home is affecting their child's learning.

7. *Give interested parents opportunities to participate in policy-making decisions.* For instance, ask parents to help create school-playground rules, develop snack guidelines, or generate ideas for specific classroom practices.

Collaborating with parents in evaluating classroom materials as well as commercially available equipment or programs are other appropriate ways of giving parents decision-making powers in early childhood education.

8. *Show genuine pleasure in every parent's attempts, no matter how small, to support their children's education.* Continually let parents know how much you appreciate the time and effort they put into their child's education, not just because their help allows you to do a better job, but because the children benefit so greatly (Berclay, 1977). Extend your personal thank you often. In addition, acknowledge parent contributions in classroom newsletters or community newspapers. Parents also may be officially recognized at program events or with tangible tokens of appreciation such as pins, certificates, plaques, or thank-you notes from the children (Kostelnik et al., in press).

Providing Parent Education

1. *Conduct a simple needs assessment of parental concerns and interests related to parent education.* This process could be carried out for your classroom alone, among several classes, or on a programwide basis.

There are several different ways to proceed. One is to invite parents to a brainstorming session in which mutual concerns are generated. Another approach is to conduct a brief written or telephone survey in which parents identify those issues that are most important to them. A third technique is to provide parents with a broad range of potential issues that could be addressed, then asking them to prioritize those issues according to their own needs. Use the compilation of the results to provide direction for future parent education efforts.

Identify the most pressing needs for the group, and make sure to deal with them early. Having said this, a word of caution is advisable here. Avoid simply going with the notion of majority rule. Instead, look at the concerns in terms of various demographic subgroupings such as low-income families or single-parent households. Try to determine which concerns are shared by all and which may be specific to certain families. Including both types of concerns in your plan will give it the widest possible appeal and will be more sensitive to all parents served by the program.

2. *Invite parents to educational workshops that involve both them and their child.* Consider using a format in which children receive child care half of the time while their parents discuss program-related information with other parents and staff. The second half of the session could be devoted to parents and children working together, practicing skills, or creating make-it/take-it items for use at home. A sample agenda for one such workshop is offered in Figure 15.11.

3. *Carry out periodic child-study sessions.* Together with parents, observe children's physical, social, or cognitive skills, then brainstorm activity ideas for school or home. Next, engage in mutual problem solving related to children's learning and development.

4. *Help parents anticipate typical developmental changes in children's skills and other program-related behaviors.* Knowing what to expect in advance empowers parents to respond appropriately when such changes occur and makes them more confident teachers of their own children. A note home to parents, a brief discussion in the classroom newsletter, a small-group discussion, or an organized workshop on a related topic are a few ways to get this kind of information home. Chatting informally with parents individually and frequently is another valuable way to convey developmental information to parents. Such contacts are especially useful since teachers can provide appropriate information and answer questions with a specific child in mind.

5. *Provide general information about child development and learning to parents in a take-home form.* Books, pamphlets, cassettes, and videotapes could be made available through a parent lending library. In a box easily accessible to parents, file articles culled from magazines, newsletters, and early childhood journals such as *Young Children, Daycare and Early Education,* and *Childhood Education* (Bundy, 1991).

9:00–9:15	*Arrival:*	Children are taken to supervised child care rooms.
9:15–10:15	*Discussion:*	Ms. Amfit talks with parents about the development of motor skills such as throwing, catching, and skipping.
10:15–10:30		Parents pick up preschool-aged children from child care rooms, receive nametags, and go to first activity station.
10:30–11:30	*Activity stations:*	Parents and children rotate from station to station every 10 minutes, approximately 6 families per station. 1. Make it/take it: Parents and children choose to make one or more gross motor items for use at home—nylon paddles, milk jug scoops, newspaper balls; also provided are instructions and activity ideas for jump ropes, suspended balls, streamers, and pillow balls. 2. Throw/catch 3. Striking 4. Gallop/skip 5. Balance 6. Nutritional Awareness and Snack
11:30–11:40	*Closing:*	All participants gather in the rainy day room for a large-group song with movement.
This workshop will be repeated next Friday evening from 6:30 to 9 P.M.		

FIGURE 15.11
Saturday Morning Parent-Child Motor Skills Workshop

Provide more than one copy of each article so that you can recommend relevant readings and parents can take them home, with no obligation to return them. Periodically send home a note, highlighting new material that is available for parents to borrow or keep. Organize parent discussions around one or more of these or give parents a check-off sheet on which they can indicate whether they would like a particular article sent home with their child.

Facilitating Parent-to-Parent Support

1. *Arrange opportunities for parents to talk with one another informally.* Plan some casual get-togethers whose primary aim is to give parents an opportunity to build their social networks and communicate with their peers. Make sure to include an unstructured break to facilitate parent-to-parent conversation during more formally scheduled events. There is strong evidence that these informal exchanges are every bit as valuable to parents as the regularly scheduled program (Powell, 1989). In fact, for single parents, strengthening informal social networks may be the most effectual means of eliciting their involvement in their children's education (Cochran & Henderson, 1986).

2. *Work with other teachers, parents, and administrators to organize a parent-to-parent mentoring program.* Pairing new families with parents already familiar with school philosophy and practices helps ease the entree of the newcomers and gives established families a responsible, important means of involvement. Make sure to give the mentors guidelines for how to fulfill their role. Some of their duties might include

- calling new parents to welcome them and answer their initial questions,
- arranging to meet new families prior to their involvement in the program to provide a tour of the facility,
- inviting new families to accompany them to open houses or orientation sessions held early in the year, or
- checking in periodically as the year progresses to answer questions and provide information as needed.

3. *Facilitate teen, single, working, and noncustodial parent peer support groups.* Suggest that your program promote these kinds of get-togethers by providing the location for group meetings and child care during that time. If such groups are already part of your program, make sure individual parents in your class know about them.

4. *Suggest that a place in the school or center be set aside as a parent lounge.* The purpose of this room would be to encourage informal contacts among parents and between parents and the staff. It could also serve as a headquarters for parent projects. A living-room type of atmosphere seems welcoming to parents, as does a pot of coffee and a parent reference library. Parents also appreciate a large bulletin board on which are posted announcements, community news, and parent requests for child care, toys, clothing, or transportation (Palmer, 1991). Updating information often, removing out-of-date material, keeping the board neat and organized, and placing it in a visible spot also prompt parents to check it frequently.

This suggestion marks the last one focusing on effective parent involvement techniques. A compilation of all the strategies offered in this chapter is presented in Figure 15.12.

The Role of the Administrator in Promoting Parent Involvement

All of the parent involvement strategies described thus far are ones teachers could carry out on their own. However, the effectiveness of their efforts is greatly enhanced when program administrators offer support and leadership at both the building and program levels (Swick & McKnight, 1989). Thus, principals and program directors play a major role in facilitating positive home-school relations and getting parents involved in early childhood education.

Within the past few years, this facet of the administrative role has been highlighted by such organizations as the NAESP, the Association for Supervision and Curriculum Development, and the NASBE. All of these organizations have published guidelines for administrators about how to make parent involvement an integral part of their daily routine. In the interest of conserving time and space, we will not attempt to duplicate those documents here. However, the following stand-

Building a Firm Foundation for Parent Involvement

- Make *frequent* attempts to include parents.
- Create many *different* ways for parents to become involved.
- Treat parents as individuals.
- Tailor parent involvement strategies to meet parents' particular needs.
- Reflect on your potential to be a full-fledged partner in the home-school alliance.

Providing Information to Parents

- Develop written policies that emphasize the importance of parent involvement.
- Acquaint parents with the assumptions, goals, and expectations of the program.
- Familiarize parents with a typical day for children.
- Write "happy notes."
- Create a weekly or monthly newsletter to inform parents about the program and children's experiences.
- Stay in touch with parents who seem unresponsive.

Gathering Information from Parents

- Early in the year, solicit information from parents to help you better understand children's ecological contexts.
- Throughout the year, ask parents to provide anecdotes and information about their child.
- Elicit input from parents about learning goals for children.
- Ask parents for evaluative feedback throughout the year.

Establishing Two-Way Communication between Parents and the Program

- Vary the communication strategies you use.
- Establish telephone hours.
- Create an individual communication notebook to send between the program, teaching, and other settings in which a child participates.
- Structure parent conferences so that collaboration is emphasized.
- Carry out home visits.
- Make contact with noncustodial parents.

Integrating Parents into the Program

- Institute an open-door policy.
- Invite parents to visit the classroom at particular times during the school/center day.
- Involve parents in making classroom collections.
- Create home-based alternatives to on-site volunteering.
- Provide home-based learning activities for parents and children to do together.
- Give interested parents opportunities to participate in policymaking decisions.
- Show genuine pleasure in *every* parent's attempt to support their children's education.

Providing Parent Education

- Provide general information about child development and learning to parents in a take-home form.
- Help parents anticipate typical developmental changes in children's skills and behaviors.
- Carry out periodic child-study sessions.
- Conduct a simple needs assessment of parental concerns and interests.
- Develop a parent education plan each year.
- Invite parents to educational workshops that involve both them and their child.

Facilitating Parent Support

- Arrange opportunities for parents to talk to one another informally.
- Organize a parent-to-parent mentoring program.
- Facilitate teen, single, working, and custodial parent peer support groups.
- Create a parent lounge.

FIGURE 15.12
A Compilation of Parent Involvement Techniques

ards prepared by the NAESP (1990) are representative of what administrators all over the country are hearing and give a good overview of the program supervisor's evolving responsibilities related to the home-school partnership.

- The principal assures that there is regular sustained communication between home and school.
- The principal gets parents involved in their own child's schooling and in the operation of the school.
- The school provides information for parents on parenting issues and problems.
- The principal works with the home and the community toward easing transitions and addressing special needs and situations.
- Parent-teacher conferences are made integral to the early childhood education process.
- The principal works with various child-focused agencies in the community toward providing a range of services to students and their parents.

Standards such as these make clear the higher priority administrators must give to linking the home and the early childhood program in the common cause of education and providing the best for children. Thus, principals and directors in cooperation with teachers and other community agencies provide continuous support and opportunities to parents aimed at helping them in their roles of provider, nurturer, socializer, and first teacher.

SUMMARY

Practitioners and parents working together has become the hallmark of effective early childhood education. This chapter has described the aims and benefits of parent involvement in programs for young children. A variety of strategies for increasing that involvement have been suggested. The techniques described here are by no means all-inclusive but rather serve to highlight the broad repertoire of skills needed by early childhood practitioners as they strive to work more effectively with parents. While many questions remain as to how to reach and involve all parents, particularly low-income and minority parents, there is no doubt that the inclusion of the child's family will continue to remain a high priority among educators of young children. Our job as early childhood professionals is to keep investigating alternative methods of parent involvement and welcome parents as full-fledged partners in the educational process.

CHAPTER 16

Testing, Assessment, and Evaluation

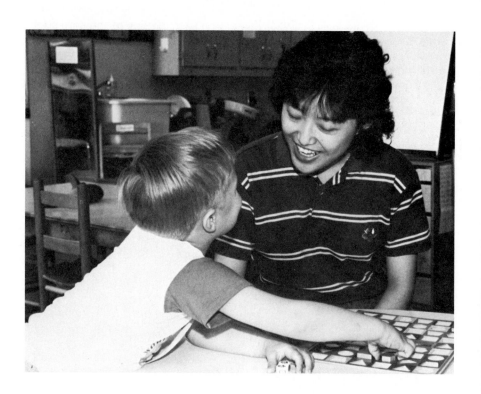

Carolyn Afree has been teaching second graders for 12 years. She has become increasingly concerned about evaluating the progress of children in her classroom. While she feels she is well aware of each child's general strengths and limitations and able to match learning tasks appropriately with children's varying abilities, standardized and "end-of-unit" tests are taking up more and more of the time she has to spend with the children. She notices that some of them seem highly stressed in the formal testing situation; others seem to attach too little importance to it, rushing through carelessly and making mistakes they do not ordinarily make when participating in classroom activity. She has spoken about it to her principal, who said, "We need to quantify children's progress somehow if we are to be accountable. Until we come up with a reasonable alternative, I'm afraid you'll have to go along with the present structure."

In another district, an early childhood education committee has been given the task of setting up a screening process for incoming kindergartners. Many of those sitting on the committee doubt the value of continuing to use standardized measures, but no one can suggest a viable alternative.

An elementary principal sits in his office, pondering about whether or not to retain 9 out of 37 kindergartners, 7 of whom are boys. He wonders if allowing them to go on with their peers to first grade might be a better decision, but he worries about erring on one side or the other. He also wonders what kinds of evaluation tools might be helpful in determining how wide the gap actually is between those nine and the other children recommended for promotion.

In this chapter, we will look at current issues related to the testing of young children, including the problems involved in using standardized tests, labeling and grouping children on the basis of such tests, and retention issues. We will also outline the basics of more authentic assessment and evaluation strategies for the early years. Included will be an overview of the purposes for testing, responsibilities of professionals conducting early childhood measurement and evaluation, selection of appropriate screening and assessment tools, data-gathering strategies, and organization and use of findings.

CURRENT ISSUES IN THE TESTING OF YOUNG CHILDREN

While the major controversy surrounding the testing of young children centers on the inappropriate use and abuse of standardized tests, other issues are also surfacing. These include the use of tests for purposes contrary to current research and developmental theory, such as the practice of denying school admission to children based on test results; assigning children to extra-year tracking, such as developmental kindergartens or pre-first-grade rooms; homogeneous grouping; retention of children; misuse of screening and readiness tests; the disproportionate number of boys, minority children, and low-income children who "fail" testing; and testing practices that drive early childhood curriculum and classroom activity, draining staff time and economic resources.

Standardized Testing

According to recent reports, approximately 55 million standardized tests of achievement, competency, and basic skills are currently administered each year to fulfill local and state mandates, with an additional 30 to 40 million given in compensatory and special education and another 2 million to screen kindergarten and prekindergarten children (Neill & Medina, 1989). Prior to 1950, standardized testing as we know it today was fairly rare in school systems and, before 1965, even less frequently seen in the early elementary grades.

Because of an influx of federal dollars during the 1960s to stem poverty and the accountability requirements that accompanied these dollars, standardized testing became an accepted feature of public education. Largely, it was a quick and easy method to document that programs were "working." Eventually, however, these tests took on a life of their own, shaping the very programs, educators, and children they were designed to evaluate.

Constance Kamii (1990), a noted early childhood educator, charges that the current overemphasis on standardized testing in the United

States is the result of grown-ups playing a series of damaging games aimed at looking good politically and maintaining jobs. The "guilty" have ranged from legislators, governors, and school board members to superintendents, principals, classroom teachers, and parents. Pressure to achieve greater "educational accountability" has gradually spawned widespread approval of such practices as teaching to the test (if not the actual test itself) and placing heavy emphasis on worksheets, drill, and other inappropriate teaching strategies in early childhood classrooms. All have been designed to get scores up because it is erroneously assumed that high scores on standardized tests equal high rates of learning in the children taking the tests.

These "games" worked so well that by 1987, average test scores in all 50 states were found to be above established norms. Did that mean American children were smarter? Or were they simply becoming smarter at taking tests? It appears that a growing number of educators are now willing to admit that the latter is true and that standardized testing as it is carried out today must be curbed in general and should be eliminated in the primary grades as a general practice.

Substantive findings of the last 15 years indicate that the "promise" of evaluation has culminated in harmful labeling and subsequent tracking, compartmentalizing rather than integrating children's learning opportunities, using restricted findings to represent broader ranges of development, employing inappropriate norming populations for comparisons with dissimilar populations, and narrowing the curriculum and experiential activity in early childhood education (Cryan, 1986). Because such variables as self-esteem, social competence, desire to learn, and self-discipline are not easily measured (particularly in young children), they have been relegated only minor importance in schools that emphasize standardized testing (Neill & Medina, 1989). Yet, in the long run, these are the very skills that children will need to sustain them in the formalized educational trek they face and—even more important—to enjoy a high-quality life thereafter.

This does not mean that all screening, assessment, and evaluation of young children should be scrapped. Indeed, screening will continue to be a necessary and important factor in the early identification of the at-risk child. In addition, appropriate evaluation strategies are essential in guiding and documenting children's developmental progress and our own professional efforts in planning effective learning experiences for them.

However, advocating an end to the "measurement-driven instruction" (Bracey, 1987) that has reduced much of education to rote learning and the drilling of children on isolated skills are such national organizations as the Association for Childhood Education International, Association for Supervision and Curriculum Development, National Association for the Education of Young Children, National Association of Early Childhood Teacher Educators, National Association of Elementary School Principals, National Council of Teachers of English, and the National Council of Teachers of Mathematics (Kamii, 1990; Wortham, 1990).

In addition to the problems already described, additional weaknesses and limitations of standardized tests include cultural bias; limited test content; inaccurate or inadequate norms; inappropriate use of results (G. Weber, 1977; Wortham, 1990); and the harmful educational, economic, and societal tracking of children (Laosa, 1977).

Test Construction. An understanding of how standardized tests are constructed is helpful in weighing the seriousness of these problems. Standardized tests used in the school setting consist primarily of criterion-referenced tests (CRT) and norm-referenced tests (NRT). CRTs are most useful for the diagnostic measuring of children's performance in specific curricular areas in which levels of difficulty have been identified and sequenced. NRTs are more commonly used to compare the overall competency of individuals or groups to that of another reference group (Cryan, 1986).

Once the purpose of the tests has been determined, a format (verbal, written, or psychomotor response; individual or group administered) is selected, and objectives are determined to spell out which skills, abilities, facts, and so forth, are to be tested. Actual test items are then prepared with an attempt to sequence difficulty of questions and/or reflect the competencies that educational experts believe should be measured.

To ensure an appropriate distribution of items, a normal curve is determined so that the scores of half a norm population would be expected to fall above the average and half below. Usually, most of the scores will be clustered somewhere around the mean and, as would be expected, more unusual scores would spread out to the left and right, theoretically forming a bell-shaped curve. This calls for establishing both a difficulty level related to each question (how many of the tryout sample correctly answers each question) and a discriminate level— that is, the extent to which a particular item distinguishes between competency or ability levels in the individuals in the experimental group (Wortham, 1990). To accomplish this, some items of limited importance may be included in the final version of a test while others of greater importance may be discarded. The difficult and time-consuming process of standardizing the test or constructing norm scores with a norm population then follows and may take anywhere from 5 to 8 years to complete (Kamii, 1990).

Included in this norming process is the development of standard or derived scores that can then be used to compare children's individual performance with that of the norm population. Kamii (1990) notes that such scores can be imprecise and subject to error; thus, they should be only *one* piece of evidence in evaluating a child's capability and not an end in themselves.

Although there is currently widespread opposition to the use of standardized testing of young children, particularly those in preschool through second grade, the use of such tests is occasionally warranted. Diagnostic assessment intended to determine conclusively whether a child has special needs requires the use of multiple types of data and sources (Meisels & Provence, 1989). Carefully constructed and valid standardized tests are legitimate tools to be considered. They are occasionally useful in ascertaining a more complete understanding of a child's strengths and weaknesses from the standpoint of evaluating performance against an established standard. Such a procedure can be useful in documenting the pre- and postinter-

vention status of groups of children who may be considered at risk because of socioeconomic factors or the geographical context in which they are reared. The tests are not intended to provide in-depth information about the ways children learn or to ameliorate learning handicaps (Sattler, 1988). However, in a relatively limited amount of time, a sample of behavior can be obtained to measure developmental status and changes or effects of remediation. The challenge is to find measures that have respectable reliability and validity, obtain a typical response from the child, and then use the data only in conjunction with other relevant information to evaluate a child's physical, intellectual, social, or psychological abilities and functioning. Michigan Department of Education curriculum and evaluation guidelines for 4- to 8-year-olds describe the following criteria for minimizing the limitations of standardized tests when used:

1. They must be designed to be individually administered. An assessment instrument that has been designed and normed for large-group administration is not appropriate.
2. They should require child responses that are mainly motoric or verbal or responses to auditory stimuli (e.g., point, construct, sort; name an object or picture; answer a question; follow directions; discriminate sound). Concrete materials and pictures should be the main media for obtaining responses. Paper and pencil should be used only as a check of perceptual motor functioning (e.g., copy a shape, write one's name).
3. They should be broad in scope. A variety of developmental domains should be covered, including emotional, social, physical, intellectual, aesthetic, language, and sensory functioning.
4. They must be relatively short to administer. Testing should take a maximum of 25 minutes.
5. They should be administered by an adult known to the child.
6. They should provide useful information for curriculum planning.
7. They should be normed on a large representative sample of children so that the norms match well with the children being tested.

8. They should be statistically valid and reliable.

LABELING, GROUPING, AND PLACING YOUNG CHILDREN ON THE BASIS OF TEST RESULTS

It is one thing to talk about the technical aspects of standardized testing. It is still another to consider that faulty decisions affecting children's futures are made because too much importance is attached to any one score, even when the test *is* a valid and reliable one. If, for example, we were to interrupt your reading of this chapter right now, have you take a test on what you have read so far, score that test, and then equate your performance with a norm group of people very much like yourself (placing you somewhere on a normal curve), you might react in one of two ways. If your performance were better than average, you might come away from the experience with a very pleased feeling. Furthermore, if decisions were to be made related to your professional life or future based on your performance on this particular test, you may feel quite relieved that your score was above the norm. If, however, your performance on the one test rated *below* average, your reaction would be quite different. You might try to explain: "But I didn't take the test seriously.... I didn't realize what was hinging on the results.... I didn't feel well.... I had a big argument with someone important recently and couldn't get it off my mind while reading the material.... I've *never* scored well on tests because I get uptight in a testing situation.... I *know* I'm better than the test indicates; in fact, I'm considered excellent in the classroom with children because I'm rather creative, and the test didn't measure any of that. The material we were tested on was presented in a boring way—I couldn't relate to it."

Fortunately, this is only a hypothetical situation, and your performance on such a test would not have an effect on your job or future. Moreover, because you are an adult and capable of interpreting your performance in light of your actual strengths or weaknesses, given the situation, you would no doubt be fairly assertive in articulating your concerns if any attempt were made to use the score in an inappropriate way.

Because of such real-life challenges, in fact, testing institutions such as the Educational Testing Service (ETS), which is responsible for overseeing such tests as the Graduate Record Exam (GRE), a test often required as part of admission criteria to graduate school, have acknowledged that any one test does not and cannot measure all the qualities that are important in predicting success and achievement. In order to protect graduate students from unfair decisions based on inappropriate use of the test, they have developed policy for general use of the GRE and have issued the following guidelines:

> Regardless of the decision to be made, multiple sources of information should be used to ensure fairness and balance the limitations of any single measure of knowledge, skills, or abilities. These sources may include undergraduate grade point average, letters of recommendation, personal statement, samples of academic work, and professional experience related to proposed study.... A cut-off score based only on GRE scores should never be used as a sole criterion for denial of admission. (*GRE Information Bulletin,* 1990–91, p. 29)

ETS has developed a similar policy for other tests they oversee, such as the Scholastic Achievement Test (SAT), a test taken by approximately 150,000 secondary students each year. Ideally, this type of policy should also govern the placement of young children in special programs. To guard against the inappropriate exclusion of children with disabilities from public school regular classrooms, Public Law 94-142 was passed in 1975 stating that, to the maximum extent possible, these children would be educated in the "least restrictive" setting. While screening, assessment, and evaluation are important tools in providing supportive services to vulnerable children and families, no decision should ever be based on the score from one test, nor should a child be labeled or said to "have a problem" because of performance on a test (Allen, 1980). Rather, as has been stated earlier, results on any test should be considered only in light of other evidence accumulated, including that from a child's parents, preschool teacher, childcare provider, or other significant adults.

However, both standardized tests as well as those reported to have no established validity or reliability are used regularly to place children in special entry programs, resource rooms, and learning groups or to bar children from school entry for an additional year. One principal proudly announced that, because of the screening methods they were using in his district, they had identified a number of children screened who were not yet "ready for kindergarten." Because the district had no other programs in place for such children, it was recommended that they wait another year to enter the system. Children and many parents may be disappointed about such outcomes but, for the most part, do not question the system. Instead, they accept decisions made as valid (particularly when supported with evidence from a standardized test) and in the best interest of the child. The consequences of such decisions can last a lifetime. There is evidence that as few as 6% of children entering special education tracks ever move completely back into the mainstream.

In the early years, males may be more vulnerable to such practices than females. Because they may be from 6 to 18 months behind their female counterparts in entering cognitive acceleration shifts, they are significantly more likely to be placed in resource rooms for the emotionally impaired and learning disabled (Soderman & Phillips, 1986) and recommended for developmental kindergarten placement, pre-first-grade rooms, or retention in kindergarten. Learning "deficits" or disabilities diagnosed in these children in kindergarten or first grade may very well be biological "deficits" (i.e., the child simply needs more time to develop the necessary myelinization, neural pathways, and other biological maturation required to make sense cognitively of abstract material that has become increasingly commonplace in kindergartens and first grade). Recent Yale University findings (Shaywitz, Escobar, Shaywitz, Fletcher, & Makuch, 1992) suggest that the numbers of children being diagnosed as dyslexic in first grade simply do not hold in third or sixth grade, that reading "problems" show year-to-year variability and may simply be the tail end of a normal reading distribution. They suggest also that because of such year-to-year variability, some of the children who appear to be functioning well at

one point may, in fact, need extra support later on and not get it. Also relevant here is the research related to maturation of the child's brain and eyes to organize incoming retinal signals. Although controversial, findings suggest that visual-perceptual problems contribute to letter reversal or letters that seem to "move about" and "run together" (Beauchamp & Kosmorsky, 1987, p. 1445).

There is increasing evidence to suggest that early academic and social differences in children are no better addressed by separating these children from their chronologically older and/or more mature peers, most differences washing out by third grade (Creager, 1990). This is not to say that developmental kindergartens have not been more comfortable placements for children less apt to achieve success in rigorously academic kindergartens. It does present proof, however, that early differences tend to disappear, and developmentally younger children can ultimately be successful when placed with children who score higher on entry measures.

There are many reasons why the practice of providing homogeneous educational placements for young children has increased. When carefully examined, few of these have to do with the long-range "best interests" of the children. More often, they may have more to do with our narrowing differences in children so that (a) planning can be more precisely targeted on specific outcomes to "prove" statistically that children are progressing and (b) children who have more "difficult problems" (i.e., out-of-step rates of learning, learning modalities, or reasoning processes) and require more of a teacher's time are outplaced so that regular classroom teachers are not expected to deal with them. Consequently, greater numbers of children are spending time in settings more highly restricted than might be necessary, which goes against the intent of PL 94-142; moreover, regular classroom teachers have lost confidence in their ability to handle such children. In most cases, children consistently benefit from spending time interacting with peers who have a broader range of skills. When the classroom climate is built on one of respect for individual differences and activities are arranged to allow for cooperative learning, high-quality interactive experiences, sequential learning, and active involvement of the teacher, all children are more highly motivated to grow. They observe what is going on in the group, pick up skills to be more like other children they admire, and contribute to or obtain help from other children in learning concepts and skills.

This is not possible, of course, in early childhood education settings in which children are closely grouped depending on what we believe they know to begin with before they ever participate in a particular setting. To the extent that the norm in an early childhood classroom is finding a correct answer and centering in on previously established facts, rather than arriving at an answer following exploration and investigation, heterogeneous grouping will be less successful. In such settings, there is a focus on avoiding wrong answers or "looking bad" that is observed by both the teacher and the children. All of this is not to suggest that every child should *always* be included in the regular classroom setting. For children who have significant organic attention deficit or psychological difficulties that would preclude their being successful in a regular classroom, a setting in which they can gain more specific one-on-one attention from the teacher and less negative stimulation from peers may be beneficial. This is what broad-based evaluation is all about. Appropriately used, it is education's comprehensive response to the uniqueness of each child (Cryan, 1986). Inappropriately used, it can cost some children opportunities that will lead to a qualitatively poorer education and, consequently, fewer opportunities to achieve in the future.

The expansion of extra-year early intervention programs (i.e., junior kindergartens, developmental first grades, and other "transition classes") to assist children with special needs has led to "serious equity issues involved in the differential rates of retention for males and minority students and in the differential ability of parents with higher incomes to provide high-quality preschool services for their children who delay entry into kindergarten" (Schultz, 1989, p. 126). Schultz suggests some policy and practice alternatives that might be more effective:

1. Postponing the use of standardized testing until children are better able to cope with test taking and results are more reliable

2. Limiting early grade testing to samples of children to obtain overall levels of achievement and trends in performance, rather than testing all children in a particular grade or school
3. Developing an assessment approach that "reduces the stakes" for both teachers and children by allowing alternatives to district retention and reward policies based on children's achievement
4. Presenting alternative methods of assessment, instruction, and classroom management so that teachers can work successfully with a variety of students
5. Legitimizing alternative efforts to replace standardized testing with documented teacher observation and work samples in a variety of content and skill areas
6. Legitimizing the time it takes away from classroom "instruction" to institute richer forms of assessment
7. Providing training to educators in evaluation and developmentally appropriate pedagogy, curriculum, and classroom management

RETENTION ISSUES

Approximately 1 million students are held back each year in all grades in the United States, at an average of $4,500 per child. Compared with their promoted peers, they are more likely to drop out, get into trouble with the law, learn less the following year, and develop more negative self-concepts. Despite this, Frymier (1989) found that 45% to 65% of teachers interviewed about the practice believed that it was an educationally sound one. Reviews of available research specifically related to kindergarten retention (Holmes & Matthews, 1984; Shepard, 1989) draw the following conclusions:

1. Retention does not improve achievement.
2. Although extra-year kindergarten programs are intended to serve both immature and slow-learner populations, there is no documented benefit to either group as contrasted with comparable control groups of children not retained. In fact, even though retained children make progress, it is not as great as that made by children who are promoted (Wortham, 1990).

3. Social-emotional outcomes on kindergarten retention indicated either no difference or some harm, with parents reporting their children had poorer attitudes toward schools, teasing by other children, a greater sense of failure, and lowered self-esteem (Bell, 1972).

The decision *never* to retain may also set some children up for certain failure. Decisions should be made on the basis of multiple data sources, specific benefits that can be obtained for the child by remaining in an educational setting or moving to another, and a complex set of other factors outlined by Light (1986): school attendance, intelligence, academic achievement, physical size, sex, siblings, previous grade retention, listing of learning disabilities, age, student's attitude toward retention, parents' school participation, and student's motivation to learn. Assessment that considers all of these factors is, of course, more complex than the most commonly used criteria to retain (i.e., the student's social maturity) (M. Curry, 1982).

APPROPRIATE AND USEFUL TESTING AND EVALUATION STRATEGIES FOR THE EARLY YEARS

Tests have been defined as systematic procedures for "comparing the performance of an individual with a designated standard of performance" and *measurement* as "the process of using numbers to describe quantity, quality, or frequency according to a set of rules" (Chase, 1978, p. 6). These two, then, are components that yield both qualitative and quantitative data that can then be judged against some established criteria. It is this aspect of attaching judgment that qualifies a procedure as *evaluation*. Others point out that evaluation is "more than tests and measurements" and calls for comprehensive, continuous, and/or periodic appraisal of children's progress and performance (Phenice & Griffore, 1990, p. 380). In the case of evaluating children, this calls for someone making use of a variety of data to gauge a child's developmental progress against an expected range of maturational behaviors, skills, readiness levels, and concept formation.

Because of the many limitations attached to the use of standardized tests, and because classroom teachers "seldom use the results of externally imposed standardized tests for their own purposes" (Raizen & Kaser, 1989, p. 719), a number of more appropriate alternatives have emerged. Although the purpose of testing is all too often simply to assign a grade, teachers can use assessment to determine what understandings children bring into a learning situation, how successful an instructional lesson has been with which children, what barriers to learning still need to be overcome, and what concepts the children still have difficulty understanding (Raizen & Kaser, p. 719). In the next section, we will provide an overview of the purposes and principles in testing young children, responsibilities of professionals who are conducting early childhood assessment and evaluation, selection of appropriate tools and methods, data-gathering strategies, and the use of findings.

Purposes and Principles in Testing Young Children

Important advantages can accrue to early childhood professionals when they systematically and professionally undertake evaluation to facilitate learning and development (Goodwin & Driscoll, 1980, p. 382; Hendrick, 1975, p. 282). Some benefits include the following:

■ Provides the educator with an increased understanding of each child
■ Increases the quality and specificity of the curriculum (by directing it toward particular skills in light of assessed strengths and weaknesses)
■ Improves the morale of the educator (by recording the early and later behavior of children and providing evidence of progress)
■ Vitalizes the process of reporting to parents (by providing detailed assessment on their child)
■ Serves as a valuable data base for reporting to funding agencies and governing agencies

Canada's Ministry of Education (*Primary Program*, 1990, pp. 154–156) has set forth a number of general principles that must be observed if evaluation is to support educators' effective decision making in planning for early childhood classroom experiences and enhancing children's learning. They are paraphrased here:

1. *Effective decision making requires systematic opportunities to observe each child's behavior.* Valid judgments about development will require that teachers encourage children to participate in a variety and number of activities that display all of the behaviors/skills of interest, including those in the social-emotional and aesthetic realms and the higher order cognitive skills.

2. *Evaluation should be based on multiple observations.* Just as one score on a standardized test is not enough to make sound decisions, specific behaviors of interest should be observed "a number of different times in a number of different contexts" (p. 154).

3. *Effective evaluation is comprehensive.* Because it is often difficult to assess outcomes related to social-emotional, aesthetic, and critical thinking, we often tend to ignore those areas and concentrate our evaluation efforts on more easily assessed areas such as the academic areas of language arts and math. In order to be effective, evaluation should cover all program goals and objectives. "It is better to make a tentative subjective decision about an important goal or outcome, than an absolute, objective judgment about a trivial one" (p. 154).

4. *Evaluation practices, strategies, and instruments must be selected in terms of program goals, objectives, and learning opportunities.* Evaluation should not be an isolated addendum to instruction. Rather, it should be integrated within the learning situations in which children have opportunity to develop the behaviors of evaluation interest.

5. *Evaluation implies that some decision will be made and that action will follow.* There is no doubt that effective evaluation takes planning and time away from other responsibilities that educators have. Unless the data will be useful in some way ultimately to make more informed instructional decisions or provide helpful feedback to the learner, it should not be undertaken. The bottom line in collecting information is to "continually ask, 'What will I do when I find out...'" (p. 154).

6. *A sound classroom evaluation program is primarily concerned with change.* Children's developmental spurts may occur at different rates and at different times, but all children do make progress that can be documented. Effective evaluation provides proof that change is taking place and some evidence of the quality of that change occurring.

7. *An effective evaluation program is constructive.* "Evaluation should support and enhance learning and development by focusing on what students can do and what they are attempting to do. When evaluation focuses on negative aspects of behavior, it becomes inhibiting and destructive, particularly in performance areas such as oral communication, emergent reading and writing, and fine arts" (p. 155).

8. *Evaluation of learning considers the processes in which children engage as well as the performances that result.* Evaluation provides opportunities for both the child and the teacher to reflect on how a child approaches a task and why he or she selects and applies particular strategies to accomplish the task.

9. *Sound evaluation of children's learning supports risk taking.* Effective evaluation not only covers children's present successes but also focuses on what they are *attempting* to learn or do. It is important not only to focus on how children are applying newly developed strategies and skills but also to look at how they are experimenting to transfer those strategies and skills to other learning.

10. *Children have an important role to play in monitoring their own learning and development.* Teachers, parents, and administrators should not be the only beneficiaries of evaluation. Children should also become aware of the processes and strategies involved in evaluation and begin to actively use them to evaluate their own learning experiences.

11. *Evaluation facilitates the transfer of learning.* When students become actively aware of the evaluation process and can begin to reflect on and evaluate their own behaviors, they develop a "metacognitive awareness" of a particular learning process, that is, the insight to begin transferring the skills gained in one learning experience to another. The same thing is true for teachers who can use what they learn

Tabita is marking where he spent his time at school and will evaluate whether his day was terrific, good, OK, sad, or terrible.

about children in one circumstance for their planning of future learning experiences in all areas of the curriculum.

12. *All evaluation is subjective.* "All evaluation procedures involve making judgments. The very process of choosing which evaluation tool to use is, in itself, subjective" (p. 156).

13. *All evaluation is subject to error.* As has been pointed out earlier in this chapter, exact and true scores related to human behaviors are impossible to obtain, given even the simplest instruments. Outcomes are always *approximations* of what the child can do and should be interpreted with this in mind.

14. *Teachers are the major instructional decision makers: assessment and evaluation are an integral part of instructional decision making.* Because the teacher is ultimately responsible for the classroom learning environment and has the greatest comprehensive knowledge of each particular child in that environment as well as each child's opportunities to practice a focused behavior, evaluation of what goes on there

should be undertaken and interpreted by the teacher, whose values and understandings are implicit in the process.

Responsibilities of Professionals Conducting Early Childhood Evaluation

Those who are implementing evaluation procedures greatly affect the outcome—by design or default. That is, assessment and evaluation will be effective only to the extent that attention is paid to (a) the relative subjectivity/objectivity and skills of the evaluator, (b) the state of the child at the time of evaluation, (c) properties of the evaluation setting, (d) timing of evaluation, (e) appropriate selection of data collection tools and strategies, and (f) thoughtful application of outcomes.

Subjectivity/Objectivity and Skills of the Evaluator. Perhaps nothing is as dangerous in the evaluation setting as the evaluator who is (a) unaware of his or her own personal traits, values, and the expectations he or she brings to the situation and projects to the child and (b) lacks evaluation know-how. The latter would include a lack of knowledge about child development as well as the ability to structure and apply appropriate evaluation strategies. Since we are advocating that evaluation in early childhood settings be carried out primarily by the classroom teacher, there is little that can be done about any effects related to differences in the teacher's and child's gender, race, ethnic background, and personality other than to have the evaluating teacher aware that establishing good rapport with individual children is a necessary prerequisite to good evaluation. The teacher must also examine as objectively as possible any expectations he or she brings into the situation and take care not to provide verbal and nonverbal reinforcement to one child that is not given just as freely to other children in the evaluation setting.

The Child.   Every effort should be made to obtain a number of samples of the child's best work, performed when the child is at ease, healthy, and motivated to undertake the task at hand, which will then be evaluated. It has been found that students, particularly those who have already developed test anxiety, perform more positively when any threat of failure is removed (Walker, Sannito, & Fireto, 1970). This includes even having evaluators encourage the student to relax and just do their best. This problem, of course, can be almost completely eliminated in early childhood classrooms in which evaluation procedures become a normal and less intrusive part of everyday activity in the classroom.

Timing of Evaluation.   There are two aspects of timing that need to be considered. One is the consistency in the scheduling of skill and behavior sampling. The other is the actual event of assessment itself. Some forms of assessment, such as vision and hearing testing and obtaining health records and family profiles, are most helpful when secured as early as possible before interaction with the child begins. Evaluation should be both formative (i.e., ongoing) and summative. The teacher should build into the program ongoing methods of collecting daily work samples and opportunities for planned observation and discussion with children; he or she must also plan for using more formal measures such as scoring oral reading tapes at specified periods during the year. Assessment of skills and behaviors should not be attempted until the teacher has established rapport with children and children have had adequate opportunity to practice the skills and behaviors to be assessed. Assessment should also not be undertaken at certain times of the school year and school day when children are more likely to be distracted, less able to concentrate, or likely to feel rushed (e.g., right before recess, on the day of a Halloween party, or after returning from vacation).

The Evaluation Setting.   Ideally, early childhood classrooms, where evaluation should take place, are pleasant environments in which attention has been paid to adequate ventilation, light, space, aesthetic qualities, minimal distractions, and modified noise levels. Realistically, of course, these factors are not always optimal. To the extent they are not, both children's learning and evaluation may be negatively affected. All of these factors should be taken into consideration when planning classroom activities that will serve as a basis for evaluation. Children should not be removed from the classroom to more unfamiliar settings for evaluation of activity and events that normally occur in the classroom, since other surroundings may be even more distracting to a child. However, every effort should be made within the classroom to see that the setting itself and ongoing activity within that setting at the time of evaluation does not distract from the child's best efforts.

Selection of Data Collection Strategies and Tools.   When we think of testing situations, we usually form a picture in our mind of people sitting quietly taking paper-and-pencil tests in group situations. That scenario in early education spells disaster and is developmentally inappropriate. First of all, young children in the primary grades are just beginning to be familiar with a paper-and-pencil format of recording information. Thus, errors on such a test may result from skill in recording rather than lack of knowledge in the content area being evaluated. Second, young children are gaining in their ability to respond to direction and may become confused in a group setting about what they need to do. Their confidence in alerting an adult to any problems they are having in the situation will depend on the rapport established with the attending adult. Third, this methodology does not match children's everyday integrated experiences in good early childhood classrooms and lends itself more to the testing of isolated skills. Tests that fall in this category are the Early Prevention of School Failure Test (Peitone), Metropolitan Readiness Test, Iowa Test of Basic Skills, Stanford Early School Achievement Test, Brigance K and 1 Screen, California Achievement Test, and Cognitive Skills Assessment Battery (Kamii, 1990). Better alternatives would consist of such methods as informal and structured observation, anecdotal records, dated work samples and portfolios, conferences, criterion-referenced checklists, descriptive inventories, and time-sample participation charts.

Application of Assessment and Evaluation Results. Findings from evaluating children's work should, first of all, *be used.* Although that may seem obvious, testing and evaluation often does not go beyond collecting scores in order to assign student grades or make comparisons across classes or schools. The process should always culminate in a plan of action on the part of the classroom teacher related to structuring learning experiences for the child. Results may also be helpful to the professional in noting where classroom instruction and/or guidance is especially strong or weak. Findings should be considered in the context of other things the teacher knows about the child and influence the timing and nature of the next evaluation effort. For example, if the child appears to be experiencing significant problems in a particular area, the teacher may want to contact other professionals for advice or follow-up diagnostic evaluation. Data should be recorded in such a way that other professionals who may need to refer to it will be able to understand the outcome, and all subjective comments should be identified as such and appear at the end of objective records. This is not to say they should not appear in a child's evaluation portfolio, since "gut-level" feelings about what may be going on with a child should be recorded so they can be checked out in future evaluation efforts. How-

ever, they should never be integrated into objective findings.

DATA-GATHERING STRATEGIES AND TOOLS

Before deciding what kind of strategies or tools are needed, the purpose of the assessment should be established. What do we want to know about this child and how specifically? Is diagnostic information needed? How will the data be used? Who else will need to see and use the data? If a federal or state granting agency or funding agency will be involved, will they accept only standardized test results, or are teacher-constructed measures considered as valid? What is there about the child or the testing situation itself that enters into our decision? How much time can be spared for the evaluation, and when and where should it take place? Will just one child be looked at or a group of children? Should a direct strategy be used that involves the child, or can an unobtrusive measure work just as well so the child is unaware of being "tested"?

Once the basic purpose and related details have been considered, there are a number of good evaluation methods that can be selected. Since standardized tests have been considered earlier in the chapter and have limited use with young children other than for diagnostic purposes, the focus in this last section of the chapter will be on measures that can be utilized by the classroom teacher in natural settings where children work and play.

Screening Procedures

One of the areas of assessment that educators are struggling with is the effective assessment of incoming kindergarten children to see if they are "ready." Many school districts have spent thousands of dollars training professionals to evaluate children's readiness and/or need for further diagnostic assessment using measures such as the Gesell, DIAL R, ABC Inventory, Brigance, Early Screening Inventory, and other standardized and nonstandardized tools. Meisels and Provence (1989, p. 14) note the need to differentiate between screening (sorting out children for whom diagnostic assessment is the "definitive next step") and "readiness" testing that looks at already acquired skills determined to be prerequisites for success in particular instructional programs.

In a recent study commissioned by Michigan's State Superintendent of Schools, it was learned that 110 different tests were being used throughout the state to assess children's entry "capabilities" (Michigan Department of Education, 1984). Fewer than 10% of the tests used had any established reliability or validity or were being used for the purposes intended. In many cases, "Frankenstein" tests had been constructed using the parts of many tests to make up what the particular district thought might tell them how successfully children would cope with what was planned for them in kindergarten.

Currently, many school districts are reassessing these earlier scrambles to identify weaknesses in children and, instead, are turning their energy toward training professionals who can cope with a wider range of skills in children. As a result, children in those districts are having a more positive first experience with what school is all about. Instead of taking a test, they are invited to come into an early childhood classroom once or twice in the spring for 1 hour just to enjoy the materials and developmentally appropriate activities planned for them. It has to be a better beginning! Parents can meet with the school principal and other professionals during this time to become better acquainted with school policy and ways in which they can work together with educators to support their child's successful orientation to school.

In addition to providing a more positive experience for children, the process just described has the advantage of allowing seasoned professionals—kindergarten teachers, Chapter I supervisors, elementary counselors and principals, speech teachers, school social workers, and psychologists—to observe the children at work and play. Some districts have the speech teacher interact purposefully with each child for a brief time during this period to get a speech/language sample. Vision and auditory screening are also scheduled to make sure these primary learning modalities are intact.

It is rarely difficult to spot the child who may have problems working with other children, adults, or materials. For those children, additional assessment is structured in addition to a private meeting scheduled with the child's parents to learn more about his or her history and present strengths and limitations.

Structured and Nonstructured Observation

One of the most underrated evaluation tools for use with the young child is observational assessment. The objective and experienced eye of someone who is knowledgeable about child development is invaluable. Observational assessment has much to offer: it is nonintrusive where the child is concerned; it yields instant, credible information that has on-the-spot utility for improving interactional and instructional strategies with children; it has heuristic value for formulating hypotheses to check out at a later date (Goodwin & Driscoll, 1980); it is a technique that can be used virtually anywhere people are behaving; and it allows the professional to capture data in natural settings that could not be obtained by other methods.

Goodwin and Driscoll (1980) define *observational measurement* as "the process of systematic recording of behavior as it occurs, or of a setting as it exists, in ways that yield descriptive and qualitative measures of individuals, groups, and settings" (p. 110). They indicate that formal observational measurement is more often used in research studies. Included here are such strategies as specimen records (continuous documentation of everything a subject does during a given time period), time sampling (noting selected behaviors or setting variables during intermittent but uniform time segments), event sampling (recording previously identified events of interest), and trait rating (subsequent rating of observed behaviors or underlying traits). Teachers frequently utilize trait rating when assessing and reporting such behaviors as cooperating and taking responsibility (Goodwin & Driscoll, 1980, pp. 116–140). In contrast, there are a number of less formal measures that can be used in understanding child behavior or planning instructional programs, and they will be the primary focus for the remainder of the chapter.

Young children are particularly good subjects for observations, since they have not yet learned to mask their feelings, thoughts, and behaviors very well. The technique also has great utility because it avoids the limitations of paper-and-pencil methods and, being fairly unobtrusive, requires no cooperation on the part of the child—and young children can be notoriously uncooperative in a testing situation. One 4-year-old who was moving through a screening process for kindergarten entry had everyone believing her name was Melissa (her name was Kate, but she preferred Melissa). She refused to answer any of the questions until her mother noted what was going on and intervened, telling her that she'd "better take things seriously and quit fooling around!" The teacher who was relating the story said, "She might have been one of our D-K kids if her mother hadn't clued us in. As it was, Kate turned out to be an exceptionally bright kindergartner."

Observation of children can be seriously flawed when bias is allowed to enter in the form of the halo effect or leniency factor. The former refers to allowing one characteristic of a child to influence perceptions of or generalize to other characteristics (Chase, 1978). For example, if a teacher observing Kate's earlier performance interpreted the behavior as a tendency to lie, she may subsequently allow that to color future observations of Kate. If, however, she viewed Kate's performance as the funny stunt of a highly creative child, she may tend to see Kate more positively in subsequent situations than might be warranted. The leniency phenomenon distorts observation in quite a different way. This observer would tend to rate not only Kate more highly than would be indicated but *all* subjects more highly; this is the phenomenon we see occurring in the case of grade inflation in secondary and postsecondary education in which entire classes of students receive a 4.0, despite distinct differences in performance.

In order to increase the reliability of observational data and minimize the limitations of the process, the following guidelines are suggested (Phenice & Griffore, 1990):

1. Be aware that the untrained observer tends to reflect an individual frame of reference, includ-

ing individual perceptions, cultural norms and developmental influence.
2. Define the problem or question one wishes to answer.
3. Scan the environment (children, adults, physical set-up) and become familiar with it before beginning the observation.
4. Prepare in advance any materials needed.
5. Develop and utilize a system for describing, counting or categorizing instances of behavior, allowing sometimes more than one observer to collect or interpret the data.
6. Observe and describe the physical setting such as space, temperature, lighting, etc.
7. Observe and describe tangible materials such as are found in the science center, pretend play area or arts and crafts center.
8. Write down your description of the visible and directly observable characteristics of individuals such as those that are directly observable through our sensory organs.
9. Write down observations immediately after you collect the data.
10. Examine observations for biases and judgments.
11. Increase accuracy of inferences by the use of more than one behavior as evidence and look for patterns and/or clusters of similar behaviors. (p. 384)

Informal observation methods most useful to early childhood educators include the use of anecdotal records, frequency counts and charts, checklists, rating scales, and participation charts.

Anecdotal Records.   Anecdotal records (see Figure 16.1) are on-the-spot descriptions of both typical and unusual behaviors in a child. These single observations, which are most conveniently written on index cards to be filed, contain sufficiently detailed descriptions of a particular behavioral event that can then be used with subsequent observations to formulate some hypotheses or conclusions about a child's behavioral functioning. Included on each card should be the child's name, date, time, and place of the observation, as well as the observer's name. A detailed description follows, providing information about the climate of the event, any known stimulus, persons involved, direct quotes if important to understanding the situation, and behavioral responses of the child. Unusual behaviors of any kind are noted. Any subjective inferences or in-

Child's Name: Gary Denzell   **Observer:** B. Miller
Date: 10/16/90   **Setting:** Kindergarten Classroom
Time: 10:17 A.M.

Children were asked by Ms. Sharpe to complete a worksheet identifying like and dissimilar objects. Gary continued to play with unit blocks until reminded by Ms. Sharpe to take his place at the table and begin working. He looked up but still did not move. When she moved toward him to get him to comply, he kicked down the block structure he had been making and walked to the table. Ms. Sharpe noted, "That's better." Gary did not respond.

Interpretation: Gary balked when asked to do seatwork. He clearly preferred playing with blocks, trucks. Would there be a better way to "teach" logicomathematical concepts than forcing him to complete ditto sheets, which he continues to have difficulty with?

FIGURE 16.1
Anecdotal Record

terpretations may be noted but must be kept separate from the observation itself.

Frequency Counts.   Frequency counts are simply behavior tallies of specified behaviors as they occur (see Figure 16.2). Sometimes we have a feeling that a particular behavior is either increasing or decreasing on a day-to-day basis with a child. Occasionally, we may want to collect baseline information before beginning purposeful intervention to alter behavior. Frequency counts can help us document whether or not our intuitions about a situation are correct and can then be charted to display the effects

of instituted treatment (see Figure 16.3). For example, a behavior of interest might be a child's aggressive interaction with other children, and a frequency count could be used to document maintenance, increase, or decrease of the behavior following intervention.

Checklists.   Checklists can range from formal criterion-referenced lists of developmental behaviors and skills to teacher-constructed inventories listing any number of behaviors of interest to the educator. They are helpful for noting both individual and group achievement and usually require a simple check (√) indicating

FIGURE 16.2
Tally of Aggressive Interactions

Child's Name: Gary Denzell
Behavior: Aggressive interaction with other children—biting, hitting, spitting, kicking
When: During center activity (9:10–10:15)
Where: Ms. Johnson's room
Observer: B. Miller
Dates: November 16–November 20, 1990

Days	Tally	Total
1	//////	6
2	////	4
3	///	3
4	/	1
5	//	2

FIGURE 16.3
Charting of Aggressive
Interactions

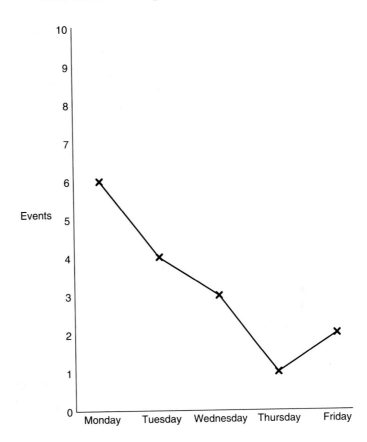

that the skill or behavior has been noted (see Figure 16.4). Teachers interested in documenting observation more than once may note the first observation by making a horizontal mark (—), the second with an added vertical mark (+), and additional crosses for subsequent observation of the skill (⟊, ✳).

Rating Scales. Rating scales are similar to checklists in that lists of behavioral variables are made. They differ in that an evaluative component is attached that qualifies behavior or skill acquisition (see Figure 16.5). Such scales can be color-coded for easier interpretation (e.g., 1 = green; 2 = blue; 3 = yellow; 4 = red).

Participation Charts. Time-sample participation charts are useful devices for recording where children are at a particular time during the school day and who they interact with most

often. Following the preparation of a coded form for documentation purposes, an observer simply notes the location of each child at a designated time. In Figure 16.6, for example, all areas of the classroom have been coded (A–J). Areas assigned to the two supervising adults in the room (Mr. Tanamato is the teacher, and Mrs. Gross is his aide) are identified. Names of children have been recorded down the left of the form, and designated times when the observations are to be made are recorded across the top. In a matter of seconds, the observer can document where each child is at that particular time. These can then be examined after a number of observations have been made to look for patterns in children's interaction with other children and adults, as well as their involvement or noninvolvement in certain activities. For example, using the participation chart in Figure 16.6, a 1-week time sample that docu-

CHILDREN'S SELF-HELP CHECKLIST

Date: 11/29/92

Teacher: Mrs. Gonzalez

	Robert	Joanna	Jerry	Larue	Donna	Gavin	Laura	Paul	Rosalie	William
Knows telephone number	✓			✓	✓	✓		✓	✓	
Can give full address	✓				✓	✓				
Buttons with no help	✓	✓		✓	✓	✓	✓	✓	✓	✓
Zips	✓			✓	✓		✓			✓
Can tie shoes	✓			✓		✓				
Puts materials away without being reminded	✓		✓		✓				✓	
Follows directions	✓		✓	✓	✓	✓			✓	
Cleans up after self	✓				✓				✓	
Asks for help when needed	✓				✓					

FIGURE 16.4

Example of Self-Help Checklist

ments where 15 children are at five different times during the morning's scheduled center activity, a teacher could obtain answers to the following points of interest:

1. You've had the feeling that too many children (more than 5 at one time) are in the art area. Do you need to structure a rule about this?
2. You suspect the boys rarely visit the language arts center. Is this true?
3. The children seem to avoid Brian (or vice versa). Is this happening?
4. Mr. Tanamato reports that he thinks Sam spends too much time in the bathroom. Does he?
5. You suspect a couple of the children may be coming to school without breakfast. Who are they?
6. What percentage of the children are visiting the science area each day?
7. The children appear to be avoiding one of the adults. What can you learn about the situation?
8. Some of the children are being dropped off late; you feel you need to document this to

SOCIAL SKILLS RATINGS SCALE

Date: ___4/10/92___

Teacher: _Mr. Lofy_

1 = Skill well developed; color code green
2 = Practical often but not always; color code blue
3 = Working on; color code yellow
4 = Rarely observed; color code red

	Juan	Jim	Sandra	Jason	Kelly	Amy	Diedra	Eric	Taylor	Regina	Elizabeth	Kerry	Ervin
Developing friendship skills	3	3	1	3	3	1	1	1	3	1	1	3	4
Initiates play/work with others	4	1	1	2	4	2	2	2	4	1	1	3	4
Makes suggestions	4	1	1	3	1	1	2	1	1	1	1	1	4
Takes suggestions	1	3	2	2	3	1	1	2	3	2	2	2	3
Negotiates conflicts (compromises)	3	3	2	3	2	1	2	1	3	2	1	2	4
Is cooperative and helpful	2	2	1	2	3	2	2	1	4	2	2	2	3
Shares materials	2	3	2	2	1	2	1	1	4	2	2	2	3
Gives assistance to others	3	4	2	2	1	2	3	2	4	2	1	2	3
Respects others and their property	2	2	1	2	2	1	2	2	3	2	1	1	3
Conforms to reasonable limits	1	2	1	1	3	2	1	1	2	1	1	1	2
Demonstrates self-control	1	2	1	2	2	2	1	2	2	1	1	2	3
Adapts to new situations	3	3	2	2	3	1	1	2	3	1	2	2	3
Terminates interactions in socially acceptable ways	2	3	1	2	1	1	2	1	3	2	1	3	3
Interacts with new people	3	3	2	3	4	1	1	1	4	1	1	2	4

FIGURE 16.5
Example of Rating Scale

FIGURE 16.6
Time-Sample Participation Chart

	Monday 8:15	8:30	9:00	9:15	9:30	Tuesday 8:15	8:30	9:00	9:15	9:30	Wednesday 8:15	8:30	9:00	9:15	9:30	Thursday 8:15	8:30	9:00	9:15	9:30	Friday 8:15	8:30	9:00	9:15	9:30
Brian	A	B	F	J	—	B	A	—	J	J	A	J	J	B	—	H	A	H	I	B	—	J	J	A	I
Amy	C	A	H	D	E	H	A	D	C	C		B	H	D	D	D	C	C	A	—	C	C	A	B	D
Kevin		B	—	E	G		A	—	B	D			F	E	E		—	—	A	D			B	E	E
Amanda	C		D	A	C	C	C	D	E	E	G	A	F	C	D	C	C	B	D	D	D	D	D	F	A
Jenny	A	I	H	D	D	A	H	D	D	F	F	E	C	C	C	A	—	C	D	D	D	G	G	E	E
Joey		E	D	D	E			A	A	C	F	D	E	D	—	H	A	D	F	C	A			F	D
Bill	D	D	C	C	G	D	B	F	A	C	D	D	B	G	G	A	D	—	F	D	G	G	G	F	D
Sam	D	B	C	C	G	D	B	F	A	C	D	D	B	G	G	A	D	—	C	F	B	B	G	H	D
Sarah	G	G	A	D	D	D	D	C	C	H	D	—	A	F	F	C	C	G	C	F	D	D	C	C	A
Erin	G	G	A	D	H	F	F	D	A	B	A		—	H	B	D	D	D	E	G	B	A	D	D	C
Tamera	G	A	D	D	G	D	A	A	C	C	—	D	C	C	C	E	F	F	G	—	A	C	C	D	G
Julio	A	D	C	B	G	D	B	C	C	C	D	A	B	G	G	A	F	—	F	D	A	G	G	H	D
Ahmad	G	G	D	E	E	E	F	F	A	D		D		G	G	B	D	D	D	A	D	G	E	E	E
Randi	D		A	G	G	G	G	D	D	A		A	C	H		F	F	C	D	A	D	E	E	B	C
Michael	B	J	D	E	E			—	A	F			—	C	C	D	D	A	F	F	B	F	D	C	F

A = snack*
B = bathroom
C = dramatic play
D = art center
E = blocks/trucks**

F = manipulatives
G = large motor**
H = science*
I = lockers
J = language arts center

*Mr. Tanamato, MWF; Mrs. Gross, TTh
**Mrs. Gross, MWF; Mr. Tanamato, TTh

talk to parents. Which children are notice-ably tardy and not arriving by 8:00?

9 Three boys are best friends. Who?

10. You found whole rolls of toilet paper in a toilet in the bathroom on Tuesday and Friday. Who may need to be watched more closely?

By examining the data collected over the 5 days in Figure 16.6, the following conclusions might be drawn in response to these questions:

1. No rule seems to be needed about too many children in the art area. Only one incident was recorded.
2. Yes, few boys appear to be working in the language arts center—only Brian every day and Michael on Monday. What can be done to stimulate their interest?
3. Yes, observation indicated that Brian and the other children are not interacting—he is often at lockers, bathroom, language arts center where there are few other children. This needs to be observed more carefully to establish cause.
4. Cannot tell whether Sam is spending too much time in the bathroom from this set of observations. Try event sampling for this question.
5. Jenny and Julio may be coming to school without breakfast. This needs to be followed up immediately by talking to the children.

6. Only 20% (3) of the children visited the science area last week.
7. Boys are avoiding areas where Mr. Tanamato is stationed, even M, W, and F snack (also science on M, W, F and blocks and large motor on T, Th). Need to follow up.
8. Kevin was tardy on M, T, W, Th, F. Joey was tardy on M, T, F; Michael tardy on T, W.
9. Bill, Sam, and Julio appear to be best friends and travel from activity to activity together.
10. Kevin and Sam are the only boys who were in the boys' bathroom on both T and F. This bears closer watching!

Self-Evaluation by the Child

Often, children are never challenged to evaluate their own progress. It is important that they do so. Besides conferencing with the teacher periodically about work they have produced, they can learn to document involvement in the classroom by using checklists that have been developed in many of the domains. For example, skills in a certain area (e.g., physical development, social-emotional development, or emergent writing) may be listed (see Figure 16.7), with a number of spaces at the right that can be dated by the teacher or student and then colored in by the child as a skill is achieved. As the year progresses, children are reminded about maintaining the skill every time they make en-

FIGURE 16.7
A Form for Child's Self-Appraisal

Date:	9/27	12/5	2/14	4/12	5/10	6/12
I can zip.						
I play and work with others.						
I share with others.						
I help clean up.						
I put materials away after using them.						
I try new things.						
I am helpful to others.						

tries and are also reinforced as they see the number of skills adding up on the checklist.

Teachers will want to produce self-evaluation checklists for children that have a range and number of skills so that every child will be able to color in at least a couple of skills accomplished in the area, right at the beginning. Those still to be obtained should be reasonably within a child's reach, given more time and practice. For children who are progressing more slowly, a checklist should be developed that breaks the skills down more finely and recognizes smaller gains in development. For younger children, the use of pictographs and a rebus is helpful.

The Ecomap

Finding out about the child's world outside the classroom can be a very useful assessment procedure, particularly when it is done early in the year, perhaps in preparation for the initial fall conference between the teacher and each child's parent(s). The ecomap (see Figure 16.8) is a paper-and-pencil exercise designed to provide a simple, visual overview of the child's life space as spent in the family and community. The teacher invites the parent(s) to participate in sketching out the child's ecomap, beginning with drawing a circle in the middle of the paper and placing the child's name in the center. Other circles representing the most salient systems in the life of that child (e.g., the immediate family members living in the household, members of the immediate family not living in the household, the extended family—grandparents, influential aunts, uncles, etc.) are then placed around the center circle and connected by lines. Other connections related to health care, recreation, extracurricular activities, parents' workplace, the child's best friends outside of school, baby-sitters, and so forth, can be added to provide more information. As the connections are drawn, the teacher may elicit extended information about any of the connections that seem to be highly problematic or supportive for either the child or parent. In this way, the teacher becomes acquainted with how children spend their time and energy outside the classroom. Also revealed is the qualitative nature of the various contexts, which provides information for a better understanding of a child's special needs

or life events that may be affecting the child's classroom performance. Parents who have participated in the exercise have reported that it allowed them to establish better rapport and feelings of collaboration. Others have said the process made them more aware that even a very young child's world can be fairly complex.

Dated Work Samples

Collecting children's work samples and putting together a comprehensive and ongoing "process-and-product" (Gardner, 1988) dossier, portfolio, or process-folio of work in language arts, mathematics, science, social studies, and other content areas is an excellent method for displaying documented academic growth in these areas, as well as "generative shifts in students' understandings in comparison to their younger selves" (Perrone, 1991, p. 59). Samples may include a child's drawings, paintings, maps, graphs, descriptions of constructions, charts, photographs of projects and friends, webs, written work, and projects. This calls for professionals to plan activities in order to have children create these products and then collect them intermittently during the school year. These can then be shared with parents at conferences and with other professionals who are interested in the child's ongoing development.

Portfolio collections may begin with the child building a collection of materials (student portfolio) and then selecting certain pieces to build a "showcase portfolio" consisting of pieces the student believes is his or her best work. Children may also contribute to a classroom "portfolio"—a bulletin board, scrapbook, videotape, or tabletop display of work produced.

In addition to the student-developed portfolios, teachers have found it valuable to keep a teacher portfolio. Contents might include copies of work the student selects or does not select for a showcase portfolio, anecdotal notes, checklists noting skills and processes observed, work samples that demonstrate progress over time, an ecomap, and anything else the teacher feels is useful in planning for the child's educational experience. Selected, representative pieces from the teacher portfolio can be added at the end of the school year to an institutional portfolio, which accompanies each child as he or she moves from

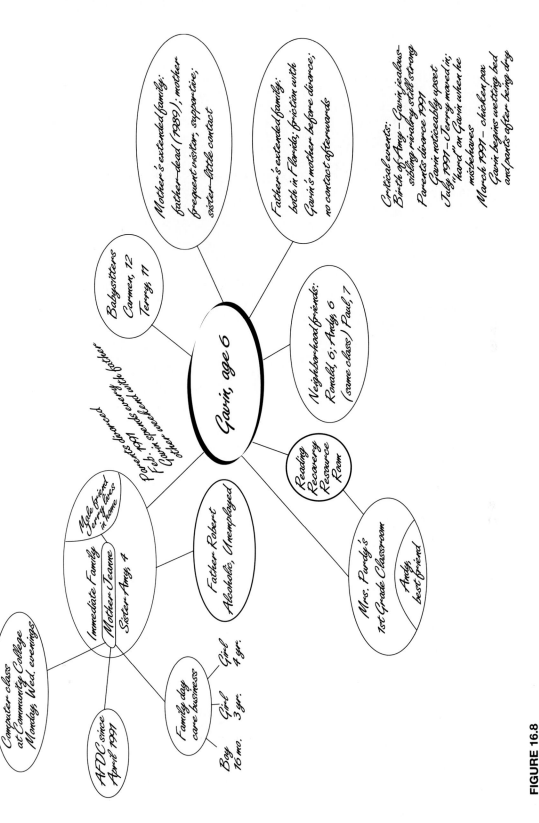

FIGURE 16.8
An Ecomap: The Child's Developmental Contexts

Portfolios are useful in noting development over time in a variety of domains.

class to class or school to school (Tierney, Carter, & Desai, 1991). In one elementary school, the folders are kept throughout elementary school and presented to the children on the evening celebrating their transition to the middle school.

As some school districts move to a literature-based approach to reading in the primary grades as an alternative to basal texts, many of them are looking for a quantitative method to document that children are making progress in reading accuracy and also their ability to recognize and correct mistakes without help. A literature-based method for obtaining samples of children's oral reading at several times during the year has been suggested (Kamii, 1990, pp. 124–129). The strategy is to offer children a selection of stories they have been introduced to in the classroom (e.g., Leo Lionni's *Fish Is Fish*), have them read one into a tape recorder, and follow up by discussing with an adult what they believe the story was all about.

The teacher, using a photocopied or typed version of the story, then listens to the tape to evaluate the quality of the child's reading, noting mistakes, number of words read, self-correc-

tions, words omitted, words added, and words reversed (see Figure 16.9). Notes are made related to comprehension, fluency and expressiveness in reading, and the nature of the mistakes made by the child.

Scoring (see Figure 16.10) consists of establishing an accuracy rate, meaningful mistake rate (mistakes that do *not* destroy syntax or meaning; e.g., *house* for *home*), self-correction rate, and a comprehension score that ranges from fragmentary understanding (1) to full and complete understanding of the story (4). Such scores, over time, provide information about whether the child is improving in accuracy and the ability to self-correct and whether more or less difficult material would be more appropriate. A summary of the process appears in Figure 16.11.

Conferences

Conferencing is an evaluation method that can be used to further follow up any of the methods described to this point. Conferences are one-on-one discussions between the teacher and child about collected samples of the child's work.

Name: Juana Perez
Date: April 4, 1991
Evaluator: Mr. Lofy

Fish Is Fish

	Word Total
AT THE EDGE OF THE WOODS THERE <u>WAS</u> A BIG	9 X/
POND, AND <u>THERE</u> A MINNOW AND A TADPOLE	17 X
SWAM AMONG THE WEEDS. THEY WERE <u>INSEPARABLE</u>	24 X
FRIENDS.	25
ONE MORNING THE TADPOLE <u>DISCOVERED</u> THAT	31 X
DURING THE NIGHT HE HAD GROWN TWO LITTLE LEGS.	40 X
"<u>LOOK</u>," he said <u>triumphantly</u>. "LOOK, I AM A FROG!"	49 /X
"NONSENSE," SAID THE MINNOW. "<u>HOW</u> COULD YOU BE A	58 X
FROG IF ONLY LAST <u>NIGHT</u> YOU WERE A LITTLE TINY FISH,	68 //
JUST LIKE ME!"	71
THEY <u>ARGUED</u> AND <u>ARGUED</u> UNTIL FINALLY THE	78 X
TADPOLE SAID, "FROGS ARE FROGS AND FISH IS FISH	87
AND THAT'S THAT!"	90
IN THE WEEKS THAT <u>FOLLOWED</u>, THE TADPOLE GREW	98 /
TINY FRONT LEGS AND HIS TAIL GOT SMALLER AND	107
SMALLER.	108

FIGURE 16.9
Analysis of an Oral Reading Sample

The teacher may ask questions to probe the child's thinking about the products, clarify concepts that are still fuzzy in the child's mind, and learn more about what the child is interested in working on in the future. Discussions that take place in small- and large-group meetings between children and the teacher also yield information about children's conceptualization that can be useful for more in-depth future planning and assessment.

ORGANIZATION AND USE OF ASSESSMENT AND EVALUATION DATA

We need to reiterate here that findings ought to be used to improve the learning climate or directly benefit the child's learning experiences. Never should assessment be structured just to gain and report a score, with no follow-up benefits to the child or educator.

Data should be recorded in a format that is most easily interpreted, and enough information should be included to ensure that time will not diminish the value of the reported material. Evaluation summaries should be written periodically (at least twice a year for each child) and should be kept confidential except for the reporting mandated by the school system or as requested by parents and professionals supporting the child's development. Assessment and evaluation data should be stored so that classroom teachers have easy access to them in program planning.

Assessment and evaluation findings should never become conversational fodder for the teacher's lounge or other public gatherings, and negative comments about a child, (i.e., points of weakness) should be considered only in light of

FIGURE 16.10
Scoring the Oral Reading
Sample in Figure 16.9

Name: Juana Perez
Date: April 4, 1991
Evaluator: Mr. Lofy
Literature Category: Level 3

A. Words read: <u>108</u>
B. Mistakes (X): <u>8</u>
C. Self Corrections (<u>/</u>): <u>2</u>
D. Meaningful mistakes(/): <u>3</u>
E. Total corrected/meaningful mistakes (<u>/</u> + /): <u>5</u>

Accuracy Score [(A–B+E) ÷A]:
$(108 - 8 + 5) \div 108 = \dfrac{105}{108} = .97$

Self-Correction Rate: [C÷E]
$3 \div 5 = .60$

Meaningful Mistake Rate: [D÷E]
$2 \div 5 = .40$

Comprehension (1 = fragmentary to 4 = full): 4

Comments: Juana's self-correction abilities are increasing (score on 2/27/91 = .22; score on 4/4/91= .60). Comprehension was excellent, and she enjoyed reading to me. According to accuracy rate, literature category is appropriate. Retest in May.

how corresponding strengths or modifications in instructional strategies can be helpful in minimizing the limitations discovered.

SUMMARY

Developmentally appropriate early childhood evaluation is necessary for documenting the growth and development of young children and providing sound information for program planning in the primary grades. Formulating an effective evaluation strategy to measure progress of children requires the following:

- Early childhood educators who have a solid understanding of the many facets of child development
- Formulation of developmental objectives in all learning domains of interest, based on child development research and theories
- A planned range of appropriate activities and experiences for children based on developmental objectives and children's abilities and interests

- A devised number of appropriate evaluation strategies to measure children's engagement in activities and developmental progress over time (e.g., conferences, criterion-related checklists, observation notation and anecdotal records, participation charts, dated work samples, self-evaluation by child, oral reading tapes, etc.)
- Thoughtful timing of individual, small-group, and large-group assessment and evaluation (time of day, spacing over school year)
- Effective use of evaluation data to improve the quality of each child's educational experiences and growth
- A useful structure for sharing obtained formative and summative information with relevant others (i.e., the children, parents, other educational staff working currently or in the future with the child and administration)

Although standardized tests can contribute to our ability to understand and plan for the special needs child, information gained from them

Analysis

1. Listen to the tape the child has made.
2. Underline *all* mistakes, writing above printed word what reader actually said.
3. Do not count the same mistake twice.
4. Indicate self-corrections by putting a *C* above the word and underlining it twice.
5. Circle any words omitted.
6. Put a caret (^) in space if an extra word is added, writing extra word above.
7. If letters or words are reversed, mark with horizontal *S* (   ).
8. Make notes on retelling, comprehension, particular qualities of reading, or problems.
9. In the right margin
    a. indicate a meaningful mistake (does not destroy syntax or meaning) by a slash (/).
    b. indicate self-corrected mistakes by underlining a slash twice (/).
    c. indicate mistakes not corrected or those that destroy meaning or syntax by a crossed slash (X).

Scoring

1. *Use the following designators:*
    A = Count total number of words read.
    B = Add total mistakes (X).
    C = Add self-corrections (/).
    D = Add meaningful mistakes (/).
    E = Total self-corrections and meaningful mistakes (/ + /).
2. *Obtain accuracy score.* From total words read, subtract uncorrected and nonmeaningful mistakes. Add self-corrections. Divide the resulting number by the total number of words read. Thus, use the following formula: [(A–B+E)÷A].

Note: If accuracy rate is below 95%, the child is likely to flounder and lose ability to use strategies ordinarily at his or her disposal. Try an easier text. If 100% accuracy, suggest a more difficult text to child.

3. *Obtain self-correction rate.* Divide number of self-corrections (/) by total of meaningful mistakes (/) and self-corrections (/). Thus, use the following formula: [C÷E].
4. *Obtain meaningful mistake rate.* Divide number of meaningful mistakes (/) by total of meaningful mistakes (/) and self-corrections (/). Thus, use the following formula: [D÷E].

Note: Both the meaningful mistake rate and self-correction rate assess a child's determination to make sense of what is being read. The higher the percentage, the more the child is gaining meaning out of reading.

5. Determine comprehension or retelling score, using the following criteria:
    1 = fragmentary understanding
    2 = partial understanding
    3 = fairly complete understanding
    4 = full and complete understanding; ability to make inferences on what is read

Note: Oral reading tapes may be passed on from one grade to another in order to assess a child's reading progress over time. It is important to use only one tape for each child, date each entry, and use the same scoring criteria across a school district so that interpretation of children's scores will be valid. Also, a school district should establish a "literature difficulty index" or category by using suggested lists such as that published in Routman's (1987) *Transitions*. It should be noted when a child is moving to a more difficult level of reading material, for it is expected that a child's accuracy and self-correction scores will fall temporarily until the child increases skills at the new level.

FIGURE 16.11
Analyzing and Scoring Oral Reading Tapes

should be used only in conjunction with other equally valid sources of information. Single scores on standardized tests should never be used in isolation to direct or redirect the lives of young children, nor should they be used to structure children into homogeneous settings when they could better be served in regular programs and with their age group of peers.

In general, it is believed that standardized testing in preschool through second grade is largely unnecessary. Alternative evaluation methods are preferred, including the use of observation and collecting of a variety of valid work samples. All assessment and evaluation findings should be carefully catalogued for future use, and information should be kept confidential except when used to support the educational experience of the young child. In the hands of professionals knowledgeable about child development, curricular planning, and early childhood assessment, effective evaluation in early childhood education can become one of the tools needed to plan advantageous beginnings for children and the kind of classroom experiences that will lead later on to sustained curiosity and a desire for lifelong learning.

CHAPTER 17

Improving Programs for Young Children through Individual and Group Change

Educators who explore principles and strategies associated with developmentally appropriate programs for young children eventually begin to wonder what it will take to

rearrange the classroom into learning centers,

shift to a more process-oriented approach to teaching,

evolve from relying on basal readers to greater use of children's narrative picture books,

replace negative rules with positive ones,

incorporate theme planning into daily routines,

find new ways to include parents in the program, or

add portfolios as a tool for assessing children's progress.

Ideas like these represent some potential innovations teachers or administrators might like to bring about in their programs. *Innovation* refers to any significant shift in philosophy, process, or aim taken by an individual or group of persons working together. To be innovative means to try something new; thus, innovations are tied to change. Such changes vary in how much they diverge from current practices. They also differ in complexity (e.g., how many changes are involved and how concrete or abstract they seem), scope (e.g., number of persons affected, amounts and types of resources required, duration, etc.), and whether they take place within the confines of a single classroom or involve programwide practices or policies. Furthermore, innovations need not be novel to others. For instance, offering children reasons for rules, collaborating with parents, and increasing children's use of manipulative materials in mathematics lessons are ideas that have been around for many years. However, to the person or persons adopting them for *the first time*, they represent new ways of thinking and doing things and so are true innovations, which demand change.

WHY CHANGE IS DIFFICULT

Change is not easy. Despite the merits or advantages of a new idea, adopting it requires people to abandon the comforts of the status quo and embrace the unknown. Both actions go against human nature. For many teachers and adminis-

trators, the *traditional way of doing things* represents security. They know what is expected and how to function within certain parameters. When those boundaries are altered, either through choice or as a product of outside forces, roles must be reformulated, old skills revised, and new skills developed. This upheaval prompts a period of disequilibrium for people despite how enthusiastic or reluctant they feel about the change. Thus, for a while, even the seasoned veteran becomes a novice again. Tynette Hills, president of the National Association of Early Childhood Specialists at State Departments of Education, reminds us that "each time we ask someone to change, we ask him or her to take a journey into incompetence" (Hills, 1991). Since most people are well aware of these uncertainties, it is not surprising that change is something with which many of us feel uncomfortable.

Besides the disquiet that comes from having one's established patterns disrupted, there are three other reasons why change is difficult (Greenman, 1988; Murphy, 1991). First, people do what they know how to do. Teachers teach as they have been taught, administrators practice the techniques they have learned and read about. Usually, individuals carry out these practices in the belief that they are doing the best they can and that what they are doing is right, so many see no good reason to change. Second, in any educational program each person's actions intertwine with others' behaviors. There is often a strong compulsion to maintain current practices. To do otherwise may alter the daily routines or challenge the beliefs or desires of colleagues, decision makers associated with the program, parents, and other influential persons in the community. A third deterrent to change is that it takes time—time to think, meet, plan, work through problems, and develop constructive relationships with others. Besides, to be sustained, change demands an investment of time over a long period. The desire for quick results and disdain of time away from the program or their personal lives often preclude teachers and administrators from devoting the hours and years necessary for real change to happen. Time is also an issue as pressures build up to tack on additional innovations before current ones are well established. This has the impact of diluting or derailing people's efforts, which can leave them with a sense of failure and disillusionment. Knowing this could happen causes many people to contemplate change reluctantly.

THE CONSEQUENCES OF AVOIDING CHANGE

Unfortunately, because change is so difficult, there is an incongruence between what we know to be good practice and what actually happens in many programs for young children (Glickman, 1991). As discussed in chapter 1, "Early Childhood Education Today," inappropriate strategies are still common practice in many schools. Some typical examples include offering workbooks and seatwork as a primary means of instruction; requiring maturity ratings, IQ or aptitude tests for the purpose of grouping children and tracking them through programs; using corporal punishment to achieve control of children's behavior; and relying on paper-and-pencil measures of achievement (Bredekamp, 1991; Siegel & Hanson, 1991). Consequently, some educators have been in the uncomfortable position of carrying out policies and practices that are not in the best interests of students. To make matters worse, the evidence is piling up that such antiquated, inappropriate practices lead to poor long-term scholastic outcomes (Peck et al., 1988; Schweinhart et al., 1986). Throughout the past decade, one gloomy report after another has decried what students do not know and what they cannot do. For the most part, these students are the product of the incongruent practices just described. There are also strong indications that developmentally inappropriate programs perpetuate inequities among children based on socioeconomic status and cultural background (Henry, 1990). The result is a growing number of youngsters who experience little success in school from an early age.

So pressing has the need for change become that people throughout society now recognize that our approach to education must be restructured, reformulated, redesigned (Brandt, 1990). Much of this restructuring will focus on making all programs for young children more developmentally appropriate. The principles of developmental appropriateness, as described in preceding chapters, offer a guide for *what* must be done. The information in this chapter will focus on *how* the process of change could begin.

THE NATURE OF CHANGE

*The teacher's lesson plans read, "Week 1, **water** in the water table. Week 2, **sand** in the water table." Tuesday of the second week, she received the following note from a parent of a 4-year-old child in the class.*

Dear Lila,

Stefan is amazed! On Sunday he learned that Jesus turned water into wine. And, on Monday he learned that you turned water into sand! Pretty miraculous!

Marina Petrovic!

Stefan had experienced a change in his classroom. He accepted that change unconditionally—even happily, and he attributed it to nothing less than a miracle.

Unlike Stefan, early childhood educators trying to implement developmentally appropriate principles in their programs and communities know that change does not come about because of miracles. On the contrary, it involves much hard work, and even then, there is no guarantee that lasting shifts in direction will occur. Yet, as difficult as the process is, individuals and entire educational programs from coast to coast are looking for better ways to teach young children. There is growing evidence, too, that some efforts can and do achieve positive results (Bellemere, 1991; Connell, 1987; Goldman & O'Shea, 1990; MacPhail-Wilcox, Forbes, & Parramore, 1990). Successful innovations range from changes in curriculum and instruction, to changes in family relationships with the program, to changes in how teachers and administrators think about themselves and one another in the workplace. They may involve one classroom or more, a single aspect of the program or several, practical or philosophical concerns. Although the variations among such programs are many, certain characteristics of change are common to all (Hord, Rutherford, Huling-Austin, & Hall, 1987):

1. *People create change.* The real meaning of every innovation lies in its human, not its material

components. Equipment, books, and packaged programs do not make change; people make change and they do it by altering their behavior.

2. *Change is a process, not an event.* It evolves out of people's experiences and is a complex endeavor that may take months or even years to do. Individuals do not assimilate change instantaneously. The notion of "sudden change" is a myth.

3. *Change is accomplished by individuals.* People create change on a person-by-person basis. Even when groups engage in innovative practices, it is only after a majority of the individuals have implemented the new idea that we can say a program has changed.

4. *Change is highly personal.* People vary. Each individual reacts differently to change. Some people accept change readily, some do not; some people make fast progress in adopting an innovation, others' rate of adoption is slower; some people fall prey to certain pitfalls, their colleagues to others. There is no one profile of change that fits everyone.

These characteristics highlight the importance people play in making change happen. It is people who cause change. And, it is they who deter-

mine whether innovations succeed or fail. Any formula for change, therefore, must consider the people whose lives are touched by it.

The Normative Sequence of Change

People about to try something new are not non-users one day and experts the next. Instead, they change their practices gradually. In fact, people go through predictable phases as they attempt to make a new strategy their own. Each phase is characterized by a particular behavioral pattern, as described in Table 17.1 (Hord et al., 1987). Potential users of an innovation proceed through the phases in an orderly fashion. Although they may spend more or less time at each phase, the sequence remains the same for everyone. In other words, an individual becomes oriented to the change before using it in a mechanized way; he or she achieves routinized comfort with the new practice before effectively refining it or collaborating with colleagues to extend the impact of the strategy throughout the program. Once a person reaches the renewal phase, such dramatic changes to the current practice may evolve that he or she reenters the sequence at the orientation or preparation level.

TABLE 17.1
The Sequence of Change

Phase	Behavioral Pattern
Nonuse	The person is unaware and uninvolved in the innovation.
Orientation	The individual makes an effort to find out about the innovation and all it entails. This desire for more knowledge may develop in response to personal needs or environmental influences.
Preparation	The person makes plans for how he or she will begin using the innovation.
Mechanical use	The innovator focuses on short-term, logistical goals. Much time is spent working out the details of the innovation and how to make it function more smoothly.
Routine use	The person stabilizes his or her use of the innovation. Once it becomes second nature, few variations are made.
Refinement	The individual begins to vary the innovation to improve its impact within his or her immediate setting.
Integration	The person collaborates with colleagues to improve the impact of the innovation throughout the program.
Renewal	The individual explores how to adapt, expand, or restructure the innovation to fit brand-new circumstances.

This begins the process all over again. What the entire sequence looks like for an individual attempting to make a change in his or her teaching practices is illustrated in Table 17.2.

Differential Rates of Change

Every person faced with change proceeds according to a personal timetable (Duke, 1990; E. Rogers, 1983). Although everyone begins as a nonuser, individuals move through the phases of change at varying rates. In addition, not all individuals in a program will enter the innovative process simultaneously. There also is no guarantee that everyone who moves beyond the nonuse phase will advance the entire way to renewal. So, few people in a group are in the same state of change at the same time.

Consider the following teachers at Salk Elementary. Cilla Hines always seems to be the first to know about the latest educational trends. Eager to try new ideas, she reads widely, goes to conferences, and keeps up with what is happening at other schools. Her colleagues look to her for fresh approaches to teaching and know she will have plenty of sug-

TABLE 17.2
An Example of One Teacher's Progress through the Varying Phases of Innovation Use

Phase	Scenario
Nonuse	Betty Jo Winston has been teaching half-day kindergarten for 3 years. For the most part she is satisfied with her daily schedule, but the "family-style" snack time is sometimes a problem because it takes so long and because the children eat at different rates. Some eat fast, some eat slow, and some do not want to eat at all. Betty Jo often struggles with trying to keep the group together as some youngsters become restless and others feel rushed by their peers.
Orientation	During a visit to another school, Betty Jo observes a preschool class in which an open snack is served as part of the free-choice time. Children are free to come at their convenience and to stay for as long or short a time as they want. She notes that some problems she has been experiencing are not evident with this snack style. Betty Jo decides to find out more about how open snack works. She talks to the preschool teacher after the session and a first-grade teacher in her school who uses the same technique. Betty Jo also reads an article in which open snack and its variations are described.
Preparation	Betty Jo decides to try open snack in her classroom. She determines what area of the room she will designate for snack as well as how she will explain the change in procedure to the children. No new materials seem necessary, so she plans to begin in January, when children return from the winter break.
Mechanical use	It takes Betty Jo 3 to 4 weeks to get the snack time to run smoothly. At first, the pitchers are so small, she is continually refilling them. Betty Jo opts for somewhat larger pitchers the children can still manage themselves, with lids to minimize spillage. When some children eat more than their share of snack, she introduces small signs on the snack baskets to remind children how much is allowed. Also, it is hard for her to remember who has had snack and who has not. Her solution is to ring a small bell 10 minutes before the end of free choice as a way to remind children who have not visited the snack area that the time to do so is almost over.
Routine use	By mid-February, open snack is well established in Betty Jo's room. Her assessment at this point is that the change in routine has been beneficial because it gives her more time in her schedule and because the children are more relaxed as they eat. For the next several weeks the procedure continues as revised with no new changes.

TABLE 17.2
continued

Phase	Scenario
Refinement	In April, while Betty Jo is observing the children at snack, she notices that some children wait near the snack table rather than busying themselves elsewhere in the room because they are fearful they will not get a turn. This takes away from their time to participate in other learning centers. During circle time, she talks about her observations with the children and asks whether the circumstances are truly problematic. Most say yes. Next, she elicits their suggestions for how to resolve the problem. Several ideas are offered. The children finally settle on having the waiting child tell one specific child already at the table that he or she would like a turn. It is the "snack child's" responsibility, once he or she has finished, to find the waiting child who might be busy elsewhere in the room and let him or her know a place is available. The children try the plan, add a "Holding" sign for empty chairs so that no one inadvertently loses his or her place while being sought out, and find it satisfactory.
Integration	The following summer, Betty Jo participates with several other teachers on a committee whose job it is to recommend how to maximize the effective use of instructional time. She suggests that the group consider instituting open snack on a programwide basis because it reduces the number of transitions during the day and meets the needs of individual children.
Renewal	Having developed an interest in computers over the past several years, Betty Jo decides to have the children record the foods they eat at snack for a month in preparation for a unit on nutrition. She reasons that the unit will be more meaningful if it is based on the children's direct experience and that children who ordinarily avoid the computer might be intrigued to participate in the project. However, she is unsure of what child-oriented computer programs might work best and so reenters the innovation cycle at the orientation phase by beginning to collect materials regarding potential software.

gestions if they are interested. Down the hall, Maria Torres is also interested in new instructional practices. Still, she feels more comfortable watching others try them first, then benefiting from their experiences. She moves cautiously but, once committed, is enthusiastic and thorough in her approach. Although seldom a leader, she has the reputation of being open to new ways of doing things. Mike Brasic, a third teacher, is aware of some innovations being tried by his colleagues but, frankly, is suspicious of change. He often waits until just about everyone else has experimented with an idea before considering it for his classroom. His timing is so slow that when finally he attempts the innovation, people like Cilla have moved on to new refinements.

Cilla, Maria, and Mike represent the natural flow of change through a group. Some people are early adopters. They actively seek challenge and often launch innovations within their organizations. This makes them strong role models as well as resources of information and advice for colleagues. Some individuals take a longer time to decide about the innovation. They manifest a wait-and-see attitude, preferring to adopt the change after it has been tested and some risks have been reduced. However, their positive attitude about the change once it occurs often is instrumental in encouraging others to try it. Late adopters trail far behind most of the group and are typically the last to become involved. Their frame of reference is the past, and their innovative decisions are based on what has gone on before. They must be somewhat certain a new idea will work before they feel they can afford to try it. Finally, without fail, there are a few people in every program who never use the innovation at all (E. Rogers, 1983).

What accounts for such variations? What makes people react to change the way they do? To answer these questions we must consider three components of change: the human elements, the characteristics of the innovation itself, and the conditions under which change occurs. These three components provide the framework for the rest of this chapter.

THE HUMAN ELEMENTS OF CHANGE

Researchers have hypothesized that internal traits such as personality, motivation, and personal concerns all influence people's responses to potential innovations.

Personality

Studies of adult development and learning reveal that certain personal attributes seem to influence the extent to which people feel comfortable with change (Glickman, 1981; E. Rogers, 1983; Shrag, Nelson, & Siminowsky, 1985). These traits typify the person in change situations as well as in many other aspects of their life. The most commonly cited characteristics are these:

- *Empathy*—the capacity to experience and understand the emotions that someone else is experiencing. Empathic people can project themselves into the role of another person. This makes them likely to be sensitive to the validity of perspectives other than their own. Consequently, they tend to be more amenable to change than individuals who are primarily self-oriented.
- *Control*—the degree to which people believe they can influence what happens to them and the world around them. Persons who feel powerless in the face of everyday events and who think the future is beyond their control tend to be less accepting of change. They believe that their successes and failures depend more on external factors such as luck or fate than on their efforts and abilities. Thus,

they prefer the status quo, which is familiar to them and within which they have learned to function. Those people who believe that they are personally responsible for their successes and failures also assume they can exert an impact on the course of change. In this frame of mind, they are more likely to accept change when it occurs.

- *Confidence*—the extent to which people feel a sense of competence and self-worth. Confident people are comfortable with who they are, with their weaknesses as well as their strengths. They treat change as an opportunity for personal growth, are less inclined to avoid things they do not do well, and are more willing to take risks. Individuals who lack confidence are more likely to assume that the process of change will be fraught with failures and that their efforts will go unrewarded.
- *Commitment*—the willingness to martial one's resources to accomplish a particular aim. Committed persons have a high degree of involvement in what they are doing. Such involvement includes investing time, effort, and personal resources. Practitioners who believe in the philosophy of the program and who are devoted to its goals are likely to be supportive of innovations designed to further those aims. On the other hand, people whose commitment is low are less willing to commit themselves to improving the program.
- *Abstract thinking*—the ability to move beyond the visual, tangible aspects of a problem or circumstance and speculate in one's mind. Change requires people to contemplate and evaluate, project and hypothesize, redefine and recategorize, generate alternatives as well as create novel solutions. Adults who exhibit high levels of cognitive development, in which abstract/symbolic thinking predominates, can better handle the complexity and flexibility related to change. Persons tied to concrete conceptual understandings are more likely to have difficulty clarifying problems. They also tend to rely on one or two habitual responses to ongoing problems and to generate incomplete solutions. These obstacles inhibit their ability to carry out change.
- *Openness to challenge*—the willingness to accept the demands, frustrations, and haz-

ards associated with achieving a particular goal. Individuals, most open to challenge, seek out new experiences and thrive on testing their knowledge and skills. They view change as an opportunity for personal growth and increased mastery. People less open to challenge consider those same conditions threatening.

- *Sociability*—how much or how little persons become involved with others. Individuals who are more sociable interact not only with greater numbers of people but with greater varieties of people as well. Consequently, they are continually adapting to others' unique characteristics. In doing so, they gain practice in how to express themselves, how to take suggestions, and how to compromise. They also learn when to retreat and when to persevere. These skills increase their adaptability to change. Less sociable people have fewer opportunities to exercise these kinds of skills and so find the process of change, which places demands on them, more difficult.

Motivation

A new policy in effect at the Maplehill Early Childhood Center was that all teachers and aides were expected to plan at least half their lessons according to a theme. Two weeks after the policy was initiated, Mrs. Bashir, the curriculum coordinator, did a "walk-through" of the program. She noted that two teachers showed little evidence of having used a theme at any time during the week. In talking to others whose use of theme planning was more evident, she discovered that one teacher had only included some theme-related activities that day because she knew she was going to be observed. Other teachers talked about their admiration for Ms. Roma, who used themes in her room and who had conducted the in-service training on themes. Their goal was to be more like her, so they intended to carry out theme planning just as she did. Only one or two teachers mentioned the children's responses to the theme. These teachers found theme planning a useful way to promote children's concept development, but they also had some ideas other than just using themes to accomplish that aim.

The teachers Mrs. Bashir observed exhibited motives for implementing policy that corresponded to the four different levels at which individuals accept change (Kelman, 1958; Peters & Kostelnik, 1981). These levels range from noncompliance, to compliance, to identification, to internalization.

Noncompliance is characterized by persons who ignore the innovation altogether. There are several reasons why noncompliance occurs. Individuals may assume the innovation does not apply to them. They may not understand, value, or agree with it. The change may be beyond their capacity to carry out, or there may be no clear advantages for doing so. Anyhow, they feel no obligation to undertake the proposed innovation.

Compliance is the next, most superficial level at which people put innovations into practice. The motivating force behind their decision is the extent to which they expect to be punished or rewarded for doing what is required. Having little understanding or interest in the rationale behind the practice or policy, they perform minimally and only under direct supervision. If ever the promise of rewards or threat of negative consequences are removed, these persons have no foundation for maintaining the innovation on their own, so they revert to their previous modes of operation.

At the *identification* level, people take on innovations that mirror ideas or strategies espoused by persons they admire. Acceptance is based on the credibility of that esteemed person, not an inherent understanding of the practice itself. This means that although the innovation can be maintained without direct supervision, the practitioner often is unable to reason out how to adapt it to changing circumstances. He or she relies on second-guessing how the original model might have dealt with the situation, because that person's behavior is the only gauge the practitioner has for making judgments about what to do. If no such evidence is available, the innovation may then be abandoned.

The most advanced and lasting level of acceptance is *internalization*. Individuals internalize new ways of thinking or doing things when they consider those ways an extension of their values and beliefs. Although the actual methods of operationalization may be very different from their current practices, when the goal of the strategy matches a goal they have already established for themselves, acceptance comes easily. Persons at this level examine the innovation very carefully. They commit themselves to it because that seems a logical way to satisfy their personal needs for mastery and competence. As a result, they make the innovation an integral part of their professional behavior and maintain its use without direct supervision. Furthermore, such persons are likely to experiment with variations and adaptations as a way to maximize potential benefits to the program and themselves.

Personal Concerns

As people make their way through the different phases of change described earlier, they experience specific, individualistic concerns about what happens each step of the way. Concerns refer to the feelings, thoughts, and reactions people have regarding the new practice or policy. There seem to be three broad categories of concerns users, or potential users, of an innovation experience. These include self-concerns, management concerns, and impact concerns (Hord et al., 1987).

Self-Concerns.   "What is this innovation all about?" "How is the innovation supposed to work?" "What kind of preparation will I receive?" "Who wants me to do this and why?" "What kinds of resources are available to me?" "How much outside preparation will this involve?" "How will this look different from what I'm doing now?" "How will I be evaluated?" "What if I make mistakes?" "Will I invest much time and energy into this program just to have it set aside for something different next year?" "What kind of support will I get in explaining this to parents?"

These questions reflect the initial concerns people have about any new idea. Just as children move from self to others in their development and learning, so, too, do adults as they contemplate change. During the initial phases of the change process, therefore, practitioners focus on how to become more aware of what the innovation involves and what that means for them personally. Only after people have fully ex-

plored these kinds of questions and been reassured by the answers can they consider more fully their management concerns.

Management Concerns.   Practical, logistical issues regarding how to carry out the innovation are the focus of people's management concerns. These concerns often surface most intensely as final preparations are being made to try the innovation and in its early stages of implementation. At this point, users and potential users become preoccupied with the nuts and bolts of the innovation. They want to know "How will I carve out time in my daily schedule to do this?" "How can I get the necessary teaching materials ready and organized?" "How can I balance this program against the other demands on my attention?" "How can I do this in the physical space I have to live with and with the materials available to me right now?" Not until these dilemmas are resolved to the practitioner's satisfaction does he or she become more fully concerned about the impact the innovation is having on its intended audience.

Impact Concerns.   Eventually teachers and administrators become intensely focused on what effect the program is having on children or parents and what can be done to improve program effectiveness. When this happens, they have reached the impact level of concern. Their attention has shifted from self to other. The questions they ask now revolve around how to carry out the innovation more efficiently, how to collaborate with others to increase the innovation's influence, and how to adapt or build on the innovation to achieve the program's goals.

Although individuals vary in the exact nature of their concerns, this general sequence parallels the phases through which people proceed in their use of each innovation (see Table 17.3). The extent to which people's concerns are satisfied influences their progress through the phases of innovation use. If a favorable resolution of concerns is made, individuals are apt to continue forward through the sequence. If the opposite occurs, their advancement could be delayed or even halted altogether, which would cause them to abandon the innovation before it

Getting organized is a typical management concern related to making changes in the classroom.

TABLE 17.3

The Relationship between People's Level of Use of an Innovation and the Nature of Their Concerns

Level of Use	Nature of Concern
Nonuse Orientation Preparation	Self-concerns
Mechanical use Routine use	Management concerns
Refinement Integration Renewal	Impact concerns

becomes an integral part of their behavioral repertoire.

Implications for Innovators

Obviously, people vary in their personalities, what motivates them to accept or reject an idea, and what innovation-related concerns become paramount. In addition, the demands of some people's job or personal life are so great at the time the innovation is proposed that just maintaining the status quo is challenge enough. During that same period, others having fewer or less strenuous responsibilities or better coping techniques may consider change a more thinkable possibility (Duke, 1990). These differences suggest that no two people will go through the change process in exactly the same way. The levels and rates at which they progress will be unique for each. Such variations are normal and should not be categorized as good or bad (Hord et al., 1987). For instance, early adopters are not necessarily better adopters than others who are more cautious in their approach. Similarly, people who are more social may have an easier time accommodating an innovation earlier than their less social peers. Yet, both may eventually advance through the normative sequence of change. This means that when an innovation is introduced into a group, it is to be expected that the group will not progress as a whole. To facilitate change, it is important to allow enough time to accommodate personal differences and make sure individual needs are addressed. Just as children cannot be rushed in their development, neither can adults be pushed through the normative sequence of change. So, eager innovators must be careful not to treat later adopters as less valued or accepted than others whose personal traits make change an easier prospect.

CHARACTERISTICS OF INNOVATIONS THAT INFLUENCE CHANGE

The personal characteristics people bring to the change process have a tremendous impact but are not the only factors in determining to what degree a new practice or policy will succeed. Certain attributes of the innovation itself also affect its adoptability. These characteristics can best be explained as principles supported by potential action guidelines (E. Rogers, 1983; Rothman, 1974). Because the principles are equally applicable to a sole innovator as well as collections of people working together to create change, we have developed guidelines to encompass both individual and group needs. Although not exhaustive, they are illustrative of what could be done.

We chose this dual approach because we knew that some of our readers would be most interested in how to alter their classroom behavior to better match principles of developmentally appropriate practice. Revising one's daily routine, integrating pretend play into the classroom, adopting a more authoritative teaching style, and promoting children's aesthetic development are potential changes someone could try autonomously.

On the other hand, certain readers might wish to promote change on a broader scale, encompassing other people in their programs. Such changes typically involve changes in program policies and procedures that cannot be accomplished alone. When the latter circumstances prevail, despite their formal role in the organization, such persons have the potential to become change leaders. People taking on that role benefit from knowing under what conditions programwide change is most likely to

occur. It is these conditions the individual could work toward developing or maintaining.

Principle 1:   Innovations people perceive as consistent with their existing values have higher rates of adoption than less congruent ones. Values permeate all aspects of human thought and action and define what human beings believe are worthwhile and desirable. As such, they underlie every change-related decision people make. It is not surprising, therefore, that change comes most easily when potential users can see a connection between their personal beliefs and those underlying the innovation (Blum & Kneidek, 1991; Deal, 1990; Rothman, 1974; Sergiovanni, 1990). The stronger the association, the more likely it is that adopters will advance to the highest levels of innovation use. This happens because their motivation to change is internalized, which causes them to make the new practice an integral part of their professional behavior and one they are committed to using for the long term.

Action Guidelines for the Individual:

- Explore your beliefs about how young children develop and learn. Use what you have learned in classes, read, and observed in real life as the basis for your reflections.
- Compare your ideas about how children develop and learn with the underlying assumptions associated with developmentally appropriate practice (refer to chap. 1 for a brief overview of these). Identify points of agreement, points about which you are not sure, and points of incongruence.
- Discuss your understandings with colleagues.
- Select for change those practices that support beliefs similar to your own.

Action Guidelines for Change Leaders:

- Begin group efforts at change, by giving people an opportunity to explore how they believe children develop and learn.
- Create an atmosphere in which people express their beliefs freely and honestly. Conduct group discussions governed by the following rules:
  1. All ideas are valuable and will be considered fairly.

2. Ideas will not be evaluated prematurely or discarded thoughtlessly.

3. Only ideas everyone in the group can live with will be committed to paper.

■ Together with others, develop a philosophy statement that represents the views of the group regarding child development and learning. Use this as a constant reference point for any actions that follow.

■ Create plans for change that build on those beliefs that are universal in the group. Address points of incongruence after people have begun to feel comfortable with one another.

■ Present ideas for change within a context of shared values. Make note of the beliefs that have evolved from the group's discussions, and link potential changes directly to the ideas expressed. For instance, if group members all seem to value children's development of self-worth, use that value as the basis for suggesting that child assessment methods be reconsidered or that staff examine the program's antibias curriculum efforts.

■ Confront differences in beliefs even-handedly. Strive for consensus rather than allow majority rule to govern such discussions. Although it is more difficult and time-consuming to develop common ground when people's views vary widely, efforts at change will come to naught if some parties to the innovation feel that their beliefs have been ignored or set aside. Talk through differences and come to an understanding that everyone can tolerate.

Principle 2: Innovations are most easily adopted when they meet innovators' current needs and when they offer personal advantages over old practices. People experience many problems in their work life. If an innovation seems to offer a solution to one or more of these, their receptivity to change increases. If, in addition, the innovation has the potential to make their job easier, more meaningful, less fragmented, or more effective, the appeal of the change becomes even greater (E. Rogers, 1983; Rothman, 1974; Walsey, 1991).

Action Guidelines for Individuals:

■ Based on your understanding of developmentally appropriate practice, identify strate-

Use common values, such as promoting children's feelings of accomplishment, as the basis for suggesting classroom changes to colleagues.

gies you use that are congruent with this philosophy. Plan how you will build on these strengths over time.

■ Identify at least one, but no more than two, current practices with which you are dissatisfied. Enter the orientation phase of change by collecting materials and observations that will help you develop a plan to alter these.

■ After you have determined what new practice might replace the old, compare the two. Identify potential benefits to yourself as well as to the program, long- and short-term pluses and minuses. Judge whether the new practice will be more advantageous than your current way of doing things. If the benefits of switching seem likely, prepare to begin implementation. Keep your list for future reference.

Action Guidelines for Change Leaders:

■ As a group, identify and make a record of mutual areas of concern. Use this as a reference when considering workshops to attend, request, or develop; visitors to invite; continuing education classes to select. Collect written materials that address the group's concerns. Circulate these widely and systematically throughout the program. For instance, some people keep a notebook of relevant journal articles selected by members of the group in the staff lounge or lunchroom. These are periodically updated, and new additions serve as discussion topics for some portion of a staff meeting.

■ Create opportunities for individuals to encounter new strategies and ideas related to developmentally appropriate practice through visits to other programs, teacher exchange days within the organization, and videotaped examples. Conduct discussions in which the innovations in question are compared to present practices.

■ Encourage program participants to exercise choices in determining what practices related to developmentally appropriate programs they would like to enact. Give priority to their selections. Offer support even when people's choices do not match the most pressing areas of concern identified by administrators or others in the group. Only after individuals have satisfied their own agendas will they be receptive to additional ideas. Thus, if teachers find discipline to be their most critical concern, they will be more amenable to change in classroom management strategies than in innovations related to parent involvement or whole-language development.

■ Work with potential innovators to identify the personal benefits they could receive from shifting to the new practice. For instance, teachers who adopt an authoritative disciplinary style eventually spend less time coping with classroom management problems. Also, they are more likely to experience cooperative relationships with the children in their charge. Such personal advantages should be highlighted early in the change process.

Principle 3:   New strategies that can be introduced gradually have a higher rate of adoption than ones requiring total implementation right away. Similarly, innovative practices that allow for experimentation on a limited basis before general installment are the most successful. Having a chance to try something in small doses before committing oneself completely removes some risk inherent in any new idea. Not only do individuals gain confidence by doing, they have a chance to modify the new technique to fit their unique circumstances. In addition, others not yet directly involved in the change benefit by observing colleagues using the innovation before implementing it themselves (E. Rogers, 1983; Rothman, 1974; Wall, McCann, & Bloomfield, 1990).

Action Guidelines for the Individual:

■ Think about the change you want to make, then break it down into manageable chunks. This can be done in one of two different ways: (a) identify the component parts of the change and then adopt them, one at a time, until all have been incorporated into your behavior; or (b) figure out logical approximations for achieving your goal, then gradually work from the least to most congruent examples. One method or the other suits most situations. Examples of each are offered in Table 17.4.

■ Avoid trying to do everything at once or too much, too soon. Create a timeline in which

TABLE 17.4
Examples of Innovations Broken Down into Manageable Chunks

Method	Ultimate Goal	Procedure
Example 1		
Accomplishing change by incorporating component parts of the innovation, one at a time, into a comprehensive whole	To develop a portfolio of materials for each child as a record of progress during the year	Fall semester—Collect samples of children's art work and writing, at least two per child per month.
		Winter semester—Collect one anecdotal record per child per week in addition to the art and writing samples.
		Spring semester—At least once per week provide children with pictograph evaluation sheets they can use to evaluate their time at school; continue the anecdotal records and the art and writing samples.
Example 2		
Accomplish change through successive approximation	To substitute storybooks and hands-on activities for the basal reader and workbook	Drop one basal story and workbook activity per week. Substitute a narrative picture book and related follow-up activity. Continue for several weeks until comfortable with the management aspects of the new procedure. Gradually extend to two stories per week, then three, and so on.

you identify approximately when you hope to achieve the steps designated earlier. Invite a colleague to review your plan's practicality. Keep this framework in mind as a guide for progress, but remain flexible, adding or taking away time or steps as necessary.

Action Guidelines for Change Leaders:

■ Use pilot programs as a mechanism for change. Asking those who are most positive about the change to try it on a small scale before soliciting a commitment from everyone provides a "shake-down" period during which the most glaring glitches can be worked out.

Enthusiasts are the least apt to abandon the innovation and the most likely to develop creative solutions for difficulties. This eases the way for later adopters, provides a model of the innovation within the organization for which it is intended, and contributes to the impression that change is not an all-or-nothing proposition.

■ Within the group, develop a long-term program plan in which the sequential implementation of the innovation is described. Work with potential innovators to identify specific activities and set a timeline for their accomplishment. An example of one such program plan is the subject of Figure 17.1.

Value Statement

Parent involvement is an integral component if we are to deal successfully with children. We feel strongly that we must do all that we can to build trust and develop a true partnership with our parents. Without those elements we cannot truly educate the whole child.

Innovation

Fairplay School will develop an extensive parent program beginning with the kindergarten class. Based on a parent questionnaire, plans will be made to develop a year-long program that will assist parents in becoming partners with Fairplay in educating their children. Each year another level will be added. For example:

1990—K, 1991—K and 1st, 1992—K and 1st and 2nd

In addition, programs will be planned for all parents based on responses to a survey sent home this spring. These programs would include such topics as child development, family math night, PE night, bring and brag night, etc.

Efforts to involve parents in a cooperative partnership will be aimed at all parents at all grade levels.

Implementation

May 1990	Develop and distribute needs assessment for K–5 parents to be used in determining program plans for coming year.
August 1990	Conduct interviews with kindergartners and parents. Distribute needs assessment to new kindergarten parents to use in planning topics of monthly meetings. Identify parents new to Fairplay and team them up with a mentor parent. Establish the location of a parent resource library, and publicize availability of resources for families. Update and add to on a regular basis.
September 1990	Hold first kindergarten parent meeting, and distribute calendar for monthly meetings with topics identified. Develop and collect evaluations for each session. Plan sessions with parents and kindergartners as well as parents-only sessions.
May 1990	Assess effectiveness of programs and begin plans for 1991. Involve parents in planning for the coming year.

FIGURE 17.1

Long-Term Program Plan for Increased Parent Involvement

Source: Adapted with permission from materials provided by the Corvallis School District, Corvallis, Oregon.

■ Realistically assess the amount of staff effort required as well as the period needed for most people to adopt the change beyond the routinized phase of use. Communicate these understandings to all persons involved in the innovation. Such estimates reduce the anxiety of some and show others what might be expected.

■ Establish an environment and a mechanism through which the gradual adoption of innovations is rewarded. Avoid creating or reinforcing the notion that people must achieve near perfection before their efforts and accomplishments are acknowledged.

Principle 4:   Tangible innovations are more easily adopted than abstract ones. The old adage "Seeing is believing" is true for adults as well as for children. Live demonstrations, videotaped illustrations, peer modeling, and opportunities for rehearsal prior to using the strategy on the job all contribute to people feeling more comfortable with the innovation. New strategies that are tangible (e.g., physically rearranging the room or putting together a portfolio) or that can be modeled are the easiest ones to adopt and the ones most likely to last over time (Kostelnik, 1990; E. Rogers, 1983; Rothman, 1974).

Action Guidelines for the Individual:

- Visit other classrooms and programs to see potential innovations in action. Ask persons experienced with the innovation to demonstrate it, in their location or yours.
- If you are considering more than one potential change, order the innovations from most concrete to most abstract. Address the concrete ones first. As you adopt these at the routinized level and beyond, gradually turn your attention to those that are less tangible.

Action Guidelines for Change Leaders:

- As a group, clearly define the innovation in concrete, practical terms. Communicate these definitions to others whose lives will be affected by it.
- Reduce chances for misinterpretation of the innovation by having individuals periodically cross-check their understanding of the new practice against those of others involved in the change. Continuously clarify people's interpretations until a universal understanding is reached.
- Create opportunities for individuals to show their understanding of the innovation in a nonthreatening environment before trying it on the job. Use these rehearsals to further clarify what the innovation involves.
- Suggest content for in-service training that goes beyond simply explaining the rationale behind developmentally appropriate programs. Although awareness is necessary, it is not sufficient to ensure that change happens. Teachers and administrators must have a clear picture of how to create such programs. They must become familiar with specific details of what a developmentally appropriate program looks like and learn the skills necessary to achieve it. Hands-on experiences in which potential innovators practice by using storybooks

to highlight reading skills, setting up learning centers, or creating antibias activities are more effective than training in which they only hear about such techniques.

PROGRAMMATIC CONDITIONS THAT FACILITATE CHANGE

Besides people's personal attributes and the characteristics of the innovation itself, the conditions under which the innovation is implemented either enhance the possibility of success or detract from it. These conditions include the extent to which people in the program are involved in the innovation, the quality of the information provided to individuals about an innovation and their involvement in it, and what kind of support they receive throughout the change process. Envision the following scenarios:

Pearl Morgan felt guilty. She, like every other teacher at the Roy Wilkins Child Development Center, had received a memo informing her that computers would become standard equipment throughout the program. A few weeks later, a brand-new computer had been delivered to her classroom. When it first arrived, even though she had no computer experience, she had high hopes that both she and the children would enjoy using it. But the computer workshop for teachers fell through, and Pearl's supervisor never got back to her about the self-teaching module Pearl had heard about. In the meantime, the computer gathered dust, while Pearl wondered what to do.

Dennis Thurman was perplexed. He had read about developmentally appropriate practice and agreed with the principle that children should have many opportunities to make decisions for themselves. He decided one way to accomplish that aim in his class was to give the youngsters a 2-hour period for self-directed learning while he got materials ready for the next day. However, things were not working out as he had hoped. Children wandered aimlessly around the room, arguments over materials and who could play with whom were frequent, and the noise level got worse each day. After the teacher in the next room complained for the third time about the chaos in Dennis's class, he decided to give up on the idea and go back to his traditional way of teaching.

The first-grade teachers were angry. Over the summer, an early childhood committee, consisting of preschool and kindergarten teachers, had put together a document entitled "Developmentally Appropriate Practice in Early Childhood." No one in first grade had seen the document, but the teachers had heard there would be no phonics instruction in kindergarten, and the children no longer would be learning the sight words required in the current basal series. Also, it was rumored that lined paper would be banished from kindergarten classrooms and that those teachers would stop showing students the proper way to hold a pencil. The angry first-grade teachers pretty much agreed their work load would certainly increase since they would have to make up for everything the preschool and kindergarten people neglected to teach in the new watered-down curriculum.

These are typical examples of what sometimes happens when people try to create change. In every instance, although the goals of the innovations had merit, the participants' efforts to make lasting alterations in their programs yielded negative results. This happened because they did not pay enough attention to the conditions necessary for innovations to succeed. These conditions are described in the principles and action guidelines that follow.

Principle 5:   The more involved people are in developing an innovation, the more likely they are to support it. Change does not happen by decree. It requires involvement by the people who will enact it. Such involvement must be genuine, not token inclusion. Meaningful participation by staff and clients maximizes organizational cohesion, minimizes dissension during periods of transition, and increases people's commitment to actions taken. This is because individuals are most willing to adopt and sustain changes they have helped to formulate. They have an ego investment in seeing that such changes succeed. For this reason, it is critical that persons who will be asked to go along with the change be given proactive roles in the process that brings it about (Hord et al., 1987; E. Rogers, 1983; Rothman, 1974). Moreover, the

broader the support base for the innovation, the more apt it is to take hold. This means people at all levels of the program should be included in some significant way as the change evolves (Brandt, 1991; Martin & McGrevin, 1990; Murphy, 1991). Such participants could include not only those in schools or centers but also parents, community leaders, neighborhood organizations and institutions, and concerned adults from all walks of life. In this way the circle of involved and invested individuals is enlarged and the pool of potential problem solvers expanded (Blythe & Gardner, 1990). Both of these conditions make potential support for the innovation stronger.

Action Guidelines for the Individual:

- Get involved in the innovation process. Move into the orientation phase of change by asking questions, talking with others further along in the sequence, and volunteering to participate in group efforts to explore the concept of developmentally appropriate programs.
- When contemplating a distinct shift in classroom practices or policies, involve other staff affected by the innovation (e.g., aides, volunteers, specialists), as well as children and their parents, in some aspect of the change process before it becomes an accomplished fact. Requests for suggestions before or during the beginning phases of change or feedback throughout a trial period are two good ways to solicit involvement and support.

Action Guidelines for Change Leaders:

- Establish formal, predictable times when people in the organization can discuss the prospect of developmentally appropriate programs for young children and what that means for your organization. This will require a commitment of resources so that all essential parties can participate.
- Involve as many relevant people as possible in discussions and decisions about the innovation.
- If the prospect of change is being handled through a committee, input to the group should span the breadth of the program. Central office and on-site administrators, teaching staff, families, specialists, nonteaching support staff, and other program decision mak-

ers need to have their views represented. Umbrella committees with working sub-groups or core committees supplemented by ad hoc task forces are two options that enhance participation without becoming too unwieldy. In either case, the expectation must be that all participate fully. Erratic membership detracts from the group's sense of cohesion, slows the decision-making process, and violates the premise of shared responsibility.

- Make sure open channels of communication with those not on the committee have been established. Provide clear information about the innovation, using a variety of ways to connect with those who will be affected by it. Verbal, written, and face-to-face communication and available media may all be used. Exchange ideas with people individually and in small and large groups.

Principle 6: The better people's informational needs are satisfied, the greater the level of innovation use and the higher the adoption rate. Three kinds of information are crucial to people contemplating change. First, teachers and administrators need access to the knowledge and skills they will need to do their jobs differently. That body of knowledge is broad and continually expanding. It includes content knowledge, pedagogy, current research, as well as group decision making and other skills demanded by the roles and responsibilities associated with change (David, 1991). A second category of necessary information includes facts about the change and people's roles in it. Potential innovators need to know what to expect, how they will be involved, and how the change will ultimately affect their work life (Hord et al., 1987). Third, people crave information about how the direction of change they have chosen compares with that selected by others in like circumstances. They want to know "Am I the only one trying this?" "Are we the only ones experiencing these feelings?" "How are other programs coping with this kind of change?" "What are other people doing to achieve more developmentally appropriate programs?" Answering these questions minimizes people's feelings of isolation and sense of risk (Kostelnik, 1990).

Action Guidelines for the Individual:

- Keep up-to-date with the field. Read, observe, ask questions, and talk to others about the notion of developmentally appropriate practice. Do not expect *all* new knowledge and skills to come to you through training provided by the program.
- Address gaps in your knowledge with the following methods:
  1. Subscribe to an early childhood journal such as *Young Children, Research in Early Childhood Education, Childhood Education,* or *Day Care and Early Education.*
  2. Read an early childhood issue of the following journals: *Principal, Journal of Curriculum and Instruction, Educational Leadership, The Arithmetic Teacher, The Reading Teacher.*
  3. Take a refresher course in child development or early childhood education.
  4. Attend at least one early childhood conference during the year.

Action Guidelines for Change Leaders:

- Provide opportunities for group members to address the gaps in their knowledge as just described.
- Promote in-service experiences aimed at helping participants learn more about child development and learning, developmentally appropriate practice, and group processes and decision making. Some efforts may involve outside speakers and workshops; others could consist of presentations and discussions featuring early adopters within the program.
- Through discussions and other means of training, provide people with information that matches their personal concerns. Help people focused on self-concerns to find out what the innovation involves and how it will affect them personally. Individuals for whom management concerns are most intense will need "how to" answers and practical solutions to the logistical problems they are most likely to encounter. At the impact level of concern, people will need opportunities to collaborate with others and expand their knowledge and skills in new directions.

■ Initiate sharing sessions in which people exchange information, personal experiences, and their interpretations of the innovation. Such sessions could center around face-to-face meetings between individuals in like circumstances from within the program or outside of it. On- and off-site observations, videos, and written materials could also be used.

Principle 7:   The more peer support an innovation enjoys within an organization, the more likely it is to be adopted. One of the greatest barriers to effectual change is the isolation people feel as they move from a state of nonuse to the more uncertain phases of the change sequence (Martin & McGrevin, 1990). Enacting change in the company of one's peers reduces this anxiety and increases people's willingness to take risks (E. Rogers, 1983; Rothman, 1974).

Action Guidelines for the Individual:

■ Go with a coworker to conferences and in-service training programs. Attend the same sessions, then compare notes on what you learned. Explore possible applications to your setting. Think of ways you might support and encourage one another should you decide to make a change in the direction suggested through the training.
■ Seek out other individuals in the organization who share job responsibilities similar to yours, and engage in informal brainstorming sessions regarding mutual concerns about how to achieve developmentally appropriate practice.
■ Seek out early adopters in your program who are willing to discuss how they dealt with their self-concerns and management issues.

Action Guidelines for Change Leaders:

■ Help people broaden their concepts of who their colleagues are. Often school or center personnel define their potential peer group too narrowly. For instance, when considering their immediate peers, kindergarten teachers might think only of other kindergarten teachers, failing to see the commonalities they share with teachers in the first or second

grades, the preschool teachers, or the after-school caregivers. Discussions and experiences that draw out the common bonds between such groups extend the breadth of available human resources.
■ As a group, identify a problem more than one person is having (e.g., including appropriate pretend play activities in the classroom). Brainstorm strategies everyone might try. Put the plan in action. Later, get together to discuss progress and refinements.
■ In forming committees, avoid appointing individuals to serve as the sole representative for a particular group (e.g., from each building, the community, the administrators, etc.). If inclusion of two or more members of each group is impossible or too cumbersome, find other ways to make connections among peers. Periodic discussions or feedback sessions within the larger peer group are possible alternatives.

Principle 8:   The more obvious the organization's commitment to change, the more likely it is that change will occur. Making innovations work takes time and money. People do not create effective change as an afterthought, or from the side of their desks, or in the wee hours of the morning when all their other job-related responsibilities are over (Simpson, 1990). Without substantive program efforts to include some time during working hours for planning, professional growth, and collaboration, most efforts at change are bound to fail (Miles & Louis, 1990). Appropriate materials and resources are also essential ingredients that cannot be overlooked. To create these necessary conditions, program decision makers must cast about for additional funds or reallocate portions of their budgets or seek in-kind donations of services. Developing internal assistance and co-ordination mechanisms are other ways to provide sustenance to adopters over the long term. Also, morale is boosted when upper-level decision makers show awareness of what developmentally appropriate programs are about and appreciation for people's efforts to achieve them. Although individuals and potential change leaders may feel that this kind of global support is beyond their means to create, there are things they can do to initiate the development of conditions favorable to change.

Action Guidelines for the Individual:

- Talk to your immediate supervisor about developmentally appropriate programs for young children. If he or she seems unaware of the concept, provide a steady but not overwhelming flow of relevant information through conversations and journal articles. Also, consider inviting him or her to accompany you to a workshop or conference focused on the topic.
- If your supervisor is familiar with the principles of developmentally appropriate programs, discuss ideas for change in your classroom within the context of those principles. Elicit his or her support in helping you achieve your goal. Such support might include additional resources as well as feedback on your progress.

Action Guidelines for Change Leaders:

- Familiarize key decision makers in your organization with the principles of developmentally appropriate programs as described here. Also, invite them to visit on-site or off-site examples of such practices in action.
- Discuss with decision makers how the principles of developmentally appropriate practice support the mission of your program. Begin exploring implications for change with them.
- Identify needs related to potential innovations, and provide program decision makers with a short report describing the time, materials, and space necessary for such changes to occur.
- Elicit the help of your immediate supervisor in obtaining support from upper-level decision makers regarding developmentally appropriate programs for children.
- Request that someone whom people at various levels of the organization respect and trust be identified as a change agent for innovations related to developmentally appropriate programs for young children. A change agent is the person responsible for shepherding the innovation through the system. Identification of such a person is a clear sign of commitment by the program.

Principle 9: Innovation adoption is favorably influenced when people receive timely, accurate, useful feedback about their efforts at change. Innovators at every stage of the change sequence benefit from knowing how congruent their performance is to that required by the innovation. They need continuous feedback to help them decide which behaviors to maintain and which to alter (LeBoeuf, 1986; Neugebauer, 1983). Without accurate, timely feedback, individuals attempting a change operate blindly, not knowing when their efforts succeed or fail. Also, when feedback is lacking, people may operate under false assumptions about how well their behavior matches the new practice and what effect it has on their work and on others. Thus, decisions to maintain or abandon certain innovations may be founded on erroneous perceptions. To avoid these negative outcomes, efforts should be made to make feedback an ongoing part of the change process.

Action Guidelines for the Individual:

- Develop a feedback partnership with a colleague you trust and respect. Identify a personal goal for change in operational terms. Ask your partner to observe you in action and provide feedback regarding your performance in relation to your goal. Use different modes of feedback, oral and written, on-the-spot and later in the day. Incorporate the elements of effective feedback outlined in Figure 17.2. Reverse roles. Continue this exchange periodically.
- Reflect on your own application of the innovation by keeping a journal or reviewing other written materials related to your goal such as lesson plans, anecdotal records, or classroom inventories. Smyth (1989) suggests that you ask yourself these questions:

"What do I do?"

"What does this mean?"

"How did I come to be this way?"

"How might I do things differently?"

- Review your performance informally with others to clarify your interpretations of appropriate practice.

Feedback should be about people's behavior, not their personality or physical characteristics.

Poor: "Your accent is hard for children to understand."
Better: "When you talk very fast it is hard for children to understand your directions."

Feedback should tell a person what to do, not what not to do.

Poor: "You shouldn't yell to children across the room."
Better: "It would be more effective if you approached the children directly and talked to them in your normal speaking voice."

Feedback should be stated as a perception, not as absolute fact.

Poor: "You make children feel uncomfortable when you hover over them."
Better: "The child looked uncomfortable when you stood over him."

Feedback should be specific, not general.

Poor: "Act more confident next time."
Better: "Act more confident. Look at him directly and speak in a normal tone of voice. Don't whisper."

Feedback should be stated in terms of "more" or "less," not "always" or "never."

Poor: "You never smile."
Better: "You only smiled once or twice during the story. Try smiling more often."

Feedback should include reasons for your reaction.

Poor: "It bothered me when you stopped the story to point out letter sounds."
Better: "It bothered me when you stopped the story to point out letter sounds. I think the children lost track of the story line."

Pitfalls to Avoid

Delaying feedback—Putting off feedback because it is uncomfortable makes matters worse. Little problems grow into big ones. Offer feedback frequently and close to the time when the behavior it is about, occurred.

Using feedback only in a crisis—Feedback should be a natural part of the daily routine. This makes it seem less threatening and more useful. Use feedback to examine day-to-day events as well as very challenging ones.

Focusing on corrective feedback only—People reject feedback that is always negative. Offer a balance of positive and corrective observations.

Giving too much feedback at once—Having too many things to change is overwhelming and may result in no change at all. Pick one skill to focus on. Start with behaviors easiest to correct (e.g., towering over children), then gradually work up to more challenging tasks (e.g., avoiding solving children's problems for them).

Not following up on feedback given or received—When getting feedback, develop a plan for making changes and determining success. When giving feedback, periodically comment on the person's progress. Compliment positive results; offer ideas and encouragement related to difficulties.

FIGURE 17.2
Guide to Effective Feedback

Action Guidelines for Change Leaders:

- Initiate opportunities for individuals to learn the skills necessary for providing effective feedback.
- Explore how a program-based mechanism for feedback to innovators could be created. Training site supervisors to give effective feedback related to the innovation is one approach. Engaging people in reflective evaluation and using peer coaching methods are two other structures that have proven successful.
- Once a mechanism for feedback is established, make a record of the state of affairs prior to introducing the innovation. This will provide an accurate basis for comparison after the new practice gets under way. People's memories are faulty, and often the "good old days" of less appropriate practices seem better than they were in light of current stresses over change.
- Plan checkpoints at logical intervals to evaluate the progress of the innovation and make adjustments as necessary.

- Devise ways to find out to what extent there is a real change in practice before attributing any effects to the innovation. Human habit is powerful. It is not unusual for individuals to believe they are carrying out the innovation when in fact they are simply thinking about it or implementing it incorrectly. Discuss and record concrete signs of progress. For example, "Have materials in the classrooms really changed?" "How many teachers have rearranged their classrooms into learning centers?"
- Arrange meetings and other more informal get-togethers to ensure a flow of feedback among people in similar circumstances (e.g., all the preschool and lower elementary teachers, or all the on-site administrators) and among the various layers of the organization (e.g., teachers, administrators, staff, parents, etc.).
- Invite outside feedback from educators external to the organization, community members, business leaders, and so forth. Provide a specific issue, document, or observation to which you would like such persons to respond.

Principle 1: Innovations people perceive as consistent with their existing values have higher rates of adoption than less congruent ones.

Principle 2: Innovations are most easily adopted when they meet innovators' current needs and when they offer personal advantages over old practices.

Principle 3: New strategies that can be introduced gradually have a higher rate of adoption than ones requiring total implementation right away.

Principle 4: Tangible innovations are more easily adopted than abstract ones.

Principle 5: The more involved people are in developing an innovation, the more likely they are to support it.

Principle 6: The better people's informational needs are satisfied, the greater the level of innovation use and the higher the adoption rate.

Principle 7: The more peer support an innovation enjoys within an organization, the more likely it is to be adopted.

Principle 8: The more obvious the organization's commitment to change, the more likely it is that change will occur.

Principle 9: Innovation adoption is favorably influenced when people receive timely, accurate, useful feedback about their efforts at change.

FIGURE 17.3
Summary of Principles of Change

We have just examined several principles of change. They transcend any particular program and so are applicable to innovations of varying complexities and organizations of differing sizes. Anyone can take steps to alter his or her behavior to better meet the needs of young children. Also, anyone can become a change leader by supporting others in their efforts to create change as we have described. The change principles that form the foundation for such actions are summarized in Figure 17.3.

CONDITIONS THAT UNDERMINE CHANGE

Obviously, there are many things people can do to increase an innovation's chances for success. Conversely, certain conditions detract from the adoptability of even the most worthy change. The following section describes these pitfalls.

Lack of Preparation, Organization, and/or Resources

Teachers from Spring Lake School attended a half-day workshop on developmentally appropriate practice. They were enthused about the concept, and Mrs. Lee, the principal, was sure she would see the idea put into practice as a result of a fine presentation. Four weeks later, a disappointed Principal Lee noted no discernible differences in the teachers' behavior. She could not understand why such a good idea had failed.

Change does not occur automatically, even when people generally agree that it is worthwhile. Mrs. Lee had provided an opportunity for the staff to enter the orientation phase of the change sequence but had stopped there, assuming the rest would take care of itself. Nothing could be further from the truth. Change requires commitment from everyone involved. This commitment takes the form of time, energy, and resources. Neither individual innovators nor groups of people working toward change can simply leap into the process unprepared or with no prospects of sustained support and expect favorable results. Individuals preparing for change are most likely to succeed when they develop a specific plan of what they are

going to change and how, when they figure out the ways in which they will allocate their time and resources to the plan, and when they recognize the sacrifices they may have to make in order to achieve their goal. Groups of people interested in enacting innovations must take into account these same factors. In addition, practitioners cannot be expected to enact major changes without organizational support. The flexible use of resources and the provision of time during normal operating hours for educators to work collaboratively are essential institutional commitments (Wilcox et al., 1990).

Too Much, Too Soon

September: Freda Forman felt excited about all the changes she was going to make in her classroom. She had attended a summer institute and was brimming with ideas. She planned to redesign her daily schedule, begin using the "project" approach to teaching, introduce literature extension activities twice a week, and "rethink" her use of circle time. She also wanted to use more creative dramatics activities with the children throughout the day.

October: Freda felt frazzled.

November: Freda felt frustrated.

December: Freda felt numb and went back to her old way of teaching just to survive.

Freda fell into a common trap experienced by eager innovators. She attempted to do too much, too quickly. The goals she set for herself were unattainable because she failed to allow herself enough time to master one innovation before trying another. Thus, Freda tried unsuccessfully to skip immediately from the orientation phase to the refinement phase in the normative sequence of change. Her actions violated a basic tenet of change, which is, *make haste slowly* (Foster, 1990). In other words, do not delay change unnecessarily, but expect full adoption to take a long time to happen. When faced with a number of potentially worthy innovations, prioritize them as best you can, then select one with which to begin. Avoid haphazardly jumping from one thing to another. Instead, develop a long-range plan in which potential entry points for new innovations are identified. Be prepared to make revisions in this schedule as new circumstances arise. Had Freda followed these guidelines, she might have chosen to first experiment with a tangible, contained activity such as circle time prior to working on more complex, pervasive changes like integrating creative dramatics throughout the day. Once she achieved success and confidence in this initial attempt at change, additional innovations could be addressed.

The pitfall of too much, too soon applies to groups as well as to individuals. In many programs an avalanche of potential innovations poses the greatest threat to the long-term success of achieving developmentally appropriate practice (Murphy, 1991). Again, being decisive about what is truly important, prioritizing, and making a commitment to a long-term plan are critical ingredients in a successful formula for change.

Overlooking People Essential to the Change Process

Anna Atcitty decided to change the way in which she structured the small-group time in her classroom. In the beginning of the year, she had grouped children by ability, but having read that children's thinking and cognitive growth were promoted via mixed ability groupings, she wanted to reconstitute the groups along those lines. On Monday she explained the change to the children and put the practice into effect. By Friday, she had received six phone calls from parents worrying or complaining about their children being switched to different groups. Anna felt beleaguered. After all, she was only doing what was best for the children.

The flaw in Anna's plan was not in its merits but in the fact that she forgot a group most likely to be affected by the change—the children's parents. Because parents were unprepared for a shift in the status quo, the result was confusion and resistance. A better approach would have been to prepare the parents for the new procedure in advance. A note home or a brief explanation in a newsletter along with a child-oriented rationale for the reformulation would have helped parents anticipate and understand why a familiar practice was being revised. Also, an invitation for them to offer observations or suggestions as the innovation was imple-

mented would have given parents a proactive role in the process. Although such measures do not guarantee support, they certainly enhance the probability of attaining it. Regardless of how narrow or far-reaching the scope of the change appears to be, it is beneficial to list all those likely to be impacted by the new practice. Finding ways to inform them and solicit input from those groups throughout the change process increases the likelihood of acceptance and long-term adoption.

Maintaining an "Us" versus "Them" Atmosphere

Nursery school people	*versus*	*child care people*
Child development people	*versus*	*education people*
Teachers	*versus*	*administrators*
Lower elementary	*versus*	*upper elementary*
School personnel	*versus*	*parents*
Innovators	*versus*	*traditionalists*

These are but a few examples of the different camps people sometimes put themselves into while exploring the notion of developmentally appropriate programs for children. Regardless of the particular labels and affiliations that differentiate the groups, the implication is always the same—"us" versus "them." Within the bounds of this definition, *us* is translated to mean *good; them* is usually translated to mean *bad* or at least *less good.* Designations of exactly who is in the two categories is always determined by "us." People in the "them" category often know who they are and tend to resist innovations suggested by "us." The existence of such groupings becomes evident when people begin to talk about "Who will be for us? Who will be against us?" "Who supports our point of view? Who does not?" "How will we get them to listen or do what we want?" "How can we get around them?" "Let's ignore them." "Our way is better than their way."

When it comes to creating effective change, the division between "us" and "them" must eventually fall away until only a group of "us" remains. That is, innovations must have support among all the potential "us" and "them" groups encompassed by an organization in order to last. Purposeful efforts must be made to create coalitions in which all voices are heard. Whenever the talk turns to "us" versus "them," people should immediately brainstorm ways of getting the "thems" somehow involved in the innovative process. From a practical standpoint, this means creating mechanisms (e.g., committees, forums, training sessions, and councils) in which varying perspectives are represented and have input into the final recommendations and procedures put into place.

The potential mistakes of (a) failing to organize or prepare adequately, (b) moving too quickly or taking on too much at one time, (c) overlooking people essential to the change process, and (d) maintaining an "us" versus "them" atmosphere can all be avoided by following the principles outlined in the preceding sections of this chapter. However, the following pitfall is one that people may inadvertently succumb to even when every effort has been made to create favorable conditions for change. For that reason, we will cover this adverse condition in detail.

Groupthink

The curriculum committee had been meeting for weeks. There had been a big flare-up a few days ago, but now the group seemed to be getting along. People were relieved. Most everyone on the committee tried hard not to disagree with anyone else's ideas. It felt better to let some things go than to stir up hard feelings. Although·a few people were uncomfortable with some of the decisions that had been made, they believed it was important for the group to present a united front, and so they kept their concerns to themselves.

The conditions undermining change we have described thus far are ones that tend to result in apathy, resistance, or rejection. Such outcomes are obvious and undesirable. There is one other negative condition, however, that transpires in a more benign, less obvious way. That unfavorable circumstance is groupthink. *Groupthink* refers to a mode of reasoning individuals employ when their desire for consensus becomes so strong that it overrides their ability to engage in critical thinking: to assess problems realistically and consider a wide range of potential solutions (Janis, 1971). Groupthink is difficult to

self-diagnose because it is often done with the best of intentions and in a spirit of sharing and cooperation.

Characteristics of Groupthink. Groupthinkers become preoccupied with preserving a sense of unanimity within the committee, the program, the district. They interpret disagreement as discord and strive to avert any conflict that might spoil the cozy feeling of togetherness they have worked so hard to attain (Janis, 1977). Over time, group members come to believe that it is disloyal to disagree and so adopt a noncritical attitude. They discount any doubts they experience by assuming that if similar objections are not voiced by others, their own conclusions are irrelevant or result from fuzzy thinking. Such individuals interpret opinions held by the majority as correct and those voiced by only one or two members as incorrect. In this way, groupthinkers suppress their objections and censure their own contributions to the decision by going along with what they perceive to be the desire of the group (Kostelnik, 1984).

The danger of groupthink is that the integrity of the decision-making process is violated and groups can blunder pell-mell into poorly formulated policies and plans. This happens when, as a result of groupthink, group members do the following things:

- Limit their discussions to only a few alternative courses of action rather than generating a broad range of options to consider.
- Continue to support a course of action preferred by the majority even when new drawbacks are discovered. No serious reexamination of the original position is made. Discarded alternatives, which in light of new information may represent viable options, are not reviewed.
- Show favorable interest in all information that supports the alternative favored by the majority, and ignore or dismiss evidence that does not.
- Exaggerate the positive aspects of the strategy they favor as a means to convince themselves that they have chosen the most worthy path in spite of the costs and risks involved. Alternately, they downplay potentially negative consequences that would otherwise

make them feel hesitant or conflicted about their decision.

- Fail to develop more than one approach to a problem, and spend little time deciding what to do should their original plan not work out.
- Make no real attempt to gain information from experts within their own organization who could give them accurate information about the pros and cons of the proposed plan.
- Rely on the belief that should worse come to worse, they can retract or negate their decision. This conviction stifles further critical assessment of the alternatives and does not take into account the social or fiscal costs of reversing the plan.
- Exaggerate the remoteness of the action to which they have committed. They agree to the plan within the group while privately concluding, "We'll never really have to do this anyway."
- Disavow responsibility for the decision being made. One way in which this happens is when each person denies that he or she personally wants to do what is being recommended but suggests that the group has been forced into the decision by circumstances beyond their control. Another manifestation occurs when group members are selective in those parts of the plan they support, assuming that any portion with which they disagree will not require their compliance.

Who Is Most Prone to Groupthink?   Almost any collection of people can fall prey to groupthink. However, the presence of certain conditions within a committee or program set the stage for such thinking to come about (Janis, 1971, 1977, 1982). These groups have the following characteristics:

- Members see themselves as fervently united in pursuit of a common goal or in opposition to a common foe.
- Cohesiveness is a predominant group value.
- Recent internal conflict has motivated group members to keep the peace at all costs.
- The first attempt to include certain groups within the decision-making structure is in response to a "crisis."
- Open communication among all persons connected to the system is usually not encouraged.

- There is a high level of stress and a low degree of hope for finding a solution better than ones proposed by influential members of the group.
- Group members feel great loyalty to a charismatic leader. Two problems may arise from this situation. First, members' admiration for the leader may cause them to concur with his or her ideas unquestioningly. Second, in their efforts to protect the leader or show their support, individuals may cut off legitimate questions and criticisms, which may have led to reconsideration or reformulation of a particular innovation or means for carrying it out.
- The group lacks leadership and flounders through the decision-making process. Desperate to come to some agreement, the group settles on a solution without carefully thinking it through.
- The timeline with which the group is faced is too brief to allow real analysis of the issues or potential solutions.

How to Avoid Groupthink.   Obviously not every group characterized by positive relations among its members or a collective sense of purpose automatically suffers from groupthink. Yet, once such states are achieved, the need to guard against groupthink increases. With this in mind, certain preventive measures can be implemented to enhance the integrity of the decision-making process (Janis, 1977, 1982; Kostelnik, 1984):

- Individuals involved in group decision making should carefully monitor themselves for groupthink tendencies. When legitimate concerns arise, they should be voiced in an honest, nonaccusing way regardless of the person's role or status in the group.
- Group facilitators and opinion leaders, both formal and informal, should take care to remain impartial whenever a new issue or suggestion is brought forward. Such impartiality is evident when such persons refrain from making their own preferences known right away, when they listen carefully to every person's point of view, when they accept criticism of their own ideas, when they acknowledge the merits of ideas that run counter to their own or those held by the ma-

jority, when they voice potential doubts or concerns that others may be reluctant to voice, and when they allow enough time for the group to discuss issues and concerns thoroughly before moving on or selecting a course of action.

- Assign more than one group to debate the same issue, each deliberating under a different leader. The results of the separate discussions could then be summarized for the consideration of the full group.

- One member of the group could take on the official role of devil's advocate, posing questions that challenge the majority opinion. Periodically, it is effective to invite an outsider to play this role.

- Plan to make decisions by consensus, not majority rule. In this way each person becomes invested in the resolution.

- Incorporate in the group discussion periodic opportunities to reexamine discarded ideas.

- Plan enough time to allow full discussions and opportunities for feedback from persons not directly involved in the group.

- Before reaching a final consensus on major issues, group representatives should return to their respective constituents and describe the group's deliberations to them. After eliciting reactions, group members can then recount their associates' responses to the group. During this time, the role of representative is one of reporter, not persuader. This demeanor ensures that opinions in conflict with the representative's own can be expressed without threat to either party.

- Institute a policy in which once consensus has been obtained, a second-chance meeting will be held at which every member of the group has the opportunity to express any residual doubts and to reconsider before committing to a final decision.

PROFESSIONAL GROWTH THROUGH CHANGE

This chapter has focused on change: what it involves, how it happens, and under what conditions it prevails. Pitfalls to avoid also have been described. Change, as noted here, is best understood as an ongoing, evolving process, characterized by uncertainty, hard work, and

commitment. It is an individual process through which every person ultimately must find his or her own way. As professionals strive to change their practices to create more developmentally appropriate programs for young children, they often ask, "How do I know if the direction in which I am going is correct?" "How can I gauge my progress?" "What milestones are reasonable to expect along the way?"

To answer questions like these, Maizie Argondizza and Jenifer VanDeusen, early elementary consultants for the state of Maine along with an advisory board to the Maine Department of Education, have created a series of self-evaluation tools. These tools depict the continuum from traditional to more developmentally appropriate practices in six areas of early childhood education: (a) philosophy, (b) the environment, (c) instructional strategies, (d) the role of the teacher, (e) classroom management, and, (f) the role of the administrator. These continuums are presented in this order in Figures 17.4 through 17.9. They represent one group's attempt to map out likely phases in the journey from nonuse to the refinement of developmentally appropriate practice. They are offered here as a reference to readers who have undertaken that same journey.

When thinking about the change process, one might wonder whether people ever arrive at a final destination, whether one can ever say, "It is finished. There is nothing left to change." For those of us involved in early childhood education, change is a way of life. The very nature of working with young children requires people to be flexible, to shift constantly in response to children's needs and ever-changing abilities and interests. New discoveries in child development and learning as well as in the pedagogy of teaching cause us to rethink our traditional beliefs and common practices. Although certain threads remain constant (e.g., children's needs to be stimulated and feel secure and competent), the details of our work continually vary as we strive to create programs that better match how children develop and learn. Thus, the impetus for change occurs each time we discover that our current practices fail to meet children's needs.

Searching for better ways to do our job, we ask questions, we gather information, we watch children more carefully and try to glean new insights from our observations. As the gap between what we come to know is best for children and what we actually do with them increases, we experience disequilibrium. In an effort to achieve a better balance, we begin experimenting with new ways of doing things, with new ways of conceptualizing what is developmentally appropriate. Eventually, practice and philosophy become more congruent, and there are periods of confidence and comfort. But it is only a matter of time before new knowledge causes us to reconsider some other aspect of our teaching. In this way, the cycle of change begins all over again.

Subsequently, we can say with confidence that change is an everpresent facet of our work. It begins in our earliest days as practice teachers and continues throughout our careers. We hope the information in this chapter will assist the reader in his or her journey through whatever change seems best to ensure that children experience the highest quality, most supportive programs human beings can envision.

Traditional ←			→ Developmentally Appropriate
Outside experts are trusted to provide curriculum for each level of skills.	The teacher is trusted to recognize needs and plan course of study.	The teacher is trusted to recognize needs; children help to plan course of action.	Children are trusted to recognize their own needs and plan own study.
The teacher has control of student learning.	The teacher is a facilitator and provider of appropriate activities.		The teacher is a questioner and guide in discovery, an equal partner in a democratic classroom.
Learning is equated with mastering skills that are predetermined by the curriculum.	The learner is active, a discoverer of knowledge.		The learner constructs own knowledge as a result of interaction with the environment.
The learner is a receiver of information passed on by the teacher.	Learning is planned with developmental stages in mind.		Learning is not only an end in itself but is also continually applied to real-life situations.
The teacher is viewed as a transmitter of information.	The teacher is a classroom manager.		The teacher uses knowledge and skills to facilitate the learning process.
Learning begins with the teaching of discrete parts.	Learning begins with the teaching of discrete parts, and builds toward understanding of the whole.	Learning begins with a whole concept, then moves to discrete parts.	Learning moves from understanding the whole to student recognition of need for learning discrete parts.
Build curriculum first, then fit children into curriculum.	Use interests of children to make set curriculum more meaningful.	Use needs and interests of the children to build curriculum.	Children actively participate in building curriculum based on their interests and needs.
Play is viewed as an outlet and is restricted to time after work is done.	Play is used with directed objects to support the learning process.	Play is viewed as necessary to social and emotional growth.	Play is viewed as essential means through which learning takes place.
Social interaction has less importance than "time on task."	There is provision for social interaction during specified times.		Social skills are emphasized and viewed as life issue.

FIGURE 17.4
Philosophy

Traditional ◄─────────────────────────────────►			Developmentally Appropriate
Desks are for individual use, may be arranged in rows or a U shape. Social interaction is minimized by room arrangement.	Desks are clustered; learning centers are located around the perimeter of room.	The room is arranged in learning centers, with teacher-selected materials and tasks, shared furniture.	The teacher/students organize the environment to facilitate social interaction and student-initiated activities.
The teacher's desk is focal point.	The teacher's desk is moved to a less conspicuous area.		The teacher's desk may give way to flexible area to be used for student conferencing, parent conferencing, record keeping. An area might be equipped with file cabinet, comfortable chairs, and shelves for professional resources.
The room remains much the same throughout the year, may be changed for variety.	Children may help the teacher plan room changes during the year.		Room arrangement and traffic patterns reflect the diverse developmental needs of children.
Basal textbooks, paper-and-pencil tasks are predominantly used. Distribution is controlled by the teacher.	Concrete materials are available; distribution is controlled by the teacher.	Concrete materials are used as needed, desired by children to assist in problem solving.	Children use concrete materials to assist in problem solving and create problems for solving.
The room is prepared with commercial or teacher-made displays for children's arrival.	The teacher has some bulletin boards prepared, reserves space for children's own work.		Wall space may be empty when children arrive; children help plan spaces and displays of their own work.

FIGURE 17.5
The Environment

Traditional ◄━━━━━━━━━━━━━━━━━━━━━━━━━━━━━━► Developmentally Appropriate			
Teacher directed and planned.	The teacher plans, but children's interests are included in planning.	Children have equal input in planning (i.e., through webbing).	Children select areas of interest and recognize skills they need to acquire.
Skills-based, time specified for each content area.	Goals-based, thematic units may be used in an interdisciplinary approach.		Interest-driven study with skills addressed as needed.
Begin with teaching parts (discrete skills) and build toward the whole concept.			Begin with whole concept; break into parts as skills acquisition is needed.
Predominantly basals, paper-and-pencil tasks	Language experience approach is used.		Individualized or small-group instruction, child's own language to build skills is used.
Predominantly whole-group instruction	Whole- and small-group instruction		Small-group and individual instruction/conferencing as well as whole-group instruction
Students work by themselves.	Interaction is provided for at specified times.		Interaction and cooperative problem solving are encouraged.
Library books may be read at specified times or when work is finished.	Library books are used to supplement the basal readers.		Reading instruction is based on children's literature and children's own writing.
Competition among children is used to motivate. Extrinsic rewards (i.e., stickers and prizes) are given.	The teacher looks for ways to minimize competition, foster cooperation.		Competition with oneself is the focus so that rewards become intrinsic. Learning is its own reward.

FIGURE 17.6
Instructional Strategies

Traditional ←——————————————————→ **Developmentally Appropriate**

Traditional		Developmentally Appropriate
Corrector—student errors are viewed as unacceptable. Errors reduce grades.	Errors are viewed as part of the learning process.	Errors are examined and used as guide to gaining new knowledge.
Imparter of knowledge		Facilitator of the learning process
The planbook is prepared several days in advance of the lesson; the teacher strives to adhere to it.	The planbook reflects goals and objectives with flexibility for activities.	The planbook reflects long-term goals and webbing of ideas generated by children.

FIGURE 17.7
The Role of the Teacher

Traditional ←——————————————————→ **Developmentally Appropriate**

Traditional		Developmentally Appropriate
Discipline is controlled and monitored by teacher.	Children begin to assume some responsibility for their own behavior.	Children practice self-discipline. Rules are established by the class and followed by all.
No choices are provided. Everyone is required to complete specified activities.	Few choices are provided, often after work is complete.	Many choices are provided. Children not only choose the center but also the activity for the center.
Conflict is settled by the teacher.		Conflict resolution skills are learned and practiced by the children.

FIGURE 17.8
Classroom Management

Traditional ←————————————————→ Developmentally Appropriate			
Requires planbooks clearly to identify approved curriculum objectives with prescribed time for each subject area	Trusts the teacher to provide plans for broader goals, allows for time flexibility	Encourages teachers to plan together and use observation and evaluation of children to guide next steps in planning	Enables staff to plan together, share ideas and resources, and observe each other's classrooms
Views role as monitor of preset curriculum		Encourages teacher to enhance adopted curriculum by incorporating the interests of children	The teacher and administrator establish goals that allow flexibility for planning classroom activities by the teacher and students.
Teacher evaluation is based on established criteria with little or no teacher input.	A committee of teachers and administrators develop criteria and process for evaluation.	Criteria are adapted to meet individual needs of teacher.	Teacher evaluation provides opportunities for teachers and administrators together to develop goals and objectives that are appropriate.
The administrative staff plans and implements inservice programs.	Staff development teams utilize teacher input to determine subjects for inservice.		All school personnel plan and implement inservice and staff development programs based on their needs.
The administrator sets the climate for the school by establishing and monitoring rules.	Teachers and administrators work together to establish a positive school climate.		The school community, including children, help with determining and monitoring rules.

FIGURE 17.9
The Role of the Administrator

References

Albrecht, K. (1991). *Quality criteria for school-age child care programs.* (Available from the American Home Economics Association, 1555 King St., Alexandria, VA 22314)

Albrecht, K., & Plantz, M. (1991). Developmentally appropriate practice in school-age child care programs. (Available from the American Home Economics Association, 1555 King St., Alexandria, VA 22314)

Alejandro-Wright, M. N. (1985). The child's conception of racial classification. In M. B. Sponcer, G. K. Brookins, & W. R. Allen (Eds.), *Beginnings: The social and affective development of black children* (pp. 185–200). Hillsdale, NJ: Erlbaum.

Alexander, K. L., & Entwistle, D. R. (1988). Achievement in the first two years of school: Patterns and processes. *SRCD Monographs, 53*(2).

All the arts for every child: Final report on the arts in general education project in the school district of University City, Mo. (1973). New York: J.D.R. III Fund.

Allen, K. E. (1980). *Mainstreaming in early childhood education.* New York: Delmar.

Allington, R. L. (1983). The reading instruction provided readers of different abilities. *Elementary School Journal, 83,* 548–558.

Almy, M. (1975). *The early childhood educator at work.* New York: McGraw-Hill.

American Medical Association. (1978). *Height-weight interpretation folder for girls; Height-weight interpretation folder for boys.* Monroe, WI: Author.

Anderson, J. A. (1988). Cognitive styles and multicultural populations. *Journal of Teacher Education, 29,* 2–9.

Arts impact: curriculum for change: A summary report. (1973). Washington, DC: Office of Education, U.S. Department of Health, Education, and Welfare.

Asher, S. R., Oden, S. L., & Gottman, J. M. (1977). Children's friendships in school settings. In L. G. Katz (Ed.), *Current topics in early childhood education* (Vol. 1, pp. 33–61). Norwood, NJ: Ablex.

Association for Supervision and Curriculum Development. (1991, November). Teaching to the Brain. *ASCD Update, 33*(8), 1–8.

Association of Childhood Education International. (1983). *Childhood educator's guidelines for teacher preparation.* Washington, DC: Author.

Balaban, N. (1985). *Starting school.* New York: Teachers College Press.

Ball, J. (February, 1989). The national PTA's stand on corporal punishment. *PTA Today, 14,* 15–17.

Balough, C. L. (1990). Mathematical concepts. In J. S. McKee (Ed.), *The developing kindergartener: Programs, children, and teachers.* (pp. 225–244). East Lansing: Michigan Association for the Education of Young Children.

Bandura, A. (1989). Social cognitive theory. In R. Vasta (Ed.), *Annals of child development.* (Vol. 6, pp. 1–60). Greenwich, CT: JAI.

Banks, J. A. (1988, Spring). Approaches to multicultural curriculum reform. *Multicultural Leader, 1*(2). Edmonds, WA: Multicultural Materials and Services Center.

Baratta-Lorton, M. (1976). *Mathematics their way.* Menlo Park, CA: Addison-Wesley.

Barbour, N. H. (1990). Flexible grouping: It works! *Childhood Education, 67*(2), 66–67.

Barbour, N., Webster, T., & Drosdeck, S. (1987). Sand: A resource for the language arts. *Young Children, 42*(2), 20–25.

Baroody, A. J. (1987). *Children's mathematical thinking.* New York: Teachers College Press.

Bateson, G. (1971). The message "This is play." In R. Herren & B. Sutton-Smith (Eds.), *Child's play.* New York: Wiley.

Battle Creek Public Schools. (1990). *Primary curriculum: Kingergarten through second grade.* Battle Creek, MI: Author.

Baumrind, D. (1967). Child care practices anteceding three patterns of preschool behavior. *Genetic Psychology Monographs, 75,* 43–88.

Baumrind, D. (1970). Socialization and instrumental competence in young children. *Young Children, 26*(2), 104–119.

Baumrind, D. (1977, April). *Socialization determinants of personal agency.* Paper presented at the biennial meeting of the Society for Research in Child Development, New Orleans.

Baumrind, D. (1978). A dialectical materialist's perspective on knowing social reality. In W. Damon (Ed.), *Moral development* (pp. 349–373). San Francisco: Jossey-Bass.

Baumrind, D. (1983). Rejoinder to Lewis's reinterpretation of parental firm control effects: Are authoritative families really harmonious? *Psychological Bulletin, 94,* 132–142.

Baumrind, D. (1988). *Familial antecedents of social competence in middle childhood.* Unpublished manuscript.

Beauchamp, G. R., & Kosmorsky, G. (1987, December). Learning disabilities: Update comment on the visual system. *Pediatric Clinics of North America, 34*(6), 1439–1447.

Becher, R. M. (1984). Parent involvement: A review of research and principles of successful practice

(Report No. 400-83-0021). Washington, DC: National Institute of Education. (ERIC Document No. ED 182–465)

Beilin, H. (1989). Piagetian theory. In R. Vasta (Ed.), *Annals of child development* (Vol. 6, pp. 85–131). Greenwich, CT: JAI.

Bell, M. (1972). *A study of the readiness room program in a small school district in suburban Detroit, Michigan.* Unpublished doctoral dissertation, Wayne State University, Detroit.

Bellemere, E. (1991). [Results of a five-year longitudinal study comparing developmentally appropriate and developmentally inappropriate classrooms in the Scarborough, Maine, public schools. Personal communication.]

Berclay, C. J. (1977). *Parent involvement in the schools.* Washington, DC: National Association for the Education of Young Children.

Bergen, D. (1988a). *Play as a medium for learning and development.* Portsmouth, NH: Heinemann.

Bergen, D. (1988b). Using a schema for play and learning. In D. Bergen (Ed.), *Play as a medium for learning and development* (pp. 169–180). Portsmouth, NH: Heinemann.

Berger, E. H. (1991). *Parents as partners in education: The school and home working together.* Columbus, OH: Merrill/Macmillan.

Berk, L. (1985). Relationships of educational attainment, child oriented attitudes, job satisfaction and career commitment to caregiver behavior toward children. *Child Care Quarterly, 14,* 103–129.

Berk, L. E. (1989). *Child development.* Boston: Allyn & Bacon.

Berns, R. M. (1989). *Child, family, community.* New York: Holt, Rinehart, & Winston.

Biber, B., Shapiro, E., & Wickens, D. (1977). *Promoting cognitive growth: A developmental interaction point of view* (2nd ed.). Washington, DC: National Association for the Education of Young Children.

Bierman, K. L. (1987). The clinical significance and assessment of poor peer relations: Peer neglect versus peer rejection. *Journal of Developmental and Behavioral Pediatrics, 8,* 233–240.

Blum, R. E., & Kneidek, A. W. (1991). Strategic improvement that focuses on student achievement. *Educational Leadership, 48,*(7), 17–21.

Bly, R. (1988). *A little book on the human shadow.* San Francisco: Harper & Row.

Blythe, T., & Gardner, H. (1990). A school for all intelligences. *Educational Leadership, 47*(7), 33–37.

Bobbitt, N., & Paolucci, B. (1986). Strengths of the home and family as learning environments. In R. J. Griffore & R. P. Boger (Eds.), *Child rearing in the home and school* (pp. 47–60). New York: Plenum.

Bollin, G. G. (1989, Summer). Ethnic differences in attitude towards discipline among day care providers: Implications for training. *Child & Youth Care Quarterly, 18*(2), 111–117.

Boneau, C. A. (1974). Paradigm regained: Cognitive behaviors restated. *American Psychologist, 29,* 297–309.

Bongiovanni, A. (1977, February). *A review of research on the effects of punishment: Implications for corporal punishment in the schools.* Paper presented at the Conference on Child Abuse, Children's Hospital National Medical Center, Washington, DC.

Borden, E. (1987). The community connection—It works. *Young Children, 42*(4), 14–23.

Bowman, B. (1991). Educating language minority children: Challenges and opportunities. In S. L. Kagan (Ed.), *The care and education of America's young children: Obstacles and opportunities. 90th yearbook of the National Society for the Study of Education* (pp. 17–29). Chicago: University of Chicago Press.

Boyer, J. B. (1990). *Curriculum materials for ethnic diversity.* Lawrence: University of Kansas Center for Black Leadership Development and Research.

Bracey, G. W. (1987). Measurement-driven instruction: Catchy phrase, dangerous practice. *Phi Delta Kappan, 68,* 683–686.

Braddock, J. H. II, & McPartland, J. M. (1990). Alternatives to tracking. *Educational Leadership, 48*(7), 76–80.

Brandt, R. (1990). Restructuring: Where is it? *Educational Leadership, 47*(7), 3.

Brandt, R. (1991). Coping with change. *Educational Leadership, 48*(7), 3.

Brandt, R., & Epstein J. (1989, October). On parents and schools: A conversation with Joyce Epstein. *Educational Leadership;* 24–27.

Branta, C. F. (1992). *Motoric and fitness assessment of young children.* In C. Hendricks (Ed.), *Young children on the grow: Health, activity, and education in the preschool setting* (pp. 89–108). Washington, DC: ERIC. Teacher Education Monograph No. 13.

Bredderman, T. (1982, September). What research says: Activity science—The evidence shows it matters. *Science and Children, 20*(1), 39–41.

Bredekamp, S. (Ed.). (1986). *Developmentally appropriate practice in early childhood programs: Servicing children from birth through age 8.* Washington, DC: National Association for the Education of Young Children.

Bredekamp, S. (1987). *Developmentally appropriate practices in early childhood programs: Serving children from birth through age 8.* Washington, DC: National Association for the Education of Young Children.

Bredekamp, S. (1991). Guidelines for appropriate curriculum content and assessment in programs serving children ages three through eight. *Young Children, 46*(3), 21–38.

Brendtro, L. K., Brokenleg, M., & Van Bockern, S. (1990). *Reclaiming youth at risk: Our hope for the future.* Bloomington, IN: National Educational Service.

Brewer, J. A. (1992). *Introduction to early childhood education: Preschool through the primary grades.* Boston: Allyn & Bacon.

Brody, G. H., & Shaffer, D. R. (1982). Contributions of parents and peers to children's moral socialization. *Developmental Review, 2,* 31–75.

Brody, J. (1984, October 24). Program reverses unhealthy trend in children. *The New York Times,* p. 14.

Bronfenbrenner, U. (1977, September). *Who needs parent education?* Paper presented at the working conference on parent education, Mat I Foundation, Flint, MI.

Bronfenbrenner, U. (1989). Ecological systems theory. In R. Vasta (Ed.), *Annals of child development* (Vol. 6, pp. 187–249). Greenwich, CT: JAI.

Brooks, M., Fusco, E., & Grennon, J. (1983, May). Cognitive levels matching. *Educational Leadership,* 4–8.

Brophy, J. (1987). Synthesis of research on strategies for motivating students to learn. *Educational Leadership, 45*(2), 40–48.

Bruner, J. S. (1983). *Child's talk: Learning to use language.* New York: Norton.

Bruner, J. S., Jolly, A., & Sylva, K. (Eds.). (1976). *Play, its role in development and evolution.* New York: Penguin.

Bryan, T., & Walbek, N. (1970). Preaching and practicing generosity: Children's actions and reactions. *Child Development, 41,* 329–353.

Bukatko, D., & Daehler, M. W. (1992). *Child development: A topical approach.* New York: Houghton Mifflin.

Bundy, B. F. (1991). Fostering communication between parents and schools. *Young Children, 46*(2), 12–17.

Burton, R. V. (1963). The generality of honesty reconsidered. *Psychological Review, 70,* 481–499.

Burton, R. V. (1984). A paradox in theories and research in moral development. In W. M. Kurtines & J. L. Gewirtz (Eds.), *Morality, moral behavior and moral development* (pp. 193–207). New York: Wiley.

Burts, D. C., Hart, C. H., Charlesworth, R., & Kirk, L. (1990). A comparison of frequencies of stress behaviors observed in kindergarten children in classrooms with developmentally appropriate versus developmentally inappropriate instructional practices. *Early Childhood Research Quarterly, 5,* 407–423.

Buss, A. H., & Plomin, R. A. (1975). A temperamental theory of personality. New York: Wiley.

Caldwell, B. (1986). Day care and the public schools: Natural allies, natural enemies. *Educational Leadership, 43*(5) 34–39.

Carle, E. (1981). *The very hungry caterpillar.* New York: Putnam.

Carlsson-Paige, N., & Levin, D. E. (1990). *Who's calling the shots?* Philadelphia: New Society.

Carman-Ainsworth Community Schools. (1986). *Stepping stones to early learning.* Carman-Ainsworth, MI: Author, Instructional Program Committee.

Carnegie Foundation for the Advancement of Teaching. (1988). *The conditions of teaching: A state by state analysis.* Princeton, NJ: Author.

Cartwright, S. (1987). Group endeavor in nursery school can be valuable learning. *Young Children, 42*(4), 8–11.

Cartwright, S. (1988, July). Play can be the building blocks of learning. *Young Children, 43*(5), 44–47.

Cartwright, S. (1990). Learning with large blocks. *Young Children, 45*(3), 38–41.

Casey, M., & Lippman, M. (1991, May). Learning to plan through play. *Young Children, 46*(4), 52–58.

Cassidy, D. (1989). Questioning the young child: Process and function. *Childhood Education, 65*(3), 146–149.

Castle, K. (1991). Children's invented games. *Childhood Education, 67*(2), 82–85.

Cavallaro, S., & Porter, R. (1980). Peer preferences of at-risk and normally developing children in a preschool mainstream classroom. *American Journal of Mental Deficiency, 84,* 357–366.

Cazden, C. (1976). Play and language and metalinguistic awareness. In J. Bruner, A. Jolly, & K. Sylva (Eds.), *Play: Its development and evolution.* (pp. 603–608). New York: Basic Books.

Ceci, S. J. (1990). *On intelligence...more or less: A bio-ecological treatise on intellectual development.* Englewood Cliffs, NJ: Prentice-Hall.

Chafel, J. (1986). Call the police, okay? Social comparison by young children during play in preschool. In S. Burrows & R. Evans (Eds.), *Play, language and socialization* (pp. 115–130). New York: Gordon & Breach.

Chance, P. (1979). *Learning through play.* New York: Gardner Press.

Chandler, L. A. (1985). *Assessing stress in children.* New York: Praeger.

Charlesworth, R., & Lind, K. K. (1990). *Math and science for young children.* New York: Delmar.

Chase, C.I. (1978). *Measurement for educational evaluation.* Reading, MA: Addison-Wesley.

Children's Defense Fund. (1991). *The state of America's children.* Washington, DC: Author.

Christie, J. (1986). Training of symbolic play. In P. Smith (Ed.), *Children's play: Research development and practical applications* (pp. 55–64). New York: Gordon & Breach.

Christie, J. (1990). Dramatic play: A context for meaningful engagements. *Reading Teacher, 43*(8), 542–545.

Chubb, P. (1903). *The teaching of English.* New York: Macmillan.

Chukovsky, K. (1971). *From two to five.* Los Angeles: University of California Press.

Clarizio, H. (1980). *Toward positive classroom discipline.* New York: Wiley.

Clayton, M. K. (Narrator). (1989). *Places to start: Implementing the developmental classroom* [Film]. Greenfield, MA: Northeast Foundation for Children.

Coburn, C. (1991, June). If only we could use it! *Early Childhood News,* 11–12.

Cochran, M., & Henderson, C. R., Jr. (1986). *Family matters: Evaluation of the parental empowerment program.* Ithaca, NY: The Comparative Ecology of Human Development Project.

Cohen, S. (1977). Fostering positive attitudes toward the handicapped: New curriculum. *Children Today, 6*(6), 7–12.

Cole, E. (1990). An experience in Froebel's garden. *Childhood Education, 67*(1), 18–21.

Combs, M. L., & Slaby, D. A. (1978). Social skills training with children. In B. Lakey & A. Kazdin (Eds.), *Advances in clinical child psychology* (pp. 129–144). New York: Academic Press.

Connell, D. R. (1987). The first 30 years were the fairest: Notes from the kindergarten and ungraded primary (K-1-2). *Young Children, 42*(5), 30–39.

Consortium for Longitudinal Studies. (1983). *As the twig is bent.* Hillsdale, NJ: Erlbaum.

Cornerstones (1989, January–February). Anger and aggression: What we hope children learn. Kansas State University Cooperative Extension Service, *1*(1), 1–8.

Crary, E. (1984). *Kids can cooperate: A practical guide to teaching problem solving.* Seattle: Parenting Press.

Creager, E. (1990, May 2). The test of time. *Detroit Free Press,* pp. 1F, 6F.

Cross, W. E. (1985). Black identity: Rediscovering the distinctions between personal identity and reference group orientations. In M. B. Spencer, G. K. Brookins, & W. R. Allen (Eds.), *Beginnings: The social and affective development of black children* (pp. 155–172). Hillsdale, NJ: Erlbaum.

Cruikshank, D., Fitzgerald, D., & Jensen, L. (1980). *Young children learning mathematics.* Boston: Allyn & Bacon.

Cryan, J. R. (1986, May–June). Evaluation: Plague or promise. *Childhood Education, 62*(5), 344–350.

Cuban, L. (1984). *How teachers taught: Constancy and change in American classrooms.* New York: Longman.

Cummings, C. (1989). *Translating guidelines into practice.* Saginaw: Mid-Michigan Association for the Education of Young Children.

Cummings, C. (1990a, November). *Developmentally appropriate practice in early education.* Address to teachers and administrators of the Midland Schools, Midland, MI.

Cummings, C. (1990b). A look at kindergarten learning environments: Combining time, space, materials, media, people, and purposes. In J. S. McKee, (Ed.), *The developing kindergarten: Programs, children, and teachers* (pp. 251–273). East Lansing: Michigan Association for the Education of Young Children.

Cummings, C. (1991a, February). *The components of developmentally appropriate practice.* Paper delivered at the Ingham Intermediate School District, Mason, MI.

Cummings, C. (1991b). [Results of the Carnegie Foundation elementary school survey and on-site visitation. Personal communication.]

Curran, J. S., & Cratty, B. J. (1978). Speech and language problems in children. Denver: Love.

Currie, J. R. (1988, Winter). Affect in the schools: A return to the most basic of basics. *Childhood Education, 65*(2), 83–87.

Curry, M. (1982). Held back in kindergarten. *Early Years, 3*–27.

Curry, N. E., & Johnston, C. N. (1990). *Beyond self-esteem: Developing a genuine sense of human value.* Washington, DC: National Association for the Education of Young Children.

Damon, W. (Ed.). (1989). *Child development today and tomorrow.* San Francisco: Jossey-Bass.

Dansky, J. L. (1980). Make believe: A mediator of the relationship between free play and associative fluency. *Child Development, 51*, 576–579.

David, J. L. (1991). What it takes to restructure education. *Educational Leadership, 48*(8), 11–15.

Dawson, M. M. (1987). Beyond ability grouping: A review of the effectiveness of ability grouping and its alternatives. *School Psychology Review, 16*, 348–369.

Day, B. (1988a). *Early childhood education: Creative learning activities.* New York: Macmillan.

Day, B. D. (1988b). What's happening in early childhood programs across the United States. In C. Waiger (Ed.), *A resource guide to public school early childhood programs* (pp. 3–31). Alexandria, VA: Association for Supervision and Curriculum Development.

Deal, T. E. (1990). Reframing reform. *Educational Leadership, 47*(8), 6–12.

Deardon, R. F. (1984). *Theory and practice in education.* London: Routledge & Kegan Paul.

Derman-Sparks, L. (1991). *Anti-bias curriculum.* Washington, DC: National Association for the Education of Young Children.

Derman-Sparks, L., & the ABC Task Force. (1989). *Anti-bias curriculum: Tools for empowering young children.* Washington, DC: National Association for the Education of Young Children.

DeVries, R. (1974). Theory in educational practice. In R. W. Colvin and E. M. Zaffiro (Eds.), *Preschool education: A handbook for the training of early childhood educators* (pp. 3–40). New York: Springer.

DeVries, R., & Kohlberg, L. (1987). *Programs of early education: The constructivist view.* New York: Longman.

DeVries, R., & Kohlberg, L. (1990). *Constructivist early education: Overview and comparison with other programs.* Washington, DC: National Association for the Education of Young Children.

Dewey, J. (1938). *Experience and education.* New York: Macmillan.

Dinkmeyer, G., & McKay, G. (1988). *S.T.E.P.: Parents handbook.* Circle Pines, MN: American Guidance Service.

Dixon, G. T., & Chalmers, F. G. (1990, Fall). The expressive arts in education. *Childhood Education, 67*(1), 12–17.

Dodge, D. (1989). Strategies for achieving a quality program. *Exchange, 67*, 43–45.

Dodge, D. (1991). *Creative curriculum for early childhood.* Washington, DC: Teaching Strategies.

Dodge, K. A., Petit, G. S., McCloskey, C. L., & Brown, M. M. (1986). Social competence in children. *Monographs for the Society for Research in Child Development, 51*(2, Serial No. 213).

Dowling, W. J., & Harwood, D. L. (1986). *Music cognition.* Orlando, FL: Academic Press.

Doyle, A., & Connolly, J. (1989). Negation and enactment in social pretend play: Relations to social acceptance and social cognition. *Early Childhood Research Quarterly, 4*, 289–302.

Doyle, R. P. (1989, November). The resistance of conventional wisdom to research evidence: The case of retention in grade. *Phi Delta Kappan,* 215–220.

Dreikurs, R., & Soltz, V. (1964). *Children: The challenge.* New York: Hawthorn Books.

Duke, D. L. (1990). Setting goals for professional development. *Educational Leadership, 47*(8), 71–76.

Durkin, D. (1990). Reading instruction in kindergarten: A look at some issues through the lens of new basal reader materials. *Early Childhood Research Quarterly, 5,* 299–316.

Dyson, A. (1990, January). Symbol makers, symbol weaver: How children link play, pictures, and print. *Young Children.*

Eastman, G. (1988). *Family Involvement in Education.* Unpublished manuscript prepared for the Wisconsin Department of Public Instruction.

Eiferman, R. (1971). Social play in childhood. In R. Herron & B. Sutton-Smith (Eds.), *Child's play* (pp. 270–297). New York: Wiley.

Eisenberg, N. (1986). *Altruistic emotion, cognition and behavior.* Hillsdale, NJ: Erlbaum.

Eisenberg, N., and Harris, J. D. (1984). Social competence: A developmental perspective. *School Psychology Review, 13,* 267–277.

Eisner, E. W. (1970). Evaluating children's art. In E. Pappas (Ed.), *Art education.* New York: Macmillan.

Eisner, E. (1981). The role of the arts in cognition and curriculum. *Phi Delta Kappan, 63*(1), 48–52.

Eliason, C. F., & Jenkins, L. T. (1990). *A practical guide to early childhood curriculum.* Columbus, OH: Merrill/Macmillan.

Elkind, D. (1976). *Child development and education.* New York: Oxford University Press.

Elkind, D. (1981). *The hurried child.* Reading, MA: Addison-Wesley.

Elkind, D. (1987). *Miseducation: Preschoolers at risk.* New York: Knopf.

Elkind, D. (1988a). Educating the very young: A call for clear thinking. *NEA Today, 6*(6), 22–27.

Elkind, D. (1988b, October). The Miseducation of young children. *Education Digest, 54,* 11–14.

Elkind, D. (1989, October). Developmentally appropriate practice: Philosophical and practical implications. *Phi Delta Kappan, 7*(2), 113–117.

Elkins, D. P. (Ed.). (1979). *Self-concept sourcebook.* Rochester, NY: Growth Associates.

Epstein, H. (1978). Growth spurts during brain development: Implications for educational policy and practice. In J. Child & A. Mersey, *Education and the brain.* Chicago: University of Chicago Press.

Epstein, H. (1979, Fall). Brain growth and cognitive functioning. *Colorado Journal of Educational Research,* 15–23.

Epstein, J. L. (1984, April). *Effects of parent involvement on student achievement in reading and math.* Paper presented at the annual meeting of the American Research Association.

Epstein, J. L. (1986). Parents' reactions to teacher practices of parent involvement. *Elementary School Journal, 86,* 277–293.

Erickson, M. F., Sroufe, L. A., & Egeland, B. (1985). The relationship between quality of attachment and behavior problems in preschool in a high-risk sample. In I. Bretherton & E. Waters (Eds.), *Growing points of attachment theory and research* (pp. 147–166). *Monographs of the Society for Research in Child Development, 50* (1–2, Serial No. 209).

Erikson, E. H. (1950). *Childhood and society.* New York: Hawthorn Books.

Evans, E. D. (1975). *Contemporary influences in early childhood education* (2nd ed). New York: Holt, Rinehart, & Winston.

Fabes, R. A. (1984). How children learn self-control. *Two to Twelve, 2*(5), 1–3.

Feeney, S., & Moravcik, E. (1987, September). A thing of beauty: Aesthetic development in young children. *Young Children,* 7–15.

Fein, G., & Stork, L. (1981). Sociodramatic play: Social class effects in integrated preschool classrooms. *Journal of Applied Developmental Psychology, 2,* 267–279.

Ferreiro, E., & Teberosky, A. (1982). *Literacy before schooling.* Portsmouth, NH: Heinemann.

Fields, M. V., Spangler, K. L., & Lee, D. M. (1991). *Let's begin reading right.* New York: Merrill/Macmillan.

Flavell, J. H. (1977). *Cognitive development.* Englewood Cliffs, NJ: Prentice-Hall.

Flavell, J. H., Green, F., & Flavell, E. (1986). Development of knowledge about the appearance reality distinction. *Monographs of the Society for Research in Child Development* (Serial No. 212), *51*(1).

Forbes, D. (1978). Recent research on children's social cognition: A brief review. In W. Damon (Ed.), *New directions for child development.* San Francisco: Jossey-Bass.

Forest Hills Public Schools. (1988). Curriculum guidelines, kindergarten through the second grade. Forest Hills, MI: Author.

Forman, G. (1987). The constructivist perspective. In J. L. Roopnarine & J. E. Johnson (Eds.), *Approaches to early childhood education* (pp. 71–84). Columbus, OH: Merrill/Macmillan.

Forman, G., & Kuschner, D. S. (1983). *The child's constructions of knowledge: Project for teaching young children.* Washington, DC: National Association for the Education of Young Children.

Foster, K. (1990). Small steps on the way to teacher empowerment. *Educational Leadership, 47*(8), 38–40.

Frank, M. (1984). *A child's brain.* New York: Haworth Press.

Franz, C. E., McClelland, D. C., & Weinberger, R. L. (1991). Childhood antecedents of conventional social accomplishment in mid-life adults: A 36-year prospective study. *Journal of Personality and Social Psychology, 60,* 586–595.

Friedrich, L. K., & Stein, A. H. (1973). Aggressive and prosocial television programs and the natural behaviors of preschool children. *Monographs of the Society for Research in Child Development, 38*(151).

Fromberg, D. P. (1987). Play. In C. Seefeldt (Ed.), *The early childhood curriculum: A review of current research* (pp. 35–74). New York: Teachers College Press.

Frost, J. (1991). *Play and playscapes.* Albany, NY: Delmar.

Fry, P. S., & Addington, J. (1984). Comparison of social problem solving of children from open and traditional classrooms: A two-year longitudinal study. *Journal of Education Psychology, 76,* 318–329.

Frymier, J. (1989). Commentary: Retention in grade is "harmful" to students. *Education Week,* p. 32.

Galen, H. (1991). Increasing parental involvement in elementary school: The nitty gritty of one successful program. *Young Children, 46*(2), 18–22.

Garcia, C. (1991). *A fieldwork study of how children learn fundamental motor skills and how they progress in the development of striking.* Unpublished doctoral dissertation, Michigan State University, East Lansing.

Gardini, L., & Edwards, C. P. (1988). Early childhood integration of the visual arts. *Gifted International, 5*(2), 14–18.

Gardner, H. (1983). *Frames of mind: Theory of multiple intelligence.* New York: Basic Books.

Gardner, H. (1988). *Assessment in context: The alternatives to standardized testing.* Unpublished manuscript prepared for the National Commission on Testing and Public Policy, Berkeley, CA.

Garvey, C. (1977). *Play.* Cambridge, MA: Harvard University Press.

Garvey, C., & Berndt, C. (1977). Organization of pretend play. *JSAS Catalog of Selected Documents in Psychology: 1.* (Ms. No. 1589)

Garvey, C., & Hagan, R. (1973). Social speech and social interaction: Egocentricism revisited. *Child Development, 44,* 565–568.

Gazda, G. M. , et al. (1991). *Human relations development: A manual for educators.* Boston: Allyn & Bacon.

Geiger, K. (1991, March). President's viewpoint: An idea whose time has come. *NEA Today,* p. 2.

George, P. S. (1987). *What's the truth about tracking and ability grouping really?* Gainesville, FL: Teacher Education Resource.

Gilbert, S. E., & Gay, G. (1985). Improving the success in schools of poor black children. *Phi Delta Kappan, 67,* 133–137.

Gilligan, C. (1982). *In a different voice: Psychological theory and women's development.* Cambridge, MA: Harvard University Press.

Gilligan, S. G., & Bower, G. H. (1984). Cognitive consequences of emotional arousal. In C. E. Izard, J. Kagan, & R. B. Zajonc (Eds.), *Emotions, cognition, and behavior.* Cambridge, MA: Cambridge University Press.

Gilmar, S., & Nelson, J. (1975, February). Resources for learning: Parents get into the act. *Childhood Education,* 208–210.

Glickman, C. (1981). *Developmental supervision.* Alexandria, VA: Association for Supervision and Curriculum Development.

Glickman, C. (1991). Pretending not to know what we know. *Educational Leadership, 48*(8), 4–8.

Goetz, E. M. (1985, Fall). In defense of curriculum themes. *Day Care and Early Education, 13,* 12–13.

Goffin, S. G. (1989). Developing a research agenda for early childhood education: What can be learned from the research on teaching? *Early Childhood Research Quarterly, 4,* 187–204.

Goldman, C., & O'Shea, C. (1990). A culture for change. *Educational Leadership, 47*(8), 41–43.

Goode, T. L., & Brophy, J. E. (1984). *Looking into classrooms.* New York: Harper & Row.

Goodlad, J. I. (1984). *A place called school.* New York: McGraw-Hill.

Goodwin, W. L., & Driscoll, L. A. (1980). *Handbook for measurement and evaluation in early childhood education.* San Francisco: Jossey-Bass.

Gootman, M. (1988, November/December). Discipline alternatives that work: Eight steps toward classroom discipline without corporal punishment. *The Humanist, 48,* 11–14.

Gordon, E. E. (1981). *The manifestations of developmental music aptitude in the audiation of "same" and "different" as sound in music.* Chicago: G.I.A. Publications.

Gordon, J. (1990, April 23). Teaching kids to negotiate. *Newsweek,* p. 65.

Gordon, T. (1989). *Discipline that works: Promoting self-discipline in children.* New York: Plume Books.

Goth-Owens, J. (n.d.). *The stress connection.* East Lansing: 4-H Youth Programs, Cooperative Extension Service, Michigan State University.

Gottman, J., Gonzo, J., & Rasmussen, B. (1975). Social interaction, social competence and friendship in children. *Child Development, 46,* 709–718.

Gotts, E. E., & Purnell, F. R. (1986). Communication: Key to school-home relations. In R. J. Griffore and R. P. Boger (Eds.), *Child rearing in the home and school* (pp. 157–200). New York: Plenum.

Greenberg, P. (1989). Parents as partners in young children's development and education: A new

American fad? Why does it matter? *Young Children, 44*(4), 61–75.

Greenman, J. (1988). *Caring spaces, learning places: Children's environments that work*. Redman, WA: Exchange Press.

Greenough, W. T. (1975, January–February). Experiential modification of the developing brain. *American Scientist, 63*, 37–46.

Grezda, M. T., Garduque, L., & Schultz, T. (Eds.). (1991). *Improving instruction and assessment in early childhood education: Summary of a workshop series*. Washington, DC: National Forum on the Future of Children and Families, National Academy Press.

Griffore, R. J., & Bulbolz, M. (1986). Family and school as educators. In R. J. Griffore & R. P. Boger (Eds.), *Child rearing in the home and school* (pp. 61–104). New York: Plenum Press.

Grossman, S. (1992). *Examining the mesosystem of the young child: An analysis of communication between teachers and providers*. Unpublished doctoral dissertation, Michigan State University, East Lansing.

Grusec, J. E., & Mills, R. (1982). The acquisition of self-control. In J. Worrell (Ed.), *Psychological development in the elementary years* (pp. 151–186). New York: Academic Press.

Gunsberg, A. (1991, Summer). Improvised musical play with delayed and nondelayed children. *Childhood Education, 67*, 4.

Halliday, M. A. K. (1973). *Explorations in the functions of language*. London: Edward Arnold.

Halliday, M. A. K. (1975). *Learning how to mean: Explorations in the development of language*. London: Edward Arnold.

Halverson, H. M. (1931). An experimental study of prehension in infants by means of systematic cinema records. *Genetic Psychology Monographs, 10*, 107–286.

Hamachek, D. (1990). *Psychology in teaching, learning, and growth*. Boston: Allyn Bacon.

Harris, J. A. (1978, September). Parents and teachers, Inc. *Teachers*, 85–87.

Harris, L., and Associates. (1987). *The American Teacher, 1987: Strengthening links between home and school. The Metropolitan Life Survey*. Washington, DC: U.S. Department of Education. (ERIC Document Reproduction Service No. ED 289-841).

Hart, L. A. (1983). *Human brain and human learning*. New York: Longman.

Hartley, R. E., Frank, L. K., & Goldenson, R. M. (1952). *Understanding children's play*. New York: Columbia University Press.

Hartup, W. W. (1978). Children and their friends. In H. McGurk (Ed.), *Issues in childhood social development* (pp. 130–170). London: Methuen.

Hartup, W. W. (1982). Peer relations. In C. B. Kopp & J. B. Krakow (Eds.), *The child development in a social context* (pp. 514–575). Reading, MA: Addison-Wesley.

Hartup, W. W. (1983). Peer relations. In P. H. Mussen (Ed.), *Handbook of child psychology* (Vol. 4, pp. 103–196). New York: Wiley.

Hartup, W. W., & Moore, S. G. (1990). Early peer relations: Developmental significance and prognostic implications. *Early Childhood Research Quarterly, 5*(1), 1–18.

Hatch, T., & Gardner, H. (1988, November/December). New research on intelligence. *Learning, 17*(4), 36–39.

Haubenstricker, J. (1991). *Motor development as a biological imperative*. Unpublished manuscript.

Haubenstricker, J. L., & Ewing, M. E. (1985). *Predicting motor performance from changes in body size and shape*. Paper presented at the annual convention of the American Alliance for Health, Physical Education, Recreation, and Dance, Atlanta, GA.

Havighurst, R. J. (1954). *Developmental tasks and education*. New York: Longman.

Hazen, N. L., & Black, B. (1989). Preschool peer communication skills: The role of social status and interaction content. *Child Development, 60*(4), 867–876.

Healy, J. M. (1989). *Your child's growing mind*. New York: Doubleday.

Heibert, E. H., & Fisher, C. W. (1990). Whole language: Three themes for the future. *Educational Leadership, 47*(6), 62–64.

Heinrich, J. S. (1977). *Native Americans: What not to teach. Unlearning "Indian" stereotypes*. New York: Racism and Sexism Resource Center for Educators.

Hendrick, J. (1975). *The whole child: New trends in early education*. St. Louis, MO: Mosby.

Hendrick, J. (1986). *Total learning*. Columbus, OH: Merrill/Macmillan.

Hendrick, J. (1990). *Total learning: Curriculum for the young child*. Columbus, OH: Merrill/Macmillan.

Hendrick, J. (1992). *The whole child: Developmental education for the early years*. New York: Macmillan.

Henry, T. (1990, July 29). Governors access education: Report asks states to redesign system. *The Burlington Free Press*, p. 1E.

Herbert, E. H., & Papierz, J. M. (1990). The emergent literacy construct and kindergarten and readiness books of basal reading series. *Early Childhood Research Quarterly, 5*, 317–334.

Herr, J., & Libby, Y. (1990). *Creative resources for the early childhood classroom*. New York: Delmar.

Hess, R. D., Block, M., Costello, J., Knowles, R. T., & Largey, D. (1971). Parent involvement in early education. In E. Grotberg (Ed.), *Daycare: Resources for decisions* (pp. 265–298). Washington, DC: Office of Economic Opportunity.

Hildebrand, V. (1990). *Guiding young children* (4th ed.). New York: Macmillan.

Hildebrand, V. (1991). *Introduction to early childhood education.* New York: Macmillan.

Hills, T. (1990, April). [Remarks made at the National Association for the Education of Young Children Leadership Conference Roundtable discussion regarding school restructuring, Washington, DC.]

Hills, T. (1991, April). [Remarks made at "School Restructuring" roundtable discussion, National Association for the Education of Young Children Leadership Conference, Washington, DC.]

Hinitz, B. F. (1987). Social studies in early childhood education. In C. Seefeldt (Ed.), *The early childhood curriculum: A review of research* (pp. 237–255). New York: Teachers College Press.

Hirsch, E. S. (1984). *The block book* (rev. ed.). Washington, DC: National Association for the Education of Young Children.

Hitz, R. (1987, January). Creative problem solving through music activities. *Young Children, 42*(2), 12–17.

Hitz, R., & Driscoll, A. (1988). Praise or encouragement? *Young Children, 43*(5), 6–13.

Hoffer C., & Hoffer, M. (1982). *Teaching music in the elementary classroom.* New York: Harcourt Brace & Jovanovich.

Hoffman, L. W. (1984). Empathy, its limitations, and its role in a comprehensive moral theory. In W. M. Kurtines & J. L. Gewirtz (Eds.), *Morality, moral behavior and moral development.* New York: Wiley.

Hoffman, M. L. (1967). Moral internalization, parental power, and the nature of the parent-child interaction. *Developmental Psychology, 5,* 45–57.

Hoffman, M. L. (1970). Moral development. In *Carmichael's manual of child psychology* (Vol. 2, pp. 262–360). New York: Wiley.

Hoffman, M. L. (1982). Development of prosocial motivation: Empathy and guilt. In N. Eisenberg-Berg (Ed.), *The development of prosocial behavior.* New York: Academic Press.

Hoffman, M. L. (1983). Affective and cognitive processes in moral internalization. In E. T. Higgins, D. N. Ruble, & W. W. Hartup (Eds.), *Social cognition and social behavior: Developmental perspectives.* New York: Cambridge University Press.

Holdaway, D. (1979). *The foundations of literacy.* Sydney: Ashton Scholastic.

Holloman, S. T. (1990, May). Retention and redshirting: The dark side of kindergarten. *Early Childhood Education,* 13–15.

Holmes, C. T. (1990). Grade level retention effects: A meta-analysis of research studies. In L. A. Shepard

& M. L. Smith (Eds.), *Flunking grades: Research and policies on retention* (pp. 16–33). New York: Falmer.

Holmes, C. T., & Matthews, I. K. M. (1984). The effects of nonpromotion on elementary and junior high school pupils: A meta analysis. *Review of Educational Research, 54,* 225–236.

Holt, B. G. (1988). *Science with young children.* Washington, DC: National Association for the Education of Young Children.

Honig, A. S. (1982, July). Prosocial development in children. *Children, 37*(5), 51–62.

Hord, S. M., Rutherford, W. L., Huling-Austin, L., & Hall, G. E. (1987). *Taking charge of change.* Alexandria, VA: Association for Supervision and Curriculum Development.

Howes, C. (1983). Caregivers' behavior in center and family day care. *Journal of Applied Developmental Psychology, 4,* 99–107.

Hunt, J. M. (1961). *Intelligence and experience.* New York: Ronald.

Hurd, P. D. (1990). Why we must transform science education. *Educational Leadership, 49*(2), 33–35.

Hyman, I. A., & D'Alessandro, J. (1984, September). Good, old-fashioned discipline: The politics of punitiveness. *Phi Delta Kappan, 66,* 39–45.

Hymes, J. (Narrator). (1980). *Hairy scary* [Film]. Silver Spring: University of Maryland.

Hymes, J. I. (1974). *Effective home school relations.* Sierra Madre: Southern California Association for the Education of Young Children.

Hymes, J. L., Jr. (1991). *Early childhood education: Twenty years in review.* Washington, DC: National Association for the Education of Young Children.

Inhelder, B., & Piaget, J. (1964). *The early growth of logic in the child.* London: Routledge & Kegan Paul.

Institute for Responsive Education. (1990). *Schools reaching out.* Boston: Author.

Instructor Magazine. (1990, September). Seven styles of learning clip-and-save chart. P. 52.

Jalongo, M. R. (1990). The child's right to the expressive arts: Nurturing the imagination as well as the intellect. *Childhood Education, 66*(4), 195–201.

Janis, I. L. (1971, November). Groupthink. *Psychology Today,* pp. 43–76.

Janis, I. L. (1977). *Decision making: A psychological analysis of conflict, choice, and commitment.* New York: Free Press.

Janis, I. L. (1982). *Groupthink.* Boston: Houghton Mifflin.

Javernick, C. (1988). Johnny's not jumping: Can we help obese children? *Young Children, 43*(2), 18–23.

Jenkins, P. D. (1980). *Art for the fun of it: A guide for teaching young children.* New York: Prentice-Hall.

Jenson, G. O., & Warstadt, T. (1990). *Ranking critical issues facing American families.* Washington, DC: U.S. Department of Agriculture.

Johnsen, E. P., & Christie, J. F. (1984). Play and social cognition. In B. Sutton-Smith & D. Kelly-Byrne (Eds.), *The masks of play* (pp. 109–118). New York: Leisure Press.

Johnson, P., & Winogard, P. (1985). Passive failure in reading. *Journal of Reading Behavior, 17,* 279–301.

Johnston, M. S. (1982). *How to involve parents in early childhood education.* Provo, UT: Brigham Young University Press.

Jorde, P. (1986). Early childhood education: Issues and trends. *Educational Forum, 50*(2), 171–181.

Kamii, C. (1985, September). Leading primary education toward excellence. *Young Children,* 3–9.

Kamii, C. (Ed.). (1990). *Achievement testing in the early grades.* Washington, DC: National Association for the Education of Young Children.

Kamii, C., & DeVries, R. (1977). Project for early education. In M. Day & R. Parker (Eds.), *Preschool in action* (2nd ed.). Boston: Allyn & Bacon.

Kamii, C., & DeVries, R. (1978). *Physical knowledge in preschool education: Implications of Piaget's theory.* Englewood Cliffs, NJ: Prentice-Hall.

Kaplan, P. S. (1986). *A child's odyssey: Child and adolescent development.* St. Paul, MN: West.

Katz, L. G. (1987) *What should young children be learning?* Urbana, IL: ERIC Clearinghouse on Elementary and Early Childhood Education.

Katz, L. G. (1988, Summer). What should young children be doing? *American Educator,* 28–45.

Katz, L. G. & Chard, S. C. (1989). *Engaging children's minds: The project approach.* Norwood, NJ: Ablex.

Katz, L. G., Evangelou, D., & Hartman, J. A. (1990). *The case for mixed-age grouping in early education.* Washington, DC: National Association for the Education of Young Children.

Katz, L. G., Rath, F., & Torres, R. (1987). *A place called kindergarten.* Urbana, IL: ERIC Clearinghouse on Elementary and Early Childhood Education.

Katz, P. (1982). Development of children's racial awareness and intergroup attitudes. In L. G. Katz (Ed.), *Current topics in early childhood education* (Vol. 4, pp. 17–54). Norwood, NJ: Ablex.

Keats, E. J. (1972). *Pet show.* New York: Macmillan.

Keeshan, B. (1989, November/December). Banning corporal punishment in the classroom. *The Humanist, 48,* 6–8.

Kellogg, R. (1969). *Analyzing children's art.* Palo Alto, CA: National Press.

Kelman, H. C. (1958). Compliance identification and internalization: Three processes of attitude change. In B. L. Hinto and H. J. Reitz (Eds.), *Groups and organizations: Integrated readings in the analysis of social behavior* (pp. 27–42). Belmont, CA: Wadsworth.

Kindergarten Curriculum Guide and Resource Book. (1985). Victoria, British Columbia: Curriculum Development Branch, Ministry of Education.

Klein, T. (1981). Results of the reading program. *Educational Perspectives, 20*(1), 8–10.

Knapp, M. S., Turnbull, B. J., & Shields, P. M. (1990, September). New directions for educating children of poverty. *Educational Leadership, 48*(1), 4–9.

Kohlberg, L. (1964). Development of moral character and moral ideology. In M. L. Hoffman & L. W. Hoffman (Eds.), *Review of child development research* (Vol. 1). New York: Russell Sage Foundation.

Kohlberg, L. (1976). Moral stages and moralization: The cognitive-developmental approach. In T. Lickona (Ed.), *Moral development and behavior* (pp. 31–53). New York: Holt, Rinehart & Winston.

Kostelnik, M. J. (1984, August). Real consensus or groupthink? *Childcare Information Exchange,* 25–30.

Kostelnik, M. J. (1989a, October). *Enabling parents to become partners in the educational process.* Keynote address, Michigan Division of Early Childhood Conference, Houghton Lake.

Kostelnik, M. J. (1989b). Trends in K–1st. *Lansing City Magazine, 3*(8), 24–27.

Kostelnik, M. J. (1990, February). *Standards of quality for early childhood education: Implications for policy makers.* Keynote address, Michigan Department of Education Early Childhood Conference, Detroit.

Kostelnik, M. J. (Ed.). (1991). *Teaching young children using themes.* Glenview, IL: Goodyear Books.

Kostelnik, M. J., Howe, D., Payne, K., Rohde, B., Spalding, G., Stein, L., & Whitbeck, D. (1991). *Teaching young children using themes.* Glenview, IL: Good Year Books.

Kostelnik, M. J., Palmer, S., & Hannon, K. (1987, November). *Theme planning in early childhood.* Paper presented at the National Association for the Education of Young Children Conference, Chicago.

Kostelnik, M. J., & Stein, L. C. (1986, November). *Effects of three conflict mediation strategies on children's aggressive and prosocial behavior in the classroom.* Paper presented at the annual meeting of the National Association for the Education of Young Children, Washington, DC.

Kostelnik, M. J., & Stein, L. C. (1990). Social development: An essential component of kindergarten education. In J. S. McKee (Ed.), *The developing kindergarten: Programs, children, and teachers.*

Saginaw: Mid-Michigan Association for the Education of Young Children.

Kostelnik, M. J., Stein, L. C., Whiren, A. P., & Soderman, A. K. (in press). *Guiding children's social development: Classroom practices.* Albany, NY: Delmar.

Kostelnik, M. J., Whiren, A., & Stein, L. (1986). Living with he-man: Managing superhero fantasy play. *Young Children, 41*(4), 3–9.

Kovalik, S. (1986). *Teachers make the difference.* Oak Creek, AZ: Susan Kovalick and Associates.

Kritchevsky, S., & Prescott, E. (1977). *Planning environments for young children: Physical space* (2nd ed.). Washington, DC: National Association for the Education of Young Children.

Languis, M., Sanders, T., & Tipps, S. (1980). *Brain and learning: Directions in early childhood education.* Washington, DC: National Association for the Education of Young Children.

Laosa, L. M. (1977). Nonbiased assessment of children's abilities: Historical antecedents and current issues. In T. Oakland (Ed.), *Psychological and educational assessment of minority children.* New York: Brunner/Mazel.

Lauer, R. M. (1990, January 31). Self knowledge, critical thinking, and community should be the main objectives of general education. *The Chronicle of Higher Education,* Sec. 2, p. 1.

Lavatelli, C. S. (1973). *Piaget's theory applied to an early childhood curriculum.* Boston: American Science and Engineering.

Lawton, J. T. (1987). The Ausubelian preschool classroom. In J. L. Roopnarine and J. E. Johnson (Eds.), *Approaches to early childhood education* (pp. 85–108). New York: Merrill/Macmillan.

Lawton, J. T. (1988). *Introduction to child care and early childhood education.* Glenview, IL: Scott, Foresman.

Lazar, I. (1981). Early intervention is effective. *Educational Leadership, 38*(4), 303–305.

Lazar, I., Darlington, R. B., Murray, H., Royce, J., & Snipper, A. (1982). Lasting effects of early education. *Monographs for the Society for Research in Child Development, 47*(2–3, Serial No. 195).

LeBoeuf, M. (1986). *Working smart: How to accomplish more in half the time.* New York: Warner Books.

Leeper, S. H., Witherspoon, R. L., & Day, B. (1984). *Good schools for young children.* New York: Macmillan.

LeFrancois, G. R. (1992). *Of children.* Belmont, CA: Wadsworth.

Lessen-Firestone, J. (1991, January). *The essence of developmentally appropriate practice.* Presentation to East Lansing K–2 teachers, East Lansing, MI.

Levitt, E., & Cohen, S. (1976). Attitudes of children toward their handicapped peers. *Childhood Education, 52,* 171–173.

Levy, A. K. (1984). The language of play: The role of play in language development. *Early Child Development and Care, 17,* 49–62.

Lewin, K., Lippitt, R., & White, R. (1939). Patterns of aggressive behaviors and experimentally created "social climates." *Journal of Social Psychology, 10,* 271–299.

Lickona, T. (1988, February). Four strategies for fostering character development in children. *Phi Delta Kappan,* 419–423.

Light, H. W. (1986). *Light's retention scale manual.* Novato, CA: Academic Therapy Publications.

Lightfoot, S. L. (1980). Families and schools: Creative conflict or negative dissonance? *Journal of Research and Development in Education, 9,* 34–43.

Lind, K. K. (1991). *Exploring science in early childhood—A developmental approach.* New York: Delmar.

Little-Soldier, L. (1989). Language learning of Native American students. *Educational Leadership, 46*(5), 74–75.

Little-Soldier, L. (1990, January). *Anthropology in education.* Keynote address, Michigan Association for the Education of Young Children, Grand Rapids.

Lowenfeld, V., & Brittain, W. L. (1965). *Creative and mental growth.* New York: Macmillan.

Luria, A. R. (1961). *The role of speech in the regulation of normal and abnormal behaviour.* London: Pergamon.

Maccoby, E. E. (1984). Socialization and developmental change. *Child Development, 55,* 317–328.

Maccoby, E. E., & Martin, J. A. (1983). In E. M. Hetherington (Ed.), *Handbook of child psychology: Socialization, personality and social development* (pp. 1–101). New York: Wiley.

Machado, J. M., & Meyer, H. C. (1984). *Early childhood practicum guide.* Albany, NY: Delmar.

MacLean, J. C. (1990). *Written schedule.* Dye Elementary School, Carman-Ainsworth School District, Carman-Ainsworth, MI.

MacPhail-Wilcox, B., Forbes, R., & Parramore, B. (1990). Project design—Reforming structure and process. *Educational Leadership, 47*(7), 22–27.

Madsen, M. C. (1971). Development and cross-cultural differences in the cooperative and competitive behavior of young children. *Journal of Cross-Cultural Psychology, 2,* 365–371.

Madsen, M. C., & Connor, C. (1973). Cooperative and competitive behavior of retarded and non-retarded children at two ages. *Child Development, 44,* 175–178.

Maeroff, G. I. (1991, December). Assessing alternative assessment. *Phi Delta Kappan, 272,* 281.

Malecki, C. L. (1990). Teaching whole science: In a departmentalized elementary setting. *Childhood Education, 66*(4), 232–236.

Manning, M. L., & Lucking, R. (1990). Ability grouping: Realities and alternatives. *Childhood Education, 66*(4), 254–258.

Marcus, F. F., & Leiserson, M. (1978, September). Encouraging helping behavior. *Young Children, 33*(6), 24–34.

Marion, M. (1991). *Guidance of young children* (3rd ed.). New York: Macmillan.

Martin, K., & McGrevin, C. (1990). Making mathematics happen. *Educational Leadership, 47*(8), 20–22.

Maslow, A. H. (1954). *Motivation and personality.* New York: Harper & Row.

Maslow, A. H. (1970). *Motivation and personality.* New York: Harper & Row.

May, R. (1981). *Power and innocence: A search for the sources of violence.* New York: Dell.

McAfee, D. (1985). Circle time: Getting past five little pumpkins. *Young Children, 40*(6), 24–29.

McDevitt, S. C., & Carey, W. B. (1978, July). The measurement of temperaments in 3–7 year old children. *Journal of Child Psychology and Psychiatry, 19*(3), 245–253.

McDonald, D. T., & Simons, G. M. (1989). *Musical growth and development.* New York: Macmillan.

McHan, J. (1986). Imitation of aggression by Lebanese children. *Journal of Social Psychology, 125*(5), 613–617.

McKee, J. S. (1986). *Play: Working partner of growth.* Wheaton, MD: Association for Childhood Education International.

McKee, J. S. (1990a). *The developing kindergarten: Programs, children, teachers.* East Lansing: Michigan Association for the Education of Young Children.

McKee, J. S. (1990b). Play-activity centers for the whole child: Invitations to play and learning engagement. In J. S. McKee (Ed.), *The developing kindergarten: Programs, children and teachers* (pp. 25–61). East Lansing: Michigan Association for the Education of Young Children.

McKee, J. S. (1991). The developing kindergartner: Understanding children's nature and nurturing their development. In J. S. McKee (Ed.), *The developing kindergarten: Program, children and teachers* (pp. 65–119). East Lansing: Michigan Association for the Education of Young Children.

McLaughlin, M. W., & Shields, P. M. (1987, October). Involving low-income parents in the schools: A role for policy? *Phi Delta Kappan,* 156–160.

McSwegin, P., Pemberton, C., Petray, C., & Going, S. (1989). *Physical best.* Reston, VA: American Alliance for Health, Physical Education, Recreation, & Dance.

Mechling, K., & Oliver, D. (1983, October). Who is killing young science program? *Science and Children, 21*(2), 16–18.

Medina, N., & Neill, D. M. (1990). *Fallout from the testing explosion: How 100 million standardized exams undermine equality and excellence in America's public schools.* Cambridge, MA: National Center for Fair and Open Testing.

Meichenbaum, D. (1977). *Cognitive behavior modification: An integrative approach.* New York: Plenum.

Meier, J. H. (1978). Introduction. In B. Brown (Ed.), *Found: Long-term gains from early intervention.* Boulder, CO: Westview.

Meisels, S., & Friedland, S. (1990). Mainstreaming young emotionally disturbed children: Rationale and restraints. In M. Jensen & Z. Chevalier (Eds.), *Issues and advocacy in early education.* Boston: Allyn & Bacon.

Meisels, S. J., & Provence, S. (1989). *Screening and assessment: Guidelines for identifying young disabled and developmentally vulnerable children and their families.* Washington, DC: National Center for Clinical Infant Programs.

Mendler, A. N., & Curwin, R. L. (1988). *Taking charge in the classroom.* Reston, VA: Reston.

Mental Health Association of Michigan. (1982). *I am loved...I am happy...I am worthwhile! The importance of self-esteem in children and some basic guides to it.* (n.p.) United Way.

Michigan Department of Education. (1984). *Superintendent's study group on early childhood education.* Lansing: Author.

Michigan Department of Education. (1986). *Michigan standards of quality and guidelines for preschool programs for four-year-olds, Lansing, Michigan.* Lansing: Author.

Midland Public Schools. (1991). *Elementary curriculum: Focus 1991.* Midland, MI: Author.

Miles, M. B., & Louis, S. K. (1990). Mustering the will and skill for change. *Educational Leadership, 47*(8), 57–61.

Miller, S. E. (1978). *The facilitation of fundamental motor skill learning in young children.* Unpublished doctoral dissertation, Michigan State University, East Lansing.

Ministry of Education, Province of British Columbia. (1988). *The primary program, Victoria, British Columbia.* Victoria, British Columbia: Author.

Minnesota Department of Education. (1989). *Model learner outcomes for early childhood education.* St. Paul: Author.

Mischel, W. (1978). How children postpone pleasure. *Human Nature, 1,* 51–55.

Mitchell, A., Seligson, M., & Marx, F. (1989). *Early childhood programs and the public schools*. Dover, MA: Auburn House.

Moles, O. C. (1982). Synthesis of research on parent participation in children's education. *Educational Leadership, 40*, 44–47.

Moore, G. T. (1987). The physical environment and cognitive development in child care centers. In C. Weinstein & T. David (Eds.), *Spaces for children* (pp. 41–67). New York: Plenum.

Moore, S. G. (1982). Prosocial behavior in the early years: Parent and peer influences. In B. Spodek (Ed.), *Handbook of research in early childhood education* (pp. 65–81). New York: Free Press.

Moore, S. G. (1986). Socialization in the kindergarten classroom. In B. Spodek (Ed.), *Today's kindergarten* (pp. 110–136). New York: Teachers College Press.

Morado, C. (1990). A look at kindergartens: Past and present practices. In J. S. McKee (Ed.), *The developing kindergarten: Programs, children, and teachers* (pp. 5–24). East Lansing: Michigan Association for the Education of Young Children.

Moran, J. D. III, & McCullers, J. C. (1984). The effects of regency and story content on children's moral judgments. *Journal of Experimental Child Psychology, 38*, 447–455.

Morrow, L. (1990). Preparing the classroom environment to promote literacy during play. *Children's Quarterly, 5*, 537–554.

Morrow, R. D. (1989, Winter). Southeast Asian child-rearing practices: Implications for child and youth care workers. *Child & Youth Care Quarterly, 18*(4), 273–287.

Moyer, J. (Ed.). (1986). *Selecting educational equipment and materials for school and home*. Washington, DC: ACE I.

Moyer, J. (1990). Whose creation is it, anyway? *Childhood Education, 66*(3), 130–131.

Mueller, M., & Strahan, D. B. (1985). Information from neuroscience, psychology, and physics: An emerging synthesis. *Transescence, 13*(2), 7–11.

Murphy, C. U. (1991). Lessons from a journey into change. *Educational Leadership, 48*(8), 63–68.

Mussen, P. H., Conger, J. J., Kagan, J., & Huston, A. C. (1990). *Child development and personality* (7th ed.) New York: Harper & Row.

Mussen, P., & Eisenberg-Berg, N. (1977). *Roots of caring, sharing, and helping: The development of prosocial behavior in children*. San Francisco: Freeman.

National Academy of Early Childhood Programs. (1991). *Accreditation criteria and procedures*. Washington, DC: National Association for the Education of Young Children.

National Association for the Education of Young Children. (1982). *Early childhood teacher education guidelines: Position statement of the National Association for the Education of Young Children*. Washington, DC: Author.

National Association for the Education of Young Children. (1984a). *NAEYC position statement on nomenclature, salaries, benefits and the status of the early childhood profession*. Washington, DC: Author.

National Association for the Education of Young Children. (1984b). Research report: Results of the NAEYC survey of child care salaries and working conditions. *Young Children, 40*(1), 9–14.

National Association for the Education of Young Children. (1986). *Early childhood teacher education guidelines for four- and five-year programs*. Washington, DC: Author.

National Association of Elementary School Principals. (1990). *Early childhood education and the elementary school principal: Standards for quality programs for young children*. Alexandria, VA: Author.

National Association of State Boards of Education. (1988). *Right from the start*. Alexandria, VA: Author.

National Council for the Social Studies. (1984). In search of a scope and sequence for social studies. *Social Education, 48*, 249–262.

National Council for the Social Studies Task Force on Early Childhood/Elementary Social Studies. (1989). Social studies for early childhood and elementary school children: Preparing for the 21st century. *Social Education, 53*, 14–23.

National Council of Teachers of Mathematics. (1989). *Curriculum and evaluation standards for school mathematics*. Washington, DC: Author.

National Council on Family Relations. (1990, January). *2001: Preparing Families for the Future* (Presidential Report). n.p.: Author.

National Research Council. (1991). *Caring for America's children*. Washington, DC: National Academy Press.

National Council of Teachers of English Committee on Elementary Language Arts Textbooks. (1991). Guidelines for judging and selecting elementary language arts textbooks. *Language Arts, 68*(3), 253–254.

National Forum on the Future of Children and Families. (1991). *Improving instruction and assessment in early childhood education*. Washington, DC: National Academy Press.

Nedler, S. E., & McAfee, O. D. (1979). *Working with parents*. Belmont, CA: Wadsworth.

Neill, D. M., & Medina, N. J. (1989). Standardized testing: Harmful to educational health. *Phi Delta Kappan, 46*(8), 688–697.

Neugebauer, R. (1983). Guidelines for effective use of feedback. In *The best of Exchange: Fostering improved staff performance* (pp. 15–18). Redman, WA: Exchange Press.

Neuman, S., & Roskos, K. (1990). Peers as literacy informants: A description of young children's literacy conversations in play. *Early Childhood Research Quarterly, 6,* 233–248.

Neumann, D. (1972). Sciencing for young children. In K. R. Baker (Ed.), *Ideas that work with young children* (pp. 137–148). Washington, DC: National Association for the Education of Young Children.

New, R. (1990, September). Excellent early education: A city in Italy has it. *Young Children, 7,* 4–8.

Newman, B. M., & Newman, P.R. (1978). *Infancy and childhood.* New York: Wiley.

Newman, J. M., & Church, S. M. (1990). Myths of whole language. *The Reading Teacher, 44*(1), 20–26.

Ney, P. G. (1988, Spring). Transgenerational child abuse. *Child Psychiatry and Human Development, 18*(3), 151–155.

Nicholls, J. G., Cobb, P., Wood, T.,Yackel, E., & Patashnick, M. (1991). Dimensions of success in mathematics: Individual and classroom differences. *Journal of Research in Mathematics Education, 21,* 109–122.

Nickelsburg, J. (1976). *Nature activities for early childhood.* Menlo Park, CA: Addison-Wesley.

Nourot, P. M., & Van Hoorn, J. (1991). Symbolic play in preschool and primary settings. *Young Children, 46*(6), 40–50.

Oakes, J. (1985). *Keeping track: How schools structure inequality.* New Haven, CT: Yale University Press.

Oakland Community Schools Early Childhood Committee. (1992). *Early childhood curriculum.* Waterford, MI: Oakland Community Schools.

Osborn, J. D., & Osborn, D. K. (1983). *Cognition in early childhood.* Athens, GA: Education Associates.

Palincsar, A. S., & Brown, A. L. (1989). Classroom dialogues to promote self-regulated comprehension. In J. Brophy (Ed.), *Advances in Research on Teaching* (Vol. 1, pp. 35–71). Greenwich, CT: JAI.

Palmer, J. M. (1990). Planning wheels turn curriculum around. *Educational Leadership, 49*(2), 57–60.

Palmer, S. (1991). [Ypsilanti public schools parent involvement strategies. Personal communication.]

Parker, J. G., & Asher, S. R. (1987). Peer relations and later personal adjustment: Are low accepted children at risk? *Psychological Bulletin, 102,* 357–389.

Parker, J. G., & Gottman, J. M. (1989). Social and emotional development in a relational context: Friendship interaction from early childhood to adolescence. In T. J. Berndt & G. W. Ladd (Eds.), *Peer relations in child development.* New York: Wiley.

Parker, W. C. (1991). *Renewing the social studies curriculum.* Alexandria, VA: Association for Supervision and Curriculum Development.

Patterson, G. R., & Stouthamer-Loeber, L. S. (1984). The correlation of family management practices and delinquency. *Child Development, 55,* 1299–1307.

Paul, R., Binkder, A. J. A., & Weil, D. (1990). *Critical thinking handbook: K–3rd grades.* Rohnert Park, CA: Foundation for Critical Thinking.

Payne, K. (1991, Spring). Principles of parent involvement in preschool classrooms. *National Organization of Laboratory Schools Bulletin, 18,* 8–9.

Pearsall, P. (1983). De-stressing children: Wellness for children. *Offspring, 25*(2), 2–9.

Peck, J. T., McCaig, G., & Sapp, M. E. (1988). *Kindergarten policies: What is best for children?* Washington, DC: National Association for the Education of Young Children.

Pellegrini, A. D. (1989). *Applied child study: A developmental approach.* Hillsdale, NJ: Lawrence Erlbaum.

Pellegrini, A. D., & Perlmutter, J. C. (1988). Rough and tumble play. *Young Children, 43*(2), 14–17.

Pepler, D. J. (1982). Play and divergent thinking. In D. J. Pepler & K. H. Rubin (Eds.), *The play of children: Research and theory* (pp. 64–78). Basel, Switzerland: Karger.

Perrone, V. (Ed.). (1991). *Expanding student assessment.* Alexandria, VA: Association for Supervision and Curriculum Development.

Perry, G. (1990). Alternate modes of teacher preparation. In C. Seefeldt (Ed.), *Continuing issues in early childhood education* (pp. 173–200). Columbus, OH: Merrill/Macmillan.

Peters, D. L., & Kostelnik, M. J. (1981). Day care personnel preparation. In S. Kilmer (Ed.), *Advances in early education and day care* (Vol. 2, pp. 20–60). Greenwich, CT: JAI.

Peterson, R., & Felton-Collins, V. (1991). *The Piaget handbook for teachers and parents.* New York: Teachers College Press.

Peterson, P. L., Fennema, E., & Carpenter, T. P. (in press). Teacher's knowledge of student's mathematical problem solving knowledge. In J. E. Brophy (Ed.), *Advances in research in teaching: Vol. 2. Teacher's subject matter knowledge.* Greenwich, CT: JAI.

Phenice, L., & Griffore, R. (1990). Assessment. In J. S. McKee (Ed.), *The developing kindergarten: Programs, children, and teachers* (pp. 373–397). East Lansing, MI: Michigan Association for the Education of Young Children.

Phillips, D., & Howes, C. (1987). Indicators of quality child care: Review of research. In D. Phillips (Ed.), *Quality in child care: What does research tell us?* (pp. 1–19). Washington, DC: National Association for the Education of Young Children.

Phillips, J. L., Jr. (1975). *The origins of intellect: Piaget's theory.* San Francisco: Freeman.

Piaget, J. (1952). *The origins of intelligence in children.* Madison, CT: International Universities Press.

Piaget, J. (1954). *The construction of reality in the child* (M. Cook, Trans.). New York: Basic Books.

Piaget, J. (1962). *Play, dreams and imitation in childhood.* New York: Norton.

Piaget, J. (1965). *The moral judgment of the child.* New York: Free Press. (Original work published 1932)

Piaget, J. (1979). *Success and understanding.* Cambridge, MA: Harvard University Press.

Plomin, R. (1989). Environment and genes: Determinates of behavior. *American Psychologist, 44,* 105–111.

Polloway, A. M. (1974). The child in the physical environment: A design problem. In G. Coales (Ed.), *Alternative learning environments.* Shoudsberg, PA: Dowdes, Hakkenson, & Ross.

Powell, R. (1989). *Families and early childhood programs.* (Research Monographs of the National Association for the Education of Young Children, Vol. 3). Washington, DC: National Association for the Education of Young Children.

Power, T. J., & Bartholomew, K. L. (1987). Family-school relationship patterns: An ecological assessment. *School Psychology Review, 16*(4), 498–512.

Preston, C. (1991). *Implementation of a school-wide discipline Okemos policy—One year after initiation.* Unpublished manuscript. Okemos, MI: Okemos Schools.

Primary Program. (1989). Victoria, British Columbia: Curriculum Development Branch, Ministry of Education.

Primary Program. (1990). Victoria, British Columbia: Ministry of Education, Curriculum Development Branch.

Provus, M. M. (1980). The discrepancy evaluation model. In W. L. Goodwin & L. A. Driscoll (Eds.), *Handbook for measurement and evaluation in early childhood education* (pp. 368–372). San Francisco: Jossey-Bass.

Pulkkinen, L. (1982). Self-control and continuity from childhood to adolescence. In P. B. Baltes & O. G. Brim, Jr. (Eds.), *Life-span development and behavior* (Vol. 4, pp. 63–105). Orlando, FL: Academic Press.

Radke-Yarrow, M. (1987, April). *A developmental and contextual analysis of continuity.* Paper presented at the biennial conferences of the Society for Research in Child Development, Baltimore, MD.

Raffini, J. P. (1980). *Discipline: Negotiating conflicts with today's kids.* Englewood Cliffs, NJ: Prentice-Hall.

Raines, S. (1990). Representational competence: Regarding presenting experiences through words, actions, and images. *Childhood Education,* 139–144.

Raizen, S. A. and Kaser, J. S. (1989, May). Assessing science learning in elementary school: Why, what and how? *Phi Delta Kappan,* 718–722.

Ramsey, P. G. (1979). Beyond "Ten Little Indians" and turkey: Alternate approaches to Thanksgiving. *Young Children, 34*(6), 28–52.

Read, K. (1966). *The nursery school: A human relations laboratory.* Philadelphia: Saunders.

Reed, D. F. (1991). Preparing teachers for multicultural classrooms. *The Journal of Early Childhood Teacher Education, 38*(12:2), 16–21.

Reifel, S., & Greenfield, P. (1983, Spring). Part-whole relations: Some structural features of children's representational block play. *Child Care Quarterly, 12*(1), 144–151.

Reuschlein, R., & Haubenstricker, J. (Eds.). (1985). *1984–1985 physical education interpretive report: Grades 4, 7 and 10.* Lansing: Michigan Educational Assessment Program, Michigan Department of Education.

Revicki, D. (1982). The relationship among socioeconomic status, home environment, parent involvement, child self-concept and child achievement. *Resources in Education, 1,* 459–463.

Reynolds, E. (1990). *Guiding young children: A child centered approach.* Mountain View, CA: Mayfield.

Rich, J. M. (1985). *Innovative school discipline.* Springfield, IL: Thomas.

Richberg, J. (1991). *Intermediate results of a school-wide discipline policy.* Paper presented to the Okemos School Board, Okemos, MI.

Ritchie, F. K., & Toner, I. J. (1985). Direct labeling, tester expectancy, and delay maintenance behavior in Scottish preschool children. *International Journal of Behavioral Development, 7*(3), 333–341.

Roberts, E., & Davies, A. (1975). A method of extending the vocal range of monotone school children. *Psychology of Music, 4*(1), 29–43.

Rogers, C. R. (1961). *On becoming a person.* Boston: Houghton-Mifflin.

Rogers, E. (1983). *Diffusion of innovations.* New York: Free Press.

Roopnarine, J. L., & Johnson, J. E. (1987). *Approaches to early childhood education.* Columbus, OH: Merrill/Macmillan.

Rosenhan, D. L. (1972). Prosocial behavior of children. In W. W. Hartup (Ed.), *The young child: Reviews of research* (Vol. 2, pp. 340–360). Washington, DC: National Association for the Education of Young Children.

Roskos, K. (1990). A taxonomic view of pretend play activity among four and five year old children. *Early Childhood Research Quarterly, 5,* 495–512.

Rothlein, L., & Brett, A. (1987). Children's teachers' and parents' perceptions of play. *Early Childhood Quarterly, 2,* 45–53.

Rothman, J. (1974). *Planning and organizing for social change*. New York: Columbia University Press.

Routman, R. (1987). *Transitions*. Portsmouth, NH: Heinemann.

Ruopp, R., Travers, J., Glantz, F., & Coelen, C. (1979). Children at the center: Final results of the National Day Care Study. Cambridge, MA: Abt Associates.

Rutter, M. (1983). School effects on pupil progress: Research findings and policy implications. *Child Development, 54,* 1–29.

Rutter, M., Maugham, B., Mortmore, P., & Ousten, J. (1979). *Fifteen thousand hours*. Cambridge, MA: Harvard University Press.

Rylant, C. (1985). *The relatives came*. New York: Bradbury.

Safford, P. L. (1989). *Integrated teaching in early childhood*. White Plains, NY: Longman.

Santrock, J. W. (1990). *Children*. Dubuque, IA: Brown.

Sapon-Shevin, M. (1983). Teaching young children about differences: Resources for teaching. *Young Children, 38*(2), 24–32.

Satir, V. (1975). *Self-Esteem*. Millbrae, CA: Celestial Arts.

Sattler, J. M. (1988). *Assessment of children's intelligence and special abilities*. Boston: Allyn & Bacon.

Schiamberg, L. (1988). *Child and adolescent development*. New York: Macmillan.

Schickedanz, J. A., Hansen, K., & Forsyth, P. D. (1990). *Understanding children*. Mountain View, CA: Mayfield.

Schickedanz, J. A., York, M. E., Stewart, I. S., & White, D. A. (1990). *Strategies for teaching young children* (3rd ed.). Englewood Cliffs, NJ: Prentice-Hall.

Schirrmacher, R. (1986). Talking with young children about their art. *Young Children, 41*(5), 3–7.

Schrader, C. (1989). Written language use within the context of young children's symbolic play. *Early Childhood Research Quarterly, 4,* 225–244.

Schrader, C. (1990). Symbolic play as a curricular tool for early literacy development. *Early Childhood Research Quarterly, 5,* 79–103.

Schultz, T. (1990, March). Testing and retention of young children: Moving from controversy to reform. *Phi Delta Kappan, 71*(2), 125–129.

Schwartz, S. L., & Robison, H. F. (1982). *Designing curriculum for early childhood*. Boston: Allyn & Bacon.

Schweinhart, L. (1985). Early childhood development programs in the eighties: The national picture (High/Scope Early Childhood Policy Papers No. 1). Ypsilanti, MI: High/Scope Educational Research Foundation.

Schweinhart, L., & Weikart, D. (1980). Young children grow up: The effects of the Perry Preschool Program on youths through age 15 (Monograph No. 7 of the High/Scope Educational Research Foundation). Ypsilanti, MI: High Scope Press.

Schweinhart, L. J., Weikart, D. P., & Larner, M. B. (1986). Consequences of three curriculum models through age 15. *Early Childhood Research Quarterly, 1*(1), 15–45.

Seefeldt, C. (1980). *Teaching young children*. Englewood Cliffs, NJ: Prentice-Hall.

Seefeldt, C. (1985, November/December). Parent involvement: Support or stress. *Childhood Education,* 98–102.

Seefeldt, C. (Ed.). (1987). *The early childhood curruculum: A review of current research* (pp. 183–236). New York: Teachers College Press.

Seefeldt, V. (Ed.) (1986). *Physical activity and well-being*. Reston, VA: American Alliance for Health, Physical Education, Recreation & Dance.

Seefeldt, V., & Vogel, P. G. (1986). *The value of physical activity*. Reston, VA: American Alliance for Health, Physical Education, Recreation & Dance.

Selman, R. L. (1976). Social-cognitive understanding. In T. Lickona (Ed.), *Moral development and behavior: Theory, research and social issues* (pp. 299–316). New York: Holt, Rinehart, & Winston.

Selman, R. L. (1980). *The growth of interpersonal understanding*. New York: Academic Press.

Selman, R. L., & Selman, A. P. (1979). Children's ideas about friendship: A new theory. *Psychology Today, 13,* 71–114.

Sendak, M. (1963). *Where the wild things are*. New York: Harper & Row.

Sergiovanni, T. J. (1990). Adding value to leadership gets extraordinary results. *Educational Leadership, 47*(8), 23–27.

Shaffer, D. R. (1989). *Developmental psychology: Childhood and adolescence*. Pacific Grove, CA: Brooks/Cole.

Shanab, M. E., & Yahya, K. A. (1977). A behavioral study of obedience. *Journal of Personality and Social Psychology, 35,* 550–586.

Sharpe, D. (1990). *Written schedule*. A hand-out for parents distributed by a teacher at Wilkshire Elementary, Haslett Public Schools, Haslett, MI.

Shaw, M. E. (1973). Changes in sociometric choices following forced integration of an elementary school. *Journal of Social Issues 29,* 143–157.

Shaywitz, S. E., Escobar, M. D., Shaywitz, B. A., Fletcher, J. M., & Makuch, R. (1992, January). Evidence that dyslexia may represent the lower tail of a normal distribution of reading ability. *The New England Journal of Medicine, 326*(3), 145–150.

Shephard, L. A. (1989). In L. A. Shepard & M. L. Smith (Eds.), *Flunking grades: Resource and policies on retention* (pp. 64–107). London: Palmer.

Short, V. M. (1991). Childhood education in a changing world. *Childhood Education, 68*(1), 10–13.

Shotwell, J., Wolf, D., & Gardner, H. Y. (1979). Exploring early symbolization: Styles of achievement. In B. Sutton-Smith (Ed.), *Play and learning* (pp. 127–156). New York: Gardner Press.

Shrag, L., Nelson, E., & Siminowksy, T. (1985, September). Helping employees cope with change. *Child Care Information Exchange,* 23–27.

Siegel, D. F., & Hansen, R. A. (1991). Kindergarten education policies: Separating myth from reality. *Early Education and Development, 2*(1), 5–31.

Siegler, R. S. (1991). *Children's thinking.* Englewood Cliffs, NJ: Prentice-Hall.

Silvern, S. B. (1988). Continuity/discontinuity between home and early childhood education environments. *The Elementary School Journal, 89*(2), 147–159.

Simpson, G. W. (1990). Keeping it alive: Elements of school culture that sustain innovation. *Educational Leadership, 47*(8), 34–37.

Sinatra, R. (1983, May). Brain research sheds light on language, learning. *Educational Leadership,* 9–12.

Slavin, R. E. (1987). Ability grouping and student achievement in elementary schools: A Best-evidence synthesis. *Review of Educational Research, 57,* 293–336.

Slavin, R. E. (1990). Achievement effects of ability grouping in secondary schools: A best-evidence synthesis. *Review of Educational Research, 60,* 471–499.

Slavin, R. E., & Madden, N. A. (1989). What works for students at risk: A research synthesis. *Educational Leadership, 46*(5), 4–13.

Slobin, D. L. (1971). *Psycholinguistics.* Glenview, IL: Scott, Foresman.

Smart, M. S., & Smart, R. C. (1972). *Children: Development and relationships.* New York: Macmillan.

Smart, M. S., & Smart, R. S. (1982). *Children: Development and relationships* (rev. ed.). New York: Macmillan.

Smilansky, S. (1968). *The effects of socio-dramatic play on disadvantaged preschool children.* New York: Wiley.

Smith, C. A. (1979). Puppetry and problem-solving skills. *Young Children, 34*(3), 4–10.

Smith, C. A. (1982). *Promoting the social development of young children.* Palo Alto, CA: Mayfield.

Smith, C. A. (1988). *I'm positive: Growing up with self-esteem.* Manhattan: Kansas State University Cooperative Extension Service.

Smith, J. (1990). *To think.* New York: Teachers College Press.

Smith, N. (1982). The visual arts in early childhood education. In B. Spodek (Ed.), *Handbook of research in early childhood education* (pp. 295–320). New York: Free Press.

Smith, T. E. (1988). Parental control techniques: Relative frequencies and relationships with situational factors. *Journal of Family Issues, 9,* 155–176.

Smyth, J. (1989). Developing and sustaining critical reflection in teacher education. *Journal of Teacher Education, 40*(2), 2–9.

Snider, M. H., & Fu, V. R. (1990). The effects of specialized education and job experience on early childhood teachers' knowledge of developmentally appropriate practice. *Early Childhood Research Quarterly, 5,* 69–78.

Snow, M. (1982). *Characteristics of families with special needs in relation to schools.* Charleston, WV: Appalachia Educational Laboratory.

Soderman, A. (1985, July). Dealing with difficult young children. *Young Children,* 15–20.

Soderman, A. (1991, May). *Facts about brain growth.* Unpublished paper delivered to the East Lansing public schools.

Soderman, A., & Greenberg, B. (1988). Television and movie behaviors of pregnant and non-pregnant adolescents. *Journal of Adolescent Research, 3*(2), 153–170.

Soderman, A., & Phillips, M. (1986, November). Education of young males: Where are we failing them? *Educational Leadership, 44*(3), 70–72.

Spier, P. (1961). *The fox went out on a chilly night.* Garden City, NY: Doubleday.

Spodek, B. (1973). *Early childhood education.* Englewood Cliffs, NJ: Prentice-Hall.

Spodek, B. (1982). *Handbook of research in early childhood education.* New York: Free Press.

Spodek, B. (1985). *Teaching in the early years* (3rd ed.). Englewood Cliffs, NJ: Prentice-Hall.

Spodek, B. (1986). *Today's kindergarten: Exploring the knowledge base, expanding the curriculum.* New York: Teachers College Press.

Spodek, B., & Robison, H. F. (1973). Are kindergartens obsolete? In B. Spodek (Ed.), *Early childhood education* (pp. 143–152). Englewood Cliffs, NJ: Prentice-Hall.

Spodek, B., Saracho, O. N., & Davis, M. D. (1991). *Foundations of early childhood education.* Englewood Cliffs, NJ: Prentice-Hall.

Sroufe, L. A., & Cooper, R. G. (1988). *Child development: Its nature and course.* New York: Knopf.

Sroufe, L. A., & Cooper, R. G. (1989). *Child development: Its value and course* (2nd ed.). New York: Knopf.

Stake, R. E. (1967). The countenance of educational evaluation. *Teacher's College Record, 68*(7), 523–540.

Starky, S. L. (1980). The relationship between parental acceptance-rejection and the academic performance of fourth and fifth graders. *Behavior Science Research, 15,* 67–80.

Staub, E. (1978). *Positive social behavior and morality: Socialization and development* (Vol. 1). New York: Academic Press.

Stein, L. C., & Kostelnik, M. J. (1984, Spring). A practical problem solving model for conflict resolution in the classroom. *Child Care Quarterly, 13*(1), 5–20.

Steinberg, A. (1990, May). Kindergarten: Producing early failure? *Principal,* 6–9.

Steinberg, L., & Belsky, J. (1991). *Infancy, childhood, and adolescence: Development in context.* New York: McGraw-Hill.

Stengel, S. R. (1982). Moral education for young children. *Young Children, 37*(6), 23–31.

Sternberg, R. J. (1983). *How can we teach intelligence?* Philadelphia: Research for Better Schools.

Stocking, S. H., Arezzo, D., & Leavitt, S. (1980). *Helping kids make friends.* Allen, TX: Argus Communications.

Strayer, J. (1980). A naturalistic study of empathic behaviors and their relation to affective states and perspective-taking skills in preschool children. *Child Development, 51,* 815–822.

Sulzby, E., & Barnhart, J. (1990). All our children emerge as writers and readers. In J. S. McKee (Ed.), *The developing kindergarten: Programs, children and teachers* (pp. 201–244). East Lansing: Michigan Association for the Education of Young Children.

Sunal, C. S. (1990). *Early childhood social studies.* Columbus, OH: Merrill/Macmillan.

Surber, C. F. (1982). Separable effects of motives, consequences, and presentation order on children's moral judgments. *Developmental Psychology, 18,* 257–266.

Sutton-Smith, B. (1971). A reply to Piaget: A play theory of copy. In R. E. Herron & B. Sutton-Smith (Eds.), *Child's play* (pp. 340–342). New York: Wiley.

Sutton-Smith, B. (1986). *Toys as culture.* New York: Gardner Press.

Swick, K. J., & Duff, R. E. (1978). *The parent-teacher bond.* Dubuque, IA: Kendall/Hunt.

Swick, K. J., & McKnight, S. (1989). Characteristics of kindergarten teachers who promote parent involvement. *Early Childhood Research Quarterly, 4,* 19–29.

Sylwester, R. (1986, September). Synthesis of research on brain plasticity: The classroom environment and curriculum enrichment. *Educational Leadership, 44*(1), 90–93.

Szekely, G. (1990, Spring). An Introduction to art: Children's books. *Childhood Education, 66*(3), 132–138.

Tauton, M. (1983). Questioning strategies to encourage young children to talk about art. *Art Education, 36*(4), 40–43.

Taylor, D. (1991). Family literacy: Text as context. In J. Flood, J. M. Jensen, D. Lapp, & J. R. Squire (Eds.), *Handbook of research on teaching the English language arts* (pp. 457–469). New York: Macmillan.

Taylor, B. (1992, January). Discipline practices: The influence of culture. *Central Michigan Association for the Education of Young Children Newsletter, 3.*

Teberosky, A. (1982). Construcción de escrituras a travis de la interacción grupal. In E. Ferreiro & M. Gomez Palaccio (Eds.), *Nueva perspectivas obre los procesos de lectura y escritura.* Mexico City: Siglo.

Tegano, D., Sawyers, J., & Moran, J. (1991, Winter). Problem finding and solving in play: The teacher's role. *Childhood Education,* 92–97.

Thatcher, R. W., Walker, R. A., & Guidice, S. (1987, May). Human cerebral hemispheres develop at different rates and ages. *Science, 236,* 110–113.

Thelen, E., Kelso, J. A. S., & Fogel, A. (1987). Self-organizing systems and infant motor development. *Developmental Review, 1,* 39–65.

Thomas, A., & Chess, S. (1977). *Temperament and development.* New York: Brunner/Mazel.

Thomas, A., & Chess, S. (1980). *The dynamics of psychological development.* New York: Brunner/Mazel.

Thomas, A., & Chess, S. (1984). *Origins and evolution of behavior disorders.* New York: Brunner/Mazel.

Thomas, A., Chess, S., Birch, H. G., Hartzig, M. E., & Korn, S. (1963). *Behavioral individuality in early childhood.* New York: New York University Press.

Thomas, R. T. (1985). *Comparing theories of child development* (2nd ed.). Belmont, CA: Wadsworth.

Thompson, C. (1990). "I make a mark": The significance of talk in young children's artistic development. *Early Childhood Research Quarterly, 5,* 215–232.

Tierney, R. J., Carter, M. A., & Desai, L. (1991). *Portfolio assessment in the reading writing classroom.* Norwood, MA: Christopher-Gordon.

Tisask, M. S., & Block, J. H. (1990). Preschool children's evolving conceptions of badness: A longitudinal study. *Early Education and Development, 4,* 300–307.

Toepfer, C. F. (1985). Suggestions of neurological data for middle level education: A review of research and its interpretations. *Transescence, 13*(2), 12–38.

Tompkins, G. E. (1990). *Teaching writing: Balancing process and product.* Columbus, OH: Merrill/Macmillan.

Tough, J. (1977). *Talking and learning.* London: Schools Council Publications.

Trad, P. V. (1988). *Psychosocial scenarios for pediatrics.* New York: Springer.

Traverse City Public Schools. (1987). *Early childhood curriculum guide: Kindergarten through 2nd.* Traverse City: MI: Author.

Trawick-Smith, J. (1988, July). Let's say you're the baby, OK? Play leadership and following behavior of young children. *Young Children,* 51–59.

Trepanier-Street, M. (1990). The developing kindergartener: Thinking and problem solving. In J. McKee (Ed.), *Developing kindergartens: Programs, children and teachers* (pp. 181–199). East Lansing, MI: Michigan Association for the Education of Young Children.

Tribe, C. (1982). *Profile of three theories.* Dubuque, IA: Kendall/Hunt.

Tudge, J., & Caruso, D. (1988). Cooperative problem solving in the classroom: Enhancing young children's cognitive development. *Young Children,* 44(101), 46–52.

Ulrich, B. D. (1989). Development of stepping patterns in human infants: A dynamical systems perspective. *Journal of Motor Behavior, 21,* 392–408.

Umansky, W. (1983, March/April). On families and the re-valuing of childhood. *Childhood Education, 59*(4), 259–266.

U.S. Department of Education. (1986). What works: Research about teaching and learning. Washington, DC: U.S. Government Printing Office.

U.S. Department of Health and Human Services (1980). *Promoting health/preventing disease: Objectives for the nation.* Washington, DC: U.S. Government Printing Office.

Van Dyke, H. T. (1984). Corporal punishment in our schools. *Education Digest, 57*(5), 296–300.

Vander-Zanden, J. W. (1989). *Human development* (4th ed.). New York: Knopf.

Vasta, R., Haith, M. M., & Miller, S. A. (1992). *Child psychology: The modern science.* New York: Wiley.

Vogel, P. G., & Seefeldt, V. (1988). *Program design in physical education.* Indianapolis: Benchmark.

Vygotsky, L. S. (1962). *Thought and language.* London: Schools Council Publications.

Vygotsky, L. (1967). Play and its role in the mental development of the child. *Social Psychology, 12,* 62–76.

Vygotsky, L. (1986). *Thought and language* (rev. ed., ed. A. Kozulin). Cambridge: MIT Press.

Walberg, H. (1984). Improving the productivity of Americans' schools. *Educational Leadership, 41,* 19–30.

Walberg, H. J. (1985). Families as partners in educational productivity. *Phi Delta Kappan, 65*(6), 397–400.

Walker, L. J., deVries, B., & Trevarthan, S. D. (1987). Moral stages and moral orientations in real-life and hypothetical dilemmas. *Child Development, 58,* 842–858.

Walker, L. J. (1989). A longitudinal study of moral reasoning. *Child Development, 60,* 157–166.

Walker, R., Sannito, T., & Fareto, A. (1970). The effect of subjectively reported anxiety on intelligence test performance. *Psychology in the Schools, 7,* 241–243.

Wall, P., McCann, J., & Bloomfield, M. (1990). *Corvallis School District elementary schools: Developmentally appropriate practices.* Corvallis, OR: Author.

Walsey, P. A. (1991). From quarterback to coach, from actor to director. *Educational Leadership, 48*(8), 35–40.

Walsh, D. J. (1991, April). Extending the discourse on developmental appropriateness: A developmental perspective. *Early Education and Development, 2*(2), 109–119.

Warger, C. (1988). *A resource guide to public school early in childhood programs.* Alexandria, VA: Association of Supervision and Curriculum Development.

Washington, V. (1988, January). Demographics: Part I. *Trends in Early Childhood Education,* 4–7.

Weaver, R. L. (1990). Separate is not equal. *Principal, 69*(5), 40–43.

Weber, E. (1984). *Ideas influencing early childhood education: A theoretical analysis.* New York: Teachers College Press.

Weber, G. (1977). *Uses and abuses of standardized testing in the schools.* Washington, DC: Council for Basic Education.

Webster, T. (1990). Projects as curriculum: Under what conditions? *Childhood Education, 67*(1), 2–3.

Weikart, D. P., Rogers, L., Adcock, C., & McClelland, D. (1971). *The cognitively oriented curriculum: A framework for preschool teachers.* Urbana: University of Illinois.

Weikart, D. P., & Schweinhart, L. J. (1987). The high/scope cognitively oriented curriculum in early education. In J. L. Roopnarine & J. E. Johnson (Eds.), *Approaches to early childhood education* (pp. 253–268). Columbus, OH: Merrill/Macmillan.

Welman, H. M. (1988). First steps in the child's theorizing about the mind. In J. Astington, P. L. Harris, & D. R. Olson (Eds.), *Developing Theories of Mind.* New York: Cambridge University Press.

Wertsch, J. V. (1985). *Vygotsky and the social formation of mind.* Cambridge, MA: Harvard University Press.

Weston, D. R., & Turiel, E. (1980). Act-role relations: Children's concepts of social rules. *Developmental Psychology, 16,* 417–424.

Whiren, A. P. (1979). Tabletoys: The undeveloped resource. In L. Adams & B. Garbeck (Eds.), *Ideas*

That Work with Young Children: Vol. 2. Washington, DC: National Association for the Education of Young Children.

Whiren, A. P. (1990). The kindergarten teacher: Roles in the classroom. In J. S. Spitler McKee (Ed.), *The developing kindergarten: Programs, children and teachers* (pp. 275–301). Ann Arbor: Michigan Association for the Education of Young Children.

Whiren, A. P. (1991, May). *Children's play and learning.* Paper presented at the Kalamazoo Association for the Education of Young Children Conference, Kalamazoo, MI.

White, S. H., & Siegel, A. W. (1976). Cognitive development: The new inquiry. *Young Children, 31*(6), 425–436.

Willar, B. (1992, April). *The full cost of quality campaign.* Paper presented at the National Association for the Education of Young Children Leadership Conference, Washington, DC.

Williams, D. L., Jr., & Chavkin, N. F. (1989, October). Essential elements of strong parent involvement programs. *Educational Leadership,* 24–27.

Williams, L. R. (1987). Determining the curriculum. In C. Seefeldt (Ed.), *The early childhood curriculum: A review of current research* (pp. 1–12). New York: Teachers College Press.

Wolf, A. D. (1984). *Mommy, it's a Renoir!* Altoona, PA: Parent-Child Press.

Wolf, D. (1991, July–August). Make believe: Why bother? *Exchange, 80,* 45–48.

Wolfgang, C. H., & Sanders, L. (1986). Teachers' role: A construct for supporting the play of young children. In S. Burroughs & R. Evans (Eds.), *Play, language and socialization* (pp. 49–62). New York: Gordon & Breach Science Publishers.

Wood, D. J., Bruner, J. S., & Ross, G. (1976). The role of tutoring in problem solving. *Journal of Child Psychology and Psychiatry, 17*(2) 89–100.

Wortham, S. C. (1984). *Organizing instruction in early childhood.* Boston: Allyn & Bacon.

Wortham, S. C. (1990). *Tests and measurement in early childhood education.* Columbus, OH: Merrill/Macmillan.

Wynne, E. A. (1988, February). Balancing character development and academics in the elementary school. *Phi Delta Kappan,* 424–426.

Yarrow, M. R., Scott, P., & Waxler, C. Z. (1973). Learning concern for others. *Developmental Psychology 8,* 240–260.

Yawkey, T. (1987). Project P.I.A.G.E.T.—A holistic approach to early bilingual education. In J. L. Roopnarine & J. E. Johnson (Eds.), *Approaches to early childhood education* (pp. 197–212). Columbus, OH: Merrill/Macmillan.

Zemach, M. (1976). *Hush little baby.* New York: Dutton.

Zigler, E. F. and Finn-Stevenson, M. (1987). *Children: Development and social issues.* Lexington, MA: Heath.

Zill, N. (1989). *Child trends: Summary report of the Select Committee on Children, Youth and Families.* Washington, DC: U.S. House of Representatives.

Zimmer, C. (1990). [Farmington Hills schools parent night successes. Personal communication.]

APPENDIX

Resources for Educators

Resources for Promoting Aesthetic Development

Lasky, L., & Mukerji, R. (1980). *Art: Basic for young children*. Washington, DC: National Association for the Education of Young Children.

Seeger, R. C. (1948). *American folk songs for children*. Garden City, NY: Doubleday.

Sullivan, M. (1982). *Feeling strong, feeling free: Movement exploration for young children.* Washington, DC: National Association for the Education of Young Children.

Warren, J. (1985). *1-2-3 Art: Open-ended art for the very young*. Everett, WA: Warren.

Resources for Promoting Affective Development

Canfield, J., & Wells, H. C. (1976). *100 ways to enhance self-concept in the classroom: Handbook for teachers and parents*. Englewood Cliffs, NJ: Prentice-Hall.

Edwards, L. C. (1990). *Affective development and the creative arts: A process approach to early childhood education*. Columbus, OH: Merrill/Macmillan.

Freeman, L. (1982). *It's my body*. Seattle: Parenting Press.

Scott, L. (1986). *Quiet times: Relaxation techniques for early childhood*. Minneapolis: Denison.

Smith, C. A. (1988). *I'm positive: Growing up with self-esteem*. Manhattan: Kansas State University Cooperative Extension Service.

Smith, C. A. (1990). *From wonder to wisdom: Using stories to help children grow*. N.p.: Nal-Dutton.

Resources for Promoting Cognitive Development

Bennett, A. B., & Nelson, L. T. (1991). *Mathematics for elementary teachers: An activity approach*. N.p.: Brown.

Burns, M. (1988). *A collection of math lessons from grades 1 through 3*. New Rochelle, NY: Cuisenaire.

Dutton, W. H. (1990). *Mathematics children use and understand: Preschool through third grade*. Mountain View, CA: Mayfield.

Harlan, J. (1988). *Science experiences for the early years.* Columbus, OH: Merrill/Macmillan.

Lind, K. K. (1991). *Exploring science in early childhood: A developmental approach.* New York: Delmar.

Seymour, D., & Beardslee, E. (1990). *Critical thinking activities.* N.p.: Seymour.

Troutman, A. P., & Lichtenberg, B. K. (1991). *Mathematics: A good beginning. Strategies for teaching children.* Pacific Grove, CA: Brooks-Cole.

Resources for Promoting Language Development

Bean, W., & Bouffler, C. (1982). *Spell by writing.* Portsmouth, NH: Heinemann.

Calkins, L. M. (1986). *The art of teaching writing.* Portsmouth, NH: Heinemann.

Calkins, L. M. (1986). *Living between the lines.* Portsmouth, NH: Heinemann.

Devine, T. G. (1982). *Listening skills schoolwide.* Urbana, IL: National Council of Teachers of English.

Dwyer, J. (Ed.) (1989). *"A sea of talk."* Portsmouth, NH: Heinemann.

Goodman, K. S., Bird, L. B., & Goodman, Y. M. (1991). *The whole language catalog.* Santa Rosa, CA: American School Publishers.

Goodman, K. S., Goodman, Y. M., & Hood, W. J. (1989). (Ed.) *The whole language evaluation book.* Portsmouth, NH: Heinemann.

Heald-Taylor, G. (1989). *The administrator's guide to whole language.* Katonah, NY: Owen.

Routman, R. (1988). *Transitions.* Portsmouth, NH: Heinemann.

Routman, R. (1991). *Invitations.* Portsmouth, NH: Heinemann.

Tompkins, G. E., & Hoskisson, K. (1991). *Language arts.* New York: Macmillan.

Weaver, C. (1990). *Understanding whole language.* Portsmouth, NH: Heinemann.

Resources for Promoting Physical Development

Barlin, A. L. (1989). *Hello toes! Movement games for children.* (1989). Pennington, NJ: Princeton.

Braley, W. T., Konicki, G., & Leedy, C. (1968). *Daily sensorimotor training activities: A handbook for teachers and parents of preschool children.* Freeport, NY: Educational Activities.

Breham, M., & Tindell, N. (1983). *Movement with a purpose.* West Nyack, NY: Parker.

Cochran, N. A., Wilkinson, L. C., & Furlow, J. J. (1981). *Learning on the move: An activity guide for preschool parents and teachers.* Dubuque, IA: Kendall/Hunt.

Dauer, V. P. (1972). *Essential movement experiences for preschool and primary children.* Minneapolis: Burgess.

Kretzschmar, J. C. (1989). *3's and 4's moving . . . Early foundations for fitness.* LEA/DECE Publication.

Thomas, J. R., Lee, A. M., & Thomas, K. T. (1989). *Physical education for children: Daily lesson plans.* Champaign, IL: Human Kinetics.

Wilkstrom, R. L. (1983). *Fundamental motor patterns.* Philadelphia: Lea & Fabiger.

Resources for Promoting Social Development

Derman-Sparks, L. (1991). *The anti-bias curriculum.* Washington, DC: National Association for the Education of Young Children.

Fry-Miller, K., & Myers-Walls. (1988). *Young peacemakers project book.* Elgin, IL: Bretheren.

Herman, M. L., Passineau, J. F., Schimpf, A. L., & Treuer, P. (1991). *Teaching kids to love the earth.* Duluth, MN: Pfeifer-Hamilton.

Kostelnik, M. J., Stein, L., Whiren, A. P., & Soderman, A. K. (in press). *Guiding children's social development: Classroom practices.* New York: Delmar.

Smith, C. (1982). *Promoting the social development of young children.* Palo Alto, CA: Mayfield.

York, S. (1991). *Roots and wings: Affirming culture in early childhood programs.* St. Paul, MN: Toys 'n' Things Press.

Resources for Promoting Pretend Play and Construction

Brokering, L. (1989) *Resources for dramatic play.* Belmont, CA: Fearon Teacher Aides.

Forman, G., & Hill, F. (1984). *Constructive play: Applying Piaget in the preschool.* Menlo Park, CA: Addison-Wesley.

Stangl, J. (1986). *Magic mixtures: Creative fun for little ones preschool–grade 3.* Carthage, IL: Fearon Teachers Aides.

Van Tassel, K., & Greiman, M. (1973). *Creative dramatization.* NY: Macmillan Threshhold Early Learning Division.

Author Index

Subject Index

ISBN 0-675-21327-4